'This volume fills a critical gap in the understanding of maritime security. It places the underappreciated maritime space into the limelight, provides the necessary clarity to an ambiguous concept, and overcomes both geographical boundaries and topical constraints to become an indispensable resource for policymakers, scholars and sailors alike.'

Jeremy Stöhs, *author of* The Decline of European Naval Forces.

'This collection of 31 essays offers an overview of some of the newest and most insightful research in the field. Topics covered range from traditional maritime security concerns such as piracy, fisheries protection and terrorism to emerging issues, including human trafficking, gender issues on the high seas and renewed great power competition in the Arctic and the South Atlantic. The authors of these essays are as diverse as the topics. They come from all over the globe and a variety of academic disciplines. For anyone interested in covering the waterfront of ideas in maritime security, I highly recommend this handbook.'

John Darell Sherwood, *naval historian and author of* War in the Shallows:
U.S. Navy Coastal and Riverine Warfare in Vietnam, *winner of*
the John Lyman Award for Excellence in Maritime and Naval History.

'This benchmark handbook presents an insightful and pluralist collection of contributions covering the full spectrum of maritime security studies. A must read for those new to the topic but also for more established observers looking to capture the state of the art in this fast evolving and increasingly important field.'

Timothy P. Edmunds, *Professor of International Security,*
University of Bristol, UK.

'This collection carries you along the entire wavelength of maritime security. In fact, it goes further, it opens the possibility of an intellectual territory yet to be charted. Whereas most Handbooks try to harmonise or define their field, the editors here have done the opposite. They have profoundly opened their field, extending it into other disciplines and new perspectives. There are essays in here that have the quality of being classics in their field.'

Timothy Doyle, *Professor Emeritus of Politics and International Relations,*
Keele University and the University of Adelaide.

ROUTLEDGE HANDBOOK OF MARITIME SECURITY

This handbook offers a critical and substantial analysis of maritime security and documents the most pressing strategic, economic, socio-cultural and legal questions surrounding it.

Written by leading international experts, this comprehensive volume presents a wide variety of theoretical positions on maritime security, detailing its achievements and outlining outstanding issues faced by those in the field. The book includes studies which cover the entire spectrum of activity along which maritime security is developing, including piracy, cyber security, energy security, terrorism, narco-subs and illegal fishing. Demonstrating the transformative character and potential of the topic, the book is divided into two parts. The first part exhibits a range of perspectives and new approaches to maritime security, and the second explores emerging developments in the practice of security at sea, as well as regional studies written by local maritime security experts. Taken together, these contributions provide a compelling account of the evolving maritime security environment, casting fresh light on theoretical and empirical aspects.

The book will be of much interest to practitioners and students of maritime security, naval studies, security studies, maritime history and International Relations in general.

Ruxandra-Laura Boşilcă is a Senior Research Fellow at Inland Norway University of Applied Sciences, Norway.

Susana Ferreira is a Lecturer at the Nebrija University, Director of the Master in Risk Management in Conflicts.

Barry J. Ryan is a Senior Lecturer in International Relations at Keele University, UK.

ROUTLEDGE HANDBOOK OF MARITIME SECURITY

*Edited by Ruxandra-Laura Boşilcă,
Susana Ferreira, and Barry J. Ryan*

LONDON AND NEW YORK

Cover image: © Getty Images

First published 2022
by Routledge
4 Park Square, Milton Park, Abingdon, Oxon OX14 4RN

and by Routledge
605 Third Avenue, New York, NY 10158

Routledge is an imprint of the Taylor & Francis Group, an informa business

© 2022 selection and editorial matter, Ruxandra-Laura Boşilcă, Susana Ferreira and Barry J. Ryan; individual chapters, the contributors

The right of Ruxandra-Laura Boşilcă, Susana Ferreira and Barry J. Ryan to be identified as the authors of the editorial material, and of the authors for their individual chapters, has been asserted in accordance with sections 77 and 78 of the Copyright, Designs and Patents Act 1988.

All rights reserved. No part of this book may be reprinted or reproduced or utilised in any form or by any electronic, mechanical, or other means, now known or hereafter invented, including photocopying and recording, or in any information storage or retrieval system, without permission in writing from the publishers.

Trademark notice: Product or corporate names may be trademarks or registered trademarks, and are used only for identification and explanation without intent to infringe.

British Library Cataloguing-in-Publication Data
A catalogue record for this book is available from the British Library

Library of Congress Cataloguing-in-Publication Data
Names: Boşilcă, Ruxandra-Laura, editor. | Ferreira, Susana de Sousa, editor. | Ryan, Barry J., editor.
Title: Routledge handbook of maritime security / edited by Ruxandra-Laura Boşilcă, Susana Ferreira and Barry J. Ryan.
Description: Abingdon, Oxon ; New York : Routledge, [2022] | Includes bibliographical references and index.
Identifiers: LCCN 2021059626 (print) | LCCN 2021059627 (ebook) | ISBN 9780367430641 (hardback) | ISBN 9781032275536 (paperback) | ISBN 9781003001324 (ebook)
Subjects: LCSH: Shipping--Security measures. | Merchant marine--Security measures. | Piracy--Prevention. | Sea control. | Security, International
Classification: LCC VK203 .R68 2022 (print) | LCC VK203 (ebook) | DDC 359/.03--dc23/eng/20211220
LC record available at https://lccn.loc.gov/2021059626
LC ebook record available at https://lccn.loc.gov/2021059627

ISBN: 978-0-367-43064-1 (hbk)
ISBN: 978-1-032-27553-6 (pbk)
ISBN: 978-1-003-00132-4 (ebk)

DOI: 10.4324/9781003001324

Typeset in Bembo
by MPS Limited, Dehradun

**dedicated to the memory of
Sam Bateman (1938–2020)**

CONTENTS

List of Figures	*xii*
List of Tables	*xiii*
List of Contributors	*xiv*

Introduction: Surveying the Seascape   1
Ruxandra-Laura Boşilcă, Susana Ferreira, and Barry J. Ryan

PART I
Perspectives on Maritime Security   15

1   Sea Power in the Transformation of States and Overseas Empires
(1500–1800)   17
Benjamin de Carvalho and Halvard Leira

2   Maritime Security in a Critical Context   27
Barry J. Ryan

3   Maritime Security: "Good Navies" and Realism Re-imagined   38
Geoffrey Till

4   Modern Maritime Strategy and Naval Warfare   49
Ian Speller

5   The Liberal Approach to Maritime Security   62
Rafael García Pérez

Contents

6 Global Maritime Security Governance   73
James Sperling

7 Maritime Security and the Law of the Sea   86
Joanna Mossop

8 Maritime Securitisation   96
Juha A. Vuori

9 Gender Perspectives on Maritime Security   106
Jane Freedman

10 Global Political Ethnography: A Methodological Approach to
Studying Maritime Security Governance   116
Jessica Larsen

11 The Politics of Piracy Numbers: The Gulf of Guinea Case   127
Katja Lindskov Jacobsen

12 Visual Representations of the Sea   139
Claire Sutherland

PART II
Practices and Norms of Maritime Security   151

13 Human Rights and Law Enforcement at Sea   153
Anna Petrig

14 Humans at Sea: Migrants, Refugees and Transnational Responses   165
Susana Ferreira

15 Contemporary Maritime Piracy and Counter-Piracy   176
Robert McCabe

16 Maritime Terrorism   189
Joshua Tallis

17 Energy Security and Maritime Security   200
Rupert Herbert Burns

18 Maritime Cybersecurity and Disruptive Technologies   214
Jeptoo Kipkech, Kristen Kuhn, and Siraj Ahmed Shaikh

Contents

19 The Nexus between Natural Resource Governance and Transnational
Maritime Crime 227
Lisa Otto

20 Fisheries Crimes, Poverty and Food Insecurity 239
Cornelia E. Nauen and Simona T. Boschetti

21 Small Island Developing States and Maritime Security 250
Christian Bouchard

22 Maritime Security and the Blue Economy 265
Anja Menzel

23 Securing Maritime Identities: The New Practices of Maritime Cultural
Heritage 276
Eliseu Carbonell

24 Non-state and Hybrid Actorness at Sea: From Narco-subs to Drone Patrols 287
Brendan Flynn

25 The Privatisation of Maritime Security: Implications for International
Security 299
Eugenio Cusumano and Stefano Ruzza

26 NATO and Maritime Security in the North Atlantic 311
Gavin E. L. Hall and Mark Webber

27 Maritime Security in the South Atlantic 323
Érico Esteves Duarte

28 Maritime Security in the Mediterranean 334
Michela Ceccorulli

29 Maritime Security in Southeast Asia 346
Kwa Chong Guan and Collin Koh

30 Maritime Security in the South China Sea 356
Chris Rahman

31 Maritime Security in the Arctic 366
Amund Botillen and Marianne Riddervold

Index *378*

FIGURES

17.1	Energy security at sea; threats and vulnerabilities	209
17.2	Energy security at sea; threat and consequences	210
21.1	Maritime political geography map of the Western Indian Ocean	255
21.2	Maritime security domains matrix (ovals and arrows), and main drivers influencing the SIDS responses to maritime security threats and risks	257
23.1	Beaching of a replica of a traditional fishing boat, April 2010	277
23.2	Ex-voto showing a shipwreck in front of Cabo Tiñoso (Spain) on the night of 24 February 1868. © Museu Marítimo de Barcelona (641F)	280
23.3	Burning the last fishing boat on 15 December 1990 (Photo: P. Sauleda archive)	283
24.1	Non-state actors across the maritime security policy cycle	289
29.1	Patrol and combat vessels of maritime forces in Southeast Asia	350
29.2	Incidences of piracy and sea robbery in the Straits of Malacca and Singapore, 1996–2010	351

TABLES

6.1	Maritime security goods	75
6.2	Regional naval capacity and maritime enforcement capability	77
6.3	Level of governance across four dimensions	80
17.1	Geopolitical insecurity levels	211
18.1	Cyber attacks on enterprise and information assets in the maritime industry	219
18.2	Cyber attacks on navigation systems in the maritime industry	220
18.3	Advanced persistent threats (APTs) in the maritime industry	220
18.4	Existing guidelines on international cyber risk management	221
21.1	SIDS selected for this chapter. GDP/PPP: Gross domestic product in purchasing power parity. Maritime domain: the ocean area from coastline to the outer limit of the exclusive economic zone	252
21.2	Bergin et al. (2019) recommendations for maritime security in the Indo-Pacific Island States	259
25.1	Pirate attacks against Panamanian-, Liberian- and Marshallese-flagged vessels 2007–2013	302
25.2	Hijackings of Panamanian-, Liberian- and Marshallese-flagged vessels by Somali pirates, 2007–2013	302
27.1	Most significant cocaine seizures in the South Atlantic, 2012–2016(kg)	325
27.2	Cocaine seizures in Argentina, Brazil and Uruguay, 2015–2018 (tons)	326
27.3	Piracy and armed robbery in West Africa and South America, 2010–2020	327
29.1	Maritime defence and security capacities of selected Southeast Asian countries	349

CONTRIBUTORS

Siraj Ahmed Shaikh is a Professor of Systems Security and is the Centre Director for the Centre for Future Transport and Cities (FTC) at Coventry University. He is Visiting Professor at the Security, Risks Management and Conflict (SEGERICO) Research Group, Universidad Nebrija, Spain. He is currently involved in the "Cyber Readiness for Boards" initiative to assess the cyber risk perception of boards in the maritime sector.

Juha A. Vuori is a Professor of International Politics at Tampere University in Finland. His research interests include securitisation theory, with a particular focus on its application in non-democratic contexts and securitisation/contestation/de-securitisation dynamics. He has also worked extensively on visual security studies, Chinese security politics and internet control, and nuclear weapons–related issues.

Ruxandra-Laura Boşilcă is a Senior Research Fellow at Inland Norway University of Applied Sciences. She holds a PhD in Political Science from the National University of Political Studies and Public Administration in co-supervision with the ARENA Centre for European Studies, University of Oslo, and was a Research Fellow at University of Bologna, Cardiff University and Institut Barcelona d'Estudis Internacionals (IBEI). Her research on EU foreign and security policies and maritime security has been published in books by Routledge and Palgrave as well as journals including *European Foreign Affairs Review*, *European Security* and the *Romanian Journal of European Affairs*, among others.

Amund Botillen is a Counsellor/Research Advisor at the Department of Research of Inland Norway University of Applied Sciences. His research interests include International Relations, transatlantic relations, security policies and governance.

Christian Bouchard holds a Ph.D. in geography (Université Laval, Québec) and is Professor Emeritus from Laurentian University (Sudbury, Canada). His research work focuses on the Indian Ocean geopolitics and the Southwest Indian Ocean, with a particular interest in maritime geopolitics and the small island states and territories of the region. He is currently Associate Editor for the *Journal of the Indian Ocean Region* (Routledge) as well as a member of the editorial boards for the *Cahiers de géographie du Québec* (Université Laval, Québec) and

Contributors

VertigO – La revue électronique en sciences de l'environnement (Université du Québec à Montréal). He is also a founding member of the Indian Ocean Research Group (IORG Inc.).

Eliseu Carbonell is a Lecturer in Social Anthropology at the University of Girona, Catalonia. He has studied and undertaken ethnographic fieldwork on maritime heritage in Quebec and Catalonia. His research focuses on artisanal fishing and intangible heritage, on which he has published three books and numerous journal articles.

Michela Ceccorulli is a Senior Assistant Professor at the University of Bologna and an Adjunct Professor at the Dickinson Center for European Studies. Her research interests lie around migration, security and security governance. Her publications include, among others, *Framing irregular immigration in security terms: the Libya case* (Florence University Press, 2014, co-edited with Sonia Lucarelli and Enrico Fassi), *The EU Migration System of Governance. Justice on the Move* (Palgrave, 2021, co-edited with Nicola Labanca), and *The EU, migration and the politics of administrative detention* (Routledge, 2014). She has widely published in many journals, among which *European Security, Contemporary Security, Mediterranean Politics, West European Politics and The International Spectator.*

Kwa Chong Guan is a Senior Fellow at the S Rajaratnam School of International Studies, Nanyang Technological University, where he works on a range of regional security issues, including maritime security. Among his publications is *Maritime Security in Southeast Asia* (Routledge, 2007, co-edited with John K. Skogan). Kwa started his career serving in the Ministries of Foreign Affairs and then Defence.

Eugenio Cusumano is a Marie Curie Fellow at Ca' Foscari University, Venice and Assistant Professor at the University of Leiden. His research on non-state actors' role in international crisis management has been published in over 20 journal articles as well as books by Oxford and Stanford University Press, Routledge and Palgrave.

Benjamin de Carvalho is a Senior Research Fellow at the Norwegian Institute of International Affairs (NUPI) in Oslo. He has written extensively on early modern Historical International Relations, and been active in the Historical International Relations section of the ISA since its inception and in a number of functions. His latest publications include *The Sea and International Relations* (Manchester University Press, co-edited with Halvard Leira), *Status and the Rise of Brazil* (Palgrave Macmillan, co-edited with Maria Jumbert and Paulo Esteves), and *The Routledge Handbook of Historical International Relations* (co-edited with Julia Costa Lopez and Halvard Leira).

Érico Duarte is an Associate Professor of Strategic Studies and International Relations at the Federal University of Rio Grande do Sul, Brazil. His research interests include military history, force design and civil-military relations.

Gavin E. L. Hall is a Teaching Fellow at the University of Strathclyde delivering a range of International Security modules. His research is focused on NATO and emerging security challenges, particularly cyber-security, and the processes involved in integrating technology and lessons learned into military strategy and doctrine.

Contributors

Cornelia E. Nauen holds a PhD in fisheries science/marine ecology from Kiel University, Germany. She worked in FAO's Fisheries Department, and later in the development cooperation and international science cooperation departments of the European Commission. Since 2010 she heads the international non-profit association *Mundus maris* – Sciences and Arts for Sustainability. She is also chair of the Board of Trustees of the scientific non-profit Quantitative Aquatics in the Philippines. Her current research interests focus on sustainable small-scale fisheries, including the essential gender and justice dimensions.

Susana Ferreira is a Lecturer at the Nebrija University and Director of the Master in Risk Management in Conflicts. She is a researcher at the Security Research, Risk and Conflict Management Group (SEGERICO-Nebrija) and associate researcher at the Portuguese Institute of International Relations (IPRI-NOVA). She has received the UNED Extraordinary Doctoral Award for her PhD thesis. Her research areas cover international migration, border management, security studies, maritime security and the Mediterranean, in which she has several national and international high-standard publications.

Brendan Flynn is a Lecturer at the School of Political Science and Sociology, National University of Ireland, Galway. He researches maritime security and defence and security studies more broadly. Recent publications include the journal article "The coming high-tech Sino-American War at Sea? Naval Guns, Technology hybridity and the 'Shock of the Old'" in *Defence Studies* (2021) and the book chapter "From hand-me-down navies to niche players? Comparing the navies of (very) small European states" in *Europe, Small Navies and Maritime Security Balancing Traditional Roles and Emergent Threats in the 21st Century* (Routledge, 2019, edited by Robert McCabe, Deborah Sanders and Ian Speller).

Jane Freedman is a Professor of Sociology at the Université Paris 8 and Director of the Centre de recherches sociologiques et politiques de Paris (CRESPPA). Her research focuses on issues of gender, violence and security, particularly in relation to conflicts and refugees. Recent publications include *Gendering the International Asylum and Refugee Debate* (Palgrave Macmillan, 2015) and *A Gendered Approach to the Syrian Refugee Crisis* (Routledge, 2017).

Rafael Garcia Perez is a Professor of International Relations at the University Pablo de Olavide in Seville, Spain. Previously he was Professor at the University of Santiago de Compostela (1995–2019). He is also professor at the Gutiérrez Mellado University Institute (Ministry of Defense – UNED). The latest books that he edited include *A extensão das Plataformas Continentais. Portugal e Espanha, perspetivas e realidades* (Porto, Fronteira do Caos, 2017), *Estrategia de Seguridad Marítima de España: una agenda de actualización* (Valencia, Tirant lo Blanch, 2019) and *Seguridad y fronteras en el mar* (Valencia, Tirant lo Blanch, 2020).

Rupert Herbert Burns is a maritime security consultant with over 20 years professional operational experience at sea. His expertise centres on providing operations and security risk management solutions for shipping, offshore and oil and gas sector clients with operations in Africa, the Middle East, Asia and Europe. Previously, he was a Director at Lloyd's Marine Intelligence Unit in Washington DC and London, has worked as a consultant to Washington DC-based geopolitical and security policy think-tanks and consultancies, and consulted for a commercial shipping practice in a leading U.S. law firm. Following re-commissioning in 2008, Herbert-Burns is currently serving as a naval staff officer in the UK

Contributors

Ministry of Defence. Dr Herbert-Burns has Master's degree in International Security Studies and a PhD in Petroleum Geopolitics from the University of St Andrews in Scotland.

Barry J. Ryan is a Senior Lecturer in International Relations at Keele University, UK. He has worked and consulted for Irish Aid, the OSCE and the United Nations Development Program. His research explores the relationship between security and governance. He traces this theme through studies of police power, spatial theory and maritime politics. His work was awarded the British International Studies Association Best Research Article Award. He is currently examining zonation at sea and its contribution to maritime security.

Jeptoo Kipkech is a Doctoral Researcher in Maritime Cybersecurity in the Systems Security Group at the Centre for Future Transport and Cities (FTC) at Coventry University. She specialises in cybersecurity in the maritime domain, which investigates all aspects of protecting the cyberspace of the blue economy.

Collin Koh is a Research Fellow at the S Rajaratnam School of International Studies, Nanyang Technological University. He primarily researches on maritime security and naval affairs focusing on Southeast Asia.

Kristen Kuhn is a Researcher in Maritime Cybersecurity in the Systems Security Group at the Centre for Future Transport and Cities (FTC) at Coventry University. She specialises in cybersecurity decision-making and maritime security. She currently works on the Cyber Readiness for Boards project, which investigates the cyber risk perception of boards in the maritime sector.

Jessica Larsen works at the Danish Institute for International Studies (DIIS) in Copenhagen. Her research revolves around maritime security and port infrastructures, particularly in the Global South. She provides policy analysis for the Danish Ministry of Defence and Ministry of Foreign Affairs on maritime security, civ-mil interventions and Danish foreign and security policy.

Halvard Leira is a Research Professor at the Norwegian Institute of International Affairs (NUPI). He has published extensively in English and Norwegian on international political thought, historiography, foreign policy and diplomacy. His most recent work includes co-editing *The Routledge Handbook of Historical International Relations* (2021) and *The Sea and International Relations*.

Katja Lindskov Jacobsen is a Senior Researcher at the University of Copenhagen in the Department of Political Science's Centre for Military Studies. Her research explores various aspects of contemporary interventionism – from stabilisation, to counterpiracy and counterterror – with a specific focus on Africa, and often with attention to maritime aspects (in the Gulf of Guinea and off the Horn of Africa) and/or the role of new technology (notably biometrics). She is the author of *Pirates of the Niger Delta* (UNODC 2021) and *The politics of humanitarian technology* (2015). Her research has also been published in *International Affairs, Security Dialogue, Cooperation and Conflict, and Global Governance*, among others.

Robert McCabe is an Assistant Professor and Director of the MA in Maritime Security Programme at the Centre for Trust, Peace and Social Relations at Coventry University. He holds a PhD in History/International Security and is the author of several books and articles addressing maritime security, governance and development topics.

Anja Menzel is a Senior Researcher at the FernUniversität in Hagen. Holding a PhD from the University of Greifswald, her expertise lies in state cooperation on the combat of piracy, with further research interests in maritime security and ocean governance. Currently, she is researching the relationship between the Blue Economy and development finance.

Joanna Mossop is an Associate Professor in the Law Faculty at Te Herenga Waka – Victoria University of Wellington. Her research focus is the law of the sea, and she has written extensively on topics such as maritime security, dispute settlement, conservation of marine biodiversity and the continental shelf.

Lisa Otto is a Senior Researcher with the SARChI Chair in African Diplomacy and Foreign Policy at the University of Johannesburg. She is interested in foreign affairs, diplomacy, conflict and security, and writes on these issues as they relate to the maritime domain.

Anna Petrig holds the Chair of International Law and Public Law at the University of Basel in Switzerland. She has widely published on maritime security from an international law perspective, with a special focus on human rights and maritime law enforcement.

Chris Rahman is a Principal Research Fellow (Associate Professor) at the Australian National Centre for Ocean Resources and Security (ANCORS), University of Wollongong. His research focuses on maritime strategy and security, strategic theory, Australian defence policy, China and the strategic relations of the Indo-Pacific.

Marianne Riddervold is a full Professor of Political Science at Inland Norway University of Applied Sciences, Research Professor at the Norwegian Institute of International Affairs (NUPI), and Senior Fellow at the UC Berkeley Institute of European Studies. Her research interests include EU foreign and security policy, EU integration theory, EU crises, maritime security and transatlantic relations. Selected publications include *The Palgrave Handbook of EU Crises* (2021, co-edited with Jarle Trondal and Akasemi Newsome), *The Maritime Turn in EU Foreign and Security Policies. Aims, Actors and Mechanisms of Integration* (2018), the Special Issue on "Transatlantic relations in times of uncertainty: crises and EU-US relations" in *Journal of European Integration* (2018, co-edited with Akasemi Newsome) and the Special Issue on "Cooperation, conflict and interaction in the Global Commons" in *International Relations* (2021, co-edited with Akasemi Newsome).

Stefano Ruzza is an Associate Professor of Political Science at the University of Turin, the co-founder and Head of Program of T.wai, the Torino World Affairs Institute, and an associate with LSE Ideas. His research focuses on conflict transformation, armed non-state actors in, and private security.

Ian Speller is an Associate Professor and Director of the Centre for Military History and Strategic Studies at Maynooth University. He also lectures at the Irish Defence Forces Military College. His main research interests are in the field of maritime strategy and naval history and he is the author of numerous works on this subject, including *Understanding Naval Warfare* (Routledge, 2018).

Contributors

James Sperling is a Professor Emeritus of Political Science at the University of Akron. His most recent publication (co-authored with Mark Weber and Martin Smith) is *What's Wrong with NATO and How to Fix it* (Polity 2021).

Claire Sutherland is a Professor of Politics at Northumbria University, Newcastle, UK.

Joshua Tallis studies maritime security and Arctic policy as a research scientist at the Centre for Naval Analyses and an adjunct professor at The George Washington University. Tallis holds a Ph.D. from the University of St Andrews and is the author of *The War for Muddy Waters: Pirates, Terrorists, Traffickers, and Maritime Insecurity.*

Geoffrey Till is an Emeritus Professor of Maritime Studies at King's College London and Chairman of the Corbett Centre for Maritime Policy Studies. Once Dean of Academic Studies at the UK Joint Services Command and Staff College, he is author of nearly 300 books, chapters and articles. Since 2009 he has been a Visiting Professor, Senior Research Fellow and Advisor at the Rajaratnam School of International Studies, Singapore. He now holds the Dudley W. Knox Chair for Naval History and Strategy at the US Naval War College, Newport, Rhode Island. His *Understanding Victory: Naval Operations from Trafalgar to the Falklands* was published by ABC-Clio in 2014 and he has recently completed the fourth edition of his *Seapower: A Guide for the 21st Century* (2018) and an edited version of Bo Hu's *Chinese Maritime Power in the 21st Century* (2019). His *How to Grow a Navy: The Development of Maritime Power* will be published by Routledge (2022).

Simona Tiziana Boschetti is a marine biologist, whose passion for the ocean started as a diver. After completing investigation on coral reefs ecology in Indonesia during her PhD, she focused on fisheries and worked in Ireland, Spain and Italy. Currently she works as a freelance scientific consultant supporting compliance to European marine directives at the European Commission. Simona is also a member of the association Mundus maris, focused on supporting sustainable fisheries projects internationally.

Mark Webber is a Professor of International Politics at the University of Birmingham, Honorary President of the British International Studies Association (2021–2022) and Senior Eisenhower Defence Fellow, NATO Defence College (2022–2023). His latest book (co-authored with James Sperling and Martin A. Smith) is *What's Wrong with NATO and How to Fix It* (Polity Press, 2021). His work on NATO, European security and transatlantic relations has appeared in *British Journal of Politics and International Relations, Defence Studies, European Journal of International Security, European Security, International Affairs, Journal of European Integration, Review of International Studies* and *West European Politics.*

INTRODUCTION: SURVEYING THE SEASCAPE

Ruxandra-Laura Boşilcă, Susana Ferreira, and Barry J. Ryan

"The sea", wrote the novelist Joseph Conrad, "has never been friendly to man. At most it has been the accomplice of human restlessness".[1] In many ways, this study of maritime security serves as the chronicle of that restlessness. The book you are reading surveys the turbulent, vast and complex political seascape of the early twenty-first century. It was conceived as a sort of testament to the coming-of-age of maritime security. It would, it was hoped, create a place where the disparate knowledges that came together to form maritime security could meet. It would document the new connections made and the openings that formed when scholars from distant disciplines gather around a problem. The book, in short, aims to mark the arrival of maritime security, celebrate its achievements and exhibit the body of knowledge it has built. The restlessness within its pages refers therefore not only to the moil of politics at sea but also to the scholarship it has generated. As we read these chapters, each surveying its own part of an impossibly difficult problem, we encounter the efforts of men and women who seek to give form, or pattern, to the unfriendly, unexplored and anarchic oceanic world. The project of seeking this form is, ultimately, the project of maritime security.

As volume editors, we sought to define this project loosely, or broadly, as some might see it. Our working understanding of the term includes any scholarship that transforms the way humankind can know and experience seaspace. This seemed natural to us – from the earliest utterings of the phrase just over a decade or two ago, maritime security has been susceptible to being an open-ended category. It was described as a "nebulous concept" (Feldt et al., 2013, p. 2), a "buzzword" (Bueger, 2015, p. 1), an "amorphous" expression (Kraska & Pedrozo, 2013, p. 6) or a phrase difficult to define as "it comprehends so much" (Till, 1996, p. 5). Its root noun, the word "maritime", is itself somewhat inscrutable. Its entry in the *Oxford English Dictionary* (2019) offers a broad array of signifiers, referring to "bordering the sea, living near the sea-coast", "relating to or dealing with matters of commerce or navigation on the sea", "intended for service at sea" or generally "pertaining to, arising from, or existing in the sea". To further complicate matters, the word to which maritime is conjoined – "security" – is so contested that there is a sub-discipline of International Relations (IR) devoted to researching its meaning and evolving practice.

With such semantic genes, maritime security was bound to always be a term open to interpretation and contextualisation. Yet, we must also consider the time into which maritime security was first coined. Security Studies throughout the Cold War had been a sub-discipline

DOI: 10.4324/9781003001324-1

of IR that was indistinguishable from Strategic Studies, and for that matter geopolitics. It was state-centric, landlocked, militaristic and represented an object of study primarily in the northern hemisphere. Even defined in terms of the survival of the state, the concept of security had a reputation for being "ambiguous" (Wolfers, 1952). In any event, the sea, lying beyond the state, relatively unexamined, symbolised the material embodiment of anarchy. As a state of nature, a site of power but not national security, the maritime sphere did not come under the scrutiny of Strategic Studies. One might readily cite Richard Ullman's (1983) article titled "Redefining Security" as the first attack on such reified constructions of security. Ullman's study "proceeds from the assumption that defining national security merely (or even primarily) in military terms conveys a false image of reality" (p. 129). His argument observed that firstly, the study of security focused only on military threats and ignored other dangers; and secondly, as an epistemology, it had led to a militarisation of IR, which contributed to international insecurity. This was a period of revolutionary change in world politics. In 1987, a United Nations sub-organisation devoted to planning a post-Cold War peace dividend produced the Brundtland Report.

> Its study of environmental and development problems focused its attention on the areas of population, food security, the loss of species and genetic resources, energy, industry, and human settlements – realising that all of these are connected and cannot be treated in isolation one from another.
> *(World Commission on Environment and Development (WCED), 1987, p. 27)*

A world no longer structured by the threat of nuclear annihilation would naturally release a range of insecurities long buried by the exigencies of national security.

Besides the reappearance of terms like "food security", in the late 1980s and 1990s, security swiftly became attached to the environment, to human rights and to socio-economic development. Unlike the natural sciences, the social sciences rarely celebrate and publicise its achievements and discoveries. This is lamentable. One such achievement was the speed and rigour with which it analysed, explored, experimented with and debated the semantic proliferation of security. The existential construction and the exceptional agency that had pervaded the term "national security" were imported into these formations of "new" security. Old school realists, to get a grip on the change, incorporated post-positivist methods associated with the study of sociology and linguistics to IR (Buzan & Hansen, 2009). They concluded that the spread of security discourse could only lead to its omnipotence, at a cost to democracy and human rights. But others argued on the contrary, the change was emancipatory (Nunes, 2012). It promised a powerful channel through which long ignored legal, political and economic projects might be relayed. It is from this ether that the phrase maritime security emerged as a medium through which the political economic order of the sea would attract much-needed attention. And yet, who first used the phrase remains an unsolved mystery.[2]

Nonetheless, the most common narrative about the origin of maritime security emanates from a national security perspective. It posits that the phrase gained currency in the anxiety that gripped the United States following attacks perpetrated by *Al-Qaida* on 9/11. In response, the US government established the Department for Homeland Security as a global intelligence hub for a powerful network of policing agencies. Its accelerated aim was to attain full domain awareness, which required real-time knowledge about everything that moved upon the planet, including the maritime domain. Homeland Security was particularly concerned about the incalculable number of container ships arriving daily to US ports. One of its first initiatives was to establish the Container Security Initiative, which dramatically altered the logistics and

Introduction: Surveying the Seascape

administration of containers shipping throughout the world. In the meantime, *via* NATO, a naval force was sent to the Mediterranean to secure it against the perceived threat of maritime terrorism. Quickly, this mission shifted to become one that policed the sea against human traffickers; eventually, it would become an anti-piracy mission.

Since then, several regulatory and policy measures have been adopted at the national, regional and international levels to improve the security of vessels at sea. While maritime terrorism was a rare occurrence, the perils posed by ship hijacking, weapon smuggling, and nuclear, biological and chemical attacks were suddenly brought into international consciousness. By the mid-2000s, a new international maritime security regime was set in place, underpinned by a broad *corpus* of regulations dealing with various aspects of safety and security in ports and at sea, notably featuring the International Ship and Port Facility Security (ISPS) Code, the amended Safety of Life at Sea (SOLAS) Convention and the revised Convention for the Suppression of Unlawful Acts against the Safety of Maritime Navigation (SUA Convention).

From this perspective, the upsurge in piracy off the coast of Somalia in 2008 provided maritime security its coveted global prominence and political urgency. Piracy became an exceptional matter for the global economy due to the strategic importance of the Gulf of Aden region: nearly 20,000 vessels, carrying as much as 12% of the world's total oil supply, transit through this critical maritime route each year (Kraska & Wilson, 2011). These developments saw a heavy engagement of a broad constellation of governments, regional organisations and private entities in naval operations, information sharing and cooperation, as well as follow-up capacity-building programs both in Somalia and neighbouring states (Bosilca & Riddervold, 2019). Efforts to contain and arrest piracy also led to innovative maritime security governance forums and policy instruments in the region, such as the Contact Group for Piracy off the Coast of Somalia, the Shared Awareness and Deconfliction mechanism and the Internationally Recommended Transit Corridor (Jacobsen & Larsen, 2019).

The decline in Somali piracy after 2012 gave way to other pressing developments at sea. Russia's annexation of the Crimean Peninsula in 2014 and the subsequent escalations between Russian border guards and the Ukrainian navy in the Kerch Strait signalled a re-emergence of the great power politics agenda and a growing relevance of maritime "hybrid" warfare. In the Global South, in the meantime, China has continued to actively pursue its claims of sovereignty in the contested waters of the South China Sea. As a direct causation of global warming, a growing number of maritime powers have now built up their military presence in the Arctic.

This narrative, it must be repeated, is perspectival. It tells one version of the origin of maritime security. A different perspective would observe that this narrative merely renames a very long custom of seignorial powers seeking to enforce their political, military and legal hegemony over oceanic space. Naval historians would see very little that is novel in the series of encounters and alliances that are forming under this version of maritime security's development. Crucially, its claim to novelty omits the very long intellectual history of order construction at sea. The first great period in modern political writing about the sea concerned debates in Europe between the great legal and strategic minds of the sixteenth and seventeenth century about its annexation, through *imperium* or *dominium*, and the possibility of creating rational rules to govern military and civilian maritime traffic. Some of the jurists who contributed their learned opinion even used the language of security. William Wellwood (1613), for instance, writing in his *Abridgement of Sea Lawes* in 1613 explicitly referred to fishermen safety and food security in an argument that sought for sovereign stewardship of the maritime space around Britain. Van Bynkershoek (1930), writing in 1737, sought to create buffer zones at sea that would supplement coastal land defences and keep neutral ports immune from war at sea (Ryan, 2019).

Moreover, in the twentieth century, the effects of the three Conventions on the Law of the Sea are not included in the national security perspective on maritime security. The third United Nations Convention on the Law of the Sea (UNCLOS III), for instance, resulted in the High Seas proximate to coastal states and islands being zoned and sub-zoned in order to bring a global rules-based system to the management of the maritime space, on the surface and on the seabed. The scientific, diplomatic and legal issues that arose during this Convention and its precursors reawakened political scientists and legal scholars to the problems of good order and security at sea, resulting in an unprecedented number of publications (Prescott, 1975; Sanger, 1986; Wenk, 1972). The Conventions additionally saw pollution and weapons of mass destruction added to the objects of security at sea that had occupied the minds of sixteenth and seventeenth-century European scholars; fishing rights, conservation, foreign vessels and warships, piracy and migration (Ryan, 2019).

UNCLOS III dramatically reanimated scholarship on the challenges of imposing a rational legal order at sea. The legal perspective addresses phenomena as diverse as piracy, hijacking and armed robbery (Kulyk, 2016); military uses of the sea (Ronzitti, 2016); maritime terrorism (Hamza, 2016); ship and port security (Kraska, 2016); smuggling and trafficking in arms, drugs and persons (Mallia, 2016; Papastavridis, 2016); the legal regime applicable to people at sea such as seafarers, pirates, stowaways, migrants and refugees (Papanicolopulu, 2018); marine pollution and environmental protection (Argüello, 2020; Harisson, 2017); and large-scale illegal fishing (Palma et al., 2010). Recently, the interest of international law scholars in maritime security has gained momentum, following the widespread media attention and growing number of cases before international courts concerning topics such as piracy and migration by sea. A prolific body of literature has examined, for instance, the international legal framework for countering piracy (Kraska, 2011), the legal constraints on the use of force against pirates (Murdoch & Guilfoyle, 2013; Proelss, 2014), as well as the international human rights law underpinning the arrest, detention and transfer of suspected pirates (Geiss & Petrig, 2011; Petrig, 2014). At the same time, maritime security has come to define the practices of coastal communities seeking to protect their traditional livelihoods and cultural heritage. For their part, environmentalists drew on the phrase as a means to conserve the oceanic flora and fauna (Germond, 2015, p. 15). Works addressing the migration and refugee crisis have focused on the tensions between security concerns and human rights law obligations (Klein, 2014), the securitisation, militarisation and criminalisation of international responses (Moreno-Lax & Papastavridis, 2017), or the contradictions between migration control policies and the application of international law (Mann, 2017). A discrete body of work on maritime security law has emerged as a "hybrid" subspecialty of international law in the borderland between various areas of legal studies (Kraska & Pedrozo, 2013, p. 2). This *corpus* has been growing since UNCLOS, clarifying, and expanding duties in safety of life and search and rescue conventions, refugee law, human rights law, labour law, criminal law and environmental law.

Too often the politics of the sea written by scholars from the Global North focuses on the restless exploits of Europeans and North Americans. Maritime security, as a narrative that arises from 9/11, is often found to be guilty of this. It needs to be said then, that long before *Al-Qaida*, it was newly decolonised states in the 1960s that advocated the most vociferously for UNCLOS III in the first place. Postcolonial states had been arguing for protections against commercial and military incursions by powerful northern Atlantic littoral states for decades (Ryan, 2013). In particular, South American and East African states were supportive of a regime that extended sovereign powers to protect their coastal waters and resources. A postcolonial narrative on maritime security can demonstrate how old colonial tensions resurface in the way new concepts like maritime security are interpreted and practiced. In important studies of the long history of

Introduction: Surveying the Seascape

efforts in Asia, South America and on the African continent to shape their proximate seas undertaken on the South China Sea (Odgaard, 2002), the Indian Ocean (Bateman, 2016), the Gulf of Guinea (Ali, 2015), the Black Sea (Sanders, 2009), or the South Atlantic (Vaz, 2015), maritime security attains an attachment to postcolonial political economy. China was one of the first states to transform its coastal seas into a "managed" blue economy. Japan has always been only too aware of the destructive power of the sea itself. Unlike European states, Japan's problematic of order at sea invokes tsunamis, earthquakes and the powerlessness of humankind in the face of climatic forces. Thus, there are different trajectories available to maritime security and these add to an origin story that foregrounds pollution, global warming, fish stock levels, transnational crime, maritime commerce, coastal community cultures and livelihoods, and many other everyday governance issues (Bennett et al., 2018; Bueger, 2015; Bueger & Edmunds, 2017; Germond, 2015). The defining aspect of the discourse associated with security governance practices is that it spreads our understanding of maritime security beyond rigid associations with war or legal regimes towards a more liquid rationale of risk management (Ryan, 2019). Security at sea can present us with a complex environment in which conventional and non-state maritime actors interact in non-linear configurations, decentralised structures and informal networks to manage a general condition of global turbulence. Bueger and Edmunds (2017) have suggested that maritime security comprises four characteristics: interconnectedness; transnationality; liminality; and its national and institutional cross-jurisdictionality. Political geographers and sympathetic scholars from IR adopt a spatial approach to maritime security to describe ocean space segmented into fungible domains, mapped according to routes and interests, and vigilantly patrolled (Cowen, 2010). Security arises where humans strive to make seaspace more homogenous, tangible and amenable to their interests (Lambach, 2021; Peters, 2020; Ryan, 2015).

The Structure of the Handbook

The most difficult question facing us as editors was how we were to organise the diversity of opinions that lay claim to the phrase maritime security? Reading the submissions, it became clear to us they were divisible into studies that describe the various *perspectives* that have emanated from maritime security, and studies that described the *practices and norms* that are emerging around it. We therefore decided to lightly partition our framing of maritime security into these two broad sections, the first which contains perspectives or approaches, and the second which is more empirical and contains the everyday politics of good order at sea. From conversations that unfold between authors within and between these sections, the Handbook presents its survey of the early twenty-first-century global seascape.

Part 1 – Perspectives

Contributors to the first section, on *perspectives*, demonstrate the variety of approaches available in the study of maritime security. Each perspective reveals itself to be different, yet connected, to other perspectives. From different epistemological positions, we are presented with a range of vantage points, each with its own version of maritime security. Although different expectations arise, there is agreement among nearly all the authors that the politics of the sea holds transformative possibilities. There is also agreement that ultimately what is at stake in maritime security is the future of planetary capitalism as it endures the dramatic effects of climate change, the rise of China, pandemics and chasmic global inequalities in wealth. All authors, from every perspective, also agree that the sea is at the centre of this turbulence. The sea is *the* political problem of the twenty-first century.

Perhaps, however, we suffer from presentism with regards to the sea, so long overlooked by the field of IR. Maybe the sea has always been at the centre of our politics? Certainly, Benjamin de Carvalho and Halvard Leira, in the opening chapter of the Handbook, would agree. Their chapter points to the pivotal role played by the sea in the evolution of European modernity. In what is certainly a theme running throughout numerous chapters, they show how public and private interests at sea together shaped the politics of land. Until the nineteenth century, de Carvalho and Leira observe, the seapower produced by these hybrid interests shaped the formation of states and empires. In Chapter 2, taking a near-historical perspective, Barry J. Ryan demonstrates how contemporary tension and cooperation between state and non-state actors at sea is embodied in the practices and norms we refer to as maritime security. Employing assemblage theory, and advocating a radically pluralist, critical epistemology, he traces a novel genesis for maritime security. It was born, he argues, on the night of 10 July 1985, in Auckland harbour, at 23:45, when the Greenpeace flagship, the *Rainbow Warrior,* was bombed. This terrorist attack by a state on a non-state actor reveals tensions in the 1980s that would eventually shape the politics forming around the post-Cold War oceanic environment.

Geoffrey Till, in Chapter 3, pursues the role of the state at sea, and examines the influence played by maritime security on traditional naval conceptions of seaspace. Till concurs to a certain extent with Ryan in the previous chapter. Both agree that maritime security has created novel maritime actors and spaces. Till is a classical realist and, as such, is dubious about the transformative potential of maritime security. Ultimately, according to him, "cooperation in maritime security, simply becomes another arena in which interstate competition is conducted" (Till, 2022, p. 46). His conclusion continues through into Chapter 4, from the vantage point of Ian Speller, who takes a geopolitical perspective. A geopolitical perspective sees maritime security as an element of a broader field of military action known as maritime strategy. His chapter places new seagoing practices and actors into a historical geostrategic context. For Speller, maritime security has altered traditional naval roles at sea by creating a "contested joint operating space" (Speller, 2022, p. 58). It has evolved maritime strategy and it has revolutionised maritime surveillance technologies. But for Speller, as for Till, the state will forever dominate the sea.

The author of Chapter 5 begs to differ. Rafael García Pérez is also aware of the ascendent position that seignorial navies enjoy in maritime space. In a chapter that seeks to identify and defend the liberalism that underwrites the project of maritime security, García Pérez argues that it represents a modern project. It is a project which seeks to govern maritime space, rather than allow it to be used as a chessboard for great power competition. Military competition will endure, but it will increasingly be deployed for policing purposes, to enforce international law through the international institutions of maritime security. Nonetheless, for so long as the persistence of sovereignty remains the "organising principle of maritime space", there will also persist "fundamental disagreements about the core content of an assumed public security good", according to James Sperling's incisive account of maritime governance in Chapter 6 (2022, p. 82). Whereas Sperling is led to conclude lamentably that the regime of maritime governance remains embryonic, Joanna Mossop's legal perspective, in Chapter 7, is more optimistic. For Mossop, UNCLOS is the legal instrument which holds the greatest possibility to bring governance to bear on the maritime sphere. As the foundation of governance, maritime law is evolving rapidly around maritime security practices. She argues that maritime security law has made two significant contributions to the project of governing the sea, namely "reducing interstate conflict in relation to maritime issues", and "a search for clear jurisdictional principles to allow states to respond to threats by non-state actors" (Mossop, 2022, p. 94).

Introduction: Surveying the Seascape

Juha A.Vuori, in Chapter 8, sets out a case for the constructivist perspective on maritime security. The constructivist methodology examines language to isolate and analyse the political import of emerging norms in a global society. Vuori views maritime security as a security continuum, where a feeling of general unease or tension bundles together several disparate problems and creates a linguistic field effect. Such is how, according to Vuori, piracy, terrorism, organised crime and migration are contrived together into one linguistic field in the norms that constitute maritime security. This occurred in the wake of an unease that circulated in the post-Cold War period, when the neat distinction between internal and external security was broken-down by seismic shifts in global political economy. Vuori calls for the desecuritisation of the maritime sphere, so that problems of order at sea might be taken from security discourse and returned to the realm of "normal" politics. One way to accomplish this might very well be to acknowledge that the sea has, since time immemorial, been surveyed from the perspective of the male gaze. In Chapter 9, Jane Freedman takes on the prevailing gendered construction of the sea, which she argues has seeped into the practices and norms of maritime security. In a harrowing account, she reveals the hidden violence experienced by women on their migratory journey across the Mediterranean. Freedman is also able to reveal gendered violence among pirate communities in Somalia to show that the referent object of maritime security ought to be the individual. And further, she insists, the project of good order at sea, if it is to be successful, needs to realise, "that these individuals are located within gendered social structures and hierarchies, which will in turn influence the ways in which they experience these security issues" (Freedman, 2022, p. 113). Jessica Larsen, in Chapter 10, proffers a methodology tailored to incorporate the perspective of human security and gender revealed by Jane Freedman. Larsen gives us the anthropological and ethnographic perspective to maritime security. Constructivist perspectives open maritime security to new voices, stories and meanings. Ethnography equivalates state with non-state, and foregrounds community and human relationships as sources of knowledge. The ethnographic perspective goes beyond language and examines the new norms of activity that emerge from maritime security. Larsen's method observes and re-cords the everyday "saying and doing, and the planning and producing" (Larsen, 2022, p. 117) that constitutes the practice of securing the sea. Hers is an argument for a cosmopolitan con-struction of maritime security, one that keeps the field open-ended and vibrant, attached to human needs and fears. Her chapter provides a technique to discover new understandings of security in the daily routines of men and women whose lives shape, and are shaped by, the contours of maritime politics.

How should a constructivist scholar, or an ethnographer, or anyone seeking to expand our understanding of the politics of the sea, address the prevailing positivist epistemology that pervades the study of maritime security? This is the question posed by Katja Lindskov Jacobsen, in Chapter 11. Drawing upon the case study of piracy statistics in the Gulf of Guinea, Jacobsen's critique exposes how "numbers serve as framing devices, contributing to the prioritisation of some issues over others" (Lindskov Jacobsen, 2022, p. 129). Numbers, she argues, are not apolitical, purely technical measuring devices; they are only the beginning of further political analysis that needs to examine the nuance and vitality of local relationships concealed within the universalism of incident reporting. The ethnographic perspective offered by Larsen and Jacobsen illustrates how maritime security is a local, historical and, above all, cultural phe-nomenon in the Global South. Claire Sutherland, in Chapter 12, agrees. She demonstrates another method to read the political cultures that shape our understanding of maritime security. Hers is a cultural representation perspective. The material aesthetics of the sea, she observes, is replete with the political history that constructs and maintains our notion of seaspace. Focusing on the materiality of sea culture, Sutherland's study demonstrates another dimension to the pragmatic constructivist perspective that is stretching and deepening our access to the ever-unfolding meanings of maritime security.

Part 2 – Practices and Norms

In the second section of the Handbook, we collated chapters that discuss the emerging *practices and norms* of maritime security, studies that enquire into how maritime security has shaped and is shaped by, contemporary oceanic politics. In this section, scholars utilise maritime security to make sense of, and to simultaneously present their version of good order to the agitated politics of seaspace. Each chapter surveys a critical aspect of maritime security. Simply put, each chapter asks how we imagine oceanic order can come about, for whom that order serves and what is required to make it happen. Moreover, they ask how humanity can itself institutionalise the ambiguity, the liquidity and the power of the sea. The sea as it lifts and pours and lives is materially antithetical to any mode of good order that emanates from a specifically land-based perspective. Maritime security is a mode of politics unto itself.

This point is reinforced by Anna Petrig in Chapter 13, where she details the extraordinary absence of human rights at sea. Petrig argues that maritime security is evolving a constabulary approach to order that is drawing on the traditional exceptionality of seaspace to skirt inter-national human rights law. Nowhere is this more evident than in what Mbembe (2019) might call the "necropolitics" of human migration. Susana Ferreira, in Chapter 14 argues that mi-gration poses a problem for the traditional rubric of security which can only be overcome by reconceptualising security around individual human rights and needs. Concurring with Petrig, she argues that territorial-based responses that use the language and practices of invasion, control, and repulsion to address this humanitarian crisis are failing. Ferreira advocates instead for a sea-based form of human security, that draws upon and develops international maritime legal instruments to protect lives at sea.

Robert McCabe, in Chapter 15, examines the way a distinctly sea-based form of con-stabulary cooperation formed around the phenomena classified under the rubric of maritime piracy. McCabe, together with Joshua Tallis, in Chapter 16, perceives maritime security as a response to "blue" criminality. Tallis's chapter explores the various manifestations of maritime terrorism and its linkages to organised crime. Maritime terrorism, in terms of its strategic aims and operational considerations differs substantially from the practices associated with terrorist groups on land and requires a specifically maritime-led response. Maritime security in this sense is a process of identifying sea-based vulnerabilities to global political economy, Rupert Herbert-Burns reports in Chapter 17 on the maritime energy sector. Oil, gas and petroleum shipping are common victims of the types of "blue" criminality documented by McCabe and Tallis, ac-cording to Herbert-Burns. The catastrophic environmental consequences of such attacks, the casualties, the commercial loss and the interstate tensions they produce, place this sector into the highest category of risk for the future of maritime security. In their contribution, Jeptoo Kipkech, Kristen Kuhn and Siraj Shaikh, in Chapter 18, outline how the future of maritime security will be increasingly defined around cyber security. Cyber-attacks obviate traditional weaponry used to perpetrate maritime crime, while extending and accentuating existing forms of martial power. In an open domain such as the sea there has always been a dependence on technology. The authors argue that the more complex this technology becomes, the more pressing the need to incorporate cyber security as a dimension of maritime domain awareness.

In Chapter 19, Lisa Otto introduces the structural factors that give rise to the blue crimes described in previous chapters. Maritime insecurity, for Otto, arises from the poor governance of natural resources ashore. In an examination of maritime insecurity in Nigerian waters, she

Introduction: Surveying the Seascape

portrays the interconnection between land and sea as a complex and expanding embodiment of criminality thriving in a field of corporate greed, extreme poverty, social exclusion, radical ideology and profound corruption. Cornelia E. Nauen and Simona T. Boschetti, in Chapter 20, examine illegal, unreported and unregulated fishing from a similar blue crime perspective. Nauen and Boschetti point to a nexus of poverty, food insecurity, gender discrimination and weak governance to account for illegal fishing practices. They conclude that a two-pronged, land–sea, approach is required to create a more integrated and inclusive form of maritime security; the provision of health, education and other social services; and a more robust enforcement of maritime laws by littoral states.

In Chapter 21, Christian Bouchard explores the problems faced by small island developing states in attaining a measure of maritime security. Facing the same problems as larger littoral states, small islands are surrounded by vast maritime domains, and often lack the capacity to address them. Generally, the more military-inclined conceptualisation of maritime security is irrelevant to these states for whom, as Bouchard notes, the sea is more immediately the source of economic and societal well-being. The survival of these states is not only threatened by man-made climate change but it is also dependent upon their capacity to "participate in comprehensive regional maritime security frameworks". Anja Menzel, in Chapter 22, delves deeper into the economic aspect of maritime security with the rise of blue economies. For Menzel, as for Bouchard, Otto, Nauen and Boschetti, socio-economic maritime development is in itself a mode of security, albeit one that is vulnerable to external shocks. Global warming is certainly increasing the potency of these shocks. Moreover, Menzel admits, blue economies often suffer from similar short-termism and social exclusion as their counterparts on land. Her conclusion echoes what many commentators in this Handbook have been observing; the oceans are an integrated space where good order is only possible with coordination and cooperation between diverse security and economic agents.

Eliseu Carbonell, in Chapter 23, adds further to a pluralist understanding of maritime security by apprehending it through a materialist perspective. In a further application of Claire Sutherland's visual and repsentational epistemology in Chapter 12, Carbonell introduces the importance of cultural heritage to the problem of good order at sea. He concludes that heritage is vital for the rejuvenation of communal identities in the face of globalisation. Identity forms a bond around coastal societies, which prevents them from fragmentation. Securing heritage therefore, seen in its most instrumentalist light, is a means towards supporting resilient coastal communities with a stakehold in good order at sea. It is a quite convincing argument.

Chapter 24, by Brendan Flynn also resonates with themes found in section one of the Handbook. Flynn's study of "hybrid actorness" at sea provides the reader with a contemporary empirical study of the intensity of relations between state and non-state actors at sea. Leira and de Carvalho in Chapter 1, Ryan in Chapter 2 and Till in Chapter 3, to mention a few, all observed that maritime security is shaped and maintained by relations between state and non-state actors. Flynn's study draws on rich examples to demonstrate the continuity of constant interaction between naval and non-governmental actors; sometimes in rivalry, sometimes in conflict and other times in cooperation. Eugenio Cusumano and Stefano Ruzza, in Chapter 25, zoom-in on one of the most pressing issues that arise when non-state actors work with state actors. A uniquely maritime legal disparity arises where small flag states, such as Panama, with whom a high percentage of vessels are registered, have neither the military capacity nor the diplomatic leverage to secure their fleet. In response, private military contractors hired to fill this gap, initially to combat piracy, have since embedded themselves as a new norm in maritime security, even on board the ships of militarily powerful states. The privatisation of force at sea was an issue in the time of Hugo Grotius, whose rise to fame occurred while defending violence perpetrated by the Dutch East India Company upon a Portuguese carrack (Ryan, 2013). However, its contemporary manifestation promises to dramatically alter the nature of maritime security, according to Cusumano and Ruzza.

The final five chapters in the Handbook describe new norms and practices in maritime security from a regional point of view. In Chapter 26, Gavin E. L. Hall and Mark Webber outline NATO's efforts to exert its influence over the increasingly contested space in the North Atlantic. In Chapter 27, Érico Esteves Duarte's study of the South Atlantic describes a maritime region that is profoundly insecure. Michela Ceccorulli, in Chapter 28, analyses the Mediterranean as a maritime region filled with tensions. She points to the tensions between environmental and human security phenomena and militarised statist responses to external actors' incursions to the region, refugees fleeing conflicts in the Middle East and North Africa and energy disputes. In Chapter 29, Kwa Chong Guan and Collin Koh, survey maritime security in southeast Asia. Taking a postcolonial perspective, Guan and Koh demonstrate the centrality of maritime boundary marking to the causes of insecurity in the region. Chris Rahman, in Chapter 30, focuses on the South China Sea, which he defines as the world's most politically contentious body of water. This representative sample of regional maritime politics is rounded off by Marianne Riddervold and Amund Botillen in Chapter 31. Physically emerging from global warming, this maritime region contains the potential to witness great power strategic cooperation in the field of maritime security, according to Riddervold and Botillen.

The Seascape of Maritime Security

This Handbook was compiled during the Covid-19 pandemic. At the time of writing this introduction, 4.55 million people have died of the virus. Each chapter was written under conditions of uncertainty, tragedy and lockdown. Indeed, we have decided to dedicate the book to Professor Sam Bateman, a veteran of oceanic politics, and Vale Commodore Professor at the University of Wollongong, Australia. Professor Bateman was preparing a chapter for this Handbook when he died in October 2020.

While the effects of the pandemic on global politics are still undecided, one can say with a measure of certainty that it has transformed humanity's understanding of threat. It has enlarged our sense of insecurity. A virus makes military power obsolete. It demands every community to act in concert against an existential danger which thrives in the closeness of human life. Undoubtedly, it has made us rethink the very nature of security. Many of the authors in the Handbook, writing during this historical caesura in the flow of global political economy, are preparing us for a world where security is a far more complex aspiration than traditionally conceived. At sea, threats come from all directions. The unpredictability of the climatic conditions, the degree of visibility, the pitch and roll of wave and even the seaworthiness of the craft constitute a security threat as much as the potential for piracy or hijack. Covid-19 has revealed to us that insecurity falls upon us differentially. It is not a universal blanket of evil; it is relative experience and some are more vulnerable than others. Maritime security, as a scholarly pursuit and as a practical application of politics, has similarly outgrown its military origins and, in a mark of its becoming, has enmeshed itself within the politics of everyday survival. It remains a project of good order at sea, but the means to this order, the various way of defining it and the forms it may take have become open to contestation. Pressing upon our shores is an ocean embodying the effects of climatic changes that will determine the fate of life on the planet. It is the hope of the editors, that in compiling this Handbook, we contribute to security thinking that engages with the panoply of phenomena that face us as a life form. While it may never have been friendly to us, humankind in all its restlessness must be more attentive than ever to the politics of the sea.

Introduction: Surveying the Seascape

Notes

1 The full quote is more political. "For all that has been said of the love that certain natures (on shore) have professed to feel for it, for all the celebrations it had been the object of in prose and song, the sea has never been friendly to man. At most it has been the accomplice of human restlessness and playing the part of dangerous abettor of worldwide ambitions" (Conrad, 1906, pp. 226–227).
2 We can trace to this time the first use of the term "maritime security", coined by Michael Pugh (1994) in a book that argued the UN needed to create a maritime peacekeeping naval force. However, Pugh's conception of the term differs substantially from its contemporary usage.

References

Ali, K. D. (2015). *Maritime Security Cooperation in the Gulf of Guinea: Prospects and Challenges*. Brill Nijhoff.

Argüello, G. (2020). *Marine Pollution, Shipping Waste and International Law*. Routledge.

Bateman, S. (2016). Maritime security governance in the Indian Ocean region. *Journal of the Indian Ocean Region, 12*(1), 5–23.

Bennett, N. J., Kaplan-Hallam, M., Augustine, G., Ban, N., Belhabib, D., Brueckner-Irwin, I., Charles, A., Couture, J., Eger, S., Fanning, L., Foley, P., Goodfellow, A. M., Greba, L., Gregr, E., Hall, D., Harper, S., Maloney, B., McIsaac, J., Ou, W., ... & Bailey, M. (2018). Coastal and Indigenous community access to marine resources and the ocean: A policy imperative for Canada. *Marine Policy, 87*, 186–193.

Bosilca, R. L., & Riddervold, M. (2019). EU-NATO inter-organizational relations in counter-piracy operations off the Horn of Africa. In J. Karlsrud and Y. Reykers (Eds.), *Multinational Rapid Response Mechanisms: From Institutional Proliferation to Institutional Exploitation* (pp. 155–171). Routledge.

Bueger, C. (2015). What is maritime security? *Marine Policy, 53*, 159–164.

Bueger, C., & Edmunds, T. (2017). Beyond seablindness: A new agenda for maritime security studies. *International Affairs, 93*(6), 1293–1311.

Buzan, B., & Hansen, L. (2009). *The Evolution of International Security Studies*. Cambridge University Press.

Conrad, J. (1906). *The Mirror of the Sea*. Harper and Brothers Publishers.

Cowen, D. (2010). A Geography of logistics: Market authority and the security of supply chains. *Annals of the Association of American Geographers, 100*(3), 600–620.

Feldt, L., Roell, P., & Thiele, R. D. (2013). Maritime security: Perspectives for a comprehensive approach. *ISPSW Strategy Series: Focus on Defense and International Security, April*(222), 1–25.

Freedman, J. (2022). Gender perspectives on maritime security. In R. L. Bosilca, S. Ferreira & B. J. Ryan (Eds.), *The Handbook of Maritime Security* (pp. XX–XX). Routledge.

Geiss, R., & Petrig, A. (2011). *Piracy and Armed Robbery at Sea: The Legal Framework for Counter-Piracy Operations in Somalia and the Gulf of Aden*. Oxford University Press.

Germond, B. (2015). *The Maritime Dimension of the European Security*. Palgrave Macmillan.

Hamza, R. (2016). Maritime terrorism and the illicit trafficking in arms. In M. Fitzmaurice, N. A. Gutiérrez & R. Hamza (Eds.), *The IMLI Manual of International Maritime Law, Volume III: Marine Environmental Law and Maritime Security Law* (pp. 414–427). Oxford University Press.

Harisson, J. (2017). *Saving the Oceans through Law: The International Legal Framework for the Protection of the Marine Environment*. Oxford University Press.

Jacobsen, L., & Larsen, J. (2019). Piracy studies coming of age: A window on the making of maritime intervention actors. *International Affairs, 95*(5), 1037–1054.

Klein, N. (2014). Maritime space. In J. Sperling (Ed.), *Handbook of Governance and Security* (pp. 388–407). Edward Elgar.

Kraska, J. (2011). Contemporary Maritime Piracy: International Law, Strategy, and Diplomacy at Sea: International Law, Strategy, and Diplomacy at Sea. ABC-CLIO.

Kraska, J. (2016). Ship and port facility security. In M. Fitzmaurice, N. A. Gutiérrez & R. Hamza (Eds.), *The IMLI Manual of International Maritime Law, Volume III: Marine Environmental Law and Maritime Security Law* (pp. 442–458). Oxford University Press.

Kraska, J., & Pedrozo, R. (2013). *International Maritime Security Law*. Koninklijke Brill NV.

Kraska, J., & Wilson, B. (2011, February 23). *Combating Piracy in International Waters*. World Policy. http://www.worldpolicy.org/blog/2011/02/23/combatting-piracy-international-waters

Kulyk, M. Z. (2016). Piracy, hijacking, and armed robbery against ships. In M. Fitzmaurice, N. A. Gutiérrez & R. Hamza (Eds.), *The IMLI Manual of International Maritime Law, Volume III: Marine Environmental Law and Maritime Security Law* (pp. 387–410). Oxford University Press.

Lambach, D. (2021). The functional territorialization of the high seas. *Marine Policy, 130*, 10.1016/j.marpol.2021.104579

Larsen, J. (2022). Anthropological and ethnographic perspectives on maritime security. In R. L. Bosilca, S. Ferreira & B. J. Ryan (Eds.), *The Handbook of Maritime Security* (pp. XX–XX) Routledge.

Lindskov Jacobsen, K. (2022). Maritime security and the politics of numbers: The case of Gulf of Guinea. In R. L. Bosilca, S. Ferreira & B. J. Ryan (Eds.), *The Handbook of Maritime Security.* (pp. XX–XX). Routledge.

Mallia, P. (2016). The human element of maritime crime: Stowaways, human trafficking, and migrant smuggling. In M. Fitzmaurice, N. A. Gutiérrez & R. Hamza (Eds.), *The IMLI Manual of International Maritime Law, Volume III: Marine Environmental Law and Maritime Security Law* (pp. 491–510). Oxford University Press.

Mann, I. (2017). *Humanity at Sea: Maritime Migration and the Foundations of International Law.* Cambridge University Press.

Mbembe, A. (2019). *Necropolitics* (Steven Corcoran, Trans.). Duke University Press.

Moreno-Lax, V., & Papastavridis, E. (2017). *"Boat Refugees" and Migrants at Sea: A Comprehensive Approach: Integrating Maritime Security with Human Rights.* Brill.

Mossop, J. (2022). Maritime security and the law of the sea. In R. L. Bosilca, S. Ferreira & B. J. Ryan (Eds.), *The Handbook of Maritime Security.* (pp. XX–XX). Routledge.

Murdoch, A., & Guilfoyle, D. (2013). Capture and disruption operations: The use of force in counter-piracy off Somalia. In D. Guilfoyle (Ed.), *Modern Piracy: Legal Challenges and Responses* (pp. 147–171). Edward Elgar.

Nunes, J. (2012). Reclaiming the political: Emancipation and critique in security studies, *Security Dialogue, 43*(4), 345–361.

Odgaard, L. (2002). *Maritime Security between China and Southeast Asia: Conflict and Cooperation in the Making of Regional Order.* Ashgate.

Palma, M. A., Tsamenyi, M., & Edeson, W. (2010). *Promoting Sustainable Fisheries: The International Legal and Policy Framework to Combat Illegal, Unreported, and Unregulated Fishing.* Martinus Nijhoff.

Papanicolopulu, I. (2018). *International Law and the Protection of People at Sea.* Oxford University Press.

Papastavridis, E. (2016). The illicit trafficking of drugs. In M. Fitzmaurice, N. A. Gutiérrez & R. Hamza (Eds.), *The IMLI Manual of International Maritime Law, Volume III: Marine Environmental Law and Maritime Security Law* (pp. 463–489). Oxford University Press.

Peters, K. (2020). The territories of governance: Unpacking the ontologies and geophilosophies of fixed to flexible ocean management, and beyond. *Philosophical Transactions of the Royal Society B. 375*, 1814. 10.1098/rstb.2019.0458

Petrig, A. (2014). *Human Rights and Law Enforcement at Sea: Arrest, Detention and Transfer of Piracy Suspects.* Martinus Nijhoff Publishers.

Prescott, J. R. V. (1975). *The Political Geography of the Oceans.* David & Charles.

Proelss, A. (2014). Piracy and the use of force. In P. Koutrakos & A. Skordas (Eds.), *The Law and Practice of Piracy at Sea: European and International Perspectives* (pp. 53–66). Hart Publishing.

Pugh, M. (Ed.). (1994). *Maritime Security and Peacekeeping: A Framework for United Nations Naval Operations.* Manchester University Press.

Ronzitti, N. (2016). Military uses of the Sea. In M. Fitzmaurice, N. A. Gutiérrez & R. Hamza (Eds.), *The IMLI Manual of International Maritime Law, Volume III: Marine Environmental Law and Maritime Security Law* (pp. 541–566). Oxford University Press.

Ryan, B. J. (2013). Zones and routes: Securing a western Indian Ocean. *Journal of the Indian Ocean Region, 9*(2), 173–188.

Ryan B. J. (2015). Security spheres: A phenomenology of maritime spatial practices. *Security Dialogue, 46*(6), 568–584.

Ryan, B. J. (2019). The disciplined sea: A history of maritime security and zonation. *International Affairs, 95*(5), 1055–1073.

Sanders, D. (2009). Maritime security in the Black Sea: Can regional solutions work? *European Security, 18*(2), 101–124.

Sanger, C. (1986). *Ordering the Oceans: The Making of the Law of the Sea.* Zed Books.

Introduction: Surveying the Seascape

Speller, I. (2022). Modern maritime strategy and naval warfare. In R. Bosilca, S. Ferreira & B. J. Ryan (Eds.), (pp. XX–XX). *The Handbook of Maritime Security*. Routledge.

Sperling, J. (2022) Global Maritime Security Governance. In Bosilca, R. L., Ferreira, S. & Ryan, B. J. (Eds.), The Handbook of Maritime Security. (pp. xx) Routledge.

Till, G. (1996). *Seapower: A Guide for the Twenty-First Century*. Routledge.

Till, G. (2022). Maritime strategy: "Good navies" and realism re-imagined. In R. Bosilca, S. Ferreira & B. J. Ryan (Eds.), (pp. XX–XX). *The Handbook of Maritime Security*. Routledge.

Ullman, R. H. (1983). Redefining security. *International Security, 8*(1), 129–153.

Van Bynkershoek, C. (1930) [1737]. *Quaestionum Juris Publici Libri Duo* (Vol .1). Photographic Reprint. Clarendon Press.

Vaz, A. C. (2015). Brazilian approaches to maritime security cooperation in IBSA and the prospects for an Atlantic-Indian maritime security governance. *Journal of the Indian Ocean Region, 11*(2), 170–183.

Wellwood, W. (1613). *An Abridgement of all Sea-Lawes*. London. Compiled and edited by Colin McKenzie 2011. http://maritimelawdigital.com/uploads/PDFs/Welwod-Sea_Laws.pdf accessed on October 25, 2018.

Wenk, E. Jr. (1972). *The Politics of the Ocean*. University of Washington Press.

Wolfers, A. (1952). "National security" as an ambiguous symbol. *Political Science Quarterly, 67*(4), 481–502.

World Commission on Environment and Development (WCED). (1987). [The Bruntdland Report], *Our Common Future*. Oxford University Press.

PART I

Perspectives on Maritime Security

PART I

Maritime Security

1

SEA POWER IN THE TRANSFORMATION OF STATES AND OVERSEAS EMPIRES (1500–1800)[1]

Benjamin de Carvalho and Halvard Leira

In the words of Charles Tilly, "war made the state and the state made war" (Tilly 1975, p. 42). Explicitly restricted to European states, to Tilly the wars in question were landed wars on the continent. However, it could well be argued that the pivotal moments in the development of the English polity between 1066 and 1940 occurred in 1588, when the Spanish Armada was beaten back at sea, and in 1757, when forces in the pay of the British East India Company beat a combined Indian and French force for the upper hand in the Indian subcontinent. Both of these battles relied on a capacity to project power on and across water, both of them involved violence-providers which were not strictly speaking state-controlled and both of them finally also were closely related to the English desire to establish a presence outside of the British Isles, to empire. The English trajectory has special traits, but it is not unique. In the Dutch case, the survival of the initial revolt against Habsburg rule depended on the *Watergeuzen* (the sea beggars) gaining control over the local sea and eventually also footholds on land, while the *Vereenigde Oostindische Compagnie* (VOC) was, for a time, probably the largest company in the world and vital cog in the machinery of the Dutch polity. Similar patterns, with variations in scale, can be found for the French, Danish and Swedish polities in the seventeenth and eighteenth centuries, while the Iberian polities followed somewhat different patterns, as did Russia, but all with an undeniable reliance on sea power and all with imperial traits. Here lies a number of paradoxes in the literature on state-formation.[2]

In this chapter, we want to explore these paradoxes and highlight some of the developmental processes which have been given too little attention (Kaspersen & Strandsbjerg, 2017). Lost in Tilly's pithy summary of fiscal-military (or "bellicist") state-formation in the early-modern period are three core features. *First*, many of the polities in question were not only states, and not primarily states, but also empires, more specifically overseas empires. Furthermore, other European states desperately wanted to become empires as well. Yet in spite of the centrality of empires during the period, it is the state that has been the main object of study of historical sociologists, and the backbone of most theorising about large-scale political change – at the expense of empires. Relying heavily on accounts of state formation from historical sociologists in the Weberian tradition such as Charles Tilly, the state is seen to have emerged victoriously from the Thirty Years War in 1648 at the expense of empires. While de Carvalho et al. (2011)

DOI: 10.4324/9781003001324-3

and Osiander (2001) have argued against this view, states emerged at the expense of empires, the story goes, and the key driver of change was warfare. As Charles Tilly famously posited, the experience and consequences of warfare were key drivers in the making of states, as well as in shaping and transforming them (Tilly, 1992).

The origins of this argument lie in foundational sociological accounts such as Max Weber, Otto Hintze and Norbert Elias and their work on the formation of states in early-modern Europe, which have been transposed to make sense of processes of state formation on other continents, and at different times. Following this body of work – what we may call the "bellicist model" of the origins of states – the model of the state spread across Europe at the expense of empires because states repeatedly defeated empires, and because rulers themselves came to recognise the superior qualities of the state organisation to handle not only the business of war but also the business of rule (Spruyt, 1996). Accounts of macro-historical change accounts for state formation and imperial decline, not the emergence of new (forms of) empires. The imperial part of the large-scale political transformation that changed the world between 1500 and 1800 only comes to light when taking into account the sea.

The desire for empire is for us a key background variable. The twin-processes of state-formation and empire-formation must be thought in conjunction, not only for each polity, but just as much for the relations between polities. In line with the original bellicist literature, we do argue for the close interrelationship between the formation of polities and the formation of the entire system of polities. This duality of state and overseas empire, combined with the system-wide interrelations between polities, ties in crucially with the next core feature; sea power.

Secondly, also largely ignored by Tilly, was all the warfighting which took place on water. Naval warfighting was far more costly than warfare on land, and if war did indeed make states (and empires), then surely naval wars must be given pride of place in the equation. The trajectories of state- and empire-formation of core European polities were quite simply crucially shaped by the polities' ability to raise and maintain sea power. The sea is, however, generally poorly understood, little researched and conspicuously absent from International Relations.

Finally, lost in the bellicist explanations of state formation are the hybrid roles of the polities in question. In many cases, the above-mentioned sea power (and its landed or hybrid component) was not under exclusive state control. A narrow focus on landed power can lead to a teleological reading of ever-tighter state control and capacity, while a broader view, which includes sea power, highlights processes were what we could anachronistically call "public-private partnerships" were drivers of processes where state control and capacity waxed and waned.

We hasten to say that the factors we highlight here have not been forgotten, and we draw extensively on the relevant literatures throughout the chapter. Nevertheless, we do argue that these different processes have not been fully synthesised before, and that bringing them together will demonstrate their interrelation. Although significantly less pointed than the original quote, we would suggest that in a process where the European polities forced themselves upon the world, and other parts of the world responded in kind, war remade polities, and polities and others remade war in the process.

Even though we believe strongly that the three above-mentioned factors are tightly interrelated, for analytical purposes the chapter deals with them in partial separation. The first section briefly lays out how the striving of polities to become and remain empires relates to their processes of state-formation and the key role of the sea. The second section turns to sea power, laying out how the building, maintenance and projection of naval power was a key driver in processes of both state- and empire-formation. The third and final section explores the fuzzy boundaries of states, empires and sea power, by looking specifically at the hybrid forms of "non-state" and "partial-state" power allowing for state- and empire-formation at sea. The discussion here is centred upon the practice of privateering.

Polities, States and Empires

If there has been such a thing as a "normal" ideal-typical polity-form in recorded history, it is probably the empire (Burbank & Cooper, 2010). Even the early-modern processes which were later dubbed as "state-building" were steeped in imperial imagery and language (Pagden, 1995). Throughout the early modern period, a key player in inter-polity affairs in Europe was the Holy Roman Empire, and monarchs eager to reject the emperor's claims to superiority, were all too eager to stress the imperial qualities of their own polities. As the English Act in Restraint of Appeals put it: "This Realm of England is an Empire, and so hath been accepted in the world [...]" (24 Hen VIII c. 12).

While religious fragmentation was a key factor in strengthening polities in Europe, what really drove the proliferation of empires in the plural was the overseas expansion starting in the late fifteenth century. The Treaty of Tordesillas (1494) in principle divided the world between the Spanish and the Portuguese. Where the Treaty of Tordesillas established Iberian empire through religious papal authority, a more secular conception of empire based on the emerging law of nations (*ex iure gentium*) provided challengers such as the French, Dutch and English with legal backing for their ambitions to trade freely where legal claims grounded in papal authority were not backed by effective occupation. As pointed out in the introduction to this volume, the sea could be seen both in terms of *dominum* and of *imperium*. Where the Spanish and Portuguese wanted *dominum* over the sea (as did later empires as soon as they believed they had the power to sustain it), the challengers relied on *imperium* at sea (Benton, 2009).

Unless established on previously uninhabited land, terrestrial force has had to deal with someone claiming some sort of right to the land. Although the early European overseas empires tried to establish similar rights to the ocean, these were never enforceable. The sea thus introduces a qualitatively different variable into the statist accounts. While one might rightfully argue that ocean-going force was typically launched from some specific piece of land, it was nevertheless typically utilised in a space above and beyond state control, in a space where there would be inter-polity governance, hegemonic governance or no governance at all. It follows from this that whereas terrestrial private force mattered as much as, or more than, maritime private force for the emergence of states, maritime private force is of particular importance for the emergence and character of empires and "the international" system. This is illustrated masterfully in Glete's (2000) discussion of the transformation in naval warfare between 1500 and 1650, and how it related to not only state-building but to systemic interaction within and outside of Europe.

The French, British and Dutch in short did not become empires by fighting one another (or the Spanish and the Portuguese) at Barfleur and La Hougue or Blenheim, they became empires largely by overseas interactions, some initiated from the centre, others in the peripheries; some by the polities themselves, others by other agents. Likewise, even if polities like Scotland and Courland failed to create overseas empires (and failed to sustain themselves as independent polities) and the Danish and Swedish overseas ventures were extremely modest in comparison to the Spanish, Portuguese, French, English and Dutch, there is no denying the aspirations of these polities. At the same time as they were conducting what we would analytically call state-formation, partially by bumping into one another in Europe, they were conducting what we would analytically call empire-building, by bumping into one another across the globe. And the key vehicle, for preying on already established empires, for establishing an imperial presence overseas, and for protecting imperial bridgeheads after they had been established, was sea power.

Sea power and Polity-Formation

Making sense of the emergence and consolidation of European empires beyond European shores from 1500 onwards requires us to take into account the sea and seaborne violence, but the *prima facie* case for this when it comes to making sense of state formation in Europe is weaker. Yet, just as the sea was crucial to the development of both, there are equally glaring omissions of this perspective in both cases in the dominant accounts of large-scale political transformation (de Carvalho & Leira, 2022c). In fact, there seems to be a convention among historical sociologists to disregard the sea and seaborne actors altogether when seeking to make sense of the processes which lead to the emergence and consolidation of what is often called the "modern state". In spite of having played a central role in Europe's drive for overseas imperial possessions, the sea itself rarely figures as a variable in accounts of large-scale political transformation (e.g., state formation, empire building). While the sea figures as a background to these processes, few studies have taken on the fact that making sense of how the sea contributed to these processes requires us to reconceptualise much of our commonplace theoretical ballast (de Carvalho & Leira, 2022b).

State Formation

Few theoretical statements on state formation take the sea into account, and if sea power figures into the equation it is either treated *as* land power, its extension, or, seen as operating along the same logic (Tilly, 1992, p. 94). For the most part, it is ignored or obliterated as a transport leg. This is not to say that sea power does not figure in accounts of international conflicts, for instance, but on the whole the sea is seen as an extension of land, and sea power and auxiliary of or conduit for land power (Steinberg, 2001). One notable exception to this is Carl Schmitt, who tackles the land/sea divide head-on in his writings on the long-term trends in state formation and civilisation. The key element to Schmitt in explaining large-scale transformation and the emergence of the global order of modernity was the extent to which humans managed to master the sea (Schmitt, 2006, 2015). And while there is no shortage of historical studies of sea power, these have tended to take as their starting point the emergence of state navies in the mid-1600s (Blakemore, 2013), long after the emergence of the first colonial polities.

Staring at the sea in IR is not an innocuous act, but one that fundamentally challenges dominant ontologies and accounts of political transformation in the field. As the historian Jan Glete has emphasised, in order to make sense of the importance of the sea, we must relax our understanding of the fiscal-military model of state-formation and understand the role of ruling state elites more in terms of their ability to *organise* than to rule (Glete, 2002). Doing so makes it possible to grasp not only how the state emerged, but how it transformed from an early site of political struggle to an organisation able to harness sophisticated means of violence in its pursuit of capital (Glete, 2010). Doing so also opens our empirical focus to understanding how states sought to address different organisational challenges, and how these tasks, in turn, contributed to the introduction and further development of increasingly complex forms of bureaucratic management. This is especially true in the case of the sea, for as Glete convincingly argued, mobilising means of seaborne violence was inherently different from mobilising armies on land (Glete, 2000). In fact, where rulers could relatively easily mobilise armies of mercenaries on short notice – given sufficient capital – seaborne violence required years, if not decades, of planning. The construction and maintenance of ships required organising the timber trade, and ships required trained military forces able to navigate. In consequence, organising war at sea had lasting implications for the emergence of state bureaucracies to the extent that war on land simply did not have.

A telling example is the extent to which the Republic of Venice – by most seen as a city with a large navy – in fact relied on vast adjacent territories for their timber supply, and how organising this process largely led to the development and political transformation of the Republic. Karl Appuhn (2009) has shown Venice's need for lumber drove the Venetian Republic to develop new and innovative techniques for governing nature, changing in the process the relationship between the Republic and the space surrounding it. Through the development and implementation of novel techniques of governance and administration of forests, Venice became "inextricably entwined with its mainland state" developing from an insular city state to a regional state (Appuhn, 2009, pp. 1–19). As Appuhn (2009, p. 158) points out, "the combination of new reserves [of lumber], new laws, and the ever-expanding geographical scope of Venice's reach for critical forest resources irrevocably altered the manner in which Venetian officials conducted forest inspections". In showing how this change took place, Appuhn problematises political space and the techniques to govern it, showing how these changes happened step by step and how they were the result of processes of gradual imposition and resistance. In fact, he argues that between 1471 and 1548 the piecemeal imposition of new techniques and modes of administration on the governance of forests and the "imposition of laws restricting local practices" (p. 142) eventually gave these innovations, and Venice's rule over forests far beyond its centre, a taken-for-granted quality. Measures that in 1471 were contentious and required long and detailed elaborations and justifications required none in 1548: "they simply took them for granted" (Appuhn, 2009, pp. 146–142).

The current state of research in Historical Sociology and International Relations does not account in detail for the extent to which the development of state navies, which took place throughout Europe between 1650 and 1800, influenced state-building. Yet, it requires no stretch of the imagination to understand that the development of navies and the globalisation of the world – both economically and politically through European imperialism – required the mobilisation of large organisational resources from all states in question, and played a central role in the development of permanent bureaucracies aimed at dealing with the large-scale and long-term provision of resources necessary to such endeavours.

Empire Formation

Just as studies of large-scale political transformation have remained largely on land, they have also on the whole remained surprisingly state-centrist. As a result, these accounts shy away from analysing the means through which states became builders of overseas empires, as understanding the connection between states and colonialism requires sustained attention to sea power. For as empires have been the most common polity form throughout history, the sea has been central to most long-distance travel and transportation of goods.

Thus, while we assume that empires emerged through the deployment of European state power, we have few cues as to how this power was deployed, and what type of power this was. As a consequence, while it is well known that European powers from the Iberian Peninsula to Scandinavia established overseas empires, we have little knowledge as to *how* these empires were built and transformed more concretely. We address this below, in our discussion of modes of power at sea and privateering. Making sense of this large-scale political transformation of the world requires us to take into account the sea and different forms of maritime predation and trade to an extent that the literature thus far has evaded. While it is not our claim that privateering was *the* most important factor in explaining these developments, it was important enough that an account of the emergence, consolidation and demise of colonial empires in the Americas requires sustained attention to the institution of privateering and its effects at different times and places.

As it stands, the literature on the emergence of empires, while capturing important workings of empires, still cannot fully account for how European colonial empires emerged in the first place. The coercion-based type of explanation overlooks the fact that imperial agents were for the most part outnumbered, while a focus on process, prevalent in much of the global history literature, tends to overlook the coercive element of empire-building. It also tends to overlook the interactions between centre and peripheries, and how different types of interaction resulted in different features of empires.

The act of establishing overseas holdings required primarily seagoing capacity, but as soon as more than one polity got involved, sea power was needed to protect and expand holdings and trade, or to fight one's way into territory and trade. Sea power was needed not only for fighting set-piece battles navy *versus* navy, but for protecting trade against privateering in wartime and pirates in times of relative peace (Earle, 2003). And even though there would be ebbs and flows in the prioritising of sea power, there was no questioning its relative importance. During the latter half of the eighteenth century, it is for instance estimated that the shore establishment of the British navy was "at least in terms of physical plant, finance and labour force, by far the largest industrial unit in eighteenth-century Britain and, probably, in the entire western world" (Scott, 1992, p. 454).

Hybrid Power at Sea: The Different Guises of Privateering

As noted above, engaging in seaborne violence was bound to take its economic toll on any state coffer. To some states, the spoils of early imperialism could sustain further explorations and increasing political control over dominions far from their shores. This was especially true of Portugal and Spain, who by early papal edicts were legitimised in their extra-European seaborne adventures to an extent that was never the case for northern European powers. Unable and unwilling to invest in the seaborne capabilities required to match their southern counterparts, these states, most notably France, England and the Netherlands, overcame their disadvantages through organising their seaborne efforts differently. Most notably, these efforts were less driven by states, but by "non-state" parties: aristocratic families with important coastal presence in England, the Huguenots, largely based in the Atlantic coast, in France, and the Protestant warring party in the Netherlands. Nevertheless, the process had strong implications for further state-building and political transformation in all three countries. Most notably, though, was their early adoption of organisational modes only indirectly controlled by the state, namely the practice of privateering. Our reason for delving into and dwelling on privateering here is not that it was necessarily the most important mode of seaborne violence during the period (Phillips & Sharman, 2020), but that it is the one that most explicitly shows how acknowledging the role of the sea requires us to rethink taken-for-granted concepts and theories, and reassess extant explanations of large-scale political change in light of the sea.

For the purpose of this text, privateering can be broadly defined as maritime predation authorised by someone with recognised legitimate (sovereign) authority. Despite being a common violent practice for around 600 years (from the thirteenth century to 1856), what we here refer to as "privateering" is a woefully little-understood phenomenon. While "piracy" has been studied and celebrated in academe as well as in popular culture, privateering, which was a much more significant phenomenon, has been left largely alone, and even presumed to be simply a variety of the former; namely "legalised piracy". While the term "privateer" and "private-man-of-war" are terms which emerge only in the late 1600s (Pennell, 2001, p. 70), the activity and legal foundation of the activity dates to the thirteenth century and the custom of reprisal.

Privateering is also of particular interest given that it is the most thoroughly institutionalised form of private violence. The practice was for several centuries couched in legal terms of rights and privileges and provided one of the foundations for Grotius' theorising of early international law. Privateering was also at times part of the ideological struggles over the construction of the ocean. Could the oceans be divided in the same way as territory, sanctioned by religious credo, or were the oceans in principle free? Could neutrals carry goods to belligerents, or were such goods generally contraband? When challenging existing notions of legality and legitimate authority at sea, states would often turn to privateers. By shadowing into piracy, privateering enabled plausible deniability by the challenging states, while the very act of issuing privateering-commissions undercut claims to supreme political and/or religious authority.

At any rate, the rules and practices of privateering remained relatively stable until the end of the sixteenth century, as the activity of French and English seafarers was still on the whole contained to the seas surrounding Europe. Thus, both the activity of privateering and the rules governing it survived the discovery of the New World, and even the first voyages beyond European waters by Iberian powers. What came to dramatically change this was thus not the fact that the European horizon had opened up, but the fact that powers who had been denied taking part in the spoils of colonial expansion by the Treaty of Tordesillas came to demand their share of it. In so doing, they were met with strong resistance from both Spanish and Portuguese ships. As French, English and Dutch seafarers ventured beyond European waters, the practices of privateering would change dramatically, even though the medieval rules governing it remained relatively unchanged (de Carvalho & Leira, 2022a).

One of the reasons why privateering – after having been a relatively stable practice in European waters – came to change in character was that the practice no longer worked in favour of consolidating princes or "states". Until the 1550s, as Cheyette (1970) has emphasised, the increasing rulemaking and regulation of "privateering" worked in favour of monarchs. It not only gave monarchs authority over the seas, but it also worked to increase their projection of sovereignty on land. Now, this had changed. France, England and the Dutch – the three European powers with arguably the most experience in "privateering" – had been excluded from the New World by the Treaty of Tordesillas. In order to make it into distant waters, relatively weak financially after prolonged religious conflicts, these states turned to privateering. Huguenot privateering was temporally the first, but it lasted for a shorter time, and was different by virtue of being part of a civil war as well as the broader struggle (de Carvalho & Paras, 2015). However, the Huguenots were crucial both in providing harbour for Dutch and English privateers, and, perhaps even more importantly, teaching them the trade about sailing and plundering on the high seas and in the Americas.

Seaborne violence was thus more prevalent than what is assumed in both International Relations and Historical Sociology, albeit in a different form than through national navies and pirates. In fact, throughout the period c. 1500–1750 privateering ships outnumbered pirates dramatically (Lunsford, 2005), and proper national navies were not established before the late seventeenth century. Until then and beyond most of the activity at sea, including those of states, took the shape of some form of cooperative venture with private merchants and shipowners; often through the guise of privateering.

Although privateering took different forms and fluctuated over time both in scale and impact, there are discernable patterns and peaks. From the mid-1500s and into the mid-1600s, privateering was an important tool to anti-Iberian powers. This was obvious across the board. The Huguenot stronghold of La Rochelle served as base for Huguenot privateers, while the Dutch *Watergeuzen* were key to the Dutch Revolt. Private ships drove the initial overseas explorations of English, French and Dutch alike. This included poaching Iberian prizes, but also a push for setting up trading posts (Emmer & Gastra, 1996). Dutch privateers were for instance central in capturing São Salvador da Bahia in 1624 from the Portuguese in Brazil (de Carvalho, 2015), and a key means to gaining control over the Indian Ocean.

The mid-1600s saw the emergence of Caribbean buccaneering, licensed by English and French governors in Jamaica and Tortuga. In 1662, Jamaica alone counted 1800 full-time buccaneers (Starkey & McCarthy, 2014). These attacked Spanish shipping and settlements, mounting effective defenses against Spanish aggression (Zahedieh, 1990). And although privateering based in the colonies did not bring in any direct revenue to European powers, it still served their interests by weakening Spanish control and generating capital for developing plantations and investments in trade.

In the 1690s, privateering of the *guerre de course* became the main naval strategy of the French against the Anglo-Dutch alliance (Symcox, 1974). Privateering was also central to England fighting against French and Spanish properties overseas during the War of Austrian Succession (1744–1748) and for both sides during the Fourth Anglo-Dutch War (1780–1781). Finally, privateering became a tool of revolutionaries in the American War of Independence (1775–1783) against British shipping, as well as by the USA in the War of 1812 (Kert, 1997). From there, privateering spread south, the *corsarios insurgentes* licensed by South and Central American revolutionaries counting over 1,000 ships (1813–1830) (Head, 2008).

During the seventeenth century, privateering played a more ambiguous role than previously, developing and consolidating overseas colonies through "inter-peripheral" trade and defense (Mulich, 2013). When English, French and Dutch established trading companies, most of the funding and necessary knowledge came from privateering (Andrews, 1984). And when "exporting" their "home" institutions, the first core institutions which were replicated in imperial peripheries tended to be admiralty courts and prize courts. By the time the practice was outlawed in 1856, northern European empires had already established their control over large overseas empires, largely lost it in the Atlantic, and the second wave of colonisation – driven by the states themselves this time – was well under way.

Privateering allowed polities many advantages over building up their own navies. Firstly, it was relatively inexpensive, as the main burden lay in private hands. Secondly, it allowed these endeavours to venture into forbidden seas – how else were they to capture Iberian prizes? Thirdly, it allowed these states plausible deniability, as the state was not directly involved. Finally, and perhaps most importantly, in spite of all this, it was controlled by the state, albeit at a distance. Thus, privateering became the principal means of challenging the Catholic construction of the sea as a different kind of space, where control was granted by the Pope. Privateering was the weapon of choice of the challengers and came to reinforce both their ambitions for overseas influence, their penetration of the colonial trade, and their own colonial ambitions.

Conclusion

Understanding modes of seaborne violence and their historical importance in the great political transformation of states and empires forces upon us a reconceptualisation of theories of political transformation. For, while early modern "inward-looking" states turning to overseas empire-

Seapower, states and overseas empires

building may seem paradoxical, on the face of it, states introducing "non-state" practices – privateering – as their main maritime strategy also defies key accounts of state monopolisation of violence (Thomson, 1994). Understanding this requires us to rethink the role of private agents and the way they interacted with states and impacted upon them, but also to critically assess key dichotomies which have informed our understanding of political transformation.

Most of our knowledge of macro-political transformation is predicated on the transition from one category to another. In fact, much of the scholarly debate underpinned by these dichotomies have been a matter of determining the question of whether developments or actors belonged to one category or another, or when the importance shifted from one category to another or a combination of both, as in the case of capital-intensive and coercive-intensive strategies posited by Charles Tilly (1992). As a case in point stands Janice Thomson's (1994) influential argument that the rise of the sovereign state happened with the elimination of private violence, and that states, willingly or unwillingly, had to address the "problem" of private force, and in the end eliminate it. Modern political structures are seen to have risen against the private notion of political authority which International Relations associates with the Middle Ages and of the ashes of private violence, so to speak. Yet, recent scholarship has sought to go beyond these dichotomies in analysing macro-political change. Benton (2009) and Trim & Fissel (2006) have called for rethinking the spatial dimension of violence through focusing on amphibious power; Kathleen Davis (2012) has recently called for doing away with the key temporal division between the "medieval" and the "modern". In a promising move, Patricia Owens, for instance, has drawn attention to the fact that the distinction between private and public violence has never been "solidly fixed" (Owens, 2010, p. 18). And finally, Andrews (1984) has pointed to the extent to which both coercion and capital coexisted in early modern seaborne enterprises. Staring at the sea thus forces us to critically reassess the dichotomous modes of theorising underlying much of the (landed) fields of IR and historical sociology.

Notes

1 The research for this chapter was financed by Research Council Norway, under the project EMPRISE, project number 262657.
2 Our exploration in this chapter is made in contrast to an existing Eurocentric literature. We aspire to a more global account of polity-formation, where agency was widely dispersed and there was significant pushback against European incursions. However, the explicit focus on naval force here necessitates a continued focus on European polities. Even though other actors challenged European supremacy, in both the Indian Ocean and the Mediterranean, the overall story of the Early Modern period is one of growing European naval supremacy.

References

Andrews, K. (1984). *Trade, Plunder and Settlement*. Cambridge University Press.
Appuhn, K. (2009). *A Forest on the Sea: Environmental Expertise in Renaissance Venice*. Johns Hopkins University Press.
Benton, L. (2009). *A Search for Sovereignty: Law and Geography in European Empires, 1400–1900*. Cambridge University Press.
Blakemore, R. J. (2013). British Imperial Expansion and the Transformation of Violence at Sea, 1600–1850: Introduction. *International Journal of Maritime History, 25*(2), 143–145.
Burbank, J., & Cooper, F. (2010). *Empires in World History: Power and the Politics of Difference*. Princeton University Press.
Cheyette, F. L. (1970). The Pirates and the Sovereign. *Speculum, 45*(1), 40–68.
Davis, K. (2012). *Periodization and Sovereignty: How Ideas of Feudalism and Secularization Govern the Politics of Time*. University of Pennsylvania Press.

de Carvalho, B. (2015). The Modern Roots of Feudal Empires: The Donatary Captaincies and the Legacies of the Portuguese Empire in Brazil. In S. Halperin & R. Palan (Eds.), *Legacies of Empire: Imperial Roots of the Contemporary Global Order* (pp. 128–148). Cambridge University Press.

de Carvalho, B., & Leira, H. (2022a). Challenging Order at Sea: The Early Practice of Privateering. In B. de Carvalho & H. Leira (Eds.), *The Sea and International Relations*. Manchester University Press.

de Carvalho, B., & Leira, H. (2022b). Introduction: Staring at the Sea. In B. de Carvalho & H. Leira, (Eds.), *The Sea and International Relations*. Manchester University Press.

de Carvalho, B., & Leira, H. (Eds.). (2022c). *The Sea and International Relations*. Manchester University Press.

de Carvalho, B., Leira, H., & Hobson, J. M. (2011). The Big Bangs of IR: The Myths That Your Teachers Still Tell You about 1648 and 1919. *Millennium – Journal of International Studies, 39*(3), 735–758.

de Carvalho, B., & Paras, A. (2015). Sovereignty and Solidarity: Moral Obligation, Confessional England, and the Huguenots. *The International History Review, 37*(1), 1–21.

Earle, P. (2003). *The Pirate Wars*. Thomas Dunne Books.

Emmer, P., & F. Gastra (Eds.). (1996). *The Organization of Interoceanic Trade in European Expansion*. Ashgate.

Glete, J. (2000). *Warfare at Sea, 1500–1650. Maritime Conflicts and the Transformation of Europe*. Routledge.

Glete, J. (2002). *War and the State in Early Modern Europe: Spain, the Dutch Republic and Sweden as Fiscal-Military States, 1500–1600*. Routledge.

Glete, J. (2010). *Swedish Naval Administration 1521–1721: Resource Flows and Organizational Capabilities*. Brill.

Head, D. (2008). A Different Kind of Maritime Predation: South American Privateering from Baltimore, 1816–1820. *International Journal of Naval History, 7*(2). https://www.ijnhonline.org/wp-content/uploads/2012/01/Head.pdf

Kaspersen, L. B., & Strandsbjerg, J. (Eds.). (2017). *Does War Make States? Investigations of Charles Tilly's Historical Sociology*. Cambridge University Press.

Kert, F. M. (1997). *Privateering and Naval Prize in Atlantic Canada in the War of 1812*. Research in Maritime History, no. 11. St John's Newfoundland International Maritime Economic History Association.

Lunsford, V. (2005). *Piracy and Privateering in the Golden Age Netherlands*. Palgrave.

Mulich, J. (2013). Microregionalism and Intercolonial Relations: The Case of the Danish West Indies, 1730–1830. *Journal of Global History, 8*(1), 72–94.

Osiander, A. (2001). Sovereignty, International Relations, and the Westphalian Myth. *International Organization, 55*(2), 251–287.

Owens, P. (2010). Distinctions, Distinctions: 'Public' and 'Private' Force?. In Colas, A. & Mabee, B., (eds). Mercenaries, Pirates, Bandits and Empires, 15–32, London: Hurst & Company.

Pagden, A. (1995). *Lords of All the World. Ideologies of Empire in Spain, Britain and France c.1500–c.1800*. Yale University Press.

Pennell, C. R. (2001). *Bandits at Sea: A Pirates Reader*. New York University Press.

Phillips, A., & Sharman, J. C. (2020). *Outsourcing Empire: How Company-States Made the Modern World*. Princeton University Press.

Schmitt, C. (2006). *The Nomos of the Earth*. Telos Press.

Schmitt, C. (2015). *Land and Sea*. Telos Press.

Scott, H. M. (1992). Review Article: The Second 'Hundred Years War', 1689-1815, *The Historical Journal, 35*(2), 443–469.

Spruyt, H. (1996). *The Sovereign State and Its Competitors: An Analysis of Systems Change*. Princeton University Press.

Starkey, D. J., & McCarthy, M. (2014). A Persistent Phenomenon Private Prize-Taking in the British Atlantic World, c. 1540–1856. In S. E. Amirell & L. Müller, (Eds.), *Maritime Violence and State-Formation in Global Historical Perspective*. Palgrave Macmillan. 10.1057/9781137352866_7

Steinberg, P. E. (2001). *The Social Construction of the Ocean*. Cambridge University Press.

Symcox, G. (1974). *The Crisis of French Sea Power, 1688–1697*. Springer.

Thomson, J. E. (1994). *Mercenaries, Pirates, and Sovereigns: State-Building and Extraterritorial Violence in Early Modern Europe*. Princeton University Press.

Tilly, C. (Ed.). (1975). *The Formation of National States in Western Europe*. Princeton University Press.

Tilly, C. (1992). *Coercion, Capital, and European States, AD 990–1992*. Blackwell.

Trim, D. J. B., & Fissel, M. C. (Eds.). (2006). *Amphibious Warfare 1000–1700*. Brill.

Zahedieh, N. (1990). A Frugal, Prudential and Hopeful Trade. Privateering in Jamaica, 1655–89. *The Journal of Imperial and Commonwealth History, 18*(2), 145–168.

2

MARITIME SECURITY IN A CRITICAL CONTEXT[1]

Barry J. Ryan

Being such an expansive and intensive constellation of parts, it is impossible to define where maritime security begins and where it ends. When we look at the fish on our dinner plate, we are encountering maritime security. When fighter jets take off from aircraft carriers to launch attacks on cities in Iraq or Syria, we are also encountering maritime security. The electricity that lights our homes; the internet that connects us to the World Wide Web; armed pirates aboard container ships; starving fishing communities; the drowned bodies of asylum seekers: all inhabit the sphere of maritime security. Maritime security is moreover a term that emerged during a particular period of accelerated globalisation. So, not only does the term embody the political economy of the maritime planet, but also the kinetic relationships between sea, land and air-space. To be asked to contextualise, to weave together into one vestment, this nexus of social, political, commercial, legal and military activity is certainly challenging. Indeed, the complexity of the phenomenon lends itself to being categorised as what Tim Morton (2013) might term a "hyperobject". This is the term Morton gives to constellations so multidimensional and unruly that they remain beyond human empirical capacity.

That said, these very attributes of maritime security tend to make it very amenable to a critical enquiry. By its very nature, maritime security is a set of practices that are only accessible through perspectival interpretation. In other words, how we experience the sea determines our understanding of what should be secured, or not secured. While the term "maritime security" may be vague and conceptual, the context around which these perspectival interrelationships contend is certainly very real. The practices of maritime security are treated in this chapter as a set of entangled interrelationships of things and humans that are simultaneously productive and destructive. In other words, maritime security is a relational concept, it concerns relationships and hence generates change by bringing these things and humans together. This also means that maritime security is unstable, perpetually evolving and unpredictable. Its context can be found in the distribution of forces that shape and reshape it. Accordingly, the approach I take assumes the *context* of maritime security is discernible in the historical set of power relations that first gave birth to it. Context is to be found where opposing tendencies contest and give rise to the definition of a novel problem. I seek it in an event that is foundational to all subsequent events within the meaning of maritime security. Thus, in this chapter I shall follow the directions given by Deleuze and Guattari (2011, p. 33) who observe the "task of philosophy, when it creates concepts, entities, is always to extract an event from things and beings".

DOI: 10.4324/9781003001324-4

The presence of a contestation is key to creating the context from which an event happens. The noun "context" translates from the Latin *contextus*, a joining together. It originally derived from the past participle of *contextere*, to weave together. This directs us to seek for the contemporary origins of maritime security where opposing forces first assemble. It should be pointed out that the verb "contest" descends from the latin *contestari*, to call to witness, to bring action. In order then to understand the context of maritime security, we need to find a political event wherein the problem is first testified, when witnessing is enacted. This irruption, or discontinuity, when found in the normal flows of global politics, signals that a new set of relations, different from the past, has emerged.

Regarding maritime security, I argue that maritime politics had always been constructed as a state-centric problematic. With a few exceptions, the historiography of the sea is a record of state-to-state relations. One can struggle to find a maritime history written in the nineteenth or twentieth century from the perspective of nonstate actors. (We turn to literature for that vantage point.) For centuries the state system has dominated the way humans encounter oceanic space. The irruption from which we might deduce a context to maritime security emerges when this construction alters, and the perspectives of new actors, with contrary visions of the good life, become politically attested. It occurs when the sea ceases being solely a performance of interstate relations and becomes something radically more. With this in mind, I propose that the sinking of the Rainbow Warrior in 1985 is an event to which we might fruitfully point as a contender for the birthplace of maritime security. It is at this moment a maritime nonstate actor contests the historical state centricity of maritime political economy, and by so doing, exposes the problem of order in the sea.

Thomas Nail (2019), whose ontology of movement draws deeply from the physics of waves and the motion of sea, argues that such historical events result amidst a confluence of heterogenous flows, or currents that have merged. He writes moreover, "An event produces a new intersection of flows that can also become the site of a new cycle" (Nail, 2019, p. 91). In this sense, on the night the French Secret Service bombed the Greenpeace flagship, Rainbow Warrior, several strong global political, military and economic currents came together and a new intersection, or place of assembly, resulted. The first and most obvious of flows in the confluence was the swelling political presence of international non-governmental organisations, such as Greenpeace and Amnesty International. Contiguous to this there was at time the emergence of wider social movements in the fields of human rights, nuclear disarmament and environmentalism. Anti-Soviet unions, like Solidarity in Poland, were growing in power throughout Eastern Europe. All of these movements were increasingly turbulent and were directly challenging the nuclear status quo in the 1980s (Davies, 2014). Concomitantly, and just as important, the superpowers in 1985 were at the height of their *détente* during the Cold War. It is the year Ronald Reagan, sworn into office for a second term as President of the USA, met with Mikhail Gorbachev, newly elected as general secretary of the Communist Party of the Soviet Union. And yet despite the thaw, each of the great powers continued to regularly test nuclear warheads in deserts and at sea. In the meantime, Europe was in an economic slump, and 1985 produced unemployment figures on par with the Great Depression (McCallum, 1986). Concurrently, the period experienced the rise of neoliberal policies that elevated private actors to the centre of the global north's political economy (Chamayou, 2021).

In the academy, change was also emerging within the dusty field of security studies. This traditionally realist field of International Relations began to garner the interests of social constructivists, environmentalists, students of peace and development studies and post structuralist scholars. In 1983 for instance, Barry Buzan published *People States and Fear: The National Security Problem in International Relations*. The Copenhagen Peace Research Institute was established in 1985. From here a new focus on post-Cold War non-traditional security "threats" would alter the study of security beyond recognition. More hawkish commentators were simultaneously scanning the horizon for the next existential enemy. Samuel Huntington's Clash of Civilizations (1993) was typical of its time in that it foresaw turbulence in the emergence of non-state ideologies.

We need also be aware that only three years previously the Third United Nations Convention on the Law of the Sea (UNCLOS III) had been signed, after 11 years of successful diplomatic deliberation. This Convention sought to position the UN, an international organisation, as steward of the High Seas. Yet, as a regime of order at sea, it too was in its infancy.

Only 25 countries, including landlocked Zambia, and nearly all postcolonial, had ratified the Convention by 1985.[2] This is telling, as we need to see UNCLOS as an Agreement[3] very much driven by the spirit of decolonisation. Littoral states in South America had been seeking sovereign rights over their proximate seas throughout the twentieth century (Ryan, 2013). The era of decolonisation strengthened this cause, and in Africa it was led by maritime states, such as Kenya. The Convention therefore had to negotiate between the security interests of states of the global south, who sought protection from the navies and merchant fleets of the global north. But it also had to incorporate the global north's insistence that its security is derived from absolute freedom of movement at sea. This same freedom was the source of the global south's insecurity. The compromise zonal regime that resulted managed to weave together these historical constructions of the maritime sphere (Ryan, 2019a). Freedom of the sea was sanctified for military and commercial actors, while sovereign responsibilities and duties were projected from land onto seaspace with specific enforcement powers (Klein, 2011). This arose in a manner that had long seemed incommensurate to purist notions of maritime freedom of movement.

Although the Agreement on the Law of the Sea did not come into force until 1994, ratification of the Convention itself would have created a security problem for coastal countries. The Convention passed legal responsibilities and duties to states which, mostly, did not have the naval power to enforce them. It established new vast swathes of liquid territory which required resources to police and administer. Thus, we can say that the Exclusive Economic Zone brought new state actors into the assemblage of global maritime politics from the early 1980s. However, while UNCLOS was a force for change, it was also an entirely state-centric claim to good order at sea. Its presence expanded the number of actors who sought a state-led, legally enforceable definition of security at sea that served commercial exploitation. While undoubtedly UNCLOS is an event that influences maritime politics in a new way, it does not alone account for the emergence of the discourse of maritime security.

I argue that an attack by one of the former colonial seignorial states on an unarmed maritime non-state actor in the southern hemisphere demonstrated to the world that there was radically different way to perceive the global sea in relation to land. In addition, it revealed that the state saw this alternative order as a threat. Within this event the currents of change that were happening around our social construction of the sea assemble. The security produced by nonstate actors enters maritime politics. It creates an immediate tension between visions of good order. Not only is there a new symbiotic relationship between state and nonstate, but also present is a fixed land logic merging with a nomadic and unruly maritime one. Nonstate actors such as Greenpeace in the 1980s, challenged the tendency towards *stasis* or equilibrium in the maritime realm. They sought radical change. On the other hand, old powers, like France, were complying to the military-commercial rationality that had prevailed at sea since modernity, and before. This rationality was ascendent and undergirded by the international law decision of 1969 which affirmed that, "the land dominates the sea" (Lathrop, 2015, p. 69).[3]

From its vantage point, a vessel was threatening to enter a zone of sea that France was securing as its territory. Despite this zone having questionable support in international law, the presence of the Rainbow Warrior within it was treated as though it was a violation of state sovereignty, an incursion. The reaction was purely militaristic; to eliminate. The military-commercial nexus that had constructed our understanding of the sea had created an imagination of order at sea that could only be maintained using a technocratic mode of governance that was enforced with violence (Steinburg, 2001, p. 179). As a maritime technocracy, the nexus was primarily interested in securing its freedom to control the sea. This technocratic order contrasted sharply with the radical democratic ethics that constituted the nonstate vision of what ought to be secure at sea. The encounter between France and the Rainbow Warrior introduced nonstate actors and a range of new problems to the field of maritime politics. Whether as sources of turbulence, or as force multipliers for a state, nonstate actors have since shaped what we now refer to as maritime security. In all respects, nonstate actors are the reason we have maritime security. They are the context that emerges from the historical flows. From their perspective, contrary to the 1969 decision of the International Court of Justice, the sea dominates the land.

The Maritime Assemblage

This chapter takes a relational perspective, famously utilised by Fernand Braudel, whose *History of the Mediterranean [1949]* (2000) remains the most impressive study of land-sea relations written. A relational approach treats maritime security as being the sum of its parts. Braudel ignored the traditional dichotomy between land and sea and instead focussed upon connections, proving land and sea fluent with one another.

Assemblage theory updates Braudel's epistemology. We can better navigate the hyper-complexity of contemporary practices subsumed by the concept of maritime security by referring to it as an assemblage. Theorised in depth by Gilles Deleuze and Félix Guattari (2008, 2011), it provides a way to explore maritime security through the heterogeneous connections that perform the politics of the sea. Everything is connected and interrelated within an assemblage; it is a field of tensions that produces power. The tensions I point to in this chapter are between a static and a non-static encounter that is mediated by the dynamism of sea. More specifically, I observe that much of maritime politics occur in the tension between a technocratic mode of security and an alternative, nomadic mode of security.

This is not to say that states always seek *stasis* or that nonstate actors are always ethical revolutionaries. In fact, it is the very opposite, any actor within the assemblage can produce (in) security. Both state and nonstate actors project onto ocean space the nihilism of organised crime, the greed of smuggling and commercial crime, the fascism of terrorism. State and nonstate create pollution, piracy and engage in criminal fishing. It needs to be said that there are also nonhuman elements in the assemblage of maritime security. The sea itself, with all the marine flora and fauna it houses, is deeply entangled in the politics of maritime security (Ryan, 2019b). In sum, there is a multiplicity of *antistasis* imaginaries of sea active within the assemblage.

Assemblage theory has been recently used effectively by Ryan (2014), Gould (2017), Bueger (2018), Jacobsen and Larsen (2019) and Bueger and Edmunds (2021). Each of these pragmatic studies has been highly innovative, revealing key attributes of maritime security. Jacobsen and Larsen (2019), for instance, shine light on the contingent nature of counter-piracy operations. In a departure from these studies, I shall draw on Deleuze and Guattari's assemblage theory in this chapter which, according to Adkins (2015) is monadic and undergirded by ontological continuity. This means everything, everyone is included as a thing within the assemblage. Using a radical pluralist epistemology, Deleuze and Guattari describe how things move and interact around the assemblage. And in agreement with Jacobsen and Larsen's findings (2019), all movement is contingent and relational. This implies that the activity of, for example, pirates, and the activity of NATO are symbiotic, indivisible.

For maritime security, although the moral concepts of security and insecurity are very certain and staid, their practical application in the physical world is less stable and clear-cut. In fact, in the real sea security and insecurity form a continuum of practices. They are not discrete phenomena: one does not exist without the other. They are relational, interdependent, interchangeable practices. An assemblage therefore is a tool that gives us a particularly pragmatic holistic approach to the sum of interconnections gathered around a series of related problems. The assemblage houses continuous contestations between things that define and secure order and things that escape and redefine it. In this sense, if we accept that security as a set of practices, is not a stable concept, we must accept that our understanding of order is equally unstable. Afterall, order today is different than it was this day last year. In the Deleuzian assemblage, equilibrium itself is always shifting. As Jacobsen and Larsen (2019) point out, everything is contingent. This monadic approach to assemblage is a liquid understanding of politics particularly suited to the study of maritime security. Deleuze and Guattari (2008, pp. 528–532), in fact, explore the maritime model as an exemplar problem space.

Our assemblage then, in lay terms, can be grasped if we think of huge waves in a storm lashing against tall rocky cliffs. The waves and the cliffs are always shaping each other and are changing in the process. While the waves are more unpredictable and move faster, the cliffs change imperceptibly and slower. However, one sudden powerful swell can destabilise the cliffs and cause an avalanche. The fallen detritus will in turn alter the flow of the waves. This suddenness contains the novelty, and indeed, the context we seek. Deleuze and Guattari (2008, pp. 6–7) compare the way an assemblage grows to a rhizome. Examples of rhizome are found in the growth structures of potatoes or grass. A root-like growth, it describes a thing that grows unpredictably and has no centre, no essence. Roots spurt randomly, adventitiously.

Maritime security is similarly rhizomatic. It rises up contingently between forces that are unmoored and entropic and forces that seek stability and equilibrium. I argue here that the birth of maritime civil society is an adventitious random root that shot out of the hierarchical, ancient military-commercial maritime assemblage. It was the sudden wave unexpected by the cliff. Deleuze and Guattari, attuned to the dynamics of complex assemblages, focus upon the interplay between tendencies of *stasis* and change. In their pluralist approach novelty is wrought by the actors of disequilibrium. Shaping the maritime sphere are the alternative trajectories of pirates, human smugglers, terrorists and revolutionaries. The entanglement of all things, solid and liquid, meet, often violently, to create novelty in an assemblage that we need to accept is always "becoming", and wherein change is immanent and non-teleological.[4]

Critical Security Studies, for the past 30 years, has incorporated this more monadic and pluralist approach (Walker, 1993). Actually, from its opening gambit, with Buzan's (1983) argument that national security produced international insecurity, the entanglement is foundational. This approach differs ethically and epistemologically from scholarship that presumes security is an entirely separate phenomenon to insecurity. Such studies are able to work from their logic that security is a solution to threats or risks at sea, insecurity. This makes security calculable, quantifiable and subject to cost/benefit analysis.

Critical theory, on the other hand, with its monist relational ontology, would observe that security is not a purely *reactive* morally correct phenomenon. On the contrary, critical theory claims that security practice and discourse is an *active* architect of maritime space.[5] Through (in) security the sea is governed, managed and shaped. In this sense, any alteration in the relations that constitute (in)security implies a change to the way the seaspace is imagined and experienced. An event which breaks down the old routines and introduces novel themes, experiences, and norms, awakens us to this change. The sudden arrival of a powerful *antistasis* actor with the capability to hold traditional claims over seaspace up to public scrutiny, in the mid-1980s, created just such an existential security event.

Maritime security, as a Deleuzian assemblage, can only be experienced as a perpetual interplay between, what Deleuze and Guattari (2008, p. 25) refer to as perceptual "semiotic flows" of security and insecurity. As they would observe, this implies that there is nothing purely secure, the sea is always becoming insecure. Likewise, there is nothing purely insecure, the sea is always becoming secured. By further implication, when examining the interrelationships between actors in the maritime arena, there is no outside from which to take an objective divine position. The assemblage is constituted by its discourses and practices. Everything is contained within it; every actor is performing (in)security. Any position occupied within this field of action is a political position. To put it bluntly, we are complicit things within the assemblage. We all have our own stake in maritime security. As writer and reader, as much as does the pirate and the frigate, together we produce and continue to reproduce the politics of maritime security.

It is notable that the Oxford English Dictionary lists the first meaning of the adjective "secure" as "fixed or fastened so as not to give way, become loose, or be lost".[6] This first meaning is given preference over its second meaning; "certain to remain safe or unthreatened". Immanent to the word "secure" therefore is a will to fix and make certain; to not allow escape. When placed into the maritime sphere, in the episteme of *stasis*, at least, the sea is always at risk of escaping equilibrium. From this perspective, the ocean world's innate adventitious chaos produces "threats" that challenge an order which aims to keep it still and constant and safe. The maritime world is restless and chaotic. To contain it is to secure a space always threatening to become something else.

Certainly, Plato considered this to be the case. His "ship of state" passage in *The Republic* rails against the sea, castigating it as the source of corrupt democracy and dissensus, and subversive to his creed of enlightened authoritarianism (Plato, 2000, p. 488; Rancière, 2007). Writing a couple of millennia later, two contemporary philosophers aired similar suspicions about the sea. Deleuze and Guattari, contrary to Plato, describe the maritime sphere as an authoritarian space of freedom. Something drastic had obviously happened to the way we encounter sea since Plato had known it. Exploring it, Deleuze and Guattari (2008, pp. 528–532) focus on the interrelationship between the sea and the order of the city/state as an interaction between smooth and striated space. The continual historical encounter between these two tendencies structures the history of maritime space. They write, "It is as if the sea were not only the archetype of all smooth spaces but the first to undergo a gradual striation, gridding it one place, then another, on this side and that" (Deleuze & Guattari, 2008, p. 529) The technologies of navigation, the invention of the compass, the development of cartography and the mathematics of longitude helped inscribe an early modern matrix of order and certainty of land onto the smoothness of the oceans. The emergence of globalisation, however, challenged the state's unworkable territorial-obsessed methods. It arises to produce a sea space that is conducive to movement, a space of freedom for trade, information and military flows to circulate without friction. Deleuze and Guattari argue that this required a different mode of control, a novel mode of governance. This was made possible with the technologies of submarine, satellite and communication, which made the sea seem smooth again, ripe for freedom. The sea itself became secondary to state-based economic and military needs. "The sea", they write, "then the air and the stratosphere become smooth spaces again, but in the strangest of reversals, it is for the purpose of controlling striated space more completely" (2008, p. 529). The freedom of the seas, on these terms, is a formative political technology of late modernity. Moreover, it is one seriously invested in by the technocratic forces of *stasis* and certainty. This same freedom of the sea, ironically, also produces (in)security; it allows the forces of disequilibrium to roam and reshape the world. Evidently, Plato was justified all along to cast the irruptive sea as the source of disorder on land.[7]

The Birth of Maritime Security

The sinking of the Rainbow Warrior was a violent attack on a vanguard agent of disequilibrium. On the night of 10 July 1985, in Auckland harbour, at 23:45, with nearly all crew aboard, French secret service operatives placed limpets that exploded open the hull of the Greenpeace flagship, Rainbow Warrior. It sank within minutes into the harbour. The boat's photographer Fernando Pereira was killed (Veitch, 2010). The headline the next day on The New Zealand Herald read, "Terrorism Strikes". The New Zealand Prime Minister called it "sordid act of international state-backed terrorism" and an "unprecedented affront to sovereignty" (Robie, 2015, p. 128). This event reveals the point where the prevailing order of seaspace, and the emergence of a new actor, a sort of roaming, watchful, critical maritime civil society, which enacts its own form of (in)security. The boat had come to Auckland from the Marshall Islands where it had assisted the evacuation of a small island's inhabitants, exposed to radiation by US nuclear testing.

It is here a new antagonism within the assemblage of maritime politics forms a new set of relationships. If one accepts that Auckland harbour might be a contender for the original event of maritime security, it needs to be also accepted that the assemblage was born when the most extreme and static embodiment of maritime order met with its ethical, nomadic other. The Rainbow Warrior had in the past (in 1973 and 1982), and was planning to in the very near future, enter the exclusion zone declared by France to allow it test weapons of mass destruction. By regarding the carelessness of the operatives who carried out the attack, it is evident that the sinking was undertaken as an act of war. The agents did not attempt to cover their tracks. In no way was it be perceived to be criminal by the 13 DGSE operatives,[8] or by the French government.[9]

It is instructive to regard how the event is experienced by Greenpeace. In a promotional video it's explained that the boat had been "rammed, raided and bombed", in its mission to "be a witness to environmental destruction, to be our eyes and ears" (Greenpeace, 2005). This is an act of attestation. We need to recognise, however, that the watchful eye of the Rainbow Warrior was different from the eyes of surveillance operating on behalf of equilibrium on the maritime sphere. The Rainbow Warrior's eye is human-centric and performative of the conscience of humanity. The significance that the victim of the bombing was a photographer hardly needs pointing out. A witness and an attestor, Pereira drowned trying to retrieve his evidence: a camera in a room below the deck.

There is overlap in the way security is practiced by various actors in the assemblage. Today, NATO is primarily a watcher in the Mediterranean. At sea, contemporary stasis-seeking actors interact to gather, process and distribute intelligence that will increase their maritime domain awareness. We must note that in these surveillance operations NATO's eye is machinic and global. It is technocratic and performative of control.

Another overlap is found in the exceptional right to intervention claimed by actors within the assemblage. In an environment relatively lawless compared to the land, security at sea acts according to its own logic and intuition. In the promotional Greenpeace (2005) video this claim is asserted when the narrator says of the Rainbow Warrior, "when bearing witness isn't enough, she takes action". Later the achievements of the boat are listed; "… she helped end nuclear testing in the Pacific, blocked coal ports to call attention to climate change, closed down destructive fishing operations, stopped the illegal transfer of timber from the Amazon". The assemblage of maritime (in)security, we can say coheres around the premise that, in the name of order, or of change, exceptional action is always justified. Contingency has been embedded within the assemblage from the beginning.

The Buzzword

Years later, when the concept, or the promise, of maritime security appeared – Bueger's (2015) "buzzword" –, it emerged in the High Seas as a force for order. It described extra-legal security activities justified in the name of the United States' declaration of a war on terror. This was a war waged against the idea of a malign and existentially threatening nonstate actor. It is of course a war without a specific enemy. As Caygill (2001) observes, security in the post-Cold War is waged on the general condition of turbulence.

Fortunately, there was little terrorist activity detectable on the Mediterranean and the NATO fleet gradually began policing the region for more banal crimes, indicatively, human trafficking. Innovatively, the freshly declared territorial seas around the Mediterranean were used during Operation Active Endeavour to police the High Seas. NATO would "shadow" suspected vessels into the nearest EEZ where jurisdiction to search and seize awaited.[10] The Mediterranean operation in fact proved an excellent training ground for NATO for when it was despatched to protect ships from being taken hostage by armed raiders off the coast of Somalia (Ryan, 2014). A uniquely maritime, universal crime, piracy conveyed a threat to global political economy by interfering with what Khalili (2020) and Cowen (2014) describe as the conveyor belt of capital at sea.

Piracy in the waters off Somalia was initially a last resort for a coastal community whose fishing waters had been polluted by toxic waste and depleted of stock by illegal fishing. This was a desperate act of (in)security by nomadic nonstate actors. In response, what Gould (2017, p. 408) refers to as a "private-public assemblage" evolved quickly, zones of safe passage were established and an alliance of state actors unlikely ever to cooperate on land formed *ad hoc* coalitions to police them. The turbulence of piracy dramatically influenced the way by which the new term maritime security was understood. Like an echo of the sinking of the Rainbow Warrior, piracy was another force of entropy, of change, that in contesting with the force of equilibrium, produced novelty. Each encounter between the forces of turbulence and change, whether state or nonstate, ethical, nihilist or capitalist, shapes and reshapes the assemblage of maritime security.

At this present time of writing, there are two turbulent *antistasis* actors challenging the tendency toward equilibrium at sea. One is China. The other is the most profoundly nonstate human actor that exists: the asylum seeker. While the contest in the South China Sea continues, a demonstrably turbulent China is currently utilising a nomadic merchant fishing fleet that sometimes acts as a buccaneering militia force (Ford, 2020). This flotilla openly and aggressively transgresses the Law of the Sea, and countless other Conventions. It is one of several disruptive nonstate entities contested by nonstate actors which tend towards equilibrium. Much of the surveillance and reporting of these activities have been undertaken by what Brendan Flynn in Chapter 24 of this volume refers to as "hybrid actors", environmentalist and humanitarian nonstate bodies, such as Global Fishing Watch,[11] supported by state and corporate funding. It's not just China. The United States is also looking at the speed, ethical outlook and nomadic flexibility of maritime NGOs to supplement its quest for maritime domain awareness. A recent article in Maritime Executive argues that:

> Volunteer organizations have the ability to make immediate impacts in a significantly shorter time period, at a fraction of the cost, than it would take to stand-up and equip instruments of a nation's maritime forces for global enforcement duties. Organizations like Sea Shepherd and Greenpeace are crewed by volunteers and operate on donations from private donors spanning the globe. Maritime experts have argued for greater interagency and international cooperation in combating illegal and unregulated fishing before. Similar to the role of Coastal Patrol during WWII, their primary function would be to contribute to regional maritime domain awareness.
>
> *(Phillips-Levine et al., 2020)*

More entangled still, nonstate policing of statist and commercial maritime security practices has been the hallmark of the humanitarian response to the deaths of asylum seekers on the Mediterranean Sea. Organisations such as the Ocean Viking, SOS Mediterranee, Sea-Watch and Médecins Sans Frontières are independent actors of dissensus which operate in and around the humanitarian-technocratic response to human migration on the Mediterranean (Striel, 2018). As had the Rainbow Warrior, this deviant offshoot of maritime civil society sees its role as attestation and intervention, and to bear witness to the strategies of *stasis* and the (in)security they generate at sea.

Conclusion

To conclude, I argue that the originary context is present in the events that continue to form and reform the "hyper object" that is maritime (in)security. The interplay lies between the tendency to bring certainty; to fix in place the dynamism of seaspace; and the tendency to escape this matrix, to evade or to attest and challenge the security it embodies. This is the fractal tension, the unique pattern running through all activities in the assemblage of maritime security. It produces constant novelty. It means maritime politics is as unpredictable as the sea itself.

I have drawn upon the metaphor of the rhizome to describe this protean turbulence as the outgrowth of violent encounters between equilibrium and entropy, between contingent ordering and adventitious deviance. The advantage of using assemblage theory is that it disallows a risk-based construction of the maritime sphere. It compels us to grapple with the difficulty of pluralism, where maritime risk is perspectival and is rarely perceived to hold universally true. Assemblage theory brought us to the night the Rainbow Warrior was bombed, and a Greenpeace activist was killed. It finds that night replayed again and again in the events that have shaped maritime security. It is found in the tension between Italian coastguards and humanitarian NGOs, between illegal fishing boats and environmentalists, between Somali fishermen and the merchant fleets of Europe. By placing it into its context, assemblage theory tells us that maritime (in)security is a continuously changing, highly unstable phenomenon. By exploring its context, we are also encountering the origins of a novel mode of maritime civil society, and perhaps, the early beginnings of a maritime democracy.

Notes

1 *In memoriam* Fernando Pereira, photographer (1950–1985).
2 Fiji, in 1982; Bahamas, Mexico, Namibia, Jamaica, Belize, Egypt, Ghana and Zambia, in 1983; The Philippines, Côte D'Ivoire, Cuba, Senegal and Gambia, in 1984; Bahrain, Cameroon, Iceland, Mali, Tanzania, Guinea, Iraq, St Lucia, Sudan, Togo and Tunisia in 1985.
3 *North Sea Continental Shelf (Federal Republic of Germany v Denmark; Federal Republic of Germany v Netherlands)(Judgement)* [1969] International Court of Justice (ICJ) Rep.3, [96].
4 It is notable that 1985 also hosted the first maritime terrorist event, the *Achille Lauro* attack. The hijackers were planning to attack the port of Ashdod, Israel, but were caught by a cabin boy preparing their weapons aboard the cruise liner *en route*. This is an event in maritime security, certainly. However, it is minor as the political outgrowth it created was not wholly maritime in nature. It remains, however, a good example for Deleuzians of novelty's immanence and nonrational emergence.
5 Positivist and critical theories are similarly not dichotomous but binary and interdependent.
6 *Oxford Dictionary of English*, second edition, (2003, p. 1596).
7 For an interesting reading of the philosophy at issue, see Farrell Krell (2019).
8 *Direction Générale de la Sécurité Extérieur*.
9 The President of the French Republic was aware of the attack. In addition, the persons convicted never served their sentences and were treated as heroes in France (Veitch 2010). Pugh (1987, p. 659) agreed, writing, "It is doubtful whether the French agencies involved in the plot had considered justifying their anticipatory action in legal terms". For more accounts, see Scott Davidson (1991).
10 Retrieved 1st April 2021 from https://www.nato.int/cps/en/natohq/topics_7932.htm
11 https://globalfishingwatch.org/

References

Adkins, B. (2015). *Deleuze and Guattari's A Thousand Plateaus*. Edinburgh University Press.
Braudel, F. [1949] (2000). *The Mediterranean and the Mediterranean World in the Age of Philip II* (Siân Reynolds, Trans.) (Vols. 1–3). The Folio Society.
Bueger, C. (2015). What is Maritime Security? *Maritime Policy, 53*, 159–164.
Bueger, C. (2018). Territory, Authority, Expertise: Global Governance and the Counter-Piracy Assemblage. *European Journal of International Relations, 24*(3), 614–637.
Bueger, C., & Edmunds, T. (2021). Pragmatic Ordering: Informality, Experimentation, and the Maritime Security Agenda. *Review of International Studies, 47*(2), 171–191.
Buzan, B. (1983). *People, States and Fear: The National Security Problem in International Relations*. Wheatsheaf.
Caygill, H. (2001). Perpetual Police? Kosovo and the Elision of Police and Military Violence. *European Journal of Social Theory, 4*(1), 73–78.
Chamayou, G. (2021). *The Ungovernable Society*. Polity Press.
Cowen, D. (2014). *The Deadly Life of Logistics; Mapping the Violence of Global Trade*. University of Minnesota Press.
Davies, T. (2014). *NGOs: A New History of Transnational Civil Society*. Oxford University Press.
Deleuze, G., & Guattari, F. (2008). *A Thousand Plateaus: Capitalism and Schizophrenia* (Brian Massumi, Trans.). Continuum.
Deleuze, G., & Guattari, F. (2011). *What is Philosophy?* Verso Press.
Farrell Krell, D. (2019). *The Sea. A Philosophical Encounter*. Bloomsbury.
Ford, A. (2020). Illegal Chinese Fishing in the Galapagos: A Threat to the Biodiversity of the Latin American Pacific. *Open Democracy*, 19th December. Retrieved 1st April 2020, from https://www.opendemocracy.net/en/democraciaabierta/
Gould, A. (2017). Global Assemblages and Counter-Piracy: Public and Private in Maritime Policing. *Policing & Society, 27*(4), 408–418.
Greenpeace. (2005). *The Boat and the Bomb*. Retrieved 31st March 2021, from https://www.youtube.com/watch?v=2uw8tg9_BU4
Huntington, S. (1993). The Clash of Civilizations? *Foreign Affairs*, Summer, *72*(3), 22–49.
Jacobsen, K. L., & Larsen, J. (2019). Piracy Studies Coming of Age: A Window on the Making of Maritime Intervention Actors. *International Affairs, 95*(5), 1037–1054.
Khalili, L. (2020). *Sinews of War and Trade*. Verso.
Klein, N. (2011). *Maritime Security and the Law of the Sea*. Oxford University Press.

Lathrop, C. G. (2015). Baselines. In D. R. Rothwell, A. G. Oude Elferink, K. Scott, & T. Stephens (Eds.), *The Oxford Handbook of the Law of the Sea* (pp. 69–90). Oxford University Press.

McCallum, J. (1986). Unemployment in OECD Countries in the 1980s. *The Economic Journal*, *96*, 942–960.

Morton, T. (2013). *Hyperobjects; Philosophy and Ecology after the End of the World*. University of Minnesota Press.

Nail, T. (2019). *Being and Motion*. Oxford University Press.

Phillips-Levine, T., Phillips-Levine, D., & Mills, W. (2020, October 20). How NGOs Can Help Keep Tabs on China's Illegal Fishing Activity. *Maritime Executive*. Retrieved 1st April 2020, from https://www.maritime-executive.com/editorials/how-ngos-can-help-keep-tabs-on-china-s-illegal-fishing-activity

Plato. (2000). *The Republic* (G. R. F. Ferrari, Ed.). Cambridge University Press.

Pugh, M. (1987). Legal Aspects of the Rainbow Warrior Affair. *International and Comparative Law Quarterly*, *36*(3), 655–669.

Rancière, J. (2007). *On the Shores of Politics*. Verso.

Robie, D. (2015). *Eyes of Fire: The Last Voyage of the Rainbow Warrior*. Little Island Press.

Ryan, B. J. (2013). Zones and Routes: Securing a western Indian Ocean. *Journal of the Indian Ocean Region*, *9*(2), 173–188.

Ryan, B. J. (2014). A Mediterranean Police Assemblage. In J. Bachmann, C. Bell, & C. Holmqvist (Eds.), *War, Police and Assemblages of Intervention* (pp. 147–163). Routledge.

Ryan, B. J. (2019a). The Disciplined Sea: A History of Maritime Security and Zonation. *International Affairs*, *95*(5), 1055–1072.

Ryan, B. J. (2019b). Zones at Sea and the Properties of Connectivity: (A)Roundness, (Imm)Unity and Liquidity. In L. Lobo-Guerrero, S. Alt, & M. Meijer (Eds.), *Imaginaries of Connectivity: The Creation of Novel Spaces of Governance* (pp. 89–108). Rowman and Littlefield.

Scott Davidson, J. (1991). The Rainbow Warrior Arbitration Concerning the Treatment of the French Agents Mafart and Prieur. *The International and Comparative Law Quarterly*, *40*(2), 446–457.

Steinburg, P. E. (2001). *The Social Construction of the Ocean*. Cambridge University Press.

Striel, M. (2018). A Fleet of Mediterranean Border Humanitarians. *Antipode*, *50*(3), 704–724.

Veitch, J. (2010). A Sordid Act: The "Rainbow Warrior" Incident. *New Zealand International Review*, *35*(4), 6–9.

Walker, R. J. B. (1993). *Inside/Outside: International Relations as Political Theory*. Cambridge University Press.

3

MARITIME SECURITY: "GOOD NAVIES" AND REALISM RE-IMAGINED

Geoffrey Till

The basic, traditional concepts of maritime strategy were first clearly and substantially elucidated at the end of the 19th and beginning of the 20th century by Admiral Alfred Thayer Mahan, (US Navy) and, in the UK, Sir Julian Corbett and have been reflected in naval behaviour ever since.[1] This chapter explores the extent to which their ideas and most naval activity conforms to the assumptions, conclusions and recommendations of the so-called Realist School of international relations. But it will then show that navies have other preoccupations too and have usually had to strike a balance between their war-fighting roles and their "softer" tasks, including Maritime Security. It will show that the world's drift into an era of renewed great power competition will increase the dilemmas faced by its naval planners, and that this shape future perceptions of Maritime Security.

Mahan and Corbett were both "realists" in the sense that they would have been entirely comfortable with the ideas expressed with clarity and punch by Hans Morgenthau some 50 years later in his seminal *Politics Among Nations: the Struggle for Power and Peace.* They assumed that international politics was basically a struggle over who gets what, when and how. The struggle could be about political influence, economic advantage, resources, values or territory and the contestants were the leaders of traditional nation states. Neither would have had difficulty in agreeing in theory with Thucydides that in the absence of overweening authority, states naturally compete and that "the strong do what they can and the weak suffer what they must" (Strassler, 1996, p. 416). Accordingly, like Morgenthau, they would have agreed that "the objectives of foreign policy must be defined in terms of national interest and must be supported with adequate power" (Morgenthau, 2007, p. 7). For this, military/naval forces were the main instruments of policy; they needed to be invested in and used intelligently if the country's interests were to be served.

In practice, however, their policy advice would have been tempered with considerations of expediency and of what was likely to work. But, theirs was an age of what later analysts have called "Social Darwinianism" – an era in which competition between nation states was not only regarded as fundamentally unavoidable but, in some quarters at least, as being a requirement for progress. National competition expressed identity and social cohesion and in a multitude of ways generated improvement in the human condition. Because military and naval forces were regarded as the chief expression of the identity and power of the nation state, naval policy

38

DOI: 10.4324/9781003001324-5

closely reflected its political leaders' conceptions of their country's interests and what needed to be done to protect them.

No time better exemplified this than did the presidency of Theodore Roosevelt (1901–1909). A navalist, Roosevelt was personally heavily engaged in the Spanish-American war of 1898, that 'splendid little war, begun with the highest motives, carried on with magnificent intelligence and spirit, favoured by that fortune which loves the brave'.[2] Ready to engage in coercive naval diplomacy whenever necessary (as against Colombia in its possible venture against Panama in 1903) and keen to display American naval power around the world with the famous cruise of the Great White Fleet 1907–1909, Roosevelt's philosophy was that the United States should "speak softly and carry a big stick". Formerly Assistant-Secretary of the US Navy and friend, admirer and colleague of Mahan, his view was that "A good Navy is not a provocation to war. It is the best guaranty of peace" (Roosevelt, 1902). By "good", of course, he meant "strong", because the deterrence of potentially malign adversaries and the defence of a beneficial peace depended absolutely on the credibility provided by the perceived capacity to prevail in conflict.

This inevitably led to a set of naval requirements – appropriate for what would now be called "peer competition" in which great power was pitted against great power, navy against navy in what was essentially a symmetrical contest of "like against like". In turn, a preoccupation with the potential threat posed by the world's other navies dominated national policy towards the size and shape of your own fleet and translated into a 'mission set' of required capabilities.

The Geopolitical Angle

Many of these "missions" were half-determined by a nation state's geographic circumstances. Geography was the first "element" of sea power that Mahan explored. Proposing that sea-based trade is safer, quicker and easier than its land-based alternatives, he argued that countries with easy access to the sea and a coastline helpfully endowed with convenient harbours have a major advantage over those that don't (Mahan, 1890, p. 25). Mahan also made the point that it was also very advantageous if a country's coastline was continuous rather than separated by territory held by other countries since this would make the "concentration of its forces" much more difficult. France and Spain with their two or three distinct fleet areas were unfortunate in this respect (Mahan, 1890, p. 27). Russia with its four separate fleets (or five counting the Caspian) was even more so, especially as its access to the open ocean was, and largely remains, climatically challenging and subject to degrees of control by often unsympathetic neighbours. Such geographic features in the containing effect of the so-called "First Island Chain" makes the "stepping out" of the Chinese navy difficult too (Bo, 2019, pp. 47–60, 61–78).

Mahan acknowledged that outgoing states with maritime aspirations would increasingly also have such problems the further they went from home but the danger could be offset by the establishment of chains of bases and colonies able to support the operations of both the merchant fleet and the navy – provided, that those bases or colonies were sufficiently well-defended, and did not become strategic liabilities in themselves.

The nature and extent of the territory held could be a factor too, Mahan thought. He partly attributed the uneven development of French maritime power to its pleasant climate, ample resources and productive agriculture, maintaining that such riches at home undermined the urge to seek them through alternative maritime endeavour. In fact, Mahan worried that this might apply to the United States too. If the Americans could satisfy all their needs like this, why should they bother to go to sea in any serious way? Finally, Mahan was clear that a country's geographic situation could be changed – for better or worse – by specific state action, often by means of naval power.

All these geographic characteristics were likely to shape a nation's political and social culture, and its foreign policy behaviour especially in the extent to which they engaged in sea-based trade. This would make some nations much more "maritime" than others. These latter more "Continental" states might be able to assemble the resources to construct navies that could seek to exploit a maritime adversary's dependency on trade, but they would not prevail. A maritime state determined to invest sufficiently in its sea power would always be able defend its trade dependency and exploit the huge advantages in economic cost, general security provided by maritime transportation. Moreover, the sea covered three-quarters of the world's surface and this offered limitless prospects for decisive strategic manoeuvre. For both reasons, maritime states would prosper in peace and prevail in war more than their more land-bound adversaries.

These geographically based observations were closely linked to the equally "realist" pre-occupations of what has become known as the "geopolitics school" exemplified by the British Geographer Sir Halford Mackinder. He and later colleagues such as Klaus Haushofer and Nicholas Spykman (Spykman, 1944) argued for the behaviour of all states to be determined in large measure by their physical position, resources and nature. Such geopolitical writers all argued that the human and material resources of extensive "continental" powers such as Russia and the Third Reich were potentially decisive. Where they differed amongst themselves and with the maritime school as represented by Mahan and the rather more judicious Corbett was in where they situated individual states in the Maritime-Continental spectrum and in the re-lative power relationships between both "kinds" of states. Here the essential question was the balance of advantage to be found between the enormous resources of the land-bound con-tinental state when set against the benefits that access to the rest of the world gave the mar-itime.[3] In large measure, a state's competitive behaviour was likely to be shaped by such considerations.

The Roles of the Traditional Navy

From these initial observations, Mahan went on to articulate what later analysts would call a navy's "mission set" whether it was confronting a maritime rival or "continental" challenger. First and foremost, amongst these was the requirement to develop the forces needed to secure, maintain, or at least contest the "command of the sea" – or "sea control" as it increasingly became known – because it was this that allowed you to set the "rules of the game", and to enjoy much greater freedom of action. Superiority at sea meant you could defend your territory and national possessions overseas while potentially threatening his; you could advance and defend your sea-based trade and threaten his. In war consequently, you were likely to prevail, at least at sea. In peace, your international influence and capacity to defend your national interests would be all the greater. "Control of the sea", declared Mahan simply "by maritime commerce and naval supremacy means predominance in the world ... [and] is the chief amongst the material elements in the power and prosperity of nations" (cited, Livesey, 1981, p. 42). This was the supreme advantage of a maritime power as opposed to a continental one. The latter aimed only at denying its adversary's capacity to control the sea and to exploit its strategic potential rather than seek those benefits itself. Its strategy in short was the negative one of "sea denial" rather than the positive alternative of "sea control" (Till, 2018, pp. 183–99, 200–231).

The capacity to prevail in what the Soviet Union's Admiral Gorshkov used to call "fleet v fleet engagements" demanded proficiency in the deadly capacity to disable or preferably sink the adversary's battlefleet (Gorshkov, 1979). If that was not possible, perhaps because it was stronger than yours in any particular area, then at least it should be neutralised to the extent possible by some kind of naval defensive or fleet-in-being strategy. All these missions in turn required, in contemporary naval parlance, a focus on high-intensity open-ocean capabilities including submarine and anti-submarine operations, the ability to attack enemy forces with gunfire, anti-ship missiles or air attack and the capacity to defend yourself against them. If you needed to operate in close proximity to the shore in the very different sea conditions to be found there, these same capabilities might need to take on a very different form. Varied as these capabilities all were, they were and remain similar in being both technologically demanding and usually very expensive. Only the richest and most advanced of nation states could afford the first-class battlefleet that was both an expression of national power and, according to Mahan at least, the way of becoming or remaining one.

Mahan's emphasis on maritime commerce as a major peacetime form of national strength gave it in his eyes a special priority in war. "[T] he necessity of a navy", he went so far as to say in a possibly unguarded moment, "springs from the existence of a peaceful shipping, and disappears with it"[4] (Cited, Westcott, 1919, pp. 16, 18). Shipping was the basis of a country's economy, he thought, and so provided the resources and the means for naval strength. In times of conflict, shipping supported the war economy and allowed you to move your forces and military supplies around as strategically necessary. Accordingly, there was hardly anything more important than the capacity to defend your "sea lines of communication" and the shipping on which they relied, and to be able to threaten those of your adversary. But all of this depended absolutely, Mahan claimed, on naval predominance.

Naval predominance also allowed you to project power ashore, both in peace and in war and to deny the adversary the ability to do likewise. Historically, this could be done by raiding the enemy's coast, by launching amphibious operations designed either simply to inflict damage or to intimidate and indeed to open up new axes or fronts of strategic attack. The traditional role of bombardment from the sea by the mid-20th century began to morph into missile attack of land targets and the whole deadly philosophy of nuclear deterrence. The capacity to defend yourself against anything the adversary might do in this regard rested on the capacity to destroy such forces while they were still moving to positions of attack and these days, to intercept their missiles before they were hit by some form of missile defence system.

These wartime capabilities had their value in peacetime too, firstly on the basis of preserving peace through deterrence as Roosevelt had claimed. This line of argument was based on the tradition of Vegetius' classic dictum of *Si vis pacem, para bellum*, if you want peace, prepare for war. In the late 19th and very early 20th centuries, this line of reasoning was broadly accepted. Those same perceived capabilities also had the apparent benefits of allowing strong naval powers to influence the shape and nature of the peace and if necessary to mould it to suit their particular interests, in a manner entirely consistent with the Thucydidean approach discussed earlier.

By performing these war and peacetime roles successfully, navies would provide maritime security (without the capital letters) for their particular nation; as a result, it and its vital interests would be secure against all enemies foreign and domestic.

The Effect on Navies of the Realist Approach

Nonetheless, there had been voices raised against what later scholars would call the Realist approach to international relations even before the First World War and the experience of that terrible conflict greatly reinforced them. Naval forces were seen by many to be a part of the problem rather than a solution to international rivalries. Indeed, the naval arms race between

Britain and Germany between 1908 and 1912 was widely blamed for poisoning the diplomatic atmosphere and precipitating the very situation it was designed to prevent.[5] Reinforced by the undeniable fact that battlefleets were extremely expensive in times of economic strain, such views lay behind the specific focus on naval disarmament during the interwar period that started with the Washington Naval treaty of 1921–1922. By the late 1930s, this led to a lack of naval preparedness in the Western allies that those of a "realist" persuasion argued was in part responsible for the onset of the Second World War. Choosing *not* to participate in a naval arms race, they considered, was far more dangerously de-stabilising than maintaining what Roosevelt would have considered a "good" navy.

Unsurprisingly, that conflict saw the navies of the protagonists exercising all the traditional roles that the great masters of maritime strategic expected of them. Further, the final triumphant success of Allied seapower provided the essential conditions under which the war was won (Gray, 1992, pp. 230–262). Indeed, by its conclusion, as one recent writer has put it, the US Navy, sweeping all resistance before it, had become "the ultimate Mahanian expression of sea power" adding, rather more contentiously, "Had the American public been willing to spend much more on defence at a much earlier stage, willing to show it was ready to go to war, it would never have had to" (Celander, 2018, pp. 198–199).

The apparent triumph of this decidedly "Realist" conception of naval activity carried on into the post-war years and through the Cold War too, if initially rather less confidently because of the perceived challenge posed to its dominance by strategic airpower centred on land-based aircraft and missiles armed with nuclear weapons. Two points need to be made about this. Firstly, the apparent rise of strategic airpower in no sense undermined realist expectations about the centrality of military force as an instrument of policy, it simply suggested the substitution of one form of military power for another. Secondly, once navies were able to get over what the Soviet Unions' Admiral Sergei Gorshkov described as the "atomic shock" (Gorshkov, 1979, pp. 156–212) and demonstrate that they too could get into the nuclear business, their continued importance was re-confirmed. Indeed, by offering through the delivery of nuclear-propelled submarines armed with ballistic missiles a more secure and credible form of strategically decisive strike "from multiple axes", they could be argued to have ushered in a second major triumph for traditional Mahanian conceptions of seapower. Even the unrealised capacity to do so could determine the outcome of great power conflict.

This was certainly the view of the architects of *The Maritime Strategy* of 1986 which was based on the proposition that by surging northwards through the Greenland-Iceland-UK gap to take on and defeat the Soviet Navy in what it might otherwise have regarded as its home waters, US and NATO navies would also wrest the strategic initiative from the massive Soviet Army and Rocket Forces and secure "escalation dominance" (Watkins, 1986; Baer, 1994, pp. 428–444). Better still, the mere prospect of this happening would force an adversary already in significant economic trouble into a major internal crisis in its attempts to keep up with the naval technological advances made by a much more economically powerful Western alliance. And so, realists such as Secretary of the Navy John Lehman proclaimed the case proven (Lehman, 2018). In effect, the "good" navies of the West had played a major role in winning the Cold War and securing a world which could prosper in peace.

In peacetime, alongside the remorseless demands of maintaining the war-fighting capabilities needed for general deterrence, navies and other agencies of maritime law enforcement found the time necessary for the maintenance of good order at sea and the conduct of naval diplomacy, coercive and otherwise, but these were secondary considerations – and in the main not what navies were designed for.

Alternative Perspectives on Naval Roles

Things did not turn out quite as expected and many varied challenges remained for navies to grapple with. And in fact, things were never as simple as this brief review of naval realism might suggest. Navies have always done more than simply counter each other. The Royal Navy's long and demanding 19th-century campaign against the slavery trade exemplified the more benign potential of what was then the world's most powerful naval force. The desire to help the people of Cuba and the Philippines in their struggle against Spanish colonialism were amongst those "highest motives" to which Ambassador Hay alluded above, and to preserve the newly found independence of Panama can likewise be seen as proceeding in part from those same humanitarian impulses. Moreover, maritime law enforcement and supporting the internal development of their country have both been secondary, if not primary, duties for many navies.

Nonetheless, these non-realist approaches were hardly front and centre to global naval development, especially in times when great power competition was the chief defining characteristics of the international order. In the immediate aftermath of the catastrophic wars of the 20th century, there were brief flickers of an aspiration for a maritime world more cooperative and collective in its approach. These were, most obviously evident in the discussions about limiting or even outlawing war and about the role and power successively of the League of Nations and the United Nations Organisation (which even went so far as to raise the prospect that these organisations might have their own powerful navies). But it was only after the end of the Cold War that such other ways of thinking about navies and sea power really emerged.

The key aspect of this was the widening of the concept of security at sea to comprise much more than the defence of a nation's territory and vital interests against largely hostile state action.[6] Now enjoying capital letters, Maritime Security as shown elsewhere in this book, is generally understood as being principally focused on the maintenance of what was previously known as Good Order at Sea, against a large variety of non-state-based threats such as maritime crime, over-fishing, environmental degradation and so on. If unchecked these potentially destabilising threats might well undermine national or international security as traditionally understood.

With the end of the Cold War, globalisation seemed to have arguably become the determining characteristic of the international order. Believers in the traditions of the 19th century British Manchester school welcomed the onset of globalisation, hoping that it would usher in an era of peace and plenty by replacing earlier, competitive, aggressive balance-of-power politics with a much greater sense of mutual need and common interest and of international community, based essentially on the mutual benefits of international sea-based trade and distributive manufacture. The world would become increasingly borderless and be dominated instead by a supranational "system" in which its national constituents would have diminished willingness, need, or indeed capacity to disturb.

Using the taxonomy of Robert Cooper, these "post-modern" nation states would, in due course, generate post-modern naval forces whose chief preoccupation would be to band together to deal with common and emerging threats to the new international order, to the system and to the peace and prosperity of all (Cooper, 2004). This was in strong and obvious contrast to the "modern" navies whose roles and priorities were dominated by the earlier, competitive, aggressive balance-of-power traditions of "modern" states politics, as discussed earlier.

The nature of this globalised trading system together with the growth of the "blue" component of many national economies around the world would help determine the nature and roles of the "post-modern" navy. Firstly, because the system depended on economically important shipping, sea-lines of communication and sea-based resources (fish, oil and gas), the good order at sea on which these depended had also to be protected against such threats of piracy, maritime terrorism, drugs and people smuggling and illegal fishing. These threats to maritime security were often transnational and so required transnational collective responses such as the international anti-piracy campaigns in the Straits of Malacca, off Somalia and in the Gulf of Benin. Further, it provided those navies with necessary experience, skills and resources to help build maritime security capabilities in the smaller navies of Africa, Southeast Asia, the South Pacific, the Gulf and Central/South America.

These "post-modern" naval preoccupations even led to something of a re-appraisal of the core concept of traditionally realist naval thinking, namely command or control of the sea. "Where the old maritime strategy focused on sea control", said Admiral Mike Mullen, the Chief of Naval operations, US Navy in 2006, "the new one must recognise that the economic tide of all nations rises not when the seas are controlled by one but rather when they are made safe and free for all" (Mullen, 2006). In this case, "control" had connotations of shared supervision or monitoring and protection rather than military dominance.

Secondly, because the system was borderless, instability anywhere in the system was likely to affect all its constituents. Accordingly in the words of British Prime Minister Tony Blair,

> The frontiers of our security no longer stop at the Channel. What happens in the Middle East affects us … The new frontiers for our security are global. Our Armed Forces will be deployed in the lands of other nations far from home, with no immediate threat to our territory, in environments and in ways unfamiliar to them.
>
> *(Blair, 2007)*

This required navies previously focussed on local defence, such as those of Scandinavia, to generate the capacity to participate in collective expeditionary operations against anything, potentially anywhere, that threatened stability and good order at sea and ashore upon which trade, and the conditions for trade, depended. These therapeutic interventions could well include dealing with humanitarian disasters whether man-made or not, which as the early 21st century unwound became almost routine. This provided a significant extra justification for the construction of amphibious warfare ships, logistics vessels and other such units that seemed particularly useful for the purpose.

Balancing Modern and Post-modern Perspectives

Several things need to be said straightaway about this apparent juxtaposition of traditional "modern/realist" naval concepts and the less familiar "post-modern" ones that for a while seemed to be succeeding them. The first caveat is a theoretical one. Neither the Realist nor the Liberal alternative approach should simply be seen as mutually exclusive opposites. Instead, both are positions on a spectrum with various shaded mixtures between them. For instance, it is possible to distinguish between a purely Liberal approach on the one hand and a so-called "Liberal Hegemonist" on the other. The former would advocate maritime cooperation for its own sake, the latter more as a means of advancing national interest (Campbell, 2019). Arguably the West's Liberal hegemonism sparked the otherwise Westphalian Vladimir Putin into Russia's subsequent "grey zone operations" (Redman, 2019). The same fine distinctions can be seen amongst "Realists" too. Even the otherwise notably hard-nosed US Admiral Ernest J. King was also perfectly capable of espousing liberal causes such as support for anti-colonialism and the League of Nations, quite apart from squalid calculations of national interest.[7]

Secondly, and more practically, the juxtaposition between hard and soft security pre-occupations is not new, although the precise balance struck between them might be. Historically, navies have always performed these non-traditional security tasks to some degree.

For example, Mahan was perfectly aware that shipping for all its benefits needed to be predictable, traceable, compliant with detailed pick-up and delivery schedules and secure. This shipping dependency provided, he saw, both an opportunity and a challenge; sea-based globalisation was and remains potentially vulnerable to disruption. He warned us of this well over a century ago:

> This, with the vast increase in rapidity of communication, has multiplied and strengthened the bonds knitting together the interests of nations to one another, till the whole now forms an articulated system not only of prodigious size and activity, but of excessive sensitiveness, unequalled in former ages.
>
> *(Mahan, 1902, p. 144)*

The "excessive sensitiveness" that Mahan had in mind derives from the fact that interdependence, and indeed dependency of any sort, inevitably produces targets for the malign, whether criminals or hostile states, to attack. Because he thought, the "...commercial interest of the sea powers [... lies...] in the preservation of peace", he advocated multinational action in defence of such commercial interest and "righteous ideals" (Mahan, 1900, pp. 99–100; Sumida, 1997).

Today's deep and extended version of globalisation depends on a supply-chain philosophy of "just enough, just in time" that increases the system's vulnerability to disruption, particularly given the lamentably low reserve stocks of life essentials such as oil and food that most countries maintain. The marine transportation system's tendency to produce fewer but much larger tankers and container ships and to concentrate on nodal hub-ports intended to supply the needs of regions may also provide the malign with particularly fruitful targets as in the Straits of Malacca, for example. Many in fact would argue that the manifold threats to good order at sea are increasing faster than the world's agencies of law enforcement can keep up with (Urbina, 2019).

Thirdly, and as a result, the juxtaposition of the modern/ realist and postmodern approaches to maritime strategy does not represent a binary divide in which navies have to choose between either. For them all, it is instead a question of a mix of the two that best serves their strategic requirements. Diplomats and statesmen after all are not just narrowly concerned about their nation but also about its place in the system. Accordingly, within the limits of their resources, navies seek to deploy a fleet with capabilities that are balanced between the various demands of hard and soft security at sea.

Fourthly, the nature of that balance reflects changes in the international environment and so the mix of approaches is a dynamic one. Illustrating the point, Jeffery Frieden argues that there was high degree of globalisation in the late 19th century, but this was threatened by the rise of nationalism that led inevitably to highly competitive navalism (Frieden, 2006, p. 16). In the First World War, Niall Ferguson adds, the result was the destruction of 13 million tons of merchant shipping, the chief agent of globalisation (Ferguson, 2006, p. 73). The consequent depression and economic protectionism of the interwar years had their effect on the construction of fleets and helped lead to renewed war as previously discussed. With the end of that conflict and the run-down of the Cold War, however, a golden era globalisation encouraged a major shift especially in Western navies towards postmodern conceptions of their functions and nature.

But more recently the tide seems to be turning again as globalisation loses its glitter (especially for those which have benefitted from it the least) and with the re-birth of nationalism and great-power competition (Maull, 2019; Mearsheimer, 2019). From a Western perspective, widespread disorder at sea, the remorseless rise of Chinese maritime power and the apparent truculence of Russia culminating in 2022 invasion of Ukraine all suggested the emergence of a more troubled and competitive world. In consequence, the world's navies have recently been heavily investing – or in most Western navies re-investing – in the traditional, high-intensity war-fighting capabilities advocated by Mahan and Corbett. New technologies such as unmanned and autonomous systems, cyber operations, artificial intelligence, machine-learning and hypersonics may be transforming the ways in which the naval battle for supremacy at sea is conducted, but its essential strategic character remains. It will still be the precondition for the capacity to attack and defend shipping and to project military power against the shore. As though symbolically to underline the return to conventional/realist thinking about sea power, the US 2nd Fleet was reactivated in May 2018 to defend NATO's control of the Atlantic and took as its mission "'Ready to' Fight" so we don't have to (BBC News, 2018).

The result is a swing back to modern/traditional/realist conceptions of what navies are basically for. This is also exemplified in the US Navy's doctrinal formulations. In 2007 there appeared *A Cooperative Strategy for Twenty-first Century Seapower*. Even at the time this was controversial for its post-modern tone, for its emphasis on the idea of a global maritime partnership, and for the elevation of the hitherto subordinate functions of Maritime Security on the one hand and Humanitarian Assistance and Disaster Response on the other. By contrast, the second "refreshed" version of this strategy which appeared in 2015 put the struggle to assure access and to maintain a forward presence at the top of its priority list for the US Navy (Conway et al., 2008; Dunford et al., 2015). Subsequent doctrines, fleet planning and exercises in China, Russia, the United States and nearly all its allies and partners, together with many bystanders, have confirmed a striking return to traditional and competitive conceptions of naval purposes.

This does not mean, however, that the softer dimension of naval activity has disappeared, merely that it now commands less attention than it did. There is still recognition of the extent to which threats to good order at sea and to stability ashore may menace the current international order. Sometimes soft, cooperative ventures might simply be part and parcel of larger policies, such as the humanitarian sea-based rescues of civilians such as Operations *Passage to Freedom* of 1955 and *Frequent Wind* 20 years later in the Vietnam War. There is, additionally, obvious diplomatic advantage in being *seen* to behave as a cooperative state.

Moreover, recognition of the likely disastrous consequences of major inter-state war, even for the victors (if any), encourages the tendency for international rivalry and competitiveness to find expression in so-called "grey-zone" operations in the uneasy maritime shadowlands between peace and war and between hard and soft security. Many see the current disputants in the East and South China Seas making extensive use of liberal means for realist purposes, for example through manipulation of Maritime Security institutions and through the provision of help to maritime capacity building to weaker states (Yoshimatsu & Trinidad, 2017). China's Belt and Road Initiative, with its important maritime security components, can likewise be interpreted at least in part as a means of producing a Sino-centric "community of shared destiny" which serves the country's security interests (Callahan, 2016). Paradoxically, in all these cases, cooperation in Maritime Security, simply becomes another arena in which interstate competition is conducted.

The general increase in the level of great power competition, taken together with the extent to which realist thinking can leach into the institutions and conduct of Maritime Security operations, suggest that the traditional realist approach will continue to dominate the maritime scene, despite a greater awareness of the need for navies and coastguards to grapple with emerging non-traditional threats at sea. In sum, Maritime Security Operations seem likely to continue to be conducted in a space set by traditional naval preoccupations.

Notes

1 Both wrote extensively. Their most influential works were Mahan (1890) and Corbett (1911). Although there were many significant differences between them, both agreed on the core principles of maritime strategy. Corbett was more cautious about the feasibility and influence of power at sea and more focussed on its effects on land.
2 As described by John Hay, US Ambassador in London and quoted in Friedel (2002, p. 1).
3 For an introduction to Geopolitics see Gray and Sloan (1999).
4 Cited in Westcott, A, (ed) *Mahan on Naval Warfare* (Boston: Little, Brown & Co., 1919) pp. 16, 18.
5 Modern historiography tends to a more nuanced conclusion, making the point that the race effectively ended in 1912 with Germany's concession of defeat, and that relations between the two navies in 1914 were significantly more cordial than they had been before.
6 The literature on this is extensive. Buzan et al. (1998) provide a useful introduction.
7 See his essay 'The Influence of the National Policy on the Strategy of a War' dated 7 Nov 132 in the Archives of the US Naval War College, Newport. I am grateful to my colleague Professor Dave Kohnen for pointing this out to me.

References

Baer, G. W. (1994). *One Hundred Years of Sea Power: The U. S. Navy, 1890-1990.* Stanford University Press.

BBC News. (2018, May 5). *US Navy Resurrects Second Fleet in Atlantic to Counter Russia,* https://www.bbc.com/news/world-us-canada-44014761

Blair, T. (2007). *Reflections on 21st Century Security: Speech on HMS Albion.* Plymouth. 12 January 2007.

Bo, H. (2019). *Chinese Maritime Power in the 21st Century: Strategic Planning, Policy and Predictions.* Routledge.

Buzan, B., Weaver, O., & de Wilde, J. (1998). *Security: A New Framework for Analysis.* Lynne Rienner Publishers.

Callahan, W. A. (2016). China's "Asia Dream": The Belt Road Initiative and the New Regional Order. *Asian Journal of Comparative Politics, 1*(3), 1–18.

Campbell, C. (2019). Review of Stephen Walt's The Hell of Good Intentions. *Journal of Strategic Studies, 42*(3–4), 557–565.

Celander, L. (2018). *How Carriers Fought: Carrier Operations in World War II.* Casemate Publishers.

Conway, J. T., Roughead, G., & Allen, T. W. (2008). A Cooperative Strategy for 21st Century Seapower. *Naval War College Review, 61*(1). Department of the Navy. 1–19.

Cooper, R. (2004). *The Breaking of Nations. Order and Chaos in the Twenty-first Century.* Atlantic Books.

Corbett, J. S. (1911). *Some Principles of Maritime Strategy.* Longmans, Green & Co.

Dunford, J. F., Greenert, J., & Zukunft, P. F. (2015). *A Cooperative Strategy for 21st Century Seapower: Forward, Engaged, Ready.* Department of the Navy.

Ferguson, N. (2006). *The War of the World: Twentieth-century Conflict and the Descent of the West.* Penguin Books.

Friedel, F. B. (2002). *The Splendid Little War.* Burford books.

Frieden, J. A. (2006). *Global Capitalism: Its Fall and Rise in the Twentieth Century.* W.W. Norton.

Gorshkov, S. G. (1979). *The Sea Power of the State.* Pergamon Press.

Gray, C. (1992). *The Leverage of Sea Power: Strategic Advantage of Navies in Major Wars.* The Free Press.

Gray, C. S., & Sloan, G. (1999). *Geopolitics, Geography and Strategy.* Frank Cass.

Hu, B. (2019). Chinese Maritime Power in the 21st Century: Strategic Planning, Policy and Predictions. Routledge.

Lehman, J. (2018). *Oceans Ventured: Winning the Cold War at Sea.* W. W. Norton.

Livesey, William W. E. (1981). *Mahan on Sea Power.* University of Oklahoma Press.

Mahan, A. T. (1890). *The Influence of History Upon History 1660-1783.* Little, Brown and Company.

Mahan, A. T. (1900). *The Problem of Asia and its Effect on International Policies.* Sampson Low, Marston & Co.

Mahan, A. T. (1902). *Retrospect and Prospect*. Sampson Low, Marston & Co.

Maull, H. W. (2019). The Once and Future Liberal Order. *Survival*, *61*(2), 7–32.

Mearsheimer, J. (2019). Bound to Fail: The Rise and Fall of the Liberal International Order. *International Security*, *43*(4), 7–50.

Morgenthau, H. (2007). Six Principles of Political Realism. In R. J. Art, J. Robert and R. Jervis (Eds.), *International Politics, Enduring Concepts and Contemporary Issues* (pp. 34–38). Pearson, Longman.

Mullen, M. (2006). Principles for a Free and Secure Global Maritime Network. *The RUSI Journal*, *151*(1), 24–39.

Redman, N. (2019). Moscow Rules. *Survival*, *61*(3), 247–254.

Roosevelt, T. (1902, December 2). Second Annual Message to Congress. UVA Miller Center, https://millercenter.org/the-presidency/presidential-speeches/december-2-1902-second-annual-message.

Spykman, N. (1944). *The Geography of the Peace*. Harcourt, Brace & Co.

Stephen, T. (2006). USN Seeks Wider Seapower Definition. *Jane's Navy International*, July–August 2006.

Strassler, R. B. (1996). *The Landmark Thucydides: A Comprehensive Guide to the Peloponnesian War*. The Free Press.

Sumida, J. T. (1997). *Inventing Grand Strategy and Teaching Command: The Classic Works of Alfred Thayer Mahan Reconsidered*. Johns Hopkins University Press.

Till, G. (2018). *Seapower: A Guide for the Twenty-first Century* (4thed.). Routledge.

Urbina, I. (2019). *The Outlaw Ocean: Crime and Survival in the Last Untamed Frontier*. The Bodley Head.

Watkins, J. D. (1986). The Maritime Strategy. *Proceedings 112/1/1995 Supplement*. U.S. Naval Institute.

Westcott, A., (Ed.). (1919). *Mahan on Naval Warfare*. Little, Brown & Co.

Yoshimatsu, H., & Trinidad, D. (2017). Realist Objectives, Liberal Means: Japan, China, and Maritime Security in Southeast Asia. In S. B. Rothman, U. Vyas & Y. Sato (Eds.), *Regional Institutions, Geopolitics and Economics in the Asia-Pacific: Evolving Interests and Strategies* (pp. 127–143). Routledge.

4

MODERN MARITIME STRATEGY AND NAVAL WARFARE

Ian Speller

Maritime strategy and naval warfare have been recorded, discussed and debated for thousands of years and the diligent historian or strategist has a large back-catalogue of texts to consult. However, and despite the occasional nod towards Thucydides, for most commentators today engagement begins with the outpouring of works on this topic that occurred in the late nineteenth and early twentieth centuries. This period might reasonably be called a "golden age" of writing on maritime strategy, with publications by a variety of naval and civilian authors helping to identify, codify and popularise ideas and concepts that had previously been more apparent in practice than discussed in theory. In doing so, they transformed maritime strategy from an arcane subject, of interest mostly to those with salt in their beards, to an important topic that was within the mainstream of political-strategic discourse. They created a new language and a form of understanding that would set the terms of future debate and that have impacted on the way navies have thought and fought ever since. The concepts that they advanced remain current in modern naval strategy and doctrine, and are taught in most naval academies and staff colleges. That strategy in the digital age should be influenced by work written in the era of the coal-fired battleship, by people studying war in the age of sail, requires some explanation. This chapter aims to provide this and to introduce the reader to the core principles of maritime strategy and naval warfare today.

Traditional Maritime Strategy

The two most influential writers of the "golden age" were an American, Alfred Mahan (1840–1914), and an Englishman, Julian Corbett (1854–1922), although many others wrote on broadly similar themes and often with similar conclusions. Both Mahan and Corbett adopted an historical approach, seeking to derive enduring principles from the study of past campaigns. Mahan was an unreliable historian and presented ideas with a force that did not always allow for balanced analysis. He was fortunate in that his work was opportune. His first books appeared at a time (1890s) of growing interest in naval affairs. For many Mahan appeared to have captured essential and timeless truths about maritime strategy. His ideas had global impact within his lifetime and continue to impact on theory and practice today (Holmes, 2019).

Mahan's main "big idea" was that history had demonstrated the central importance of mastery at sea as a route towards national power and prosperity. His vision of "sea power" was

DOI: 10.4324/9781003001324-6

49

both economic and strategic, incorporating civilian and military uses of the sea. The link between the two was close. Maritime trade created wealth, but it also sponsored the generation of maritime resources (shipbuilding, port facilities, experienced seafarers, maritime focused policy makers) that supported the maintenance of a powerful navy that was required to protect that trade and could also be used to launch naval strikes and raids, support expeditions, seize colonies or bases, and strangle an adversary's economy by cutting their maritime communications. This was all founded on the key role of the sea as a vast connected manoeuvre space, a "global common", over which goods and military forces could move far more quickly and reliably than they could by land. Thus, he argued, "control of the sea by maritime commerce and naval supremacy means predominant influence in the world; because nothing facilitates the necessary exchanges as does the sea" (Mahan, 1894, p. 559).

For Mahan, the key to success lay in gaining mastery or command of the sea, the ability to protect maritime communications in peace and to control them in war. This was best secured by removing those things that threatened it, meaning the enemy navy, and his work strongly emphasised the need to concentrate naval forces, to achieve superior numbers at the decisive point, and to aggressively bring the enemy to battle. Once command was assured, navies would be free to focus on exploiting the sea for strategic and economic effect. He applied a Napoleonic paradigm of decisive battle to war at sea, describing offensive action to destroy the enemy fleet as a "fundamental principle" of naval warfare (Mahan, 1890, 1892, 1911).

Corbett's analysis was more nuanced than Mahan's and was grounded in a more professional approach to history. His conclusions tended to be more sophisticated and to be more reflective of the limitations, as well as the strengths, of maritime power. This, and his emphasis on the need for navies to cooperate with armies to achieve strategic effect, did not always endear him to those wearing dark blue. In particular, his tendency to argue that victory in battle might be difficult to force on a weaker foe (who could simply elect not to fight) and that such victory might not even be necessary, outraged those with more conventional views. Drawing on his reading of Clausewitz, Corbett recognised that maritime strategy was a sub-set of national strategy, it was not driven by its own logic, and that battle was just a means to an end. If that end could be achieved by a means other than battle, then it was foolish to accept an engagement on anything other than very favourable terms (Corbett, 1911).

Despite their differences, Mahan and Corbett can be identified as belonging to a dominant "blue-water" tradition of maritime strategy, that focused on the value of securing and exploiting command of the sea beyond local waters. Command did not mean physical occupation of the environment, as it might on land, as the sea cannot be occupied in this way. Rather, it related to the ability to control activity at sea. Defined by some in rather absolute terms, both Mahan and Corbett were clear that command would always be limited in time, space and degree. No navy had ever been able to command all of the sea all of the time, nor had they needed to. This is reflected in the modern phrase "sea control", usually defined as the condition where one has the freedom of action to use a particular area of the sea for a period of time and, if necessary, to deny its use to an opponent.

These ideas were relevant not only to large navies, small navies able to prevail against their peers might be able to reap major rewards through a traditional sea control approach, as did the Chilean Navy in the War of the Pacific (1879–1883). Here victory in battle eventually gave Chile control of the relevant seas, that could then be exploited to protect trade, blockade the enemy, move troops and to launch expeditionary operations that proved critical to final victory. The number of ships involved was small, but the impact was great, and the route and results fit the classic paradigm very well.

Modern Maritime Strategy and Naval Warfare

Traditional ideas, as discussed above, have tended to dominate discourse on maritime strategy. Henry Stimson may have been exaggerating, in the 1940s, when he argued that the US Navy Department frequently "seemed to retire from the realm of logic into a dim religious world in which Neptune was God, Mahan his prophet and the United States Navy his only true church" (Crowl, 1986, p. 444), but he may not have exaggerated much. This may have suited major navies, or navies (like that of Imperial Germany) that aspired to greatness, but Mahan's work offered rather little for those who were critically inferior to their likely enemies.

Historically, the most obvious route for a weaker navy was not to fight a losing battle to control the sea, but rather to pursue to lesser objective of denying such control to an enemy. This might revolve around the maintenance of a "fleet-in being"; whereby a significant naval force would be held in readiness, but avoid battle on unfavourable terms, on the assumption that its presence would reduce the enemy's options and, at the very least, force a substantial diversion of effort to guard against the threat posed by this fleet. Alternately, or in addition, weaker navies often focused on commerce raiding, sending individual ships or small squadrons to prey on enemy trade, without any attempt to gain command, adopting a form of guerrilla warfare at sea, as was advocated by the French "Jéune Ecole" in the late nineteenth century (Roksund, 2007). Such attacks tended not to have the strangling impact of blockade, but they could inflict costs on the enemy, disrupt their trade and force the diversion of significant assets to hunt down the raiders.

The development of new technology in the late nineteenth century promised to give new options to weaker navies. Long-range coastal artillery, sea mines, small fast torpedo boats and, in the twentieth century, submarines and aircraft, offered credible options to deny control even to those without a major navy. The successful Ottoman defence of the Dardanelles in 1915, using a system of mines, fixed coastal artillery and mobile howitzers, demonstrated how effective this could be, albeit in very confined waters. Similarly, submarines, mines and aircraft enhanced the options for commerce raiding, although experience in both world wars tended to reinforce the belief of traditionalists in the superiority of blockade over raiding undertaken without command of the sea.

In the inter-war years, the Soviet New School argued for an approach based on coastal defence and local sea denial, useless for imperial adventures but well suited to challenging the kind of western maritime intervention that the Soviets had suffered in 1918–1919 (Ranft & Till, 1983). Similarly, in the 1950s Communist China dealt with the threat of enemies superior at sea through the adoption of principles of guerrilla warfare at sea. The People's Liberation Army (Navy)'s first commander, Admiral Xiao Jinguang, described this as "sabotage warfare at sea", using surprise, deception, offensive spirit, unorthodox and unexpected methods to gain a series of incremental victories at sea as a means to defeat and deter enemy forces in local waters. In 1956 this was codified into the concept of "active defence" and remained PLA(N) policy until the adoption of the more ambitious "near seas defence" in the 1980s (Murphy & Yoshihara, 2015).

New technology has continued to provide options for weaker naval forces. The development of superior mines, cheap and efficient diesel-electric submarines and effective anti-ship missiles, have all seemed to reinforce the sea denial capacity of small navies in local waters. "Sabotage warfare at sea" was and is an option pursued by many, particularly those who fear attack by larger "sea control" navies. It is notable, however, that the Soviet Union abandoned the advice of their New School in the 1930s, adopting a more traditional approach to sea power, more suited to great power status. During the Cold War the weakness of their position relative to the United States reinforced this point, encouraging a process of expansion under Admiral Gorshkov, whose writings on maritime strategy (1974, 1979) sit comfortably within the tradition of Julian Corbett. Coastal defence might have suited a weak and beleaguered state, but a superpower required naval forces able to fulfil a range of missions far from home. One could argue, too, that China is on the path away from this alternative route, towards a much more traditional idea of maritime power and strategy, as is discussed below.

The classic works of maritime strategy generally focused on military roles and on the employment of navies in times of conflict, where the primary threat to control was other navies. Non-naval threats may not have been ignored entirely, but they were not the major area of interest. This tended also to be reflected in the ways in which navies (particularly larger navies) envisaged themselves, as organisations whose major purpose was to fight other navies. Navies did often find it useful to stress their utility as instruments of national power in situations short of war, and this generated considerable academic interest during the Cold War (See Cable, 1971; Luttwak, 1975; Booth, 1977). More mundane constabulary roles tended to receive much less attention and were discussed, when they were noticed at all, under the rubric of "good order at sea" (Till, 1982).

That situation changed somewhat after the end of the Cold War. Western navies were faced with a situation where, in the absence of a credible conventional enemy, they had an opportunity to prioritise different things and a need to do so in order to justify their share of diminishing defence budgets. The initial response for many was to emphasise power projection and crisis management far from home, and this led to a major re-emphasis on capabilities, such as amphibious ships, that could support such actions; note, for example, the US Navy's strategic concepts "... From the Sea" (1992) and "Forward ... from the Sea" (1994) (Haynes, 2015). In the early years of the new century "maritime security" gained prominence in naval thinking, not least because of US fears that instability at sea could be exploited by terrorists, within the context of the "global war on terror". The challenges that they faced, and the need to appear relevant, forced navies to place increased emphasis on non-traditional security threats and to cooperate with other agencies, and other navies, to deal with complex and often unpredictable problems.

This prompted a shift in the policies and priorities of many navies, who chose to focus on what Geoffrey Till (2018) described as "post-modern" roles, revolving around cooperative engagement with other navies to deal with transnational challenges, such as piracy, terrorism or human trafficking. This was reflected in the US 2007 "Co-operative Strategy for 21st Century Seapower", where the navy, marines and coast guard together emphasised the need to build maritime partnerships, supporting the notion of a global "1,000 ship navy" made up of allies, partners and friends cooperating to deal with common threats (US Department of the Navy, 2007). This did not represent a fundamental change in approaches to naval warfare, or to maritime strategy, but it did reflect a broader view of security and a new emphasis on the full range of maritime roles. It is important to note, however, that the 2015 update of that strategy returned to a more traditional interpretation of naval priorities and inter-state rivalry (US Department of the Navy, 2015).

Contemporary Naval Doctrine and Maritime Strategy

The works of traditional maritime strategy continue to influence discourse today. Academic commentary in this field tends to begin with a discussion of the relevance, or otherwise, of such work and, even in cases where the authors are not referred to directly, the analysis is often presented in terms that they helped to define. Mahan and Corbett remain the most prominent. Both are quoted on the first page of Geoffrey Till's influential study of "Seapower" (2018) and their work provides the starting point for other enquiries into contemporary maritime strategy and naval warfare (Speller, 2018; Holmes, 2019). Even those who dispute the value of Mahan's ideas have often felt the need to devote significant time to discussing them, for example note Andrew Lambert's recent work on "Sea Power States" (2018).

Traditional approaches to maritime strategy are taught in most western naval academies and staff colleges, and most naval officers have at least a passing acquaintance with the key writers, although in this author's experience the majority appear to limit their engagement to those extracts, they are required to read in preparation for lectures and seminars. Current western naval doctrine and strategy are built on core ideas that were laid down in the classic works. UK Ministry of Defence (2017) presents ideas about sea control, maritime communications and the importance of joint operations that are reflective of Corbett's ideas. The same is true of the published doctrine and strategy of other navies, including, for example, those of Australia (2010, 2017), India (2015) and the Netherlands (2014).

Mahan is not cited in the latest US maritime strategy, published in December 2020, but it is not difficult to detect his influence (US Department of the Navy, 2020). The sea is defined in traditional terms as "a competitive space that has served as both a strategic buffer and a vital connection to the world" and the strategy provides a powerful call to arms, emphasising the need for long term investment in "all domain naval power" to meet the challenge posed, primarily, by state-base rivals. China is identified as providing the main threat, particularly in the context of the exponential growth of its navy, coast guard and maritime paramilitary forces, and also through the challenge that it apparently poses to a "rules-based international order". The strategy explains the need for a renewed emphasis on sea control and notes the importance of an offensive capacity to achieve such control within the context of high-intensity war fighting. It also notes the challenge posed by maritime security threats and by state-sponsored hybrid threats below the threshold for war, and explores ways in which the navy, marines and coast guard can cooperate, with allies and partners, in response. In this respect it offers a more rounded vision of maritime strategy than might have been offered during the Cold War, reflecting on the need to meet challenges across the "continuum of conflict".

US naval doctrine, updated in 2020, also discusses naval warfare in terms that are decidedly Mahanian, and notably more so than the previous edition published a decade earlier (US Navy, 2010, 2020). "Command of the sea" is described as a "fundamental strategic pillar of our nation, necessary for the security and prosperity of our citizens". The document repeatedly emphasises the importance of sea control, described as the "manifestation of lethality afloat", as the key activity that "enables all other functions". It stresses the significance of aggressive offensive action and a willingness to engage the enemy as key enablers in the battle for such control and illustrates with reference to past campaigns. The doctrine does not neglect maritime security, which is listed as one of five "enduring functions" of the naval service (alongside power projection, deterrence, sealift and sea control). However, there is a clear emphasis on hard security roles (Drennan, 2020).

Even the title of the US Navy's "Design for Maintaining Maritime Superiority" (2018) reflects a traditional emphasis on mastery at sea. That document focuses explicitly on great power competition, on the challenge posed by other navies and on the central importance of being able to compete for sea control in order to protect sea lines of communication, assure access to markets and enable global power projection. The manner in which this will be achieved differs greatly from that discussed by Mahan, reflecting changes in technology and of wider context. The emphasis today is on "Distributed Maritime Operations" (DMO), seemingly in contrast to Mahan's emphasis on the need for concentration. DMO reflects a response to the growing challenge of anti-access technologies, but also to the growing potential for advanced data links to network dispersed assets into a deadly, coherent whole. Under

DMO, ships may not be concentrated physically, but the idea is that they can concentrate their effect, where it matters, to engage and defeat enemy systems. The mechanism has changed since the battleship era, but the idea appears distinctly Mahanian. The US Navy's "Surface Forces Strategy" (US Commander Naval Surface Forces, 2017) is even more clearly within this tradition. Subtitled "return to sea control" the document articulates the requirement to re-focus on the battle for sea control, to enhance the offensive and defensive capacity of all US Navy vessels, on the principle that "if it floats, it fights".

US naval policy is grounded in a general approach to the strategic utility of the sea, and the requirement for offensive operations to secure sea control, that is redolent of Mahan, and also Corbett, given the emphasis placed on the need to cooperate fully with joint forces to deal with threats that may originate on land, at sea, in the air, space, cyberspace or through the electromagnetic spectrum. Of course, noting the congruence between traditional writings and current practice does not necessarily mean that the latter is inspired directly by the former. Current US strategy reflects an appreciation of the ends, ways and means required to meet national requirements today. But these are viewed through a filter that is influenced, consciously or otherwise, by ideas about maritime strategy that were codified and popularised over a century ago and that form the basis of teaching in most western naval academies and staff colleges. Thus, Professor James Holmes of the US Naval War College has argued that Mahan's "fundamental ideas" are "encoded into the sea services DNA" (Holmes & Delamer, 2017).

It may be the case that some navies follow the "logic" of these ideas even in the absence of a credible enemy. The Brazilian Navy's pursuit of nuclear-powered attack submarines (Olivares, 2018) appears to be driven by a very traditional desire to impact the contest for sea control in the Atlantic Ocean even in the absence of any obvious adversary, and despite more immediate challenges much lower down the spectrum of conflict. This does not stop Brazil contributing to maritime security missions at home and overseas but does represent a very major investment of scarce capital in an advanced war-fighting capability, despite the absence of any obvious conventional adversary.

It is important to note that many navies do not follow a traditional route. The latest version of Russian Maritime Doctrine emphasises the importance of activity at sea and the need to secure and protect access. However, the focus is less on maintaining and exploiting wartime control in a traditional sense, and more on deterring attack, or punishing transgressions, through an ability to deny local seas and to launch devastating responses using sea-based strike systems, such as the Kalibr missile (Davis, 2015). In peacetime, the Russians wish to exploit the military, economic and political potential of the seas in a multi-dimensional way, and they have proved adept at exploiting the grey area between war and peace to bring pressure to bear on Ukraine, through low-level maritime aggression. In terms of major conflict, they seem less interested in gaining mastery at sea, and to focus more on disputing and mitigating the impact of their rival's maritime capabilities. It reflects a different tradition to that of the US Navy.

The recent growth in the size, reach and capability of the PLA(N) has prompted much discussion about the extent to which China has been influenced by traditional concepts, usually identified with Mahan. Some authors have argued that China is self-consciously influenced by his work, following a strategy focused on command and on securing and exploiting access from the sea (Kane, 2002; Yoshihara & Holmes, 2018). Others contest this idea, pointing to a lack of firm evidence of such influence, and to the lack of any obvious value to China of Mahan's approach (Cheng, 2011).

In recent years the PLA(N) has emphasised the need to establish "command of the sea" in waters important to China, defining such command as "control over a given maritime area, for a given period", in terms that resemble current western definitions of sea control. Thus, in

2017, the commander of the PLA(N) argued that "command of the sea is the eternal topic of the navy ... [it] must always be the main focus of its construction of core military capabilities" (Martinson, 2020, p. 12). It appears likely that the PLA(N) aims in future to be able to challenge the US Navy for control within the "first island chain", with heavy support from land-based systems, and to reduce US capacity to project power into the region by denying control further afield, notably in the Philippine Sea, through a denial approach described in 2014 by the then commander of the PLA(N) as "far seas sabotage-raid warfare" (Martinson, 2020, p. 10). If not necessarily in the tradition of Mahan, it is an approach that recognises the strategic importance of the sea and critical importance of sea control and denial against major state rivals.

It is impossible to generalise on the maritime strategy and policy of the world's many small navies (Mulqueen et al., 2014; McCabe et al., 2018). Some have very limited capabilities and focus primarily on maritime security roles within their own EEZ, including, for example, most navies of Sub-Saharan Africa. Others focus on maritime security and also seek to contribute to collaborative security missions or to peace-keeping operations further afield, and the Irish Naval Service and Royal New Zealand Navy provide examples of these. On the other hand, some small navies exist in areas where they feel that their safety might be threatened by "hard se-curity" challenges, and these often then focus on matters of sea control and denial that reflect the traditional model. Thus, during the Cold War the navies of Denmark, Norway and Sweden focused primarily on the apparent threat posed by the Soviet Union and tailored their approach towards local sea denial and self-defence. When the threat abated in the 1990s, with the collapse of their potential adversary, all three re-focused on maritime security and collaborative en-gagement to deal with non-traditional threats beyond local waters. However, policy has changed once again, with renewed focus on the challenge posed by Russia. This does not mean that broader security tasks are no longer relevant, but they are trumped in terms of naval policy and strategy by the more immediate threat to the east (Olsen, 2017; Granholm, 2018). The small navies of east and southeast Asia face similar challenges, in the context of their proximity to China (Till, 2017).

New Challenges and Old Concepts

The essence of traditional maritime strategy is that control of the sea confers strategic advantage through the capacity to strangle enemy trade whilst protecting one's own, and through the potential to exploit (or deny) for military purposes a manoeuvre space that covers two-thirds of the planet. It is not impossible that some political, legal or technological development could make the traditional concepts irrelevant, but this has not happened yet.

Globalisation makes the sea more not less important, as international trade flows primarily by maritime means and inter-continental internet traffic is carried largely by under-sea cables. At a time where states may be reluctant to base troops overseas on foreign soil, or to host such bases, the sea continues to provide a medium that gives global access to those military forces that can use it. Changes in maritime geography cause by climate change, such as the opening of new routes through the arctic, may shift the location of some naval activity and will cause con-frontation in spaces that were previously relatively benign, but this is likely to reinforce rather than to change any fundamental principles of naval warfare and maritime strategy.

Developments in maritime law, notably through the widespread acceptance of the 1982 UN Convention on the Law of the Sea, impact on maritime rights and responsibilities and have created new challenges for navies in terms of protecting or disputing claims of maritime jur-isdiction. However, these have not yet had a profound impact on the ability of navies to use the seas. Fears about the impact of creeping territorialisation of the sea, which could undermine the entire basis of current strategy, by challenging freedom of manoeuvre, have prompted a robust response. Thus, for example, Chinese attempts to assert greater maritime rights in the South China Seas have prompted the US to challenge their interpretation through frequent "Freedom of Navigation" cruises through disputed waters (Bateman, 2020).

For the foreseeable future, navies will continue to operate in a medium that offers them global reach and access without the need to cross international boundaries or to infringe on the sovereignty of others. This helps them to provide flexible options for military intervention, both benign and aggressive, making balanced navies immensely useful tools for diplomatic signalling and for the application of limited military force in situations short of war (Le Miere, 2014; Rowlands, 2018).

The military advantage gained from use of the sea, and thus the value in disputing such use, has been demonstrated across the spectrum of conflict from the dawn of time to recent operations in Libya, Syria and Yemen. The value is not limited to conventional navies. The sea has always been exploited for criminal purposes and non-state groups have also used it for political ends, to move people and goods, to launch attacks and to deny access. That some non-state groups can possess relatively sophisticated sea denial capabilities was demonstrated by successful attacks at sea by the Liberation Tigers of Tamil Eelam, during the Sri Lankan Civil War, and more recently by successful missile and rocket attacks undertaken by Hezbollah in Lebanon and by Houthi rebels in Yemen.

In terms of major conflict, it seems likely that sea control and denial will continue to be important in enabling or inhibiting activity such as strikes from the sea, maritime transportation, expeditionary operations, and blockade and interdiction, and this is reflected in contemporary strategy and doctrine. Commerce raiding may be problematic as the internationalised nature of global maritime trade would make it very difficult to limit the impact of this activity only to the belligerent states. On the other hand, it would be naïve to assume that this alone means that such a campaign can never take place, and the Tanker War in the Gulf during the 1980s demonstrates both the capacity for states (or others) to deliberately attack neutral shipping and the associated need for naval intervention to protect trade. Recent Iranian harassment of ships around the Strait of Hormuz reinforces the point. Attempts by pirates or politically motivated actors to attack or hijack ships also pose a threat to commercial activity, and often require a military response, as is discussed in detail elsewhere in this volume. Blockade, legal or otherwise, remains a viable weapon in both war and peace; note the Israeli blockade of Gaza and the Saudi blockade of Houthi held territory in Yemen, and also maritime interdiction operations conducted in support of UN sanctions (Elleman & Paine, 2006; Fink, 2017).

Sadly, there seems to be little or no chance that the sea will cease to be a contested space within the foreseeable future. Use of the sea confers advantage in conflict situations, meaning that if states and other groups find reasons to fight, they will find reasons to fight at and from the sea. That fight may often be very one-sided, as in the case of NATO intervention in Libya in 2011, or Russian strikes during the Syrian Civil War, or it may be more evenly fought, particularly in areas where the weaker navy can exploit local conditions and rely on the support of land-based forces to deny control within regional waters.

The potential for groups to launch "hybrid attacks", operating just below their adversary's threshold for the use of military force, exploiting the grey area between war and peace, figures prominently in current academic and professional discourse (Stoker & Whiteside, 2020). This is true also of the maritime environment, where actors may launch unclaimed or false flag attacks designed to deny access, to create instability or to sow discord in support of some aim. Tools might include

Modern Maritime Strategy and Naval Warfare

covert deployment of mines, attacks by "little blue sailors" with military-grade weapons and training but without identification flags or insignia, deniable attacks on cables and under-sea infrastructure, state-sponsored terrorism against ships or shore infrastructure, or cyber-attacks on infrastructure and critical enablers such as satellite-based communications and aids to navigation (Stavridis, 2016). The propensity of the Chinese to use their fishing fleet as an undeclared tool of national policy, and a potential trigger for coastguard or naval intervention, reflects another aspect of this. Navies thus need to be able to provide responses to challenges that bridge the gap between peace and war, and to be able to cooperate closely with coastguards and other maritime agencies, to respond to complex challenges that do not easily sit within the traditional paradigm of war and peace. It is a point that is reflected in western military thought and practice, prompting a renewed emphasis on a capacity for flexible response across the whole spectrum of conflict.

New Technology

There is, and always has been, a vibrant debate about the extent to which new technology has made traditional concepts obsolete. In the twentieth century new weapons, including sub-marines, aircraft and anti-ship missiles, appeared to challenge established ideas based on securing control. However, the challenges were more tactical than strategic. New technology prompted new approaches to meet new challenges. The cost of getting the response wrong could be very high, and usually involved people getting wet. However, despite frequent claims to the contrary, naval fundamentals did not change. Navies still sought to gain or deny control, and to exploit that control in ways that were broadly reflective of past practice, and that exploited new technology to increase their range and reach. Techniques and technology changed, sometimes dramatically, but key principles remained. Even nuclear weapons, the most disruptive tech-nology of all, did not make navies irrelevant, as was soon proven by experience during the Cold War (Speller, 2018).

Recent and evolving technology may both enable and inhibit naval activity. New weapon systems, including electromagnetic rail guns, directed energy weapons (especially lasers and microwave weapons), "piloted" drones and autonomous unmanned systems, all have the po-tential to increase both the offensive and defensive power of advanced navies. At the same time, the wider availability of anti-ship weapons, and particularly the proliferation of mines, rockets and anti-ship cruise missiles, allied to the development of new and more deadly systems, such as hypersonic cruise missiles, hypersonic glide weapons and anti-ship ballistic missiles, challenge survivability, particularly of surface ships which are necessary platforms for a range of important activities. In terms of high-end warfighting, we are likely to see a continuation of the action-reaction cycle whereby developments in one field are met by countermeasures in another. Thus, for example, lasers may provide a counter to hypersonic weapons and offer defence against attacks by swarming autonomous drones. Piloted drone attacks may be defeated using electro-magnetic countermeasure. Improved offensive submarine capabilities may be matched by improved anti-submarine warfare, seabed detection systems, and by the continued use of submarines to hunt submarines and so on. The result is not pre-ordained, but it is far from clear that anything has happened, or is likely to happen, to make navies redundant in the near future.

On the other hand, today even some sub-state groups have access to sophisticated anti-ship weaponry. Houthi attacks on Saudi and other shipping off the coast of Yemen, using rather basic rockets, drones and remotely piloted unmanned vehicles, demonstrate some capacity to challenge their adversary's use of the sea (Reuters, 2020). The successful attack conducted by Hezbollah on an Israeli corvette off the coast of Lebanon using an anti-ship cruise missile, in

2006, demonstrates a greater degree of capability and it is reasonable to expect continued proliferation of such weapons. Future navies will have to show a greater degree of caution when approaching a conflict zone and will require an array of rather expensive defensive capabilities if they are to do so in safety. They will also need to be aware that some threats, including ballistic missiles, terrorist/special forces operations and cyber-attacks may challenge them even in their home base.

Anti-Access/Area-Denial (A2/AD)

Current debate often revolves around the challenge to control that can be represented by anti-access and area denial (A2/AD) techniques and technology. This represents a fusion of old and new technology, allied to new techniques designed to challenge access across all domains (land, sea, air, cyber, space, electromagnetic spectrum). It is argued that new technology can give even relatively weak adversaries the ability to challenge access to particular areas or to degrade freedom of movement within a theatre. Well-equipped opponents may be able to challenge access to the extent that some sea areas may be simply too dangerous to enter, particularly for large valuable (and therefore scarce) assets such as aircraft carriers (Tangredi, 2013). This may mean that such assets have to keep out of the most dangerous areas, placing a premium on the capacity to project power from over the horizon and also on the utility of stealth. It may also increase the utility of smaller, cheaper and less personnel intense assets, including unmanned drones, whose loss would not be mission-critical. In many respects this is a return to the historical norm; even dominant navies have usually had to accept that there were places they did not go.

Current US naval plans make clear that they expect to have to fight to secure sea control in any future conflict against a significant adversary. That also represents a return to the norm after three decades of unprecedented hegemony at sea. It is now generally recognised that the fight for control must involve all services, and also include engagement with partners and allies. Only a synergistic joint (i.e., inter-service) response can meet the multi-dimensional challenges that all armed forces face. The point is well reflected in US naval policy and in the policy and doctrine of the other services, hence the current focus on "multi-domain operations" (US Army, 2018; USAF, 2020). The US Navy also recognises the need to work as closely as possible with partners and allies, in a world where naval superiority is no longer assured (US Department of the Navy, 2020).

The requirement today is for "commons control" across all warfighting domains; sea control alone is not enough to secure all-domain access in a contested joint operating environment (US Joint Forces Command, 2016). One should also note the "return to sea control" of some European navies who have shifted back to emphasising the capacity to meet potential Russian aggression at sea, as they did during the Cold War, after a period where cooperative engagement in support of maritime security tasks had been accorded a higher priority (Olsen, 2017; Granholm, 2018).

This will have implications lower down the spectrum of conflict, where navies undertaking maritime security missions may need to be aware of the possibility that some actors may have access to weapons that can place friendly assets in grave danger. Effective counter-measures, even to relatively cheap mines and missiles, imply the presence of expensive defensive capabilities which lie beyond the reach of many "non-war fighting" navies. In future, these may find that their ability to operate within even a moderately contested environment is dependent on the cover provided by those with deeper pockets. There is a further point worthy of note here. Many of these threats (missiles, rockets, etc.) are best countered by strikes to destroy the launchers before they are in a position to initiate an attack. This may be problematic where rules of engagement deny the right to launch a pre-emptive defensive strike, increasing the need for expensive defences systems for ships that may have to grant the first strike to their adversaries, or else for a robust attitude towards risk.

Conclusion

Traditional approaches to maritime strategy and naval warfare are based on the belief in the strategic importance of the sea, for economic and military purposes, and on the importance of gaining, maintaining and exploiting sea control or in denying such control to an adversary. For many writers and practitioners, the key to naval warfare was victory in battle aggressively pursued to secure mastery at sea by destroying assets capable of challenging control. More nuanced analysis identified that sea control was a means to an end, rather than an end in itself, and that battle was not the only means of securing control, which meant no more than the ability to use the sea and to deny that use to others. This was linked to the understanding that maritime strategy was a subset of national strategy and as such must serve national interests and priorities that would differ in time and place.

Classic works of maritime strategy did not devote much time to maritime security issues. Today maritime security is generally recognised to be an important element within a much broader view of what is encompassed by "maritime strategy". Indeed, for a period in the 2000s maritime security gained a notable prominence within such strategy. Today, for many navies, the greater emphasis is once more on traditional concerns of sea control and denial in the context of great power competition. This may reflect a return to their comfort zone for some admirals and commentators who, one suspects, are happy to focus once again on the things that they always felt were important after a period where expediency forced them to emphasise something different.

It appears that nothing, in terms of the way in which the sea is conceived and used, has altered the central importance of established ideas about sea control and sea denial. The globalised world economy is even more dependent on the sea than it was in Mahan's time, and the maritime domain continues to represent a medium that can be exploited for strategic effect. Technological advances will entail tactical responses, as they always have, but do not appear to have driven any fundamental change in strategic principles insofar as they relate to naval warfare.

Today, the basic principles of maritime strategy still apply or, at least, most navies still believe that they apply, and this is reflected in both theory and practice. Of course, the manner in which principles apply will change. Mahan formulated ideas about concentration and offensive battle at a time when that suited the tactics and technology. Today concentration is more likely to be of effect rather than of location. Intelligent strategy may require navies to forego the offensive in certain conditions, and to be circumspect about where they go. It is also important to recognise that many navies will not follow the dominant blue-water tradition. For them, the best route may be to focus on denial. For those that pursue "sabotage warfare at sea", Xiao Jinguang may be more relevant than Mahan. There is nothing new about this. Different navies will do different things to meet different needs, or at least they should do if maritime strategy is to serve national policy. What is certain is that people will continue to try to gain strategic advantage from the sea, and that navies will be employed in support or denial of this.

References

Bateman, S. (2020, January 21). *Freedom of navigation and the law of the sea. Asia and the Pacific Policy Society.* https://www.policyforum.net/freedom-of-navigation-and-the-law-of-the-sea/

Booth, K. (1977). *Navies and foreign policy.* Croom Helm.

Cable, J. (1971). *Gunboat diplomacy. The political application of limited naval force.* Praeger.

Cheng, D. (2011). The influence of sea power on China, or the influence of Mahan on Yoshihara and Holmes? *Asia Policy, 12,* 142–146.

Corbett, J. (1911). *Some principles of maritime strategy.* Longmans.

Crowl, P. (1986). Alfred Thayer Mahan: The naval historian. In P. Paret (Ed.), *Makers of modern strategy from machiavelli to the nuclear age* (pp. 444–477).Princeton University Press.

Davis, A. (Trans.). (2015). *Maritime doctrine of the Russian federation.* US Naval War College.

Drennan, J. (2020, August 6). Naval warfare 2010–2020: A comparative analysis. *Center for International Maritime Security.* http://cimsec.org/naval-warfare-2010–2020-a-comparative-analysis/45129

Elleman, B., & Paine, S. (2006). *Naval blockades and seapower: Strategies and counter-strategies, 1805–2005.* Routledge.

Fink, M. (2017). Naval blockade and the humanitarian crisis in Yemen. *Neverlands International Law Review, 64,* 291–307.

Gorshkov, S. (1974). *Navies in war and peace.* Naval Institute Press.

Gorshkov, S. (1979). *The seapower of the state.* Pergamon.

Granholm, N. (2018). Small navies and naval warfare in the Baltic sea region. In R. McCabe, D. Sanders, & I. Speller (Eds.), *Europe, small navies and maritime security* (pp. 71–88). Routledge.

Haynes, P. (2015). *Towards a new maritime strategy: American naval thinking in the post-Cold War era.* Naval Institute Press.

Holmes, J. (2019). *A brief guide to maritime strategy.* Naval Institute Press.

Holmes, J., & Delamer, K. (2017). Mahan rules. *US Naval Institute Proceedings, 143*(5). https://www.usni.org/magazines/proceedings/2017/may

Indian Navy. (2015). *Indian maritime doctrine: Naval strategic publication 1.1.* Integrated Ministry of Defence India. (2015). https://www.indiannavy.nic.in/content/indian-maritime-doctrine-2015-version

Kane, T. (2002). *Chinese grand strategy and maritime power.* Frank Cass.

Lambert, A. (2018). *Seapower states: Maritime culture, continental empires and the conflict that made the modern world.* Yale University Press.

Le Miere, C. (2014). *Maritime diplomacy in the 21st century: Drivers and challenges.* Routledge.

Luttwak, E. (1975). *The political uses of sea power.* Johns Hopkins University Press.

Mahan, A. T. (1890). *The influence of sea power upon history, 1660-1783.* Little Brown & Co.

Mahan, A. T. (1892). *The influence of sea power upon the French revolution and empire, 1793–1812.* Little Brown & Co.

Mahan, A. T. (1894). Possibilities of an Anglo-American reunion. *The North American Review, 159*(456), 552–573.

Mahan, A. T. (1911). *Naval strategy.* Little Brown & Co.

Martinson, R. D. (2020). Counter-intervention in Chinese naval strategy. *Journal of Strategic Studies, 44*(2), 1–23.

McCabe, R., Sanders, D., & Speller, I. (2018). *Europe, small navies and maritime security.* Routledge.

Mulqueen, M., Sanders, D., & Speller, I. (Eds.). (2014). *Strategy and policy for small navies in war and peace.* Routledge.

Murphy, M., & Yoshihara, T. (2015). Fighting the naval hegemon. Evolution in French, Soviet and Chinese naval thought. *Naval War College Review, 68*(3), 13–28.

Olivares, P. (2018, December 14). *Brazil takes its first step in program to join nuclear powered sub club.* Reuters. https://www.reuters.com/article/us-brazil-submarine/brazil-take-first-step-in-program-to-join-nuclear-powered-sub-club-idUSKBN1OD2CV

Olsen, J. A. (2017). *NATO and the North Atlantic. Revitalizing collective defence.* RUSI.

Ranft, B., & Till, G. (1983). *The sea in Soviet strategy.* Macmillan.

Reuters. (2020, August 30). *Saudi-led coalition destroy explosive laden drone, boat launched by Yemen's Houthis.* https://www.reuters.com/article/saudi-security-yemen-idAFL8N2FW0QO

Roksund, E. (2007). *The Jeune Ecole.* Brill.

Rowlands, K. (2018). *Naval diplomacy in the 21st century.* Routledge.

Royal Australian Navy. (2010). *Australian maritime doctrine*. https://www.navy.gov.au/sites/default/files/documents/Amd2010.pdf

Royal Australian Navy. (2017). *Australian maritime operations*. https://www.navy.gov.au/media-room/publications/australian-maritime-operations-2017

Royal Netherlands Navy. (2014). *Fundamentals of maritime operations. Netherlands maritime military operations.* https://english.defensie.nl/downloads/publications/2014/02/13/netherlands-maritime-military-doctrine

Speller, I. A. (2018). *Understanding naval warfare* (2nd ed.). Routledge.

Stavridis, J. (2016). Maritime hybrid warfare is coming. *US Naval Institute Proceedings, 132* (12). 30–33.

Stoker, D., & Whiteside, C. (2020). Blurred lines: Gray-zone conflict and hybrid war—Two failures of American strategic thinking. *US Naval War College Review, 73*(1). https://digital-commons.usnwc.edu/nwc-review/vol73/iss1/4/

Tangredi, S. (2013). *Anti-access warfare: Countering A2/AD strategies.* Naval Institute Press.

Till, G. (1982). *Maritime strategy and the nuclear age.* St. Martin's Press.

Till, G. (2017). *Asia's naval expansion: An arms race in the making?* Routledge.

Till, G. (2018). *Seapower: A guide for the twenty-first century* (4th ed.). Routledge.

UK Ministry of Defence. (2017). *Joint doctrine publication 0-10. Maritime power* (5th ed.). DCDC.

USAF. (2020, March 5). *Air force doctrine note 1–20. USAF role in joint all domain operations.* https://www.doctrine.af.mil/Portals/61/documents/Notes/Joint%20All-Domain%20Operations%20Doctrine--CSAF%20signed.pdf

US Army. (2018, August 9). *The US army in multi-domain operations 2028.* Retrieved August 10, 2020, from https://www.tradoc.army.mil/Portals/14/Documents/MDO/TP525-3-1_30Nov2018.pdf

US Commander Naval Surface Forces. (2017). *Surface force strategy. Return to sea control.* https://www.public.navy.mil/surfor/Documents/Surface_Forces_Strategy.pdf

US Department of the Navy. (2000). *Advantage at sea: Prevailing with integrated all-domain naval.* Department of the Navy.

US Department of the Navy. (2007). *A cooperative strategy for 21st century sea power.* Department of the Navy.

US Department of the Navy. (2015). *A cooperative strategy for 21st century sea power.* (2nd (revised) ed.). Department of the Navy.

US Joint Forces Command. (2016). *Joint operating environment 2035. The joint force in a contested and disordered world.* https://www.jcs.mil/Portals/36/Documents/Doctrine/concepts/joe_2035_july16.pdf?ver=2017-12-28-162059-917

US Navy. (2010). *Naval doctrine publication No. 1. Naval warfare.* Department of the Navy.

US Navy. (2018). *A design for maintaining maritime superiority. Version 2.* Department of the Navy.

US Navy. (2020). *NDP 1. Naval doctrine.* Department of the Navy.

Yoshihara, T., & Holmes, J. (2018). *Red star over the Pacific: China's rise and the challenge to U.S. maritime strategy* (2nd ed.). Naval Institute Press.

5

THE LIBERAL APPROACH TO MARITIME SECURITY

Rafael García Pérez

The sea is a recurring scene of international confrontation. Diplomatic encounters between maritime states are persistent and at least a third of these disagreements reach a military dimension (Frederick et al., 2017).

Nowadays, several countries have open maritime disputes. China has engaged in ten diplomatic conflicts, many with its neighbours (among them Senkaku/Diaogu, Spratly or Paracels), in one of the regions with the greatest naval tensions today, the South China Sea. Russia with nine open contentious issues, being the most serious one the confrontation with Ukraine in the Kerch Strait in 2018; or Turkey, which starred in an incident off Greece and Cyprus in 2020, due to the expansion of its continental shelf in the Mediterranean. In the modern age, this type of confrontation takes place more frequently at sea than on land.

The liberal perspective of maritime security tries to avoid the militarisation of these conflicts through diplomatic management and the establishment of a normative framework, protected by international institutions that guarantee freedom of navigation, free trade and the preservation of global common goods. Furthermore, the establishment of security regimes contributes extensively to conflict management and disputes resolution.

Empirical evidence demonstrates that states with greater naval capabilities tend to claim greater maritime areas on the high seas. Actually, these conflicts tend to materialise more frequently between developed states, even within democracies, and there is greater success in solving them through the application of international norms and the participation and involvement of multilateral institutions (McLaughlin Mitchell, 2020).

But naval conflicts go beyond territorial disputes. Climate change driven by global warming also exacerbates the risk of conflict. The foreseeable rise in sea level threatens coastal communities that represent half of the world population, with a population density much higher than average (García Pérez, 2019). Warming ocean waters has dramatic effects on fish stocks given its impact in rising water acidity. With this, mortality escalates and migration patterns change. Therefore, access to fishing grounds will represent a growing element of dispute in the near future (Caverley & McLaughlin Mitchell, 2021).

A liberal approach to maritime security craves to manage conflict through the application of institutionalised international norms in a multilateral framework of global governance (Nemeth et al., 2014). Although sharing the fundamental principles of liberalism in security studies (Baldwin, 1993), there has been no systematic attempt to transfer its postulates to the theoretical

62

DOI: 10.4324/9781003001324-7

plan of maritime security (Rahman, 2009, p. 3). In fact, some of its theories do not find application in this area. For example, the theory of democratic peace upheld by the premise that democracies do not engage in war with each other (Owen, 2018), does not find an empirical translation to the maritime domain. As studies by McLaughlin Mitchell and Prins (1999) and Daniels and McLaughlin Mitchell (2017) have shown, democracies have not avoided maritime territorial conflicts with their democratic peers.

Still, other aspects of liberalism, such as the concept of human security, have in fact been transferred to the field of maritime security (Liotta & Owen, 2006). Human security, understood as a complex of societal security, environmental security, food security and economic security (Martin & Owen, 2013), is more connected to the concept of development than to the traditional theoretical frameworks associated with security and defence. However, the relationship between human security and maritime security has not yet received much attention in academic literature, although there is a close relationship between the two on several dimensions: the vulnerability of coastal populations as well as regarding those who work and transit the sea (Bueger, 2015). In any case, the concept of human security applied to maritime security offers a holistic perspective of the management of security problems by collectively addressing the legal, institutional, economic and social conditions that contribute to reducing illegal activities carried out in the marine environment. In certain settings, such as the Gulf of Guinea, regulatory developments in maritime security adopted by coastal states are specifically anchored in the notions of human security, disarmament, development, the eradication of poverty and environmental protection (Yaoundé Code of Conduct, 2013).

Nevertheless, the liberal approach has reached greater development and impact in the normative dimension, becoming the main pacifying factor of coexistence at sea and the foundation of ocean governance. In this sense, the liberal conception of security permeates the architecture of maritime security built after the Second World War in at least two domains: in regulatory development and the creation of governance regimes in the maritime domain, by applying a spatial criterion.

These two dynamics have fuelled great progress in the conception of security in the marine environment. First, there has been an expansion of the jurisdiction of the coastal states over their adjacent waters. At the same time, there has been increasing governance over international spaces, understood as spatially delimited material entities (such as, but not limited to, the oceans) (Young, 2011). These international spaces are regions, and resources, that are outside the jurisdiction of the states. Their singular economic, political and environmental importance, and the need to protect them from international competition aimed at conquest, allowed for the construction of a new legal notion for protection: the "common heritage of humanity" (International Ocean Institute, 2018).

The traditional conception of these spaces and resources, considered as *res communis*, defends the idea that they are available for use and exploitation by any state acting on its own authority. However, the liberal conception affirms that the members of international society have authority as a collective to establish rules that govern the use of these international spaces.

This has been widely accepted, resulting in the adoption of constitutive agreements that regulate governance of the oceans, the most significant of which is the United Nations Convention on the Law of the Sea (UNCLOS, 1982), defined as "the constitution of the oceans" (Koh, 1982).

The set of rules and procedures articulated in UNCLOS provides the framework to establish the foundations of governance for the marine environment, but they do not satisfy security needs on concrete issues that must be specifically addressed (Oude Elferink, 2005). Substantive issues such as the safety of maritime transport, discharges, contamination from land sources or the eradication of illegal fishing, unreported and unregulated fishing (IUU), require operational rules adopted by organisations such as the International Maritime Organisation or the development of agreements such as the London Convention (International Maritime Organization, 2003), on the prevention of marine pollution, or those relating to the prevention of IUU fishing.

To understand the application of these notions to maritime security, the first section of this chapter examines the influence of liberalism on its normative definition through the development of conventional structures that constitute the "law of the sea". It also analyses the contribution of liberalism to the creation of maritime zones of jurisdiction through the zoning of the sea as a fundamental instrument for the management of security at sea. The second section examines how the liberal conception of maritime security has broadened its research agenda in material areas that were not previously considered relevant by traditional security studies. It addresses the contribution of liberalism to the operational field of security at sea through cooperation structures (both formal and informal, between national and international, civil and military, as well as public and private authorities) by creating regional security regimes that are more or less institutionalised. Finally, it exposes the unique contribution that the liberal approach offers to a modern and expanded conception of maritime security.

The normative definition of maritime security and its spatial conceptualisation: The zoning of the sea

The doctrinal influence of the liberal approach on the normative definition of maritime security is very much relevant to the international community's undertaking of shaping the concept of security at sea. UNCLOS demonstrates the strong doctrinal influence of liberalism (Freestone, 2013). All states have the responsibility to adhere to UNCLOS, and even if they do not do so (as is the case with the United States) they assume compliance with this vast set of precepts on which the good governance of the sea is based, making this document globally accepted. However, the contribution of the liberal perspective goes beyond the extraordinary normative instrument that is UNCLOS. It inspires the principle of collaboration between all actors present at sea through the shared responsibility of contributing to maritime security through common rules.

A truly unique contribution of the liberal conception has been to conceive maritime security through the control of the marine space: understanding the sea as a global environment made up of contingent, interconnected, overlapping and multifunctional areas that regulate uses and movements through it (Ryan, 2015). In this way, zoning has become the key to the current existing maritime governance structure.

Zoning of the sea began in the eighteenth century with the British "Hovering Acts", which allowed for the formation of a spatial order at sea. As Barry Ryan (2019, p. 1057) pointed out, this normative development entailed overcoming the concepts of "*imperium*" and "*dominium*" that until then had framed the conception of security at sea. The notion of "*imperium*" held that the sea constituted an essentially different sphere from the terrestrial one, and was only subject to minimal structure from the government. It was an open space that could be strategically controlled through force. Contrastingly, the notion of "*dominium*" was aimed at territorialising the sea, projecting legal and permanent sovereignty from a coastal state to the adjacent sea as a barrier against threats to security from the sea. Both cases followed a working militarised logic of modern state security in which the sea was an extension of the land in defensive terms, acquiring the same rights of possession over it as when conquering territory.

The distance covered by a cannonball fired from the coast established the scope of the territorial authority of a coastal state on the adjacent strip of sea.

The "Hovering Acts" legitimised state action in matters of security beyond the territorial sea. This led to defining maritime zones built on the principles of risk containment and resource management, applying a principle of order that was no longer based on the notions of sovereignty and power. The expansion of *"Pax Britannica"* on the oceans in the nineteenth century advanced this legal formula capable of being applied everywhere. It promoted a liberal universalism in which security was not limited to containing traditional state enemies but also included putting a stop to forces that threatened the freedom of navigation, or represented other uses of the maritime space considered barbaric or savage such as piracy, the slave trade, illegal trade, or protectionism. In this way, the new concept of maritime security replaced the notion of "enemy" with that of "criminal" as its backbone, and the high seas came to be understood as a space that should be protected against the risks posed by these disruptive forces that threaten the freedom of navigation and commerce. A governance regime over a global space, universally applicable and defined by ethical criteria had emerged. As a consequence, the British navy became a policing force whose function was to maintain the global order that supported the material basis of the empire (Gough, 2014, p. 6).

In the twentieth century, the right of states to exercise their jurisdiction beyond their territorial waters in times of peace was enshrined. The zoning principle, sanctioned by UNCLOS, resulted in the creation of maritime zones defined under security criteria. The territorial sea, up to 12 nautical miles (nm), was consolidated as an area of territorial sovereignty of the coastal state. Over the contiguous zone, between 12 and 24 nm, the state exercises a purely policing function, while in the Exclusive Economic Zone (EEZ), between 12 and 200 nm, the state is allowed to exert sufficient power to protect economic resources (mainly against illegal fishing and pollution) and to regulate the nature of the ships (and their cargoes) that cross this zone. Beyond that, up to 350 nm, in the case of expansion into the continental shelf, the coastal state exercises jurisdictional powers over the seabed and subsoil.

UNCLOS gave states legitimacy to prosecute crimes that threatened land security or affected the economic potential of the sea (the biological and environmental conservation of living resources and the seabed), creating a maritime security logic focused on criminals, rather than on enemies, and based on spatial criteria (zoning) and not on strategic considerations (Ryan, 2019, p. 1066).

The new maritime security practices of the twenty-first century have created governance frameworks that occasionally integrate civilian actors, and have functions closer to policing actions rather than military power. A maritime order has also been created in which the actions of the states, to be legitimate, must be consistent with the new maritime security agenda fundamentally built around the identification of unconventional threats. Zoning has also been established as a continually expanding spatial framework. For example, Marine Protected Areas (MPAs) have been adopted as the main instruments for the conservation and rehabilitation of marine biodiversity. If in 2000 these covered 3.2 million km^2, in 2020 they represent 26.9 million km^2 (7.4%) and were estimated to reach 50% of the global sea surface by the middle of the century (Duarte et al., 2020, p. 40).

Along with the spatial conception of maritime security, the liberal approach has also contributed to the institutionalisation of international organisations that play an essential role in containing threats in the maritime domain. The most important of these organisations is the International Maritime Organisation (IMO), a specialised agency of the United Nations created in 1959. IMO has carried out outstanding work in the field of maritime safety (human safety at sea) promoting such relevant regulatory developments such as the ISPS Code and the SOLAS

Convention, the most important maritime security convention in force (Hesse, 2003). It also assumes the function of providing cooperation mechanisms between governments for the prevention and control of pollution of the marine environment by ships (Karim, 2015) and has promoted regimes to combat piracy such as the Djibouti Code of Conduct (DCoC).

A liberal agenda for maritime security

The traditional conception of security at sea has centred on preserving freedom of navigation, promoting trade and maintaining good practices for coexistence. In periods of strategic conflict, prior to World War I and during the Cold War, the focus was on the continued rivalry between the great powers for control of maritime space.

Since then, under the stimulus of the liberal vision, the field of maritime security has continued to grow, adding an enormous variety of contents to the research agenda. This does not mean, however, that an alternative liberal agenda centreing on strategic and geopolitical issues has been created separate from the traditional agenda. Simply, the scope of study has broadened to take into consideration threats that, from a terrestrial perspective, had previously received less consideration but that now have been substantiated thanks to a more comprehensive approach (Feldt et al., 2013) to the study of maritime security promoted by the liberal vision.

In this vein, the issues added to the maritime security agenda have not stopped growing. There are traditional threats such as acts of piracy and armed robbery at sea, terrorism, contraband, illicit trafficking (of people, drugs or weapons), but also acts against underwater cultural heritage, intentional and illicit damage against the marine environment, including the over-exploitation of living resources from illegal fishing, and of course the impact of climate change (UN General Assembly, 2008: Section VI). Natalie Klein (2011, p. 11) offers a definition that reflects the holistic conception that maritime security has now taken on: "the protection of a state's land and maritime territory, infrastructure, economy, environment and society from certain harmful acts occurring at sea". The liberal approach to maritime security encompasses everything, taking into account the security interests of states, both against threats posed by other actors (state or non-state) as well as other natural risks, such as the preservation of the marine environment, which is considered a global public good. This expansion of the research agenda has turned maritime security into an ubiquitous concept or "buzzword" (Bueger, 2015, p. 159) whose content and attributes have not ceased to extend their limits.

In a sense, the term maritime security itself is a consequence of the prevailing liberal vision of security since the end of the Cold War (Buzan et al., 1998). Its development followed the emergence of new unconventional threats: maritime terrorism, piracy off the coast of Somalia, organised crime in the Gulf of Guinea as well as all forms of illicit trafficking. This is in addition to the fact that, generally, the protection of the marine environment and the management of natural resources also face tensions due to the development of the so-called "blue economy" (Silver et al., 2015). The liberal maritime security agenda broadens the scope and nature of security at sea, both in its practical and conceptual dimensions. It includes both traditional issues related to security and the application of international law, as well as new issues associated with economic development or environmental conservation. And it integrates the relationships that all these interconnected areas maintain by adopting a comprehensive approach. Moreover, it proposes a cooperative form of management that involves the participation of international organisations, public agencies, private shipping companies, port facilities, contracted private security personnel and, in general, all actors that operate in the maritime environment.

These new threats were incorporated into the strategic documents that states and other intergovernmental organisations began to publish in the first decade of the twenty-first century. NATO (2011), European Union (2014), African Union (2014) and a long list of states around the world developed their own strategic maritime documents where they take into account these new threats along with the traditional threats derived from strategic rivalries and present in such settings such as the Indian Ocean, the South China Sea or the Arctic regions. These strategic documents share a series of common ideas, such as the need to contain threats beyond the limits of the maritime areas of national jurisdiction (Riddervold, 2018). Another element of coincidence is the concept that links internal and external security, between land and sea, establishing a continuum between them (Wolff, 2012). The relationship between threats of a non-military nature and national economic development is also highlighted, given the strategic consideration that is generally attributed to the development of the "blue economy" (Bueger et al., 2020).

A renewed interest in maritime affairs has fuelled a revitalised maritime security agenda concerned with creating a maritime order consistent with globalisation (Moran & Russell, 2016). This new agenda is not conceived of as an alternative to, or in competition with, traditional content. In fact, the traditional vision of the sea as a scenario for the projection of geopolitical power is still fully in force. This is illustrated by the numerous studies dedicated to analysing the effects of the projection of maritime influence by new rising powers (Holmes & Yoshihara, 2008). In any case, the influence of the liberal vision on maritime security has resulted in an expanded and deepened research agenda that incorporates a larger set of problems than traditionally addressed (Bueger & Edmunds, 2017).

The increasing attention paid by states to the world's oceans is a consequence of the possibilities opened up by technological developments that allow for the exploitation of resources previously unattainable to humans. The development potential of the "blue economy" also highlights the fragility of the marine environment and turns economic activities carried out at sea into threats to security if they are not carried out under strict protocols to reduce their environmental impact.

A paradigmatic example is the regulation of fishing activity. Fishing, partly as a consequence of the development of new technologies, acts as a critical node (De Sombre, 2019) around which different dimensions of maritime security interact: territorial conflicts over ensuring access to fishing areas; acts of piracy, especially in the Indian Ocean off the coast of Somalia; and, of course, the environmental impact caused by indiscriminate fishing practices.

One of the most significant regulatory developments to address this threat is the forthcoming Agreement on the Conservation and Sustainable Use of Marine Biological Diversity of Areas Beyond National Jurisdiction (BBNJ), which has been under United Nation's negotiation since 2018. The content of the document under negotiation (BBNJ Agreement, 2020) draws on experiences from the Regional Fisheries Management Organisations (RFMOs) and the high seas protected maritime areas created under the Convention for the Protection of the Marine Environment of the North-East Atlantic (OSPAR) and the Convention on the Conservation of Antarctic Living Marine Resources (CCAMLR). This ambitious project will improve the protection of BBNJ areas through mandatory regulatory mechanisms that will regulate activities directly related to marine pollution and fishing, the mitigation of the effects of deep-sea mining and the collection of marine genetic resources (De Santo, 2018).

The liberal perspective seeks to offer normative and functional cooperative instruments to address and overcome the tensions and rivalries that hinder cooperation among maritime actors. In this sense, the contribution of the liberal perspective in constructing a maritime security agenda has been crucial. The perception of marine security as a set of interrelated challenges comprised of national, environmental, economic and human security issues has been widely accepted and applied through multiple instruments of international cooperation.

The influence of the liberal vision in the management of conventional threats at sea

Expectations raised by the wealth potential of the "blue economy" have also revitalised the geopolitical tensions that are developing at sea. The possibility of exploiting the riches of the seabed and subsoil at great depths has increased tensions between states to reclaim areas of jurisdiction, to build artificial islands (Chan, 2018) or air grievances regarding the extension of the continental shelf beyond 200 nm. Oceanic regions such as the Arctic (Conde & Iglesias, 2016) or the South China Sea (Tran et al., 2019) have become ideal settings for these clashes. Also, the surge in maritime trade in recent decades and the critical role it plays in the globalised economy have given rise to ambitious naval programs in an effort to ensure freedom of navigation and access to natural resources.

The need to neutralise threats derived from piracy, terrorism or illicit trafficking has been added to these difficulties. The proliferation of these tensions, rivalries and conventional threats has revived the traditional security agenda. That said, neither the geopolitical disputes nor the regulatory developments associated with the implementation of UNCLOS exhaust the operational and conceptual tools needed to tackle the challenges that maritime security entails today. The liberal vision favours coastal countries managing their maritime interests collectively and cooperatively by establishing governance regimes, mainly at the regional level (Damayanti, 2019), not only for the sustainable use of the oceans but also for the security of trade and the states themselves.

The notion of "security communities" (Pouliot, 2008) helps to understand the development of cooperative maritime governance structures that operate mainly at the regional level, despite the difficulties involved in identifying common security interests among coastal states. In regions such as the Indian Ocean, the lack of sufficient state power, the absence of fora for regional cooperation, and the political, economic and development differences between coastal states have prevented the institutionalisation of formal structures of cooperation in security matters. However, the perception of shared risks along with the vulnerabilities manifested by societies with very limited naval military resources have allowed the establishment of collaborative security structures that lay the foundations for emerging regionalism (Cordner, 2018).

These "security communities" can take on organisational forms with different purposes and intensities (Bueger & Stockbruegger, 2013). They are groups with a high level of agreement where diplomatic dialogue predominates as a means to achieve coordination between the policies applied by the participants (Brosig, 2013). Bueger (2013) points out the keys that allow identifying the evolution from a maritime security regime to a security community: a) the establishment of shared commitments (mutual engagement) beyond the formal institutions of regional security, through the creation of new collaboration platforms both at the regional, subregional or interregional level; b) the adoption of shared repertoires (protocols, meetings, conferences or statements that allow connecting actors and institutions of a diverse nature); c) the assumption of joint enterprises (legislative developments, good governance practices, port management, joint scientific research on the marine environment or common fishing policies); and d) an increasing process of securitisation through the shared identification of common threats. In regions such as East Africa, for example, there has been an emergence of embryonic security communities that follow increasingly convergent patterns of interaction (Potgieter, 2013).

The practical way to execute these actions is through multinational operations of very diverse nature. In the context of maritime security, operations are the set of measures carried out by various kinds of authorities necessary to counter threats and mitigate the risks of illegal activities in the maritime domain (Feldt et al., 2013). The objective is to enforce the law of the sea, to protect citizens and the marine environment and to safeguard national and international interests. These forms of collaboration have been successfully applied to the fight against piracy. Unlike the traditional vision of military cooperation based on hierarchical command structures and unity of action, multinational naval operations carried out in the Indian Ocean (Rumley, 2015), both off the coast of the Horn of Africa (Percy, 2016) and in the Strait of Malacca (Lee & McGahan, 2015), have adopted unique forms of collaboration based on network structures, equality between participants, and informal types of military cooperation.

In other regions, such as the Gulf of Guinea, regional cooperation in maritime security is facing greater difficulties. Given the scarcity of resources of the coastal states, and the transnational nature of most of the threats they face, regional cooperation is offered as the necessary and inclusive response to face regional maritime insecurity. The way in which the cooperation itself is organised is as relevant as the means that are made available to achieve operational efficiency. It is necessary to strengthen the governance of regional maritime security so that the efforts invested achieve anticipated results (Ali, 2015, p. 226).

The African maritime environment (mainly the Mediterranean, the Horn of Africa and the Gulf of Guinea), face serious maritime security challenges that require demanding operational responses with the participation of all stakeholders. The 2050 Africa's Integrated Maritime Strategy (2014) is a promising step in the creation of a regional maritime security regime. This document takes on many of the developments offered by the liberal perspective to maritime security, for example, by strengthening political cooperation (through the creation of specialised regional associations), as well as legislative and judicial cooperation (by promoting the incorporation of international legal instruments into national laws and harmonising judicial procedures). It also addresses zoning as a maritime security strategy (envisioning the creation of a Conventional Exclusive Economic Zone for Africa), prioritises the containment of unconventional threats (such as environmental security) and contemplates the development of permanent operational structures such as the creation of an integrated network of coast guards (Vrancken, 2018).

The operational execution of the liberal vision of maritime security is based on the multilevel cooperation of very diverse actors. A shared perception of threats and a shared commitment (mutual engagement) are necessary to face both the implementation of operations as well as capacity building and the adoption of collective action standards. The concept of a "security community" reflects that aspiration. Understood as a collective in whom the members construct securitisations with one another (Buzan & Wæver, 2009, p. 254), it represents an ideal type of collaboration whose relevance lies more in the efforts invested in its development than in the effectiveness of potential results achieved from first steps. Multilevel cooperation and a comprehensive approach constitute the axes on which to implement the operational execution of the liberal vision of maritime security.

Conclusion: A new conception of maritime security

The liberal conception of maritime security provides a transdisciplinary and holistic dimension that has allowed new content to be incorporated into the security agenda. It offers an analytical perspective that integrates the legal, political, economic, social and environmental dimensions so as to generate a response that contributes to reducing or neutralising the risks that threaten the marine environment. The normative instruments inspired by this conception promote cooperation between all the actors involved and the collective responsibility to contribute to maritime security by accepting compliance with common rules: a governance regime over a global space, of universal application and defined by ethical criteria.

The influence of liberalism on maritime security is substantive in at least two areas: in normative and institutional development, and in the creation of governance regimes that apply spatial criteria. Perhaps its most unique contribution is the conception of the high seas as an international space, a common heritage of humanity.

Bueger and Edmunds (2017, p. 1300) also highlight the liminal conception of security at sea that cannot be confined to an isolated space, naval or land. It is an interspatial, transnational and interjurisdictional conception.

The liberal vision of maritime security provides an integrated conception of the interconnected factors that act in this security complex. It offers innovative responses to ocean governance. Finally, it works to normatively institutionalise coexistence and joint actions between the different maritime actors.

References

African Union. (2014). *2050 Africa's Integrated Maritime Strategy.* African Union. http://pages.au.int/maritime/documents/2050-aim-strategy-0

Ali, K. D. (2015). *Maritime Security Cooperation in the Gulf of Guinea: Prospects and Challenges.* Brill.

Baldwin, D. A. (1993). Neoliberalism, neorealism, and world politics. In D. A. Baldwin (Ed.), *Neorealism and Neoliberalism: The Contemporary Debate* (pp. 3–28). Columbia University Press.

BBNJ Agreement. (2020). *Textual proposals submitted by delegations by 20 February 2020, for consideration at the fourth session of the Intergovernmental conference on an international legally binding instrument under the United Nations Convention on the Law of the Sea on the conservation and sustainable use of marine biological diversity of areas beyond national jurisdiction (A/CONF.232/2020/3).* https://www.un.org/bbnj/sites/www.un.org.bbnj/files/textual_proposals_compilation_-_28_feb_2020.pdf

Brosig, M. (2013). Introduction: The African security regime complex—Exploring converging actors and policies. *African Security, 6*(3–4), 171–190.

Bueger, C. (2013). Communities of security practice at work? The emerging African maritime security regime. *African Security, 6*(3–4), 297–316.

Bueger, C. (2015). What is maritime security? *Marine Policy, 53,* 159–164. 10.1016/j.marpol.2014.12.005

Bueger, C., & Edmunds, T. (2017). Beyond seablindness: A new agenda for maritime security studies. *International Affairs, 93*(6), 1293–1311. 10.1093/ia/iix174

Bueger, C., Edmunds, T., & McCabe, R. (2020). Into the sea: Capacity-building innovations and the maritime security challenge. *Third World Quarterly, 41*(2), 228–246. 10.1080/01436597.2019.1660632

Bueger, C., & Stockbruegger, J. (2013). Security communities, alliances, and macro-securitization: The practices of counter-piracy governance. In M. J. Struett, J. D. Carlson, & M. T. Nance (Eds.), *Maritime Piracy and the Construction of Global Governance* (pp. 99–124). Routledge.

Buzan, B., Waever, O., & Wilde, J. (1998). *Security: A New Framework for Analysis.* Lynne Rienner.

Buzan, B., & Wæver, O. (2009). Macrosecuritisation and security constellations: Reconsidering scale in securitisation theory. *Review of International Studies, 35*(2), 253–276. 10.1017/S0260210509008511

Caverley, J., & Mclaughlin Mitchell, S. (2021, 25 February). A liberal case for seapower? *War on the Rocks.* https://warontherocks.com/2021/02/a-liberal-case-for-seapower/

Chan, N. (2018). 'Large ocean states': Sovereignty, small islands, and marine protected areas in global oceans governance. *Global Governance, 24*(4), 537–555. 10.1163/19426720-02404005

Conde, E., & Iglesias, S. (Eds.). (2016). *Global Challenges in the Arctic Region Sovereignty, Environment and Geopolitical Balance.* Routledge. 10.4324/9781315584768

Cordner, L. (2018). *Maritime Security Risks, Vulnerabilities and Cooperation: Uncertainty in the Indian Ocean.* Springer.

Damayanti, A. (2019). Indo-Pacific maritime cooperation: ASEAN mechanisms on security towards global maritime governance. *Global & Strategis, 13*(1), 7–11. 10.20473/jgs.13.1.2019.1-44

Daniels, K., & McLaughlin Mitchell, S. (2017). Bones of democratic contention: Maritime disputes. *International Area Studies Review*, *20*(4), 293–310. 10.1177/2233865917740269

De Santo, E. M. (2018). Implementation challenges of area-based management tools (ABMTs) for biodiversity beyond national jurisdiction (BBNJ). *Marine Policy*, *97*, 39–40. 10.1016/j.marpol.2018.08.034

De Sombre, E. R. (2019). The security implications of fisheries. *International Affairs*, *95*(5), 1019–1035. 10.1093/ia/iiz140

Duarte, C. M. (2020). Rebuilding marine life. *Nature*, *580*, 39–51. 10.1038/s41586-020-2146-7

European Union. (2014). *European Union Maritime Security Strategy*. European Union. https://register.consilium.europa.eu/doc/srv?l=EN&f=ST%2011205%202014%20INIT

Feldt, L., Roell, P., & Thiele, R. D. (2013). *Maritime Security – Perspectives for a Comprehensive Approach*. Institut für Strategie-Politik-Sicherheits- und Wirtschaftsberatung (ISPSW Strategy Series, n° 222). www.files.ethz.ch/isn/162756/222_feldt_roell_thiele.pdf

Frederick, B. A., Hensel, P. R., & Macaulay, C. (2017). The issue correlates of war territorial claims data, 1816–2001. *Journal of Peace Research*, *54*(1), 99–108. 10.1177/0022343316676311

Freestone, D. (Ed.). (2013). *The 1982 Law of the Sea Convention at 30: Successes, Challenges and New Agendas*. Koninklijke Brill NV.

García Pérez, R. (2019). *Retos para la seguridad marítima en el horizonte 2050*. Instituto Español de Estudios Estratégicos. http://www.ieee.es/Galerias/fichero/docs_investig/2019/DIEEEINV05-2019Seguridad_maritima.pdf

Gough, B. (2014). *Pax Britannica: Ruling the Waves and Keeping the Peace before Armageddon*. Palgrave Macmillan.

Hesse, H. G. (2003). Maritime security in a multilateral context: IMO activities to enhance maritime security. *The International Journal of Marine and Coastal Law*, *18*(3), 327–340.

Holmes, J. R., & Yoshihara, T. (2008). *Chinese Naval Strategy in the 21st Century: The Turn to Mahan*. Routledge.

International Maritime Organization. (2003). London Convention 1972 : Convention on the Prevention of Marine Pollution by Dumping of Wastes and Other Matter, 1972 and 1996 Protocol / International Maritime Organization. London: International Maritime Organization.

International Ocean Institute (Ed.). (2018). *The Future of Ocean Governance and Capacity Development. Essays in Honor of Elisabeth Mann Borgese (1918-2002)*. Brill Nijhoff.

Karim, M. S. (2015). *Prevention of Pollution of the Marine Environment from Vessels: The Potential and Limits of the International Maritime Organisation*. Springer.

Klein, N. (2011). Two fundamental concepts. In N. Klein (Ed.), *Maritime Security and the Law of the Sea* (pp. 1–22). Oxford University Press.

Koh, T. T. B. (1982). *A Constitution for the Oceans*. Remarks by Tommy T.B. Koh, of Singapore. President of the Third United Nations Conference on the Law of the Sea. United Nations. https://www.un.org/depts/los/convention_agreements/texts/koh_english.pdf

Lee, T., & McGahan, K. (2015). Norm subsidiarity and institutional cooperation: Explaining the straits of Malacca anti-piracy regime. *The Pacific Review*, *28*(4), 529–552. 10.1080/09512748.2015.1012537

Liotta, P., & Owen, T. (2006). Why human security? *Whitehead Journal of Diplomacy and International Relations*, *7*(1), 37–55.

Martin, M., & Owen, T. (Eds.). (2013). *Routledge Handbook of Human Security*. Routledge.

McLaughlin Mitchell, S. (2020). Clashes at sea: Explaining the onset, militarization, and resolution of diplomatic maritime claims. *Security Studies*, *29*(4), 637–670. 10.1080/09636412.2020.1811458

McLaughlin Mitchell, S., & Prins, B. (1999). Beyond territorial contiguity: Issues at stake in democratic militarized interstate disputes. *International Studies Quarterly*, *43*(1), 169–183.

Moran, D., & Russell, J. A. (Eds.). (2016). *Maritime strategy and global order: Markets, resources, security*. Georgetown University Press.

NATO. (2011). *Alliance Maritime Strategy*. North Atlantic Treaty Organization. https://www.nato.int/cps/en/natolive/official_texts_75615.htm.

Nemeth, S. C., McLaughlin Mitchell, S., Nyman, E. A., & Hensel, P. R. (2014). Ruling the Sea: Managing Maritime Conflicts through UNCLOS and Exclusive Economic Zones. *International Interactions*, *40*(5), 711–736. https://doi.org/10.1080/03050629.2014.897233

Oude Elferink, A. G. (Ed.). (2005). *Stability and Change in the Law of the Sea: The Role of the LOS Convention*. Brill.

Owen, J. M. (2018). Liberal approaches. In A. Gheciu & W. C. Wohlforth (Eds.), *The Oxford Handbook of International Security* (pp. 100–115). Oxford University Press.

Percy, S. (2016). Counter-piracy in the Indian Ocean: A new form of military cooperation. *Journal of Global Security Studies*, *1*(4), 270–284. 10.1093/jogss/ogw018

Potgieter, T. (2013). Notes on regional leadership and maritime security. *Journal of African Union Studies*, *2*(3-4), 65–77. https://www.jstor.org/stable/26893588

Pouliot, V. (2008). The logic of practicality: A theory of practice of security communities. *International Organization*, *62*(2), 257–288. 10.1017/S0020818308080090

Rahman, C. (2009). *Concepts of Maritime Security: A Strategic Perspective on Alternative Visions for Good Order and Security at Sea, with Policy Implications for New Zealand.* Centre for Strategic Studies – Victoria University of Wellington. https://ro.uow.edu.au/cgi/viewcontent.cgi?referer=https://www.google.com/&httpsredir=1&article=1087&context=lawpapers

Riddervold, M. (2018). *The Maritime Turn in EU Foreign and Security Policies: Aims, Actors and Mechanisms of Integration.* Palgrave Macmillan.

Rumley, D. (2015). The emerging Indian Ocean landscape: Security challenges and evolving architecture of cooperation – An Australian perspective. *Journal of the Indian Ocean Region*, *11*(2), 184–204. 10.1080/19480881.2015.1069491

Ryan, B. J. (2015). Security spheres: A phenomenology of maritime spatial practices. *Security Dialogue*, *46*(6), 568–584. 10.1177/0967010615598049

Ryan, B. J. (2019, September). The disciplined sea: A history of maritime security and zonation. *International Affairs*, *95*(5), 1055–1073. 10.1093/ia/iiz098

Silver, J. J., Gray, N. J., Campbell, L. M., Fairbanks, L. W., & Gruby, R. L. (2015). Blue Economy and Competing Discourses in International Oceans Governance. *The Journal of Environment & Development*, *24*(2), 135–160. 10.1177/1070496515580797.

Tran, T. T., Welfield, J. B., & Le, T. T. (Eds.). (2019). *Building a Normative Order in the South China Sea: Evolving Disputes, Expanding Options.* Edward Elgar Publishing.

UNCLOS. (1982). *United Nations Convention on the Law of the Sea.* https://www.un.org/Depts/los/convention_agreements/texts/unclos/unclos_e.pdf

UN General Assembly. (2008). *Oceans and the Law of the Sea: Report of the Secretary-General*, 10 March 2008, A/63/63. https://documents-dds-ny.un.org/doc/UNDOC/GEN/N08/266/26/PDF/N0826626.pdf?OpenElement

Vrancken, P. (2018). The African perspective on global ocean governance. In: D. J. Attard, D. M. Ong, & D. Kritsiotis (Eds.), *The IMLI Treatise on Global Ocean Governance, vol. 1: UN and Global Ocean Governance* (pp. 216–231). Oxford University Press.

Wolff, S. (2012). *The Mediterranean Dimension of the European Union's Internal Security.* Palgrave Macmillan.

Yaoundé Code of Conduct. (2013). *Yaoundé Code of Conduct Concerning the Repression of Piracy, Armed Robbery against Ships, and Illicit Maritime Activity in West and Central Africa*, signed in Yaoundé, 25 June 2013. https://wwwcdn.imo.org/localresources/en/OurWork/Security/Documents/code_of_conduct%20signed%20from%20ECOWAS%20site.pdf

Young, O. R. (2011). Governing international spaces: Antarctica and beyond. In Berkman P. A., Lang, M. A., Walton, D. W. H. & Young, O. R. (Eds.), *Science Diplomacy: Antarctica, Science and the Governance of International Spaces.* Washington, DC: Smithsonian Institution Scholarly Press. https://doi.org/10.5479/si.9781935623069.287

6

GLOBAL MARITIME SECURITY GOVERNANCE

James Sperling

Introduction

The *de facto* status of maritime space remains as vexing today as it did in the 17th century. Hugo Grotius (1916) established the doctrine of *mare liberum* in 1609, which John Seldon challenged with his defense of *mare clausum* in 1663. The problem of maritime security governance (MSG) would have been significantly simplified had Seldon prevailed: if littoral states (or a hegemonic maritime power) were to have been assigned sovereignty over the entirety of maritime space and thereby effected the complete enclosure of the maritime commons, the scope of MSG would be reduced to the problem of recognising territorial boundaries, respecting those boundaries, establishing mechanisms for adjudicating conflicts between littoral states, and assessing the ability of littoral states to govern their maritime territory. *Mare liberum* prevailed as a firmly established principle of customary international law by the mid-18th century (see de Vattel 1916). The *de jure* result was limited maritime territoriality and a weakly governed (Klein, 2014; Voicu & Bosilca, 2015), if not anarchical (Sloggett, 2013, pp. 35–36), strategic space on the high seas. The desire to extend or restrict maritime territoriality in the contemporary international system does not reflect a preference for weaker or stronger governance but rather a tension, in the first instance, between littoral states with limited maritime capabilities and maritime powers wishing to maximise their freedom of action in exclusive economic zones (EZZ) comparable to that enjoyed on the high seas as historically demarcated; and in the second, between *status quo* and revisionist maritime powers, the latter seeking to restrict the prerogatives of the former and displacing them with a more congenial regional governance regime – more times than not in ways that deprive the *status quo* powers of their maritime prerogatives and power projection capabilities (Suárez de Vivero & Rodríguez Mateos, 2010, pp. 973–976). Each provides a different challenge to the task of MSG. The first reflects the efforts of *status quo* maritime powers to enforce the United Nations Convention on the Law of the Sea (UNCLOS) and customary maritime law more generally in the face of revisionist state challenges to UNCLOS; the second manifests as the growing unwillingness of *status quo* and revisionist states alike to act in a manner consistent with established international law and norms or to accept the jurisdiction of international institutions in the settlement of disputes.

Security governance is a well-established analytical construct that explains the management of security in regions where the post-Westphalian state has emerged or is in a state of becoming (Sperling, 2009; Lucarelli, 2019; Sperling & Webber, 2019). Yet when maritime governance

DOI: 10.4324/9781003001324-8

has been investigated with respect to regional seas and oceans (Rochette et al., 2015; Mahon & Fanning, 2019) or to specific maritime institutions (Bateman, 2011; Aarstad, 2017), these analyses are not rigorously disciplined by a theory of "security governance". MSG is compromised as an empirical and theoretical matter by several factors. First, the question remains open whether the high seas are in fact anarchical or weakly governed and therefore susceptible to a stronger system of institutionalised governance and a corresponding sacrifice of existing sovereign prerogatives. This question cannot be settled here. But UNCLOS and the range of international institutions that claim a governing function are sufficiently developed to proceed *as if* MSG exists. Second, maritime space itself resists a binary assessment of the existence or absence of security governance. It has both vertical (seabed to superjacent airspace) and horizontal (inland waters to high seas) dimensions. Their intersection yields several discrete spaces that are treated differentially in international law, are contested differentially by maritime powers and littoral states, and have weak to strong to non-existent systems of security governance. Third, the securitisation process defining maritime threats is not uniform spatially, a condition circumscribing the number of global maritime public security goods requiring collective action. The content of maritime security varies significantly between regionally defined seas and thus makes any claim that there is a global system of MSG a dubious proposition empirically. Arguably a regional approach to MSG would be superior to a global one insofar as it would differentiate zones of effective governance from those that are weak or non-existent and profit from the theory of regional public goods (Sandler, 1998). It would also provide an analytical alternative to the orthodox treatment of the ocean as a global common (Posen, 2003; Sperling, 2011). Nonetheless, the UNCLOS regime provides the base-line definition of maritime threats: an encroachment on, or violation of, the unimpeded access to the sea lines of communication (SLOC), freedom of navigation, right of innocent passage or transit, and the protection of surface and submarine infrastructures among others. The blue economy constitutes a fourth complication. There is a widespread tendency to conflate rather than differentiate between the blue economy and maritime security. Their differentiation is essential owing to the uneven and asymmetrical processes of regional maritime securitisation. Some littoral states treat the blue economy as a problem of managing common-pool resources in order to maximise the extraction of ocean resources without depleting those (renewable) resources, whereas for others, the over-exploitation or fouling of the blue economy does not merely threaten economic loss but represents an existential threat to national food security. The blue economy and maritime security are virtually identical for the littoral states of Africa, but are separable in EU-governed waters owing to the dense institutionalisation of the blue economy, the effective mechanisms for conflict resolution, and its status as an economic rather than security challenge.[1]

MSG therefore faces empirical and theoretical challenges that raise five questions: What maritime domains are threatened and what are the nature of those threats? What are the necessary conditions requiring an effective system of MSG to emerge? What are the components of a system of MSG? Does the current governance system meet the criteria defining a system of security governance? The answers to these questions lead to a disappointing conclusion for security governance scholars: the system of global MSG is weak and underdeveloped at best. It also suggests that a more fruitful line of empirical (and theoretical) enquiry would focus instead on regional maritime security governance as a pathway to constructing a global system of MSG.

Securitisation of the Maritime Commons

The literature on maritime security fuses two separable phenomena: threats from or on the sea that affect the systemic or regional maritime milieu; and maritime threats that are the negative

Global Maritime Security Governance

Table 6.1 Maritime security goods

		Excludable	
		Yes	*No*
Rival	*Yes*	***National good*** Territorial waters Inland waters Seabed resources in EEZ and continental shelf	***Common pool resource*** Submarine power, telegraphic and Fibre-optic cables
	No	***Club good*** Regional maritime orders	***Public good*** SLOC Right of innocent passage and transit Freedom of navigation Effective search and rescue

externalities of terrestrial disorder or insecurity. This tendency occurs most frequently in analyses of piracy (Vreÿ, 2009, pp. 23–25; Kamal-Deen, 2015, pp. 97–98). If the "security" in MSG is going to have meaning, the focus must be on the first category of threat. There are four separable categories of maritime security goods. The literature has treated the security of the maritime commons as a public good; namely, a good with the characteristics of non-rivalness and non-excludability. There are, however, three additional categories of maritime security good that impinge directly or indirectly upon MSG: national security goods (rival and ex-cludable); club security goods (non-rival but excludable); and common-pool security goods (rival, but non-excludable). This typology of security goods can be used to map the range of threats susceptible or resistant to a system of MSG (see Table 6.1).

A systemic investigation of MSG would begin with public and common-pool security goods in three discrete maritime spaces – the seabed, surface waters and superjacent air rights –inviting or resisting a global system of MSG. The seabed is a common-pool resource and a newly securitised domain, the importance of which has increased exponentially with the onset of the digital age: fibre-optic cables carry over 95% of the world's digital communications. They are not only the core infrastructure of the global communications, financial and economic systems, but for great- and medium-sized powers are critical enablers of national armed forces. The submarine infrastructure also presents critical vulnerabilities arising from (un)intentional dis-ruptions by state and non-state actors alike. The intentional severing of submarine fibre-optic (and power) cables poses a grave risk to national security for states highly dependent on net-centric warfare and globally integrated financial markets or communications systems (UN General Assembly, 2016b; Office of Director of National Intelligence, 2017, pp. 6–8, 11). Submarine oil and natural gas pipelines are similarly critical to national or regional energy security and susceptible to submarine disruption. Yet, as is generally the case with fibre-optic cables, intentional disruptions are easier to accomplish at landing stations although submarine infrastructures are less resilient and more difficult to repair. Nonetheless, as offshore wind power provides a greater share of national energy requirements, threats to submarine power cables and surface platforms constitute an increasing source of disquiet in national and systemic security discourses (see NATO, 2019; Sunak, 2017, pp. 19–27; Clark, 2016, pp. 235–236).

The mitigation of most maritime threats poses a collective action problem. The 2016 UN Secretary General's Report, *Oceans and Law of the Sea*, identified the most pressing maritime threats as "piracy and armed robbery at sea, transnational organised crime and terrorism in the maritime domain, trafficking in persons, the smuggling of migrants, illegal, unreported and unregulated fishing and other maritime activities that threaten global stability, security and prosperity" (UN General Assembly, 2016a, para 37); a 2016 General Assembly Resolution subsequently expanded the range of threats to include "terrorist acts against shipping, offshore installations and other maritime interests" (UN General Assembly, 2016b, para. 109). Yet international law and littoral state incapacity complicate the mitigation of threats that transnational terrorists or criminal organisations pose. The complex rules governing the interdiction and boarding of vessels on the high seas, particularly with respect to jurisdiction and the appropriate forum for prosecution, make enforcement difficult (Guilfoyle, 2015, pp. 219–223). As important, many littoral states are unwilling or unable to fulfil their constabulary obligations in territorial and contiguous zone waters or to monitor effectively the search and rescue areas assigned them by international convention (see Saint-Mézard, 2015, pp. 9–11). These barriers to effective enforcement, which reflect a system-wide unwillingness to compromise sovereign prerogatives over commercial or naval vessels, provide a permissive context for trafficking small arms and the weapons of mass destruction or enforcing sanctions against a state actor.

There are three additional major threats to maritime security that affect the systemic milieu: encroachments on the freedom of navigation for warships and commercial vessels; the denial or constriction of access to SLOC; and piracy on the high seas and robbery in territorial waters. The freedom of navigation, right of transit or right of innocent passage for warships (and commercial vessels) in another nation's territorial waters (12 nautical miles from the coast), contiguous zone (24 nautical miles from the coast), exclusive economic zone (up to 200 nautical miles), archipelagic waters and straits connecting two parts of the high seas, and the high seas constitute the core disputes between the *status quo* and revisionist naval powers. Russia and China, particularly, wish to place limits on the right of innocent passage either by making unlawful excessive territorial claims, requiring prior notification of naval warships in violation of the right of innocent passage, or adopting anti-access and area denial strategies that inhibit freedom of navigation, particularly as it pertains to naval force projection consistent with international law.[2] These encroachments are increasingly treated as a category of hybrid warfare by "quasi-revisionist states" in maritime gray zones (Morris et al., 2019, p. 4). There is a connected, secondary maritime threat arising from state and non-state interference with the primary maritime routes between commercial ports and naval bases. Of particular concern is the potential closing of critical sea lane choke points (e.g., Gulf of Hormuz, Malacca Straits, and Bab el-Mandab) that could seriously compromise the functioning of the global economy: 61% and 80% of oil and merchandise trade are, respectively, sea-borne (US Energy Information Agency, 2019; Cerdeiro et al., 2020, p. 4).

Piracy and armed robbery have received a substantial amount of attention in the last 20 years, largely owing to the collapse of littoral states around the Horn of Africa, other littoral states lacking the maritime capacity to prevent piracy in the Bay of Bengal, Gulf of Thailand, and Celebes Sea, and the piratical preference for ships carrying oil from the Persian Gulf or the Gulf of Guinea (Stable Seas, 2020a, 2020b). Piracy suppression has been by necessity largely left to the efforts of the major maritime powers, notably those members of the European Union, NATO and US naval partners in the Indo-Pacific, notably Australia and Japan. Stable Seas presents a fairly dismal portrait of littoral state naval capacity, particularly in East Africa, the Gulf of Guinea, South China Sea and Indian Ocean. Of the 71 countries of the Indian Ocean Basin, the littoral states of western Africa, and the Levant and North Africa, only eight (Egypt, India, Iran, Israel, Saudi Arabia, South Africa, Singapore and the UAE) are classified as regional naval powers able to execute the entire range of naval tasks outside their EEZ and only five (Nigeria, Indonesia, Malaysia, Thailand, Vietnam) are able to operate to the limits of the national EEZ.

Global Maritime Security Governance

Table 6.2 Regional naval capacity and maritime enforcement capability

	Indian Ocean	Persian Gulf	South China Sea	East Africa	Gulf of Guinea	Levant and North Africa
Naval capacity	45	70	52	27	36	63
Maritime enforcement	52	61	50	55	53	58

Source: Stable Seas (2020b). Author's calculations.

The remaining 50 lack the capacity to fulfil their SAR responsibilities or more demanding constabulary duties (Stable Seas, 2020a, p. 11, 2020b). More generally, an index for regional naval capacity and maritime enforcement below 70 indicates a regional inability to secure regional seas with the possible exception of the Persian Gulf states (see Table 6.2). But even in the Persian Gulf, the US-led International Maritime Security Construct (IMSC) and European-led Maritime Surveillance Mission in the Strait of Hormuz (EMASOH) are essential for the protection of merchant vessels and oil tankers (Embassy of France, 2020; Saab, 2020).

Superjacent airspace has a strategic significance intimately connected to disputes about the right of innocent passage for warships in foreign EEZs. The right of overflight in the EEZ of any country is guaranteed in Article 87 of the UNCLOS (Guilfoyle, 2015, p. 206), but those states demanding pre-notification when warships enter EEZ waters have sought to place similarly illegal restrictions on foreign aircraft entering the national air defense identification zone (ADIZ) or have defined the ADIZ in such a way that it makes an indirect territorial claim at sea. Superjacent airspace is also essential for the purposes of acquiring maritime domain awareness (MDA), defined as "the art of obtaining actionable understanding of anything in the oceans that could affect the safety, security, economy, or environment at sea" (Kraska, 2011, p. 217). Naval powers, the US particularly, view MDA as essential for the purpose of projecting naval power owing to the digitalisation of information and the multidimensionality of warfare at sea (the intersection and networking of surface warships, submarines, drones and aircraft, as well as securing the electromagnetic spectrum upon which that networking depends).

These maritime threats are aligned with the entire range of security governance policies: protection, prevention, assurance and compellence (Kirchner & Sperling, 2007). Policies of maritime protection fall predominately in the category of a national security goods. However, there are a limited number of protection policies that constitute collective goods insofar as effective national control over inland and territorial waters consistent with international best practices (e.g., the International Ship and Port Facility Security Code or Container Security Initiative) minimises opportunities for criminal organisations and terrorist groups to exploit maritime commerce. Policies of maritime prevention include precautionary measures that raise the cost of piracy and armed robbery at sea or trafficking, such as the LRIT system which has virtually eradicated piracy for commercial vessels and oil tankers in excess of 300 tons (Kraska, 2011, pp. 218–219; Vespe et al., 2015); and the creation of quasi-institutionalised multilateral maritime hubs – the EU Critical Maritime Routes Programme, the Singapore-based Information Sharing Centre and Information Fusion Centre, and the Australian-initiated Pacific Fusion Centre – have improved information sharing (Payne, 2018; ASEAN Regional Forum, 2019, pp. 147, 162; EU, 2021). Assurance policies were initially conceived as collective efforts to create an institutional framework that enhanced third-party state capabilities in a post-conflict environment. Although this governance category is less relevant in the maritime domain, there are three policies of maritime assurance: first, Australian, British, French, Japanese and American freedom of navigation operations challenge excessive territorial claims on littoral states lacking an effective naval capability; second, the presence of EU and NATO-led anti-piracy operations assure commercial vessels (and those insuring them) that SLOC will remain open irrespective of a specific ship's flag, ownership or crew; and lastly, international institutions (e.g., International Tribunal for the Law of the Sea and International Court of Justice) have undisputed jurisdiction in the adjudication of maritime disputes. The traditional preserve of policies classified as maritime compellence consists of enforcing customary international law (e.g., the IMSC and EMASOH in the Persian Gulf) and sanctions regimes (e.g., EU Operation IRINI in the Mediterranean) as well as projecting force in accordance with UN-mandated military operations or UN peacekeeping operations, although the latter do not figure prominently or at all in most UN operations.[3]

An effective system of MSG that institutionalised these four categories of security governance policies would enhance the prospect of providing an optimal supply of systemic maritime security *and* meeting the challenges attending the technologies of public goods production specific to each. These policies (and the threats generating them) raise collective action problems for all nations regardless of their status as a global or regional maritime power or as a littoral state with limited maritime assets or a landlocked nation owing to the importance of the seas for communication and commerce. There is a well-defined legal regime governing maritime space, but it remains an open question whether it constitutes a system of MSG.

Maritime Security Governance: Necessary and Sufficient Conditions

Security governance was a response to developments in the international system that required an analytical shift from a state-centred conception of security policy in a densely institutionalised geostrategic space. It requires both "the development of complex, overlapping arrangements (institutional, legal and normative) of monitoring and regulation" (Sperling & Webber, 2019, p. 6) and agreement on what differentiates a security "good" from a security "bad". A system of security governance emerged in Europe, particularly, in response to five developments: the emergence of the late- or post-Westphalian state; a growth in the number of non-state security actors (as agents of threat or as security providers); a proliferation of new security pathologies that require a broad range of policy instruments bridging the internal-external divide in combination with external cooperation to achieve domestic goals; and the transformation of heretofore national security goods into (impure) public security goods owing to an increasing interaction density between states and societies.

These permissive conditions do not hold strongly or at all in the global maritime space. First, the majority of the states in the international system are not late- or post-Westphalian states, but rather traditional Westphalian states that resist any transfer of sovereignty to international institutions or failed and failing states that lack *de facto* territorial sovereignty, let alone *de facto* sovereignty in territorial or contiguous waters (see Behr et al., 2013, pp. 8–9). There has been a rapid growth in the number of non-state security actors: commercial vessels increasingly rely upon private security firms as an added layer of security when traversing sea lanes plagued by piracy (Aarstad, 2017, pp. 318–321); regional security organisations increasingly accept the necessity of governing the seas for the purposes of disciplining state behaviour with respect to the demarcation of territorial waters and EEZs as well as encouraging regional naval cooperation to execute constabulary duties to thwart terrorist groups and criminal organisations (Pandya et al., 2011; Zou, 2015, pp. 636–639; Anozie et al., 2019, pp. 198–200). The securitisation of the seas, the increasingly salience of non-state actors, and the projection of sea-borne criminal and terrorist activities into sovereign territory have required and produced rising cooperation among states towards mitigating those kinds of threats, but that cooperation does not compromise existing sovereign prerogatives (Council of the European Union, 2014, pp. 3–10; US Navy, 2014).[4] Maritime interaction density has steadily increased and is mediated on or beneath the waves: trade as a share of global GDP increased from 27% to 60% between 1970 and 2019 (World Bank, 2020); global internet traffic has risen from 1.6 to 70.5 thousand gigabits per second between 2006 and 2014 (Manyika et al., 2016); and the volume of daily transactions on currency markets has grown from just under $1.6 trillion in 1995 to over $8.3 trillion in 2019 (BIS, 2019, p. 66). These developments have generated sea-borne security concerns. National security objectives and the systemic imperative of milieu security require states inside or outside institutions to defend against sea-borne threats to submarine infrastructures and SLOC. This imperative has transformed heretofore private security goods into impure public goods, thereby increasing the challenge of collective action in maritime space.

Yet, a reparative system of MSG remains elusive. There are three formidable barriers to its emergence and, by extension, a resolution of impediments to collective action. First, there is no agreement on the content of the public goods to be provided and rising naval powers, particularly China, openly contest key features of the UNCLOS regime (Freeman, 2019, pp. 1–7; CRS, 2020, pp. 3–8). Second, the production technologies of public goods and common-pool resources in the maritime domain pose significant barriers to the optimal supply of either (Sperling, 2011). The weakest link technology pertains to piracy insofar as the least capable littoral state along a major SLOC will determine the aggregate level of maritime security from piracy or trafficking. The best shot technology is most relevant for security of submarine infrastructures and suggests that states collectively invest in a single actor – such as the International Maritime Organisation or the International Telecommunications Union – to govern that security domain. Although customary international law with respect to submarine infrastructures is well established (Saito, 2019, pp. 110–116), Davenport (2012, p. 222) notes that "there is no international governmental agency responsible for submarine cables". Moreover, the littoral states of the Indo-Pacific contest third party rights on the EEZ seabed, and the emergence of these infrastructures as the targets of hybrid warfare diminishes the prospect of creating a resilient system of security governance (Clark, 2016, pp. 235–236).

The summation technology of collective goods provision, where the public security good supplied is equal to the summed contributions of the relevant actors, is highly problematic in the current maritime environment. The regional maritime powers in conjunction with the global maritime powers possess sufficient capabilities to provide the range of maritime security goods identified. The problem – again – is China and Russia: their contributions to freedom of navigation operations, for example, have tended to violate the provisions of UNCLOS rather than reinforce them – as when Chinese or Russian naval vessels have intentionally entered, respectively, Japanese or Swedish territorial waters (Panda, 2018; Reuters, 2020). Both view the US, US-led, and NATO FONOPs as inimical to their interests since it ensures the US and allied ability to project power in regional seas of vital interest to both; and regional maritime powers (e.g., Iran or India) are as unlikely to view US FONPs any more favourably (Brewster, 2017, pp. 278–280; Morris et al., 2019, pp. 14–33).

As an empirical matter, the level of security governance and the contribution of littoral states to the provision of collective maritime security goods is anemic: the indices for rule of law and maritime enforcement fall outside the effective range, for international cooperation (defined as signatories to international conventions) the index is fair, and the index for piracy indicates that only two of the six regional seas are relatively free from it (see Table 6.3). The combined fleets of the global and regional maritime powers could enforce the UNCLOS provisions *if* all treated

Table 6.3 Level of governance across four dimensions

Regional sea/ocean	Rule of law	International cooperation	Maritime enforcement	Piracy and armed robbery	Security governance average [*]
East Africa/Horn of Africa	39	63	36	85	61 (43 to 77)
Gulf of Guinea	47	76	44	55	58 (39 to 82)
Indian Ocean	52	77	50	74	67 (38 to 81)
Mediterranean Basin	49	63	58	99	73 (58 to 84)
Persian Gulf	46	67	67	99	78 (71 to 85)
South China Sea	59	75	60	52	63 (38 to 82)

Source: Stable Seas (2020b). Author's calculations.

Note:
[*] Range of governance scores for individual littoral states in parentheses

UNCLOS as intrinsic to their interests. But they do not and maritime security is correspondingly diminished.

Conclusion: A Global System of Maritime Governance?

An effective and dense system of MSG exists if the following conditions hold: there has been either a significant loss or transfer of sovereign prerogatives to international or regional security institutions that produce heterarchical authority structures; norms and laws are highly developed and intrinsic rather than extrinsic to state calculations of interest and national policy choices; national conceptions of security are directed towards the system or milieu rather than another state; states willingly accept binding arbitration within highly institutionalised frameworks; and the security dilemma is attenuated and there exists relatively high levels of amity (Sperling, 2014, pp. 590–593). These characteristics are largely absent in the global maritime security space.

Sovereign prerogatives: The existing legal regime and institutional fora governing maritime security remain predicated upon the existence, demarcation and preservation of sovereignty and sovereign prerogatives. Multilateral (large- or small-n), regional, or bilateral maritime arrangements are relied upon to address specific maritime threats and those arrangements do not entail any marked loss or pooling of sovereignty. In some instances (e.g., the EEZ and the laws governing the boarding or seizing of ships), the purpose of the governing treaty or convention is to *guarantee* the exercise of sovereignty without regard to their naval capability to do so. Thus, authority relationships within the maritime domain remain hierarchical and have so far resisted the emergence of the heterarchical authority structures – an essential and distinguishing characteristic of any system of security governance.

Security referents. The maritime security referents for most states are external or systemic. The systemic referents include freedom of navigation, open access to the SLOC, innocent passage and maritime territoriality. Those referents frame the maritime objectives and foreign policy purposes of the EU and NATO states, for example, whereas they are challenged by the revisionist maritime powers (China and Russia) and littoral states that view UNCLOS as an instrument of western maritime dominance. The challenges to the precise meaning of those systemic referents have generated maritime policies with external referents, the most serious of which include Sino-American and Russo-American maritime conflicts in the South China Sea

Global Maritime Security Governance

and Arctic Ocean, respectively, as well as between China and the vast majority of South China Sea littoral states. MSG would require all maritime powers and littoral states not only to lack external referents in their maritime policy assessments but also agree on the content of the systemic referents to be realised and preserved.

Interaction context. The interaction context in the Indo-Asia Pacific is inimical to a functioning system of security governance. An intense security dilemma has arisen, largely owing to the rapid expansion of the Chinese navy, excessive Chinese territorial claims that would, if recognised, restrict the freedom of navigation and innocent passage in much of the South China Sea, and to the US unwillingness to accept any limitations on its freedom of navigation (and ability to project power) in China's neighbourhood. The threatened enclosures of the maritime commons in the South China Sea and Arctic Ocean, particularly, have heightened the level of enmity and security dilemma among the *status-quo* and revisionist maritime states: US and allied FONOPS directly challenge Chinese maritime claims; the US has declared China (along with Russia) as adversaries; and the Chinese view the US inflexibility in interpreting UNCLOS as an effort to preserve its naval presence and regional dominance (Ramal, 2014, pp. 19–24; US Department of Defense, 2015, pp. 5–14; People's Republic of China, 2019, pp. 15ff). The $1.4 billion Pacific Deterrence Initiative included in the 2021 Senate federal budget proposal is direct evidence of that enmity and represents an effort to enhance the US naval presence in the Indo-Pacific (US Senate, 2020, pp. 935–941).

Norms and rules. Since 1884, states have concluded over 100 international, multilateral and bilateral treaties, conventions and agreements with a maritime dimension (Rothwell et al., 2015, pp. xix–xlv). Just as there can be no doubt that there exists a highly developed legal regime that identifies the rights and obligations of states on the high seas, the EEZ, the contiguous zone and territorial waters, it is also the case that compliance with those obligations is high and the decisions of international courts are generally accepted as binding (see below). Yet obligations impinging upon freedom of navigation, the right of innocent passage and the level and kind of sovereignty a maritime state can exert are heavily caveated (US Navy, 2021). It suggests that the rules and norms of the maritime legal regime are extrinsic to the definition of national interests and adherence to either are instrumental rather than substantive for most littoral states (particularly in the Indo-Pacific and Southeastern Atlantic). It is also the case that the traditional maritime powers, particularly Australia, France, Japan, the US and the UK, treat the maritime legal regime as intrinsic to their definition of the national maritime interest and substantive rather than merely instrumental.

Regulator of conflict. The UNCLOS provides a compulsory dispute settlement mechanism institutionalised by the International Tribunal for the Law of the Sea (ITLOS). The convention holds that state signatories "give their consent to the jurisdiction of the dispute settlement bodies set out under Article 287" and unlike the International Court of Justice, where both parties must agree that the court has jurisdiction in a dispute, "any state can unilaterally invoke the dispute settlement procedures *without* having to take any extra step" (italics in original) (Nguyen, 2018, p. 107). This dispute mechanism has enabled states to resolve outstanding maritime disputes by mutual consent or allowed states facing the predatory claims of a major power to appeal to the court without that state's prior consent. Yet, there are two major weaknesses of the ITLOS dispute resolution mechanism. First, the most important sources of conflict as it pertains to security – territoriality and military exercises – are under the jurisdiction of the International Court of Justice. Second, the decisions of the ITLOS are legally binding, but there is no effective enforcement mechanism (Oxman, 2015, pp. 398, 406–407). The *South China Sea Arbitration* (2016) is a case on point: China refused to accept binding arbitration with respect to its excessive territorial claims in the South China Sea despite its ratification of the treaty; second, the tribunal found in favour of the Philippine claims against China; and third, the Chinese government declared that it "neither accepts nor recognizes" the decision (McDorman, 2016). Although the matter of China's claims regarding the nine-dash line in the South China Sea is resolved legally, as a matter of practice the Chinese position on its prerogatives and claims have not changed. The enforcement of the *South China Sea Arbitration* decision has taken the form of US or US-led freedom of navigation operations.

The fundamental problem in constructing a robust system of MSG is the persistence of sovereignty as the key organising principle of maritime space. Rather than trending towards pooling sovereignty or the delegation of sovereignty to international institutions to tackle collectively the entire range of maritime threats identified, states seek to expand their sovereign prerogatives and territory, particularly in regional seas. The second major problem is the conflict between revisionist and *status quo* maritime states that reveals fundamental disagreements about the core content of an assumed public security good. In other words, it is difficult to resolve a collective action problem if the security good that is undersupplied means different things to different stakeholders. The system of security governance that emerged in the European geostrategic space reflects the transition from the Westphalian state to post-Westphalian state. The states of the Indo-Pacific and South Atlantic are more interested in consolidating sovereignty than giving it up. A global system of maritime security governance is, at best, in an embryonic state.

Notes

1 The UN has identified environmental degradation of the world's oceans, a key component of the "blue economy", as a security threat in 2008 (Klein, 2014, p. 391; UN General Assembly, 2020, pp. 2/19–7/19). This specific category of threat, which is largely (although not exclusively) a by-product of terrestrial activities, generally falls outside the ambit of MSG.
2 At least 17 states require prior notification for the innocent passage of warships or the conduct of military operations in the EEZ (see US Department of Defense, 2020, pp. 3–6). Over 60 states have placed restrictions or regulations on naval warships entering the EEZ or contiguous zone (see Kaye, 2008, pp. 8–12). For a comprehensive list of states restricting navigation (and overflight) inconsistent with customary international law, see US Navy (2021).
3 The first maritime peace-keeping operation took place in 2006 when a UN Maritime Task Force was a formal component of the UN Interim Force in Lebanon (United Nations, 2015, p. 4).
4 Partial exceptions include several US initiatives, notably the Container Security Initiative, the Proliferation Security Initiative and the Customs-Trade Partnership Against Terrorism (see Chalk, 2008, pp. 38–39).

References

Aarstad, A. K. (2017). Maritime security and transformations in global governance. *Crime Law Social Change, 67*, 313–331.

Allied Command Transformation. (2011). *Assured Access to the Global Commons: Maritime/Air/Space/Cyber. Findings and Recommendations.* https://www.act.nato.int/images/stories/events/2010/gc/aagc_recommendations.pdf

Anozie, C., Umahi, T., Onuoha, G., Nwafor, N., & Alozi, O. J. (2019). Ocean governance, integrated maritime security and its impact in the Gulf of Guinea: A lesson for Nigeria's maritime sector and economy. *Africa Review, 11*(2), 190–207.

ASEAN Regional Forum. (2019). *Annual Security Outlook.* Thailand: Ministry of Foreign Affairs.

Bateman, S. (2011). Solving the "wicked problems" of maritime security: Are regional forums up to the task? *Contemporary Southeast Asia, 33*(1), 1–28.

Behr, T., Aaltola, M., & Brattberg, E. (2013). *Maritime Security in a Multipolar World: Towards an EU Strategy for the Maritime Commons.* Finnish Institute of International Affairs.

BIS. (2019). *Triennial Central Bank Survey. Global Foreign Exchange Market Turnover in 2019.* https://www.bis.org/statistics/rpfx19_fx_annex.pdf

Brewster, D. (2017). Silk roads and strings of pearls: The strategic geography of China's new pathways in the Indian Ocean. *Geopolitics, 22*(2), 269–291.

Cerdeiro, D. A., Komaromi, A., Liu, Y., & Saeed, M. (2020). *World Seaborne Trade in Real Time: A Proof of Concept for Building AIS-Based Nowcasts from Scratch.* IMF Working Paper, No. 20/57. https://www.imf.org/en/Publications/WP/Issues/2020/05/14/World-Seaborne-Trade-in-Real-Time-A-Proof-of-Concept-for-Building-AIS-based-Nowcasts-from-49393

Chalk, P. (2008). The Maritime Dimension of International Security. Rand Corporation. https://www.rand.org/content/dam/rand/pubs/monographs/2008/RAND_MG697.pdf

Clark, B. (2016). Undersea cables and the future of submarine competition. *Bulletin of the Atomic Scientists, 72*(4), 234–237.

Council of the European Union. (2014). *EU Strategy on the Gulf of Guinea.* Foreign Affairs Council Meeting, 17 March, Brussels. https://www.consilium.europa.eu/media/28734/141582.pdf

CRS. (2020). *US-China Strategic Competition in South and East China Seas: Background and Issues for Congress.* CRS Report R42784. https://sgp.fas.org/crs/row/R42784.pdf

Davenport, T. (2012). Submarine Communications Cables and Law of the Sea: Problems in Law and Practice. *Ocean Development & International Law, 43,* 201–242.

De Vattel, E. (1916). *Le droit des gens, ou, Principes de la loi naturelle.* Carnegie Institute.

Embassy of France. (2020). EMASOH – Joint Communiqué on the European Maritime Awareness in the Strait of Hormuz. 1 October. https://www.diplomatie.gouv.fr/en/french-foreign-policy/europe/news/article/emasoh-joint-communique-on-the-european-maritime-awareness-in-the-strait-of

EU. (2021). *Critical Maritime Routes Programme.* https://criticalmaritimeroutes.eu/mission/

Freeman, C. P. (2019). An uncommon approach to the global commons: Interpreting China's divergent positions on maritime and outer space governance. *The China Quarterly, 241,* 1–21.

Grotius, H. (1916). *Freedom of the Seas or the Right Which Belongs to the Dutch to Take Part in the East Indian Trade.* Oxford University Press.

Guilfoyle, D. (2015). The high seas. In D. R. Rothwell, A. G. Oude Elferink, K. N. Scott, & T. Stephens (Eds.), *The Oxford Handbook of The Law of the* Sea (pp. 203–225). Oxford University Press.

Kamal-Deen, A. (2015). The anatomy of Gulf of Guinea piracy. *Naval War College Review, 68*(1), 93–118.

Kaye, S. (2008). *Freedom of Navigation in the Indo-Pacific Region.* Papers in Australian Maritime Affairs, no. 22. Sea Power Centre, Australian Department of Defence.

Kirchner, E. & Sperling, J. (2007). *EU Security Governance.* Manchester University Press.

Klein, N. (2014). Maritime space. In J. Sperling (Ed.), *Handbook on Governance and Security* (pp. 388–407). Edward Elgar.

Kraska, J. (2011). *Maritime Power and Law of the Sea: Expeditionary Operations in World Politics.* Oxford University Press.

Lucarelli, S. (2019). The EU as a securitizing agent? Testing the model, advancing the literature. *West European Politics, 42*(2), 413–436.

Mahon, R., & Fanning, L. (2019). Regional ocean governance: Polycentric arrangements and their role in global ocean governance. *Marine Policy 107,* 1–13.

Manyika, J., Lund, S., Bughin, J., Woetzel, J., Stamenov, K., & Dhingra, D. (2016). *Digital Globalization: The New Era of Global Flows.* McKinsey Global Institute Report. https://www.mckinsey.com/business-functions/mckinsey-digital/our-insights/digital-globalization-the-new-era-of-global-flows#

McDorman, T. L. (2016). The South China Sea Arbitration. *ASIL Insights, 20*(17). https://www.asil.org/insights/volume/20/issue/17/south-china-sea-arbitration

Morris, L. J., Mazarr, M. J., Hornung, J. W., Pezard, S., Binnendijk, A., & Kepe, M. (2019). *Gaining Competitive Advantage in the Gray Zone: Response Options for Coercive Aggression Below the Threshold of Major War.* RAND Corporation. https://www.rand.org/pubs/research_reports/RR2942.html

NATO. (2019). *Strategic Importance of, and dependence upon undersea cables.* NATO CCDCE. https://ccdcoe.org/uploads/2019/11/Undersea-cables-Final-NOV-2019.pdf

Nguyen, L. N. (2018). The UNCLOS dispute settlement system: What role can it play in resolving maritime disputes in Asia? *Asian Journal of International Law, 8,* 91–115.

Office of Director of National Intelligence. (2017, September 28). *Threats to Undersea Cable Communications.* https://www.dni.gov/files/PE/Documents/1---2017-AEP-Threats-to-Undersea-Cable-Communications.pdf

Oxman, B. H. (2015). Courts and tribunals: The ICJ, ITLOS, and arbitral tribunals. In D. R. Rothwell, A. G. Oude Elferink, K. N. Scott, & T. Stephens (Eds.), *The Oxford Handbook of The Law of the Sea* (pp. 394–415). Oxford University Press.

Panda, A. (2018, January 16). Japan Identifies Chinese Submarine in East China Sea. *The Diplomat.* https://thediplomat.com/2018/01/japan-identifies-chinese-submarine-in-east-china-sea-a-type-093-ssn/

Pandya, A. A., Herbert-Burns, R., & Kobayash, J. (2011). *Maritime Commerce and Security: The Indian Ocean.* Henry L. Stimson Center. https://www.stimson.org/wp-content/files/file-attachments/Section_1_-_Maritime_Commerce_and_Security_The_Indian_Ocean_1.pdf

Payne, M. (2018, September 5). *Australia to Support New Pacific Fusion Centre.* Australian Minister for Foreign Affairs. https://www.foreignminister.gov.au/minister/marise-payne/media-release/australia-support-new-pacific-fusion-centre

People's Republic of China. (2019). *China's New Defense in the New Era.* http://www.xinhuanet.com/english/2019-07/24/c_138253389.htm

Posen, B. (2003). Command of the commons: The military foundation of US hegemony, *International Security, 28*(1), 5–46.

Ramal, F. (2014). *Access to the Global Commons and Grand Strategies: A Shift in Global Interplay,* Etude de l'IRSEM n°30. Institute for Strategic Research of the École Militaire.

Reuters. (2020, September 23). *Sweden Calls In Russian Diplomats to Protest Breach of Its Waters.* https://www.reuters.com/article/us-sweden-security-russia/sweden-calls-in-russian-diplomats-to-protest-breach-of-its-waters-idUSKCN26E2LF

Rochette, J., Bille, R., Moenaar, E. J., Drankier, P., & Chabason, L. (2015). Regional oceans governance mechanisms: A review. *Marine Policy, 60*(1), 9–19.

Rothwell, D. R., Oude Elferink, A. G., Scott, K. N., & Stephens, T. (Eds.). (2015). *The Oxford Handbook of The Law of the Sea.* Oxford University Press.

Saab, B. Y. (2020, January 28). Trump's curious multilateralism. *Foreign Policy.* https://foreignpolicy.com/2020/01/28/trumps-curious-multilateralism/

Saint-Mézard, I. (2015). *The French Strategy in the Indian Ocean and the Potential for Indo-French Cooperation.* Nanyang Technological University.

Saito, Y. (2019). Reviewing law of armed conflict at sea and warfare at new domain and new measures: Submarine cables, merchant missile ships and unmanned marine systems. *Tulane Maritime Law Journal, 44*(107), 107–124.

Sandler, T. (1998). Global and regional public goods: A prognosis for collective action. *Fiscal Studies, 19*(3), 221–247.

Sloggett, D. (2013). *The Anarchic Sea: Maritime Security in the Twenty-First Century.* Hurst & Company.

Sperling, J. (2009). Security governance in a westphalian world. In C. Wagnasson, J. Sperling, & J. Hallenberg (Eds.), *European Security Governance: The European Union in a Westphalian World* (pp. 1–16). Routledge.

Sperling, J. (2011). NATO and the global commons: A perspective on emerging challenges. In R. Alcaro & S. Lucarelli (Eds.), *Managing Change: NATO's Partnerships and Deterrence in a Globalised World.* https://www.act.nato.int/images/stories/events/2011/managing_change_hr.pdf

Sperling, J. (2014). European Union. In J. Sperling (Ed.), *Handbook on Governance and Security* (pp. 588–617). Edward Elgar.

Sperling, J., & Webber, M. (2019). The European Union, security governance and collective securitization. *West European Politics, 42*(2), 228–260.

Stable Seas. (2020a). *Stable Seas Maritime Security Index: Codebook.* One Earth Future.

Stable Seas. (2020b). *The Stable Seas Maritime Security Index.* One Earth Future.

Suárez de Vivero, J. L., & Rodríguez Mateos, J. C. (2010). Ocean governance in a competitive world. The BRIC countries as emerging maritime powers—building new geopolitical scenarios. *Marine Policy, 34*(5), 967–978.

Sunak, R. (2017). *Undersea Cables: Indispensable, Insecure.* Policy Exchange. https://policyexchange.org.uk/publication/undersea-cables-indispensable-insecure/

UN General Assembly. (2016a). *Oceans and Law of the Sea: Report of the Secretary General.* (6 September) UN Doc. A/71/74/Add.1. https://documents-dds-ny.un.org/doc/UNDOC/GEN/N16/278/87/PDF/N1627887.pdf?OpenElement

UN General Assembly. (2016b). *Resolution Adopted by the General Assembly on 23 December 2015, 70/235. Oceans and the Law of the Sea.* https://www.un.org/en/development/desa/population/migration/generalassembly/docs/globalcompact/A_RES_70_235.pdf

UN General Assembly. (2020). *Oceans and Law of the Sea: Report of the Secretary General, UN Doc.* A/75/70, 16 March. https://documents-dds-ny.un.org/doc/UNDOC/GEN/N20/068/85/PDF/N2006885.pdf?OpenElement

United Nations. (2015). *United Nations Peacekeeping Missions: Military Maritime Task Force Manual.* http://repository.un.org/handle/11176/387297

US Department of Defense. (2015). *The Asia-Pacific Maritime Security Strategy: Achieving U.S. National Security Objectives in a Changing Environment.* Department of Defense.

US Department of Defense. (2020). *Annual Freedom of Navigation Report. Fiscal Year 2020.* Department of Defense.

US Energy Information Agency. (2019). *World Oil Transit Chokepoints Analysis Brief.* https://www.eia.gov/international/content/analysis/special_topics/World_Oil_Transit_Chokepoints/wotc.pdf

US Navy. (2014). *Maritime Stability Operations, NWP 3-07.* Department of the Navy.

US Navy. (2021). *Maritime Claims Reference Manual.* https://www.jag.navy.mil/organization/code_10_mcrm.htm

US Senate. (2020). *S.4049—National Defense Authorization Act for Fiscal Year 2021,* 116th Congress, 2nd Session (2019–2020). https://www.congress.gov/bill/116th-congress/senate-bill/4049?q=%7B%22search%22%3A%5B%22Pacific+deterrence%22%5D%7D&s=1&r=9

Vespe, M., Greidanus, H., & Alverez, M. (2015). The declining impact of piracy on maritime transport in the Indian Ocean: Statistical analysis of 5-year vessel tracking data. *Marine Policy, 59,* 9–15.

Voicu, A., & Bosilca, R. L. (2015). Maritime security governance in the fight against piracy off the coast of Somalia: A focus on the EU response. Proceedings of the EURINT Conference 2015, Alexandru Ioan Cuza University, vol. *2,* 371–386.

Vreÿ, F. (2009). Bad order at sea: From the Gulf of Aden to the Gulf of Guinea. *African Security Review, 18*(3), 17–30.

World Bank. (2020). Trade (% of GDP). https://data.worldbank.org/indicator/NE.TRD.GNFS.ZS

Zou, K. (2015). The South China Sea. In D. R. Rothwell, R. Bille, E. J. Moenaar, P., Drankier & L., Chabason (Eds.), *The Oxford Handbook of The Law of the Sea.* Oxford University Press.

7

MARITIME SECURITY AND THE LAW OF THE SEA

Joanna Mossop

Introduction

Maritime security is inextricably linked to the law of the sea. Security concerns are at the heart of the 1982 United Nations Convention on the Law of the Sea (UNCLOS) and related legal instruments. The situation that existed prior to UNCLOS was one of conflict between states over the appropriate extent of maritime zones and rights and obligations in those zones. Concern about the "creeping jurisdiction" of coastal states meant that naval powers saw the benefit of a single treaty that brought together the key rules about navigation and resource exploitation. It was seen as desirable to resolve the heated disputes, which had the potential to undermine security.

UNCLOS contributes to maritime security in several ways. It successfully reduced tensions by providing certainty on maritime zones, and rights within those zones. In particular, the rights of navigation for military and other vessels were clearly protected and outlined. It also built on established jurisdictional principles to determine the control that states can exert over vessels in various zones. A dispute settlement process that involved compulsory disputes settlement for some types of disputes was intended to ensure that disagreements could be resolved peacefully.

The law of the sea encompasses more than UNCLOS. Customary international law rules as well as other treaties have played a part in developing legal principles. This is particularly the case when the international community has had to respond to new and emerging maritime security issues, such as terrorism. Thus, the law relating to maritime security can justify a book length treatment (e.g., Klein, 2011; Kraska & Pedrozo, 2013; Galani & Evans, 2020).

The goal of this chapter, rather than addressing all the legal developments on all maritime security issues, is to situate the issue of maritime security in its international legal context. The chapter begins with a discussion of the meaning of maritime security from an international law perspective and the limitations of international law in resolving inter-state disputes. It then focuses on two ways in which the law of the sea plays a fundamental role in maritime security (Klein, 2015, p. 582). First, one goal of the law of the sea is to reduce inter-state conflict caused by disagreement about the legal principles applicable to uses of the oceans. Second, the law of the sea establishes the jurisdictional basis for states to undertake law enforcement in respect of maritime activities by non-state actors. In respect of each of these functions, the law has had a certain level of success, but disputes continue in which the content of the law is contested.

DOI: 10.4324/9781003001324-9

International law and maritime security

A legal definition of maritime security?

International lawyers, as in other disciplines, have defined maritime security in different ways. The concept is not legally defined in any binding international instrument, possibly reflecting a broader lack of consensus about the scope of the topic. However, common elements can be identified as underpinning a legal approach to maritime security.

UNCLOS directly mentions security in only a few articles. The preamble to the Convention notes that it recognises "the desirability of establishing ... a legal order for the seas and oceans", to among other things, "promote the peaceful uses of the seas and oceans". The phrase "maritime security" does not appear in UNCLOS. "Security" is used primarily to denote the fundamental rights of a state to protect itself from hostile action or other acts that undermine the good order of the state. For example, passage of foreign vessels through the territorial sea is only permitted "so long as it is not prejudicial to the peace, good order or security" of the coastal state (art. 19(1)). The list of activities considered to be prejudicial to the peace, good order and security of the coastal state includes fishing, pollution and unloading of goods or people contrary to the laws of the state (art. 19(2)). States can suspend temporarily innocent passage in their territorial sea "if such suspension is essential for the protection of its security, including weapons exercises" (art. 25(3)). Therefore, although security is usually referenced in relation to military security, it can also be seen as a broader concept because of the inclusion of non-military activities, such as fishing, that are included in art. 19(2) (Kaye, 2006, p. 349). As will be argued later in this chapter, although there is a lack of direct reference to maritime security in UNCLOS, security concerns lay behind its negotiation.

In the absence of an authoritative definition, it is difficult to identify a legal definition of maritime security. Many scholars focus on the threats or goals that are the focus of maritime security. Galani and Evans (2020, p. 8) have suggested that there is no single definition, but that maritime security is the focus of a blend of threats and activities by state and non-state actors. Similarly, Klein (2011, p. 9) focuses on "the protection of a state's land and maritime territory, infrastructure, economy, environment and society from certain harmful acts occurring at sea".

Instead of attempting to define maritime security as a single concept, for the purposes of this chapter it is useful to consider what a legal approach to maritime security might entail. First, the "rule of law" is a key principle in international as well as domestic law and applies to maritime security. Kraska and Pedrozo (2013, p. 1) define maritime security as "the stable order of the oceans subject to the rule of law at sea". At its simplest, this requires a response to threats based on legal rules adopted by the international community, found in customary international law, or negotiated through international treaties. Informal, non-binding rules can also contribute to this goal. In this way, law is a "normative standard against which behaviour can be assessed" (Scott, 2018, p. 629) and provides "a degree of order, predictability and stability" to the international community (Charney, 1993, p. 532). The legal approach to maritime security is concerned with identifying and developing rules governing behaviour at sea and the jurisdictional basis for a response to activities that threaten security. A number of sub-disciplines of international law may be involved beyond the law of the sea, including international criminal law, international human rights law and the law of naval warfare (Kraska & Pedrozo, 2013, p. 2). The contribution of the law of the sea is that it establishes the international legal boundaries within which states can respond to maritime security threats by state and non-state actors.

The relationship between the rule of law and maritime security goes beyond identifying and developing rules. The rule of law can also be considered to be a source of legitimacy for state actions (Guilfoyle, 2019, p. 1001). The rhetorical appeal of justifying action as lawful is to establish the validity of that action. This has been referred to as an ideology, the observance of which is a criteria for membership of the international system (Scott, 1994, p. 322). Thus, international law and international politics cannot be fully separated (Klein et al., 2010, p. 9).

Second, a legal approach often takes a functional approach (Klein et al., 2010, p. 10). This involves developing legal tools to address particular threats perceived to undermine maritime security. These have been the focus of significant legal scholarship. Topics include piracy, terrorism, smuggling of people and goods, other illegal activities at sea including illegal fishing and wilful environmental pollution or degradation. Taking a functional approach to maritime security can lead to diverging definitions, because the meaning of maritime security depends on the perception of the person or institution interacting with it (Barnes & Rosello, 2020, p. 52). Nevertheless, the functional approach remains the primary lens through which much legal analysis occurs.

Third, international law often seeks to build cooperation to achieve community goals of security for all users of the ocean (Kraska & Pedrozo, 2013, p. 10). Klein (2011, p. 16) has identified that maritime security engages "exclusive interests" – benefitting individual states – and "inclusive interests" – accommodating all states. Exclusive interests in maritime security include the interest of a state in controlling its border and detecting and punishing illegal activities that impact on its own security. Inclusive interests are those involving cooperation to achieve shared interests in security, such as the cooperation against terrorism and smuggling of illegal weapons (Klein, 2011, p. 17). This focus on cooperation is often a goal of international legal instruments.

Finally, international law emphasises the need to find peaceful resolutions to disagreements between states with incompatible ideas about their rights and obligations under international law. Dispute settlement provisions are features of many treaties and are often seen as a counter to the power of certain states (Steinberg & Zasloff, 2006, p. 65; Churchill, 2017, p. 218). Disputes between states that are not able to be resolved peacefully undermine maritime security.

Challenges for legal approaches to maritime security

There are limitations on the ability of international law to respond effectively to maritime security challenges. First, a "rule of law" approach may assume a common set of rules. That assumption is not always reflected in reality. For example, UNCLOS is frequently lauded as establishing a "constitution for the ocean". However, it was never intended to contain the totality of international law applicable to the ocean. Instead, it was envisaged that other international law instruments would develop the law in new ways to respond to changing circumstances. Thus, rules are fragmented among different legal sources and, due to the operation of *pacta tertiis*, apply differently to states depending on whether they have acceded or ratified the relevant treaty.

The process of international law-making requires the identification of common interests among states. In an increasingly pluralised international community, common interests can sometimes be difficult to identify. The process of negotiating international instruments is usually slow and often problematic, as common interests are weighed against the national interests of states. Although international law has a formal rule of equality of states, the reality is that more powerful states have a disproportionate influence on the outcome of treaty-making processes. Thus, establishing a common set of rules in the face of new threats to maritime security is not easy and requires political will (Gibson, 2009, p. 69).

Second, the interpretation of existing rules is a potential source of conflict between states (Kraska & Pedrozo, 2013, p. 7). For example, different interpretations of UNCLOS have heightened tensions between states at times. Some familiar issues include: whether the right of innocent passage permits foreign warships to navigate through territorial seas without the permission or consent of the coastal state; the rights of foreign militaries to undertake hydrographic and other surveys in the exclusive economic zone (EEZ); and whether certain features are capable of generating an EEZ and continental shelf (*South China Sea* arbitration). These disputes can be exacerbated by different approaches to international law depending on the cultural background of the participants (Roberts, 2017, p. 6).

Third, dispute settlement processes are not capable of resolving all legal issues. UNCLOS excludes certain disputes from the jurisdiction of third-party dispute settlement processes (UNCLOS, arts. 297 and 298). These types of dispute, such as maritime delimitation or military activities, are often at the core of sovereign interests, making them more likely to spike controversy among states, undermining maritime security.

Over the last decade, states and others are increasingly referring to the need for a 'rules-based order' in international discourse (Breuer & Johnston, 2019, p. 440). This phrase has been deployed in relation to maritime security, particularly when there is a perception that states may not be abiding by their international obligations and has most often been used in respect of activities by China and the United States. The question is whether there is any implication from the use of this phrase as opposed to, for example, calls for compliance with international law. Some commentators seem to equate a rules-based order with one based on international law (e.g., Raymond, 2019, p. 222). However, others have suggested that the phrase is used by states that seek to create new rules that may not be based on international law, or that rely on sources that go beyond law such as general principles or soft law (e.g., Scott, 2018, p. 641). Indeed, some consider international law as a source of legitimacy rather than representing the totality of the rules-based order (Hall & Heazle, 2018, p. 21). Thus, although there is some overlap, caution must be used before equating statements expressing support for a rules-based order to support for an order based on international law.

Law of the sea and inter-state maritime security

If maritime security has the goal of creating a legal order for the oceans, absent from conflict or illegal behaviour, then the peaceful relationship between states is key to this outcome. Over centuries, states (or their predecessors, such as monarchs) have competed with each other at sea. Since the development of the modern international law system, with the principle of non-aggression and peaceful settlement of disputes at its core, the amount of warfare conducted at sea has greatly diminished, although it has not disappeared completely. However, this has not prevented disagreements between states arising over different perspectives of their legal rights that have the potential to lead to conflict of various types. Therefore, one role of the law of the sea has been to create rules that reduce these disagreements and thus aid in creating order at sea as between states. This has not been easy however, and even the negotiation of UNCLOS has not prevented states from disputing other states' interpretation of rules. The dispute settlement system has not always been able to resolve these disputes.

Maritime security and the development of the law of the sea

The origins of the modern law of the sea are often traced back to Hugo Grotius' seminal work *Mare Liberum*, although other contemporary authors were also advocating the doctrine of freedom of the seas (Vieira, 2003). This idea was in contrast to the view, promoted by Portugal and Spain, that the oceans were *mare clausum*, or closed seas (Papastavridis, 2011). Grotius and his peers argued that no one could subject the seas to sovereignty, and that each state could use the oceans without harming others. Navigation and fishing, in particular, would be free for all ships, which would be subject only to the control of their home state. The freedom of the seas was rapidly accepted as the dominant approach to the law of the sea. Navies and merchants in particular came to rely heavily on freedom of navigation, which they fiercely defended.

A major exception to the freedom of the high seas was the declaration of territorial seas, over which coastal states claimed sovereignty and the right to enforce their laws against ships. This concept was the antithesis to the freedom of the seas, although a right of innocent passage developed which protected shipping from interference by coastal states. Passage through the territorial sea would be permitted so long as it did not impinge on the peace, security and good order of the coastal state. Over time, a number of disagreements arose as to the acceptable distance from shore that a coastal state could claim sovereignty over. For example, some argued that a state could exert sovereignty over the distance from shore that a canon could be fired (and sink a ship), giving rise to the cannon-shot rule. Naturally, the development of technology allowing canons to fire greater distances made that approach too uncertain to maintain. Instead, states asserted control over the sea based on nautical miles from shore, although no consensus was reached as to how many miles the territorial sea could extend.

Over the course of the twentieth century, a variety of claims were made to jurisdiction over parts of the ocean which, when challenged, posed a risk of conflict between states. The key tension arose from as a tendency for coastal states to claim control over increasingly large areas of the ocean adjacent to their coastlines, a phenomenon termed "creeping jurisdiction" (Klein, 2011, p. 7). Examples included disputes over the extent of the territorial sea, extended fisheries zones and the declaration of sovereign rights over continental shelves. These claims by coastal states narrowed the available part of the ocean that was high seas, in which all states had freedom of navigation and other freedoms such as fishing and marine scientific research. Disputes involving contested claims to rights over ocean space had the potential to reduce overall security at sea if they escalated.

The international community attempted to resolve some of these issues by negotiating international treaties in 1958. Four law of the sea treaties were concluded in Geneva addressing the territorial sea, continental shelf, high seas and fishing respectively. Two problems emerged from this development. First, agreement on the extent of the territorial sea could not be reached. Second, states were picking and choosing between the four conventions to only ratify those that benefited them. A second international conference was held in 1960 which attempted to reach agreement on a 6-mile territorial sea and a 6-mile fisheries zone. However, this attempt failed by a narrow margin.

UNCLOS' contribution to maritime security

The negotiation of UNCLOS between 1973 and 1982 was an enormous diplomatic achievement. In order to avoid the piece-meal approach generated by the 1958 Conventions, states agreed to work on a "package deal". Under this method, no part of the Convention was agreed until all was agreed. No reservations would be permitted, ensuring that states had to agree to the entirety of the Convention or none (Harrison, 2011).

Although security is mentioned explicitly only in passing in UNCLOS (Kaye, 2006, p. 348), it was very successful at resolving most debates over the extent of, and rights in, various maritime zones. The Convention went well beyond the modest claims to territorial sea and fisheries zones that were at issue in 1960. Under UNCLOS, coastal states could claim 12-mile territorial seas, and the concept of the EEZ, in which coastal states had sovereign rights to resources up to 200 miles from shore, rapidly became widely accepted.

At the same time, powerful states were keen to ensure that the freedom of navigation was protected, both for commercial shipping and to ensure the movement of navies around the world (Richardson, 1980, p. 911). The right to undertake innocent passage was clarified, with specific activities listed that transiting vessels could not undertake (art. 19). The expansion of territorial seas from 3 to 12 miles necessitated detailed provisions protecting the right of passage through international straits that would otherwise be within the territorial sea of states, and thus subject to temporary closure.

Finally, the Convention included a detailed dispute settlement procedure. Given the fractious history of international disputes arising from different interpretations of the law of the sea, a system to resolve those disputes was seen as crucial to maintaining a uniform interpretation and hence the stability of the new regime (Klein, 2005, p. 21). An unusual feature of the dispute settlement procedure was the ability for states, in many disputes, to require another state party to submit to third-party dispute settlement. The adoption of such a system reflects the ambition for UNCLOS to promote peaceful settlement of disputes.

Challenges for the law of the sea and maritime security between states

As discussed above, the negotiation of treaties is a complex process in which states attempt to create legal rules around a common interest. This is reflected in the way that UNCLOS was formed.

The dispute settlement process has not proven to be as effective as it could be at resolving disputes between states over the interpretation of UNCLOS. The exclusions from the compulsory dispute settlement process (including exercise of coastal state jurisdiction, maritime delimitation and military activities, see arts. 297 and 298) have lessened the ability of courts and tribunals to take jurisdiction over some arguments. Additionally, where issues have been perceived as central to the exercise of sovereignty, states are often reluctant to bring the dispute to third party settlement, for fear of losing control of the outcome of the disagreement.

Although UNCLOS resolved many legal issues, it failed to resolve some existing issues and even created new problems. Disputes over maritime boundaries are a good example. Maritime delimitation is a core issue of sovereignty as it determines the physical extent of a state's jurisdiction. UNCLOS contains some limited provisions relating to the negotiation of maritime boundaries (e.g., arts. 74 and 83). States wished to retain control over the outcome of such disputes, and so they can be excluded from compulsory dispute settlement (UNCLOS, art. 298). These disputes are difficult to resolve because of the promises of wealth from living and non-living resources for the successful state (Schofield, 2014, p. 120).

One difficulty identified above is the use of deliberate ambiguities in treaties. Such ambiguities arise when states cannot agree on the precise legal obligation and wording is designed to be acceptable to all parties. This allows states to adopt legal interpretations that support their position. The relevance of deliberate ambiguity in the law of the sea is enhanced by the fact that states are not permitted to enter reservations to any part of UNCLOS (UNCLOS, art. 309). This restriction does not apply to many other relevant international law instruments.

There are many ambiguities in UNCLOS that arguably have impacted on maritime security because they have led to tensions between states. One example is article 121 which establishes whether a small feature in the sea can generate an EEZ and continental shelf. Following lengthy debates about what factors would exclude a feature from generating these zones, delegates agreed that "rocks which cannot sustain human habitation or an economic life of their own shall have no exclusive economic zone" (art. 121(3). This allowed states to interpret the relatively vague criteria in ways that have given rise to disputes between states, most problematically in the South China Sea (e.g., Guilfoyle, 2019).

Another area of dispute relevant to maritime security has been the respective rights of coastal states and flag states in the EEZ. For example, there is disagreement among states over the right of foreign states to undertake military activities in the EEZ (Rothwell & Stephens, 2016, p. 100). Such activities are not explicitly prohibited in the Convention, and a number of naval powers maintain that such activities are part of the "other internationally lawful uses of the sea" protected in article 58 (Van Dyke, 2004, p. 35). Other states, including China, have argued that such activities are not peaceful, threaten their national security and do not fit within the freedom of navigation which is preserved by article 58 (Ma, 2019, p. 246).

One of the key strengths of UNCLOS was its clarification of maritime zones including the creation of the EEZ and the extent of the continental shelf. However, the creation of new sovereign rights by UNCLOS has also led to further disputes among states who need to delimit the boundaries between their new entitlements. It is arguable, for example, that recent issues in the South China Sea were partly provoked by a Chinese response to a claim to an extended continental shelf lodged with the Commission on the Limits of the Continental Shelf in 2009 (Beckman, 2013, p. 154).

Law of the sea and non-state actors

The key role of the law of the sea in relation to illegal activity by non-state actors is to establish the rules of jurisdiction: under what circumstances can a state take steps against a vessel flagged to another state if the crew or passengers of a vessel are engaged in unlawful conduct? The rules relating to jurisdiction over vessels allocate responsibility and rights to states, depending on the location of the vessel.

Flag state responsibility lies at the heart of the law of the sea regime. States must exercise jurisdiction and control over vessels flying their flag (UNCLOS, art. 94). Vessels are expected to have a "nationality", reflecting the state to which the vessel is registered (art. 91). Although article 91 requires a genuine link between the state and the ship, this is not uniformly applied in practice. Indeed, the phenomenon of "flags of convenience" is commonplace. Flags of convenience usually have open registers, which require minimal evidence of connection to the flag state before issuing registration to a vessel. A number of security issues arise from this, including a lack of transparency of ownership of vessels or scrutiny by the flag state (Marcopoulos, 2007). Poor flag state control and exclusive flag state jurisdiction on the high seas is a cause of frustration for law enforcement activities at sea (Galani & Evans, 2020, p. 5).

Vessels undertaking unlawful activities at sea often fly no flag at all. These stateless vessels are vulnerable to boarding and inspection at any point, although the ability of the boarding state to arrest the vessel, especially beyond national jurisdiction, is disputed (Churchill & Lowe, 1999, p. 213).

Maritime security in areas under national jurisdiction

In maritime zones which confer some rights or jurisdiction on a coastal state, the Convention has sought to achieve a balance between freedoms of navigation and coastal state interests. In the territorial sea, a foreign vessel has a right of innocent passage which should not be hampered by the coastal state (UNCLOS, arts. 17–19, 24). However, in relation to activities excluded from innocent passage, the coastal state can enforce its laws against the foreign vessel, with some exceptions (UNCLOS, art. 21). There are limitations on the ability of a coastal state to exercise criminal jurisdiction against persons on board a foreign vessel passing through the territorial sea (UNCLOS, art. 27). In ports, coastal states have the right to set conditions for entry into port and can exercise criminal jurisdiction over vessels and their crews and passengers (Tanaka, 2019, p. 96).

In the EEZ the coastal state has sovereign rights over resources as well as a right to enforce its laws relating to living resources against foreign vessels (UNCLOS, arts. 56, 73). However, to the extent that UNCLOS does not give jurisdiction to the coastal state, the high seas freedoms apply and the flag state retains exclusive jurisdiction (UNCLOS, art. 58). As already mentioned, states do not always agree on the appropriate balance between coastal state and flag state rights. Such disagreements can lead to disputes among state parties to UNCLOS about the exercise of jurisdiction in certain cases.

Maritime security in areas beyond national jurisdiction

UNCLOS provides clear guidelines for state jurisdiction in areas beyond national jurisdiction. While on the high seas (which includes the EEZ to the extent the coastal state does not have jurisdiction over an activity – see UNCLOS, art. 58), the vessel is exclusively subject to the jurisdiction of the flag state (UNCLOS, art. 92). Therefore, on the high seas there are limited circumstances in which a state can board and inspect a foreign vessel.

UNCLOS provides for a right to board if a state has engaged in the hot pursuit of a vessel from within national jurisdiction to an area beyond its jurisdiction (UNCLOS, art. 111). In addition, article 110 provides a right of visit, in which states can board and inspect foreign vessels for limited purposes. These include where the ship has engaged in piracy, slave trading, unauthorised broadcasting, to verify the vessel's nationality, or where the ship is without nationality. However, a right of visit does not permit the boarding state to exercise enforcement jurisdiction over (in other words, arrest) the foreign vessel. Only piracy (UNCLOS, art. 105) and unauthorised broadcasting (UNCLOS, art. 109) permit states to arrest foreign ships. Therefore, in respect of the high seas, the flag state has almost exclusive authority to take enforcement action against a vessel.

Several factors have caused strain to the law in relation to foreign vessels in areas beyond national jurisdiction. For example, terrorist groups became much more active from the 1990s, and the attack on the United States on 9 September 2001 sharpened attention on this activity. The growth in flags of convenience over time raised concerns that illegal activity would not be adequately monitored and punished. The smuggling of irregular migrants became a bigger issue for developed states including the European Union members and Australia (Papanicolopulu, 2018). The limited exceptions to exclusive flag state jurisdiction in UNCLOS article 110 meant that states had to work within the existing legal framework or seek to develop new rules.

The global response to terrorism highlighted issues that were not directly addressed in UNCLOS and is a good example of the development of the law of the sea in response to specific threats. In particular, restrictions on the ability of states to board foreign vessels suspected of being engaged in criminal behaviour in support of terrorism became problematic for some states. The development of the Proliferation Security Initiative (PSI) by the United States was a key example of this. The PSI was a coalition of states under United States' leadership, with the goal of preventing the transportation of weapons of mass destruction and terrorists at sea. The stated aim was to use existing law to support the law enforcement efforts. However, some states remained suspicious that the interdiction principles stretched the boundaries of international law (Klein, 2011 p. 198). Although the PSI was not underpinned by a multilateral treaty, the United States entered into agreements with some flag states, such as Liberia and Panama, to allow for the US to board their vessels in certain circumstances (Kaye, 2006, p. 358).

At the same time, the International Maritime Organisation began negotiations for a protocol to the Convention for the Suppression of Unlawful Acts against the Safety of Maritime Navigation 1988 (SUA Convention). The SUA Convention criminalises a range of behaviours including hijacking or damaging a ship in a way that is likely to endanger the safety of a ship. States parties are required to prosecute or extradite accused offenders found in their territory. The protocol completed in 2005 updated the Convention to deal with new threats, namely the use of ships to transfer or discharge biological, chemical or nuclear weapons (BCNWs) and other hazardous substances as part of a terrorist act. Although the United States wanted a right to board foreign vessels suspected of transporting BCNWs, this was considered too great an imposition on the freedom of the high seas. Instead, state parties to the 2005 Protocol can give permission in advance for vessels to be boarded.

The example of terrorism shows the international legal system responds to new and emerging threats through a variety of approaches. These can include interpreting existing law to cover the new issue, negotiating new instruments or agreements, using existing organisations to elaborate regulatory responses, or even taking bilateral approaches to achieve order at sea.

Conclusions

The law of the sea plays a fundamental role in maritime security as a discipline and field of research. UNCLOS and other treaties and arrangements provide the parameters within which states can respond to threats from non-state actors as well as set the ground rules for inter-state cooperation. An approach to maritime security based in international law acknowledges the importance of establishing order at sea based on a cooperative rule of law that is appropriate for the issues at hand and provides for peaceful settlement of disputes. As the concept of maritime security has expanded to include a wider range of topics (such as illegal fishing and environmental degradation), so the realm of applicable law has also expanded.

It is impossible in the space provided to explore the topic in detail given the myriad of legal instruments that impact on this field in addition to UNCLOS. Instead, this chapter has identified two key contributions that international law makes to maritime security: reducing inter-state conflict in relation to maritime issues; and a search for clear jurisdictional principles to allow states to respond to threats by non-state actors.

It can be seen that UNCLOS provided a great deal of clarity around issues that had been problematic for the international community, including the extent and nature of maritime zones. However, treaties are not capable of resolving all issues and disputes that may arise in the future. The expanding concern about terrorist activities at sea after 9/11 is a good example of the fact that UNCLOS was considered by some states to be inadequate to respond to serious new threats by non-state actors. Instead, states look to develop new rules and interpretations through state practice, negotiating new instruments and dealing with issues on a regional or bilateral basis.

References

Barnes, R., & Rosello, M. (2020). Fisheries and maritime security: Understanding and enhancing the connection. In M. D. Evans & S. Galani (Eds.), *Maritime security and the law of the sea: Help or hindrance?* (pp. 48–82). Edward Elgar.

Beckman, R. (2013). The UN Convention on the Law of the Sea and the maritime disputes in the South China Sea. *American Journal of International Law, 107*(1), 142–163.

Breuer, A., & Johnston A. I. (2019). Memes, narratives and the emergent US–China security dilemma. *Cambridge Review of International Affairs, 32*, 429–455.

Charney, J. I. (1993). Universal international law. *American Journal of International Law, 87*, 529–551.

Churchill, R. (2017). The general dispute settlement system of the UN Convention on the Law of the Sea: Overview, context, and use. *Ocean Development and International Law, 48*, 216–238.

Churchill, R. R., & Lowe, A. V. (1999). *The law of the sea* (3rd ed.). Manchester University Press.

Galani, S., & Evans, M. D. (2020). The interplay between maritime security and the 1982 United Nations convention on the law of the sea: Help or hindrance? In M. D. Evans & S. Galani (Eds.), *Maritime security and the law of the sea: Help or hindrance?* (pp. 1–24). Edward Elgar.

Gibson, J. (2009). Maritime security and international law in Africa. *African Security Studies, 18*, 60–70.

Guilfoyle, D. (2019). The rule of law and maritime security: Understanding lawfare in the South China Sea. *International Affairs 95*, 999–1017.

Hall, I., & Heazle, M. (2018). Resolving contradictions: US primacy and the 'rules-based' order. In M. Heazle & A. O'Neil (Eds.), *China's rise and Australia-Japan-US relations* (pp. 18–44). Edward Elgar.

Harrison, J. (2011). *Making the law of the sea: A study in the development of international law.* Cambridge University Press.

Kaye, S. (2006). Freedom of navigation in a post 9/11 world: Security and creeping jurisdiction. In D. Freestone, R. Barnes, & D. Ong (Eds.), *The law of the sea: Progress and prospects* (pp. 347–364). Oxford University Press.

Klein, N. (2005). *Dispute settlement in the UN Convention on the Law of the Sea.* Cambridge University Press.

Klein, N. (2011). *Maritime security and the law of the sea.* Oxford University Press.

Klein, N. (2015). Maritime security. In D. R. Rothwell, A. G. Oude Elferink, K. N. Scott, & T. Stephens (Eds.), *The Oxford handbook on the law of the sea* (pp. 582–603). Oxford University Press.

Klein, N., Mossop, J., & Rothwell, D. R. (2010). Australia, New Zealand and maritime security. In N. Klein, J. Mossop, & D. R. Rothwell (Eds.), *Maritime security: International law and policy perspectives from Australia and New Zealand* (pp. 1–21). Routledge.

Kraska, J., & Pedrozo, P. (2013). *International maritime security law.* Martinus Nijhoff.

Ma, X. (2019). Military activities in foreign exclusive economic zones: Identification and the application of the law. In M. H. Nordquist, J. N. Moore, & R. Long (Eds.), *Cooperation and engagement in the Asia-Pacific region* (pp. 238–294). Koninklijke Brill NV.

Marcopoulos, A. J. (2007). Flags of terror: An argument for rethinking maritime security policy regarding flags of convenience. *Tulane Maritime Law Journal, 32*(1), 277–312.

Papanicolopulu, I. (2018). *International law and the protection of people at sea.* Oxford University Press.

Papastavridis, E. (2011). The right of visit on the high seas in a theoretical perspective: Mare liberum versus mare clausam revisited. *Leiden Journal of International Law, 24*, 45–70.

Raymond, G. V. (2019). Advocating the rules-based order in an era of multi-polarity. *Australian Journal of International Affairs, 73*, 219–226.

Richardson, E. L. (1980). Power, mobility and the law of the sea. *Foreign Affairs, 58*(4), 902–919.

Roberts, A. (2017). *Is international law international?* Oxford University Press.

Rothwell, D. R., & Stephens, T. (2016). *The international law of the sea* (2nd ed). Hart Publishing.

Schofield, C. (2014). The 'El Dorado' effect: Reappraising the 'oil factor' in maritime boundary disputes. In C. Schofield, S. Lee, & M.-D. Kwon (Eds.), *The limits of maritime jurisdiction* (pp. 111–126). Martinus Nijhoff.

Scott, S. V. (1994). International law as ideology: Theorizing the relationship between international law and international politics. *European Journal of International Law, 5*, 313–325.

Scott, S. V. (2018). The decline of international law as a normative ideal. *Victoria University of Wellington Law Review, 49*, 627–644.

Steinberg, R. H., & Zasloff, J. M. (2006). Power and international law. *American Journal of International Law, 100*, 64–87.

Tanaka, Y. (2019). *The international law of the sea* (3rd ed.). Cambridge University Press.

Van Dyke, J. M. (2004). Military ships and planes operating in the exclusive economic zone of another country. *Marine Policy, 28*, 29–39.

Vieira, M. B. (2003). Mare liberum vs. mare clausum: Grotius, Freitas, and Seldon's sebate on Dominion over the seas. *Journal of the History of Ideas, 64*, 361–377.

8

MARITIME SECURITISATION

Juha A. Vuori

The study of maritime securitisation focuses on the politics of making maritime concerns issues of security. This approach can be used to examine both traditional military and geopolitical issues as well as comprehensive and broad security concepts. Both military and non-traditional security issues can have implications for regional and international security dynamics. At the same time, sectors of security issues can be interdependent and form complexes (Buzan & Wæver, 2003). Securitisation theory is apt for investigating what it means to, for example, use military means to deal with matters that have previously been civilian or constabulary concerns.

I begin this entry in the handbook by briefly introducing securitisation theory as an approach to the study of security generally and maritime security specifically. I will then focus on three of the most prominent aspects of the previous maritime securitisation literature, namely geopolitics and maritime regional security, piracy and maritime transnational crime, and maritime immigration. I conclude with some views on possible openings in the study of maritime securitisation.

Securitisation Theory

Securitisation as a keyword or notion has become very enticing, even to the degree that it is used in articles to do things without any references to the securitisation studies literature. There seems to be something self-explanatory in the term as such. Intuitively, securitisation is about how security politics comes about. As such, security means different things to different societies, as the core fears of any group or nation are unique and relate to vulnerabilities and historical experiences (Wæver, 1989, p. 301). Yet, despite this historical contingency, security tends to be portrayed as something "good", as being or feeling safe from harm or danger, which corresponds with its everyday (non-expert) meaning as something of positive value. Perhaps paradoxically, in the realm of international politics though, security is often understood as a more negative concern since it is about blocking unwanted developments. Concomitantly, security arguments in effect reproduce insecurities; security arguments tend to promise more than they can deliver.

The notion of securitisation captures the performative power politics of the concept "security" and has shown how issues acquire the status of security through intersubjective

96

DOI: 10.4324/9781003001324-10

Maritime Securitisation

socio-political processes. Although many things can threaten the existence of valued referent objects, such threats do not come with labels – they require political action to gain the deontic rights, duties, obligations, requirements and authorisations that come about by "performing and getting others to accept" (Searle, 2011, p. 85) securitisation speech acts. The aim of securitisation studies is to gain an increasingly precise understanding of who (securitising actors) can securitise (political moves via speech acts) which issues (threats), for whom (referent objects), why (perlocutionary intentions/how-causality), with what kinds of effects (interunit relations) and under what conditions (facilitation/impediment factors) (Vuori, 2017).

The approach combines the study of what securitisation does (what it "triggers") with political constellations, or who or what does securitisation (what "triggers" it) (Guzzini, 2011, pp. 336–337). The effects of securitisation on society, process and polity can be studied in three stages (Wæver, 2015), where:

1 Aspirations of actors are related to societal conditions;
2 Political codifications that constitute particular relationships are analysed through speech act theory;
3 Effects on political, legal and socio-psychological life are examined.

The model contains several important elements (Buzan et al., 1998): The general script or plot of security entails priority and utmost importance of the particular issue; the existence of a valued referent object is at stake and under threat. The model as such has seven variables (Vuori, 2017):

1 A securitising actor (that which or who makes the move towards a new, or to alter an existing issue of security in accordance with particular conventions and grammars);
2 A referent object (that which is to be secured);
3 A threat (that which threatens the referent object);
4 An audience (the necessary relation needed to produce the deontic modality of security or those who have to be "convinced" for securitisation to be satisfied);
5 Felicity conditions (rules and conventions of the speech act and its consequences);
6 Facilitation factors (factors that can facilitate or impede the acceptance of the securitisation move; social conditions that relate to social positions of the actor and audience as well as the threat);
7 Functional actors (actors that are neither the securitising actor, the threat, nor the referent object, but still have some bearing on the process).

Securitisation can have multiple political functions (Vuori, 2011): it can be used to raise an issue onto the security agenda, legitimise future or past actions, control subordinates or to deter opponents. Securitisation can be used to change the status of an issue, but it can also be used to gain moral support without recourse to actual security actions (Balzacq et al., 2016). Securitisation can happen through speech acts in "high politics", but it can also happen "diffusely" through security practices, techniques and technologies (Huysmans, 2014). The referent objects of security can range from societal and identity questions to global or macro-level issues that concern the physical survival of most of humanity (Buzan & Wæver, 2009; Vuori, 2010). Finally, securitisation processes can be contested or resisted (Vuori, 2015), and how issues become security issues or are removed from security agendas is dynamic (Bourbeau & Vuori, 2015).

Maritime Securitisation

As the theory of securitisation suggests, not even maritime threats are *security* issues without political moves that make them so. Indeed, there are multiple ways particular maritime threats can be dealt with. Deterrence (Vuori, 2016) is one avenue for dealing with potential threats that are also mentioned in the maritime securitisation literature as a goal of specific policies (e.g., Pugh, 2004; Bueger & Stockbruegger, 2013, p. 102). Threats can be judicialised, which makes constabulary actions relevant for dealing with them (Åtland & Ven Bruusgaard, 2009). Issues can also be politicised rather than securitised, and they can be dealt with in terms of international diplomacy (Piedade, 2016). This means that securitisation has its own domestic and international costs and effects, and is not an inevitable feature of any policy or practice, but a political choice. Securitisation can also work in tandem with other logics for dealing with threats, such as risk management (Lobo-Guerrero, 2008), and it can be used to combine disparate issues together into security continuums and fields of practice (Bigo, 1994).

Indeed, according to Christian Bueger (2015, p. 159) the notion of maritime security gained traction from the fear over the threat of maritime terrorism following the 9/11 attacks and was solidified through the issue of Somali piracy in the latter half of the decade. The number of states that have accepted the consideration of piracy as a security issue (rather than being merely criminal) and that have participated in joint naval operations has expanded significantly with this development (Bueger & Stockbruegger, 2013, p. 102). The concept draws together a semiotic field of a number of maritime issues into a "maritime security complex" that includes elements from maritime safety, economic development, resilience and seapower (Bueger, 2015, p. 161). Accordingly, the literature on maritime securitisation has dealt with a great number of specific threats that state and international actors have securitised in their documents and activities. Indeed, securitisation theory allows for the study of traditional maritime security issues (such as sea-lines of communication and geopolitics) and non-traditional maritime security issues (like piracy and people smuggling) within the same framework.

Securitisation theory can be deployed to study specific processes to see what kind of maritime issues have been securitised and what the elements the theory directs analytical attention to in them are. It allows to, for example, ask how and why traditional and non-traditional issues such as fishery disputes escalate and de-escalate, what kinds of political levels are involved in this, what kind of actors and measures are involved and what impacts the success or failure of such processes (Åtland & Ven Bruusgaard, 2009, p. 335). When used together with regional complex theory (Buzan & Wæver, 2003), such individual processes can be combined together to see what kinds of issues, sectors, levels and dynamics of security are at play in maritime regions. In this way, securitisation theory makes it possible to connect divergent political claims with interests and ideologies (Bueger, 2015, p. 160), get a grasp on visions of the political that securitising speech and practice contain (Huysmans, 2014), and to do ethical interventions into issues and processes after their contingency and political nature have been discerned (Vuori, 2014, pp. 156–162).

While securitisation theory has much to offer for the study of maritime security, some of the maritime securitisation literature has also engaged in theoretical discussions regarding elements of the general theory and securitisation dynamics. For example, desecuritisation and subsequent resecuritisation (Åtland, 2008; Hellmann & Herborth, 2008), counter-securitisation, as well as the failed securitisation of issues like fisheries and fishing disputes have been discussed in the literature (Åtland & Ven Bruusgaard, 2009). Indeed, the types of actors that are involved in the securitisation of a specific incident (e.g., hot pursuit of an illegal trawler) or a whole field of activity (e.g., piracy) as (de)securitising actors (e.g., politicians, militaries, ministries, IGOs,

NGOs) and audiences (e.g., constituencies, officials, governments, IGOs) have a bearing on whether the issue is escalated, de-escalated, (un)successfully securitised or desecuritised. States can also avoid the securitisation of an issue that could be framed in security terms. These kinds of elements have also been present in the three main strands of the literature I discuss here.

Geopolitics and Maritime Regional Security

Maritime securitisation is part and parcel of regional security in many parts of the world. Regional security complex theory (Buzan & Wæver, 2003) allows for the analysis of more traditional geopolitical maritime issues with a constructivist ontology together with a multi-sectorial approach to security. Maritime security can be considered a national (e.g., sovereignty and interdiction at sea), a regional (e.g., transnational crime), or even a global issue of concern (global flows) (Bueger & Stockbruegger, 2013; Piedade, 2016, p. 80). Similarly, maritime issues can be about political (island disputes), social (irregular migration), economic (transportation of goods, use of maritime resources, smuggling and trafficking), military (terrorism, inter-state disputes) and environmental (oil spills, overuse of fisheries) issues (cf. Emmers, 2004; Piedade, 2016, p. 77). In the geopolitical maritime securitisation literature, matters that relate to the security of sea-lines of communication, regional patterns of securitisation and desecuritisation, as well as island disputes have been the focus of most attention (e.g., Garcia & Breslin, 2016). For example, the freedom of sea-lines of communication has been a major concern for the US, but states like India and Japan have also securitised the issue (Chand & Garcia, 2017, pp. 318–320).

The South China Sea (SCS) is one example of a maritime region that has been viewed through the lens of securitisation. The natural resources, the scale of traffic through its sea-lines, and the disputed ownership of the hundreds of reefs, shoals and islets in the area make the SCS opportune for securitisation particularly as China's activities there have been a source of worry for many littoral states in the region for decades. Indeed, island and maritime border disputes relate to state sovereignty and securitisation can be used to galvanise consensus towards policy actions (Garcia & Breslin, 2016, p. 271; Chand & Garcia, 2017).

The SCS has not been the only island dispute discussed in the literature though. There are also securitised island disputes between China and Japan, and South-Korea and Japan (Garcia & Breslin, 2016), where China has deployed non-state actors in the securitisation of its island dispute with Japan, which has subsequently been desecuritised by official actors (Danner, 2014). The securitisation dynamics of such issues not only bears on how the dispute is handled but on how the general image and impression of the states involved are perceived in the regional security complex (RSC). In other words, such disputes are an important part of the patterns of securitisation and desecuritisation within RSCs. For example, in Southeast Asia, the desecur-itisation of Japan, securitisation of China and non-securitisation of India follow patterns of securitisation within maritime issues (Chand & Garcia, 2017, pp. 315–316). Such patterns can also cut across or spill over from one security sector to another. For example, desecuritisation through management in non-military sectors of maritime security had a positive effect in de-fusing tensions in the military sector in late Cold War arctic relations (Åtland, 2008, p. 306).

Non-traditional security issues such as piracy can also have regional or even global effects on how security is organised (Bueger, 2013; Bueger & Stockbruegger, 2013, p. 102). Issues such as transnational crime, terrorism, piracy and boat migration can have both national and regional implications (Emmers, 2004). Here, piracy has been a driving force in Africa. For example, the Djibouti Code of Conduct concentrated on anti-piracy efforts (Bueger, 2013, p. 305). In Southeast Asia, island disputes and terrorism have been more central (Lobo-Guerrero, 2008).

Fishing disputes in the SCS have also been securitised and feared to spark geopolitical conflicts as the use of "fishing militias" are viewed as having ulterior motives (Zhang & Bateman, 2017, pp. 289–290). Such "tactical" use of securitisation in regard to the SCS fisheries raises public attention regarding the issue yet can justify increased US military presence or even involvement in the SCS dispute, and most crucially reduces operational trust among the disputants (Zhang & Bateman, 2017, pp. 302–305). While economic issues could be a source of increased co-operation and trust in the region, securitisation works against these kinds of developments.

Maritime securitisation has been instrumental in the formation of nascent maritime security regimes that are informed by regional security identities, practices, institutions and infra-structures. Some countries go further in their bilateral cooperation in maritime security issues than the measures adopted in multilateral fora, like the cooperation between Malaysia and Singapore compared with that within ASEAN generally (Emmers, 2003, 2004). Joint opera-tions are not always a sure way to build confidence though. For example, the securitisation of piracy in the Gulf of Aden with human security, economic interests and terrorism as the main referents has had implications for Sino-Indian relations. Here, joint operations and other efforts in this field were seen to work as a platform for confidence building by China, yet China using antipiracy as a guise for ulterior naval motivations has remained a continued source of concern in India (Gippner, 2016, pp. 108, 127). As such, maritime security regimes tend to deal with security in a multi-sectorial mode and are about more than traditional military security issues by linking various types of threats and issues together into continuums or lists.

Securitisation of Piracy and Maritime Transnational Crime

The concept of security continuums comes from Didier Bigo's (1994, p. 164, 2000) studies of the internal security field in Europe. In a security continuum, a general feeling of unease or insecurity is linked to a group of issues e.g., terrorism, organised crime and immigration, as they have often been listed together in official European documents without any overarching jus-tification for doing so. As a field effect, this grafts the fear of terrorism onto issues of migration, for example. These kinds of continuums are also present in the securitisation of irregular maritime migration particularly in Australia, and in the EU (Ghezelbash et al., 2018; Moreno-Lax, 2018).

Security continuums can also be found in the Asian context, for example, in Singapore where piracy and terrorism have been conflated in public official statements (Young & Valencia, 2003; Mak, 2006) – a move which failed for the International Maritime Bureau in Malaysia, but succeeded for the Mahathir administration which linked pirates, foreign terrorists and "illegal migrants" (Mak, 2006). International insurance companies have also included the threat of terrorism and piracy in the Malacca Strait in their war lists to push littoral states to police the area more effectively (Lobo-Guerrero, 2008). "Illegal migration" has also been connected to terrorism in Australia (Emmers, 2004; Huysmans, 2005; McDonald, 2011). ASEAN too has combined other forms of transnational crime together with terrorism in its policy declarations (Haacke & Williams, 2008).

Security continuums can be used to facilitate securitisation moves. Indeed, it is easier to securitise some types of issues than others. Linking an issue into a continuum of prevalent security issues provides a sense of plausibility for the claims of the securitisation actor who is intent on labelling a new issue or token as a security problem. The securityness of one issue can be "grafted" onto another. Indeed, J.L. Mak's (2006) analysis of the "partial success" of se-curitising piracy in Malaysia and Singapore shows how the multiple relevant audiences he studied reacted in various ways to the securitisation moves of different actors. Indeed, just as securitisation moves can have several audiences and several forms, an act of securitisation can also function on multiple levels either in terms of actors, referents, threats, or audiences. For example, the Singaporean terrorism discourse works on at least five levels of securitisation: the individual, institutional, state, the macro-level and the international level (Mak, 2006, pp. 88–90). Maritime-based terrorism has also been responded to in the UK through the securitisation of its ports (Malcolm, 2016). This is part of the trend of securitising piracy, terrorism and drug trafficking in formal maritime strategies of the UK, the African Union and the European Union, yet the securitisation of ports in the UK is specifically tied to the global war on terror and the protection of "a civilized way of life" (Malcolm, 2016, pp. 444, 446). Constructing UK ports as target and a vulnerable node for terrorist acts resulted in new legislation and regulations as well as institutional structures, infrastructure developments and working practices where the increased use of surveillance cameras and visual reminders of security measures were the most visible changes (Malcolm, 2016, pp. 451, 453).

The International Maritime Bureau has discussed the issue of piracy for some time (Emmers, 2004; Mak, 2006), yet Somali piracy was the instance that got the issue onto the agenda of the UN Security Council (Oliveira, 2018, pp. 515–517) and a number of other international security actors like NATO (Bueger & Stockbruegger, 2013, pp. 99–100). Indeed, piracy has been a major security concern in Somalia and West Africa, which has resulted in the formulation of maritime strategies and building of institutions that can be considered a nascent "regime complex" (Bueger, 2013, pp. 298–299) that also deploys a security continuum (Lehr, 2009). The shared, regional maritime threat package includes illegal resource exploitation, transnational organised crime, piracy, environmental pollution and terrorism (Tsvetkova, 2009; Vreÿ, 2010; Bueger, 2013, p. 310), which are subsumed under the label of "good order at sea" (Piedade, 2016, p. 76). Such maritime issues have been discussed within, for example, the Intergovernmental Authority for Development where piracy, smuggling, illegal fishing and waste dumping, as well as terrorism have been on the agenda (Bueger, 2013, p. 307). Like in Southeast Asia, such securitisation has resulted in the establishment of Maritime Domain Awareness centres (Bueger, 2013, p. 308). Interestingly, the securitisation of piracy has not been as effective in the Gulf of Guinea as extra-regional actors have undermined the process (Piedade, 2016).

Beyond the establishment of nascent maritime security regimes and the sharing of information to form awareness and common stocks of knowledge, the securitisation of transnational crime like piracy and terrorism has formed transnational fields of maritime security experts (cf. Bigo, 2000). While regional integration in for example ASEAN and the African Union is not near the level of the EU, the separation of inside and outside issues and practices have already been merged in the maritime security field where, for example, navies have taken on constabulary tasks (Oliveira, 2018, p. 521). In the African context, the increased use of force against piracy in response to the securitisation of Somali piracy has been relevant as the issue shifted away from being considered criminality to one of the security of the international system that was dealt with military force (Oliveira, 2018, p. 518). A shift in the use of naval military forces for previously civilian tasks is evident in the field of maritime irregular migration too.

Securitisation of Maritime Immigration

The securitisation of immigration is one of the most studied topics within securitisation studies. This issue is also a major part of the maritime securitisation literature. The initial case of interest here was Australia that has interjected boat migrants off its coasts since 2001 justified with securitisation (Emmers, 2004; McDonald, 2011). This resulted in the Migration Amendment

Act of 2001 removing Australia's offshore territories from its "asylum zone" (Pugh, 2004, p. 60). The physical interception and deflecting of migrant ships with naval forces have also been done in secret on grounds of operational matters, which made it difficult to assess whether Australia has abided by search and rescue (SAR) provisions and hindered other forms of democratic oversight (Ghezelbash et al., 2018, pp. 329, 342). More recently, the EU and the situation in the Mediterranean have become a focus of attention here. Both the Australian and European cases display similar effects in terms of what securitisation does to humanitarianism and respect for maritime international law (Ghezelbash et al., 2018; Moreno-Lax, 2018).

Beyond customary international law regarding the sea, the contemporary SAR regime is based on the International Convention for the Safety of Life at Sea from 1974, the International Convention on Maritime Search and Rescue from 1979, and the United Nations Convention of the Law of the Sea from 1982. The norms of this SAR regime give no regard to the identity of either rescuers or those being rescued, nor to the zonal status of the waters where the rescue is taking place (e.g., territorial sea, EEZ, or high seas) (Pugh, 2004, p. 51; Ghezelbash et al., 2018, p. 322). Securitisation of migration in the maritime field conflates interdiction and SAR, which side-lines the humanitarian requirements of the international SAR regime (Ghezelbash et al., 2018; Moreno-Lax, 2018, p. 122).

The presentation of "boat people" (the term originates from the 1970s and was used to designate people fleeing Vietnam) as threatening has resulted in responses in coastal states that undermine humanitarianism in the cosmopolitan space of the sea (Pugh, 2004, p. 51). As such, control of state borders and hospitality are considered key elements of sovereignty, and have been crucial elements of the political securitisation of irregular migration under the label of "illegal immigration". In the EU, the focus of fear has moved from the irregular element of migration to its uncontrollability (Moreno-Lax, 2018, p. 130). Similarly, the unknown background of individuals has been considered dangerous and a way to disguise criminals or even terrorists (Ghezelbash et al., 2018, p. 330). Like with the securitisation of on land irregular migration, maritime migrants are portrayed as endangering lifestyles, economy and culture, irrespective of whether they were brought to a country due to distress at sea or whether they intended to enter the country irregularly (Ghezelbash et al., 2018, p. 330).

The EU's response to maritime migration has not been to develop the humanitarian elements or to deal with push factors involved, but to fight people trafficking and smuggling through FRONTEX operations like Triton and Sophia (Moreno-Lax, 2018, pp. 126–128). The shift away from SAR missions in these operations towards border security partly resulted in the large numbers of asylum seekers and irregular migrants lost in the Mediterranean (e.g., 5,000 of the 7,700 world total in 2016) (Ghezelbash et al., 2018, pp. 318, 334). European states have also had disputes over to which ports boats carrying migrants in distress should go and where they should be allowed to disembark, which has resulted in the loss of life as people were denied access to medical assistance (Ghezelbash et al., 2018, p. 316).

Michael Pugh (2004) argues that securitisation challenges humanitarian values of the maritime regime that have a millennia-long pedigree in the form of solidarity among seafarers. Emphasising border security pushes the humanitarian goals of SAR aside, increases militarisation and criminalisation, and makes accountability more difficult (Ghezelbash et al., 2018). At the same time, humanitarian vocabulary can be used to hide the exercise of power in divesting people of their rights in the name of "protection" (Moreno-Lax, 2018, p. 133). Overall, securitisation turns unfamiliar strangers from those offered hospitality into sources of unease and potential enemies (Pugh, 2004, p. 53), and the presentation of securitised boat people makes the issue appear apocalyptic (Methmann, 2014; Moreno-Lax, 2018).

At the same time, the securitisation of boat migration has been justified both in Australia and in the EU with its intended deterrence effect (Pugh, 2004, p. 56; Ghezelbash et al., 2018). In this imaginary, the risks of being interdicted and turned back, or placed in internment camps for years outweigh the risks involved in beginning the perilous sea-journey in the first place. In other words, securitisation here aims at deterrence by raising the risks of irregular migration, even while ostensibly protecting those being smuggled (Moreno-Lax, 2018, p. 133; cf. Vuori, 2011; 2016). This has turned the issue into one of border control and even littoral defence, where warships are deployed to stop migrant boats (Pugh, 2004, p. 57). The securitisation of migration has also resulted in pre-emptive risk calculations about migrants overwhelming Europe that has been addressed with the deployment of visual technologies to monitor migrants and to construct elaborate data-doubles on them (Madörin, 2020, pp. 703, 707).

The study of these securitisation processes has called for the desecuritisation of asylum seekers and boat people in destination states so that the perceptions that concern these people can be transformed into ordinary people in extraordinary circumstances rather than sources of danger and threat (Pugh, 2004, p. 65). Similarly, Ghezelbash et al. (2018, p. 350) call for rescuing the humanitarian essence of SAR from its current securitised and militarised connotations both in Australia and the EU. As the situation in Europe in the latter half of the 2010s shows however, the trend of securitisation has not been reversed, quite the opposite.

Conclusions and Openings

The securitisation of transnational crime like piracy and terrorism has had the effect of joining the inside and outside of states in maritime security issues where navies have taken on constabulary tasks in regard to piracy. The securitisation of boat migration in turn has turned rescue at sea into an issue of border control. Security continuums have been in operation here (piracy and terrorism are conflated as is irregular migration and terrorism), and even non-traditional security concerns have seen as affecting regional politics, where the securitisation of fisheries can maintain distrust, yet also contrarily desecuritisation in civilian sectors can spill over to military fields. The securitisation of criminality has also resulted in the privatisation of maritime security (Oliveira, 2018, p. 523), including maritime insurance as global risk management (Lobo-Guerrero, 2008).

Much of the analyses of maritime security through the securitisation framework shows how certain issues have been securitised, and how this securitisation has affected policies, strategies, institutions and practices. What is often missing though is the critical push of securitisation studies where in addition to showing how some process has taken place it is possible to show how things could have been different, which is an opening for ethical interventions into the issue. There are studies that call for the desecuritisation of for example boat migrants (Pugh, 2004; Ghezelbash et al., 2018), or fisheries in the SCS to minimise power abuses (Zhang & Bateman, 2017, p. 306), as securitisation reduces trust and cooperation that are required to deal with the tragedy of the commons in the field of fisheries. There could be more studies that focus on desecuritisation though. Indeed, some scholars even use the securitisation framework to promote certain threat narratives rather than producing critique of their politics (e.g., Tsvetkova, 2009; Vreÿ, 2010).

There is also an opening for visual maritime securitisation studies (cf. Vuori, 2013; Andersen et al. 2015; Vuori & Andersen, 2018). Some of the existing literature already touches upon visual aspects of maritime securitisation. For example, the arrival of boat people is presented visually and imagined in visual media in similar apocalyptic terms as other types of migrants and asylum seekers (Pugh, 2004, p. 53; cf. Methmann, 2014). This works to remove the human right and other humanitarian needs of such people in jeopardy and transforms them into dehumanised threats that arrive as uninvited "floods", "tides", "flows", or "Waves" (Pugh, 2004, p. 54) instead. This racial securitisation of boat migrants is also part of the visual-digital securitisation nexus (Madörin, 2020, p. 700). Similarly, the securitisation of UK ports in the war on terror has resulted in an increase of surveillance and identification practices towards preparation, protection and verification (Malcolm, 2016, p. 455). Visual reminders of the threat narratives were also used to justify these practices (Malcolm, 2016, p. 454). Such examples show how it is worthwhile to study visual maritime securitisation systematically.

References

Andersen, R. S., Vuori, J. A., & Mutlu, C. E. (2015). Visuality. In C. Aradau, J. Huysmans, A. Neal & N. Voelkner (Eds.), *Critical Security Methods: New Frameworks for Analysis* (pp. 85–117). Routledge.

Åtland, K. (2008). Mikhail Gorbachev, the Murmansk Initiative, and the Desecuritization of Interstate Relations in the Arctic. *Cooperation and Conflict, 43*(3), 289–311.

Åtland, K., & Ven Bruusgaard, K. (2009). When Security Speech Acts Misfire: Russia and the Elektron Incident. *Security Dialogue, 40*(3), 333–353.

Balzacq, T., Léonard, S., & Ruzicka, J. (2016). "Securitization" Revisited: Theory and Cases. *International Relations, 30*(4), 494–531.

Bigo, D. (1994). The European Internal Security Field: Takes and Rivalries in a Newly Developing Area of Police Intervention. In M. Anderson & M. den Boer (Eds.), *Policing Across National Borders* (pp. 161–173). Pinter.

Bigo, D. (2000). When Two Become One: Internal and External Securitisations in Europe. In M. Kelstrup & M. C. Williams (Eds.), *International Relations Theory and the Politics of European Integration: Power, Security and Community* (pp. 171–204). Routledge.

Bourbeau, P., & Vuori, J. A. (2015). Security, Resilience, and Desecuritization: Multidirectional Moves and Dynamics. *Critical Studies on Security, 3*(3), 1–16.

Bueger, C. (2013). Communities of Security Practice at Work? The Emerging African Maritime Security Regime. *African Security, 6*(3–4), 297–316.

Bueger, C. (2015). What is Maritime Security? *Marine Policy, 53*, 159–164.

Bueger, C., & Stockbruegger, J. (2013). Security Communities, Alliances, and Macrosecuritization: The Practices of Counter-Piracy Governance. In M. J. Struett, J. D. Carlson & M. T. Nance (Eds.), *Maritime Piracy and the Construction of Global Governance* (pp. 99–124). Routledge.

Buzan, B., & Wæver, O. (2003). *Regions and Powers.* Cambridge University Press.

Buzan, B., & Wæver, O. (2009). Macrosecuritization and Security Constellations: Reconsidering Scale in Securitization Theory. *Review of International Studies, 35*(2), 253–276.

Buzan, B., Wæver, O., & de Wilde, J. (1998). *Security: A New Framework for Analysis.* Lynne Rienner.

Chand, B., & Garcia, Z. (2017). Power Politics and Securitization: The Emerging Indo-Japanese Nexus in Southeast Asia. *Asia & the Pacific Policy Studies, 4*(2), 310–324.

Danner, L. K. (2014). Securitization and De-Securitization in the Diaoyu/Senkaku Islands Territorial Dispute. *Journal of Alternative Perspectives in the Social Sciences, 6*(2), 219–247.

Emmers, R. (2003). ASEAN and the Securitization of Transnational Crime in Southeast Asia. *The Pacific Review, 16*(3), 419–438.

Emmers, R. (2004). *Non-Traditional Security in the Asia Pacific: The Dynamics of Securitisation.* Marshall Cavendish International.

Garcia, Z., & Breslin, T. A. (2016). Biting the Cow's Tongue: Securitization and Capacity Building in the South China Sea. *Journal of Asian Security and International Affairs, 3*(3), 269–290.

Ghezelbash, D., Moreno-Lax, V., Klein, N., & Opeskin, B. (2018). Securitization of Search and Rescue at Sea: The Response to Boat Migration in the Mediterranean and Offshore Australia. *International & Comparative Law Quarterly, 67*(2), 315–351.

Gippner, O. (2016). Antipiracy and Unusual Coalitions in the Indian Ocean Region: China's Changing Role and Confidence Building with India. *Journal of Current Chinese Affairs, 45*(3), 107–137.

Guzzini, S. (2011). Securitization as a Causal Mechanism. *Security Dialogue, 42*(4–5), 329–341.

Haacke, J., & Williams, P. D. (2008). Regional Arrangements, Securitization, and Transnational Security Challenges: The African Union and the Association of Southeast Asian Nations Compared. *Security Studies, 17*(4), 775–809.

Hellmann, G., & Herborth, B. (2008). Fishing in the Mild West: Democratic Peace and Militarised Interstate Disputes in the Transatlantic Community. *Review of International Studies*, *34*(3), 481–506.

Huysmans, J. (2005). *What is Politics?* Edinburgh University Press.

Huysmans, J. (2014). *Security Unbound: Enacting Democratic Limits*. Routledge.

Lehr, P. (2009). Somali Piracy: The Next Iteration. *Perspectives on Terrorism*, *3*(4), 26–36.

Lobo-Guerrero, L. (2008). "Pirates," Stewards, and the Securitization of Global Circulation. *International Political Sociology*, *2*(3), 219–235.

Madörin, A. (2020). "The View from Above" at Europe's Maritime Borders: Racial Securitization from Visuality to Postvisuality. *European Journal of Cultural Studies*, *23*(5), 698–711.

Mak, J. N. (2006). Securitizing Piracy in Southeast Asia: Malaysia, the International Maritime Bureau and Singapore. In M. Caballero-Anthony, R. Emmers & A. Acharya (Eds.), *Non-Traditional Security in Asia, Dilemmas in Securitisation* (pp. 66–92). Ashgate.

Malcolm, J. A. (2016). Responding to International Terrorism: The Securitisation of the United Kingdom's Ports. *The British Journal of Politics and International Relations*, *18*(2), 443–462.

McDonald, M. (2011). Deliberation and Resecuritization: Australia, Asylum-Seekers and the Normative Limits of the Copenhagen School. *Australian Journal of Political Science*, *46*(2), 281–295.

Methmann, C. (2014). Visualizing Climate-Refugees: Race, Vulnerability, and Resilience in Global Liberal Politics. *International Political Sociology*, *8*(4), 416–435.

Moreno-Lax, V. (2018). The EU Humanitarian Border and the Securitization of Human Rights: The 'Rescue-through-Interdiction/Rescue-without-Protection' Paradigm. *JCMS: Journal of Common Market Studies*, *56*(1), 119–140.

Oliveira, G. C. (2018). The Causal Power of Securitisation: An Inquiry into the Explanatory Status of Securitisation Theory Illustrated by the Case of Somali Piracy. *Review of International Studies*, *44*(3), 504–525.

Piedade, J. (2016). From Politicization to Securitization of Maritime Security in the Gulf of Guinea. *Croatian International Relations Review*, *22*(75), 69–85.

Pugh, M. (2004). Drowning Not Waving: Boat People and Humanitarianism at Sea. *Journal of Refugee Studies*, *17*(1), 50–69.

Searle, J. R. (2011) [2010]. *Making the Social World: The Structure of Human Civilization*. Oxford University Press.

Tsvetkova, B. (2009). Securitizing Piracy Off the Coast of Somalia. *Central European Journal of International and Security Studies*, *3*(1), 44–63.

Vreÿ, F. (2010). African Maritime Security: A Time for Good Order at Sea. *Australian Journal of Maritime and Ocean Affairs*, *2*(4), 121–132.

Vuori, J. A. (2010). A Timely Prophet? The Doomsday Clock as a Visualization of Securitization Moves with a Global Referent Object. *Security Dialogue*, *41*(3), 255–277.

Vuori, J. A. (2011). *How to Do Security with Words – A Grammar of Securitisation in the People's Republic of China*. Annales Universitatis Turkuensis B 336. University of Turku.

Vuori, J. A. (2013). Pictoral Texts. In M. B. Salter & C. E. Mutlu (Eds.), *Research Methods in Critical Security Studies: An Introduction* (pp. 199–202). Routledge.

Vuori, J. A. (2014). *Critical Security and Chinese Politics: The Anti-Falungong Campaign*. Routledge.

Vuori, J. A. (2015). Contesting and Resisting Security in Post-Mao China. In T. Balzacq (Ed.), *Contesting Security: Strategies and Logics* (pp. 29–43). Routledge.

Vuori, J. A. (2016). Deterring Things with Words: Deterrence as a Speech Act. *New Perspectives: Interdisciplinary Journal of Central & East European Politics and International Relations*, *24*(2), 32–50.

Vuori, J. A. (2017). Constructivism and Securitization Studies. In M. D. Cavelty & T. Balzacq (Eds.), *The Routledge Handbook of Security Studies* (2nd Edition) (pp. 64–74). Routledge.

Vuori, J. A., & Andersen, R. S. (Eds.). (2018). *Visual Security Studies: Sights and Spectacles of Insecurity and War*. Routledge.

Wæver, O. (1989). Conflicts of Vision — Visions of Conflict. In O. Wæver, P. Lemaitre & E. Tromer (Eds.), *European Polyphony: Perspectives beyond East- West Confrontation* (pp. 283–325). Macmillan.

Wæver, O. (2015). The Theory Act: Responsibility and Exactitude as Seen from Securitization. *International Relations*, *29*(1), 121–127.

Young, A. J., & Valencia, M. J. (2003). Conflation of Piracy and Terrorism in Southeast Asia: Rectitude and Utility. *Comparative Southeast Asia*, *25*(2), 269–283.

Zhang, H., & Bateman, S. (2017). Fishing Militia, the Securitization of Fishery and the South China Sea Dispute. *Contemporary Southeast Asia*, *39*(2), 288–314.

9
GENDER PERSPECTIVES ON MARITIME SECURITY

Jane Freedman

There are so far very few gender analyses of maritime security issues, but like other areas of security studies this is one which merits the use of a gendered lens. The absence of a gender analysis may in part be explained by the relatively recent emergence of maritime security as an area of research in international relations (Bueger, 2015) and also a lack of consensus over the exact definition of what is included within this security domain (Klein, 2011; Kraska & Pedrozo, 2013; Bueger, 2015). Whatever the reasons, maritime security has not featured widely in academic discussions of the Women, Peace and Security agenda of the United Nations (Kirby & Shepherd, 2016) or in other research or policymaking in the domain of gender and security. However, if we understand maritime security to concern the safety and security of individuals in maritime spaces (Papanicolopulu, 2018) then it follows that we should be interested in who these individuals are, and their social positioning within categories and hierarchies of gender, class, race, ethnicity, etc. The individuals whose lives and livelihoods depend on safety and security in maritime spaces are men and women whose experiences and opportunities within these spaces are determined by social, economic and political structures of gender inequality. These gendered realities have often been overlooked. Fishing activities, for example, have been seen as primarily male activities, and the important role of women within these industries has been ignored in much research (Schwerdtner-Máñez & Pauwelussen, 2016; Alami & Raharjo, 2017). This in turn means that the particular risks and insecurities that fisherwomen face are also ignored (Anna, 2012). Women make a major contribution to food security of their communities through fishing activities, but decisions on management and governance of maritime fisheries are generally taken by men (Rohe et al., 2018). Similarly, issues of gender-based forms of violence against women seafarers are also overlooked because "sailing the oceans has been considered a male profession for a long time" (Pineiro & Kitada, 2020, p. 1). Thus, the differential security of women and men during sea journeys and crossing maritime borders are often not taken into account. Whilst it would be impossible in a limited space such as this to provide an exhaustive gendered analysis of all elements of maritime security, this chapter will provide a more in-depth look at some particular issues, examining the ways in which social constructions of gender, in intersection with other social categorisations, impact on questions of maritime rescue and the role of maritime security in migration and refugee "crises". It will then go on to discuss gender mainstreaming in maritime security strategies and the limitations of what this has achieved thus far.

106

DOI: 10.4324/9781003001324-11

Gender, Migration and Maritime Borders

One issue within maritime security which has received particular attention in recent years is that of the securitisation of maritime borders in the face of what some governments have portrayed as an immigration or refugee "crisis" (Freedman, 2019a). The interconnections between gender, migration, violence and insecurity have been highlighted by research in various regions of the world (Marchand, 2008; Freedman, 2012). Different push and pull factors, migration control regimes, as well as social and economic conditions in countries of origin, transit and destination create varying types of insecurity and violence for men and women, depending on their varying social and economic positions and the relations of power between them. As Marchand argues: "It goes without saying that the migration–violence nexus is gendered. Men and women are affected in different ways and the violence to which they are exposed is related to their position with respect to the migration–violence nexus" (Marchand, 2008, p. 1387). This is also true for the migration-violence nexus at sea, where particular forms of gender-based violence and insecurity may be produced. Recent research has also highlighted the physical risks of border crossing for women, and the higher rate of mortality at the borders for women than for men (Pickering & Cochrane, 2013). And again, this is true of sea borders, where mortality rates are proportionally higher for women than men. As one report states:

> On the ships, women and children are often placed below deck by their male family members in order to protect them during the crossing. But this location can quickly become a trap, often with tragic consequences. Rescue teams coming to the aid of capsized ships often find women and children who have suffocated from toxic exhaust fumes or drowned by incoming waters. Women often have poorer swimming skills compared to men, and their attempts to save their children often also lead to their higher risk of drowning. When rescuers discover drowned women, they often find them with heavier clothing that pulled them under the water.
>
> *(Plambech, 2017)*

When listening to the stories of migrants and studying their experiences, it does seem clear that migration does entail considerable threats to human security and that individual security is particularly threatened by the contemporary efforts to control migration. This seems to support an argument for reconceptualisation of security in multidimensional and multilevel terms (Tickner, 1992, p. 128) and of a reanalysis of the relationship between migration and security beyond that of the threats that migration poses to states. To move beyond a state-centric approach to the insecurities of migration, a gender-informed approach to human security such as that proposed by Hoogensen and Stuvøy (2006) seems a productive one. This type of approach can, its proponents argue, "offer a great deal in opening human security up to voices from below" (Hoogensen & Stuvøy, 2006, p. 217), stressing the need to make visible relations of dominance and to identify the ways in which insecurities develop as a result of these relationships. The prioritisation of an epistemological approach based on a concern with "peopling IR" (Pettman, 1996) and with dealing with contextually dependent practices and relationships also seems to us highly relevant in the study of migration. As Hoogensen and Stuvoy explain: "The theoretical concern with the activities and experiences of average people, referred to as "everyday feminist theorizing" (Sylvester, 1996, p. 236), institutes an empirical focus of gender IR on the experiences of marginalised people, among them women, for the purposes of bringing new insights on the interconnections between everyday practices and international politics" (Hoogensen & Stuvøy, 2006, p. 223).

Gender and Insecurity in the Mediterranean

One maritime arena which has been particularly central and visible in public and political debates on migration and maritime borders is the Mediterranean, which has become a focus for European efforts to control or limit migration, provoking major debates over responsibilities for protection of refugees and for responsibilities for rescue at sea. In 2015, over one million refugees arrived by boat in the European Union, leading to major public and political debates over a so-called refugee "crisis". The increase in sea crossings to Europe via what have been identified in policy as the three main Mediterranean routes (Western, Central and Eastern) can be attributed both to continuing conflict and instabilities in countries of migrant origin such as Syria, Afghanistan, Iraq or Somalia, but also to the closure or restriction of other migration routes to Europe (Andersson, 2016), forcing refugees into dangerous and increasingly expensive crossings by sea. The variations in arrival through each route is also attributable to the EU's attempt to close down each route, so that the European Union's agreement with Turkey in March 2016 (European Council, 2016) which entailed the return of all "illegal" arrivals on the Greek islands to Turkey, can be seen as a factor in limiting arrivals via the Eastern Mediterranean route and increasing those via the Central Mediterranean route from Libya to Italy. The highly risky nature of the sea crossing is demonstrated by the rates of death at sea, which in 2016 were estimated to reach 5,143 people (IOM Missing Migrants Project, 2019). And these figures are highly likely to be severely underestimated. Weber and Pickering (2011, 2014) report that it has been estimated that for every body found in the Mediterranean between two and ten go undiscovered. In 2019, the IOM estimated that 0.9% of estimated crossings resulted in death (IOM Missing Migrants Project, 2020), leading to the claim that the route from Libya to Europe is the migration route with the highest death toll in the world (UN News, 2019). European responses to the deaths in the Mediterranean have been paradoxical. On the one hand, lamenting the loss of life and the insecurities for migrants; and, on the other, limiting search and rescue missions and reinforcing securitised and militarised sea borders, in what has been labelled "organised hypocrisy" (Cusumano, 2019). On 23 April 2015, at the beginning of the current refugee "crisis", the European Council held a special meeting in response to the crisis situation in the Mediterranean during which they acknowledged that the situation in the Mediterranean is a "tragedy", and promised to take measures including strengthening the EU's presence at sea, fighting against traffickers, preventing illegal migration flows and reinforcing international solidarity and responsibility. The EU's approach has been heavily criticised, however, by human rights groups and migrant support groups for its focus on repression of trafficking and prevention of irregular migration rather than on protecting the rights and lives of migrants who are desperate to reach Europe (Costello & Giuffré, 2015). Since 2015 the EU's approach to search and rescue operations in the Mediterranean has been characterised by a gradual disengagement from these search and rescue operations by the EU and its member states, pushbacks or refoulements of refugees attempting the sea crossing, delegation of responsibility for "pushback" to Libyan or Turkish coastguards, closure of European ports to boats carrying refugees, and an increasing criminalisation of NGOs involved in their own search and rescue operations (Carrera & Cortinovis, 2019). The delegation of responsibility and orchestrating of intermediaries for sea border control by the EU has been argued to be a calculated attempt to escape its legal responsibilities in this area (Müller & Slominski, 2020). As the EU pushes a policy of deterrence and repression, the insecurities of refugees attempting to reach Europe are heightened (Zamatto et al., 2017). And as argued above, these insecurities must be considered through a gendered lens to take account of the differential social positioning of the individual refugees involved.

Gender Perspectives on Maritime Security

Whilst the majority of those attempting the crossing have been men, there have been increasing numbers of women and children amongst arrivals by sea across the Mediterranean. And although fully accurate gender-disaggregated data is still missing. The UNHCR estimates that in 2020, 16.2% of sea arrivals have been women and 25.1% children (UNHCR, 2020). Proportionally far more women than men die crossing the Mediterranean by boat. One estimate suggests that for every five men who drown, six women also die (Plambech, 2017). There are various reasons for this. Women are generally less likely to be able to swim than men, and also more likely to be wearing clothing which impedes them from swimming and makes it more difficult to stay afloat until they are rescued. Women may also drown whilst trying to save their children who are travelling with them (Plambech, 2017). Figures also suggest that increasingly women who make this journey are likely to be pregnant, often as a result of rape or sexual violence on the journey (Grotti et al., 2018; Sahraoui, 2020), and this may also mean that they are more likely to drown if their boat capsizes. One study in Italy found that 14% of women arriving by sea were pregnant (Trovato et al., 2016). Paradoxically, in some situations, women may be encouraged or even forced to become pregnant before attempting a sea crossing, because it is believed that boats containing visibly pregnant women are more likely to be helped by maritime rescue services (Tyszler, 2018, 2019). The perception of women as vulnerable, and the belief that they will access protection and help more easily is also used by the smugglers and those arranging journeys. Refugees reported, for example, that during the sea crossing from Turkey to Greece, women were placed at the front and on the outside edges of the crowd of refugees in each boat. This was a deliberate strategy to ensure that the boat was more likely to be rescued by coastguards as they would be more inclined to help these vulnerable women, and far less likely to leave the boat to sink if they saw women on board (Freedman, 2019b).

Some research has pointed to the different gendered impacts of the Mediterranean crossing on men and women. Women interviewed in Greece after arrival by boat from Turkey described their experiences as highly traumatic. One woman who had been in a boat that broke down and was left floating for nine hours before being rescued by the Greek coastguard, explained that: "I would never do that again, I thought I was going to die, and my children too. It was the worst experience of my life. I would never do that again" (cited in Freedman, 2016, p. 9). An MSF psychologist reinforced the idea that women seemed more traumatised by the experience of the sea crossing than men, or that women would express this trauma more readily than men would (Freedman, 2016). Securitisation of the Mediterranean Sea routes has also increased risks of sexual and gender-based violence for women travelling on these routes. There are many sources of violence. Women have recounted being victims of sexual violence and rape by coastguards, but also by smugglers. And there are many stories of smugglers demanding sexual relations from women as a price for being able to get onto a boat (Freedman, 2016). The EU has claimed that "smuggling of migrants" is one of the major risks to its maritime security as we will discuss further below. But despite this, and despite EU maritime security operations such as Triton, Poseidon and Sophia possessing a mandate which prioritises the "disruption of the business model of human smuggling and trafficking networks" (European Council, 2015), there have been no real efforts to understand and act upon the gendered insecurities that exist for these migrants.

Gendered Paradigms of Maritime Border Security: An Australian Example

Australia is another country which has securitised their maritime space to try and prevent sea arrivals of asylum seekers and refugees. And research has shown that migrant women attempting to reach Australia by sea face the same dangers and insecurities as those attempting the Mediterranean crossing:

> For those women who take dangerous voyages at sea facilitated by people smugglers in an attempt to reach Australia, similar experiences to migrants crossing the Mediterranean Sea to reach Europe and those crossing the Andaman Sea in South East Asia reveal the vulnerabilities that women face. Cramped conditions aboard the boat, limited access to food and water (including for their children), starvation, dehydration, poor hygiene and privacy and the ongoing threat of gender-based sexual and domestic violence are parallel experiences for irregular women migrants who take boat journeys to Australia and for those who journey by the same means in Europe and South East Asia.
>
> *(Pickering & Powell, 2017, p. 119)*

Pickering (2014), analyses the way in which Australia's border regime operates in maritime spaces, and the roles and functions of maritime customs vessels which have become "floating carceral spaces". As she describes "they operate across a vast maritime space and following interception asylum seekers can be held on the vessel for days, sometimes even weeks, until disembarkation into the immigration detention network is possible" (Pickering, 2014, p. 188). As in the European case, Australian migration officials have noted an increasing number of women travelling by sea to Australia both alone or as part of family groups. In her article Pickering (2014) describes how the Maritime Enforcement Officers (MEOs) working on board maritime customs vessels have seen their role change as they are asked to intercept, detain and transport refugees to offshore detention centres. A strongly gendered element emerges in these MEOs perception and representation of these various roles that they are expected to play in rescue and custody of the refugees they intercept. Representations of heroic masculinity were implicit in the ways that the MEOs described sea rescues in difficult and dangerous conditions. Furthermore, they showed more ambivalent attitudes to what were perceived as the more feminine tasks of post-rescue custodial arrangements, including assuring the welfare of the refugees on board. One issue which emerged from interviews with the MEOs, was the problem that their boats were not adapted for holding refugees in custody, and even less adapted for female refugees. There were no separate spaces where women could be held apart from men, and not enough showers and toilet facilities for women to be assigned their own separate facilities. As Pickering concludes: "With increasing numbers of women seeking asylum by boat, the micro-politics of border controls played out – above and below the decks of customs vessels – in the minutiae of the tensions of the security–humanitarianism–rights nexus" (Pickering, 2014, p. 202). This security-humanitarianism-rights nexus is similar to that being played out in the Mediterranean and in other maritime spaces across the world. And in a similar fashion, policymakers who prioritise the security element of this nexus, have ignored the gendered realities of those who are caught up in its centre.

Gender and Piracy: A Forgotten Perspective

Another area of maritime security within which gender has been largely ignored, is that of preventing international piracy. Whilst piracy may seem at first glance a rather different problem to that of refugees and maritime border security, there is an argument that in this case as well, the prioritisation of a militarised and securitised approach and the ignoring of the human, social and gendered elements of the problem, have led to a failure to find an adequate solution.

Gender Perspectives on Maritime Security

The phenomenon of Somali piracy gained much international attention in the early years of the twenty-first century with high-profile attacks on commercial shipping in the Gulf of Aden (Winn & Lewis, 2017). The threat to global trade and to maritime security in general has led to counter-piracy initiatives being placed high up on the agendas of the African Union (AU), the United Nations Office on Drugs and Crime (UNODC), the North Atlantic Treaty Organization (NATO), the European Union (EU), and others (Winn & Lewis, 2017). However, as some researchers have argued, the securitisation of the counter-piracy debate and the way it has been framed as a question of arresting and prosecuting "extremely dangerous individuals" (Rothe & Collins, 2011), rather than a more general discussion of the social, political and economic conditions in Somalia which produce piracy, has led to a failure of policies put in place (Samatar et al., 2010).

Gender analysis is almost completely absent from any research or policy on piracy and counter-piracy, but Gilmer (2017) has carried out research which highlights what she calls "narratives from the margins" on piracy, including new gendered narratives. Her interviews with Somali women showed their frustration with what they perceived as their marginalised role in the fight against piracy. They argued that the fact that women, and particularly young women, were the principal victims of pirates was being overlooked because women's voices were not heard in the debate. In fact, young women were being lured into sexual relationships by pirates, who then exploited them and distanced them from family and community. One woman interviewed explained:

> Puntland pirates come to Somaliland and bring their ransom money. They come and marry Somaliland women and partake in soliciting prostitution. Piracy is bad for girls and women in Somaliland. One woman left her husband and children to go marry a pirate. Only the pirate didn't end up marrying her and when she tried to return to her husband, he would not take her back. Now she has no family and no money.
>
> *(cited in Gilmer, 2017, p. 7)*

The women Gilmer talked to asked that their voices be heard in international dialogues on piracy, so that these real-life stories of women being tricked and exploited by pirates could be made public, and lead to reaction from the international community to prioritise the protection of women, and not just global trade, from piracy.

A second marginal narrative explored was that of pirates who had been imprisoned for their piracy activities. These prisoners stressed the importance of fulfilling their masculine roles as husbands and breadwinners for their families, and the need to have money to be able to marry and support a family. Thus, they believed that they were "good men" who had no choice but to break the law to fulfil their expected masculine roles. As Gilmer explains:

> The piracy prisoner self-narrative of piracy tells a story of respectable men who wanted to be good workers and providers but failed to do so because of the dire local political economic realities being further compounded by the actions of real pirates.
>
> *(Gilmer, 2017, p. 11)*

Whilst these men's narratives should also perhaps be understood in the context of them wishing to rehabilitate themselves and to gain greater social acceptance of the crimes for which they had been imprisoned, they too speak to the importance of understanding the influence of gender roles and norms in constructing social conditions for the emergence of piracy and the gendered impacts of piracy on Somali society. And as Gilmer concludes:

These new narratives can help push beyond understandings of piracy off the coast of Somalia as a "man's crime" that should be addressed by men. rather, it opens up the possibilities for onshore responses to piracy that recognise the importance of making women equal partners in the fight against piracy and creating counter-piracy approaches that acknowledge and address piracy as a gendered experience.

(Gilmer, 2017, p. 13)

This research provides another example of the importance of incorporating a gendered perspective and gendered analysis into maritime security policies and strategies, and of listening to the women and men who are impacted by maritime security issues.

Mainstreaming Gender into Maritime Security Strategies

The examples above lead to the question of what is or is not being done to integrate gender concerns more convincingly into maritime security policies and research. One method of integrating gender concerns into policy is through a gender mainstreaming strategy. Gender mainstreaming can be defined as "the (re)organisation, improvement, development and evaluation of policy processes so that a gender equality perspective is incorporated in all policies at all levels and at all stages, by the actors normally involved in policy making" (Council of Europe, 2019). In line with a general commitment to gender mainstreaming at national, regional and international levels (as evidenced for example by the commitment to gender mainstreaming by the United Nations, the African Union or the European Union and by many national governments), gender should be integrated into Maritime Security Strategies. However, those analyses of Maritime Security Strategies which exist, show a failure to significantly take gender issues into account. In her analysis of the Spanish National Maritime Security Strategy (SNMSS) and the European Union Maritime Security Strategy (EUMSS), Lirola-Delgado (2019) finds that neither adequately mainstreams gender equality issues. The recent EUMSS (European Council, 2014) does contain references to areas which are particularly relevant in terms of gender equality, for example by highlighting that "cross-border and organised crime, including trafficking of human beings and smuggling of migrants, and organised criminal networks facilitating illegal migration" are some of the major risks to European maritime security. However, the document fails to go on to describe the consequences of these risks for individuals, consequences which are themselves highly gendered, especially if we note that women make up the large majority of victims of trafficking of human beings to the EU (Lirola-Delgado, 2019; Mussi, 2019) and that increasingly migrants and refugees arriving in the EU by sea are women as shown above. This failure to take into account human consequences of maritime security issues can be seen as typical of an approach which prioritises technical (Germond, 2018) and state-centric approaches over the situations and needs of individuals. There is also a failure to integrate gender in the systems set up to monitor the EUMSS. A first Action Plan on the EUMSS was developed in 2014, followed by two implementation reports in 2016 and 2017. The reports gathered information from Member States but did not assess the activities reported by each State and none of the reports from Member States included information on gender issues (Lirola-Delgado, 2019). Moreover, a failure "to include a specific fundamental rights-related operational objective in Frontex joint operations (…) has resulted in a lack of age- and sex-disaggregated data collection" (Lirola-Delgado, 2019). This is an important omission because one of the key requirements of gender-mainstreaming is to have adequate sex-disaggregated data to be able to understand the situation of men and women and

Gender Perspectives on Maritime Security

to plan policies and programmes to respond to their specific situations. Lirola-Delgado (2019) also compares the EUMSS to other national maritime security strategies and finds that none of the four national strategies of the UK, France, the USA or India refer to gender equality. By contrast, another regional maritime security strategy, the African Integrated Maritime Strategy (2050 AIM Strategy) (African Union, 2012) places an important emphasis on the human security aspects of maritime security and as a consequence includes a clear gender dimension. The 2050 AIM Strategy thus for example refers specifically to women and children whilst discussing human trafficking. One of the problems with this AIM Strategy is that there is a general lack of capacity and resources for implementation in many African States and at regional level (Walker, 2017). However, part of the content of the AIM Strategy has been transformed into an international legal obligation through the adoption of the African Charter on Maritime Security and Safety and Development in Africa, otherwise referred to as the Lomé Charter. This Charter outlines the obligation of each state party "to develop and implement sound migration policies aimed at addressing the trafficking of human beings, especially women and children" (Lirola-Delgado, 2019). The fact that the AIM Strategy and Lomé Charter are the only national or regional maritime security instruments which incorporate a gendered dimension highlight the need to push other national and regional governments and institutions to make further progress in integrating gender into their maritime security strategies. Until it is recognised that these strategies are not only technical, bureaucratic and state-centric documents, but strategies which concern and have consequences on the security of gendered individuals, then their capacity for making real change will be severely limited.

Conclusions

This chapter has highlighted the continuing absence of gender analysis in contemporary research and policy on maritime security. Although there is not space to consider all elements of maritime security which is a diverse and complex field, the examples provided demonstrate the ways in which a prioritisation of state-centred and militarised solutions to maritime security problems are limited and problematic, because they fail to fully take into account the impacts on individuals of maritime security policies and strategies. And it is vital to remember that these individuals are located within gendered social structures and hierarchies, which will in turn influence the ways in which they experience these security issues.

Women and men face differing security risks during sea journeys and maritime border crossings, for example, with women being particularly at risk of sexual and gender-based violence and of mortality and drowning because of structural gender inequalities, such as economic inequalities, or their caring responsibilities for children. But the maritime security strategies put in place do not adequately address these issues and in fact sometimes act to increase insecurities and risks for women in these circumstances, particularly when they are devised within a framework of "securing" state borders. Strategies aimed at fishing industries or coastal communities also frequently fail to take into account the differentiated impacts on men and women in these locations.

Gender inequalities interact with other social categorisations which are the basis of structural discriminations such as race, nationality, ethnicity, class, etc. When reflecting on a gendered approach to maritime security, we need to argue therefore, for a real consideration of the situation of individuals, and of the intersections of social constructions of gender, race, class, etc. to have a concrete impact on improving their own personal security and rights.

References

African Union. (2012). 2050 Africa Integrated Maritime (AIM) Strategy. https://au.int/en/documents-38

Alami, A. N., & Raharjo, S. N. I. (2017). Recognizing Indonesian fisherwomen's roles in fishery resource management: Profile, policy, and strategy for economic empowerment. *Journal of the Indian Ocean Region, 13*(1), 40–53.

Andersson, R. (2016). Europe's failed "fight" against irregular migration: Ethnographic notes on a counterproductive industry. *Journal of Ethnic and Migration Studies, 42*(7), 1055–1075.

Anna, Z. (2012). The role of fisherwomen in the face of fishing uncertainties on the North Coast of Java, Indonesia. *Asian Fisheries Science Special Issue, 25S*, 145–158.

Bueger, C. (2015). What is maritime security? *Marine Policy, 53*, 159–164.

Carrera, S., & Cortinovis, R. (2019, June). Search and rescue, disembarkation and relocation arrangements in the Mediterranean. Sailing away from responsibility? *CEPS Paper in Liberty and Security in Europe* 2019-10.

Costello, C., & Giuffré, C. (2015). Drowning refugees, migrants, and shame at sea: The EU response. *Blog in Two Parts, 27*, 247–280.

Council of Europe. (2019). What Is Gender Mainstreaming? https://www.coe.int/en/web/genderequality/what-is-gender-mainstreaming

Cusumano, E. (2019). Migrant rescue as organized hypocrisy: EU maritime missions offshore Libya between humanitarianism and border control. *Cooperation and Conflict, 54*(1), 3–24.

European Council. (2014, June 24). European Union Maritime Security Strategy. Brussels, 11205/14.

European Council. (2015). Council Decision (CFSP) 2015/778 of 18 May 2015 on a European Union Military Operation in the Southern Central Mediterranean (M1 EUNAVFOR MED Operation SOPHIA). European Council.

European Council. (2016, March 18). EU-Turkey Statement. https://www.consilium.europa.eu/en/press/press-releases/2016/03/18/eu-turkey-statement/

Freedman, J. (2012). Analysing the gendered insecurities of migration: A case study of female Sub-Saharan African migrants in Morocco. *International Feminist Journal of Politics, 14*(1), 36–55.

Freedman, J. (2016). Engendering security at the borders of Europe: Women migrants and the Mediterranean "crisis". *Journal of Refugee Studies, 29*(4), 568–582.

Freedman, J. (2019a). A gendered analysis of the European refugee "crisis". In C. Menjívar, I. Ruiz, & E. Ness (Eds.), *The Oxford handbook of migration crises* (pp. 705–720). Oxford University Press.

Freedman, J. (2019b). The uses and abuses of «vulnerability» in EU asylum and refugee protection: Protecting women or reducing autonomy? *Papeles del CEIC, International Journal on Collective Identity Research*, (1), 1–15.

Germond, B. (2018). Clear skies or troubled waters: The future of European ocean governance. *European View, 17*(1), 89–96.

Gilmer, B. (2017). Hedonists and husbands: Piracy narratives, gender demands, and local political economic realities in Somalia. *Third World Quarterly, 38*(6), 1366–1380.

Grotti, V., Malakasis, C., Quagliariello, C., & Sahraoui, N. (2018). Shifting vulnerabilities: Gender and reproductive care on the migrant trail to Europe. *Comparative Migration Studies, 6*(1), 1–18.

Hoogensen, G., & Stuvøy, K. (2006). Gender, resistance and human security. *Security Dialogue, 37*(2), 207–228.

IOM Missing Migrants Project. (2019). *Latest Global Figures.* https://missingmigrants.iom.int/

Kirby, P., & Shepherd, L. J. (2016). The futures past of the women, peace and security agenda. *International Affairs, 92*(2), 373–392.

Klein, N. (2011). *Maritime security and the law of the sea.* Oxford University Press.

Kraska, J., & Pedrozo, R. (2013). *International maritime security law.* Martinus Nijhoff Publishers.

Lirola-Delgado, I. (2019). Maritime security strategies from a gender perspective: Implications for United Nations SDG 5 implementation. *WMU Journal of Maritime Affairs, 18*(4), 537–555.

Marchand, M. H. (2008). The violence of development and the migration/insecurities nexus: Labour migration in a North American context. *Third World Quarterly, 29*(7), 1375–1388.

Müller, P., & Slominski, P. (2020). Breaking the legal link but not the law? The externalization of EU migration control through orchestration in the Central Mediterranean. *Journal of European Public Policy, 8*(6), 1–20.

Mussi, F. (2019). Migration at sea: Some gender-related remarks on the United Nations protocols on smuggling and trafficking. In I. Papanicolopulu (Ed.), *Gender and the law of the sea* (pp. 260–278). Brill Nijhoff.

Papanicolopulu, I. (2018). *International law and the protection of people at sea.* Oxford University Press.

Pettman, J. J. (1996). *Worlding women: A feminist international politics.* Routledge.

Pickering, S. (2014). Floating carceral spaces: Border enforcement and gender on the high seas. *Punishment & Society, 16*(2), 187–205.

Pickering, S., & Cochrane, B. (2013). Irregular border-crossing deaths and gender: Where, how and why women die crossing borders. *Theoretical Criminology, 17*(1), 27–48.

Pickering, S., & Powell, R. (2017). Death at sea: Migration and the gendered dimensions of border insecurity. In *A gendered approach to the Syrian refugee crisis* (pp. 105–124). Routledge.

Pineiro, L. C., & Kitada, M. (2020). Sexual harassment and women seafarers: The role of laws and policies to ensure occupational safety & health. *Marine Policy, 117,* 103938.

Plambech, S. (2017). Drowning mothers/ As refugees try to cross the Mediterranean sea - women are more likely to drown. *Open Democracy.* https://www.opendemocracy.net/en/beyond-trafficking-and-slavery/drowning-mothers/

Rohe, J., Schlüter, A., & Ferse, S. C. A. (2018). A gender lens on women's harvesting activities and interactions with local marine governance in a South Pacific fishing community. *Maritime Studies, 17,* 155–162.

Rothe, D. L., & Collins, V. E. (2011). Got a band-aid? Political discourse, militarized responses, and the Somalia pirate. *Issues in Criminal, Social, and Restorative Justice, 14*(3), 329–343.

Sahraoui, N. (2020). Gendering the care/control nexus of the humanitarian border: Women's bodies and gendered control of mobility in a European borderland. *Environment and Planning D: Society and Space, 38*(5), 905–922. 10.1177/0263775820925487.

Samatar, A. I., Lindberg, M., & Mahayni, B. (2010). The dialectics of piracy in Somalia: The rich versus the poor. *Third World Quarterly, 31*(8), 1377–1394.

Schwerdtner-Máñez, K., & Pauwelussen, A. P. (2016). Fish is women's business too: Looking at marine resource use through a gender lens. In K. S. Máñez, & B. Poulsen (Eds.), *Perspectives on oceans past: A handbook of marine environmental history* (pp. 193–211). Springer.

Sylvester, C. (1996). The contributions of feminist theory to international relations. In S. Smith, K. Booth, & M. Zalewski (Eds.), *International theory: Positivism and beyond* (pp. 254–278). Cambridge University Press.

Tickner, J. A. (1992). *Gender in international relations: Feminist perspectives on achieving global security.* Columbia University Press.

Trovato, A., Reid, A., Takarinda, K. C., Montaldo, C., Decroo, T., Owiti, P., Bongiorno, F. & Carlo, S. D. (2016). Dangerous crossing: Demographic and clinical features of rescued sea migrants seen in 2014 at an outpatient clinic at Augusta Harbor, Italy. *Conflict and Health, 10*(1), 14.

Tyszler, E. (2018). Sécurisation des frontières et violences contre les femmes en quête de mobilité. *Migrations Société, 173*(3), 143–158.

Tyszler, E. (2019). From controlling mobilities to control over women's bodies: Gendered effects of EU border externalization in Morocco. *Comparative Migration Studies, 7*(1), 1–20.

UNHCR. (2020). *Mediterranean Situation.* https://data2.unhcr.org/en/situations/mediterranean

UN News. (2019, January 30). "World's deadliest sea crossing" claimed six lives a day in 2018: UN refugee agency. https://news.un.org/en/story/2019/01/1031582

Walker, T. (2017). Reviving the AU's maritime strategy. Institute for Security Studies. *Policy Brief, 96.* http://issafrica.s3.amazonaws.com/site/uploads/policybrief96.pdf

Weber, L., & Pickering, S. (2011). *Globalization and borders: Death at the global frontier.* Springer.

Weber, L., & Pickering, S. (2014). Counting and accounting for deaths of asylum seekers en route to Australia. In T. Brian, & F. Laczko (Eds.), *Fatal journeys: Tracking lives lost during migration* (pp. 177–203). International Organization for Migration.

Winn, N., & Lewis, A. (2017). European Union anti-piracy initiatives in the Horn of Africa: Linking land-based counter-piracy with maritime security and regional development. *Third World Quarterly, 38*(9), 2113–2128.

Zamatto, F., Argenziano, S., Arsenijevic, J., Ponthieu, A., Bertotto, M., Donna, F. D., Harries, A. D. & Zachariah, R. (2017). Migrants caught between tides and politics in the Mediterranean: An imperative for search and rescue at sea? *BMJ Global Health, 2.* 10.1136/bmjgh-2017-000450

10

GLOBAL POLITICAL ETHNOGRAPHY: A METHODOLOGICAL APPROACH TO STUDYING MARITIME SECURITY GOVERNANCE

Jessica Larsen

Maritime security studies is an interdisciplinary collection of academic work that has been burgeoning in the last decade. It has grown concurrently with the increasing attention paid to the maritime domain in international relations (Wilson, 2018). Studies of maritime governance emanate in particular from the disciplines of Law and International Relations (IR). In different combinations, these studies use legal analysis and case law, statistical projections, policy and organisational analysis, and to a lesser extent interviews and observations to discuss and estimate the efficacy, relevance and complications of the laws, policies and organisational structures that are in place to address maritime insecurity. In this way, maritime security studies possess a distinct policy relevance for states, organisations and the private sector with an interest in maritime governance to learn from these insights and ensure security at sea.

Less prevalent in maritime security studies are sociology and anthropology (Bueger & Larsen, 2020). Or more precisely: the classical qualitative methodology associated with sociology and in particular anthropology, namely ethnography, remains underutilised to study maritime security governance. Ethnography is commonly associated with qualitative methods like interviews, participant observation and other fieldwork activities taking place on-the-ground in specific contexts of relevance to the subject of study. It has the advantage of studying the complex processes of for instance putting law into practice and implementing policy. While maritime security has thus enjoyed much analytical attention in terms of clarifying and problematising maritime security governance *structures*, hereunder its laws, policies, mandates and organisation, its governance *practices* remain a limited area of study, i.e., that which is observable when people, organisations, technologies, concepts, etc. interact in everyday doings. This is a crucial gap, in so far as analysis and policy stand to benefit from being informed by actual experiences on the ground. It leaves a window of opportunity to examine what happens when structures of maritime security governance are translated into intended (and unintended) activities.

116

DOI: 10.4324/9781003001324-12

Global Political Ethnography

This chapter maps how maritime security governance has been approached in recent years and explores the analytical purchase of adding ethnography as a complimentary methodology to understanding it. The case of Somali piracy is used as an illustration, which has enjoyed a veritable explosion of publications since 2008.[1] Given that the chapter speaks to maritime security studies emanating from Law and IR, which focus on governance, the chapter likewise focuses on the rich *counter*-piracy literature, i.e., maritime security governance, leaving studies of the crime itself for another discussion. The chapter introduces *global political ethnography*, a trend emanating from the social and political sciences, as a valuable means to studying maritime security governance. Global political ethnography takes its point of departure in ethnographic methods to unpack the dynamics of international policy processes (Stepputat & Larsen, 2015). It combines practice perspectives from interviews and participant observation with document analysis (e.g., laws, policies, etc.) to gain a holistic understanding of the field. In other words, it is a form of analytical order-making, which allows the enquiry to start with practice, while also drawing on laws, policies and organisational structures to develop an understanding of the empirical field. It retains a focus both on the structures and the practices: it moves between saying and doing, planning and producing, intention and action. This approach holds potential as a contribution to existing studies because it goes beyond analysing the laws, policies, organisations, etc. and unpacks which meanings and effects they produce in practice, in the process of implementation. Insights of this type are of both academic and policy relevance.

The aim of the chapter is thus to establish ethnography more firmly as a track within maritime security studies. And while ethnography is certainly a methodology in its own right, it is important to stress that the chapter does not argue for a replacement of dominant approaches coming from law and IR. Rather, ethnography can add value to existing maritime security studies by complementing them to understand contemporary maritime security governance at top levels more fully from bottom-up perspective.

The empirical field of maritime security related to Somali piracy is elaborated elsewhere in this Handbook (McCabe, 2022). Suffice to say, that the counter-piracy field is characterised by a high degree of complexity. It encompasses a multitude of laws (national and international), policies (civilian and military), actors (state and private) and organisations (international and regional), that are each involved in different parts of the law enforcement architecture across land and sea. International security and development organisations, alongside state actors, co-ordinate governance interventions, and since the high seas comprise over 60% of the world's oceans, it is clear why maritime security is fundamentally an international endeavour. Piracy spills across maritime borders, and it requires transboundary collaboration which, in turn, develops distinct governance spaces across land and sea. Maritime security as an empirical field is, in other words, perpetually dense and layered. As we shall see, this condition poses particular requirements of a methodological approach to capture maritime security governance in all its complexity, which ethnography is apt at doing.

The chapter is organised as follows. Section two situates the chapter's enquiry by briefly examining contributions to maritime security studies from a methodological perspective. It focuses on the abundant academic literature published over the past decade, which analyses the case of Somali counter-piracy. Finding ethnography an under-represented approach, section three introduces global political ethnography and explores how it may supplement existing studies and mainstream debates by generating different and context-specific findings through a bottom-up approach. Section four elaborates on central aspects of relevance to the study of maritime security to suggest a future qualitative research agenda in maritime security studies. Section five provides some concluding remarks.

Jessica Larsen

Methodological approaches to the study of maritime security governance

First a look at existing studies of maritime security governance and their methodology. Here, law is a fundamental aspect since the threats to security and the governance of the oceans are spelled out in various regulatory regimes. In the case of Somali piracy, all thinkable challenges of a legal nature have been subject to academic assessment. Studies discuss legal concepts and estimate regulatory challenges. Accordingly, characteristic of their methodology is that they are based on analysing law, whether focusing individual legal articles, a comparison of entire legal regimes, or discussing concepts of the law. In this way, studies address legal problems held in the definition of piracy (Guilfoyle, 2008; Eggers, 2013), the relation between piracy and terrorism in legal clauses (Burgess, 2006; Kontorovich, 2010), and human rights regimes in the case of piracy (Guilfoyle, 2010; Petrig, 2014). Studies analyse overlapping piracy regulation (Joyner, 2009), the concept of universal jurisdiction over piracy (Kontorovich & Art, 2010; Garrod, 2014) – and lack of proper jurisdiction at all (Shu, 2014). Legal restrictions in maritime policing have been analysed (Fink & Galvin, 2009; Gosalbo-Bono & Boelaert, 2014), hereunder wording on states' use of force (Treves, 2009; Murdoch & Guilfoyle, 2013), and clauses governing private armed guards (Kraska, 2013). Regarding law enforcement, studies discuss crime scene investigations and evidentiary challenges (Fouche & Meyer, 2012; Lorenz & Paradis, 2015), legal options for prosecution (Guilfoyle, 2012; Sterio, 2012) and the legality of transfer of suspects between states (Laraia, 2012). Analyses of national counter-piracy laws are likewise prevalent, covering western state perspectives (Feldtmann, 2011), regional state perspectives (Narain, 2013; Larsen, 2015), and both (Sterio, 2015; Larsen, 2017). In short, a vast and detailed array of legal issues is addressed. The methodological focus on legal texts is of course natural in legal studies, and important questions are discussed and often solved. However, a fundamental question left unanswered by these studies is: what are the actual problems encountered, not in law, but in the process of the implementation of these legal regimes? We return to this below.

Since the empirical field of maritime security governance, as mentioned in the introduction, is so rich with actors and organisations, another main line of enquiry in academic research is found in IR. In the case of Somali piracy, it analyses the constellation of governance actors and the implications for maritime security. The methodology remains predominantly a textual approach, i.e., mapping policies, programmes, institutional frameworks and the network of stakeholders with mandates to address maritime (in)security. Thus, studies have analysed the proliferation of governance bodies addressing piracy (Bueger, 2013; Percy, 2016). It has provided actor-specific analyses within the network of maritime security governance, e.g., the mandate of the EU (Germond, 2015; Riddervold, 2016a) and the role of private sector (Liss, 2013; Cusumano & Ruzza, 2020). It has discussed the complexity of governance structures, e.g., inter-organisational coordination (Riddervold & Boşilcă, 2019), the relation between organisations and legal frameworks (Roach, 2010; Struett et al., 2013) and between policies and laws (Guilfoyle, 2013). These studies provide pertinent overviews of the counter-piracy policy regime by disentangling governance structures while pointing to new forms of cooperation and concerns of overlaps in mandates, as well as identifying norm development in international relations. Yet, as in the legal studies above, a major question that remains open for debate is: what are the actual problems encountered in the process of policy implementation and in which ways are they negotiated or solved? To answer such questions about maritime security governance, stepping from deskwork to fieldwork brings promise.

In sociology and anthropology, which commonly base analyses on ethnography, studies of maritime security governance are relatively fewer than in law and IR – and themes revolve around the nature of and circumstances surrounding Somali piracy itself, rather than the activities related to countering it.[2] However, small and important pockets do exist that base analyses on a mix of ethnographic methods, such as interviews and participant observation – often in combination with legal or policy analysis – to base studies on both the structures and the actual practices that make up this particular case of maritime security governance. This essentially corresponds to global political ethnography, which is treated in more detail in the next section.

The existing ethnographic studies merit detailed attention. While they are few, their findings yield significant contributions to our understanding of maritime security governance. One ethnographically informed study presents empirical observations from policy meetings of how global governance is produced through the specific micro-level practices of international actors cooperating around maritime security (Bueger, 2018). It is clear from this study that cooperation is characterised by being politicised, something policy analysis may appreciate but cannot wholly document and analyse without empirical data to back it up. Another study is an analysis based on multi-year observations and interviews in different fields of counter-piracy activity generating observations of how capacity-building activities allow the establishment of certain roles – or yield so-called constitutive identity effects – of capacity-building actors (Jacobsen & Larsen, 2019). Such a sensitive diagnostic cannot be read in policy documents but requires field-specific observations of the subtle and various ways actors through time and space seek to position themselves via their counter-piracy activities. A study has also provided interview-based insights into how the European Commission influenced the EU's counter-piracy mandate beyond its delegated powers (Riddervold, 2016b). Uncovering this behind-the-scenes development requires building trust and having multiple conversations with EU representatives to detect such delicate manoeuvring. One study has used interviews with insurers and call transcripts to map and understand the tricky dynamics of kidnap for ransom (Shortland, 2019). This shadowy world is little-known to even the most avid counter-piracy observers and requires access to persons holding otherwise restricted information. Finally, an analysis based on interviews and observations exists of the practices of counter-piracy law enforcement actors, finding that legal issues such as the problem of defining piracy in *law* meets quite different challenges in law *enforcement* and uncovers how states use counter-piracy as a catalyst to position themselves on the international stage (Larsen, 2017). Such practice-specific studies can bring nuance to debates in legal literature and detect the highly politicised nature of international law, which again cannot be read in for instance UNCLOS.

Judging by the sheer number of references, it seems that ethnography as an approach to studying maritime security is still relatively rare compared to other methodologies. But, as shown above, it holds the potential to critically assess how the laws and policies are translated into practice by applying methods like interviews and participant observation. The examples above suggest that ethnography can to some extent contribute to suggesting answers to the questions left open by law and IR – what the actual problems are in the processes of implementing law and policy – to arrive at an understanding of the implications and effects of maritime security governance. We might say that the difference between analysis in law and IR versus ethnography is that the former rightly identifies certain problems, tensions and power struggles, while the latter can uncover how these tensions and struggles are overcome and negotiated in practice – in turn pointing to yet other and new problems, which the researcher could not have discovered without closer inspection of practical doings of counter-piracy. Both sides have value and, certainly, combining them could have many advantages. To reap the benefits of ethnographic perspectives, the next section suggests a methodological approach that may help shape, broaden and anchor ethnography in maritime security.

Jessica Larsen

Bringing global political ethnography to the maritime domain

Ethnography, with its qualitative data collection, particularly through interviews and participant observation, is traditionally coupled with the discipline of anthropology. However, in recent decades it has found its way into the interpretative and constructivist arms of political science and IR as a fruitful way of studying policy processes in the context of international governance. This trend has been termed "global political ethnography" (Stepputat & Larsen, 2015) and, as we shall see below, is an apt approach to unpack the dynamics of the maritime security field.

Global political ethnography seeks to bring out the inner workings of international governance, for instance public institutions such as states and international organisations, as they interact on various policy issues (Sharma & Gupta, 2006; Abélès, 2011), but also agents of civil society and the private sector engaging in "global" or "transnational" activities (Cunningham, 1999; Tsuda et al., 2014). A prevalent feature is the focus on formal and informal practices of power and authority, when policies travel across space and interact in the international domain (Wedel et al., 2005; Shore & Wright, 2011). This is based on the realisation that adopting a law or writing a policy does not equal, or guarantee, its implementation. In the context of maritime security studies, global political ethnography thus promises to help direct attention towards the ways in which actors, policies, laws and organisations produce, or even co-constitute, the maritime security field (Jacobsen & Larsen, 2019).

Thus, for instance, when legal studies conclude that the legal definition of piracy holds various problems or that law enforcement suffers from overlapping legal regimes, what do we make of the fact that an elaborate law enforcement set-up actually exists – despite legal complications – to counter Somali piracy? And how do we learn from the problem-solving processes that must have taken place to overcome these challenges in practice? Or, when the vast and complex organisational field of maritime security governance is mapped, and the fragmented institutional mandates are identified in IR – which rightly leads to concerns of lacking coordination – how do we learn what counter-piracy actors do to mitigate the mandate issues in their work? And what are the actual problems with, and effects of, the lacking coordination in the maritime domain? Based on these yet unanswered questions, it would seem that there is still untapped potential to dig into the empirical field of maritime security governance through ethnography to learn from what happens in practice.

To do so, there are concretely three key features of global political ethnography relevant to guide the study of maritime security. Firstly, global political ethnography, indeed ethnography as such, presupposes an insistence on practice as a primary conveyor of knowledge. It implies a distinct attention to various social processes in the field. This requires collecting first-hand knowledge of the field. But contrary to common expectations of what ethnography is, this first-hand knowledge does not only imply "being there" (Hannerz, 2003), i.e., in the field. This is why the methods repertoire in the global political ethnography toolbox essentially *combines* the classical ethnographic methods, like participant observation and interviews, with other forms of knowledge generation about the field – including a broad range of document analysis, such as archival research and analyses of relevant laws, polices, media articles, speeches, court transcripts and statistics, to mention a few (see Stepputat & Larsen, 2015 for a discussion). As alluded to above, this mixed-methods approach can help answer relevant questions about maritime security governance. Comparing and contrasting observations of everyday experiences with textual analysis of field-specific documents, it is possible to oscillate analytically between saying and doing, planning and producing, intentions and actions.

Secondly, global political ethnography often entails "studying up" (Nader, 1969). In other words, conducting research on – and among – positions of authority. Sometimes representatives of states, international organisations and multinationals, other times moving among the "street level bureaucrats" (Feldtmann, 2011) as they carry out, indeed make sense of, policies from above. Studying up means engaging the executive level, policy-making and the inner workings of power (Abélès, 2011). This often implies manoeuvring in a field that is politically charged, as public and private stakeholders seek to carry out their interests through policy initiatives, strategies, etc. Such features are common to the field of maritime security with its wealth of especially state actors, international organisations but also private actors engaged in law enforcement, capacity-building, insurance, not to mention the shipping industry itself.

Thirdly, global political ethnography – just like the maritime security field – is often multi-sited. It involves a combination of disparate locations that are all relevant to the enquiry. Multi-sited fieldwork has been defined as the ethnographer following for instance the thing, the people or the metaphor as they transverse time and space (Marcus, 1995). In a maritime security context, this could be following the relevant legal articles across space from a warship to the prison and courtroom (Larsen, 2017). When ethnographers of multi-sited fieldwork move between diverse actors and activities in different positions and locations, they are faced with various normative orders, historical trajectories and political agendas (Collier & Ong, 2005). This offers a further link to maritime security governance, as it, too, consists of multiple spaces of interaction, which are related through e.g., law enforcement cooperation and capacity-building relationships (Larsen, 2017), states competing for recognition and roles in the international community (Jacobsen & Larsen, 2019), or in more direct opposition to one another such as the criminal networks versus legal fields of activity. These multiple sites are relational. They exist in part as a prerequisite or a consequence of the other, and ethnography promises to lift out and connect their specificities in the context of broader maritime security policy and governance processes. But how to do it in practice? Next, some concrete strategies are suggested to help apply ethnography to the field of maritime security – a research agenda to be tested and refined as the ethnography of maritime security studies go forward and matures.

Managing complexity, mitigating politics

If global political ethnography is practice-oriented, studies "up" and is multi-sited, there are two immediate issues of importance to consider when applying it to the study of maritime security governance. Firstly, because global political ethnography, indeed the study of maritime security in practice, lends itself to a multi-sited research endeavour, it produces a multi-vocality in the empirical data, in other words multiple voices, positions, agendas, norms, etc., by virtue of spanning different states or sites and, within these, different professional environments among the multiple types of stakeholders involved in counter-piracy. To manage such complexity analytically requires consideration of the relations and positions that produce a specific multivocality, because it is ultimately what defines that which is studied – defines the field.

In policy studies, it has been suggested that the field be considered "not a particular people or organisation" – far less a reified policy itself – but as a "social and political space articulated through relations of power and systems of governance" (Shore & Wright, 2011, p. 11). In other words, the field is defined in an organic and fluid process sorting through its complex relations around a given policy issue. It would thus seem that multivocality is a condition in the ethnographic approach. To order the complexity, indeed to operationalise the slippery endeavour to define a complex "field", Bourdieu (1991) offers a way. His practice theoretical approach conceptualises the field as the relations between actors with varying levels of power that draw on different types of human capital. The actors not only interact but also compete to define the norms and rules within the field. This conceptual structuring can be used to identify a topology of the field and order the complexity. And it can serve as a point of departure to analyse the specific norms, practices and positions within the field of maritime security governance. Think about the sheer number and types of maritime security actors involved in law enforcement to counter Somali piracy; as a field, it is impossible to study the totality of actors. Bourdieu's concept of the field may support the selection of certain relations of power and aspects of governance that converge around the given policy area to be studied.

Another possible way of managing complexity is by drawing on assemblage theory (Latour, 2005; DeLanda, 2006). It approaches social phenomena – this could be maritime security governance – as connections of heterogeneous components in the empirical field that continually shift into different constellations. The convergence of components is what defines the particular object of study, i.e., the field. In maritime security, it could for instance be the distinct junctures of law enforcement activities in the maritime domain, in which particular people(s), things, ideas, practices, technologies, policies, laws, discourses and institutions connect in the specific process of producing security. Thus, where Bourdieu focuses on actors or positions of power, an assemblage approach brings a range of other aspects into the centre of attention and does not focus solely on power relations. The assemblage allows for the study of empirical articulations of practical processes related to the production, or contestation, of policies, norms, discourses, etc., through studying social interactions. This provides a flexible research strategy to open up the field and order its complex, dense and layered components.

Turning to the other issue in need of consideration as global political ethnography is drawn into the maritime domain is the ethical effects of "studying up". It is an exercise of mitigating the politics of the field. For an ethnographer coming from the outside with no direct purpose in the field and no direct importance to its actors, her endeavour may seem inconvenient to the ranks of public or private authority under ethnographic scrutiny – or simply as snooping. For instance, in maritime security governance, law enforcers, the guardians of justice, move in professional communities representing state institutions. Information collected by the ethnographer can potentially uncover irregularities in law – e.g., through participant observation becoming aware how compromises to piracy suspects' *habeas corpus* is carried out at sea. Or inadvertently it may burst a sensitive political balloon – e.g., gaining knowledge through interviews of one state's backchannel diplomacy on a certain issue, which, if made public, can hurt it *vis à vis* another state.

Thus, when actors in the field are engaged as objects of study, they may feel concerned about making mistakes or revealing legal irregularities. They may even seek to control the ethnographer's knowledge production, as has been studied in comparable environments (Pouliot, 2008, p. 285). Either way, it requires attention to bias in the data, but more fundamentally draws in the question of ethics, posing a responsibility on the ethnographer to use responsibly any sensitive information which might come to light. Strategies to avoid causing conflicts include signing informed consents at the beginning of fieldwork to set the parameters and boundaries for information-sharing, and furthermore member checking can be used after fieldwork, where the ethnographer ensures with stakeholders in the field that facts have been understood correctly (Stepputat & Larsen, 2015, p. 20). This is also a question of legacy and how the field is left for the next ethnographer to visit. But, most importantly, it is a basic principle in ethnographic ethics: do no harm (AAA, 2012). Just as ethnography is apt to speak truth to power, it should respect both truth and power. Thus, whether possessing information on sensitive state practices or tensions in transnational collaborations etc., data collection becomes an exercise of mitigating politics even before the analysis can begin.

Conclusion

Ethnography is still a marginal methodological approach to the study of maritime security governance. This chapter discussed its analytical purchase and use, first mapping existing methodological approaches to maritime security, then drawing the trend of global political ethnography into the orbit of existing studies to argue how it may push our knowledge further of this particular field. The chapter showed that while existing studies point to a range of pertinent issues and challenges in maritime security governance, it is examined primarily from the perspective of the laws, policies, organisational structures and mandates, while less from the point of view of how these dimensions of maritime security are actually translated into practice. There are obvious reasons for the lack of ethnography in studying maritime security governance – issues of access, including security and gatekeeping, not to mention often limited resources for extensive fieldwork. But these restrictions make access a lengthy process rather than unattainable. And so far, it has left analytical insights with a certain blind eye.

The chapter argued that global political ethnography is a valuable methodological approach which can be used to fill the existing gap. Established, yet diverse, global political ethnography is characterised by being practice-oriented (focusing on everyday interactions), studying "up" (engaging the power ranks that be) and multi-sited (connecting field sites across space). It works from the assumption that the world is complex and that understanding the words of a policy, or a law is not equivalent to knowing *a priori* how it is implemented. Indeed, the value of ethnography is keeping an eye on the intentions of the laws, policies, actions, etc. governing for instance maritime security but following them through to the governance practises that these (textual) frameworks generate. It observes concrete activities, working from practice and out toward the formal structures through methods like interview and participant observation and combining this with textual analysis. Practice theory and the assemblage were offered as research strategies to select and connect otherwise disparate – and potentially endless numbers of – physical locations, power positions, regulatory frameworks, etc. collected in one exploration. And it was discussed how to manage the complexity and mitigate the politics that it inevitably entails with regards to defining the field and maintaining ethical standards when studying multi-sited and politically sensitive settings.

Compared to the abundance of publications emanating from law and IR, more ethnographic studies are surely welcome. While legal and IR approaches set the scene and bring order to the formal side of maritime security governance, ethnography can shed light on how the informal, or everyday, practices also produce and shape maritime governance. Global political ethnography renders actual the law, it brings out the implications of policy, and personifies the formal positions of state and non-state actors. It provides windows onto how laws and policies take on lives of their own in the process of implementation and bring to the fore the subtle power and problem-solving dynamics, which shape the maritime security field as much as the formal structures do. It therefore promises bring nuance, and to potentially correct, existing scientific narratives. The different sets of approaches nesting within maritime security studies are thus highly complementary and are not a question of either/or. They draw out the structures of law and policy and the practices of their implementation when it comes to the pressing issue in maritime security governance. Combined, they allow the pairing of saying and doing, planning and producing, intentions and actions to grasp more fully the maritime security field. Combined, such insights hold the potential for theory development, as well as legal revision and enhancing policy. There is yet a fruitful opportunity waiting to be explored regarding the contextualisation of the legal and policy studies available in maritime security studies. The potential reaches beyond Somali piracy to other forms of maritime governance, be it in the Indian Ocean or in other waters around the world.

Notes

1 For a literature review of maritime security studies more broadly covering all crimes and their responses, see Bueger and Larsen (2020).
2 For example, with respect to its root causes (Pham 2010; Hastings & Phillips, 2018), types of attacks (Twyman-Ghoshal & Pierce 2014) and level of organisation (Hansen 2009; Percy & Shortland, 2013). Piracy motivations are discussed as either greed (Keating, 2013), grievance (Klein, 2013) or cultural practices (Dua, 2013). Owing to the obvious security issues related to collecting empirical data through ethnography on the topic of Somali piracy, few of these studies are based on fieldwork – with Hansen (2009) and Dua (2013) being notable exceptions.

References

AAA. (2012). *Code of Ethics of the American Anthropological Association.* American Anthropological Association. https://www.americananthro.org/LearnAndTeach/Content.aspx?ItemNumber=22869&navItemNumber=652

Abélès, M. (Ed.). (2011). *Des anthropologues à l'OMC. Scène de la gouvernance mondiale.* Editions du CNRS.

Bourdieu, P. (1991). *Language and Symbolic Power.* Harvard University Press.

Bueger, C. (2013). Responses to contemporary piracy: Disentangling the organizational field. In D. Guilfoyle (Ed.), *Legal Challenges and Responses* (pp. 91–114). Edward Elgar Publishing.

Bueger, C. (2018). Territory, authority, expertise: Global governance and the counter-piracy assemblage. *European Journal of International Relations, 24*(3), 614–637.

Bueger, C., & Larsen, J. 2020. Maritime insecurities. In F. Hampson & A. Ozerdem (Eds.), *The Routledge Handbook of Peace, Security and Development* (pp. 149–163). Routledge.

Burgess, D. R. (2006). *Hostis Humani Generi*: Piracy, terrorism and a new international order. *University of Miami International and Comparative Law Review, 13,* 293–341.

Collier, S. J., & Ong, A. (2005). Global assemblages, anthropological problems. In S. J. Collier & A. Ong (Eds.), *Global Assemblages. Technology, Politics and Ethics as Anthropological Problems* (pp. 3–21). Blackwell Publishing.

Cunningham, H. (1999). The ethnography of transnational social activism: Understanding the global as local practice. *American Ethnologist: The Journal of the American Ethnological Society, 26*(3), 583–604.

Cusumano, E., & Ruzza, S. (2020). *Piracy and the Privatisation of Maritime Security.* Palgrave Macmillan.

DeLanda, M. (2006). *A New Philosophy of Society: Assemblage Theory and Social Complexity.* Bloomsbury.

Dua, J. (2013). A sea of trade and a sea of fish: Piracy and protection in the Western Indian Ocean. *Journal of Eastern African Studies, 7*(2), 353–370.

Eggers, P. M. (2013). What is a pirate? A common law answer to an age-old question. In D. Guilfoyle (Ed.), *Modern Piracy. Legal Challenges and Responses* (pp. 250–267). Edward Elgar Publishing.

Feldtmann, B. (2011). Should we rule out criminal law as a means of fighting maritime piracy? - An essay on the challenges and possibilities of prosecuting Somali pirates. In U. W. Andersson, C. Hansen & H. Örnemark (Eds.), *Festskrift till Per Ole Träskman* (pp. 179–188). Norstedts Juridik.

Fink, M. D., & Galvin, R. J. (2009). Combating pirates off the coast of Somalia: Current legal challenges. *Netherlands International Law Review, 56*(03), 367–395.

Fouche, H., & Meyer J. (2012). Investigating sea piracy: Crime scene challenges. *WMU Journal of Maritime Affairs, 11,* 33–50.

Garrod, M. (2014). Piracy, the protection of vital state interests and the false foundations of universal jurisdiction in international law. *Law, Diplomacy and Statecraft, 25*(2), 195–213.

Germond, B. (2015). *The Maritime Dimension of European Security: Seapower and the European Union.* Palgrave Macmillan.

Gosalbo-Bono, R., & Boelaert, S. (2014). The European Union's comprehensive approach to combating piracy at sea: Legal aspects. In P. Koutrakos & A. Skordas (Eds.), *The Law and Practice of Piracy at Sea. European and International Perspectives* (pp. 81–166). Hart Publishing.

Guilfoyle, D. (2008). Piracy off Somalia: UN security council resolution 1816 and IMO regional counter-piracy efforts. *International and Comparative Law Quarterly, 57*(03), 690–699.

Guilfoyle, D. (2010). Counter-piracy law enforcement and human rights. *International and Comparative Law Quarterly, 59*(01), 141–169.

Guilfoyle, D. (2012). Prosecuting Somali pirates. A critical evaluation of the options. *Journal of International Criminal Justice, 10,* 767–796.

Guilfoyle, D. (2013). Policy tensions and the legal regime governing piracy. In D. Guilfoyle *Modern Piracy. Legal Challenges and Responses* (pp. 325–336). Edward Elgar Publishing.

Hannerz, U. (2003). Being there... and there... and there! Reflections on multi-site fieldwork. *Ethnography, 4*(2), 201–216.

Hansen, S. J. (2009). Piracy in the greater Gulf of Aden. Myths, misconceptions and remedies. *NIBR Report* 2009:29. Norwegian Institute for Urban and Regional Research.

Hastings, J., & Phillips, S. (2018). Order beyond the state: Explaining Somaliland's avoidance of maritime piracy. *The Journal of Modern African Studies, 56*(1), 5–30.

Jacobsen, K. L., & Larsen, J. (2019). Piracy studies coming of age: A window on the making of maritime intervention actors. *International Affairs, 95*(5), 1037–1054.

Joyner, C. (2009). Navigating troubled waters. Somalia, piracy, and maritime terrorism. *Law & Ethics, 10*(2), 83–91.

Keating, T. (2013). The political economy of Somali piracy. *SAIS Review, 33*(1), 185–191.

Klein, A. (2013). The moral economy of Somali piracy - Organised criminal business or subsistence activity? *Global Policy, 4*(1), 94–100.

Kontorovich, E. (2010). "A Guantanamo on the sea": The difficulties of prosecuting pirates and terrorists. *California Law Review, 98*, 243–276.

Kontorovich, E., & Art, S. (2010). An empirical examination of universal jurisdiction for piracy. *American Journal of International Law, 104*(3), 436–453.

Kraska, J. (2013). International and comparative regulation of private maritime security companies employed in counter-piracy. In D. Guilfoyle (Ed.), *Modern Piracy. Legal Challenges and Responses* (pp. 250–267). Edward Elgar Publishing.

Latour, B. (2005). *Reassembling the Social. An Introduction to Actor-Network-Theory.* Oxford University Press.

Laraia, M. (2012). Piracy is an international problem that needs a multi-prong solution. *Regent Journal of International Law, 9*, 105–143.

Larsen, J. (2015). Towards maritime security in the Indian Ocean: The case of Seychelles. *Island Studies – Indian Ocean/Océan Indien, 3*(3), 50–59.

Larsen, J. (2017). *Conceptualising the Legal Assemblage. An Anthropological Analysis of Counter-piracy Law and Practice off the Coast of Somalia.* Faculty of Law, Copenhagen University.

Liss, C. (2013). Private military and security companies in maritime security governance. In A. P. Jakobi & K. D. Wolf (Eds.), *The Transnational Governance of Violence and Crime. Non-State Actors in Security* (pp. 193–213). Palgrave Macmillan.

Lorenz, F., & Paradis, K. (2015). Evidentiary issues in piracy prosecutions. In M. Scharf, M. A. Newton & M. Sterio (Eds.), *Prosecuting Maritime Piracy: Domestic Solutions to International Crimes* (pp. 207–241). Cambridge University Press.

Marcus, G. E. (1995). Ethnography in/of the world system: The emergence of multi-sited ethnography. *Annual Review of Anthropology, 24*, 95–117.

McCabe, R. (2022). Contemporary maritime piracy and counter-piracy. In R. Bosilca, S. Ferreira & B. J. Ryan (Eds.), *The Handbook of Maritime Security* (pp. xx–xx). Routledge.

Murdoch, A., & Guilfoyle, D. (2013). Capture and disruption operations: The use of force in counter-piracy off Somalia. In D. Guilfoyle (Ed.), *Modern Piracy. Legal Challenges and Responses* (pp. 147–171). Edward Elgar Publishing.

Nader, L. (1969). Up the anthropologist: Perspectives gained from studying up. In D. Hymes (Ed.), *Reinventing Anthropology* (pp. 284–311). Pantheon.

Narain, A. (2013). Preparing for piracy trials in Mauritius. *Commonwealth Law Bulletin, 39*(1), 53–58.

Percy, D. (2016). Counter-piracy in the Indian Ocean: A new form of military cooperation. *Journal of Global Security Studies, 1*(4), 270–284.

Percy, S., & Shortland, A. (2013). The business of piracy in Somalia. *Journal of Strategic Studies, 36*(4), 451–578.

Petrig, A. (2014). *Human Rights and Law Enforcement at Sea: Arrest, Detention and Transfer of Piracy Suspects.* Brill Nijhoff.

Pham, P. (2010). Putting Somali piracy in context. *Journal of Contemporary African Studies, 28*(3), 325–341.

Pouliot, V. (2008). The logic of practicality. *International Organization, 62*(2), 257–288.

Riddervold, M. (2016a). Et spørsmål om legitimitet. Hvorfor Norge valgte EU foran NATO i kampen mot somaliske pirater. *Norsk statsvitenskapelig tidsskrift, 4*, 363–382.

Riddervold, M. (2016b). (Not) in the hands of the member states: How the European Commission influences EU security and defence policies. *Journal of Common Market Studies, 54*(2), 353–369.

Riddervold, M., & Boşilcă, R. L. (2019). EU–NATO inter-organizational relations in counter-piracy operations off the Horn of Africa. In J. Karlsrud & Y. Reykers (Eds.), *Multinational Rapid Response Mechanisms. From Institutional Proliferation to Institutional Exploitation* (pp. 155–176). Routledge.

Roach, J. A. (2010). Countering piracy off Somalia: International law and international institutions. *The American Journal of International Law, 104*(3), 397–416.

Sharma, A., & Gupta, A. (2006). *The Anthropology of the State. A Reader*. Blackwell Publishing.

Shore, C., & Wright, S. (2011). Conceptualising policy: Technologies of governance and the politics of visibility. In C. Shore, S. Wright & D. Però (Eds.), *Policy Worlds. Anthropology and the Analysis of Contemporary Power* (pp. 1–26). Bergham Books.

Shortland, A. (2019). *Kidnap: Inside the Ransom Business*. Oxford University Press.

Shu, Y. (2014). Establishing an effective mechanism of the jurisdictions over piracy. *International Journal of e-Education, e-Business, e-Management and e-Learning, 4*(2), 154–159.

Stepputat, F., & Larsen, J. (2015). *Global Political Ethnography: A Methodological Approach to Studying Global Policy Regimes*. DIIS Working Paper 2015:01.

Sterio, M. (2012). Piracy off the coast of Somalia. The argument for pirate prosecutions in the national courts of Kenya, The Seychelles, and Mauritius. *Amsterdam Law Forum, 4*(2), 104–123.

Sterio, M. (2015). Incorporating international law to establish jurisdiction over piracy offenses. A comparative examination of the laws of the Netherlands, South Korea, Tanzania, India, and Kenya. In M. P. Scharf, M. A. Newton & M. Sterio (Eds.), *Prosecuting Maritime Piracy. Domestic Solutions to International Crimes* (pp. 75–100). Cambridge University Press.

Struett, M. J., Nance, M. T., & Armstrong, D. (2013). Navigating the maritime piracy regime complex. *Global Governance, 19*, 93–104.

Treves, T. (2009). Piracy, law of the sea, and use of force: Developments off the coast of Somalia. *European Journal of International Law, 20*(2), 399–414.

Tsuda, T., Tapias, M., & Escandell, X. (2014). Locating the global in transnational ethnography. *Journal of Contemporary Ethnography, 43*(2), 123–147.

Twyman-Ghoshal, A., & Pierce, G. (2014). The changing nature of contemporary maritime piracy. Results from the contemporary maritime piracy database 2001-10. *British Journal of Criminology, 54*(4), 652–672.

Wedel, J. R., Shore, C., Feldman, G., & Lathrop, S. (2005). Toward an anthropology of public policy. *The Annals of the American Academy of Political and Social Science, 6000*(1), 30–51.

Wilson, B. (2018). The Turtle Bay pivot: How the United Nations security council is reshaping naval pursuit of nuclear proliferators, rouge states, and pirates. *Emory International Law Review, 33*(1), 1–90.

11

THE POLITICS OF PIRACY NUMBERS: THE GULF OF GUINEA CASE

Katja Lindskov Jacobsen

Introduction

According to the International Maritime Bureau (IMB), Gulf of Guinea (GoG) piracy surged (again) in the third quarter of 2020, with "132 attacks since the start of 2020".[1] Not only the IMB but also a range of other public and private agencies count and report the number of piracy attacks, including when such attacks occur in what is currently the world's most piracy-affected waters. The GoG accounts for "95% of global kidnappings", including incidents in an area spanning from the Ivory Coast to Congo.[2] Much has been said about "piracy counting", also pertaining to the GoG region. One familiar debate is the longstanding discussion about underreporting and different agencies' diverging incident reporting (Lombardo, 2014; Sow, 2018; Pichon, 2019). For 2020, the IMB for example reported 84 incidents of piracy and armed robbery at sea in GoG,[3] whilst the MICA Centre reported 114 incidents of piracy and armed robbery at sea in the region for the same period.[4] Breaking this further down, IMB reported 35 incidents recorded in Nigerian waters alone, whilst MICA reported a number of 42.[5] Whilst acknowledging debates about underreporting as well as more recent discussions about over-reporting, this chapter argues that the "politics of numbers" in relation to GoG piracy goes beyond divergent metrics. For example, asking too narrowly about whether the number of "incidents" has increased or decreased risks paying insufficient attention to nuances surrounding these numbers. What goes unnoticed, what is missing or made unavailable, and what does that mean for counter-piracy engagements in this region?

Another debate about what goes unnoticed in the counting of piracy is that focusing too much and too narrowly on piracy numbers risks rendering invisible the prevalence of other types of maritime insecurity. As used in this chapter, invisibility does not refer to absolute invisibility (i.e., something that cannot be seen) but to how specific practices and assumptions make visible certain aspects, while others are concealed or obscured. In that sense, invisibility emerges from "a set of practices and ideas that order the world and its politics", also in the realm of maritime (in)security (Van Veeren, 2018). From the perspective of GoG states and populations, piracy is neither the only nor necessarily the most pressing maritime security challenge. Piracy is better understood as a "squeezed" priority, which is high on the agenda of numerous external actors whilst often competing for funding and attention both with other types of maritime crime as well as with various onshore security challenges. Besides piracy, other

DOI: 10.4324/9781003001324-13

127

maritime crimes affect the GoG region, from drugs trafficking[6] and weapons smuggling[7] via maritime routes, to illicit arms trafficking to illegal, unreported and unregulated (IUU) fishing affecting coastal communities' livelihoods and food security (Okafor-Yarwood, 2019). Yet, narrower attention to piracy incidents may unintentionally risk downplaying the extent and significance of other crimes and related security challenges at sea. Not only should this range of maritime challenges not be forgotten in current debates about piracy numbers, but from the point of view of regional actors, piracy is not considered the most pertinent maritime threat, like the kidnapping and release of expatriate seafarers once the ransom has been negotiated has few immediately negative implications for communities in which hostage camps are hosted.[8] There is thus a risk that these different security priorities will remain unaddressed given the overwhelming focus on piracy numbers; indeed, no other maritime crime is counted with the same amount of attention.

This chapter looks at the regional case study of the GoG through the theoretical lens of the politics of piracy numbers. From this perspective, the chapter adds to current cautionary debates about how "piracy data" as an "indicator of general maritime security in the Gulf of Guinea" (Okafor-Yarwood et al., 2021) may invisibilise underlying divergences in maritime security priorities. Notably, external counterpiracy actors' emphasis on piracy data may unintentionally confer invisibility or lower priority to other maritime security challenges (like IUU or illicit weapons trafficking) – which, from a regional perspective, are considered important with reference to the type of insecurity they cause or feed into. More specifically, this chapter adds to current debates about piracy and maritime security in the GoG in two main ways: a) by shifting attention from problem-side invisibilities to solution-side invisibilities; and b) by shifting attention from maritime counting to questions about critical onshore aspects of GoG piracy, of relevance also to other issues of maritime insecurity. As such, the chapter contributes to existing debates about the politics of piracy numbers both through its focus on how piracy counting risks conferring invisibility onto other maritime challenges in the GoG region, and through its focus on how, in contrast to the attention given to counting offshore piracy, little is known about most onshore dimensions of GoG piracy.

In terms of method, the findings presented in this chapter are based on readings of official documents (like the Yaoundé Code of Conduct), on participant observations in policy fora (such as G7++ Friend of the Gulf of Guinea) as well as on interviews with regional and international actors including industry representatives, security experts, policy makers and practitioners of counter-piracy. This wide range of interviewees is key to shedding light into the diverse perspectives through which the politics of numbers can be uncovered.

The politics of numbers as a lens onto GoG-piracy and maritime crime

"Missing" numbers: Solution-side invisibilities and onshore invisibilities

Missing numbers are not necessarily synonymous with straightforward knowledge gaps or methodological and/or access challenges, but sometimes tied to broader interests in maintaining a level of invisibility. Besides the issue of invisibilities of other maritime security challenges, this chapter argues that the "politics of missing numbers" is also a useful lens onto dynamics on the "solution-side" of maritime security, including counter-piracy. To illustrate this, it looks at the counting (or absence thereof) of various maritime security capacity-building programmes in the GoG-region. Indeed, so many different capacity-building engagements exist that no one has a comprehensive picture of these activities.[9] More systematised efforts have been made to provide an overview of capacity-building engagements of US AFRICOM in Nigeria, but even that picture is "messy" (Østensen et al., 2018). The lack of recording of capacity-building engagements has also been raised in various settings, including in meetings of the G7++ Friends of the Gulf of Guinea Group, a forum, which is co-chaired by a regional and an external partner, currently Gabon and the US, and whose purpose is to support the Yaoundé Architecture.[10]

Acknowledging this gap leading to duplication and coordination challenges in the area of capacity-building efforts in the region (e.g., overlaps, duplication), Oceans Beyond Piracy provided a free database that actors could use to report their activities. Yet, as an interviewee noted, "very few external actors had an interest in more transparency regarding their own programmes so it was never really used by anyone".[11] Thus, whilst piracy incidents at sea are counted by numerous actors, no mechanism has been set up to keep track of the numerous externally funded counter-piracy engagements in various GoG states and at various levels in the inter-regional Yaoundé structure. What, then, is the politics of this example of missing numbers? For now, this absence seems linked to power relations, as seen from debates about whose job it would be to produce such an overview, and which actors would find themselves privileged and powerful enough not to report. As mentioned, not all actors may be equally interested in such a mapping exercise, and not all actors are equally concerned about overlaps. As argued by one interviewee, many of the external actors involved in GoG counter-piracy have their own agendas, or are only superficially engaging "to show that I am doing something".[12]

Which other numbers are obscured, and what political dynamics, like donors prioritising "countable" engagements (e.g., number of training sessions, headcounts, etc.) over less tangible ones (e.g., addressing corruption, poverty, etc.) may affect the broader politics of missing (counter)-piracy numbers? Again, though numerous actors report on piracy incidents in the GoG, little is known about most onshore dimensions of this phenomenon or other types of maritime crime. For instance, how much profit has been made from piracy ransom payments? Such numbers are not readily available, though they of course exist: negotiators, shipping companies, and local actors would be expected to know how much money has been dropped off to pirates in the Niger Delta. Indeed, numerous unanswered questions emerge once we attend critically to the politics of missing piracy numbers ashore.

Ballooning effects and a missing category

Shifting the focus to another aspect of the politics of numbers, Andreas and Greenhill (2010) note: "to measure something – or at least claim to do so – is to announce its existence and signal its importance and policy relevance". The issue of maritime piracy is commonly debated with reference to numbers as being at the heart of claims about its importance (or not). This notion of a "politics of numbers" highlights how numbers serve as framing devices, contributing to the prioritisation of some issues over others (Jacobsen, 2017). A case in point is the seeming inability of external actors to attend to the importance of GoG piracy and Somali piracy simultaneously. As an interviewee noted, it seems that attention goes where reporting is highest once piracy attacks off Somalia plummeted attention shifted to the GoG.[13] This is of course also another take on the issue of invisibility mentioned above: crimes at sea (IUU, smuggling, etc.) that pose challenges to the GoG region but are not counted with the same attention as piracy incidents are automatically signalled as less important and thus less policy relevant. Hence, current debates about regional reporting centres and the focus of such mechanisms should not be regarded merely as a technical but rather as a deeply political discussion.

What do relatively stable incident numbers, when viewed from a statistical birds-eye perspective, tell us about GoG piracy? Critics argue that the constant number of reported incidents reveals the failure to address GoG piracy for almost a decade. Yet, whilst some numbers show continuity, other numbers convey changes that offer a more nuanced explanation of how and in what sense some of the counter-piracy efforts have faced challenges in combatting GoG piracy. Some of these changes are explored with reference to the notion of the so-called "ballooning effects" (Jacobsen & Carrasco, 2018; Jacobsen, 2018). Other changes become visible by looking more closely at the incidents that are reported and counted. This chapter uses the politics of numbers as a framework to unpack incident reporting. With this framework attention is for example drawn to the question of whether to include another category of "maritime crime" incidents, which in turn qualify to what extent "incident numbers" in themselves may be indicative of the level of piracy threat in the GoG.

These are the two focus points which structure the analysis of GoG piracy as one component of much wider maritime insecurity complexes as a regional case study. Specifically, this analysis follows the two sections above by first looking at "missing numbers and invisibilities", and then at "ballooning effects and missing incidents categories". The politics of numbers is a unifying lens through which these two issues become part of a common story by bridging two distinct bodies of policy-oriented body of works: the literature on the politicisation of numbers and the studies on the GoG piracy, respectively.

This lens has already provided interesting perspectives on other policy areas. Examples include refugee studies (Crisp, 1999) and the global war on terror – e.g., calling attention to whose lives are counted or not in casualty statistics of US drone strikes (Suchman, 2020). This chapter draws upon these and related analyses to further develop the notion of the "politics of numbers" into a practical analytical framework. Jeff Crisp (1999), for example, used the concept to examine how attention to the political use of numbers in the realm of refugee assistance is about much more than the often-heard stories about host country governments and "inflated refugee numbers". He shows that the reverse situation sometimes occurs, with under-reporting explained either as a result of diplomatic niceties and a "wish to avoid antagonizing each other" or as a way to discourage "military reprisals from the country of origin" (Crisp, 1999, p. 10). Bearing this in mind and shifting our focus to the politics of piracy numbers, is there perhaps a case for devoting more analytical attention to the issue of under-reporting. What politics would become visible if we were to explore in more detail which cases go unreported and why – notably where this is not only due to lack of awareness that an incident took place. Are there overlooked cases actually showing the contrary, i.e., over-reporting?[14]

The politics of "missing" piracy numbers: What is not counted?

After briefly introducing the "politics of numbers" as an analytical lens that brings forth often-overlooked aspects of piracy and other types of maritime crime, this section focuses on the regional case study of the GoG. It argues that besides the prioritisation of piracy over other forms of maritime crime reporting, another type of number gap is equally important:[15] in contrast to the numerous and highly visible counting of piracy incidents at sea, there is little publicly available information on the onshore dimension of this phenomenon.

The politics of missing onshore numbers: Pirate groups

Numerous sources indicate that "kidnapped crewmembers are normally taken ashore in the Niger Delta region where KFR groups demand ransom payments in exchange for the safe return of the crewmembers" (US Department of Transportation, 2021; see also Jacobsen, 2021). Yet, little published knowledge can be found about various important onshore dimensions of GoG piracy, including for example Kingpins and pirate groups operating out of Nigeria's Niger Delta region, but also the broader webs and enabling structures within which these actors operate on land. Maritime security experts hold different views on the actual number of such groups. Some interviewees estimated that 15 pirate groups "currently terrorize the waters" of the GoG,[16] while for others the numbers were significantly lower.[17] Still others question the usefulness of the notion of "pirate group", pointing to the fluidity of these loose structures, and to how individuals may become involved in different types of illicit activity alongside piracy, both at sea and on land.[18]

Crucially, disagreements exist and unconfirmed stories and rumours[19] often fill the gap in reliable publicly available information about onshore aspects of GoG piracy, including the number of pirate groups based in the Niger Delta. By contrast, in Somalia, pirate groups were "counted" even when piracy was at an all-time low after NATO declared its fight against piracy a success and ended its mission in the region. For instance, "two main Pirate Action Groups (PAGs) [were] still active in Somalia," though they were "not exclusively engaged in piracy," at that point in time (Jacobsen & Carrasco, 2018). One PAG was "run by Issa Yuluh and Aragoste, who profited greatly from past hijackings", and another was "run by Garfanje out of Hobyo in Galmudug" (Jacobsen & Carrasco, 2018). Although several incidents continue to take place in the GoG region little publicly available data exists about similar onshore dimensions of GoG pirate groups.

The politics of missing onshore numbers: Complicity

As noted, missing numbers are not always synonymous with lack of knowledge, but may sometimes be a result of politics, i.e., when making certain numbers invisible serves the pursuit of specific objectives of key actors. Numbers indicating the size of the "collusion economy" that seems closely adjacent to the GoG piracy business is another example of "missing numbers". Pointing in this direction are accounts about the benefits gained by different Nigerian authorities from their invisible involvements in the crimes (piracy and illegal oil refinery) that they are meant to fight. Only very few reports, however, thoroughly address this issue.

Already in 2012, critical scholars argued that actors involved in oil bunkering "must pay a fee to the Navy and have to "settle" (bribe) the local communities to have access to oil theft opportunities" and to ensure that they "are not disturbed by a naval presence" (Pérouse de Montclos, 2012, pp. 534–535).[20] A more recent report, published by Transparency International in 2019, similarly argues that in some cases "benefit comes from providing 'protection' – both ensuring military, security forces and other officials turn a blind eye to illegal activity and protecting oil thieves' access to extraction points from rivals – in exchange for financial bribes". Zooming into Nigeria's Joint Task Force (JTF), the report further notes that "there have been indications that some JTF members are complicit in, and often benefit from, precisely the pursuit they are mandated to eradicate: the illicit oil industry" (Transparency International, 2019).

Also highlighting these onshore challenges, Østensen, et al. (2018) revealed that "the Joint Task Force and the Navy, the two main law-enforcement bodies tasked with combating oil theft, were themselves heavily involved in facilitating medium- and largescale illegal bunkering". Likewise, a report published by the Stakeholder Democracy Network (2015, p. 5) showed that "rogue actors within the JTF actively participate in and profit from theft and illegal refining". Under the heading "official complicity", a Chatham House report also described examples of collusion between officials and the pirates whose business they were supposed to disrupt. The authors note that "security and oil company sources report having seen ships engaged in oil theft pass freely through maritime checkpoints, in full view of military patrols" (Katsouris & Sayne, 2013, p. 5). More than turning a blind eye, JTF officers were reportedly seen "standing guard at illegal tap points and providing armed escort to ships loaded with stolen crude" (Katsouris & Sayne, 2013, p. 5).

Furthermore, most of the training in anti-corruption and good governance in Nigeria was of "limited value" in addressing this often-overlooked dimension of GoG piracy. While the issue has been briefly covered in the past by a handful of reports, detailed knowledge about onshore collusion structures is still largely missing; moreover, the onshore dimensions of the piracy business have not been the main focus of counter-piracy engagements up until now.[21] Whilst research on onshore enabling structures is often limited to the topic of piracy and oil bunkering in Nigeria, the value of an analytical lens that attends to missing figures (also concerning on-shore collusion structures) goes beyond these limitations – and can shed light into other GoG states as well as other types of maritime insecurity.

Beyond continuity: Ballooning effects and missing category

The second part of this analysis takes the "politics of numbers" framing as an invitation to look more closely at incident reporting and seeming continuity in overall levels of GoG piracy. At least two changes become visible by doing so. The first change is the shifts in the offshore geography of GoG piracy. The second change that is commonly overseen by incident reporting is what this chapter refers to as "inter-crime attacks", with incidents reported as piracy attacks likely being linked to other types of criminal activity (Siebels, 2021).

Double offshore ballooning

Piracy continues to remain a threat to maritime security in the GoG region, despite numerous efforts seeking to address the problem. Yet, at the same time, GoG piracy has changed over the course of these years, shifting from "petro-piracy" to kidnap-for-ransom piracy. Adding to this, pirates operating in the GoG have more recently proven capable of adapting to the changing security environment, e.g., to counter-piracy measures put in place. I describe this below via the term "ballooning effects", which has also been used to depict similar tendencies in the case of Somali piracy (Jacobsen, 2018; Jacobsen & Carrasco, 2018). As used here, ballooning refers to the risk that law enforcement activities targeting piracy along a particular route may cause a relocation of criminal business to other geographical spaces, rather than addressing the issue.[22] Focusing exclusively on overall statistics may result in insufficient attention to such ballooning effects within the GoG region.

a   Geographical ballooning: Outside Nigerian water

The birds-eye image of statistical continuity comes at the expense of overlooking important geographical changes. For example, "recent attacks show that pirates are [...] moving their operations to where easy targets can be found" (Oceans Beyond Piracy, 2018). What we have seen more recently can be described as geographical ballooning, with GoG pirates increasingly operating outside Nigerian waters. As noted by the US Maritime Administration authority: "During the first half of 2020, pirates and armed robbers operated off at least eight countries in the Gulf of Guinea (Nigeria, Benin, Cameroon, Equatorial Guinea, Ivory Coast, Ghana, Togo and Gabon)." Within Cameroonian waters, six incidents were recorded between January and June 2020.[23] In Benin, an attack in July 2020 represented "the seventh reported incident off

The Politics of Piracy Numbers

Cotonou so far this year [2020]."[24] When compared to Nigeria, pirate attacks are far more "unusual off the Gabonese coast". Yet, in May 2020, two fishing vessels were attacked near Libreville, and prior to that, two attacks were reported in December 2019. In Togo, attacks were also reported in December 2019, with 20 Indian crew kidnapped (Al Jazeera, 2019). Interestingly, the Indian authorities took up the issue with Nigerian authorities,[25] which suggests that, even when kidnappings occur beyond Nigerian waters, such attacks are perpetrated by Nigeria-based pirate groups. The maritime security consultancy Dryad Global similarly assessed that "perpetrators of the most serious incidents likely come from Nigeria," and further corroborating this, various sources indicate that "pretty much all hostages are released in the Niger Delta."[26]

Such "ballooning" of piracy incidents beyond Nigerian waters is caused by a combination of factors, including increased security measures adopted by states and industry alike. Furthermore, one interviewee noted that several GoG states are now handling more cargo than before, with port traffic increasing and ships spending longer time at anchor, which makes them more vulnerable to attack.[27] Indeed, recent attacks show that pirates are following the merchant traffic and moving their operations to "soft spots" where easy targets can be found. By June 2020, more incidents were taking place outside of Nigerian waters than within (28 and 45, respectively), a trend observed since November 2019.[28] Yet, at the same time and as we shall see below, there is a risk that such observations might be based to some extent on incident reporting that may not represent "genuine" piracy attacks.

b   Geographical ballooning: Further offshore

In addition to attacks moving beyond Nigerian water, another trend is that incidents occur increasingly further from the coastline (Jacobsen, 2021). Security experts argue that various "security means deployed by vessels when in Nigeria waters" contribute to reducing the likelihood of a successful pirate attack. However, rather than reducing piracy incidents, this and other factors seem to have "pushed pirate's group to continue to look for easy targets [...] very deep offshore." Several examples illustrate this, among them is the attack on DAVIDE B in March 2021) which occurred more than 210 nm south of Benin.[29] Other sources similarly note "an increase in deep offshore incidents" (Dryad Global, 2020). Taken together, these two ballooning effects highlight how important nuances become visible once we dig deeper into statistics and numbers that at a first glance portray a picture of continuity.

"Hidden" incident type

Other nuances that incident reporting risks overlooking are a) an increase in the number of hostages per incident, and b) a type of incident, which differs from both kidnap-for-ransom piracy, petty theft, and oil theft.

a   Steady number of kidnap and ransom (K&R) incidents, but more individuals being kidnapped

For some time now, we have witnessed a shift in the modus operandi of GoG piracy. Following the drop-in oil prices, illicit activities shifted away from theft of oil products to increasingly focusing on kidnap for ransom attacks (Jacobsen, 2021; Kamal-Deen, 2020). Moreover, even if the number of reported K&R incidents has been somewhat steady (with 16 kidnapping cases in the first half of 2020 largely corresponding to the number of kidnappings for the same period in

2019), a closer look at individual cases reveals an important change: the number of kidnapped individuals per pirate attack has increased. While during the first half of 2019, 62 people were abducted by pirates, this number reached 98 for the same period in 2020. In other words, GoG pirates are now capable of capturing more hostages per incident.[30] This might reveal a certain level of confidence on the part of the pirate groups in the low risk of encountering law enforcement officials to disrupt their kidnapping business (Jacobsen, 2021). Moreover, there are also indications of a shift in the type of vessel being targeted by pirates. One interviewee noted that "it would seem that at least, one pirate group decided to aim fishing boats as a sweet target".[31] It is thus important to look beyond numbers and take into account the significance of onshore dimensions of GoG piracy.

b   Piracy's many faces – Adding a new category

GoG-piracy has many faces. Besides kidnap for ransom piracy, other related aspects are a) large-scale theft of oil products, and b) "petty theft" (Jacobsen & Nordby, 2015), with "petty thieves" operating around Lagos anchorage[32] but also in other countries across the region.[33] Yet, these petty criminals do not have the "operational sophistication of the pirate rings" (Akinsola, 2015, p. 5). Indeed, scholars have categorised piracy in different ways (e.g., Hastings, 2012; Peters, 2020). Adding to these efforts, this chapter suggests that by paying careful and critical attention to numbers and incident reporting, more facets of GoG-piracy can be uncovered beyond those suggested by current categorisations and incident reporting. A common theme across reported incidents is that not all incidents may be "genuine" piracy attacks. Instead, some seem more connected to what this chapter terms "inter-crime rivalry" an emerging incident type with "product tankers and fishing vessels seemingly involved in other types of maritime crime, now being targeted" and reported as piracy.[34] Put differently, some of the incidents that are counted as "piracy" may be better understood as a different type of incident, with a distinct type of risk profile vis-à-vis international shipping. Such incidents differ not only in the "threat" profile but also in the type of countermeasures required. Thus, one blind spot that calls for further exploration (rather than continued mislabelling) is the question of the type of attacks being counted as "piracy". An example pointing in this direction is a recent news story about how what "seemed to be just another opportunistic ransom kidnapping" turned out to be linked to "a disagreement between two criminal groups" (Ponniah, 2020). In May 2020, the Nigerian navy "publicly accused the tanker company of being involved in the transport of stolen crude oil from the Niger Delta to Ghana", and according to the Nigerian navy, the attack and the kidnapping were provoked by a dispute between rivalling criminal groups (Ponniah, 2020). Adding to this, one interviewee noted that there were cases of "product tankers being targeted that are clearly involved in dodgy activities, and the same is true for fishing vessels like those targeted off Gabon". Another interviewee mentioned cases of "pirates" attacking a ship involved in oil bunkering transfers, with the likely aim of getting hold of the huge amount of cash stored on ships involved in these activities.[35] Finally, another interviewee explained how attacks sometimes relate to the "amount of cash" involved in a particular business practices surrounding IUU fishery, referred to locally as "saiko" (i.e., when local fishers buy "trashed fish" from vessels conducting IUU fishery).[36]

While none of these statements offers solid evidence, they nevertheless draw the contours of one or more incident types that remain hidden in current reporting, which in turn illustrates the relevance of attending to the politics of missing numbers when analysing a complex and evolving phenomenon such as GoG piracy. That politics infuses the way "piracy" is defined should come as no surprise. This matter was also debated when attention was directed at piracy off the coast of Somalia.[37] Yet, the question of what eludes categorisations and how this affects our appreciation of complex phenomena is a question that requires renewed attention for each context, as well as over time. The politics of missing numbers offers a lens that attends to precisely these kinds of questions and sensitivities, and will thus be relevant for analysing other aspects of the maritime insecurity complexes in the GoG.

Conclusion

It is both a virtue and a vice that piracy numbers and empirics are valuable in and of themselves, not only for policy and industry, but also when filling knowledge gaps about a phenomenon with dimensions that are still under-studied. It is a virtue that many empirical findings concerning GoG piracy often receive attention in scholarly and practitioners' circles. Yet, at the same, this interest in research that uncovers new empirical dimensions may risk becoming a vice if critical attention to questions about the broader significance of these empirics slide into the background (Jacobsen & Larsen, 2019). The literature on "the politics of numbers" (Andreas & Greenhill, 2010) provides a useful framework for analysing GoG piracy, revealing important changes, such as "ballooning effects" like piracy moving beyond Nigerian waters, an increasing focus on kidnap for ransom attacks, and a growing number of individuals kidnapped per incident. These and other crucial nuances – like the emergence of "inter-crime" attacks – risk being lost if current studies remain confined to the logic of overall statistics and unquestioned reporting numbers and categories.

This initial analysis of "the politics of piracy numbers" is certainly not meant as an exhaustive list of topics when exploring GoG piracy. Instead, the aim of this chapter was to illustrate how these mechanisms can help guide analytical attention to questions that are not simply about numbers, but also about the politics of missing empirics and the politics of sources and categories that these numbers are based on. New questions emerged from this analysis, such as to which extent counter-piracy efforts are bound to remain at the periphery of the problem if these gaps in knowledge and missing numbers remain invisible, or how current counting reinforces a focus on GoG piracy that only address the top of an iceberg, whose depths actually starts and ends on land.

Notes

1 According to UNCLOS, piracy refers to incidents – "illegal acts of violence or detention, or any act of depredation [...] against a ship" – "on the high seas," which differ from incidents that occur in territorial waters, referred to as "armed robbery at sea" (United Nations, Division for Ocean Affairs and the Law of the Sea, 2010).
2 See Kamal-Deen, 2020; Jacobsen, 2021.
3 Angola: 6; Benin: 11; Equatorial Guinea: 3; Gabon: 2; Ghana: 9; Guinea: 5; Ivory Coast: 3; Liberia: 2; Nigeria: 35; Sao Tome & Principe: 2; The Congo: 3: Togo: 3 (GoG) + Mozambique: 4 (IMB, 2020, p. 6).
4 MICA Center, 2020.
5 Adding to these reporting differences, recent figures presented by the Nigerian Navy accentuate the discussion of "true" piracy numbers. In February 2021, former Nigerian Chief of Navy staff reported that between 2015 and 2020, 214 piracy attacks had been recorded in Nigerian waters plus an additional 107 incidents of sea robbery. Even if broken down into estimated annual figures, these piracy numbers by far exceed those reported by IMB and MICA.
6 Indicative of the maritime challenges beyond piracy are for example various recent news about cocaine seizures (Reuters, 2021).
7 Mangan and Nowak (2019).

8 This was also highlighted during interviews with an intentionally diverse array of actors – from the Captain on a Navy ship used for maritime capacity-building, to managers of large donor-funded programmes and regional maritime security experts.

9 Anonymous interview with two senior project managers of a large external institution funding various maritime capacity- building projects in the GoG region. Skype, December 2020. This further corresponds to participant observation made during a large, recurring meeting of donors and regional actors in the GoG, 2019.

10 GoGIN Watch (2019).

11 Anonymous interview with capacity-building practitioner based in Abuja, Nigeria, and with many years of field experience from capacity-building projects in various GoG states. Skype, November 2020.

12 Anonymous interview with capacity-building programme manager, managing projects in Nigeria, Ghana, and at regional level, October 2020.

13 Anonymous interview with capacity-building practitioner based in Abuja, Nigeria, and with many years of field experience from capacity-building projects in various GoG states. Skype, November 2020.

14 Occasionally, Nigeria has complained about over-reporting, and adding to that are current debates about the recently expanded "Listed Area" by the Joint War Committee, in September 2020. With this decision, the insurance industry expanded the area where additional premiums can be charged, based on reporting and numbers showing an apparent spread of incidents. Though partly true, this chapter at the same time uses the "politics of numbers" lens to show how not all reported incidents may be "genuine" piracy attacks.

15 An exception to this is "Pirates of the Niger Delta", which explicitly focuses on various onshore dimensions of Niger Delta-based piracy (Jacobsen, 2021).

16 https://shippingwatch.com/carriers/article12695802.ece

17 See Jacobsen, 2021.

18 Anonymous interview with maritime security and risks analysis expert, October 2020.

19 See Sandor (2020) on the role of rumours in neighbouring Sahel.

20 See also Hastings and Phillips (2015).

21 The more recent shift from oil theft to kidnap for ransom, further aggravates this knowledge gap insofar as past reports on "collusion" have focused mainly on this issue in relation to oil theft and illegal refinery, not on collusion structures related to kidnap for ransom piracy.

22 There is a rich literature on this, which unfortunately I am not able to unfold in this chapter. Please see: Jacobsen, 2018.

23 In some cases, responded to in an objectionably heavy-handed manner. Cameroun's BIR maritime patrol is for example reported to have "killed 6 [suspected] sea pirates on board their speed boat in the creeks SW Bakassi Peninsula".

24 On 24 June 2020, the PANOFI FRONTIER was attacked by several gunmen on board a speedboat. After a successful boarding, the pirates left the vessel with six crew members.

25 "Our Mission in Abuja has taken up the matter with the Nigerian authorities, as also with the authorities of the neighbouring countries", the ministry said in a statement (Al Jazeera, 2019).

26 The Maritime Executive, 2020.

27 Anonymous interview with maritime security and risks analysis expert, October 2020.

28 Anonymous interview with maritime security and intelligence expert, June 2020.

29 Safety4Sea, 2021.

30 IMB, 2020.

31 Anonymous interview with maritime security analyst, August 2020.

32 I.e., "low-level maritime security incidents, such as robberies" (Dryad Global, 2020).

33 Anonymous interview with maritime security and intelligence expert, June 2020.

34 Anonymous interview with maritime security and risks analysis expert, October 2020.

35 Anonymous interview made with regional maritime security expert based in Ghana, December 2020.

36 Anonymous interview with regional maritime security expert, October 2020.

37 As an interviewee note: "for the HOA it is almost impossible to internationally agree on reporting categories." One example of this is when IMO created a definition of piracy as occurring within the territorial waters, since the UNCLOS definition does not cover that.

References

Akinsola, J. (2015). *Lethal Violence Offshore in Nigeria.* IFRA Nigeria Working Papers Series, No.51 WP2Jimoh.pdf (nigeriawatch.org).

Al Jazeera. (2019, December 17). *India Says 20 Crew Kidnapped from Tanker off Togo.* https://www.aljazeera.com/news/2019/12/17/india-says-20-crew-kidnapped-from-tanker-off-togo

Andreas, P., & Greenhill, K. M. (Eds.). (2010). *Sex, Drugs, and Body Counts: The Politics of Numbers in Global Crime and Conflict.* Cornell University Press.

Crisp, J. (1999). "Who has counted the refugees?" UNHCR and the politics of numbers. *New Issues in Refugee Research*, Working Paper No. 12. UNHCR. https://www.unhcr.org/research/working/3ae6a0c22/counted-refugees-unhcr-politics-numbers-jeff-crisp.html

Dryad Global. (2020, July 15). The impact of piracy in West Africa with Dryad Global. https://www.ship-technology.com/features/impact-piracy-west-africa-dryad-global/

GoGIN Watch. (2019, July 1). G7++ group of friends of the Gulf of Guinea meets in Brussels. *GoGIN. The Gulf of Guinea Inter-regional Network.* https://www.gogin.eu/en/2019/07/01/g7-group-of-friends-of-the-gulf-of-guinea-meets-in-brussels/

Hastings, J. V. (2012). Understanding maritime piracy syndicate operations. *Security Studies, 21*(4), 683–721.

Hastings, J. V., & Phillips, S. G. (2015). Maritime piracy business networks and institutions in Africa. *African Affairs, 114*(457), 555–576.

IMB. (2020). *Annual Piracy Report 2020.* https://www.icc-ccs.org/reports/2020_Annual_Piracy_Report.pdf

Jacobsen, K. L. (2017). Maritime security and capacity building in the Gulf of Guinea: On comprehensiveness, gaps, and security priorities. *African Security Review, 26*(3), 237–256.

Jacobsen, K. L. (2018). Poly-criminal pirates and ballooning effects: Implications for international counterpiracy. *Global Policy, 10*(1), 52–59.

Jacobsen, K. L. (2021). *Pirates of the Niger Delta.* UNODC Report. https://www.unodc.org/res/piracy/index_html/UNODC_GMCP_Pirates_of_the_Niger_Delta_between_brown_and_blue_waters.pdf

Jacobsen, K. L., & Carrasco, J. (2018). *Navigating Changing Currents: A Forward-Looking Evaluation of Efforts to Tackle Maritime Crime off the Horn of Africa.* Centre for Military Studies, University of Copenhagen.

Jacobsen, K. L., & Larsen, J. (2019). Piracy studies coming of age: a window on the making of maritime intervention actors. *International Affairs, 95*(5), 1037–1054. https://doi.org/10.1093/ia/iiz099

Jacobsen, K. L., & Nordby, J. R. (2015). *Maritime Security in the Gulf of Guinea.* Royal Danish Defence College Publishing House.

Jimoh, A. (2015). *Maritime Piracy and Lethal Violence Offshore in Nigeria.* IFRA-Nigeria Working Papers Series, no. 51. http://www.nigeriawatch.org/media/html/WP2Jimoh.pdf

Kamal-Deen, A. (2020). Gulf of Guinea piracy: The old, the new and the dark shades. *CEMLAWS Africa, 2*(1), 1–20.

Katsouris, C., & Sayne, A. (2013). *Nigeria's Criminal Crude: International Options to Combat the Export of Stolen Oil.* Chatham House Report. https://www.chathamhouse.org/sites/default/files/public/Research/Africa/0913pr_nigeriaoil.pdf

Lombardo, N. (2014). *Underreporting of Crimes at Sea. Reasons, Consequences, and Potential Solutions.* Oceans Beyond Piracy, Discussion Paper. https://oneearthfuture.org/research-analysis/underreporting-crimes-sea-reasons-consequences-and-potential-solutions

Mangan, F., & Nowak, M. (2019). *The West Africa- Sahel Connection. Mapping Cross-border Arms Trafficking.* Small Arms Survey Briefing Paper. http://www.smallarmssurvey.org/fileadmin/docs/T-Briefing-Papers/SAS-BP-West-Africa-Sahel-Connection.pdf

MICA Center. (2020). *Biannual Report.* https://www.mica-center.org/download/Bilan_annuel_MICA_CENTER_2020.pdf

Oceans Beyond Piracy. (2018). *The State of Maritime Piracy 2017.* https://oceansbeyondpiracy.org/reports/sop/west-africa

Okafor-Yarwood, I. (2019). Illegal, unreported and unregulated fishing, and the complexities of the sustainable development goals (SDGs) for countries in the Gulf of Guinea. *Marine Policy, 99*, 414–422.

Okafor-Yarwood, I., Walker, T., & Reva, D. (2021). *Gulf of Guinea Piracy: A Symptom, Not a Cause, of Insecurity.* ISS. https://issafrica.org/iss-today/gulf-of-guinea-piracy-a-symptom-not-a-cause-of-insecurity

Østensen, A. G., Brady, S., & Schütte, S. A. (2018). *Capacity Building for the Nigerian Navy: Eyes Wide Shut on Corruption?* U4 Anti-Corruption Resource Centre. Chr. Michelsen, U4 Issue 4. https://www.u4.no/publications/capacity-building-for-the-nigerian-navy-eyes-wide-shut-on-corruption

Pérouse de Montclos, M. A. (2012). Maritime piracy in Nigeria: Old wine in new bottles? *Studies in Conflict and Terrorism, 35*(7–8), 531–541.

Peters, B. C. (2020). Nigerian piracy: Articulating business models using crime script analysis. *International Journal of Law, Crime and Justice, 62*, 1–17. https://doi.org/10.1016/j.ijlcj.2020.100410.

Pichon, E. (2019, March 19). *Piracy and Armed Robbery off the Coast of Africa: EU and Global Impact.* EPRS in-depth analysis. https://www.europarl.europa.eu/thinktank/en/document.html?reference=EPRS_IDA(2019)635590

Ponniah, K. (2020, May 10). *The Day the Pirates Came.* BBC News. https://www.bbc.com/news/world-asia-52295222

Reuters. (2021, February 26). *Ivory Coast Gendarmes Seize Record Haul of Cocaine.* https://www.reuters.com/article/us-ivorycoast-drugs-idUSKBN2AQ0OS

Safety4Sea. (2021, March 12). *15 Crew Kidnapped from Tanker off Benin.* https://safety4sea.com/15-crew-kidnapped-from-tanker-off-benin/?__cf_chl_jschl_tk__=pmd_PR3RTTk.zsJTnpAbqDpVMUFtMzqa1tljEP.BF478Cw4-1631436696-0-gqNtZGzNAfujcnBszQgl

Sandor, A. (2020). The power of rumour(s) in international interventions: MINUSMA's management of Mali's rumour mill. *International Affairs, 96*(4), 913–934.

Siebels, D. (2021, January 26). *Attacks at Sea Aren't All Linked to Piracy. Why It's Important to Unpick What's What.* The Conversation. https://theconversation.com/attacks-at-sea-arent-all-linked-to-piracy-why-its-important-to-unpick-whats-what-153591

Sow, M. (2018). *Figures of the Week: Piracy Increasing in the Gulf of Guinea.* Brookings Series Africa in Focus. https://www.brookings.edu/blog/africa-in-focus/2018/08/02/figures-of-the-week-piracy-increasing-in-the-gulf-of-guinea/

Stakeholder Democracy Network. (2015). Communities not Criminals. Illegal oil Refining in the Niger Delta. CommunitiesNotCriminals.pdf (stakeholderdemocracy.org).

Suchman, L. (2020). Algorithmic warfare and the reinvention of accuracy. *Critical Studies on Security, 8*(2), 175–187.

The Maritime Executive. (2020, July 27). *Nigerian Pirates Release Kidnapped S. Korean Fishermen.* https://www.maritime-executive.com/article/nigerian-pirates-release-kidnapped-s-korean-fishermen

Transparency International. (2019). Military Involvement in Oil Theft in the Niger Delta. Discussion paper, June 2019. https://ti-defence.org/wp-content/uploads/2019/05/Military-Involvement-Oil-Theft-Niger-Delta_WEB.pdf

United Nations, Division for Ocean Affairs and the Law of the Sea. (2010, September 9). Legal Framework for the Repression of Piracy Under UNCLOS. Retrieved June 15, 2021 from https://www.un.org/Depts/los/piracy/piracy_legal_framework.htm

US Department of Transportation. (2021). Gulf of Guinea-Piracy/Armed Robbery/Kidnapping for Ransom. Retrieved June 15, 2021, from https://www.maritime.dot.gov/msci/2021-002-gulf-guinea-piracyarmed-robberykidnapping-ransom

Van Veeren, E. (2018). Invisibility. In R. Bleiker (Ed.). *Visual Global Politics* (pp. 196–200). Routledge.

12

VISUAL REPRESENTATIONS OF THE SEA

Claire Sutherland

Maritime security is a contested concept but conjures a sense of threat that needs to be addressed and controlled. It is instructive, therefore, to consider some of the visual representations that have conveyed that sense of threat over time and sought to project control over the seas. While maritime security has come to greater prominence since the attacks on the World Trade Centre in New York on 11 September 2001, naval seapower and the management of maritime trade and the environment are certainly not new. Western colonialism was key to the establishment and enforcement of maritime security networks. Across the Pacific, for example, sixteenth-century Spain, Portugal and the Netherlands "sought to create mercantile monopolies via military bases and pacts with local rulers rather than significant territorial control" (Douglas, 2018, p. 132).

Today, maritime security can encompass everything from the so-called blue economy, involving shipping, smuggling and pollution, through maritime resource management, to state seapower, including the European Union (EU) and its member states' controversial "modes of political abandonment" regarding seaborne migration across the Mediterranean (Vaughan-Williams, 2015, p. 12). Despite differences in international organisations' and other security actors' strategic understandings of maritime security, "the importance of maritime power projection" (Bueger, 2015, p. 160) clearly has not waned across the centuries, and can be traced through visual representations of the sea. As testament to human hubris, images of marine life choking on plastic waste and rubbish bobbing on warming oceans provide poignant evidence of the impact and insufficiencies of ocean governance in the age of the Anthropocene.

The chapter shows that visual representations of the sea often depict it as an accessory to human endeavour, to be crossed or exploited, but that other representations of the sea's own materiality exist. Addressing themes of colonial cartography, nationality, materiality and migration in turn, it first discusses how the sea became a site of human heroism, conquest and overcoming fear of the unknown. The chapter then shows how the sea is often "flattened" into a two-dimensional, geometric space, thereby losing any sense of its material fluidity in favour of a focus on its strategic uses. It explores maritime representations, which are often constitutive of and fundamentally "Other" to national imaginings, before looking at how the sea can be a nationalist accessory but also a source of unease, both literally and figuratively. The discussion contrasts the maritime "space as it is perceived or lived [with] the abstractions of the mapmaker" (Padrón, 2014, p. 211). Abstract, cartographic modernity has made claims to universality, often drowning out alternative visions, but as this chapter concludes, artistic representations of the sea

DOI: 10.4324/9781003001324-14

139

nonetheless have strong potential to subvert colonially inflected nationalist imaginings and make us think critically about the power projections underpinning maritime security constructs.

Colonial Cartography

An understanding of the colonial antecedents of maritime security helps inform "analysis of the political process by which threats are constructed and issues are lifted on the security agenda" (Bueger, 2015, p. 160). Visual representations and celebrations of economic, scientific and military mastery of the seas, encapsulated in the imperial conceit of "Britannia rule the waves", served to consolidate both European colonialism and nationalism in the nineteenth and twentieth centuries. As Miles Ogborn (2008, p. 7) shows, every chapter in England and then Britain's modern history involved the sea:

> Elizabethan England's forays into trade, empire and colonialism; settlement in early North America; trade with the East Indies; trade in the Atlantic world; the organisation of maritime labour; the changing forms of piracy; the transatlantic slave trade; plantation slavery in the Caribbean; the movement to abolish the slave trade; and the voyages of "discovery" in the Pacific Ocean.

When explorers like James Cook encountered the "native seas" (Salesa, cited in Douglas, 2018, p. 131) of Pacific Islanders, European "discovery" of one of the last areas on earth to be comprehensively mapped went hand in hand with its Euroamerican colonisation and control. Maritime maps are often segmented into exclusive economic zones and criss-crossed by shipping lanes which, in some cases, are overlaid on an iconography of ancient seafaring, but Pacific islanders' nautical charts offer an alternative visual mapping of the sea which effectively renders it in terms of movement and flux.

Medieval European *mappae mundi* were the work "of ecclesiastical mapmakers more interested in orienting the soul toward heaven than in directing the body through the physical world" (Padrón, 2014, p. 211). Stylised seas and oceans featured in depictions centred around Jerusalem or biblical figures. Similarly, Thongchai Winichakul (1994) discusses a late eighteenth-century Siamese map of Southeast Asia that combines a territorial representation of the region with symbolic elements from Buddhist cosmography. Here, the sea represented a spiritual connection between two "incorrectly" situated countries, as shown by two sages travelling across it. Thongchai (1994, p. 26) argues that the "artist deliberately put the map into a larger framework of description [...] For the artist and his audience, it correctly signifies the genesis of local Buddhism".

The "positive emptiness" (Padrón, 2014, p. 212) of the sea, as opposed to a blank zone beyond human knowledge, emerged with the development of European geometric maps from the beginning of the sixteenth century. At the same time, the decorative practice of filling seascapes on the margins of maps with monsters, serpents and other mythological creatures testifies to the ongoing connotations of the seas with a sense of dread, even as they were being progressively charted and explored (Galata Museo del Mare, 2015, pp. 10–11). As Natalie Klein (2011, p. 2) notes in her discussion of maritime security and the law of the sea, security "may be seen as an emotive term, extending to a sense of safety and hence freedom from fear". Visual representations of the sea are often a projection of those human hopes and fears. Cartography is thus more closely bound up with the cultural and political significance of ocean journeys than the materiality of the sea itself. For example, Carla Lois (2014, p. 29) traces the process by which the Atlantic Ocean was reimagined as a vertical axis, or "backbone" of the Western world as a consequence of European colonialism, when it had previously been depicted in a variety of more peripheral forms. Now the dominant depiction of the world, based on the sixteenth century Mercator projection, this was the origin of Western-centric imaginaries and "ontological imperialism" (Levinas, cited in Jackson, 1995, p. 87). As such, it provided an initial basis for a range of "legislative, executive, judicial, military and police actions – designed to respond to a collective need for order and protection from internal and external threats" (Klein, 2011, p. 2) that would eventually come to be associated with maritime security.

Nautical charts are navigational aids, which themselves need not always conform to the principles of geometric mapping. Chinese seafarers, for example, who traded across what is now known as the South China Sea for many centuries before the age of European imperialism, developed coastal charts reproducing landmarks along a straight line, to be read from right to left (Thongchai, 1994, p. 30). These itinerary maps find a parallel in late medieval Mediterranean "portolan charts" produced with the aid of a compass, and then further refined into the grid-patterned maps that accompanied European navigators as they sought to find routes through the oceans. This can be understood as the beginning of a controlling or "taming" process, at a time when "the spaciousness and tracklessness of the sea is an object of dread" (Padrón, 2014, p. 233). Mapping the seas was part of the colonial mindset of expansion, settlement, trade and one means among many of exerting control (Smith, 2014, pp. 266–267). As such, it contributed to a European aesthetics of subjugation and the maintenance of a national "imagined community" (Anderson, 1991). In the early seventeenth century, for example, the Dutch were acknowledged as the preeminent cartographers in Europe at around the same time as their colonial conquests reached their apogee (Schmidt, 2014). This dominance also extended to the arts.

The Dutch golden age of painting included many seascapes reflecting their leading role in maritime trade at the time. Subjects ranged from historical scenes to depictions of naval battles, complete with very detailed renderings of ships and a corresponding fascination with ship-wrecks (Thompson, 2014). As such, visual representations of the sea both projected national glories and told cautionary morality tales to guard audiences against courting disaster (Scott, 2014, p. 168; Thompson, 2014, p. 134). Interest in marine art waxed and waned with European colonial countries' conquests and naval warfare, and was combined with a taste for the picturesque. For example, the late eighteenth and early nineteenth panoramic views of the newly settled British colony of Sydney cove in Australia displayed an "aesthetic with great appeal to a maritime people, a social order whose empire depended on control of the seas" (Smith, 2014, p. 275). These coastal scenes were deliberately painted to resemble English views, to encourage a sense of familiarity and promote emigration. By the 1920s, British ocean liners were plying routes visually marketed as "Highways of Empire" (Cusack, 2014, p. 5).

Historical maps continue to play a part in power politics, including some of today's most prominent and intractable maritime security conflicts. For example, they feature in the long-running dispute between the People's Republic of China (PRC) and Vietnam, among other Southeast Asian states, over control of the South China Sea. Vietnam has laid out its credentials as a "sea-oriented" nation (Roszko, 2015) with long-standing cultural and trading links to the seas, in order to underpin its claim to the Paracel and Spratly islands and the natural resources found around these rocky outcrops. Part of Vietnam's strategy has been to mount frequent exhibitions of historic maps to substantiate its narrative. For example, a temporary exhibition held in the central Vietnamese town of Da Nang in 2017 displayed a series of maps in the local museum foyer, with captions in Vietnamese, English and Mandarin suggesting its target audiences. The English language label on a reproduction of a European map dated 1613 and titled *India Orientalis* states "The coast of Central Vietnam facing these archipelagos was named as *Costa de Pracel*. This proves that the author of this map recognised the close ties between

Vietnam's territory and Pracel (It then included both the Paracel and Spratly Archipelagos)". The exhibition also displays twentieth-century U.S. maps of the PRC stretching only as far south as its undisputed territory of Hainan Island, truncating the rest of the South China Sea. Again, the accompanying captions suggest that the South China Sea should not be considered Chinese. By contrast, one of the watermarks on PRC passports features a map including the so-called "nine dash line" that delineates its claim to most of the South China Sea. These conflicting visual representations show polarised and highly politicised perspectives that project notions of bounded territorial sovereignty onto the seas. This is a key feature of state maritime security strategies that seek exclusive control over marine resources and maritime trade routes (Klein, 2011, p. 3). However, not all maps render the sea in this way.

One alternative cartography of the sea is the stick charts produced by Marshall Islanders in the Pacific Ocean. They are nautical representations of the sea itself, with its different wave patterns and swells, and were always intended to be teaching aids rather than used on board (Romm, 2015; Langlois, 2016). Together with hours spent blindfolded in canoes learning to feel the motion beneath them, these charts helped budding seafarers understand the sea, not in relation to atolls that are so low-lying as to be often invisible on the horizon, but on its own terms: "Instead of going landmark to landmark, you go seamark to seamark" (Genz cited in Brown, 2019, online). In this sense, these charts stand perhaps in starkest contrast to cartographies that aim to capture the sea measurably and relationally within a geometric framework. They diverge from the conventional focus by placing the sea and its currents at the centre, with small cowrie shells to pinpoint land. Unlike nautical charts made to be unfurled and consulted at sea, these abstract, subjective renderings needed to be explained by an experienced mariner. As such, they upend many prevailing assumptions around nautical charts and Eurocentric perspectives on maritime cartography more generally.

Epeli Hau'ofa (1993, pp. 7-8) contrasts how Pacific islanders "played in [the sea] as soon as they could walk steadily, they worked in it, they fought on it. They developed great skills for navigating their waters" to "Europeans and Americans, who drew imaginary lines across the sea, making the colonial boundaries that, for the first time, confined ocean peoples to tiny spaces". To take another example, the boat-dwelling peoples commonly known as sea nomads who live on South-East Asia's seas challenge the very idea of belonging to a territorially bounded nation-state (Chou, 2012). Their vision of the South-East Asian region is of a borderless world delimited only by the extent of their maritime mobility, with different eras of colonial and postcolonial control washing over but not effacing their alternative world view. This points to a different understanding of *mare liberum* (Klein, 2011, p. 2) to the colonial mindset, which considered the seas a space to be mastered and managed, rather than an entity to be respected and enjoyed as part of a maritime way of life. Conceptions of maritime security arguably continue to display a tendency to carve up the sea according to state interests and perceived threats that are more redolent of the former conception. In British maritime museums, for example, post-imperial imaginings still prevail.

Maritime Nationality

Maritime museums are the corollary to the aquarium; they tend to represent human stories relating to the sea rather than the life of the sea itself (Sutherland, 2017). This institutional separation already does much to distance maritime museums from the sea's materiality and fluidity. For example, boats are quite often exhibited without any visual or textual reference to the actual waters in which they sailed. Despite their association with the sea, then, national maritime museums largely project the spatiotemporal framing of the nation onto their specialist

Visual Representations of the Sea

subject. That is, they are a corollary of maritime security frameworks in that they often reproduce territorial understandings of conflict and control, rather than adopting a seaborne perspective. For example, exhibits on naval battles and local fisheries primarily reflect national politics and economics. It is therefore instructive to consider how even maritime museums mirror state-centric perspectives, as a way of critically challenging how maritime security maps state concerns onto the sea, rather than necessarily displaying concern for the sea.

Maritime museums located in ports connect primarily to the human activity that starts from the harbourside. Harbours are linked most often to fishing, trade and exploration and sometimes to sport, recreation and tourism. In turn, most of these activities are framed in the national mode. For example, a national fishing fleet, sportspeople representing their country, national naval exploits, especially in wartime, and seafarers expanding colonies and commerce in the name of their national sponsors all come under the standard purview of maritime museums. That is, the sea is still often represented today as an accessory to human endeavour, and national maritime museums play an important part in maintaining the "imagined community" of the nation (Anderson, 1991). Similarly, maritime security is closely bound up with human security, but this is frequently filtered through a national security lens. As such, maritime museums can be likened to a political landscape in miniature, reflecting evolving national identities and relationships to history in the stories they choose to tell.

Australia's National Maritime Museums in Sydney and Perth, for example, were conceived as part of larger national celebrations, namely the bicentenary of Australia's European settlement and millennium celebrations, respectively. Although the Sydney Museum marked the bicentenary, it was not subject to the same public debates and controversy as Canberra's National Museum of Australia (Taylor, 2012). Instead, it appeared to fit less prominently but no less powerfully into a conventional linear chronology of "'natural' progression: from aboriginal landscape to colonial port, to booming nineteenth-century docklands then finally to a redundant industrial wasteland" (Burns cited in Taylor, 2012, p. 403). The aboriginal relationship to the sea appeared to be downplayed overall, relegated to a closed off section in the Perth Museum that suggests ongoing marginalisation as opposed to integration into the museum's aim of "defining Australia" (Taylor, 2012, p. 409) through its social history, its material culture and its role in European navigation and colonisation. It is not hard to see how attention to Aboriginal cosmography would destabilise a fundamentally Western-centric national perspective primarily focused on land and territorial property, when Aboriginal "dreaming paths" continue from land to sea and combine spiritual, cultural and material sustenance in ways that the rest of Australian society still finds hard to understand. Jackson (1995, p. 94, emphasis in original) notes the coining of awareness-raising terms like sea–country and

> *salt-water* country as an analogy with the well-established relationship and sense of belonging indigenous people have to the land and the role of land as the source of origin and spirituality with that of the sea, thus conveying Aboriginal concepts of the sea to non-indigenous Australians.

The United Kingdom's National Maritime Museum in Greenwich is reinterpreting its collections in response to current debates around the legacy of Empire for British belonging. It also nods to the materiality of the sea in some of its newest galleries, opened in 2018. For example, an exhibit entitled *Sea Things* invites visitors to "Explore objects, share stories, find your connection to the sea", set against a filmed backdrop of gently lapping blue water. This may be intended to shift visitors' perspectives on Britain as well as themselves, since the exhibit notes that "over 6,000 islands make up the British Isles". Another recently installed exhibit entitled *Pacific Encounters* opens strikingly with a large wooden wave curling over visitors' heads. However, the materiality of the sea soon recedes into a more conventional historical account of exploration, exploitation and tradition focused on the British-Pacific Island nexus, though it does make some effort to include Pacific Islanders' perspectives and interrogate colonial representations. Nevertheless, other permanent exhibits such as *Nelson, Navy, Nation* indicate that national heroes and histories are still very much a part of the museum's visual representations of the sea. Similarly, a huge Mercator map of the world covers the floor of the central atrium, with the land coloured green, the seas in blue and Europe at the centre.

As is to be expected of a British national museum, conventional cartography dominates, thereby missing an opportunity to encourage visitors to think differently about their view of Britain in the world. What is more, the Mercator map is overlooked by four statues of late eighteenth and early nineteenth naval commanders captioned "Monuments for the nation". Lest we forget, the accompanying information panel notes that when "they were made, Britain's navy was the largest and most powerful in the world: its past achievements were a source of national pride and its great fighting commanders were widely recognized". The colonial context underpinning their exploits is not addressed, other than to evoke a spirit of adventure; "To join the Navy was quite literally an opportunity to see the world". Some correctives to this can be discerned, however. The life-size, full-length portraits of local community members who worked with the museum on its new gallery interpretation, and who represent a diversity of organisations and voices, are placed near the naval statues, presumably to offset these and signal the museum's attempt to be more inclusive (National Maritime Museum Greenwich, no date). Elsewhere in the museum, the gallery on the East India Company offers an unvarnished view of its impact on India and the Opium Wars with China. Nevertheless, the sea itself is not centre stage. Rather, the museum offers another angle on the national imaginary, with the sea employed as a sort of mirror image to reflect the industrial and imperial glory of Britain's maritime history.

The tone of the Scottish Maritime Museum in the west coast town of Irvine near Glasgow is similarly celebratory, but with a different emphasis. Instead of naval exploits, it focuses on Scotland's contribution to the shipbuilding, commerce, engineering and invention that made imperial Britain the workshop of the world. The museum adopts an overarching narrative of "enterprise culture" (Taylor, 2012, p. 412) characterised by seafaring as a symbol of mobility, change and exchange, focusing on the working-class industrial heritage of shipbuilding in Glasgow and on the river Clyde, while barely sketching out the imperial endeavour that it fuelled. The museum is located on a coastal estuary, but the sea seems far removed from the industrial machinery and small pleasure boats on display in the museum's vast space, itself a nineteenth-century engine works dismantled and moved to the site. According to an exhibition panel, Glasgow's access to the Atlantic "started a pattern of progress which saw Glasgow rise from a provincial town to become the second city of the British Empire". Yet the colonial context of its commercial success is barely touched upon, whereas the visual impact of much hulking, obsolete heavy machinery is very strong.

In both Greenwich and Irvine's maritime museums, the materiality of the sea itself is hard to fathom. Even in the Greenwich exhibition entitled *Atlantic Worlds*, which traces slavery, trade and migration across three continents against a black and white backdrop of roiling waves, the focus is on "the movement of people, goods and ideas across and around the Atlantic Ocean from the seventeenth to the nineteenth century". That is, the Atlantic connotes the "positive emptiness" (Padrón, 2014, p. 212) of the sea, ready to be inhabited by human experience, rather than the sea itself. In his book of the same name, Paul Gilroy (1993, p. 4) used the term *Black Atlantic* to denote the "fractal structure of a transcultural, international formation" that

Visual Representations of the Sea

could transcend U.S. and British national boundaries to connect black cultural studies across them. This could be used to frame the remaking of identity that enslaved Africans like Olaudah Equiano endured on crossing "the liminal space of the Atlantic" (Cusack, 2014, p. 5) in the eighteenth century, for example, even though Africa "sits mostly silent" in Gilroy's analysis (Shilliam, 2015, p. 10). Conversely, nineteenth-century black Americans like Frederick Douglass experienced greater freedom on crossing the Atlantic to Europe, as did the native American Oglala Lakota Chief Red Shirt, who was living on an Indian Reservation.

Emily Burns (2014, p. 41) suggests that *The Atlantic Storm* (1876) by John Singer Sargent, an expatriate American born in Florence who did not visit the United States until he was 20, captures some of the emotional (as well as physical) turmoil these men endured on their sea-crossings. In a departure from his usual portraiture, Sargent's focus on the ocean swells themselves suggests an alternative visualisation of the sea with its own analytical potential. In an extension to their work on *Wet Ontology* (Steinberg and Peters 2015), Kim Peters and Phil Steinberg (2019) adopt the concept of Hypersea to capture the relationship of co-dependence between air, water, earth and life. A possible parallel and a radical departure from state-centric conceptions would be an inclusive and cooperative understanding of maritime security that foregrounds the needs of the sea itself.

The nineteenth-century English artist J.M.W. Turner's many seascapes also reflect an artistic preoccupation with the sea's materiality. Turner increasingly engaged with the power and majesty of the sea itself as his career progressed. His late works became increasingly abstract and impressionistic, as "the anonymous, unrelenting churn of the sea became the focus of deep self-reflection" (Johns, 2013, online). Although famous and feted in his own time, Turner's con-temporaries did not appreciate such maritime representations, for in "Western Picturesque terms, the ocean was thought too featureless to form a view" (Cusack, 2014, p. 4). Nevertheless, the French artist Gustave Courbet was also fascinated by the sea itself and painted a large series of wave studies from 1865 to 1870 that sought to convey their intensity and power using thickly applied paint. The paintings echo the well-known Japanese print *the Great Wave off Kanagawa* by Katsushika Hokusai, who himself drew on both Japanese and European, specifically Dutch, influences. All of these depictions foreground the sea and act as a reminder today that dwindling fish stocks, pollution and plastic waste blight its beauty. Maritime security will struggle to get to grips with the sustainability and security of the sea itself until it becomes sea-centric, as opposed to state-centric. Contemporary artists have also used the sea's materiality to draw attention to the plight of migrants, who are defined as such by the very nation-state borders that national maritime museums work to uphold.

Migration and Materiality

This chapter has shown how the sea has always been a cipher for danger and the unknown. For example, recovered silver coins from the ancient Mediterranean Phoenician civilisation depict their ships sailing alongside a sea monster known to the Ancient Greeks as a hippocamp, a winged creature with a horse's head and a fish's body (Abulafia, 2011). These monsters em-bodied the dangers of navigation, but also the projection of fears of the unknown and horrific events, a tradition that can be traced through to popular film culture with the success of Ishirō Honda's 1954 film *Godzilla* and Steven Spielberg's 1975 blockbuster *Jaws* (Galata Museo del Mare, 2015, p. 47). This tension was captured in Genoa Maritime Museum's 2015 exhibition entitled *Mare Monstrum*, a play on the Mediterranean's Latin name, *mare nostrum* ("our sea"). Billed as an exploration of how the sea is both admired and feared, it ranged from depictions of giant sea monsters, such as the squid-like Kraken – which also features in the dioramas of its permanent exhibition – to tracing the genesis of contemporary fears conjured by migrants crossing the Mediterranean. The exhibition confronted the racialisation of those fears by tracing "Othering" at sea, from the horrors of slave ships to the frequent and continuing loss of black migrants' lives at sea.

Nick Vaughan-Williams (2015, p. 12) has pointed to securitisation "situations in which some 'irregular' migrants are endangered precisely by the authorities associated with humanitarian border security" in the Mediterranean. At sea as on land, the language of crisis is frequently used to assert national or European interests over those of migrants (De Genova et al., 2016). Reversing this approach to maritime security would mean that "the mobility of people is reinterpreted as ontologically prior to any attempts by border security authorities to control them" (Vaughan-Williams, 2015, p. 8; see also Brubaker, 2015, p. 132; Sutherland, 2019). The slogan used by Mediterranean migrants and their allies "We are here because you were there" (cited in De Genova et al., 2016), encapsulates the postcolonial legacy underlying the security situation in the Mediterranean, one that reached "crisis point" in the summer of 2015 but has yet to be resolved.

Artists and critics alike have sought to use visual representations of the sea to draw attention to the ongoing, frequent deaths of migrants and refugees crossing the Mediterranean in overcrowded craft (Stierl, 2016). For example, the critic Jonathan Jones (2015) drew parallels between Théodore Géricault's *Raft of the Medusa*, painted in 1818 to show the scandalous abandonment of shipwrecked passengers off the coast of Africa, and migrants at the mercy of unseaworthy vessels today. Similarly, Turner's 1840 masterpiece *Slave Ship (slavers throwing overboard the dead and dying: typhoon coming on)* depicted a captain's murderous jettisoning of slaves to collect insurance money in 1781, set against the lowering red skies of nature's fury. Barely seaworthy cargo vessels nicknamed "coffin ships" also transported Irish famine victims to the 'New World' in the 1840s, losing an average of one in five on route (Cusack, 2014, p. 6).

Géricault's painting was unusual for the time in focusing on the suffering of "the socially and racially marginalised" as blameless victims (Scott, 2014, p. 170). Géricault reportedly travelled from Paris to Normandy to study the sea and the sky, and the unrelentingly sombre tones of the painting help to convey the desperation and danger his subjects faced; "Standing before it you feel the sea surge towards you. In this disturbing experience of looking, the anguish of the people on the raft becomes vivid and immediate. We are there beside them" (Jones, 2015). What is striking about this quote is the distancing use of the word "we" at the same time as urging empathy and compassion with this image of suffering, and by extension that of modern-day migrants crossing the Mediterranean. Like the seaborne perspective discussed in the previous section, the painting evokes an alternative way of seeing the sea that is not centred on state interests or EU border security. A parallel could be drawn with the so-called "grief activism" that sought to stand in solidarity with Mediterranean migrants and against the predominant securitisation discourse (Stierl, 2016).

Jonathan Jones (2015) is presumably using the pronoun "we" to refer to the left-leaning, liberal British readers of the *Guardian* newspaper for which he was writing, but the pronoun rather counter-productively serves to limit any solidarity those readers might feel, evoking a politics of pity instead. Solidarity can be defined as a principle "that leads to the establishment of a community of interest" in pursuit of what is right or good, as opposed to a politics of pity that emanates from hierarchies of power and fundamental inequality (Cheah, 2014, p. 79). Contemporary artists continue to use water, both physically and on film, to try to engage the viewer in the experience of being a migrant, and the waters of the Mediterranean have become a frequent reference point for artists and scholars commenting on the European Union's so-called refugee "crisis" (De Genova, 2017; Sutherland, 2017, p. 52). What is more, water's

Visual Representations of the Sea

fluidity and changeability offers an excellent medium for thinking through *Wet Ontology* (Steinberg & Peters, 2015) as an alternative to state-centric politics and international relations, not least maritime security itself.

Philip Steinberg and Kim Peters (2015, p. 250) define wet ontology as "a perspective that problematises accepted notions of time, space, mobility and materiality". Far from fetishising fluidity, wet ontology can be used as a different means of thinking identity and belonging through mobility, as opposed to the static, bounded basis of the nation-state. It offers an explicit counterpoint to the "ontological imperialism" cited at the outset of this chapter (Levinas, cited in Jackson, 1995, p. 87). Such an approach is particularly well-adapted to capturing migrant "statuses that are temporary, uncertain and non-linear", and thus go beyond the simplistic binaries of citizen and foreigner, and legal or illegal immigrants (Gonzales & Sigona, 2017, p. 7; see also Hepworth, 2015; Ni Mhurchu, 2014). In this instance, the sea is not simply the mirror image of territorial sovereignty, trade and conquest and the national interests these reflect, as is frequently envisioned in maritime security. Rather, the materiality and fluidity of the sea itself can be used as visual challenges to simplistic dichotomies of self and other, native and migrant, us and them that evoke not pity, but solidarity. As Nguyễn-Võ (2018, p. 346) notes in the context of the American civil rights movement and the Vietnam War, such an approach does not take part in the "co-optation of abject forms of existence and their 'diverse' expressions in culture but is an act of radical re-examination of how we think, speak, write, or even make revolution predicated on the joint social location of people of colour". For example, wet ontology can be used as a basis to refuse national identities implicitly or explicitly imagined as ethnically exclusive in their calls for unity and community. The artworks in the "Disappearance at Sea" exhibition demonstrate one way of visually representing this approach in practice.

The temporary art exhibition entitled "Disappearance at Sea-Mare Nostrum", held at the Baltic Art Gallery in Newcastle upon Tyne, North-East England, from 27th January to 14th May 2017, brought together fourteen works of art by a range of artists to draw attention to the humanitarian disaster continuing to unfold in the Mediterranean. What was particularly arresting about the exhibition was the darkened main room, which offered an immersive experience that recalled being under water. This was heightened by the fact that four of the five artworks in the space were large-screen video installations filmed on or under water, so that the visitor felt completely surrounded by the medium. For example, Hrair Sarkissian's film entitled *Horizon* (2016) invited viewers to imagine themselves as migrants about to embark on a boat plying the short Mycale strait between Turkey and Greece, and to cross the sea from their perspective. According to the artist, this work "evokes the danger of being surrounded by water, showing the dark and mysterious depths of the sea, and its unpredictability" (Sarkissian, 2016, online). Similarly, Nikolaj Bendix Skyum Larsen's work entitled *End of Dreams* (2015) also evoked bodies at the mercy of the sea, much like Géricault's *Raft of the Medusa* created two centuries before.

As a reflection on the many refugees and migrants drowning in the Mediterranean, Larsen submerged wrapped, corpse-like concrete sculptures in the sea to "acquire a patina of sea organisms" (Larsen, 2015, online). This was a variation on an earlier work entitled *Ode to the Perished* (2011). However, a storm unexpectedly ripped the sculptures from their moorings and they were variously sunk, washed ashore, or lost. From the artist's viewpoint, the "intervention of nature brought the process of the work's production even closer to the feelings of trauma and peril he was trying to express" (Larsen, 2015, online). He photographed the lacerations on the pieces he could retrieve and in 2015 created an installation in Rome, which completely surrounded the visitor with five large-screen videos of underwater scenes and sculptures strewn across the floor. The video of the submerged forms exhibited in Newcastle was one element of this larger piece and was shown alongside Larsen's *Reflections from Meriç* (2013). This work consisted of a four-minute video, again focused exclusively on footage of water, and accompanied by a voiceover chronicling the frequent deaths of migrants trying to "defy the forces of nature" by crossing a river bordering Greece and Turkey. Collectively, these pieces commented on the materiality of water as a dangerous medium that is impossible for human bodies to control completely, echoing the sense of dread associated with the sea that has continued down the ages.

Part of the fourth water-based work in the Baltic exhibition, Jackie Karuti's *There are Worlds out There They Never Told You About* (2016), used water itself as a medium, in the form of paper boats bobbing across a map of the world on a water-filled plinth. In an interview with the artist, Neo Musangi (2016, online) frames Karuti's work in terms of the relationship "of human imagination to linear temporalities and spatial limitations." In her own commentary, Karuti (cited in Musangi, 2016, online) states that "the work also hints at migration, displacement, and the idea of home and what that means". All these are issues we talk about on a daily basis in the "real" world. At the same time, Karuti sees her work as encouraging people to imagine alternative homes and alternative ways of being and seeing. What links this assemblage of works is their use of the materiality of water to comment on mobility, and migrant mobility in particular, across taken-for-granted national borders. This section has argued that these artistic expressions chime with attempts to use the constantly churning materiality of seas and oceans themselves as an alternative starting point for theory-building (Peters & Steinberg 2019).

Conclusion

"Mapping maritime security" (Bueger, 2015, p. 163) conceptually is a complex and contested undertaking. A focus on visual representations of the sea serves to highlight some of the entrenched assumptions underlying depictions of the maritime space, that in turn help to unpack some of maritime security's conceptual connotations. This chapter has shown how the sea is variously depicted as a marginal or liminal space-dependent for its meaning on human crossing and control, a reflection of land-based national imaginaries, and a potential site of solidarity with migrants who seek to cross constructed nation-state boundaries. Different representations of the sea thus have significant implications for how maritime security and ocean governance are understood and performed.

The section on colonial cartography explored the origins of "ontological imperialism" (Levinas, cited in Jackson, 1995, p. 87) and the perceptions of threat and fear that extended to the very concept of *mare liberum* itself (Klein, 2011, p. 2). The thought of the sea as a wild and untamed space was considered inherently deficient by those explorers and colonisers who sought to bring it under control by capturing it cartographically and criss-crossing it empirically with shipping lanes ferrying migrants and trading cargo, including human cargo. These ships made Empires real, and the evolving parameters of state control, such as illegal smuggling set against legitimate maritime trade, represent the antecedents of maritime security principles today. At the same time, there have always been other ways of imagining and representing the sea that do not conform to two-dimensional cartography and Mercator projections, suggesting that maritime security could always be reimagined to be less state-centric and more inclusive and cooperative (Klein, 2011, p. 3).

The section on maritime nationality argued that maritime museums contribute to representations of the sea as both constitutive of and fundamentally "Other" to many national imaginings. This offers thought-provoking parallels as to how maritime security may connect with the legacy of colonialism in latent, unacknowledged ways, and how it might be reimagined to foreground the security of the sea itself. In a climate emergency created by the

Anthropocene, this would seem an urgent and necessary endeavour. Dominant cartographies of land and sea require a "sea-change" (Kelly, 1998, p. 853) in conventional understandings of political space – and by extension maritime security – in order to escape their colonial connotations with the development of Western imperialism, control and subjugation.

The section on migration and materiality offered one possible means of transcending conventional conceptions of maritime security by focusing on the very materiality of the sea. Wet Ontology (Steinberg & Peters, 2015) and its elaboration (Peters & Steinberg, 2019) offer ways of reimagining and reinterpreting maritime security around the security of the sea itself, rather than that of the states controlling and exploiting it to the point of planetary exhaustion. At the same time, visual representations of the sea which seek to capture its materiality can bring the viewer closer to empathising with the migrant experience, while refusing dichotomies of "us" and "them" and the hierarchies of power these often entail. The contemporary artists discussed above are rising to that challenge by engaging with the materiality of the sea itself and the experiences of "Others" embarking on treacherous waters in fear and desperation. Like the sea monsters of old, Mediterranean migrants seem to embody a deep-seated fear of the unknown that must be confronted in order to be understood and overcome. Similarly, maritime security's connections to these fundamental fears and perceptions must be acknowledged, critiqued and if possible overcome. Visual representations of the sea offer one starting point for this political project.

References

Abulafia, D. (2011). *The Great Sea: A Human History of the Mediterranean*. Penguin.

Anderson, B. (1991). *Imagined Communities: Reflections on the Origin and Spread of Nationalism*. Verso.

Brown, M. (2019). Marshall islands stick chart. *Archaeology*. May/June. https://www.archaeology.org/issues/338-features/maps/7551-maps-marshall-islands-stick-chart

Brubaker, R. (2015). *Grounds for Difference*. Harvard University Press.

Bueger, C. (2015). What is maritime security? *Marine Policy, 53*, 159–164.

Burns, E. (2014). The old world anew: The Atlantic as the liminal site of expectations. In T. Cusack (Ed.), *Framing the Ocean: 1700 to the Present. Envisaging the Sea as a Social Space* (pp. 37–54). Ashgate.

Cheah, P. (2014). "The world is watching": The mediatic structure of cosmopolitanism. In L. Chouliaraki & B. Blaagaard (Eds.), *Cosmopolitanism and the New News Media* (pp. 72–82). Routledge.

Chou, C. (2012). *The Orang SukuLaut of Riau, Indonesia: The Inalienable Gift of Territory*. Routledge.

Cusack, T. (2014). Introduction: Framing the ocean, 1700 to the present: Envisaging the sea as social space. In T. Cusack (Ed.), *Framing the Ocean: 1700 to the Present. Envisaging the Sea as a Social Space* (pp. 1–20). Ashgate.

De Genova, N. (2017). Introduction. The borders of "Europe" and the European question. In N. de Genova (Ed.), *The Borders of "Europe": Autonomy of Migration, Tactics of Bordering*. Duke University Press.

De Genova, N., Fontanari, E., Picozza, F., Soto Bermant, L., Spathopoulou, A., Stierl, M., Suffee, Z., Tazzioli, M., Van Baar, H. & Yildiz, C. (2016). "Migrant crisis"/"refugee crisis" in New Keywords Collective.(Ed.), *New Keywords of "the Crisis" in and of "Europe"*. http://nearfuturesonline.org/europecrisisnew-keywords-of-crisis-in-and-of-europe-part-3/

Douglas, B. (2018). Imagined futures in the past: Empire, place, race, and nation in themapping of Oceania. In W. Anderson, M. Johnson & B. Brookes, (Eds.), *Pacific Futures: Past and Present* (pp. 131–156). University of Hawaii Press.

Galata Museo del Mare. (2015). *Mare Monstrum: L'immaginario del mare trameraviglia e paura*. Il Geko.

Gilroy, P. (1993). *The Black Atlantic*. Harvard University Press.

Gonzales, R., & Sigona, N. (2017). Mapping the soft border of citizenship: An Introduction. In N. Sigona (Ed.), *Within and Beyond Citizenship. Borders, Membership and Belonging* (pp. 1–16). Routledge.

Hau'ofa, E. (1993). Our sea of islands. In V. Naidu, E. Waddell & E. Hau'ofa (Eds.), *A New Oceania: Rediscovering Our Sea of Islands*. University of the South Pacific.

Hepworth, K. (2015). *At the Edges of Citizenship*. Ashgate.

Jackson, S. (1995). The water is not empty: Cross-cultural issues in conceptualising sea space. *Australian Geographer, 26*(1), 87–96.

Johns, R. (2013, November 15). JMW turner: Master of the ocean. *The Guardian*. https://www.theguardian.com/artanddesign/2013/nov/15/jmw-turner-sea-paintings-national-maritime

Jones, J. (2015, August 11). The 200-year-old painting that puts Europe's fear of migrants to shame. *The Guardian*. https://www.theguardian.com/artanddesign/jonathanjonesblog/2015/aug/11/the-200-year-old-painting-that-puts-europes-fear-of-migrants-to-shame

Kelly, J. (1998). Time and the global: Against the homogeneous, empty communities in contemporary social theory. *Development and Change, 29*, 839–871.

Klein, N. (2011). *Maritime Security and the Law of the Sea*. Oxford University Press.

Langlois, K. (2016, February 2). Science and tradition are resurrecting the lost art of wave piloting. *Smithsonian Magazine*. https://www.smithsonianmag.com/arts-culture/science-and-tradition-are-resurrecting-lost-art-wave-piloting-180958005/

Larsen, N. (2015). End of dreams. *Nikolaj Bendix Skyum Larsen*. https://www.nbsl.info/end-of-dreams-image

Lois, C. (2014). From *Mare Tenebrorum* to Atlantic Ocean: A cartographical biography (1470-1900). In T. Cusack (Ed.), *Framing the Ocean: 1700 to the Present. Envisaging the Sea as a Social Space* (pp. 23–36). Ashgate.

Musangi, N. (2016). Interview, Jackie Karuti: There are worlds out there they never told you about. *Contemporary And (C&)*. https://www.contemporaryand.com/magazines/there-are-worlds-out-there-they-never-told-you-about/

National Maritime Museum Greenwich. (no date). *Creating a More Inclusive Museum*. https://www.rmg.co.uk/sites/default/files/creating%20a%20more%20inclusive%20museum.pdf

Nguyễn-Võ, T.-H. (2018). Articulated sorrows: Intercolonial imaginings and the national singular. *Canadian Review of American Studies, 48*(3), 327–351.

Ni Mhurchu, A. (2014). *Ambiguous Citizenship in an Age of Global Migration*. Edinburgh University Press.

Ogborn, M. (2008). *Global Lives: Britain and the World 1550–1800*. Cambridge University Press.

Padrón, R. (2014). Mapping plus ultra: Cartography, space, and hispanic modernity. In M. Jay & S. Ramaswamy (Eds.), *Empires of Vision: A Reader* (pp. 211–245). Duke University Press.

Peters, K., & Steinberg, P. (2019). The ocean in excess: Towards a *more-than-wet* ontology. *Dialogues in Human Geography, 9*(3), 293–307.

Romm, C. (2015, January 26). How Sticks and shell charts became a sophisticated system for navigation. *Smithsonian Magazine*. https://www.smithsonianmag.com/smithsonian-institution/how-sticks-and-shell-charts-became-sophisticated-system-navigation-180954018/

Roszko, E. (2015). Maritime territorialisation as performance of sovereignty and nationhood in the South China Sea. *Nations and Nationalism, 21*(2), 230–249.

Sarkissian, H. (2016). "Horizon". http://hrairsarkissian.com/work/horizon/

Schmidt, B. (2014). Mapping an exotic world: The global project of Dutch geography, circa 1700. In M. Jay & S. Ramaswamy (Eds.), *Empires of Vision: A Reader* (pp. 246–266). Duke University Press.

Scott, Y. (2014). Reconstructing the Raft; Semiotics and memory in the art of the shipwreck and the raft. In T. Cusack (Ed.), *Framing the Ocean: 1700 to the Present. Envisaging the Sea as a Social Space* (pp. 165–180). Ashgate.

Shilliam, R. (2015). *The Black Pacific*. Bloomsbury.

Smith, T. (2014). Visual Regimes of Colonization: European and Aboriginal seeing in Australia. In M. Jay & S. Ramaswamy (Eds.), *Empires of Vision: A Reader* (pp. 267–280). Duke University Press.

Steinberg, P. & Peters, K. (2015). Wet ontologies, fluid spaces: Giving depth to volume through oceanic thinking. *Environment and Planning D, 33*(2), 247–264.

Stierl, M. (2016). Contestations in death – The role of grief in migration struggles. *Citizenship Studies, 20*(2), 173–191.

Sutherland, C. (2017). *Reimagining the Nation; Togetherness, Belonging and Mobility*. Policy Press.

Sutherland, C. (2019). Stop the clock! Taking the nation out of linear time and bounded space. *Time and Society* (online first). 29(3), 727–749. 10.1177/0961463X19873792

Taylor, W. (2012). Bound by sea and pressed for time: Geographical and transient dimensions of seafaring heritage in two Australian maritime museums. *International Journal of Heritage Studies, 18*(4), 400–417.

Thompson, C. (2014). Shipwrecks, mutineers, and cannibals: Maritime mythology the political unconscious in eighteenth-century Britain. In T. Cusack (Ed.), *Framing the Ocean: 1700 to the Present. Envisaging the Sea as a Social Space* (pp. 133–148). Ashgate.

Thongchai, W. (1994). *Siam Mapped: A History of the Geo-Body of a Nation*. University of Hawaii Press.

Vaughan-Williams, N. (2015). *Europe's Border Crisis: Biopolitical Security and Beyond*. Oxford University Press.

PART II

Practices and Norms of Maritime Security

PART II

Nature and Norms of Maritime Security

13

HUMAN RIGHTS AND LAW ENFORCEMENT AT SEA

Anna Petrig

Introduction

Despite the controversy and uncertainty surrounding the concept of "maritime security", the elevated position of transnational crime at sea among contemporary maritime security threats can hardly be overlooked. Quite naturally then, maritime law enforcement is key to ensuring safe and unimpeded navigation on the seas and oceans. Yet, similar to policing on dry land, enforcement of the law in the maritime environment is an activity disposed to interfering with the human rights of those upon whom enforcement measures are imposed, not least because it may involve coercion and sometimes even the use of (deadly) force. The linkage between maritime security, transnational crime at sea, maritime law enforcement and human rights is thus patently obvious.

However, until rather recently, safeguards and limitations constraining at-sea enforcement has not received a great deal of scrutiny – neither in doctrine nor in practice. This is hardly surprising if we consider the idiosyncrasies of the two legal bodies that primarily govern policing in the maritime domain: the law of the sea and international human rights law (IHRL). The law of the sea, where we find the relevant authorisations to counter transnational crimes amounting to maritime security challenges, is in large part "human rights blind" and only exceptionally and rather erratically limits enforcement powers exercised at sea. IHRL, in turn, which is supposed to fill the gaps left by the law of the sea, has until recently suffered from a serious "seablindess".

As a result of this unfortunate combination, the analysis of the legal protection of persons subject to enforcement measures at sea remained unexplored until roughly a decade ago. Interestingly enough, it was the first truly international maritime law enforcement operation – the various counter-piracy missions off the coast of Somalia, the first of which was deployed in 2008 – that finally brought momentum to the discussion. They turned a spotlight on the looming, but also actual, human rights violations occurring in the course of policing operations at sea. With this, legal analyses of maritime law enforcement through a human rights lens began to flourish, and various states and international organisations started harbouring a practical interest in the issue. At the same time, however, the very characteristics of these operations pose considerable, but generally not insurmountable, challenges to the application of IHRL – many of which have not yet been sufficiently scrutinised from both a theoretical and operational point of view.

DOI: 10.4324/9781003001324-16

153

The linkage between maritime security and human rights

The term "maritime security" has acquired firm footing in the vocabulary of persons and institutions dealing with the seas and oceans. Yet, despite being widely used, there is little agreement over its exact meaning (Boşilcă et al., 2022). Indeed, definitions of the concept are actor, context and region-specific: they are reflective of the interests of those crafting them and shaped by the purpose behind their adoption as well as the circumstances prevailing in a given area at a given time (Klein, 2011). Not only is there no agreed definition of what "maritime security" is, but even the definitional approaches differ considerably and notably span from positive to negative conceptualisations of the term. The former approach "projects a certain ideal-typical end state that has to be reached" (Bueger, 2015, p. 159); in this vein, legal doctrine has defined maritime security, for instance, as "a stable order of the oceans subject to the rule of law at sea" (Kraska & Pedrozo, 2013, p. 1). By contrast, the negative conceptualisation of the term rests on an understanding of maritime security as the absence of specific threats. It is usually complemented and further specified by a list of threats deemed to amount to security challenges at sea – hence, the origin of the term "laundry list" approach (Bueger, 2015, p. 159).

Regarding the specific threats enumerated in these "laundry lists", it is noteworthy that Till's observation that "the phrase 'maritime security' comprehends so much" (Till, 1996, p. 5) has not lost in currency despite being 25 years old. Maritime security continues to be "an inclusive term of uncertain boundaries" (Klein et al., 2020, p. 729) even today. However, it is equally true that – despite the many variations – virtually every contemporary definition of maritime security comprises one type of threat: transnational crimes committed at sea. Indeed, the very consolidation and mounting popularity of the concept of maritime security is intrinsically linked to "incidences of breaking the law" (Percy, 2018, p. 610): while the term first emerged in the 1990s, it came into the public's view following a spate of terrorist attacks against vessels occurring in the wake of 9/11, before definitely entering the common vocabulary with the rise of Somali-based piracy after 2006 (Boşilcă et al., 2021). Today, transnational crimes at sea – despite being referred to as "unconventional" security challenges (Percy, 2018, p. 607) – occupy a central place in the maritime security framework. They usually complement more "conventional" challenges gravitating around, *inter alia*, territorial integrity, freedom of navigation and access to resources (Percy, 2018).

From the finding that transnational crime ranks very high among contemporary challenges to a stable order of the oceans, it is only a further small step to conclude that law enforcement constitutes a "critical tool" in the quest to ensure maritime security (Sonnenberg, 2012, p. 10). Indeed, given that these unconventional menaces are "criminal in nature or linked to criminals", they "are most appropriately addressed by law enforcement" (Sonnenberg, 2012, p. 11). While the term "maritime law enforcement" is not defined in positive international law, doctrine offers various definitions. Quite instructive is the one by Wilson, according to whom maritime law enforcement "refers to customs, police, or other law enforcement action that seeks to detect, suppress, and/or punish violations of law in the maritime environment" (Wilson, 2016, p. 244). Equally useful is the definition by Tondini (2017), who suggests that the concept indicates "all police-type operations conducted by warships and other state-owned vessels against criminal, or otherwise prohibited, activities at sea", which "implies the interception of merchant vessels with the purpose of subjecting them to the control of the intercepting vessel's flag state and possibly imposing criminal or administrative sanctions" (Tondini, 2017, p. 254).

The latter definition already insinuates the specific measures that may be taken in the course of maritime law enforcement operations. First of all, given the vastness of the maritime commons and the resulting anonymity, the detection and localisation of illegal conduct at sea often hinges on the gathering of intelligence and sharing of information between relevant actors (Klein, 2010). If a ship suspected of engaging in criminal conduct is ultimately identified, potential measures against it may include its stopping, boarding and searching at sea or diversion to a port or other place for inspection and further investigation. Moreover, a vessel used for the commission of a crime, as well as illicit cargo and crime paraphernalia found on board, may potentially be seized and destroyed or disposed of in another way (e.g., sold). Persons on board who are suspected of engaging in illegal activity, in turn, may be searched, interrogated, arrested and detained and, if suspicion hardens, transferred for prosecution to the land territory of the seizing state or to a third state (Guilfoyle, 2009; Klein, 2011; Papastavridis, 2013). The taking of these and further enforcement measures is only lawful if it can be based on a relevant legal authorisation, which are *inter alia* conferred by treaties – such as the UNCLOS or suppression conventions dealing with specific transnational crimes – and United Nations Security Council resolutions (McLaughlin, 2016).

From this broad-brush overview accrues that maritime law enforcement is – similar to other forms of policing – a "highly interventionist process" (McLaughlin, 2016, p. 467). Indeed, the enforcement measures just depicted are vertically imposed by the seizing state, meaning that coercion and, as a last resort, (deadly) force may be used in cases of non-compliance. From this plainly follows that the interests and values protected by IHRL may be at stake: life, physical integrity, liberty, security, privacy and property – to name but a few. As per Batsalas (2014), human rights may be affected in all phases that a law enforcement operation at sea generally involves. Prior to interdiction, intelligence, surveillance and reconnaissance activities must be considered in light of the right to private life. When gaining access to a ship, specifically in cases of opposed boarding, the right to life and physical integrity may be at stake. Finally, upon boarding – when the ship and its cargo is searched, and persons interrogated and possibly even arrested and ultimately transferred for prosecution – yet another set of rights may attach, notably the right to liberty, various procedural safeguards and the prohibition of *refoulement*. If the cargo and/or the vessel is destroyed or disposed of in another way, the right to property is at stake (Batsalas, 2014). It is against this backdrop that Article 2 of the UN Code of Conduct for Law Enforcement Officials stipulates that "[i]n the performance of their duty, law enforcement officials shall respect and protect human dignity and maintain and uphold the human rights of all persons". However, as we will see next, the law of the sea, which authorises enforcement action at sea, is certainly not a body of law imbued with the idea of IHRL. At the same time, the concept of human rights was not firmly moored in the maritime security framework until recently as a result of the "seablindness" from which it long suffered.

The "human rights blindness" of the law of the sea

In an ideal world, legal instruments authorising enforcement measures at sea would include a detailed and comprehensive list of safeguards, which specify and thus operationalise abstract human rights norms for policing activity in the maritime domain. Moreover, these safeguards would be framed as rights belonging to persons directly or indirectly affected by at-sea enforcement measures. The reality though is a different story.

The primary reference point in terms of (enforcement) jurisdiction at sea is the UNCLOS. The UNCLOS negotiations extended from 1973 to 1982 (Rosenne & Gebhard, 2008) – and what may appear to be an impressive time span is put in perspective by the equally impressive mandate of the Conference, which was "to adopt a convention dealing with all matters relating to the law of the sea" (UNGA 3067 (XXVIII), para. 3). In view of this broad mandate and the fact that IHRL took a giant leap forward during the period the UNCLOS was being drafted – as evidenced by the entry into force of the two UN human rights covenants in 1976 – Haines astutely surmises that there must have been "a measure of mutual influence" (Haines, 2021, p. 19). Yet, he swiftly concludes that this was not the case. Indeed, the UNCLOS – also dubbed the "Constitution for the Oceans" (Koh, 1983, p. xxxiii) – does not contain a bill of rights, as one might expect from a document with a "constitutional" aspiration; nay not even a "general principle establishing the duty to protect people at sea" (Papanicolopulu, 2018). Moreover, its provisions governing transnational crime at sea remain markedly silent in terms of the rights of persons upon whom enforcement measures are imposed. Symptomatic in this respect are the eight provisions dealing with piracy – seemingly the most densely regulated crime in the entire UNCLOS – none of which confer rights to piracy suspects (Petrig, 2014). It is against this backdrop that UNCLOS' limitations become clear, namely its struggle to conceptualise persons as rights-holders (Papanicolopulu, 2012).

It would nonetheless be wrong to conclude that the UNCLOS is indifferent to people at sea and criminal suspects more specifically. Rather, as Treves succinctly put it, "concerns for human beings, which lie at the core of human rights concerns, are present in the texture of its provisions" (Treves, 2010, p. 3). In this vein, Oxman argued that because authorisations to enforce the law in the UNCLOS are precisely circumscribed and "far from unqualified" (Oxman, 1998, p. 403), they are "deterring excessive zeal" (Oxman, 1998, p. 404) and thus protect liberty interests. A handful of UNCLOS provisions convey human rights concerns even more explicitly by setting specific limitations on enforcement powers. Exemplary in this respect is Article 73 UNCLOS, where the drafters counterbalanced the conferral of far-reaching enforcement powers over violations of fisheries laws with a series of safeguards: the coastal state is *inter alia* barred from imposing corporal punishment as a sanction; in case of arrest or detention of a foreign vessel, it must promptly inform the flag state of any action taken and penalties imposed; and it is obliged to promptly release an arrested vessel and its crew upon the posting of a reasonable bond.

While the practical importance of provisions of this kind cannot be underestimated – indeed, the majority of cases adjudicated by the International Tribunal for the Law of the Sea turned on prompt release of vessels as provided for in Article 73 UNCLOS (Petrig & Bo, 2019) – two caveats are in order. First, provisions of the UNCLOS that usher concerns for human beings are framed as obligations of states and do not attribute any rights directly to individuals, which has repercussions on "standing and options for redress" (Papanicolopulu, 2018, p. 55). Second, the UNCLOS provisions setting limitations on the exercise of enforcement powers are few and far between, which means that considerable protective gaps remain. Particularly striking is the absence of a rule governing the use of force – and this was not an oversight. Shearer (1998), who attended the UNCLOS negotiations as a delegate, somewhat ironically comments on this lacuna by stating that provisions authorising enforcement action "appear to assume that the delinquent vessel will meekly submit" to the respective measures (Shearer, 1998, p. 440). He goes on to explain that the protective gap was due to "a disinclination" during the negotiations "to discuss such distasteful matters" (Shearer, 1998, p. 440) and the prevailing perception among delegates that "customary international law already governed the exercise of force" sufficiently (Shearer, 1986, p. 341). The latter proposition is reflective of the idea expressed in the preamble of the UNCLOS, according to which "matters not regulated by this Convention continue to be governed by the rules and principles of general international law". As Anderson perceptively concluded, "[p]olicing at sea is one of those matters" (Anderson, 2013, p. 234). This, together with the earlier observations about the protection of suspects by the UNCLOS, implies that IHRL continues to occupy a central role in limiting enforcement powers.

The same conclusion can be drawn as regards legal instruments governing transnational crimes at sea – the so-called "suppression conventions" – even though they contain, to different extents, safeguards limiting enforcement action. Considering these treaties on a timeline, one can observe an expansion over time of provisions dedicated to the protection of persons affected by enforcement measures at sea. While the 1988 UN Convention Against Illicit Traffic in Narcotic Drugs and Psychotropic Substances obliges the states engaged in at-sea enforcement action to "take due account of the need not to endanger the safety of life at sea, the security of the vessel and the cargo" (Article 17) – a clause replicated in the 2000 Migrant Smuggling Protocol (Article 9) and 1995 Fish Stock Agreement (Article 21) – the latter regulates, in addition, the use of force (Article 22). The 2005 SUA Protocol, which was adopted in the aftermath of the 9/11 attacks to counter terrorism and non-proliferation of weapons of mass destruction at sea, is even more comprehensive. Next to listing the safeguards known from earlier suppression conventions, it builds a bridge to IHRL by requiring that persons against whom enforcement measures are taken "are treated ... in compliance with the applicable provisions of international law, including international human rights law" (Article 8*bis*(10)(a)(ii)). The importance of IHRL is further emphasised through a non-prejudice clause stipulating that the 2005 SUA Protocol shall in no way affect rights and obligations arising under IHRL. This heightened awareness of the role of IHRL in countering transnational crime is due to the zeitgeist prevailing when the treaty was negotiated; indeed, its preamble refers to a UN General Assembly resolution reaffirming the obligation of states to "ensure that any measure taken to combat terrorism complies with their obligations under international law, in particular international human rights law".

Although the other mentioned suppression conventions do not feature the link between norms authorising enforcement measures and human rights as prominently as the 2005 SUA Protocol, IHRL plays an important – complementary but also self-standing – role in the quest to limit the exercise of enforcement powers at sea. It is complementary because important protective gaps remain: while the conventions emphasise the safety and treatment of persons, they lack procedural safeguards, such as the right to be informed about the reason of the arrest, the right to be brought promptly before a judge, and the right to formulate a *non-refoulement* claim and have it assessed on an individual basis (Petrig, 2014). IHRL has, in addition, a self-standing role: since the safeguards in suppression conventions are framed as obligations of states, it "not always clear who owns the equivalent rights" (Papanicolopulu, 2018, p. 55) – a question that, by contrast, can be clearly answered in IHRL where human beings are the holders of rights.

Finally, IHRL is also key for the protection of criminal suspects subject to enforcement measures authorised by the UN Security Council – as it did, for instance, regarding armed robbery at sea off the coast of Somalia or the smuggling of migrants from Libya. While earlier resolutions remained mute in terms of strictures attaching to the exercise of authorised enforcement powers, newer ones tend to include germane phraseology, according to which the exercise of authorised powers must be "in full compliance with ... international human rights law, as applicable" (UNSCR 2292 (2016), para. 4). Hence, rather than setting out the specific safeguards that must be observed by states or regional and international organisations acting upon granted authorisations, the Security Council refers to the "applicable" IHRL. Besides the fact that this "referential approach" is problematic because of the uncertainties regarding whether, when and to what extent human rights apply in the at-sea enforcement context (to which we turn in the last section of this chapter), the Security Council follows this path more erratically than consistently (Petrig, 2018).

To conclude, while the law of the sea does not directly attribute any (human) rights to suspects, it at least obliges states to observe specific limits when exercising enforcement powers at sea. Yet, these safeguards are far from complete and important protective gaps remain. IHRL thus, as a matter of circumstance, plays a key role in protecting persons subject to enforcement measures at sea from unwarranted and arbitrary state action. What is more, the law of the sea recognises this complementary or self-standing role of IHRL by relying on various legal techniques – notably by stating in the preamble of the UNCLOS that matters not regulated by the convention are left to international law, through the non-prejudice clauses or express linkages with IHRL included in suppression conventions, or by pursuing a referential approach as does the UN Security Council. True, IHRL would also apply without the law of the sea building these bridges. Yet the linkage has a practical and symbolic importance as it renders the liaisons between these two bodies of law – which led a separate existence for a (too) long time – more visible.

The "seablindness" of human rights law

It sounds like a truism that "the right to have rights" (*Hirsi Jamaa v Italy*, Concurring Opinion Judge Pinto de Albuquerque, 2012, p. 59) under IHRL belongs to both people on land and people at sea and cannot "depend on the place where a person happens to be" (Papanicolopulu, 2018, p. 4). Yet, the idea that criminal suspects at sea are – just like perpetrators on land – entitled to rights and freedoms espoused in IHRL has only started taking hold in the past decade. In practice, considerable differences between land and sea persist; even in states which, in a land-based context, are the "model pupils" in terms of human rights implementation, such as Denmark (Petrig, 2014). While the "move beyond seablindness" (Bueger & Edmunds, 2017, p. 1294) took place quite late in international security studies (Boşilcă et al., 2022), it occurred even later in the field of human rights law, the reasons for which are manifold and interrelated.

That the maritime dimension of human rights (and the human rights dimension of the law of the sea) has long been overlooked has much to do with the people who draft, interpret and apply the law. Oxman (1998) got to the heart of the matter when writing that "[v]iewed from afar, all lawyers constitute a single guild" and lawyers themselves tend to perceive international lawyers as belonging to "a single guild" (Oxman, 1998, p. 399). Yet, when zooming in, it becomes apparent that two different epistemic communities engage with the law of the sea and IHRL respectively and that "the gulf between them is real" (Oxman, 1998, p. 400). Treves similarly observes the emergence of specialised fields of international law "with clusters of scholars, organisations and sometimes courts and tribunals" (Treves, 2010, p. 1) among which interaction is limited. Against this backdrop it is hardly surprising that the law of the sea and IHRL largely developed "in isolation from each other" (Oxman, 1998, p. 400) and the sizable community of IHRL lawyers tended to "forget about the existence of the sea" (Papanicolopulu, 2018, p. 8) – both of which resulted in a body of IHRL scholarship with a palpable land bias.

The neglect of the maritime dimension of IHRL can further be observed at the institutional level. Organs set up to monitor human rights compliance, such as the UN Human Rights Council and treaty body system, primarily focus their attention on states' human rights performance on dry land. Conduct of states in the maritime environment, by contrast, is far from comprehensively and systematically scrutinised; nor is the seascape at the centre of the otherwise commendable efforts of NGOs and civil society organisations relating to the implementation and actual realisation of human rights. Only rarely is there a dedicated workstream for human rights abuses occurring at sea; and the first NGO that uniquely but comprehensively deals with rights of persons in the maritime environment – the UK-based charity "Human Rights at Sea" – was only established in 2014 (Haines, 2021).

Human Rights and Law Enforcement at Sea

A further explanation for the modest awareness about the human rights of people at sea is to be found in the law itself. Norms comprised in IHRL instruments are formulated with a high degree of abstraction and generality. They neither mention specific geographical contexts nor categories of persons since, as a general rule, human rights are supposed to apply to everybody everywhere as long as the person is under the jurisdiction of a state party to the respective treaty (Article 1 ECHR, Article 2(1) ICCPR). An important means for refining and translating general IHRL norms for or to specific contexts and/or categories of persons is the development of soft law instruments (Lagoutte et al., 2016). Yet, for the maritime space, and the rights of criminal suspects at sea specifically, this process has started only of late.

The fact that the maritime dimension of IHRL remained largely underexplored opened up space for the claim that human rights do not apply to policing activities at sea. Indeed, in a case before the European Court of Human Rights involving a violation of the right to liberty of suspects arrested by a French navy vessel in the course of counter-drug operations at sea, France argued that the ECHR would be inapplicable *ratione materiae* "for want of any provisions in the Convention ... concerning maritime matters" (*Medvedyev v France*, para. 49). This objection – which is emblematic of the difficulty to conceive IHRL as a body of law restricting police activity at sea – was one that the Court was not prepared to accept, and France was found to have violated the rights of the suspects arrested at sea. The ruling probably would not have attracted so much interest had it not come at a very sensitive moment – when the first truly international law enforcement operation, which was deployed to counter piracy off the coast of Somalia, was in full swing, resulting in numerous foiled attacks and dozens of arrests of suspects. These operations marked the turning point as regards the rights of persons subject to policing measures at sea and contributed to the emergence of the concept of human rights at sea more generally (Papanicolopulu, 2018; Haines, 2021).

This high-profile constabulary response to Somali-based piracy, to which an unprecedented number of states and, initially, three multinational missions contributed (Geiss & Petrig, 2011), attracted a great deal of media attention. With this, police operations at sea, including the risk for human rights violations they entail, swung into public view (Haines, 2021). For the contributing states, as well as regional and international organisations, the issue of human rights at sea was no longer merely theoretical but suddenly a tangible and imminent political and operational concern (Treves, 2009; Treves, 2010).

It goes without saying that these operations, including the human rights issues they involve, also attracted the attention of the legal community. According to Papanicolopulu (2018, p. 1), "an unprecedented flourishing of legal literature" on counter-piracy law enforcement and human rights could be witnessed. Indeed, a series of articles (e.g., Treves, 2009; Guilfoyle, 2010), chapters (e.g., Geiss & Petrig, 2011; Batsalas, 2014) and even entire books (e.g., Petrig, 2014) began chartering these relatively unknown waters.

What is more, the ongoing operations led to renewed interest from academics and practitioners alike in the (handful) of international court rulings comprising pronouncement on human rights and law enforcement at sea. They also gave rise to new cases before domestic and international courts that, mainly or tangentially, involved human rights issues. According to Wilson, this judicial involvement implied that "[j]udges are now ruling on maritime law enforcement issues previously under the sole ambit of government officials and operational commanders" (Wilson, 2016, p. 245). The more than a dozen judgments involving maritime interdiction and human rights issued between 2009 and 2015 were even said to "signal a new period in jurisprudence" (Wilson, 2016, p. 245), which was previously primarily concerned with human rights abuses on dry land.

The counter-piracy operations off the coast of Somalia where thus a watershed moment for the idea that police activity at sea must abide by human rights standards. Moreover, the developments in this specific field served as a catalyst for the establishment of the concept of human rights at sea more generally and, with this, a clear rejection of the idea of the seas and oceans as a "zone de non-droit" where IHRL could be overlooked altogether (Grobson, 2017).

Conclusion

Roughly a decade ago, Treves (2010) wrote that the law of the sea and IHRL are "not separate planets rotating in different orbits", but rather two that "meet in many situations" (Treves, 2010, p. 13). Indeed, as this chapter demonstrates, the law of the sea builds various bridges to IHRL, and it is increasingly accepted that IHRL applies not only at land but also in the maritime environment. Yet, the legal issues arising at the interface of these two bodies of law have only recently been uncovered and many have not yet been fully explored from a theoretical and operational point of view, let alone decided by courts or human rights bodies. As regards law enforcement operations to counter maritime security threats specifically, relying on answers developed in the context of policing the land may provide a useful starting point, but will often be insufficient as every single feature of these operations – the maritime environment, actors involved, cooperative approach and informality – poses intricate challenges as regards the protection of suspects through IHRL.

In terms of the operational environment, it seems no longer contested that human rights apply in the maritime domain; instead, the questions have become more subtle, namely whether the "wholly exceptional circumstances" (*Medvedyev v France*, para. 105) reigning at sea may justify a modified standard. So far, these circumstances have been invoked to justify lower standards than those applicable on land – for instance, a more generous interpretation of the concept of bringing a suspect "promptly" before a judge (Batsalas, 2014). It is posited that the "wholly exceptional circumstances" may, in specific situations, require adherence to a stricter standard than on land. As Papanicolopulu (2018) rightly stressed in a more general context, people at sea "find themselves in a hostile environment, not intended to accommodate humans, and in areas that are often far off from land and the possibility to apply for protection" (p. 2). Overall, the "maritime situation" (Treves, 2010, p. 8) in which suspects – and enforcers alike – are present, must be taken into account when interpreting IHRL norms; and this may ultimately result in a more lenient or stricter standard compared to that developed for policing the land. A "context-free" application of human rights (Wilson, 2016, p. 319), by contrast, entails the risk of the law being "incompletely or inefficiently or even incorrectly" applied (Papanicolopulu, 2018, p. 8).

In terms of actors, the law of the sea plainly foresees a role for the navy in policing the sea, notably by stipulating that only warships (next to other specific state crafts) are authorised to enforce the law at sea. In various states though, domestic law does not (yet) fully account for this role of the navy and the fact that warships are used as "lawships" (Bateman, 2014); and domestic law plays a pivotal role in (multinational) law enforcement operations at sea, including for the protection of suspects as it translates the abstract human rights norms into concrete operational rules to be followed (Petrig, 2020). That domestic law does not sufficiently take into account the policing role of the navy may manifest itself in the fact that the personal scope of application of key domestic legal acts only extends to the police (and maybe coast guard) but not the navy. Further, the territorial scope of application of relevant legal acts, such as codes of criminal procedure or police laws, may be such that it only covers waters under the sovereignty of the coastal state but not the high seas. Finally, counter-piracy operations evidenced that certain states follow an "extraordinary suspect approach", taking the stance that suspects deprived of their liberty at sea are not "ordinary" criminal suspects (such as those arrested by these states on land) to which domestic criminal law and the respective procedural safeguards apply. They only exceptionally apply domestic law and its protections to suspects seized at sea, namely in the (very rare) case they decide to prosecute them in their own domestic courts. In the standard case, however, where suspects are transferred to third states for prosecution, they are not granted the procedural rights that seizing states usually grant to persons arrested on dry land (Petrig, 2014).

The cooperative approach to law enforcement at sea is yet another source for intricate legal human rights issues. Of major complexity is, for instance, the question of attribution of violations in a setting where states interact with their counterparts and, oftentimes, with international organisations (Geiss & Petrig, 2011). Moreover, views differ as to which state is responsible for granting a specific right in the first place. On land, as a general rule, one and the same state arrests, detains and prosecutes a suspect; and this state is responsible for safeguarding the human rights of the person subject to the respective measures. In multinational operations, such as the counter-piracy missions, the measures of arrest, detention, transfer and prosecution are often taken by different states. This may lead to confusion as to which state must ensure specific rights, which can be illustrated at the example of the right to be brought promptly before a judge: is it the seizing state and/or the (regional) state to which the person is ultimately transferred for prosecution which must bring them before a judge? Some argue that a "judge is a judge", regardless of the state to which they belong and that it suffices if the suspect is brought before a judge upon their transfer to a third state for prosecution, which at times takes place weeks after the arrest. Yet, good legal reasons – extensively discussed by the present author previously (Petrig, 2013) – exist for maintaining that the *seizing* state's courts must oversee the legality of the arrest and detention taking place at sea.

Lastly, concerns regarding human rights also result from the "turn to informality" (Guilfoyle, 2021, p. 293) witnessed in the response to Somali-based piracy and likely to become a feature of maritime security operations more generally (Bueger & Edmunds, 2017). Reliance on informal processes instead of well-established legal procedures specifically, may entail great practical benefits but come with the risk "to sequester maritime security measures away from ordinary oversight or interaction with human rights norms" (Guilfoyle, 2021, p. 309). The phenomenon of "transfers" to bring suspects within the jurisdiction of the prosecuting state in counter-piracy operations in the Indian Ocean is quite illustrative in this respect. As seizing states were reluctant to bring arrested suspects before their domestic courts, at times resulting in their release, it proved impossible to implement the basic tenet of every law enforcement operation – to bring alleged offenders to justice. To solve the problem, the EU and several states concluded transfer agreements with states of the region in which the latter declared their general willingness to accept piracy suspects for prosecution. Hence, rather than relying on extradition, which is the most obvious legal mechanism to move suspects from the jurisdiction of the arresting state to that of the prosecuting state, seizing states opted for "transfers". The two processes differ considerably, notably in terms of human rights protection. Extradition is a surrender taking place in execution of a decision issued by an administrative and/or judicial body in a formalised procedure prescribed by law in which the suspect is a party. By contrast, transfers are the result of negotiation and cooperation between relevant stakeholders in informal fora without participation of the suspect. Hence, in extradition proceedings, suspects can exercise procedural rights, most notably formulating a *non-refoulement* claim and requesting the judicial review of the decision – possibilities that are inexistent when transfers are used (Petrig, 2014).

This cursory overview suffices to demonstrate that the features of (multinational) law enforcement operations to counter maritime security threats pose particular challenges in granting suspects seized at sea the same rights as are granted to their peers on land. Many of these challenges have not yet received sufficient attention in doctrine and practice. Thus, further scrutiny of the phenomenon of maritime law enforcement through the analytical lens of "human rights at sea" is necessary in order to fully realise the idea that human rights do not end at the shore but extend fully to the sea and oceans. If successful, international maritime security law – which "has emerged as a 'hybrid' subspeciality of international law in the borderland between various areas of legal studies" (Boşilcă et al., 2022, p. 4) – will live up to its claim to include international human rights law – not only on paper but in the operational reality too.

References

Literature

Anderson, D. H. (2013). Some Aspects of the Use of Force in Maritime Law Enforcement. In N. Boschiero, T. Scovazzi, C. Pitea & C., Ragni (Eds.), *International Courts and the Development of International Law* (pp. 233–243). T.M.C. Asser Press.

Bateman, S. (2014). Regional Navies and Coastguards: Striking a Balance between "Lawships" and "Warships". In G. Till & J. Chan (Eds.), *Naval Modernisation in South-East Asia: Nature, Causes and Consequences* (pp. 245–262). Routledge.

Batsalas, D. (2014). Maritime Interdiction and Human Rights. In E. Papastavridis & K. Trapp (Eds.), *La criminalité en mer/Crimes at Sea* (pp. 429–456). Martinus Nijhoff.

Boşilcă, R.-L., de Sousa Ferreira, S. R., & Ryan, B. J. (2021). Introduction. In R.-L. Boşilcă, S. R. de Sousa Ferreira & B. J. Ryan (Eds.), *The Routledge Handbook of Maritime Security* (pp. 1–13). Routledge.

Bueger, C. (2015). What is Maritime Security? *Marine Policy, 53*, 159–164.

Bueger, C., & Edmunds, T. (2017). Beyond Seablindness: A New Agenda for Maritime Security Studies. *International Affairs, 93*(6), 1293–1311.

Geiss, R., & Petrig, A. (2011). *Piracy and Armed Robbery at Sea: The Legal Framework for Counter-Piracy Operations in Somalia and the Gulf of Aden.* Oxford University Press.

Grobson, S. (2017). Droit de la mer et protection internationale de l'individu. In M. Forteau & J.-M. Thouvenin, *Traité de droit international de la mer* (pp. 1099–1118). Editions Pedone.

Guilfoyle, D. (2009). *Shipping Interdiction and the Law of the Sea.* Cambridge University Press.

Guilfoyle, D. (2010). Counter-Piracy Law Enforcement and Human Rights. *International and Comparative Law Quarterly, 59*(1), 141–169.

Guilfoyle, D. (2021). Maritime Security. In R. Geiss & N. Melzer (Eds.), *The Oxford Handbook of the International Law of Global Security* (pp. 291–309). Oxford University Press.

Haines, S. (2021). Developing Human Rights at Sea. *Ocean Yearbook Online, 35*(1), 18–51. 10.1163/2211 6001_03501003.

Klein, N. (2010). Intelligence Gathering and Information Sharing for Maritime Security Purposes under International Law. In N. Klein, J. Mossop & D. R. Rothwell, *Maritime Security: International Law and Policy Perspectives from Australia and New Zealand* (pp. 224–241). Routledge.

Klein, N. (2011). *Maritime Security and the Law of the Sea.* Oxford University Press.

Klein, N., Guilfoyle, D., Karim, S. M., & McLaughlin, R. (2020). Maritime Autonomous Vehicles. *International and Comparative Law Quarterly, 69*, 719–734.

Koh, T. (1983). "A Constitution for the Oceans". In United Nations, *The Law of the Sea: Official Text of the United Nations Convention on the Law of the Sea.* United Nations New York.

Kraska, J., & Pedrozo, R. (2013). *International Maritime Security Law.* Martinus Nijhoff Publishers.

Lagoutte, S., Gammeltoft-Hansen, T., & Cerone, J. (2016). Introduction: Tracing the Roles of Soft Law in Human Rights. In S. Lagoutte, T. Gammeltoft-Hansen & J. Cerone (Eds.), *Tracing the Roles of Soft Law in Human Rights* (pp. 1–13). Oxford University Press.

McLaughlin, R. (2016). Authorizations for Maritime Law Enforcement Operations. *International Review of the Red Cross, 98*(2), 465–490.

Oxman, B. H. (1998). Human Rights and the United Nations Convention on the Law of the Sea. *Columbia Journal of Transnational Law, 36*, 399–429.

Papanicolopulu, I. (2012). The Law of the Sea Convention: No Place for Persons? *The International Journal of Marine and Coastal Law, 27*, 867–874.

Papanicolopulu, I. (2018). *International Law and the Protection of People at Sea*. Oxford University Press.

Papastavridis, E. (2013). *The Interception of Vessels on the High Seas: Contemporary Challenges to the Legal Order of the Oceans*. Hart Publishing.

Percy, S. (2018). Maritime Security. In A. Gheciu & W. C. Wolforth (Eds.), *The Oxford Handbook of International Security* (pp. 607–618). Oxford University Press.

Petrig, A. (2013). Arrest, Detention and Transfer of Piracy Suspects: A Critical Appraisal of the German *Courier Case* Decision. In G. Andreone, G. Bevilacqua, G. Cataldi & C. Cinelli (Eds.), *Insecurity at Sea: Piracy and Other Risks to Navigation* (pp. 161–167). Giannini Editore.

Petrig, A. (2014). *Human Rights and Law Enforcement at Sea: Arrest, Detention and Transfer of Piracy Suspects*. Martinus Nijhoff Publishers.

Petrig, A. (2018). The Role Accorded to Human Rights in Security Council Maritime Resolutions. In K. Neri (Ed.), *Le Conseil de sécurité des Nations Unies et la mer – United Nations Security Council and the Sea* (pp. 43–71). Editoriale Scientifica.

Petrig, A. (2020). Multinational Military Operations at Sea. In R. Geiss & H. Krieger (Eds.), *The "Legal Pluriverse" Surrounding Multinational Military Operations* (pp. 345–369). Oxford University Press.

Petrig, A., & Bo, M. (2019). The International Tribunal for the Law of the Sea and Human Rights. In M. Scheinin (Ed.), *Human Rights Norms in "Other" International Courts* (pp. 353–411). Cambridge University Press.

Rosenne, S., & Gebhard, J. (2008). Conferences on the Law of the Sea. In A. Peters (Ed.), *Encyclopedia of Public International Law* (online edition). https://opil.ouplaw.com/home/mpil.

Shearer, I. (1986). Problems of Jurisdiction and Law Enforcement Against Delinquent Vessels. *International and Comparative Law Quarterly, 35*, 320–343.

Shearer, I. (1998). The Development of International Law with Respect to the Law Enforcement Roles of Navies and Coast Guards in Peacetime. *International Law Studies, 71*, 429–453.

Sonnenberg, D. C. (2012, March). *Maritime Law Enforcement: A Critical Capability for the Navy?* Unpublished M.A. thesis, Naval Postgraduate School. https://calhoun.nps.edu/handle/10945/6873.

Till, G. (1996). Developments in Maritime Security. In P. Cozens (Ed.), *A Maritime Nation: New Zealand's Maritime Environment and Security* (pp. 5–27). Centre for Strategic Studies.

Tondini, M. (2017). The Use of Force in the Course of Maritime Law Enforcement Operations. *Journal on the Use of Force and International Law, 4*(2), 253–272.

Treves, T. (2009). Piracy, Law of the Sea, and Use of Force: Developments off the Coast of Somalia. *The European Journal of International Law, 20*(2), 399–414.

Treves, T. (2010). Human Rights and the Law of the Sea. *Berkeley Journal of International Law, 28*, 1–14.

Wilson, B. (2016). Human Rights and Maritime Law Enforcement. *Stanford Journal of International Law, 52*(2), 243–319.

Legal instruments

Agreement for the Implementation of the Provisions of the United Nations Convention on the Law of the Sea of 10 December 1982 relating to the Conservation and Management of Straddling Fish Stocks and Highly Migratory Fish Stocks, adopted 4 August 1995, entered into force 11 December 2001, 2167 U.N.T.S. 3 (Cited as 1995 Fish Stock Agreement).

Code of Conduct for Law Enforcement Officials, adopted by General Assembly Resolution 34/169 of 17 December 1979 (Cited as UN Code of Conduct for Law Enforcement Officials).

Convention for the Protection of Human Rights and Fundamental Freedoms (European Convention on Human Rights, as amended), signed 4 November 1950, entered into force 3 September 1053, E.T.S. 5 (Cited as ECHR).

International Covenant on Civil and Political Rights, adopted 16 December 1966, entered into force 23 March 1976, 999 U.N.T.S. 171 (Cited as ICCPR).

Protocol against the Smuggling of Migrants by Land, Sea and Air, Implementing the United Nations Convention against Transnational Organized Crime, adopted 15 November 2000, entered into force 28 January 2004, 2241 U.N.T.S. 507 (Cited as 2000 Migrant Smuggling Protocol).

Protocol of 2005 to the Convention for the Suppression of Unlawful Acts against the Safety of Maritime Navigation, adopted 14 October 2005, entered into force 28 July 2010, IMO Doc. LEG/CONF.15/21 (Cited as 2005 SUA Protocol).

United Nations Convention against Illicit Traffic in Narcotic Drugs and Psychotropic Substances, adopted 20 December 1988, entered into force 11 November 1990, 1582 U.N.T.S. 95.

United Nations Convention on the Law of the Sea, adopted 10 December 1982, entered into force 16 November 1994, 1833 U.N.T.S. 3 (Cited as UNCLOS).

United Nations, General Assembly Resolution 3067 (16 November 1973) UN Doc. A/Res/ 3067(XXVIII) (Cited as UNGA 3067 (XXVIII)).

United Nations, Security Council Resolution 2292 (14 June 2016) UN Doc S/RES/2292 (Cited as UNSCR 2292 (2016)).

Case-law

Hirsi Jamaa and Others v Italy App no 27765/09 (Grand Chamber, ECtHR, 23 February 2012).

Medvedyev and Others v France App no 3394/03 (Grand Chamber, ECtHR, 29 March 2010).

14

HUMANS AT SEA: MIGRANTS, REFUGEES AND TRANSNATIONAL RESPONSES

Susana Ferreira

Over the last decade, the maritime environment has increasingly become a site of human emergency and crisis. The maritime dimension of migration has thus emerged as a modern security risk as well as a humanitarian concern given the rising toll of death across different maritime spaces, including the Mediterranean. The so-called "migratory crisis" has made visible the maritime character of irregular migration. Although, seaborne migration is not a new phenomenon in itself, its contemporary aspects are related to two specific factors. First, the crisis revealed irregular maritime migration is increasingly composed of "mixed flows" that include both "forced and voluntary movements" (Ferreira, 2019b); second, it showed the growing importance of the business of migrants' smuggling and trafficking within maritime routes.

As individuals have to rely on alternative perilous routes to reach a safe haven, undertaking dangerous journeys by sea, the maritime dimension of migration came to the centre of recent academic and political discussions regarding transnational flows by sea. In this sense, literature from across different fields has addressed transnational movements of people by sea offering a variety of theoretical frameworks, engaging with different preoccupations concerning the challenges posed by the seascape to human mobility. How to integrate a human security focus on maritime security? What are the challenges posed by the maritime environment to migration? And, what are the approaches adopted by states to address these flows? These are some of the questions that this chapter aims to shed light on. With this starting point in mind, the chapter contributes to the field by presenting a comprehensive conceptualisation of maritime migration, moving beyond the regional approaches that mostly focus on policy practices.

A paradigm shift in migration: Between human security and maritime security

Safe and secure seas are axiological for guaranteeing freedom of navigation, protecting marine resources and the environment, and ensuring the rule of law. The escalation of threats to the maritime domain has pushed maritime security to the forefront of international political debates and policy agendas. As maritime themes have acquired particular relevance over recent years, as highlighted in this Handbook, the academic community has not been indifferent to the complex phenomenon of seaborne migration.

A common, although controversial, approach to migration in the maritime environment has been to frame it within a logic of securitisation, based on governments' approaches to address

DOI: 10.4324/9781003001324-17

this phenomenon. As highlighted by Vuori's chapter on "Maritime Securitisation" in this Handbook, maritime migration has been conceptualised as a threat to state's external and internal security. In this sense, a significant body of research within securitisation studies has focused on seaborne migration through the lens of securitisation (Huysmans, 2000; Bourbeau, 2011; Gerard, 2014).

These theoretical frameworks mostly focused on the "uncontrollability" of these movements and their connections to criminal activities, which has translated into the adoption of urgent deterrence measures to control migration flows, particularly by the European Union (EU) and its member states, the United States (US) or the Australian government. Images of overloaded migrants' boats portrayed by mass media reinforce these narratives, focusing on anonymous flows of people crossing the seas. Consequently, the emphasis is placed on the dimension of dissuasion through the reinforcement of border surveillance systems. In the European context, "the EU uses a deterrence strategy based on minimum common denominators to manage migration in its Southern border" (Ferreira, 2019b, p. 198). Thus, the "standard" (but contested) literature on maritime migration has been dominated by a perception of threat posed by "boat-migrants".

However, as stressed by Bueger (2015, p. 164), "[u]nderstanding migration as threat has undermined economic or humanitarian understandings, led to often extreme measures of border control and silenced the humanitarian tragedies that cases of illegal migration might imply". This conceptualisation has translated into securitised approaches that hinder refugee protection and humanitarianism within the sea space (Pugh, 2004; see also Vuori in this Handbook).

In more recent discourses of maritime security, the individual has taken central place, capturing the attention of several authors (Azad, 2008; Ralby, 2016; McAuliffe & Mence, 2017; Moreno-Lax & Papastavridis, 2017). Therefore, the human security dimension of maritime security emerges as a paradigm shift, moving towards a comprehensive understanding of security and including a wide range of issues related to the safeguarding of people's safety and security (Azad, 2008).

Nonetheless, this is still a rather neglected field by academic literature, despite the proliferation of academic works on the securitisation of migration that we have seen with the "refugee crisis" of 2015. As McAuliffe and Mence (2017) correctly note, theorising about irregular maritime migration can be a daunting task despite the high profile and visibility of these flows. First, this is a highly sensitive subject and migrants or refugees might not be willing to openly engage with researchers. Second, the growing connection between irregular maritime migration and human smuggling and trafficking networks might translate into greater information gaps due to difficult access to government classified information. Third, the polarised discourses on irregular migration often limit the adoption of a balanced and critical approach. Moreover, I would add, the difficulties in accessing reliable data overall on irregular migration, becomes even more challenging in a maritime context.

Another narrative thread developed by Azad (2008) explores why the human dimension of the maritime domain has been left unattended so far. This can be explained by a strong and narrow land-centric perspective, as conceptualisations of security are often associated with the construction of nation-states and inextricably tied to the idea of territoriality. There is therefore a general need of a more comprehensive understanding of spatial demarcation that takes into account the marine sphere. The adoption of a traditional conceptualisation of maritime security often overlooks "low intensity conflicts" or issues that have a direct or indirect impact on people's lives and wellbeing, as well as the human presence in the marine environment.

Studying migrants at sea requires a move beyond a territorial notion of human security, and an exploration of its interlinkages with violence, maritime crimes, or food and health security, to fully grasp its manifestations in the maritime and oceanic domains. Azad's work (2008) presents an extensive analysis of the different fields of human security connected with maritime security, which range from threats to fishery or coastal communities to human smuggling and trafficking. Still, "(...) a direct comprehensive work on the subject is still lacking" (Azad, 2008, p. 3).

The world's seas currently face political instability, insecurity and lack of order, which pose severe concerns to human security. Piracy and maritime terrorism, human trafficking and smuggling of human beings, trafficking in arms and drugs or the deterioration of the marine environment, all have significant repercussions in the different aspects of human security (Azad, 2008, p. 21). In this sense, seaborne migration is associated with particular risks. The risks of travelling across the sea include the hazard of drowning and the exposure to extreme weather conditions during sailing. Furthermore, the unseaworthy conditions of overcrowded vessels, with migrants having access to limited supplies and insufficient life jackets often triggers situations of high distress, while these individuals often have limited swimming capacities, creating greater tensions (Jumbert, 2018).

The notion of human security privileges the security and safety of the individual and is based on the understanding that "(...) the security needs of the people are different from the security needs of the state, and therefore need to be addressed directly" (Ralby, 2016). The international community is thus responsible for the individual's security, along the line of a broader approach focused on the "freedom from want" to a narrower approach, "the freedom from fear".

To advance on the study of maritime migration is essential to take into account the intersection of migration profiles within the routes and the complex nature of these flows, with categories merging and mingling within single individuals. Such mixed flows include refugees or people in need of assistance, minors, trafficking victims or torture survivors, with personal circumstances being critical for determining the rules applicable to each individual (Moreno-Lax & Papastavridis, 2016, pp. 5–6).

These accounts reveal not only how complex the maritime environment is, but they also show the fluidity of the seascape and how criminal networks take advantage of this situation. In fact, criminal networks have developed increasingly more advanced systems of migrant smuggling and human trafficking by sea, posing huge challenges to maritime security, migration management and law enforcement (Moreno-Lax & Papastavridis, 2016, p. 6).

Irregular migrants and refugees repeatedly fall into the clutches of these networks, due to their vulnerability. In this sense, their eagerness to survive and reach a safer harbour may lead them to resort to smuggling, thus engaging in "survival crimes" and jeopardising their own human security. Smuggling is increasingly associated with serious human rights violations and deaths. As highlighted by the UNODC's report "Global Study on Smuggling of Migrants 2018", "[e]very year, thousands of migrants die during smuggling activities. Accidents, extreme terrain and weather conditions, as well as deliberate killings have been reported along most smuggling routes" (UNODC, 2018, p. 9). Thus, migrants' human security is threatened as they are deprived of their fundamental rights (Ferreira, 2019b, p. 42).

From a legal standpoint, "smuggling of migrants is a criminal offence that relates to facilitating the passage of irregular migrants across an international border for profit", which is "a crime preying on people's dreams of a better life" (UNODC, 2018, p. 38). This has severe implications for individual's human rights, with smuggled migrants often being vulnerable to various forms of violence, exploitation, extortion and kidnapping.

In essence, maritime migration poses a conceptual challenge to security. Devising irregular maritime movements as a threat to states' security has shaped maritime policies and strategies, often colliding with the protection of fundamental principles (Mallia, 2013, p. 5; Moreno-Lax & Papastavridis, 2016, p. 4). A human security approach to seaborne migration, moving within a sea-land nexus, therefore provides a conceptual framework that takes into account the interaction between human rights and maritime law (Goodwin-Gill, 2016, p. 31).

Humanitarian regime at sea

Maritime migration comes with a set of specific legal commitments under international law. Similarly to the land domain, issues related to the human aspect of maritime security are formulated within the wide sphere of ocean governance, which provide the principles and tools to address those issues (Azad, 2008).

As highlighted in the previous section, the mixed character of maritime movements, involving refugees and persons with different migratory profiles requires an intricate regime that involves the distinct areas of international law, encompassing international law of the sea, international human rights law, international refugee law, international humanitarian law and international criminal law (UNHCR, 2011). In essence, "the humanitarian regime at sea can be defined as a composite of maritime laws, norms and practices operated with high consistency by states and seafaring communities (including ship owners, insurers and maritime unions)" (Pugh, 2004, p. 58). While the International Maritime Organisation (IMO) has limited powers in advocating, employing and monitoring the application of laws and conventions, the ultimate responsibility for enforcing compliance with the regime lies with states (Pugh, 2004, p. 58).

Providing assistance to those in distress at sea is a longstanding maritime obligation, which has become an intrinsic part of the international maritime law and is enshrined in several conventions (UNHCR, 2002), namely: The United Nations Convention on the Law of the Sea (UNCLOS), 1982; the International Convention for the Safety of Life at Sea (SOLAS), 1974, as amended; the International Convention on Maritime Search and Rescue (SAR), 1979, as amended.

These agreements enshrine the obligation to aid those in peril at sea, the principle of Search and Rescue (SAR). The SAR obligation applies to anyone at sea, regardless of their nationality, legal status or the circumstances in which they are found. According to paragraph 2.1.10 of Chapter 2 of the Annex to SAR, 1979: "Parties shall ensure that assistance be provided to any person in distress at sea. They shall also do so regardless of the nationality or status of such a person or the circumstances in which that person is found".

The legal framework codifies the responsibilities of the different actors and how they interrelate within such a convoluted scenario. The obligation of ship masters to provide assistance to those in distress at sea is firmly rooted in customary law and was first codified in 1910 and later incorporated to Article 98 of UNCLOS and the SOLAS regulation (UNHCR, 2002). Although flag states are bound by international maritime law, in practice responsibilities can often be difficult to pinpoint due to the so-called flags of convenience. That is particularly problematic regarding the treatment of stowaways,[1] where the current practice is often to hold ship owners accountable regardless of the flag state. In addition, coastal and port states have the obligation to establish search and rescue centres to rescue persons in distress found in their coastal areas, as stipulated in the SOLAS Convention and the SAR Convention. Moreover, the SAR state has an obligation to provide urgent assistance, as well as to disembark rescued people to a place of safety.

While the principle of SAR is axiomatic and considered to be a sacred duty, there is uncertainty and confusion in international maritime law in the criteria for defining the "place of safety" in disembarkation. The conceptualisation of the "place of safety" within common practices, legal opinion and the UNHCR itself, has been associated with the "next port of call", which is not necessarily the most convenient port nor the nearest one (Pugh, 2004, p. 61). This is in fact contrary to the legislation but politically expedient. Thus, several aspects should be taken into account when considering the question of disembarkation: compliance with legal obligations; functional, humanitarian and security concerns; as well as, commercial interests (UNHCR, 2002). In order to overcome some of these difficulties, IMO, UNHCR and the International Chamber of Shipping have adopted a Guide for Rescue at Sea, entitled "Rescue at Sea. A Guide to Principles and Practice as Applied to Refugees and Migrants" (IMO, UNHCR & International Chamber of Shipping, 2015) to regulate disembarkation processes. Still, a major concern arises, since there is no mandatory obligation for states to accept disembarkation, apart from a humanitarian concern, and it is a state's traditional prerogative to regulate the admission of non-citizens. In this sense, "[i]n the case of rescue or interception by public ships (that is, a State's naval or equivalent vessels), flag-State responsibility should indeed be the starting point (…)" (Goodwin-Gill, 2016, p. 26). The Italian case is very illustrative on this regard, with the former Interior Minister Matteo Salvini facing a possible indictment with charges of kidnapping, for refusing a migrant rescue ship to dock at a Sicilian port, leaving it stranded at sea for more than two weeks, in 2019. Although the case was dismissed later in May 2021, it highlights the raising concerns with the fulfilment of maritime law and human rights law while implementing policies and practices of deterrence.

Furthermore, rescue operations have to comply with the principle of *non-refoulment* that is the prohibition of expulsion or return of a refugee or asylum-seeker to a territory where his life or freedom is at risk. Article 33 of the Refugee Convention of 1951 consecrates this principle:

> No Contracting State shall expel or return ("refouler") a refugee in any manner whatsoever to the frontiers of territories where his life or freedom would be threatened on account of his race, religion, nationality, membership of a particular social group or political opinion.
>
> *(The Refugee Convention, 1951)*

This refers not only to the country of origin but any territory where the migrant's life might be at risk. In practice however, this principle is frequently violated, and people are returned to transit or origin countries where their lives are threatened and the right to seek asylum is obstructed.

International refugee law should guide the humanitarian regime at sea. States' responsibility to ensure international protection, as conveyed by the 1951 Convention relating to the Status of Refugees, is triggered once asylum-seekers are found among those rescued. In this sense, the Convention specifies who is subject of protection, although not specifying procedures, and settles fundamental principles such as non-penalisation for illegal entry and *non-refoulment*. Such provisions under the convention are activated once asylum-seekers are present in the territory and fall straightforwardly onto the receiving state. However, states have devised a dubious approach to the concept of "presence in the country", distinguishing between physical and legal presence, based on subjective decisions on the limits of their sovereign territory in order to evade the provisions of the Convention (Pugh, 2004, p. 60).

Maritime interception operations conducted by states to halt or prevent the arrival of irregular migrants through maritime channels often fail to uphold these obligations. Interception operations deployed on the high seas or in the territorial water of other states[2] adds to the concerns regarding the safeguarding and protection of these principles.

Still, combating migrant smuggling and human trafficking deserves considerable attention from states worldwide and international agencies, given its transnational scale and scope. In this sense, the Protocol Against the Smuggling of Migrants by Land, Sea and Air (United Nations, 2000a), dedicates a chapter to the "Smuggling of Migrants by Sea", defining a set of measures and safeguarding clauses. In the context of sea-rescue, as enshrined in Article 19, even when smuggled, asylum-seekers and refugees should not be deprived from international protection. Furthermore, the Protocol to Prevent, Suppress and Punish Trafficking in Persons, Especially Women and Children (United Nations, 2000b) provides special protection to victims of human trafficking (Article 6), and foresees the repatriation of the victims (Article 8), but ensuring that it is done "without prejudice to any applicable bilateral or multilateral agreement or arrangement that governs, in whole or in part, the return of victims of trafficking in persons" (Article 6.6, United Nations, 2000b).

Given the complex nature of the humanitarian regime at sea, the implementation and compliance with these norms not only binds states parties to the international treaties but also international agencies and the international community as a whole (UNHCR, 2002). International actors, such as the International Maritime Organisation (IMO), UNHCR and the International Organisation for Migration (IOM) have clear-cut responsibilities. IMO is directly responsible for supervising the evolution and implementation of maritime law, while the UNHCR is committed to providing assistance, guidance and monitoring the application of refugee protection responsibilities. In turn, IOM is in charge of assisting on broader topics related to migration, and on the specificities of migrants at sea. Furthermore, the international community should take action on the development of cooperative frameworks of action to ensure the implementation of comprehensive mechanisms, based on a responsibility-sharing approach (UNHCR, 2002).

Overall, the constituent elements of the humanitarian regime at sea emerge from overlapping, but complementary, regimes that deal with critical dimensions of seaborne migration, particularly rescue at sea, maritime interception and delivery or return to a place of safety. While the regime is based on a set of well-rooted principles which are commonly accepted, there are still significant gaps and uncertainties regarding the operationalisation of these principles that expose migrants to greater vulnerabilities.

Historical evolution: From "boat people" to "irregular maritime migrants"

Far from unprecedented, the maritime scenario has marked the development of human history, going back to the period after the late-Holocene advent of the sail. Actually, maritime migration in the pre-industrial era has shaped demographic trends and cultural approximations, thanks to the development of seafaring technology (Anderson et al., 2006, p. 1).

In the modern era, the establishment of the asylum regime after World War II created a framework to ensure international protection for refugees. However, several events will highlight the challenges of protection at sea and the perils of the journey, particularly the Indochina crisis that will bring along the conceptualisation of "boat people".

The academic community has not been indifferent to this phenomenon and there is an expanding body of literature on "boat people" (Pugh, 2004; Mann, 2016; Moreno-Lax & Papastavridis, 2016; Fitzgerald, 2019). Authors have taken migrants' embarking on those dangerous sea routes to the core of their concerns in order to conceptualise about the logics of control (Moreno-Lax & Papastavridis, 2016), the national and multilateral approaches adopted, the technologies implemented, although often failing to give a voice to migrants themselves.

Their approaches have focused mostly on regional practices, particularly in regards to the Indochina crisis and the European situation.

The end of the war in Vietnam in 1975 led to the largest exodus after 1945, with thousands of people trying to escape the country devastated by the conflict. The term "boat people" was used to refer to those individuals who "fled Indochina in fishing boats after the Vietnam war. Thousands perished at sea, many at the hands of pirates in the Gulf of Thailand" (Pugh, 2004 p. 51). These unregulated movements crossing the South Pacific, throughout the 1970s and 1980s, were seen with high concern by neighbouring countries, particularly by Australia (Schloenhardt, 2000, p. 33).

While some of these individuals found asylum in neighbouring countries, many other Asian nations refused to accept refugees from Vietnam. This reaction of regional actors resembles today's reality in the Mediterranean, regarding states refusal to accept a certain number of refugees. While Vietnam did little to prevent the exodus, it also took the international community some time to realise the dimension of the humanitarian crisis. Nevertheless, after an intense period of negotiation, mediated by the United Nations, a resettlement framework was established, in which several countries participated, including Australia (Schloenhardt, 2000, p. 33).

Similar movements have followed since:

> movements of Cubans and Haitians across the Caribbean followed since the early 1980s; Albanians took the Adriatic Sea for most of the 1990s; and sub-Saharan Africans have headed to the shores of Spain, Malta and Italy throughout the 2000s. Afghans have also employed the sea route taking the Bay of Bengal to escape persecution, as have done Eritreans and Somalis across the Gulf of Aden, or Iraqis towards the Greek islands from the early 2000s.
>
> *(Moreno-Lax & Papastavridis, 2016, p. 3)*

Nowadays, we see a paradigm shift from Indochina's "boat people" to the concept of "irregular maritime migrants", moving beyond a conceptualisation of "boat migrants" as a globalised threat to state's internal security, as well as to the identities and western societies' lifestyles. In the end, this eventually led to a growing securitisation of irregular migration and the adoption of more restrictive policies.

The powerful image of the arrival of migrants in boats depicted by mass media channels has shaped current discourses and translated into a reframing of the representation of migrants and asylum-seekers. The visual image of "boat people" is used to portray migrants as individuals with no territorial homeland, the "gypsies of seas" (Pugh, 2004, p. 54), representing "stateless wanderers" impeded to reach coastal water worldwide (Pugh, 2004, p. 53).

This depiction of irregular maritime migrants projects the fabricated threat, correlating to the securitisation of migration as addressed in the first section, inverting the risk and the referent object, rather than focusing on the hazards faced by those individuals. As highlighted by Pugh (2004, p. 55): "For it is actually the boat people who are at the mercy of tides, waves, shipwreck and drowning". Still, this negative representation is problematic, since it informs and shapes policies and strategies, emphasising discourses where arrivals are conceived as a "burden", translating into the adoption of the "burden-sharing" policy concept (Pugh, 2004, pp. 64–65).

The geography of today's maritime migration is spread across different hotspots, through a complex web of mobility patterns. Maritime migration channels design spatial linkages, connecting shores through different flows (humans, trade or cultural exchanges). Several hotspots can be identified across different seas, motivated by various forces that range from political and social instability, inequalities and insecurity to economic reasons and prosperity (Ferreira, 2019a, pp. 129, 134).

The Mediterranean is currently the world's deadliest migratory corridor, with migratory pressure having intensified during this last decade, reaching its peak in 2015 with over 1.8 million detections in the EU's southern border and a death toll of over 4,000 people in that same year (FRONTEX, 2019; IOM, 2021). The migratory pressure in the Caribbean, turns it into an important hub for transit movements to the American continent, with migrants from Haiti, Cuba and the Dominican Republic attempting to reach the US shores. Moreover, since the mid-1970s, Australia has seen an increase in the number of irregular arrivals, reaching over 20,700 arrivals in 2013, although registering a significant drop ever since. Moving to the African continent, the Gulf of Aden and the Red Sea between the Horn of Africa to Yemen, is characterised by an increasing maritime mobility of migrants from Ethiopia and Somalia (McAuliffe & Mence, 2017, pp. 24–28). Another relevant hotspot can be found in South-East Asia, mostly involving Rohingya refugees fleeing conflict and persecution in Myanmar and trying to reach the coasts of Bangladesh (UNHCR, 2019).

The geographies of maritime migration tend to be clandestine and are the result of migrants' impotence in accessing regular channels and safe routes, precipitating a significant number of people to reach for alternative, dangerous pathways. Therefore, as highlighted by McAuliffe & Mence (2017, p. 28): "The true scale of this movement is thought to be substantial (…) although the numbers are difficult to track and there is limited data to report".

Political approaches: Lessons and perspectives

Over the last years, the debate on border management has thrived with the surge in boat migrants crossing the Mediterranean Sea, particularly since 2013. This has spurred the discussion between the humanitarian and securitarian challenge at the Western countries' borders and the dilemma of how to safeguard internal security while preventing the loss of human lives at sea.

The mechanisms put in place by receiving states, from Australia to the US and the EU, have primarily focused on legal and administrative restraints to asylum and migration (Schloenhardt, 2000, pp. 40–41). These mechanisms have facilitated the establishment of a Catch-22, which traps individuals through a set of contradictory rules and restrictions. The logic of deterrence prevails in the national and regional approaches, rescuing what Fitzgerald (2019) conveys as medieval concepts of dome, moat, buffers, caging and barbicans, which are interrelated as part of a continuum of coercion that goes from the lightest (the dome) to the most extreme (the barbicans) in the externalisation of borders. Within this vision, the sea has been transformed into a moat to keep unwanted people out, intercepting vessels that carry passengers in an irregular situation. Still, throughout the oceans, patrols and military operations have been deployed to monitor and intercept vessels and prevent the disembarkation and readmission of those individuals intercepted at sea. In addition, states have pushed control away from their maritime borders and turned to the work of third countries as border guards (Fitzgerald, 2019).

Portraying maritime migration through the imaginary of "boat migrants" has triggered a securitisation process, through the use of war aphorisms – the idea of a "littoral invasion" –, to address the potential threat posed by these "undetected intruders" crossing the seas (Pugh, 2004, p. 57). Thus, national authorities have spawned a sense of emergency to support the adoption of interdiction policies and deterrence measures.

The management of human mobility at sea has become increasingly more technological, and is currently based on a set of high-tech devices, such as computers, scans, radars and other IT instruments, operated by a network of highly skilled agents. These technologies facilitate the deployment of SAR missions, and often have an early warning character, providing a "situational awareness picture at the sea border" (Jumbert, 2018).

While the development of sophisticated surveillance tools and information exchange systems help secure the frontier and detect potential risks, the unregulated use of these systems might also turn them into instruments of exclusion, facilitating detection and interception. Actually, there is greater awareness among academics regarding the "humanitarian" usages of these technologies, which might grant them far-reaching legitimacy. Despite their deterrence character, surveillance systems are critical for facilitating the detection of situations of distress at sea and deployment of SAR operations (Jumbert, 2018). At the same time, they also expedite the monitoring and supervision of the seascape to detect and address potential criminal activities.

Another crucial element has been the deployment of rescue operations to safeguard lives at sea, given the unfit and overcrowded vessels used during these dangerous crossings. Nevertheless, "rescue at sea is different to the act of maritime enforcement amounting to interception, differing in both intention and purpose, the two sometimes overlap" (Mallia, 2013, p. 9). In this sense, interception is a state enforcement exercise to exert power in the maritime domain, which may in turn avert a rescue operation. During recent years, interception operations have been strongly condemned, by the public and international NGOs, such as Amnesty International, but also by judicial bodies such as the European Court of Human Rights, which repeatedly called for the "full implementation of member states' obligations under international maritime law, human rights law and refugee law" (Council of Europe, 2019), regarding return operations from Italy to Libya.

More recently, however, the focus has gradually shifted towards traffickers, rather than refugees or migrants, with greater attention being paid to the importance of decriminalising migrants. Regional courts have played an important role in this regard and countries have devised strategies and approaches to address this phenomenon. Take for instance the implementation of EUNAVFOR MED Operation Sophia (now replaced by Operation Irini), a military mission focused on the identification and disruption of smugglers' networks and patrol of international waters, mandated to search and seize suspected vessels at sea. Nonetheless, the operation has been subject to numerous critiques given its military character, stressing humanitarian concerns due to the lack of opportunities offered to migrants in terms of legal channels (Riddervold, 2018; Boşilcă et al., 2020).

Overall, Western countries have chosen to implement a continuum of coercion in order to detain and bring maritime movements to a halt. These actions, however, have been largely unsuccessful in curtailing the number of arrivals, having led instead to changes in the patterns of migrant routes or to the shift to more dangerous ones.

Maritime migration is a cross-cutting issue that affects both countries of origin, transit and destination, as well as the international community. Given the complex character of the phenomenon, a comprehensive approach is required, grounded on the principles of cooperation and coordination (Mallia, 2013, p. 5). A number of authors have emphasised the need to develop and adopt a regulatory framework that ensures that states comply with international law, protect human lives at sea, and take action to prevent and fight the smuggling of migrants and trafficking in human beings (Mallia, 2013; Moreno-Lax & Papastavridis, 2016). This should envision a holistic approach to the challenges posed to and by irregular maritime movements, taking into account the full migration cycle and engaging all stakeholders as contemplated in the Global Compact on Migration.

Conclusion

The research agenda on maritime migration has expanded as the sea continues to be a site of humanitarian crisis. Associating "boat migrants" with a fear of invasion has securitised human mobility at sea, which has translated into the adoption of deterrence emergency measures.

National strategies aiming to manage maritime irregular migration were set up to conduct border management tasks, through the deployment of naval operations and the development of new technologies to facilitate early detection. These measures reveal a strong preoccupation with matters of internal security and have direct policy implications with the creation of logics of control and dissuasion.

This chapter advocates that a human security approach offers a different interpretation of this complex phenomenon, as it enables states to cope with international law obligations, while safeguarding human lives. Seaborne migration places various challenges to maritime security and human security. Still, despite ongoing crises such as the one in the Mediterranean and the existence of a Global Compact for Safe and Orderly Migration, states, and the international community, have still not been able to implement the mechanisms necessary to avoid these humanitarian emergencies, as states' national interests prevail over the adoption of mechanisms of cooperation.

In the end, addressing the challenges posed by irregular maritime movements requires a move beyond policies and practices of control based on a language of invasion and repulsion. Thus, a sea-based approach to human security is a critical element in the protection of lives at sea. In that sense, the adoption of a "comprehensive approach", as argued by Moreno-Lax and Papastavridis (2017), has to draw upon human rights and international maritime legal instruments, considering the entire migration cycle and involving all stakeholders. Since the challenges of today are either the opportunities or threats of tomorrow, we are faced with the need to unload the tensions between security concerns and human rights to create a comprehensive framework to address current and future trends.

This chapter, thus, argues for a comprehensive approach to this phenomenon, where the ultimate goal is deconstructing threats and desecuriting migrants and asylum seekers, while complying with international law obligations.

Notes

1 A stowaway "is a person who secretly boards a vehicle, such as an aircraft, bus, ship, cargo truck or train, to travel without paying" (UNHCR, 2011, p. 4).
2 United Nations Security Council Resolution 2240 of the 9th October 2015, on cooperation to combat human trafficking and smuggling of migrants in Libya's territorial sea and on the high seas off the coast of Libya.

References

Anderson, A., Chappell, J. , Gagan, M. & Grove, R. (2006). Prehistoric maritime migration in the Pacific islands: An hypothesis of ENSO forcing. *The Holocene, 16*(1), 1–6. 10.1191/0959683606hl901ft

Azad, A. K. (2008). The marine dimension of human security: Implications for Bangladesh. *BIISS Journal, 29*(1), 1–40.

Boşilcă, R. L., Stenberg, M., & Riddervold, M. (2020). Copying in EU security and defence policies: The case of EUNAVFOR MED Operation Sophia. *European Security, 30*(2), 218–236.

Bourbeau, P. (2011). *The Securitization of Migration: A Study of Movement and Order.* Taylor & Francis.

Bueger, C. (2015). Learning from piracy: Future challenges of maritime security governance. *Global Affairs, 1*(1), 33–42. 10.1080/23340460.2015.960170

Council of Europe. (2019, November 15). Commissioner publishes observations on alleged human rights violations of migrants returned from Italy to Libya. Commissioner for Human Rights. https://www.coe.int/en/web/commissioner/-/commissioner-publishes-observations-on-alleged-human-rights-violations-of-migrants-returned-from-italy-to-lib-1

Ferreira, S. (2019a). Connecting shores: Migration and human security in the Atlantic basin (pp. 129–148). In N. S. Teixeira & D. Marcos (Eds.), *Evolving Human Security Challenges in the Atlantic Space*. Jean Monnet Network on Atlantic Studies and Brookings Institution Press.

Ferreira, S. (2019b). *Human Security and Migration in Europe's Southern Borders*. Palgrave Macmillan.

Fitzgerald, D. S. (2019). *Refuge beyond Reach. How Rich Democracies Repel Asylum Seekers*. Oxford University Press.

FRONTEX. (2019). *Risk Analysis for 2019*. Frontex.

Gerard, A. (2014). *The Securitization of Migration and Refugee Women*. Routledge.

Goodwin-Gill, G. S. (2016). Setting the scene: Refugees, asylum seekers, and migrants at sea – The need for a long-term, protection-centred vision. In V. Moreno-Lax & E. Papastavridis (Eds.), *"Boat Refugees" and Migrants at Sea: A Comprehensive Approach*. Brill Nijhoff.

Huysmans, J. (2000). The European Union and the securitization of migration. *Journal of Common Market Studies, 38*(5), 751–777.

IMO, UNHCR & International Chamber of Shipping. (2015). *Rescue at Sea. A Guide to Principles and Practice as Applied to Refugee and Migrants*. IMO, UNHCR & International Chamber of Shipping.

IOM. (2021). *Missing Migrants. Tracking Deaths along Migratory Routes*. https://missingmigrants.iom.int/

Jumbert, M. G. (2018). Control or rescue at sea? Aims and limits of border surveillance technologies in the Mediterranean Sea. *Disasters*, Overseas Development Institute. *42*(4), 674–696. 10.1111/disa.12286.

Mallia, P. (2013). The challenges of irregular maritime migration. *Jean Monnet Occasional Paper*, 4/2013. https://www.um.edu.mt/library/oar/bitstream/123456789/18177/1/JM%20Occasional%20Paper%20no.%204%20final%20as%20re-uploaded.pdf

Mann, I. (2016). *Humanity at Sea. Maritime Migration and the Foundations of International Law*. Cambridge University Press.

McAuliffe, M., & Mence, V. (2017). Irregular maritime migration as a global phenomenon (pp. 11–48). In M. McAuliffe & K. Koser (Eds.), *A Long Way to Go. Irregular Migration Patterns, Processes, Drivers and Decision-Making*. Australian National University Press.

Moreno-Lax, V., & Papastavridis, E. (2016). 'Boat Refugees' and Migrants at Sea: A Comprehensive Approach. Leiden: Martinus Nijhoff.

Moreno-Lax, V., & Papastavridis, E. (2017). Tracing the bases of an integrated paradigm for maritime security and human rights at sea. In V. Moreno-Lax & E. Papastavridis (Eds.), *"Boat Refugees" and Migrants at Sea: A Comprehensive Approach. Integrating Maritime Security with Human Rights* (pp. 1–16). Brill Nijhoff.

Pugh, M. (2004). Drowning not waving: Boat people and humanitarianism at sea. *Journal of Refugee Studies, 17*(1), 50–69.

Ralby, I. M. (2016). Maritime security cooperation in the Gulf of Guinea: Prospects and challenges, by Kamal-Deen Ali. *Naval War College Review, 69*(3), 9.

Riddervold, M. (2018). A humanitarian mission in line with human rights? Assessing Sophia, the EU's naval response to the migration crisis. *European Security, 27*(2), 158–174.

Schloenhardt, A. (2000). Australia and the boat-people: 25 years of unauthorised arrivals. *UNSW Law Journal, 23*(3), 33–55.

The Refugee Convention. (1951). https://www.unhcr.org/4ca34be29.pdf

UNHCR. (2002). *Background Note on the Protection of Asylum-Seekers and Refugees Rescued at Sea*. UNHCR. https://www.unhcr.org/3e5f35e94.pdf

UNHCR. (2011). *Rescue at Sea, Stowaways and Maritime Interception. Selected Reference Materials* (2nd Edition). UNHCR. https://www.refworld.org/docid/4ee087492.html

UNHCR. (2019). *Refugee Movements in South-East Asia. Searching for Safety. January 2018–June 2019*. UNHCR. https://www.unhcr.org/5d91e2564.pdf

United Nations. (2000a). *Protocol against the Smuggling of Migrants by Land, Sea and Air, Supplementing the United Nations Convention against Transnational Organized Crime*. https://www.refworld.org/pdfid/479dee062.pdf

United Nations. (2000b). *Protocol to Prevent, Suppress and Punish Trafficking in Persons, Especially Women and Children, Supplementing the United Nations Convention against Transnational Organized Crime*. https://www.ohchr.org/en/professionalinterest/pages/protocoltraffickinginpersons.aspx

UNODC. (2018). *Global Study on Smuggling of Migrants 2018*. United Nations.

15

CONTEMPORARY MARITIME PIRACY AND COUNTER-PIRACY

Robert McCabe

Introduction

Piracy is a crime that has existed in some form for centuries. This has manifested in different regions, in different contexts and in profoundly different ways. Episodes of piracy are not only contextually unique across the geographic divide but also regionally distinctive during different historical periods. It can be linked to discourses as diverse as naval history and maritime strategy (Speller, 2014; Till, 2016), politics and International Relations (Struett et al., 2014; Bueger et al., 2019), business and economics (Anderson, 1995; Fu et al., 2010; Sergi & Morabito, 2016), to development studies (Bueger et al., 2019; Okafor-Yarwood, 2020) international law (Rubin, 1988; Guilfoyle, 2009; Roach, 2010), and conflict and security studies (Murphy, 2007; Chalk, 2008).

The vulnerability of shipping to attack has long been a feature of the maritime environment. The ocean is a vast, empty and largely ungoverned space that offers a fluid highway for various legitimate and illegitimate activities. In modern times, piracy and armed violence at sea have tended to manifest in spaces with certain static and shifting traits. These include proximity to merchant trade routes, porous coastal geography, volatile socio-economic conditions ashore, regions with a propensity for conflict and states that lack a national maritime consciousness and enforcement capability.

Historically, the phenomenon of piracy has been linked to statecraft and warfare through commerce raiding, has experienced periods of legitimisation as privateering during the sixteenth century, and has played a central role in the development of international maritime law. More recently, maritime piracy resurged in the late twentieth century in a distinct manner to previous historical eras. This related to the unique political, social and economic context of the period, such as the fallout from large regional conflicts, a growth in seaborne trade coupled with a decline in global naval power following the Cold War, and increased economic hardship in coastal regions despite a more globalised and interconnected economic system.

This chapter will examine contemporary piracy and responses to it. As a starting point, definitions, conceptualisations and broader consequences will be briefly discussed to place piracy within the modern political and security context. This is followed by an overview of causal factors, manifestations as well as regional and international efforts initiated to suppress piracy in the western Indian Ocean, Southeast Asia and the Gulf of Guinea. The final section will explore

176   DOI: 10.4324/9781003001324-18

some lessons and perspectives from insights into modern piracy and counter-piracy. These include the changing role of private security, the effectiveness of informal governance, the enduring utility of navies, the interlinkages of maritime crime, as well as the relationship between security and blue growth.

Definitions, conceptualisations and consequences

While the provenance of the term "piracy" can be traced back to the ancient Graeco-Roman world,[1] in a modern context, it was not until the decades after the First and Second World Wars that any meaningful attempt was made to codify, define and conceptualise piracy and maritime criminality. Collectively, these efforts – such as the volume published by Harvard Law school in 1932 and the Geneva Convention on the High Seas of 1958 – led to the United Nations Convention on the Law of the Sea of 1982 (UNCLOS). According to Article 101 of UNCLOS, piracy consisted of any of the following:

> (a) any illegal acts of violence or detention, or any act of depredation, committed for private ends by the crew or the passengers of a private ship or a private aircraft, and directed: (i) on the high seas, against another ship or aircraft, or against persons or property on board such ship or aircraft; (ii) against a ship, aircraft, persons or property in a place outside the jurisdiction of any State; (b) any act of voluntary participation in the operation of a ship or of an aircraft with knowledge of facts making it a pirate ship or aircraft; (c) any act of inciting or of intentionally facilitating an act described in subparagraph (a) or (b).

It should be noted that codifying maritime piracy was not the primary motivation behind the drafting of UNCLOS (it is addressed in just seven articles out of 320). Therefore, despite offering the principal internationally endorsed legal definition of piracy (it attracted 119 signatories), UNCLOS led to a lack of clarity around issues of jurisdiction, "hot pursuit", the "private ends" motivational clause, the "two vessel" requirement and its failure to impose a legal obligation on states to suppress piracy in their territorial waters. Some of these limitations were rectified in proceeding conventions such as the Convention for the Suppression of Unlawful Acts of Violence Against the Safety of Maritime Navigation of 1988 and the UN Convention against Transnational Organized Crime of 2000.

By limiting acts of piracy to those committed outside the jurisdiction of a state's maritime boundary, UNCLOS inadvertently created two separate definitions of what was essentially an identical crime perpetrated in a different maritime space. This was problematic as most of these types of attacks, as well as other forms of maritime criminal activity, tended to occur in anchorages, ports and littoral sea spaces. To compensate for this (and for the purposes of gathering more accurate statistics), various international organisations, such as the International Maritime Bureau (IMB), created broader definitions of piracy by grouping it with armed robbery in territorial waters. This defined piracy as, "An act of boarding or attempting to board any ship with the apparent intent to commit theft or any other crime and with the apparent intent or capability to use force in the furtherance of that act" (IMB, 2002). This reflected a broader consensus that in practice piracy and armed robbery are interchangeable phenomena, particularly from a victim impact perspective (McCabe, 2018, p. 106).

Indeed, acts of piracy are frequently conflated with other forms of maritime criminality such as terrorist activity, smuggling and fisheries crime. This is an important consideration as piracy is often just one type of act that a maritime criminal engages in when it is most likely to generate more revenue and less risk than, for example, smuggling people, weapons, or drugs. Piracy and terrorism are different. While the modus operandi is often similar (e.g., kidnap for ransom), the motivation, targeting and levels of violence are largely distinct. This adds a layer of geostrategic complexity to piracy and, as Murphy (2009, p. 6) notes, makes it all the harder to eliminate.

Piracy is therefore a phenomenon that impacts well beyond the immediate act itself. It can have ramifications for the shipping industry, the safety of its personnel and the global supply chain, the security and economic resilience of coastal communities, as well as a negative impact on the blue economic prospects of littoral states.

Causes and responses

To understand how modern piracy manifests, it is important to examine the context in which it occurs and how states respond to it in different regions, some of which are explored elsewhere in this volume. This section highlights the distinctiveness of causes and responses to piracy in three regions and illuminates why, despite the universality of the term, piracy means different things to different actors in different space and time settings.

Context matters

The escalation of Somali-based piracy after 2005 brought the issue to the attention of the international community and captured the public imagination unlike manifestations in other parts of the world. The genesis of modern Somali piracy can be traced back to the Civil War and the subsequent collapse of the central government of Siad Barre in 1991, although maritime criminality including piracy, smuggling and hostage-for-ransom kidnappings had featured along the coast of Somalia and in the Gulf of Aden since at least the early eighteenth century (Anderson, 2009, p. 2). The collapse of state institutions and the lawlessness that ensued after 1991 provided ample opportunity for criminal enterprise particularly in the more isolated coastal communities. An organised and capable maritime criminal network developed along the coast of Somalia after 2005 as a result of favourable geography, combined with financial incentive, access to weaponry, entrepreneurial acumen, community support, extreme poverty, limited regional maritime enforcement infrastructure and a low risk of arrest (Murphy, 2009, pp. 24–45; Chalk, 2010, p. 92; Bueger, 2013, pp. 1813–1814; McCabe, 2018, pp. 167–168). Other drivers of Somali piracy include socio-economic and environmental grievances linked to illegal, unreported and unregulated (IUU) fishing and the discarding of contaminated waste by foreign companies exploiting an anarchic maritime environment (Hanson, 2009; Sloggett, 2013).

While acts of piracy in the western Indian Ocean made international news headlines following several high-profile incidents, the situation on the other side of the continent failed to gain traction and attract attention in the same way – despite the severity and frequency of attacks. The problem of piracy in the Gulf of Guinea has largely evolved as a symptom of the unrest created by mismanagement of the region's oil industry, alongside issues of ethnic and political "ownership" of resources in a post-conflict environment (Manby, 2003, p. 3; Berube & Cullen, 2012, p. 143). What began primarily as attacks against oil infrastructure close to the shore, extended further out to sea to oil tankers, merchant and fishing vessels after 2008. The context differed considerably from Somali piracy given the existence of a functioning government ashore in Nigeria with a maritime enforcement capability. While the motivation for attacks by Somali pirates was almost exclusively financial, a large percentage of piracy in the Gulf of Guinea was at least partly politically driven (IMB, 2008, p. 26). These robberies were facilitated by an inadequately governed sea space, primarily due to poor maritime domain awareness and an underfunded coastguard and navy to monitor and patrol maritime zones. Compounding this is an historical "seablindness", issues of corruption among local officials, poverty and economic disenfranchisement in coastal communities, and a lack of deterrence due to inadequate judicial structures ashore to investigate and prosecute those engaged in illicit maritime criminal activity (Bueger & Edmunds, 2017).

Unlike acts of piracy – including the hijacking of vessels and kidnapping of crews for ransom – in the western Indian Ocean and the Gulf of Guinea, most incidents of piracy in Southeast Asia were generally less violent and manifested at a lower, more opportunistic level. Such acts typically included armed robberies and petty thefts from vessels in ports and anchorages. Several factors, both regional and international, influenced the character of modern Southeast Asian piracy, particularly after 1997. These included increased economic, social and political marginalisation in the aftermath of the Asian financial crisis; lack of state naval capacity; corruption among local law enforcement; increase in commercial maritime trade; the legacy of regional conflict; and the impact of the attacks on the United States on 11 September 2001 (Liss, 2003, pp. 57–58; Young, 2007, p. 18; Storey, 2008, p. 106; Raymond, 2009, pp. 32–33). In addition, the expansion of the globalised system meant maritime criminals could exploit and profit from increasingly porous borders, as well as less restrictions on international travel, enhanced telecommunications, the internet and more interconnected financial markets all facilitated by a large and poorly governed maritime space (McCabe, 2018, p. 96). According to a report by the UN Office on Drugs and Crime (UNODC, 2010, p. 29), "globalisation meant that human and commercial flows are too intense to easily distinguish the licit from the illicit". Aside from piracy, several transnational crimes had a distinct maritime dimension such as the illegal trafficking of weaponry, drugs, human beings and counterfeit goods (UNODC, 2010). In 2015 and 2016, there was an increase in serious incidents of abduction of crew from ships for ransom in the Sulu-Celebes Seas and waters off Eastern Sabah. This was reportedly linked to the Abu Sayyaf Group and domestic politics in the Philippines, which highlights how local context is an important consideration in understanding how and why piracy manifests in a particular location at a specific time (Hamzah, 2016, pp. 2–3; ReCAAP ISC, 2016, p. 2). These recent incidents of maritime piracy in the region are exacerbated by weak maritime security governance capacity and cooperation more generally and a likely awareness of the profitability in ransoming a vessel and crew, mirroring to some degree the modus operandi of Somali pirates after 2008.

Cooperation and contestation – Responding to piracy

The response to Somali piracy was unprecedented. While sluggish at first, by 2008, it had evolved into a multifaceted and multinational effort. At its height, in 2011, counter-piracy assets in the western Indian Ocean comprised 32 vessels from 11 countries, with four aircraft on average, and around 1,800 personnel, costing around US$1.27 billion (Oceans Beyond Piracy, 2011, p. 27; UN Security Council, 2011, p. 8). There were multinational naval patrols launched by the European Union (EUNAVFOR Operation Atalanta), The United States and its allies (Combined Maritime Task Force 151), and NATO (Operation Ocean Shield), alongside several independent deployers such as Russia, China and Iran. Innovative approaches were adopted to maximise this naval presence, such as the creation of an Internationally Recommended Transit Corridor (IRTC) and group transit system, which afforded vessels a higher level of protection by placing them proximal to international naval assets patrolling in the corridor (McCabe, 2018, p. 214).

Given the array of naval assets, national governments and regional organisations involved in counter-piracy activity in the western Indian Ocean, new and experimental informal governance structures were also created. The Shared Awareness and Deconfliction Forum (SHADE) attempted to coordinate and deconflict the various activities of multinational naval forces, while the Contact Group on Piracy off the Coast of Somalia (CGPCS) was established as an international cooperation mechanism to act as a common point of contact between states, regional and international organisations, and other stakeholders on all aspects of combating piracy (UN Security Council, 2011, p. 9).

These efforts were buttressed by the deployment of Privately Contracted Armed Security Personnel (PCASP) and nationally-designated armed Vessel Protection Detachments on board ships alongside softer security approaches, such as five different iterations of Best Management Practice (BMP), which were conceived of and published by the shipping industry to maximise self-defence measures while transiting the High-Risk Area.[2] Experimental approaches to building maritime security capacity also emerged. These were primarily led by international actors such as the EU, UNODC and the International Maritime Organisation, and sought to develop regional law enforcement capacities, maritime patrol and surveillance systems, inter-agency and cross-national information sharing tools as well as maritime governance structures (Bueger et al., 2021, pp. 229–240). At a regional level, capacity-building projects also supported important counter-piracy frameworks such as the Djibouti Code of Conduct (DCoC), which was expanded to encompass issues beyond piracy in 2017.

The combination of these various approaches resulted in a sharp decline in successful acts of piracy in the region after 2013. The unique international response, tailored to the Somali piracy context, in particular the fact that Somalia was a failed state without the capacity to police or govern its waters, was not directly transferable to other regions, such as the Gulf of Guinea. This was due to the existence of functioning governments ashore and existing, albeit often weak, national enforcement capabilities at sea.

Unlike the Horn of Africa, where counter-piracy responses were primarily internationally led, responses in the Gulf of Guinea are conducted by regional actors as there are no failed states. International involvement here mainly takes the form of advocacy for maritime safety and security initiatives, delivering capacity-building support and conducting naval exercises, such as the annual multinational Obangame Express. International pressure, for example, hastened the Yaoundé Architecture, which included a Code of Conduct for the repression of illicit maritime activity, an interregional coordination centre and the creation of new maritime operational zones (Gulf of Guinea Interregional Network, n.d.).

Nigeria, the region's largest maritime power and the genesis of most piratical incidents, has made recent strides to address to problem including novel initiatives, such as the Deep Blue Project, which focuses on intelligence gathering, response capability through the acquisition of maritime security assets, and training of personnel to patrol Nigeria's territorial waters and Exclusive Economic Zone (Nigerian Maritime Administration and Safety Agency (NIMASA), 2020).

The widespread use of PCASP in the western Indian Ocean could not be easily replicated in the Gulf of Guinea due to a complex "patchwork of legal, security, administrative, command and control interests" (IMO, 2016, p. 7). Instead, the Nigerian Navy has responded to requests for assistance and private maritime security companies have provided escort services using private vessels with Nigerian armed forces personnel on board (Danish Ministry of Foreign Affairs, 2019, p. 7). Inspired by successes in the western Indian Ocean but recognising the unique context in the Gulf of Guinea, in March 2020, the shipping industry published a BMP document to deter piracy and enhance maritime security in West Africa (International Chamber of Shipping, et al., 2020). The IMO (2017a) also published a strategy statement in 2017 on implementing sustainable maritime security measures in West and Central Africa.

While states in the Gulf of Guinea have increased their capacity in terms of equipment and tools for monitoring, compliance and surveillance, they have failed to deal with the root causes of piracy, such as disenfranchisement and economic marginalisation in coastal communities, through, for example, improved marine spatial planning and governance. They have, however, enacted new legislation known as the Suppression of Piracy and Other Maritime Offences Act in June 2019 – which criminalises piracy, sea robbery and other maritime crimes in domestic legislation – the first country in West and Central Africa to have a standalone antipiracy law (Safety4Sea, 2019). The first suspects to be tried under this new legislation took place in July 2020.

Counter-piracy efforts in Southeast Asia were assisted by the development of new navigational and satellite technologies, such as the introduction of a mandatory Automatic Identification System in 2004. Several national, bilateral and multilateral counter-piracy initiatives were also undertaken. These included the creation of new national maritime coordination bodies and the strengthening of enforcement capacities in Indonesia, Malaysia, the Philippines and Singapore. This was in parallel to several bilateral and trilateral agreements, particularly by countries along the Malacca Strait, designed to strengthen the proliferation of intelligence, improving surveillance capacity, establishing cooperative anti-piracy frameworks and coordinating maritime surface patrols (McCabe, 2018, pp. 113–114). There was also a significant contribution from international stakeholders such as Australia, China, Japan, India and the United States in supporting regional maritime security initiatives and improving capacities.

External pressure alongside fears that direct US involvement in internal maritime security matters could undermine sovereignty prompted regional states to establish the Malacca Straits Coordinated Patrols under the banner of the Malacca Straits Security Initiative in 2004 (Baker, 2004). This was enhanced in 2005 with the introduction of a joint air-surveillance programme called "Eyes in the Sky", which resulted in a sharp decline in incidents of piracy along the Malacca Strait from 38 in 2004 to just 12 reports in 2005 (IMB, 2005, p. 5). This multilateral-driven regional counter-piracy approach reached its zenith in 2006 with the signing of ReCAAP agreement – the first regional government-to-government agreement to promote and enhance cooperation against piracy and armed robbery against ships in Asia (ReCAAP ISC, n.d.). While ReCAAP did not have a dedicated enforcement arm (this was left to the discretion of individual states), it did establish an Information Sharing Centre (ISC) in Singapore, which was instrumental in raising awareness through the promotion of information sharing, collating data, publishing guidance and recommendations, and providing a more nuanced picture into how piracy has manifested in the region since 2007.

In response to a rise in maritime kidnapping for ransom after 2015, regional states stepped up counter-piracy patrols. The Philippine Coast Guard, for example, deployed sea marshals onboard shipping vessels in high-risk areas in the Moro Gulf of the Sulu and South China Seas (Joubert, 2020, p. 20). In addition, the UNODC, in partnership with the Philippine Coast Guard, convened the first meeting of the Contact Group on Maritime Crime in the Sulu and Celebes Seas in August 2018, mirroring the CGPCS model employed in the western Indian Ocean. In the Strait of Malacca, trilateral counter-piracy cooperation was also expanded in 2015 and continued to benefit from actionable information provided by the Singapore-based Information Fusion Centre.

Mirroring guidance published in the western Indian Ocean and the Gulf of Guinea, but tailored to regional specificities, ReCAAP ISC published a "Tug Boats and Barges Against Piracy and Sea Robbery" guide in December 2012 and guidance on the abduction of crews in the Sulu-Celebes Seas and waters off Eastern Sabah in 2019. This reflects once more that cognisance of local context is critical in tailoring nuanced and effective interventions to supress piracy. As in all regions discussed in this chapter, piracy can be supressed when concerted efforts are made, but it is rarely eradicated, unless structural and systemic changes are initiated ashore, which requires long-term investment and political will.

Lessons and perspectives

The contemporary experience of attempting to counteract maritime piracy has generated different lessons and perspectives, not only in relation to best practices for tackling maritime criminality more generally but also to how states can better cooperate in governing the shared commons and benefiting from the resources of the maritime domain. A key lesson that emerged from the experience of piracy in the western Indian Ocean, for example, was the importance of a comprehensive approach that tackled the root causes ashore while addressing the symptomatic manifestations at sea and at coastal interfaces. It is clear there is no "one size fits all" approach, and that national context is critical both to understand manifestations but also to design and implement more effective responses. Despite this, broader lessons, perspectives and insights can be extracted from the experiences of piracy and acts of armed robbery against ships in different parts of the world. These include the changing role of private security providers and other non-state actors, the enduring utility and versatility of naval forces and coastguards, the interlinkages of maritime crimes, the effectiveness of informal governance approaches, the growth of capacity-building for maritime security, and, finally, the blue-turn in African coastal state policy.

Private security

PCASP on board ships are widely recognised as a force-multiplier and effective deterrent against successful acts of piracy (see for example Chapsos, 2019; McCabe, 2016, p. 26). In the western Indian Ocean, PCASP were one of the central pieces of the puzzle that stifled hijackings and contributed to a sharp decline in attempted attacks. Notwithstanding legislative challenges, it was easier to regulate private armed guards transiting Somalia due to the lack of functioning administration ashore when compared with Southeast Asia or the Gulf of Guinea. However, even though (at the time of writing) no ship that had embarked PCASP had been successfully boarded or hijacked in the western Indian Ocean, the shipping industry regards their deployment as an "exceptional response" and "neither normal nor permanent" (ICS, 2015, p. 5). This is primarily due to the complex legal issues of privately held arms moving through sovereign jurisdictions and the innocent passage of commercial shipping as well as concerns over violation of human rights and international law, and ambiguity as regards command and control of a vessel (Affi et al., 2016, p. 935). Despite these enduring difficulties, the success of PCASP in countering and deterring piracy, particularly in the western Indian Ocean, means that they will likely be a feature of maritime security in high-risk maritime zones for the foreseeable future (McCabe, 2016, p. 26). In addition, as Cusumano and Ruzza (2018, pp. 81–82) posit, "the policies undertaken to protect the shipping industry from piracy offer an ideal example of the growing hybridisation between public and private that is increasingly characterising contemporary global governance".

Naval responses

Modern piracy has highlighted the enduring utility and versatility of naval forces, despite a steady decline in the number of assets worldwide since the end of the Cold War. In addition, it has highlighted the importance of an appropriately equipped, well-trained and sustainably funded constabulary maritime policing capacity. Kenya, for example, established a coastguard for the first time in the history of the state to address a broad range of maritime criminal issues including piracy. International organisations are also trying to strengthen the capacity of African navies through the donation of boats, technical training, maintenance courses and the provision of maritime surveillance equipment and analytical software (UNODC, 2015, p. 13). The multilateral naval response to piracy in the western Indian Ocean illustrated the importance of a comprehensive approach and mirrored to some extent the concept of the "1,000 ship navy", which hypothesised a global maritime security arrangement, designed to synergise the collective maritime capabilities of allies to enhance security in the maritime domain (Uhls, 2006, p. 2). The presence of such an array of naval forces illustrated the truly global nature of the response to Somali piracy alongside a unique opportunity for foreign navies to demonstrate blue water capability and project soft power on an international stage (McCabe, 2018, p. 219). China, for example, established its first-ever foreign military base in Djibouti in 2017 under the guise of counter-piracy operations and Russia also attempted to expand its presence beyond naval operations in the region, albeit unsuccessfully (Ramani, 2020). In the Gulf of Guinea and Southeast Asia, sensitives over territorial integrity combined with an often-antiquated maritime enforcement capacity meant organising and coordinating multilateral naval patrols was and remains a more challenging undertaking. Despite this, joint and coordinated bilateral, trilateral and multilateral maritime security and counter-piracy patrols have been conducted between regional navies, alongside exercises with international navies.

Beyond piracy

Piracy typically exists alongside other criminal – often interlinked – activities in the maritime domain such as fisheries crime, smuggling of illicit material such as drugs or weapons, illegal migration, oil theft and fuel smuggling. While many of these issues do not impact seafarers directly, governments need to recognise the linkages and invest resources to address maritime insecurity in a more holistic manner. The experience of Somali piracy in particular highlighted the interlinkages of maritime crime. When the risk of capture or injury from acts of piracy became too great, pirate action groups diversified their activities to arms, narcotic and charcoal smuggling as well as human trafficking (Coker & Paris, 2013). The need to recognise piracy as one thread in a web of interlinked maritime criminal activities was clear in the Jeddah Amendment to the DCoC in 2017 for example. It was highlighted how acts of piracy and armed robbery against ships manifest alongside other transnational organised criminal activities that also threaten legitimate uses of the oceans and endanger the lives of people at sea, as well as the livelihoods and security of coastal communities (International Maritime Organization (IMO), 2017b, p. 35). Similarly, in the Gulf of Guinea, there is evidence that IUU fishing, fuel smuggling, pipeline vandalisation and acts of piracy and armed robbery are sometimes perpetrated by the same individuals and organised criminal groups (Denton & Harris, 2019, pp. 15–16; Okafor-Yarwood, 2020, pp. 125–133). In Southeast Asia, criminal syndicates have long been involved in maritime criminality ranging from piracy, armed robbery, fuel siphoning, oil bunkering, phantom ship fraud as well as narcotic, weapon and people smuggling. According to Karsten von Hoesslin (2016, p. 2), "this has been a consistent trend within Southeast Asia, which is why any counter-piracy efforts at the multinational level in the region must also include tackling other transnational maritime crimes". Recognising these interlinkages is important for tailoring appropriate operational and policy responses. Lessons learned from contemporary counter-piracy operations have had a wider applicability beyond piracy in, for example, tackling smuggling. In the Mediterranean two approaches have been replicated in an attempt to counter human smuggling and irregular migration – a naval operation designated EUNAVFOR MED Operation Sophia and a deconfliction forum known as SHADE MED.

Informal governance

In the western Indian Ocean region, the utility of informal and experimental governance approaches to address maritime crime emerged as a valuable lesson – not only for how to govern counter-piracy activities but also to potentially develop best practice approaches for broader fields of transnational governance like climate change and economic regulation (Tardy, 2014, p. 85). This approach was less significant in the Gulf of Guinea and Southeast Asia, where more formalised, traditional approaches have been favoured to mitigate and manage divergent state interests. The CGPCS is the principal example of an effective informal governance mechanism that was broadly successful in bringing together multiple regional and international stakeholders to address Somali-based piracy. According to Bueger (2014, p. 82), "The growing experimentalism was also supported by the confidence to formally invite representatives other than states...shipping associations, industry associations, humanitarian organisations and even academics were formally invited to feed their ideas and proposals into the process". However, some remain sceptical about the universal utility of this approach in other contexts. As Jakobi (2014, p. 7) contests, "the model of the Contact Group is likely to be less successful in cases where the criminal activity is more widespread, and more conflicting interests and veto-players would need to be moderated".

Maritime security capacity-building

The upsurge in modern piracy, particularly in the western Indian Ocean, resulted in a new, experimental, field of capacity building that differed from more traditional Security Sector Reform or peacebuilding approaches ashore. Maritime security capacity building incorporates a range of security concerns that move beyond institutions and individual states such as engaging transnational criminal actors and incorporating ambitious new epistemic practices and technologies such as maritime domain and situational awareness (Bueger et al., 2020, p. 231). Since 2012, it has also expanded to incorporate a wider range of maritime security concerns, including illegal fishing, trafficking at sea and marine resource protection, management and development. Core practices from the western Indian Ocean have been adopted elsewhere, including the Gulf of Guinea and in the Sulu and Celebes seas (UN Office on Drugs and Crime (UNODC), 2018, p. 45). Other regions, including the Mediterranean, Caribbean and South Pacific, have also developed initiatives derived initially from the western Indian Ocean experience (UN Office on Drugs and Crime (UNODC), 2018, pp 6–15, 42–49).

African maritime renaissance

Perhaps the greatest impact of the story of modern piracy, chiefly in Africa, is how it precipitated a turn toward the ocean in national consciousness and security policy. Kenya and Nigeria, two of the most developed coastal states on opposite sides of the continent, have recognised that, to address maritime piracy and crime in a sustainable way, the ocean economy needs to be developed and the needs of coastal communities must be considered in policy formulation. Security and blue economic concerns need to be a unified policy issue. In 2019–2020, for example, Kenyan investment in developing and coordinating the blue economy surpassed investment in all other areas including agribusiness, industrial development and business financing with an unprecedented KES3.7 billion allocated compared with just KES100 million in 2016–2017 (Development Initiatives, 2019, p. 25). The phenomena of piracy in Africa, therefore, has "opened a window of opportunity to re-organise maritime security governance and build sustainable institutions" (Bueger, 2015, p. 40). Similarly, in Nigeria, the blue economic and maritime security agenda have gained prominence, with a recognition from the Nigerian Maritime Administration and Safety Agency that piracy and armed robbery against ships need to be suppressed and maritime institutions strengthened to "put the maritime sector and the blue economy on the path of sustainable development" (Edward & Chigozie, 2017, p. 14).

Conclusion

Piracy has negative implications for the shipping industry, seafarers and the global supply chain. It undermines the security and economic resilience of coastal communities as well as the socio-economic prospects of regional states. While the phenomenon of piracy has experienced upsurges and periods of decline throughout the modern era, it has manifested differently in specific contexts. In the western Indian Ocean, piracy manifested as an organised criminal enterprise with financiers, sophisticated logistics and a willing pool of disenfranchised foot soldiers to launch attacks and hijack vessels, as well as a community infrastructure to hold seafarers for ransom. Only a combination of state and non-state intervention tailored to the distinctive context of the problem and region resulted in the suppression of incidents. While organised criminal networks were active in acts of piracy in Southeast Asia, incidents there have tended to manifest at a less organised and less violent level. In contrast to Somalia and its littoral states, Southeast Asian countries, such as Singapore, Indonesia, or the Philippines, generally have access to more resources, more functional maritime security institutions and better enforcement capacity to address piracy, particularly when they have acted in a joined up or concerted way. In the Gulf of Guinea, piracy remains a problem at the time of writing, although regional and international states are paying more attention to the problem and exploring innovative and more collaborative efforts to counter the problem such as the Deep Blue project.

What connects each region is the use of the sea and coastal interfaces as a conduit for illicit activity of which piracy and armed robbery against ships is just one manifestation. The experience of attempting to understand and address modern piracy has resulted in innovative approaches, collaborations and changes in the way international security problems are governed. There is increasing recognition that piracy is just one thread in a web of interlinked maritime criminal activities that need to be tackled in a holistic way. Experimental informal governance mechanisms, such as the CGPCS, have been broadly successful in bringing together multiple regional and international stakeholders in this regard. Modern piracy has also highlighted the enduring utility and versatility of naval forces as agents of maritime security, diplomacy and power projection, rather than simply being archaic warfighting platforms. In addition, the success of privately contracted armed security in countering and deterring piracy means that they will likely be a feature of maritime security in high-risk maritime zones for the foreseeable future.

Coastal states in Africa and Southeast Asia that have struggled economically are recognising the strategic value of the ocean economy. Continued incidents of piracy, armed robbery and maritime kidnapping, however, will stifle investment and damage the regions' reputation as a location for development, blue growth and enterprise. Piracy can be suppressed when a concerted, multilateral and situationally adapted effort is undertaken. This requires adequate enforcement capacity, political will and relevant judicial structures as well as regional cooperation. In the long term, maritime criminal activity can only be curbed by addressing the structural and systemic issues ashore that drive elements of coastal communities towards crime.

Notes

1 According to Alfred P. Rubin (1988, p. 5), the earliest time when the surviving literature in Greek uses the word *pierato* and its derivatives appears to be around 130 BC.
2 The High-Risk Area is an area within the UK Maritime Trade Operations designated Voluntary Reporting Area where it is considered there is a higher risk of piracy and within which self-protective measures are most likely to be required (IMO, 2015).

References

Affi, L., Elmi, A. A., Knight, W. A., & Mohamed, S. (2016). Countering piracy through private security in the Horn of Africa: Prospects and pitfalls. *Third World Quarterly*, *37*(5), 934–950.

Anderson, J. L. (1995). Piracy and world history: An economic perspective on maritime predation. *Journal of World History*, *6*(2), 175–199.

Anderson, D. (2009). *Somali piracy: Historical context and political contingency*. Centre for European Policy Studies. Working Paper, 33.

Baker, M. (2004, April 6). *Malaysia rebuffs US sea force plan*. The Age, Global Policy Forum. https://archive.globalpolicy.org/empire/intervention/2004/0406usmalacca.htm

Berube, C., & Cullen, P. (2012). *Maritime private security: Market responses to piracy, terrorism, and waterborne risks in the 21st century*. Routledge.

Bueger, C. (2013). Practice, pirates and Coast Guards: The grand narrative of Somali piracy. *Third World Quarterly*, *34*(10), 1811–1827.

Bueger, C. (2014). Experimental governance: Can the lessons of the CGPCS be transferred to other policy fields? In T. Tardy (Ed.), *Fighting piracy off the coast of Somalia: Lessons learned from the contact group* (78–85). EU Institute for Security Studies.

Bueger, C. (2015). Learning from piracy: Future challenges of maritime security governance. *Global Affairs*, *1*(1), 33–42.

Bueger, C., & Edmunds, T. (2017). Beyond seablindness: A new agenda for maritime security studies. *International Affairs*, *93*(6), 1293–1311.

Bueger, C., Edmunds, T., & McCabe, R. (2020). Into the sea: Capacity-building innovations and the maritime security challenge. *Third World Quarterly*, *41*(2), 228–246.

Bueger, C., Edmunds, T., & McCabe, R. (Eds.). (2021). *Capacity building for maritime security: The Western Indian Ocean experience*. Palgrave Macmillan.

Bueger, C., Edmunds, T., & Ryan, B. J. (2019). Maritime security: The uncharted politics of the global sea. *International Affairs*, *95*(5), 971–978.

Chalk, P. (2008). *The maritime dimension of international security: Terrorism, piracy and challenges for the United States*. RAND Corporation.

Chalk, P. (2010). Piracy off the horn of Africa: Scope, dimensions, causes and responses. *The Brown Journal of World Affairs*, *16*(2), 89–108.

Chapsos, I. (2019). *Maritime security*. Oxford Research Group. https://www.oxfordresearchgroup.org.uk/blog/maritime-security-an-interview-with-ioannis-chapsos

Coker, M., & Paris, C. (2013, November 1). *Somali pirates shift course to other criminal pursuits*. Wall Street Journal. https://www.wsj.com/articles/SB10001424052702304470504579165421385623670

Cusumano, E., & Ruzza, S. (2018). Security privatisation at sea: Piracy and the commercialisation of vessel protection. *International Relations*, *32*(1), 80–103.

Danish Ministry of Foreign Affairs. (2019). *Gulf of Guinea Maritime Security Programme*, 2019–2021.

Denton, G. L. & Harris, J. R. (2019). The impact of illegal fishing on maritime piracy: Evidence from West Africa. *Studies in Conflict & Terrorism*, *44*(11), 1–20.

Development Initiatives. (2019). *Kenya's 2019/20 budget and the big four agenda: A pro poor analysis*. https://devinit.org/resources/kenyas-201920-budget-and-the-big-four-agenda-a-pro-poor-analysis/

Edward, O. & Chigozie, E. (2017). Developing the blue sea economy in Africa: The Nigerian story. *The Voyage: Nigerian Maritime Administration and Safety Agency*, *5*(1), 10–14.

Fu, X., Ng, A. K. Y., & Lau, Y. Y. (2010). The impacts of maritime piracy on global economic development: The case of Somalia. *Maritime Policy & Management*, *37*(7), 677–697.

Guilfoyle, D. (2009). *Shipping interdiction and the law of the sea*. Cambridge University Press.

Gulf of Guinea Interregional Network. (n.d.). *Yaoundé architecture*. https://www.gogin.eu/en/about/yaounde-architecture/

Hamzah, B. A. (2016). Mitigating maritime violence in Sulu Sea: Regional cooperation needed. *RSIS Commentary, 303*, 2–3.

Hanson, S. J. (2009). *Piracy in the greater Gulf of Aden: Myths, misconception and remedies.* Norwegian Institute for Urban and Regional Research. NIBR.

International Maritime Bureau (IMB). (2002). Piracy and armed robbery against ships annual report 2002, ICC.

International Maritime Bureau (IMB). (2005). Piracy and armed robbery against ships annual report 2005, ICC.

International Maritime Bureau (IMB). (2008). Piracy and armed robbery against ships annual report 2008, ICC.

IMO. (2015). *Somali pirate activity: The high-risk area.* http://www.imo.org/en/OurWork/Security/PiracyArmedRobbery/Documents/HRA%20Revisions%20and%20Supporting%20Guidance%20Oct-2015.pdf

IMO. (2016). *Guidelines for owners, operators and masters for protection against piracy in the Gulf of Guinea region.* Version 2. http://www.imo.org/en/OurWork/Security/WestAfrica/Documents/GOG_Guidelines_V2_June_2016.pdf

IMO. (2017a). *Implementing sustainable maritime security measures in West and Central Africa.* http://www.imo.org/en/OurWork/Security/WestAfrica/Documents/WCA%20Strategy_English_April%202017.pdf

International Chamber of Shipping (ICS). (2015). Lessons identified from Somali Piracy. ICS. https://www.ics-shipping.org/wp-content/uploads/2014/01/lessons-identified-from-somali-piracy-2013.pdf

International Chamber of Shipping (ICS), BIMCO, IGP&I Clubs, INTERCARGO, INTERTANKO, and OCIMF. (2020). *Best management practice document to deter piracy and enhance maritime security in West Africa.* http://www.imo.org/en/OurWork/Security/PiracyArmedRobbery/Documents/BMP%20West%20Africa.pdf

International Maritime Organization (IMO). (2017b). *Strengthening maritime security in West and Central Africa.* http://www.imo.org/en/OurWork/Security/Guide_to_Maritime_Security/Documents/WEB_version_v1-01.09.17.pdf

Jakobi, A. P. (2014). *Global governance and transnational crime: Situating the Contact Group.* Cardiff University. http://www.lessonsfrompiracy.net/files/2014/10/Jacobi-Transnational-Crime.pdf

Joubert, L. (2020). *The state of maritime piracy 2019: Assessing the human cost.* One Earth Future Foundation.

Liss, C. (2003). Maritime piracy in Southeast Asia. In Singh, D. & Wah, C. K. (eds.) *Southeast Asian affairs2003.* ISEAS. 52–68.

Manby, B. (2003). The Warri crisis: Fuelling violence. *Human Rights Watch, 15*(18), 2–29.

McCabe, R. (2016). Private maritime security: Transitory measure or permanent fixture? *Seaways: International Journal of the Nautical Institute,* 24–26. July 2016.

McCabe, R. (2018). *Modern maritime piracy: Genesis, evolution and responses.* Routledge.

Murphy, M. N. (2007). Suppression of piracy and maritime terrorism. *Naval War College Review, 60*(3), 23–45.

Murphy, M. N. (2009). *Small boats, weak states, dirty money: Piracy and maritime terrorism in the modern world.* Hurst.

Nigerian Maritime Administration and Safety Agency. (NIMASA) (2020, March 1). *World shipping community confident in Nigeria's antipiracy fight.* https://nimasa.gov.ng/world-shipping-community-confident-in-nigerias-antipiracy-fight/

Oceans Beyond Piracy. (2011). *The economic cost of maritime piracy.* One Earth Future Foundation.

Okafor-Yarwood, I. (2020). The cyclical nature of maritime security threats: Illegal, unreported, and unregulated fishing as a threat to human and national security in the Gulf of Guinea. *African Security, 13*(2), 116–146.

Ramani, S. (2020, July). *Engaged opportunism: Russia's role in the Horn of Africa.* Foreign Policy Research Institute. https://www.fpri.org/wp-content/uploads/2020/06/engaged-opportunism-russias-role-in-the-horn-of-africa.pdf

Raymond, C. Z. (2009). Piracy and armed robbery in the Malacca strait: A problem solved? *Naval War College Review, 62*(3), 32–42.

ReCAAP ISC. (n.d.). *About ReCAAP information sharing centre.* https://www.recaap.org/about_ReCAAP-ISC

ReCAAP ISC. (2016). *Guidance on abduction of crew in the Sulu-Celebes seas and waters off Eastern Sabah.* ReCAAP ISC.

Roach, A. J. (2010). Countering piracy off Somalia: International law and international institutions. *The American Journal of International Law, 104*(3), 397–416.

Rubin, A. P. (1988). *The law of piracy.* Naval War College Press.

Safety4Sea. (2019, October 10). *UN applauds Nigeria's antipiracy law.* https://safety4sea.com/un-applauds-nigerias-antipiracy-law/

Sergi, B. S., & Morabito, G. (2016). The pirates' curse: Economic impacts of the maritime piracy. *Studies in Conflict & Terrorism, 39*(10), 935–952.

Sloggett, D. (2013). *The anarchic sea: Maritime security in the 21st century.* Hurst.

Speller, I. (2014). *Understanding naval warfare* (2nd ed.). Routledge.

Storey, I. (2008). Securing Southeast Asia's sea lanes: A work in progress. *Asia Policy, 6,* 95–128.

Struett, M. J., Carlson, J. D., & Nance, M. T. (2014). *Maritime piracy and the construction of global governance.* Routledge.

Tardy, T. (Ed.). (2014). *Fighting piracy off the coast of Somalia: Lessons learned from the Contact Group.* EU Institute for Security Studies.

Till, G. (2016). *Seapower: A guide for the twenty-first century* (4th ed.). Routledge.

Uhls, D. (2006). *Realizing the 1000-Ship navy. Naval war college.* https://apps.dtic.mil/dtic/tr/fulltext/u2/a463750.pdf

United Nations Convention on the Law of the Sea (UNCLOS). (1982). Treaty series, 1833(31363).

UN Security Council. (2011, October 25). Report of the Secretary-General pursuant to Security Council resolution 1950. S/2011/662.

UNODC. (2010). *The globalisation of crime: A transnational organized crime threat assessment.* UNODC.

UNODC. (2015). *Global Maritime Crime Programme: Annual Report 2015.* UN Publishing and Library Section.

UN Office on Drugs and Crime (UNODC). (2018). *Global maritime crime programme annual report 2018.* UNODC.

von Hoesslin, K. (2016). *The economics of piracy in South East Asia.* Global Initiative against Transnational Organized Crime.

Young, A. J. (2007). *Contemporary maritime piracy in Southeast Asia: History, causes, and remedies.* International Institute for Asian Studies.

16

MARITIME TERRORISM

Joshua Tallis

In the study of maritime terrorism, three debates represent a selective but diverse cross-section of the field's major areas of research:

1   *Why the maritime distinction?* What makes maritime terrorism unique and worthy of analysis separate from other forms of terrorism?
2   *Who uses maritime terrorism?* How do such groups do so and what (if any) is the relationship between terror groups and criminal networks?
3   *What future issues might drive acts of maritime terrorism and the study thereof?*

In the sections below, we take each in turn.

Why the maritime distinction?

Maritime terrorism studies face a question at its most fundamental level – academics do not study "land terrorism", so why maritime? How is maritime terrorism distinct from other forms of terroristic violence? The answer comes in two layers – that maritime terrorism is distinct from its landward cousin in both the strategic calculations it foists upon non–state organisations, and the operational considerations it imposes on individual acts of terror.

Strategic considerations – Audience and change

Terrorist organisations must integrate acts of terror into broader strategic rationales, specifically those of audience and effect. Terrorism is performative, a theatrical act in which the violence is not solely aimed at the immediate target. When terrorists attack a nightclub, those killed are tragically in service to a broader audience whom terrorists seek to influence. The further re-moved an attack is from society, the less clearly such attacks can be made visible to an audience, and the less immediately society feels the propaganda of the deed.

At sea, isolation poses strategic limitations on the use of terrorism. Organisations must identify: who is the audience for a maritime attack, and can such attacks reach that audience? Historically, distance diminished visibility, news coverage and the sense of *it could have been me* that drive social responses to terrorism. As the ability to transmit video by phone grows, the

DOI: 10.4324/9781003001324-19

reach to audiences has as well, but the underlying strategic challenge remains for maritime terrorists – who are they trying to influence?

Influence does not just require reaching an audience but also identifying how an attack at sea integrates with a strategic campaign of violence to shape societal behaviour. Terrorists employ terrorism as a tactic in part because they believe it is an effective tool to achieve a political end with limited resources (English, 2016). Sometimes, their theory of change is an economic one – do enough material damage to society and a community will demand accommodation. Sometimes, the theory of change is a provocative one – elicit an overreaction on the part of government forces and popular support for the state will erode. No matter the strategy, terrorists must consider how acts of terror at sea advance their theories of change. Can maritime attacks create systemic economic damage? Can maritime attacks provoke government overreach?

The answers are often unclear. Imposing economic costs on a national economy via attacks on shipping is challenging, with long-term effects on the economy ambiguous (Murphy, 2009). It is also difficult to draw state forces into a protracted, expensive, or unpopular conflict at sea, where the balance of power is far out of terrorists' favour. With fewer civilians on the terrain, and the audience challenge, it becomes harder to force an overreach by state forces and harder still to leverage any overreach to force political change.

The strategic questions that terrorists face in the maritime domain are not unique to operations at sea – terrorists active in all domains must think through theories of change – but their answers may be, which is our first hint at the utility of analysing maritime terrorism separately from that on land.

Operational considerations – Skills and barriers

The maritime domain imposes operational constraints on terrorist attacks that further differentiate seaward attacks from those onshore. These constraints rhyme with many that pirates face, which gives us a further clue about how to think about maritime terrorism's relationship to conventional terrorism. If one asked, "why study piracy—we don't talk about land theft?" piracy scholars would note that theft at sea capitalises on novel tactical skillsets and relies on unique operational circumstances. Likewise with maritime terrorism, which shares many of the necessary skills and circumstances that drive piracy. As Murphy (2009) notes, maritime terrorism typically requires some combination of:

- Legal and jurisdictional opportunities
- Geographical necessity
- Inadequate security
- Secure base areas
- Maritime tradition
- Charismatic and effective leadership
- State support
- Promise of reward

Some of these conditions are necessary for any act of insecurity in the maritime domain – terrorism, piracy, trafficking – but two have outsized prominence for the operational effectiveness of maritime terrorism: the role of leadership and state support.

Acts of maritime terrorism do not necessarily come to fruition even where many of the above conditions are met. It may be logical to assume that the lack of maritime attacks where conditions seem ripe is due to a lack of technical knowledge to stage them. Yet Lehr (2016) argues that barriers to entry for maritime attacks are overstated – they are high, relative to land-based terrorism but low relative to aviation terrorism, and thus do not fully explain the lack of attacks. What spurs them may in part be motivated and innovative leadership. In the case of Al-Qaeda, Abd al-Rahim al-Nashiri (the "Prince of the Sea") was to maritime terrorism as Ramzi Yousef was to aviation terrorism. Al-Nashiri was the mastermind behind the attempts on the US Navy destroyers USS *The Sullivans* and USS *Cole*, and the French tanker M/V *Limburg*. Al-Nashiri was personally motivated to develop and execute attacks in the maritime space, and that interest and force of personality were enough to push an enterprising terrorist organisation over the entry barriers and into the sea. And as Lehr notes, al-Nashiri's 2002 arrest may be a critical explanatory factor in why so few al-Qaeda attacks thereafter utilised the sea (Lehr, 2016).

State sponsorship is also an important variable in maritime terrorism, which often separates maritime terrorism from other forms of maritime insecurity. Just as acts of political violence occasionally garner state sponsorship on land, so too at sea. And because the sea can be such a complicated operational space, state sponsorship can make a big difference in a group's willingness to strike at sea and the sophistication of those attacks. This was the case in the 1980s, when US support for the Contras in Nicaragua precipitated some maritime attacks (Murphy, 2009). This remains the case with groups such as Hezbollah and the Houthis and their support from Iran.

Terrorists and positions of weakness

Terrorists face hurdles that, collectively, often dissuade the pursuit of maritime terrorism as a viable tactic because terrorists generally operate from a position of relative weakness and are thus risk-averse. Terrorist attacks cost money. The more sophisticated the attack, the more it costs. Attacks take time to plan. The longer the planning cycle, the greater the likelihood of detection. Attacks require personnel. The more complicated the attack, the more specialised the recruits. And because successful attacks are scarce commodities, terrorists often prioritise lower risk, lower cost, higher likelihood scenarios.

"This cost benefit analysis" Murphy (2009, pp. 379–380) summarises, "imposed by the strategic and operational considerations that the maritime domain uniquely imposes on the use of terrorism as a tactic, typically argues against acts of terror at sea". As a result, maritime attacks occur sparingly relative to other incidents – in one assessment, representing about 2% of all attacks (Greenberg et al., 2006).

This relative paucity of attacks has spawned a speculative vein in maritime terrorism study. As the retired US admiral James Stavridis writes, "it has famously been said that the devastating 9/11 attacks were not a failure of intelligence but a failure of imagination"; a failure to consider the novel ways that terrorist organisations could deliver violence (Stavridis, 2017). In the years after 9/11, many scholars turned to studying maritime terrorism in an exploratory manner in an effort to uncover all the possible permutations of violence that could manifest at sea. By workshopping plausible (if not always probable) scenarios of maritime terrorism, analysts were building mechanisms for characterising risk.

And yet, the imaginative drive can also create incentives to hypothesise with abandon, resulting in a strain of analysis focused on high consequence, but low probability, attack scenarios, i.e., "megaterrorism speculation" (Lehr, 2009, p. 55). This literature can quickly become unmoored from the real-world examples available for study, and which tell us directly how terrorists can and have leveraged the sea.

So, it would still be fair to ask – with acts of maritime terrorism so (relatively) rare, what are scholars of maritime violence even studying, and why?

First, as Lehr (2009, p. 55) notes, "All [the] formidable obstacles notwithstanding, acts of maritime terrorism do occur, targeting ships, ports and oil terminals. For this reason, we have to study and analyse them, to prepare ourselves for countermeasures". True, maritime terrorism is rare in relative terms. But the maritime distinction is critical to help us understand *why* terrorism at sea is infrequent, as well as why some groups break through against the odds. Without taking a distinctly maritime look, it would be difficult to measure the scale of the problem, learn under which circumstances maritime terrorism becomes a potent threat, and describe how to counteract it.

Additionally, the study of maritime terrorism helps analysts think about terrorism, broadly, from a new angle. Core questions of terrorists' strategic and operational drivers – questions like audience reach, theories of change, the role of individual skills, or the importance of leadership and state sponsorship – take on new light when considered from the sea. In that domain, scholars are forced to consider terrorist decision-making as often based in rational cost-benefit analyses of strategy and intent, which carries utility for the study of why terrorists pursue any of their strategies and attacks.

Finally, there is a practical valence to this maritime perspective in informing how states respond to political violence. Given state challenges assuring security on land, the maritime portion of terrorist threats often fall by the wayside. Yet many organisations are active at sea – either staging attacks or supporting their activities via financing or maneuver – and should not be viewed as simply operating in one domain (the sea) or the other (on land). Instead, for many non-state groups, the sea is part of an integrated whole in their operations and thus counter-terrorism would benefit from an understanding of the sea. Indicatively, a 2020 report (Curran et al., 2020) on political violence at sea catalogues 43 major non-state actors and their varying relationship to, and reliance on, the maritime space. In an operational sense, this would mean "widening the aperture to consider the litany of ways the maritime space is utilised to promote organised political violence" (Curran, 2019, p. 1). To understand how organisations integrate the sea into cross-domain campaigns of violence, it is useful to explore more directly some of the organisations involved in terrorism at sea and the ways they leverage that space.

Who engages in maritime terrorism, and is there a relationship between terrorism and other forms of maritime crime?

After outlining the obstacles that constrain terrorists' use of maritime operations, it is reasonable to ask why any organisation would commit to maritime terrorism. What does the sea provide that would be worth the risk, and how does maritime terror manifest in reality? Understanding how the maritime space can be appealing for terrorist groups helps us identify attack typologies, the organisations that pursue them and the relationship between maritime terrorism and crime.

How the maritime domain is used – Attack typologies

Terrorists capitalise on the maritime domain in four primary ways:[1]

- *The sea as a source of income:* Attacks on maritime economies – fishers, merchants, ports, etc. – in pursuit of terror financing.
- *The sea as a logistics channel:* Use of the sea to move people and materiel not in direct support of an imminent attack, such as the importation of weapons or fighters.
- *The sea as maneuver space:* Attacks on targets on land supported by tactical maneuver at sea, such as landing by boat to stage an attack on a coastal target.

- *The sea as a source of targets:* Attacks at sea, on targets tied to the maritime domain, such as shipping, offshore energy infrastructure, or military vessels.

Notably, not all the means which terrorists can use the sea are acts of terrorism. As with terrorist activities on land, some acts are directly terroristic, while others are criminal and reflect a need to finance activities or traffic in products or people. At sea, that means that some acts are functionally similar to other irregular maritime activities. Leveraging the sea as a source of income by means of violence is, on its face, no different than piracy. Leveraging the sea as a means of transporting goods or people is likewise no different than illicit trafficking. These acts take on added significance when conducted in support of terrorism, but at the operational level they should be familiar to those who study other forms of maritime insecurity.

Where maritime terrorism is unique compared to other irregular maritime issues is in the use of the sea as a maneuver space in direct support of an attack, and in actually committing politically motivated attacks on maritime targets. These two categories share some conditions that would invite their use by terrorists – limited state maritime domain awareness, poor maritime enforcement capabilities and inadequate port security, for example. The two may also separately rely on more specialised conditions – for example, secure land borders may be an important factor incentivising the use of the sea as a medium for mobility, while the availability and accessibility of targets is a distinguishing factor when staging attacks at sea (Curran, 2019).

Committing attacks at sea – of all the categories, the most directly terroristic – can be further subdivided based on target type (Murphy, 2009, p. 200):

- *Iconic targets*, e.g., warships, cruise ships, famous vessels, or vessels flying certain flags.
- *Economic targets*, e.g., tankers, oil platforms, container vessels and ports.
- *Mass casualty targets*, e.g., cruise ships and ferries.

Attacks at sea can also be subdivided by attack type. Lehr (2009, 2016, p. 203) writes of "WBIED attacks being the most frequent method … followed by conventional non-suicide IED attacks … sub-surface attacks, stand-off weapon attacks and the hijacking of ships for political reasons". In rough order of likelihood, these attacks could include:

- *Bombings*, e.g., placing a concealed explosive on a ship.
- *Small boats as weapons*, e.g., waterborne improvised explosive devises (WIEDs).
- *Subsurface concealment*, e.g., using combat divers or semi-submersibles to place explosives on vessels or infrastructure.[2]
- *Ship hijackings*, e.g., taking or killing hostages onboard a vessel or maritime installation (such as an offshore energy rig).
- *Large vessels as weapons*, e.g., oil or gas tankers rigged to detonate, or a container laden with chemical, radiological, or explosive contents.

Thus, as with acts of terrorism on land, maritime terrorism plots are diverse. Exploring some of the groups prominently active in maritime terrorism is a useful way of describing how attacks vary in practice.

Who uses the maritime domain – Prominent groups?

A look at four broad groups of actors offers a diverse cross-section of how the attack typologies above manifest in reality:

Levantine groups

Levantine groups' early foray into maritime terrorism came somewhat by accident during the MS *Achille Lauro* attack in 1985. Four members of the Palestinian Liberation Front (PLF) boarded the ship in Egypt, intending to use the vessel as transportation to stage an attack in Ashdod, Israel. While in their cabin cleaning their weapons, ship's crew discovered the assailants and in response the attackers hijacked the ship. They broadcast political demands, calling for the release of prisoners held by Israel, and separated passengers by nationality. One passenger was ultimately killed in the attack – a wheelchair-bound Jewish American man named Leon Klinghoffer. As Curran (2019) notes, Levantine groups have attempted manoeuvre the sea several times since *Achille Lauro*. In 1990, members of the PLF attempted to land near Tel Aviv from a ship boarded in Libya. In 2014, Hamas swimmers came ashore near a *kibbutz* just north of Gaza in a similar mission.

Levantine groups are also occasionally supported by state patronage, of which the 2006 strike on the Israeli Navy Ship (INS) *Hanit* is an example. On 14 July 2006, during the Israeli-Lebanese War, the Israeli corvette *Hanit* came under fire from shore-based anti-ship cruise missiles that Hezbollah likely acquired from Iran. One missile overflew the ship, striking a commercial freighter further to sea, while a second struck *Hanit* on its stern killing four sailors. The attack was a watershed in the use of sophisticated state-level technology to stage an attack at sea (Zakheim, 2013).

Liberation Tigers of Tamil Eelam

One of the most prolific efforts by a non-state group to seize the advantage of maritime operations came via a specialised arm of Sri Lanka's Liberation Tigers of *Tamil Eelam* (LTTE) – the Sea Tigers. At its high-water mark, LTTE employed more than 2,000 individuals in support of its naval wing (Dunigan et al., 2012). Often, Sea Tigers' use of the sea fell into indirect support categories, such as transporting weapons, for which the group operated a robust fleet of freight vessels. This support function was also evident in some of the attacks executed by the group and their non-military targets. In 1998, for example, the Sea Tigers hijacked the ship *Princess Kash*, which the Sri Lankan Air Force then bombed in order to prevent the group from utilising its cargo (Chatterjee, 2014).

The LTTE naval wing was particularly adept at constraining freedom of mobility for the Sri Lankan Navy around the northeastern coast of the island, where the insurgency was based, helping to secure the group from flanking and ensuring the inflow of needed material (Dunigan et al., 2012). This was often accomplished with attacks on Sri Lankan forces. In April 1995, for example, Sea Tiger divers blew up two Sri Lankan Navy gunboats in Trincomalee (Lehr, 2009). Yet the Sea Tigers, like the LTTE more broadly, is likely best known for its pioneering use of suicide attacks. "Wolf pack" tactics typically included several small boats operating in co-ordination, targeting Sri Lankan naval vessels, with one craft rigged to explode on impact. In an 18-year period, the Sea Tigers executed approximately 40 suicide missions (Dunigan et al., 2012).

Al-Qaeda and affiliates

On 3 January 2000, a small boat sank near the Yemeni port of Aden. Nearby, the American destroyer USS *The Sullivans* sat in port for refuelling. Unbeknownst to the crew, they had been spared an attack because the men launching the small boat overburdened their waterborne IED with explosives. It is a mistake they did not make twice. Nine months later, on 12 October, the same men lowered the same boat into the water, and it floated. They drove the vessel as a suicide WIED into the side of another visiting destroyer, USS *Cole*, killing 17 sailors. The attack was a success for al-Qaeda's maritime planner, al-Nashiri, who two years later used the same tactic to cripple the French Tanker MV *Limburg*, killing one onboard. The *Limburg*, like the Cole, ultimately survived the attack, but only after sustaining massive damage and dumping tens of thousands of barrels of oil off the Yemeni coast.

Lacking his leadership, al-Qaeda's interest in maritime attacks dipped following al-Nashiri's arrest. Yet periodically, efforts to stage more complicated maritime efforts continue to arise. One of the most elaborate incidents was the 2014 attack on a Pakistani frigate. In that event, militants affiliated with a then-new al-Qaeda group attempted to seize control of PNS *Zulfiqar* and ostensibly aimed to use the vessel to fire on a nearby US ship. The assault was foiled after a lengthy firefight.

Houthis

In January 2017, Yemeni-based Houthis employed the tried method of a suicide WIED against a Saudi frigate, successfully striking the ship with one boat and killing two onboard (LaGrone, 2017). That same year, the group began experimenting with remotely piloted small craft to execute similar attacks. They twice attempted to steer such a bomb towards vessels in the port of Mocha in the summer of 2017, both times seeming to miss a specific target. The group has also deployed sea mines near ports and in the spring of 2017, a Yemeni coast guard vessel struck one, killing two on board (Rowas, 2017).

However, at sea, Houthis may be best known for a series of anti-ship cruise missile strikes in October of 2016, likely a result of Iranian sponsorship. On the first of the month, the group fired a cruise missile and struck an Emirati-flagged vessel near the Bab el Mandeb. The incident prompted the US Navy to deploy several ships, including the destroyer USS *Mason*, to patrol the sea lane. *Mason* subsequently came under fire itself, facing three anti-ship missile volleys but suffering no impacts (LaGrone, 2016a–b). It remains one of the only documented cases of a US Navy vessel defending itself from cruise missiles, and the only known use of some shipboard countermeasures.

Whither the crime-terror nexus?

Many more groups have used the maritime domain to pursue terrorist objectives. The Provisional Irish Republican Army used the sea for resupply, and Chechen rebels staged occasional attacks on ferries in the Bosporus Straits (Greenberg et al., 2006). ISIS (Islamic State of Iraq and the Levant) experimented on Iraq's rivers to launch WIED attacks and move forces. Indonesian groups, from separatists like the Free Aceh Movement (GAM) to Islamists groups such as Jemaah Islamiyah, extensively relied on maritime geography. Likewise with Philippine organisations, such as the Abu Sayyaf Group (ASG), responsible for the deadliest terrorist attack in Philippine history – came the 2004 bombing of SuperFerry 14.

Some of these groups have even reportedly collaborated. In one instance, Philippine military sources alleged that Jemaah Islamiyah had invested in diving and explosives training for ASG (Curran, 2019), the latter organisation being famous for lurching from terrorism to criminality and back. This invites a brief discussion of perhaps the most perennial debate in the study of maritime terrorism: whether there is a "nexus" between terrorism and other forms of maritime crime.

As we have seen, some terrorist organisations use the sea to support their political agenda by ways that are criminal in nature. These include fundraising (narcotics trafficking, kidnapping, illegal oil bunkering, extortion, piracy) as well as moving people and supplies. Overall, more than a quarter of funding for non-state groups likely comes from narcotics trafficking alone (maritime and otherwise) (Nellemann et al., 2018). Groups such as the Moro National Liberation Front, the Moro Islamic Liberation Front and ASG have all engaged in piracy and at-sea extortion to fund campaigns of political violence (Murphy, 2009). Criminal financing schemes can become quite elaborate, as when al-Shabab utilised its control of Somali ports to garner taxes from charcoal exports (Curran, 2019). Within terrorist organisations, there is a self-evident link between criminal fundraising, criminal trafficking and terrorism.

However, the question of a crime-terror nexus is often meant to imply connectivity between organisations, not within them. As Murphy (2009, p. 380) cautions on that question, "'Nexus' is an evocative word that needs to be used with care because, in this context, it can gloss over the motivational and operational reasons that generally keep criminals and terrorists apart and imply an instrumentality that does not exist". Criminal groups thrive in the absence of state interest in, or awareness of, their efforts. Terrorists, to some extent, do not. These motivational distinctions have operational corollaries – a terrorist attack without an audience is a political failure, whereas criminal activity with an audience is a business risk. In many cases, the risks for criminal groups outweigh any immediate financial gains of partnering with terrorists. As a RAND report (Greenberg et al., 2006, pp. xxi–xxii) concludes: "There is little evidence that terrorists and piracy syndicates are collaborating".

Yet the world does not operate in absolutes. The criteria that help to explain where maritime terrorism might emerge are similar to those that predict piracy and other irregular maritime activities. As a result, maritime crime and maritime terror often coexist geographically. This can lead to the misleading impression that terrorist groups are engaged in coordinated activities with criminal groups. But it no doubt also presents real-world opportunities for individuals to move between networks or for networks to cooperate in *ad hoc* dynamics (Murphy, 2009). Therefore, the debate over a crime-terror network at sea continues, though with some well-earned skepticism.

What does the future hold for maritime terrorism and its study?

Predicting the future is a dangerous proposition, but trends offer us an empirical foundation from which we can explore dynamics that may shape maritime terrorism. Three in particular are global in scope and already influencing society: technological change, human geography and global power dynamics.

How might technology shape terror at sea?

Do new technologies offer terrorists opportunities to cultivate new methods? We have already seen Houthi militants experiment with remote explosives at sea, morphing a technology common on land into the maritime space. More broadly, terrorist groups, such as ISIS (Knoll, 2016) have a documented record of rapid innovation and may adopt new techniques or technologies quickly. What emerging technologies may expose new vulnerabilities for maritime targets, or provide modified attack methods for terrorists?

Increasingly, merchant vessels, cruise ships and ferries are going digital (even unmanned), as part of the larger internet-of-things trend. Engineers have long demonstrated the vulnerability of navigation software to hacking and manipulation (Curran, 2019). A major glitch in 2017 highlighted just how catastrophic a cyber incident could be for the maritime world (Greenberg, 2018). At this point, "there is little evidence that major violent non-state groups currently possess the capabilities to carry out cyberattacks" (Curran, 2019, p. 12). Cyber seems to remain in the purview of state actors and criminal groups. Is that a permanent condition because the attack type is not particularly flashy or physically destructive? May that change as the digital and physical worlds continue to converge? And if so, what would precipitate adoption by terrorist groups?

Questions of cyber terrorism are not novel to maritime terrorism – the relationship between technology and political violence is pervasive. But one area where technology opens a new question for maritime terrorism, in particular, is its relationship to one of the core constraints on maritime terrorism noted above – the audience barrier. Does communications technology erode the audience challenge that maritime attacks have historically faced? In some maritime attacks by Houthis, trailing boats have allegedly deployed to capture footage of the incident (Henderson & Vaughan, 2017). If that barrier continued to erode, and connectivity in open maritime spaces became ubiquitous, would that change the strategic calculus about the exposure of attacks at sea? Or would the other noted challenges – the operational hurdles, the lack of an "it could have been me" sensation for most viewers – continue to impose suitable stumbling blocks for many?

Do human geographic trends portend shifts in political violence?

Human geographic trends – urbanisation, littoralisation, human connectivity – are driving people into denser clusters along global coastlines (Kilcullen, 2013; Tallis, 2019) at the same time as countries and cities in many parts of the world struggle to provide services and security to the millions of new citizens that join their ranks every year. In places where municipal authorities fail to establish governance, rival centres of power emerge, be they criminal gangs in Brazilian *favelas* or warlords in Somalia. Norton (2003) referred to this phenomenon as feral cities. This phenomenon of ungoverned spaces seized by unconventional groups is not new, but the underlying human geographic trends that shape this dynamic continue apace. By 2050, two-thirds of people will live in cities, many (perhaps up to a billion) in slums. Right now, about 1.5 million people move to a city each week (Kilcullen, 2013). Half of the global population lives within a day's walk of the coast, as with about 75% of large cities (Tallis, 2019). How might these changes in human habitation, migration and the pressures they exert on municipal and national governments affect where violent groups emerge, or what local grievances drive that violence?

Among the many implications of these statistics, changes in human interaction and habitation patterns may also be reshaping the relationship of states to their urban centres, and urban centres to their coastlines. Cities already play clear roles in generating demand for, or creating the circumstances that facilitate, a wide variety of maritime insecurity. Cities are pull centres for the exploitation of trafficked individuals in industry or sex work, for narcotics use, and even for higher consumptions of fish protein tied to illegal, unreported and unregulated fishing (Tallis & Klaus, 2018). Cities are also targets for terrorists, and those along the coast provide fodder for terrorists, including the infamous 2008 Mumbai attack.

Targeting cities for attack from the maritime space may not be new, but the rise of cities as places of political power and security actors is a notable shift in global dynamics. What role might they play in providing structures for counteracting maritime insecurity? On other transnational issues – climate change, most notably – cities have created international organising bodies to coordinate action and drive innovation. Sister city programs provide bilateral forums for addressing shared challenges, and some large cities have unilaterally pursued global security structures (e.g., New York City) (Tallis & Klaus, 2018). With concentrations of wealth, people and power, cities may be more than targets but also spaces for security innovation with respect to maritime terrorism.

Does strategic competition among great powers portend shifts in terror trends?

As we saw throughout this chapter, state sponsorship can increase the reach of groups attempting to engage in terrorism at sea. And while some smaller national actors have faced sanction for their sponsorship of non-state groups, proxies have also long served as instruments in great power dynamics that are far harder to curtail (Rosenau & Gold, 2019). The US and Soviet uses of non-state proxies during the Cold War is a prolific if not unique example of this dynamic and the havoc it can cause as rival powers push money and materiel into local conflicts.

Today, the phrase "great power competition" is on the rise in US policy circles, filtering through to security establishments and academia abroad (Friedman, 2019). And if competition among the US, China and Russia grows in intensity, as it appears to be doing, it is feasible that competitive dynamics at the global systemic level could once again filter down into the tools, capabilities, or sponsors made available to non-state groups. How might reinvigorated US-Russia tensions shape non-state actors in the orbit of either nation? How might an even more strained relationship between Washington and Beijing do the same – not least given China's extensive distant water fishing fleet and maritime militia (Poling, 2019).

In the post-9/11 era, the study of maritime (and non-maritime) terrorism has often focused on non-state actors as threats in their own right. The resurgence of strategic competition among great powers may disrupt how states and analysts view the overall threat of maritime terrorists to national security, while at the same time shifting the resources and opportunities made available to such groups. How that changes potential hotspots or causes that may become sources of grievance and violence is a source for further study.

Conclusion

Maritime terrorism is a diverse field, with sociologists, political scientists, criminologists, anthropologists, legal scholars, regional experts and others converging on this multidisciplinary exploration of how and why political violence takes to the sea. To provide a selective overview, this chapter looked at three of the central debates in the field. First, we explored what makes maritime terrorism unique and worthy of its own field of study, what obstacles help explain its relatively infrequent use, and how those same obstacles can help us understand why and when groups would engage in acts of maritime terrorism. Following that, we turned to understand who uses maritime terrorism, how, and with what potential help from criminal groups at sea. We surveyed four prominent groups to find concrete examples of attack typologies for maritime terrorism and described the contours of the debate on the crime-terror nexus. Finally, we turned to the critical question of what is next. To ground that gaze into the future in empirical evidence, we identified three prominent global trends – technology, human geography and global power dynamics – to ask how they may shape maritime terrorism and responses to it.

Notes

1 Alternatively, one easy-to-remember framework to describe maritime terrorism is that of the "5T's": tactical support, target selection, take, trafficking and tax (Curran 2019).
2 Al-Rashim's had aspirations for a "scuba jihad" (Lehr, 2016, p. 211). Modern diving attacks stretch back at least to 1975, when Argentine guerrillas placed explosives on the hull of an Argentine Navy destroyer, damaging it to such an extent that its entry into service was delayed for up to a year (Lehr, 2009, pp. 62–63).

References

Chatterjee, A. (2014). Non-Traditional Maritime Security Threats in the Indian Ocean Region. *Maritime Affairs, 10*(2), 77–95.

Curran, M. (2019). *Soft Targets and Black Markets: Terrorist Activities in the Maritime Domain*. Stable Seas.

Curran, M., et al. (2020). *Violence at Sea: How Terrorists, Insurgents, and other Extremists Exploit the Maritime Domain*. Stable Seas.

Dunigan, M., et al. (2012). *Adversary Capabilities in Maritime Irregular Warfare, in Characterizing and Exploring the Implications of Maritime Irregular Warfare*. RAND.

English, R. (2016). *Does Terrorism Work? A History*. Oxford University Press.

Friedman, U. (2019, August 6). *The New Concept Everyone in Washington is Talking About,* The Atlantic. https://www.theatlantic.com/politics/archive/2019/08/what-genesis-great-power-competition/595405/.

Greenberg, A. (2018, August 22). *The Untold Story of NotPetya, the Most Devastating Cyberattack in History.* Wired. https://www.wired.com/story/notpetya-cyberattack-ukraine-russia-code-crashed-the-world/

Greenberg, M., et al. (2006). *Maritime Terrorism: Risk and Liability*. RAND.

Henderson, S., & J. Vaughan. (2017). The Saudi-Hothi War at Sea. *Washington Institute for Near East Policy.*

Kilcullen, D. (2013). *Out of the Mountains: The Coming Age of the Urban Guerrilla*. C. Hurst & Company.

Knoll, D. (2016, September 30). *How ISIS Endures by Innovating*. Foreign Affairs. https://www.foreignaffairs.com/articles/2016-09-30/how-isis-endures-innovating

LaGrone, S. (2016a, October 15). *CNO Richardson: USS Mason Appears to Have Come Under Attack*. USNI News October Issue. https://news.usni.org/2016/10/15/cno-richardson-uss-mason-attacked-cruise-missiles-off-yemen

LaGrone, S. (2016b, October 12). *Pentagon Pledges to Respond in "Appropriate Manner" After New Yemen Missile Attack on USS Mason*. USNI News October Issue. https://news.usni.org/2016/10/12/pentagon-respond-appropriate-manner-new-missile-attack-uss-mason-yemen

LaGrone, S. (2017, January 31). *Two Saudi Sailors Dead in Houthi Suicide Boat Attack*. USNI News. https://news.usni.org/2017/01/31/two-saudi-sailors-dead-houthi-suicide-boat-attack

Lehr, P. (2009). Maritime Terrorism: Locations, Actors, Capabilities. In Herbert-Burns, S. Bateman & P. Lehr (Eds.), *Lloyd's Maritime Intelligence Unit Handbook of Maritime Security* (pp. 56–69). Auerbach Publishers.

Lehr, P. (2016). (No) Princes of the Sea: Reflections on Maritime Terrorism. In J. Krause & S. Bruns (Eds.), *Routledge Handbook of Naval Strategy and Security* (pp. 202–204). Routledge.

Murphy, M. (2009). Murphy, *Small Boats, Weak States, Dirty Money*. Columbia University Press/Hurst Publishers.

Nellemann, C., et al. (Eds.). (2018). World Atlas of Illicit Flows. A RHIPTO-INTERPOL-GI Assessment. RHIPTO-Norwegian Center for Global Analyses, INTERPOL and the Global Initiative Against Transnational Organized crime.

Norton, R. J. (2003). Feral Cities. *Naval War College Review, 56*(4), article 8. https://digital-commons.usnwc.edu/nwc-review/vol56/iss4/8

Poling, G. (2019, June 25). *China's Hidden Navy*. Foreign Policy. https://foreignpolicy.com/2019/06/25/chinas-secret-navy-spratlys-southchinasea-chinesenavy-maritimemilitia/

Rosenau, W., & Gold, Z. (2019). *The Cheapest Insurance in the World? The United States and proxy warfare*. CNA. www.cna.org/CNA_files/PDF/DRM-2019-U-020227-1Rev.pdf

Rowas, M. (2017). *Remotely Piloted Craft Attacks off Yemen's Red Sea Coast Indicate Growing Threat to Marine Hulls and Port Infrastructure*. Jane's by IHS Markit.

Stavridis, J. (2017, June 29). *Terrorists Have Been All Too Effective by Air and Land. What If They Hit by Sea?* Time. https://time.com/4838706/what-if-terrorists-hit-by-sea/

Tallis, J. (2019). *War for Muddy Waters; Pirates, Terrorists, Traffickers, and Maritime Insecurity*. Naval Institute Press.

Tallis, J., & I. Klaus. (2018). Cities and the Sea: The Urban Role in Maritime Security. *Marine Corps University Journal, 9*(2). https://apps.dtic.mil/sti/pdfs/AD1068707.pdf

Zakheim, D. (2013). *The United States Navy and Israeli Navy*. CNA.

17

ENERGY SECURITY AND MARITIME SECURITY

Rupert Herbert Burns

At 03:12 GMT on 13 June 2019, U.S. Navy units in the Persian Gulf received a distress call from the Suezmax tanker *M/T Front Altair* as she was steaming south-east in the Gulf of Oman. The master reported she had suffered an explosion and was on fire. A U.S. Reaper UAV reported observing what were later assessed to be Iranian Revolutionary Guards Corps (Navy) [IRGC(N)] fast boats close to the *Front Altair*. Later, at 04:00 GMT, a second distress call was received from a product tanker, *M/T Kokuka Courageous*, which also reported an explosion at the waterline on the starboard side. All crew from both tankers abandoned their respective vessels. The crew from the *Front Altair* were initially rescued by a South Korean merchant vessel, *M/V Hyundai Dubai*; however, they were subsequently forced to hand them over to an IRGC(N) vessel and taken to Bandar Abbas. The crew from the *Kokuka Courageous* were picked up by a Dutch merchantman and taken to Dubai. Both attacks occurred in international waters; over 20 km off the Iranian coast.

Though suffering notable damage, neither ships sank or were rendered constructive total losses (CTL). Nevertheless, what is certain is that both attacks could have turned out very differently: the damage caused by the explosives placed by the IRGC(N) could have caused fires that could not have been brought under control, which might have resulted in the foundering of the vessels, considerable loss of life and extensive environmental damage. The tertiary effects of this would have resulted in disruption of shipping through the Gulf of Oman and Persian Gulf and raised hull and P & I insurance premiums, to say nothing of further exacerbating regional tensions. It is noteworthy that a deliberate attack against a vessel is unlikely to necessarily result in an immediate counter-action by the injured flag state or home nation of the owning company. However, such is the elevated geopolitical and economic sensitivity of locations, cargoes, vessels and infrastructure associated with petroleum, incidents such as the attacks outlined above occurring amidst other attacks in the region in a common time-frame, are likely capable of igniting wider conflict.

The purpose of this chapter is to explore the particular threats, vulnerabilities and security risks that are unequivocally intrinsic to petroleum industry shipping, the offshore sector, and coastal and littoral infrastructure; particularly when located in geographies of strategic relevance and geopolitical sensitivity.

200   DOI: 10.4324/9781003001324-20

Energy Security and Maritime Security

Threat assessment

The security calculus confronting a government or company that has responsibility for, and equity in, oil and gas producing infrastructure and/or petroleum sector shipping, must start with a sophisticated and constantly updated appreciation of the various threats that are (or could be) ranged against valued assets. In fundamental terms, threat is assessed as a factor of *intent* and *capability*: the extant or potential intent of an aggressor to target a given asset, coupled with its capability to do so. In the context of the generation of threat, these variables cannot exist in isolation. Whilst piracy and hijacking remain serious threats to tankers and to a lesser degree offshore infrastructure, particularly in the Gulf of Guinea, and will continue to be a threat in the years to come, I will not address this criminal threat in this chapter. The threat categories examined in this chapter are as listed below: (a) Conventional state action or attacks; (b) Militant/rebel forces action; (c) Terrorism.

All of the threat types to this sector have all existed in the past and several still prevail; however, not all have existed at the same time or at consistent levels. In the late 1980s, the threat was overwhelmingly from inter-state warfare (notably during the 1980–1988 Iran-Iraq War). In the 1990s, tankers fell victim to a rise in piracy and vessel hijacking in Southeast Asia, whilst other vessels and assets were targeted by Liberation Tigers of Tamil Eelam (LTTE), which was responsible for the first sophisticated methods in maritime terrorism in the coastal waters off Sri Lanka. After 9/11, during the 2003–2011 Iraq War, and the ensuing rise and decline of Islamic State's control in Iraq and Syria, the dominant threat to the petroleum sector was from terrorism; specifically, from Islamic terrorist groups such as Al Qaeda, Al Qaeda in Iraq (AQ-I), Islamic State in Syria (ISIS) and the Abu Sayaf Group (ASG). From 2007 to 2013, there was the steady rise in increasingly effective Somali piracy and hijacking attacks in the Indian Ocean. Additionally, the threat of piracy in the Gulf of Guinea, though reduced, still persists. However, since the steadily escalating tensions between the Gulf Arab states and Iran, between Iran and the US (since 2017), and the increasingly brittle relationship between the US and China, we have returned again to the possibility of state-based threats to shipping and infrastructure. These could be both symmetric and asymmetric in nature, and could also embrace phenomena explicit in "hybrid warfare", characterised by deliberately un-attributable state attacks.

Conventional state action or attacks

In examining state-generated threat, it is important to draw distinction between actions in peacetime (including periods of heightened tensions), and actions in times of open conflict. This enables inclusion of phenomena such as constabulary activity, asymmetric and symmetric approaches to threat mitigation, and the concept of "hybrid" warfare.

Constabulary actions by navies or coastguards is something that any captain of a vessel should be prepared for. A prime example of this was the sudden boarding of the Iranian-flagged VLCC, *Grace 1*, by Royal Gibraltar Police and Royal Marines Commandos on 4 July 2019. The action was taken as the tanker was *en route* to Syria lifting a cargo of oil from Iran in contravention of EU sanctions (Bateman, 2019). Despite conflicting reports regarding the conduct of the boarding forces, and the impact upon the civilian crew, the detention was judged as legitimate. However, the incident had serious consequences in that it resulted in a very similar action by Iranian IRGCN forces that boarded a British-flagged tanker, the *Stena Imperio*, in the Persian Gulf only two weeks later, an escalation in tensions in the Gulf, and the deployment of additional coalition warships.

In the same year, as a consequence of steadily escalating tensions between Iran and its Gulf Arab neighbours and the United States, and as a move intended to deliberately increase pressure on Saudi Arabia, Iran staged a daring and sophisticated UAV and missile attack on the oil processing complex at Abqaiq and Khurais in the Kingdom's Eastern Province on 14 September 2019 (Hubbard et al., 2019). The damage inflicted was extensive, which caused both facilities to be shut down, resulting in a loss of some 50% of Saudi Aramco's production and spike in global oil prices. Both of these facilities, Abqaiq in particular, process oil exported via the two largest single export terminals in the world, Ras Tanura and Juaymah. Though responsibility for the strike was initially claimed by the Yemeni-based and Iranian-aligned Houthis, post-attack analysis of the weapons used, the numbers of weapons and the direction from which they were launched, pointed to an Iranian attack (which it still denies).

The startling factor about this incident is its risk factor. Had the damage been far more extensive that it turned out to be and resulted in the destruction of Abqaiq in particular, which would very likely have caused extensive loss of life and massive disruption to the Kingdom's oil exports, a retaliatory strike against Iran may have been unavoidable. Whilst the putative consequences of a counter-attack are impossible to know, what is very likely is that any ensuing counter-strikes would have targeted other high-consequence petroleum infrastructure on both sides and possibly transiting petroleum shipping in the Gulf. The Abqaiq/Khurais attack and the strikes against tankers in the Gulf of Oman and off Fujairah in the summer of 2019 are textbook examples of "hybrid" warfare. Essentially, these were state military operations that have sufficient vector ambiguity so as to facilitate plausible deniability and sufficient doubt in the minds of the international community; rendering reprisal counter-strike less likely.

Militant/rebel forces action

The strategic value of rebel forces targeting the high-profile oil targets, such as Very large Crude Carrier (VLCC's) flying the flag of an enemy state, enables them to "punch above their weight", even if the attacks are inconclusive. In April 2018 and again in July, Houthi rebels attacked three Saudi-flagged oil tankers. While only minor damage was inflicted, the Houthis used water-born improvised explosive devices (WBIEDs) in these attempts to disrupt Saudi oil exports (Sheppard et al., 2018). In the previous year, Houthi forces attempted to strike an Aramco oil terminal, also using a WBIED (Aljazeera, 2018). During the course of the war in Yemen, Houthi maritime strike capabilities became increasingly sophisticated and effective, including the use of anti-ship cruise missiles fired from coastal batteries. The use of well-designed remotely operated WBIEDs and advanced missiles indicated substantive Iranian support for its proxy rebel ally. Had the attacks inflicted far more serious damage, the consequences in terms of loss of life and environmental damage close to a major oil chokepoint would likely have been severe.

Terrorism

Terrorist attacks against shipping and maritime environment oil infrastructure are comparatively uncommon in the history of modern terrorism, and successful attacks with notable political-economic effects rarer still. However, paradoxically, it is sometimes what did not happen that could have happened, which leaves its mark in terms of the resultant elevated risk management required, and altered perceptions of existential dangers. In this regard, an unsuccessful or inconclusive attack can have some of the lasting political and strategic effect, if not the telegenic impact, that the aggressors were seeking.

In July 2010, an Al Qaeda-aligned group (Abdullah Azzam Brigade) executed one of the most daring attacks recorded at the time in its attempt to destroy a VLCC in the Persian Gulf. Though motives and means were initially inconclusive, subsequent investigation revealed the attackers had used a WBIED to attack the laden 270,204 dwt *M/V M.Star* whilst she was underway at night in the traffic separation scheme (TSS) exiting the Gulf (BBC News, 2010). The site of the detonation was astern on the starboard side, by the main machinery spaces and the bunker service tanks. Subsequent forensic evidence found traces of low-yield TNT explosive residue on the superstructure. The blast caused considerable denting of the side of the vessel but did not breach the hull as the quantity of explosive used was insufficient. However, had the blast punched though into the engine room, the tanker could very likely have foundered in the Straits of Hormuz, causing widespread environmental damage and consequential disruption to shipping. Perhaps most significantly, such an outcome would have likely encouraged similar attempts by other terrorists, through demonstrating effect.

Though admittedly dated as an example, the attack by AQ-I against the Iraqi KAAOT and ABOT offshore oil terminals in April 2004, demonstrated the potential of an asymmetric attack against critical national infrastructure if not adequately protected in times of conflict. Prior to the attack, AQ-I was not regarded as a group with maritime strike capability, and indeed the attempt was not successful in terms of intended destructive effect (Herbert-Burns, 2008). The attacks, though of low kinetic effect, did result in a substantive allied maritime security operation (MSO) by naval units of the Royal Navy, U.S. Navy, U.S. Coast Guard, Australian Navy and Iraq Marine units.

Vulnerabilities of key petroleum infrastructure and shipping

Oil/gas fields, processing plants and tank storage farms

In the maritime realm, oil and gas fields (including those containing condensate[1]) are those situated inland (connected to coastal terminals by export pipelines), on the coast, or sited offshore. When in full production, necessitating extensive and highly vulnerable processing infrastructure, onshore and offshore oil and gas fields become significant strategic assets and present considerable security challenges to governments, national oil companies (NOCs) and international oil companies (IOCs) alike.

In-production fields, which have easily identifiable wellhead valves and inter-field pipeline infrastructure, are often spread over large areas; they are isolated and highly vulnerable to attack. Examples include the attacks by the Iraqi army against Kuwaiti fields in 1991, and rebel forces and terrorist actions against well and pumping infrastructure in the southwestern and central Libyan desert in 2013–2016 (Porter, 2015).

The most important infrastructure found near onshore fields, which is often of considerable size and strategic value, are the processing facilities and oil storage farms. Crude oil, condensate and associated gas cannot be processed and exported by sea without these. Gas oil separation plants (GOSPs) take crude direct from the wellhead (including from offshore fields) and separate out the water, associated gas and aggregate materials (such as sand). The oil or condensate is then stored for export by tanker or pipeline, and the associated gas is stored and exported (or flared if uneconomical to export). The tank storage farms are the vital linking feature that enables the field(s) to maintain constant production; even whilst exporting by sea is intervallic or disrupted. Storage farms can be vast, conspicuous and highly vulnerable to conventional military strikes, as evidenced in the Iran-Iraq War. However, militant or terrorist attacks can also be decidedly effective. In January 2016, during the civil war in Libya, IS terrorists destroyed seven tanks at Es Sider and Ras Lanuf; resulting in 18 dead, massive fires and the loss of over 1.3 million barrels of oil (al-Warfalli & Elumami, 2016). GSOPs and tank farms are particularly vulnerable to military strikes from the air, land or sea, and their large perimeter and elevated processing and storage structures also render them vulnerable to asymmetric attack by terrorists or rebel forces armed with RPGs, assault weapons and skilled in placing IEDs.

The most significant security incidents involving production facilities located on the coast were the two attacks against the Saudi Aramco oil processing facility at Abqaiq in the Eastern Province of Saudi Arabia in 2006 and 2019. Abqaiq, the largest of its kind in the world, accounts for over 50% of the Kingdom's crude production capacity, and 7% of all global production. To render this infrastructure inoperable for an extended period would have drastic consequences for the Saudi economy, and the supply disruption to the macro-oil market would reverberate globally.

The attempted suicide vehicle-borne IED attack by Al Qaeda against the facility in February 2006 was thwarted by security forces, and unsurprisingly resulted in extensive security hardening of the accesses and perimeter of Abqaiq; specifically, to defend against vehicle IEDs and ground assaults. However, ironically, this hardening is one of the reasons future attackers opted to use aerial means of attack, which inflicted far greater levels of damage. On 14 September 2019, AUV and missile strikes against Abqaiq and Khurais caused extensive damage to processing units; particularly at the former. Though the attacks were claimed by Houthi rebels fighting in Yemen far to the south, forensic evidence later revealed the attacks originated from the northeast, indicating Iranian involvement (Pamuk, 2019). Though the facilities were quickly repaired and back in production by October, the incident shows the clear vulnerability of this strategically critical infrastructure to modern means of attack. Indeed, the anti-air defences near Abqaiq had no effect upon the incoming UAVs and missiles. Ultimately, had the attack been far larger in scale, the level of destruction would have had far more serious consequences; not only in terms of lost production but also because of the very real likelihood of igniting an inter-state conflict in the Gulf.

a   *Offshore sector infrastructure and vessels*

This is a thoroughly varied sector within the oil and gas industry; with most infrastructure and vessels being technologically complex and of considerable capital value. Fundamentally, it is these drilling and production units and vessels that enable the exploration, development and production (ED&P) of oil and gas in the littoral – from nearshore through to the deep and ultra-deep waters beyond the continental shelf. Indeed, it is the very fact that modern technology enables ED&P in deep waters distant from national shorelines and situated in EEZs that are in many cases disputed, which can give rise to interstate tensions and insecurity; such as in the South China Sea, East China Sea, Eastern Mediterranean, Persian Gulf and the Gulf of Guinea.

Assets can be divided into two categories – platforms and vessels. Drilling and production platforms are either fixed to the seabed or floating, semi-submersible, platforms far offshore anchored to the seafloor or held precisely in position over the well-site by motors controlled by highly accurate differential GPS. Units include: jack-up, anchored or semi-submersible platforms for use in shallower waters; dynamically-positioned (DPS) semi-submersible drilling rigs and production platforms for use in deep and ultra-deep water, and DPS drill-ships. Vessels are in two categories: those designed for ED&P, such as drill-ships, floating production and off-loading units (FPSOs) or floating LNG (FLNG) units; and, specialised vessels such as seismic survey vessels, sub-sea construction vessels, well-intervention vessels, pipe-layers, and offshore supply vessels or anchor-handling tugs.

Energy Security and Maritime Security

From a security perspective, offshore platforms are clearly vulnerable to varying degrees due to their largely static nature, complex functionality, isolation and the considerable challenges to establishing a sufficiently effective security perimeter at sea. The establishment of security zones around drilling rigs and production platforms is only effective if there is a sizable force of patrolling naval and security vessels, which for most countries that have small maritime forces is not possible. Furthermore, they are clearly desirable as targets due to their strategic and capital value for terrorists, militants or pirates. In times of war, it is axiomatic that offshore infrastructure will be viewed as important strategic targets for opposing militaries. Offshore infrastructure is vulnerable to attacks from the air (including from UAVs), from the surface (gun and missile-armed vessels and WBIEDs), from underwater sabotage (though this kind of vector is only possible by highly trained teams), and also from within – an insider attack. There are numerous examples of different kinds of attacks against offshore infrastructure, a good example being the US attack on several Iranian platforms in the Persian Gulf in 1987 and 1988 as reprisal for attacks against US-flagged tankers, using naval gunfire and special forces (Herbert-Burns, 2011).

In 2019, drilling rigs and offshore support vessels came under increasing attacks by armed pirates operating in Mexican territorial waters and EEZ. A series of numerous attacks highlighted the vulnerability of isolated offshore jack-up oil rigs to assault (where the legs are easy to scale and the drilling hull is comparatively close to the water's surface); a vulnerability that was further amplified by the slow reaction-time and inexperience of national maritime security forces. A principal concern for the rig operators has been the considerable danger resulting from gunfire exchanges between pirates and security forces in close proximity to the assets under attack. Needless to say, both aimed and stray automatic weapon fire close to oil drill pipe and processing modules under high pressure presents a considerable threat to life. During 2018–2019, the number of attacks against platforms in the littoral reached 197; an increase of 310% according to company records (Woody, 2019).

Whilst FPSOs and drill-ships are challenging to assault due to their elevated freeboards, offshore platforms, especially jack-up rigs closer inshore in shallow water, are more vulnerable to forced boarding. Furthermore, all operational offshore platforms are problematic to protect with complex, layered anti-boarding obstacles and are manned only by unarmed civilian crews. Production platforms of all kinds have tightly packed mission-critical gas separation and processing modules operating at high pressure, massed piping arrangements, storage tanks and electrical power units. A well-placed high-yield IED could result in sequential destruction of adjacent modules and even the destruction of the entire platform (Hueper, 2005). The accidental destruction of Pipe Alpha in 1988, which killed 166 crew, is evidence of the devastation that can result from explosion and fire of oil and gas burning under high pressure.

Offshore supply vessels are highly vulnerable to assault from the sea due to their very low freeboards, slow speed, fixed routines and routes, and small crews. These vessels have been attacked by pirates routinely in areas such as the Niger delta in the Nigerian littoral in the past. Their vulnerability can only be mitigated against with very robust levels of anti-boarding protection, an armed vessel protection team, or a naval/coast guard escort. Specialised vessels, such as sub-sea construction and seismic survey vessels, are also highly vulnerable to assault when in operation as they are severely restricted in their ability to manoeuvre, and can only be ensured of adequate security by embarking armed security personnel or by a naval patrol close by.

b.   *Refineries*

The purpose of a refinery is of course to convert crude oil (including condensate) into fuels that can be widely utilised. The refining process draws in crude oil (which heats it to about 385°C), whereupon it is pumped into the crude distillation unit (CDU) to fractionalise the oil. The CDU is by far the largest and most obvious feature within the refinery and is certainly the most vulnerable feature. Aside from the CDU, key secondary modules that use chemical and thermal processes to maximise production following initial distillation, make up the other components in the refinery. The destruction of the CDU will shut down the refinery for an extended period; perhaps indefinitely. In the event of a successful sabotage, terrorist or conventional military attack, the destruction of some secondary units will not necessarily halt production for a prolonged period (Hueper, 2005). However, were the pumps and valves associated with a Fluid Catalytic Caracking unit (FCC) (that operates at over 500°C) destroyed with an IED, the potential for a catastrophic explosion and fire is certainly real.

Refineries are arguably the preeminent feature in the maritime petroleum realm from a security risk standpoint: they are highly conspicuous and very challenging to protect due to their sizable footprint and extensive perimeter (much of which is water-facing). Refineries are of immense capital value, and many of the largest throughput facilities can be considered strategic critical national infrastructure. Indeed, it would be difficult to find a better target in the context of either a conventional strike in an inter-state conflict or as part of a terrorist or insurgent campaign.

c.   *Gas processing plants*

Steady increase in the global production and conveyance of LNG in the last 20 years, and particularly within the last decade, has precipitated, and been enabled by, the development of large numbers of gas processing, LNG production and re-gasification infrastructure. Indeed, the evolution of this technology and more endemic establishment of the relevant facilities has transformed the petroleum industry. However, it has presented contemporaneous challenges to ensure the requisite security de-risking strategies in keeping with those for the crude oil and refined product trades.

Though there has yet to be a deliberate strike – military or asymmetric – against an LNG production and export facility, an accidental explosion at the LNG facility at Skikda in Algeria in 2004 provides some insight as to the potential consequences of even a partially successful attack against one of these highly vulnerable complexes. On 20 January, a leak in a pressurised gas line formed an extensive fuel-air vapour cloud within and above Skikda that ignited, causing a massive explosion. This resulted in the death of 27, the injury of 74, the destruction of three of the six production trains, and considerable damage to one of the LNG cryogenic loading jetties (OGJ Editors, 2004). At the time, the incident caused the disruption to some 2% of global supplies of LNG.

Processing plants and LNG production trains are substantial in scale and investment, and for many major producing and exporting states – such as Qatar, Australia, the US, Russia, Malaysia and Algeria – this infrastructure is of strategic economic significance. The plants are very large and highly challenging to protect against all forms of security threat. They are vulnerable to high levels of damage and the disabling of the production train if attacked kinetically in the correct way. The high operating pressures, vapour contents, multiple piping runs and valve connectors, ensures that an explosion that breaches a system under high pressure, processing volatile raw wet gas and NGLs, will highly likely result in subsequent wider conflagration and possible further explosions (if the gas were released into a confined or semi-confined space with sufficient levels of oxygen to enable combustion).

d.   *Terminals*

Oil terminals, whether handling crude oil, condensate or refined products are the enabling exporting link between tank storage farms and attending tankers. They are at once critical infrastructure, vulnerable, at elevated security risk and problematic to protect. As evidenced in the terrorist attacks against Iraq's offshore terminals – Al Basrah Oil Terminal and Khor al Amaya Terminal in 2004 examined earlier.

During the Iran-Iraq War, the Iraqi air force conducted repeated raids against Iran's oil export terminal at Kharg Island; located just 138 nautical miles from Iraq's Gulf coast. Iraqi bombing between 1980 and 1986 inflicted such extensive damage that it was eventually put out of commission. The strategic purpose of the attacks was to terminate Iran's ability to export oil and thus starve its economy of its primary means of revenue. Though it did not achieve this to the extend aspired to, the attacks resulted in considerable logistical challenges for Iran to maintain exports, and raised the risks to Iranian shuttle tankers within the "prohibited war zone" in the northern Persian Gulf (Reuters, 1985). Though the attacks against Kharg occurred over 35 years ago, and the weapons used were unsophisticated by contemporary standards, the damage inflicted evidences at once the vulnerability of maritime terminals and the consequences of attacking them. Oil export terminals are located onshore or offshore. Onshore terminals often require loading by means of extended T-jetties to enable the berthing of deep-draft tankers. The connecting trestle functions as a walkway and as support for the delivery pipelines. Alternatively, the entire berthing arrangement can be located well offshore with no connecting jetty and the oil is delivered via export pipelines laid on the sea floor. The largest and most well-known are: Ras Tanura in Saudi Arabia, Mina al Ahmadi in Kuwait, and the Al Basrah Oil terminal in Iraq (Fuller & Pitt, 2013). The Sea Island terminal at Ras Tanura being the largest in the world, and is unquestionably one of the prime examples in the world of strategically critical petroleum export infrastructure. In a peacetime context, offshore terminals are very challenging to adequately protect due to their positioning, isolation and size against terrorist or saboteur attacks. In wartime, their vulnerability to missile and gunnery attack from the sea, and particularly from the air, is indubitable.

The most vulnerable features are the high-elevation oil loading arms that connect the supply to the loading tanker's manifolds, and at the points when the export oil lines surface from the seabed and connect to the underside of the jacket structures that support the trestles and berthing dolphins. The times of by far the greatest vulnerability and attractiveness to the attacker are when multiple tankers are loading/discharging simultaneously. A successful attack directed at the seaward side of the tanker using a high-yield remotely operated WBIED approaching at high speed will be almost impossible to prevent (unless detected early and neutralised by a precisely-positioned warship equipped with high rate of fire weaponry).

The other form of offshore terminal uses single point moorings (SPM), which are large buoys moored in deep water designed to enable a sub-sea oil pipeline to surface [via the pipeline end Manifold (PLEM) and riser line] and link it to floating transfer hoses, which connect to a VLCC's manifold. Nominally, SPMs are vulnerable to sabotage due to their isolation and lack of protection. A sizable IED properly placed in the valving arrangement on top of the buoy's turn-table when oil is being transferred could likely ignite the crude flow as it spreads out on the surface around the tanker. An oil fire this close to a loading tanker and hoses would quickly endanger the vessel also, which itself is particularly vulnerable with partially filled cargo tanks and combustible vapours around the manifold.

e.   *Vessel types and vulnerabilities*

Tankers and gas carriers represent the moving parts of the maritime petroleum systemic – functioning as multiple petroleum "sea bridges", which are of clear strategic significance. Viewed another way, tankers and gas carriers arguably constitute one of the cornerstones of the health of the global economy (Herbert-Burns, 2011). Unsurprisingly, due to the wide array of different oils – crude, refined products and gases, there are a correspondingly broad range of different types and sizes of tanker and gas carrier. This results in differing levels of vulnerability and susceptibility to security risk. Tankers can be divided in the first instance into crude oil tankers, floating storage and offloading units (FSOs),[2] product tankers and chemical tankers.

VLCCs and ULCCs convey crude oil from sources of reserve and production – Saudi Arabia, Russia, Iraq, the US, UAE, Kuwait and Nigeria) to primary markets (China, the US, India, Japan, South Korea and Europe). These linkages determine the main sea lines of communication (SLOC) along which crude flows. This is clearly relevant from a security risk perspective as it reveals what geopolitical flashpoints and maritime spaces these vulnerable vessels must pass through. This, combined with the inherently vulnerable nature of oil tankers, which are slow, restricted in manoeuvrability, of low freeboard when laden, manned with small crews, and lifting volatile cargoes (some 2 million barrels in the case of a VLCC), clearly elevates their security risk (Herbert-Burns, 2011).

Tankers are most vulnerable when loading/discharging, at slow speeds in pilotage waters or anchorages, or when transiting congested chokepoints – notably the Gulf of Oman, Straits of Hormuz, Bab el Mandeb and the Suez Canal. Conversely, it is very important to note that despite their vulnerabilities to attack, crude oil tankers are not that straightforward to destroy, sink or render a constructive total loss (CTL) as evidenced during the 1984–1988 Tanker War. The combination of their considerable structural robustness, double hulls, high levels of compartmentalisation, and the fact that crude oil is comparatively stubborn to ignite means that tankers might not turn into quite the telegenic effect that a terrorist or saboteur would be hoping for. This is not to say that an attacker with the right weapons or sufficient quantities and types of explosives mounted in a WBIED could not destroy a large crude oil tanker, it is just problematic to do so.

Product tankers are said to be either "clean" (or "white") ships or "dirty" (or "black") ships. Clean tankers lift products such as: gasoline, Jet-A, kerosene, AVGAS, gasoil, diesel and naphtha. Dirty tanker cargoes include: heavy fuel oil (or residual fuel oil), bitumen and asphalts, and are less vulnerable than clean tankers from a cargo volatility standpoint. The greater volatility and often far lower flashpoint of clean products and refined fuels renders them far more vulnerable to a well-conceived attack.

Gas carriers also come in different types and displacements. LNG carriers are either Moss types (which store the liquid gas in Spherical IMO Type B containment tanks or membrane carriers). The latter are now the more common variant, with modern vessels typically built in three main size categories: Conventional (135,000 m³–152,000 m³); Q-Flex (210,000 m³–217,000 m³); and, Q-Max (263,000 m³–266,000 m³). The most strategically significant LNG export streams in the world pass through the following geopolitically sensitive areas and chokepoints: The South China Sea; the Persian Gulf/Straits of Hormuz/Gulf of Oman; the Gulf of Guinea; the Eastern Mediterranean/Suez Canal, and Bab al Mandeb.

LNG Carriers are not nearly as vulnerable to destruction as suggested in the alarmist risk assessments written in the aftermath of 9/11 and the attack on the VLCC *Limburg* in 2002. A detailed review of why this is so is more appropriately addressed in a dedicated technical study; however, in brief, gas carriers are extremely robust and resistant to kinetic effect from a WBIED. If ignited, LNG spilling from a hull breach will burn in a pool fire rather than explode. LPG cargoes are more easily ignited, but conveyed in equally robust double hulls. Nevertheless, it is important to bear in mind that gas carriers would of course be far more vulnerable to CTL or destruction by conventional missile attack in times of open conflict.

Security risk assessment

Security Risk can be defined as a factor of the conflation of credible *threat* (the *likelihood* of a threat being inflicted) and an asset's inherent physical and technical vulnerabilities. The threat is a product of the location in which the asset is located and the capability and intent of an aggressor. An intuitive means of assessing the risks associated with a given category of infrastructure or vessel type is by means of a series of visualisations that combine the following factors: threat likelihood and vulnerability; threat likelihood and consequence; and, the impact of location and environmental geopolitical causal variables.

Threat and vulnerability

The amalgamation of *threat* and *vulnerability* (Figure 17.1) renders a risk picture of the more physically and operationally vulnerable infrastructure and vessel types that have been targeted to varying extents by all actor types, and for many assets continue to be threatened – notably product tankers, VLCCs, offshore vessels, tank farms and oil and gas processing plants. It is important to note that high profile and nominally vulnerable gas sector assets that have been erroneously viewed as high risk in the past, such as LNG tankers and liquefaction facilities, are not in fact in a high-risk category. This does not mean that these assets do not require robust levels of protection; however, it does reveal where high levels of prophylactic security are essential; particularly in times of civil conflict and elevated inter-state or regional tensions.

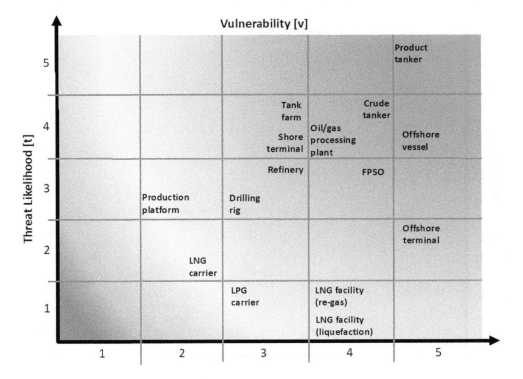

Figure 17.1 Energy security at sea; threats and vulnerabilities

Threat likelihood and consequence

The risk profile generated by the conflation of threat and consequence (Figure 17.2) reveals where the potential for increasing levels of damage, and in the case of large vessels and major infrastructure, the conceivable risks for high-impact secondary and tertiary effect. Areas of concern remain oil and gas processing facilities and tank farms and shore terminals (as seen by attacks in the Sirte Basin crescent in Libya). Whilst the putative consequences of a large military attack or a highly skilled terrorist or militant strike against a liquefaction facility would be of a very high order, the current threat remains low. To date, attacks against offshore infrastructure such as FPSOs, drilling and production units in the Gulf of Guinea has been confined to hostage and kidnapping incidents, and not, fortunately, the disastrous effects of explosive fires and conspicuous environmental damage. Additionally, attacks involving VLCCs in the Gulf of Guinea and the Southern Red Sea have resulted only limited structural damage and loss of cargo. Nevertheless, the nominal risk for these vessels is evident during times of war, as is the potential for high-consequence effect in terms of loss of life, environmental damage, trade disruption and inflammation of existential regional geopolitical tension.

Environmental context for maritime insecurity: The impact of existential geopolitical risk

When discussing maritime insecurity as it pertains to shipping and maritime-located petroleum infrastructure, it is essential to view the threats, vulnerabilities, risks and consequences of the

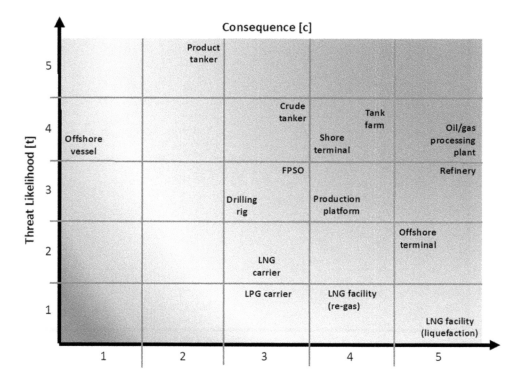

Figure 17.2 Energy security at sea; threat and consequences

Energy Security and Maritime Security

Table 17.1 Geopolitical insecurity level

Region	Score: 1 to 5
Persian Gulf and Gulf of Oman	Very High [5]
Gulf of Aden and Red Sea	High [4]
Gulf of Guinea	Medium [3]
North Africa	Medium [3]
South China Sea/East China Sea	Med-low [2]
Eastern Mediterranean	Med-low [2]
Central and South America	Low [1]
Caspian Sea	Low [1]

conflation of these variables in the context of the geographical setting in which they occur, or placed in a more clearly causal context – the geopolitical risk of the region in question. Petroleum assets that are at some form of existential risk, and operate in the spaces identified in Table 17.1, have petroleum geopolitical risk values applied that can be conflated with values derived from the other two graphs to generate a composite asset security risk value. Naturally risk levels change and must be reviewed routinely; particularly when increasing.

Geopolitical risk, in the context of this essay, can be defined as: The extent to which geopolitical forces in a given space – the latent or actively vectored power of a state or non-state actor to impose its will over the region in which it resides, and the will and actions of competing actors to counter this power in a geostrategically exceptional space – give rise to existential risk of conflict within that space. The scale of that risk is contingent upon the magnitude and persistence of the forces at work and the size of the area in which they are projected or exist. This can result in what I term *geopolitical risk amplification*. This phenomena at once shapes the potential consequences of insecurity and determines that likelihood of kinetic threat.

In the Persian Gulf, the geopolitical risk is generated by the long-term contest between Iran and the Gulf Arab States for dominance of the region, the effects of external power interests and actions, the existence of the single largest concentration of petroleum reserves on earth, and the presence of a critical trading chokepoint. In the Red Sea and the Gulf of Aden, the risk derives from the longstanding war in Yemen in which external regional powers have supported opposing sides and exacerbated destructive effect, astride a vital maritime trade route. The risk in the Gulf of Guinea is lower and is variable according to the willingness of coastal states to cooperate on security matters that can affect them all to varying extents; namely Islamic terrorism, piracy and vessel hijacking, and the effects of external power influence and corporate interests.

The Eastern Mediterranean, despite the long history of conflict in the Levant and the Arab-Israeli Wars, is in the early stages of evolving geopolitical risk in the context of petroleum resource competition. Considerable gas reserves in the EEZ waters of Israel, Egypt, Cyprus, Greece and Turkey (and potentially also Lebanon and Syria) have both exacerbated extant disputed territorial water and EEZ boundaries, generated tensions over exploration rights, and complicated means and opportunity for cooperative E,D & P. Whilst the South China Sea and the East China Sea exert geopolitical risk upon riparian states, due principally to the dominant hegemonic behaviour of China, it is the sheer scale and complexity of the territorial disputes in this space, the criticality of petroleum SLOCs, and the effect of extra-regional power projection that amplifies risk.

Conclusions and outlook

In the short to medium term, the world will continue to rely heavily on petroleum. Though the demand for oil for transportation will decline over the next two decades, there will be an endemic and more prolonged need for natural gas for power generation and for condensate for petrochemical feedstock. Clearly, this means there will continue to be assets and infrastructure as targets of value and opportunity – whether in the context of a conventional conflict, or for pirates, terrorists and insurgents. The combination of the differing levels of intrinsic vulnerability of assets, and their clear equity and often strategic value, ensures that maritime petroleum infrastructure and shipping will remain attractive targets. Nevertheless, the factor that stands out, what rings true throughout the examination, is that despite their high value and criticality, they continue to be at risk. Why? Because insufficient and ineffective risk assessments continue to be made, and insufficient steps are taken to protect them; particularly by states.

This chapter also examined the types and effectiveness of a wide range of threat vectors; thus, if the latter is conflated with the former then the petroleum sector will be at varying levels of risk for some time to come, despite improvements in levels of security. However, on the positive side, albeit not for some time, the level of security risk to the petroleum sector will likely recede as global dependency recedes and targets of opportunity and value reduce in number; likely during the 2030s, and increasingly during the 2040s.

Finally, some comments on the geopolitical security risk outlook, as there are familiar regions with enduring and developing levels of existential risk, which must continue to be monitored with intelligent and sophisticated due diligence. The ontology of the global supply and demand of oil and gas is changing; systemically and in terms of volumes and the typology of petroleum resources conveyed: The building of export-configured refineries in producing regions is resulting in the long-range lifting of larger volumes of more volatile refined fuels and petrochemicals in more vulnerable product tankers, at the expense of crude volumes; the massive expansion in LNG use for power generation in Asia and Europe; and, the surge in US oil and LNG production and exports is changing the global maritime petroleum trading dynamic.

This will have the effect of elevating the petroleum geopolitical value and risk of Asia; in particular the South China and East China Seas. Furthermore, during the remainder of this decade and into the next, the continued need for producing and processing infrastructure in the Americas, Europe, West Africa, the MENA region and Asia to be connected by tankers and gas carriers is self-evident. Thus, petroleum shipping will continue to be built and navigate through vital SLOCs along the Atlantic/Indo-Pacific "East-West-East" trading belt. These assets will continue to be at risk, and perhaps the future vectors of that risk will come from conventional, asymmetrical and hybrid *state* kinetic action as the potential for inimical geopolitical forces in regions such as the Eastern Mediterranean, the Persian Gulf and the South China Sea become an existential risk. Arguably, in a macro geo-strategic framework, the level of insecurity risk of these maritime spaces will be determined principally during the course of the next decade by the strategic contest between the world's major powers within the Indo-Pacific maritime realm – China and the United States. If we also add the inevitable developing importance of the Northern Sea Route as an emerging petroleum SLOC across the top of the world, Russia's increasing exertion of her power and influence in that most unique of maritime environments will inevitably be the decisive variable in determining geopolitical and security risk in that space.

Notes

1 Condensate (also known as *lease condensate*) is a mixture of light liquid hydrocarbons, comprising mostly natural gas liquids (NGLs) and naphtha. Upon separation from natural gas in the field processing plants, it is handled like a crude oil. It can be conveyed directly to market by pipeline/tanker as it occurs or blended at a refinery with conventional crude oil.
2 FSOs are converted VLCCs or ULCCs that are used as storage in an offshore oil field, wherein processed oil is then transferred at sea to attending tankers for transfer ashore or more distant export terminals.

References

Aljazeera. (2018, April 4). *Saudi oil tanker attacked off Hudaida port.* https://www.aljazeera.com/news/2018/4/4/saudi-oil-tanker-attacked-off-hudaida-port

al-Warfalli, A., & Elumami, A. (2016, January 21). *Islamic state attack sets storage tanks ablaze at Libyan oil terminal.* Reuters. https://www.reuters.com/article/us-libya-security-idUSKCN0UZ0P0

Bateman, T. (2019, July 30). *Royal marines used brute force, says tanker captain.* BBC News. https://www.bbc.com/news/uk-49162256

BBC News. (2010). *Japan tanker was damaged in a terror attack, UAE says.* BBC News. https://www.bbc.com/news/world-asia-pacific-10890098

Fuller, K., & Pitt, A. (Eds.). (2013). *World energy atlas* (7th ed.). Petroleum Economist.

Herbert-Burns, R. (2008). Tankers, specialised production vessels, and offshore terminals: Vulnerability and security in the international oil sector (pp. 133–158). In R. Herbert-Burns, S. Bateman & Peter Lehr (Eds.), *Lloyds MIU handbook of maritime security.* CRC Press.

Herbert-Burns, R. (2011). *Petroleum geopolitics: A framework for analysis.* PhD thesis, University of St Andrews.

Hubbard, B., Karasz, P., & Reed, S. (2019, September 14). Two major Saudi oil installations hit by drone strike, and U.S. blames Iran. *The New York Times.* https://www.nytimes.com/2019/09/14/world/middleeast/saudi-arabia-refineries-drone-attack.html

Hueper, P. (2005). *Fundamentals of energy infrastructure security: Risk management in the international environment.* Petroleum Economist Ltd.

OGJ Editors. (2004, February 18). Algerian LNG complex explosion caused by gas pipeline leak. *Oil & Gas Journal.* https://www.ogj.com/pipelines-transportation/article/17292920/algerian-lng-complex-explosion-caused-by-gas-pipeline-leak

Pamuk, H. (2019, December 19). *Exclusive: U.S. probe of Saudi oil attack shows it came from north – Report.* Reuters. https://www.reuters.com/article/us-saudi-aramco-attacks-iran-exclusive-idUSKBN1YN299

Porter, G. D. (2015, February). Terrorist targeting of the Libyan oil and gas sector. *CTC Sentinel, 8*(2), 8–10.

Reuters. (1985, September 8). Iraq reports raiding Kharg island and "large naval target". *The New York Times.* https://www.nytimes.com/1985/09/08/world/iraq-reports-raiding-kharg-island-and-large-naval-target.html

Sheppard, D., Al Omran, A., & Raval, A. (2018, July 26). Saudis suspend Red Sea oil shipments after tanker attacks. *Financial Times.* https://www.ft.com/content/f0858962-9005-11e8-b639-7680cedcc421

Woody, C. (2019, November 13). *Pirates attacked an Italian ship off the coast of Mexico – the latest sign of a growing criminal industry.* Insider. https://www.businessinsider.com/pirate-attacks-in-gulf-of-mexico-related-to-fuel-theft-2019-11?r=US&IR=T

18

CYBERSECURITY AND DISRUPTIVE TECHNOLOGIES

Jeptoo Kipkech, Kristen Kuhn, and Siraj Ahmed Shaikh

Introduction

The ocean has always been a perilous realm where ship security is uncertain. This is due to factors like weather, lack of information or technology, or an attack. Traditional attacks on marine vessels include piracy, boarding, theft and destruction. While these attacks are often successful and continuous, they are well-understood (Jones et al., 2016). Maritime security is increasingly complex due to the multidimensional nature of the maritime sphere as activities operate above, on and below the surface of the sea. Strategically, there are economic, physical, legal, political and military dimensions to the maritime environment which need to be protected (White House, 2005). Therefore, states and other actors place maritime security high on their security agendas.

The evolution of information systems and the diffusion of broadband communication has led to wide adoption of *information and communications technology* (ICT) in the maritime sector (Polemi, 2017). This has added value to industry through increased globalisation and access to new markets. In 2018, the e-commerce value alone of the maritime industry was worth £26 trillion (United Nations Conference on Trade and Development (UNCTAD), 2018). However, a drawback of making ICTs the backbone of industry is that it leaves systems vulnerable to cyber threats (Carrapico & Barrinha, 2017).

Cyber attacks are stealthier than traditional attacks, and have a range of potential implications including business disruption, financial loss, damage to reputation, damage to goods and environment (Jones et al., 2016). A 2017 study by an insurance firm found that cyber attacks cost a medium-sized company, on average, $3.79 million (Harry & Gallagher, 2018). This study ranked the transportation sector third in terms of cyber vulnerability.

Cyber threats that emerge from technological advancement pose a major risk to maritime security (United Nations General Assembly, 2008). Yet, the maritime sector has not demonstrated proportionate effort to understand cyber attacks. Efforts should reflect the weight of the matter: International shipping is a $183.3 billion industry (Tam & Jones, 2018) responsible for 90% of world trade (International Chamber of Shipping, 2020).

The speed with which technology changes, coupled with the increasing attack surface as technology is adopted, means that most cannot escape vulnerability. Cybersecurity is about managing risks – not eliminating them.

214

DOI: 10.4324/9781003001324-21

There is a need for effective cyber risk management to improve cyber preparedness. If not, the consequences of such attacks can be catastrophic and have cascading effects. Ironically, this is due to the very technologies and information used to mitigate threats, whereby increased connectivity means an attack on a single system may carry across networks.

A 2019 study that explores a hypothetical cyber attack on 15 ports across Asia Pacific estimates losses of up to $110 billion to the world economy (Cambridge Centre for Risk Studies, 2019). While this study is on ports, it is a call to action for the entire maritime industry: More must be done to address cybersecurity and disruptive technologies. The future prosperity of the blue economy depends on the ability to safeguard trade, preserve freedom and maintain good governance at sea (White House, 2005).

This chapter is organised as follows: It begins with an analysis of vessels as a cyber-physical environment. It then goes on to explore cybersecurity of vessels, including its importance and attributes. The following sections focus on threat analysis and review known cyber attacks on ships. Finally, the chapter examines efforts to overcome cyber threats to vessels and analyses cyber power in the maritime environment.

Vessels as a cyber-physical environment

Information networks and integrated systems make vessels more connected than ever before. These interdependencies introduce new cyber threats to vessels that extend along the global supply chain. Today, a single cyber attack on an ICT system can lead to crippling vessel damage and network disruption.

A *cyber-physical system (CPS)* is an integration of computation with physical processes, whereas embedded computers and networks monitor and control physical processes, usually with feedback loops (Lee & Seshia, 2016). CPSs are made up of computational entities that link the physical and virtual world to achieve a global behaviour (Monostori, 2018). They include sensors, actuators, control processing units and communication devices that enable automation (Brinkmann & Hahn, 2017; Cardenas, 2018).

The global shipping supply chain is a complex CPS system composed of interconnected *Information Technology* (IT) and *Operational Technology* (OT) systems (Polemi, 2017). While IT focuses on the use of data as information, OT deals with controlling data or monitoring physical processes (International Maritime Organization, 2017). The interaction of IT and OT elements – cyber and physical – cannot be separated and is, in a sense, an entity itself. CPS is the intersection of physical and cyber (Lee & Seshia, 2016).

To identify and respond to current threats, it is essential to be familiar with the critical systems of vessels. In this chapter, the marine vessel is referred to as "vessel" and means any component or structure intended for exposure to a marine environment, including an oil drilling platform [rig] and a navigational aid (New Jersey Department of State, 2017). Ship components vary according to vessel function and sophistication.

Indeed, a modern vessel itself may be considered a complex cyber-physical system. This dependence on technology extends the presence of a vessel in the cyber domain and heightens the risk of cyber attacks. Three factors that magnify cyber risk for vessels include a growing ship-to-shore connection, the use of outdated and diverse systems, and increased autonomy. These factors result from disruptive initiatives in the maritime industry, either new technology or the discovery of new information.

According to International Maritime Organization (International Maritime Organization, 2017), these are the five general ship components and their function:

- Automatic Identification System (AIS): This system informs the port and maritime authorities of the ship's position. It also measures the distance from the surrounding ships, ensures safety at sea by monitoring traffic and avoids collisions.
- Electronic Chart Display Information System (ECDIS): This system displays the position of the ship on a screen and provides navigational safety information.
- Global Navigation Satellite System (GNSS): This system displays the vessel's position, speed, route and time via satellites and a receiver, including global positioning system (GPS). It also enables orientation and navigation for sea, land and air.
- Integrated Bridge System (IBS): This system manages bridge components and provides centralised access to information from components.
- Voyage Data Recorder (VDR): This system analyses the circumstances that resulted in an accident, by examining the recorded data. This is the ship's "aeronautical black box."

Ship-to-shore connection

While shipboard communication is often discussed as it applies to computer networking between ships and shore facilities, it also applies to networks between ships. The *ship-to-shore connection*, in this chapter, refers to both ship-to-shore and ship-to-ship interfaces. Different communication links exist between these interfaces, including radio, satellites and computers. Therefore, one cannot ignore "the three sides of the coin": Ship, shore and their connections (International Maritime Organization, 2019b).

The harmonised collection, integration, exchange, presentation and analysis of marine information on board and ashore by electronic means is referred to as *e-Navigation* (International Maritime Organization, 2019b). Ship-borne users of e-Navigation include offshore energy vessels, fishing vessels and commercial tourism craft; shore-borne users encompass ship owners and operators, port authorities and financial organisations. By modulating a ship's journey, e-Navigation reduces delays, increases efficiency and reduces environmental pollution. However, connected systems increase vulnerability by increasing attack surface, raising the risk of cyber attacks. Further, the disruption of a single connected system can compromise its entire network.

Outdated and diverse systems

With the arrival of computers, which offer greater flexibility and sophistication, a wide array of highly efficient digital modes are available. Despite this, there is a tendency to use outdated technologies. For instance, the amateur RTTY radio is widely used (Electronics Notes, 2019). This creates vulnerabilities: For radio-based communications, signal jamming is particularly effective on ships, as they are often far from other signal sources, making those signals weak and easy to jam (Tam & Jones, 2018). Maritime pirates, who can easily intercept conversations to learn about a vessel and its cargo, exploit this technological vulnerability.

The tendency to use outdated ICT and CPS systems is motivated by the reluctance to haul ships, or repair them, as this is a timely and costly ordeal. There is general agreement that a ship only earns money when it is at sea (Oram, 1965). Re-hauls on vessels are rarely done unless necessary. Further, when re-hauls are done, they are usually extremely expensive due to the custom nature of the repairs. It is often decided to update existing software and patch vulnerable systems, rather than replace them, due to time and cost considerations. For this reason, vessels are under significant threat of cyber attacks because many carry outdated software and were not designed with cybersecurity in mind (Jones et al., 2016). A study led by Plymouth University's

Maritime Cyber Threats Research Group suggests operators could easily mitigate against such dangers by updating security systems and improving ship design (Jones et al., 2016).

Autonomous vessels

At least three organisations aim to produce and sail autonomous ships by 2020, due to developing technologies and policy that make autonomy a feasible solution (Tam & Jones, 2018). While estimates for autonomous ships show them to be cost-effective, they often ignore new risks associated with CPS systems. On the one hand, autonomy reduces the number of on-board navigation systems (Tam & Jones, 2019), therefore decreases the attack surface area. However, the addition of remote-controlled operations increases the severity and likelihood of successful exploits.

Ongoing efforts to understand new risks associated with autonomous ships and remap the cyber threat landscape invokes another industry challenge: Like traditional vessels, autonomous ships are each unique in design, which results in diverse (but no longer outdated) vessel systems. It will be a feat to develop a risk classification model inclusive of each of these vessels, but not so broad as to be rendered irrelevant in the creation of an industry standard.

A starting point to developing a risk classification model for autonomous ships is to understand that all ships will include a minimal crew on-board and operate on a spectrum of partial to full autonomy. In this sense, similarities can be drawn from trends in port automation. However, it is also something that must be constructed from scratch: Existing risk models for physical ship safety and autonomous cars (and ports) do not adequately represent the unique nature of cyber-threats for autonomous vessels within the maritime sector. Thus, it is essential to begin assessing new cyber-risk profile

Cybersecurity of vessels

What do we mean by cybersecurity?

Many vessel components are CPSs, or intersecting points between physical and cyber. The cyber environment, or *cyberspace*, includes all connected computing devices, personnel, infrastructure, applications, services, telecommunication systems, and the totality of transmitted, processed and stored data. Cyberspace is continuously shifting and therefore challenging to secure.

Cybersecurity refers to the protection of information systems, the data on them, and the services they provide, from unauthorised access, harm or misuse (UK Government, 2016). The interpretation of "cybersecurity" within the context of maritime vessels covers ship components and their cyber-physical aspects. It includes data, monitoring, control, off-ship support, hardware, ship documentation and processes. However, it is key to recognise that cybersecurity encompasses not only technology and information but also physical aspects, processes and people (Boyes et al., 2020).

Does cybersecurity matter in marine transport?

The international shipping industry is the lifeblood of the global economy. It facilitates intercontinental trade, the bulk transport of raw materials, affordable food and manufactured goods. Today, over 50,000 merchant ships transport cargo around the globe. These ships are technically sophisticated high-value assets and their operation generates an estimated annual income of over half a trillion US Dollars (International Chamber of Shipping, 2020). The critical systems in these modern vessels are generally digital systems, either industrial control systems or information systems.

Cyber-physical systems are often interconnected to form assets that provide a range of operational services, where technology plays an increasingly vital role. The loss, or compromise, of one or more of these assets has the potential to affect the health and safety of ship personnel, impact the ability of the ship to operate safely as well as influence the speed and efficiency of the ship (Kuhn, Kipkech, et al., 2020). Cybersecurity was ranked as the highest risk for the shipping sector in 2020 (Allianz Global Corporate and Specialty SE, 2020) which illustrates its relevance.

Threat analysis in the maritime sector

Digital technologies are essential to the operation of vessels and their critical systems. However, design inadequacies, system integration or maintenance, and lapses in cyber discipline may result in cybersecurity vulnerabilities. To prevent exploitation, these vulnerabilities are addressed through threat analysis, which identifies potential threat actors and their sophistication.

Threat actors

Threat actors that attempt cyber attacks on vessels all seek to achieve an aim. In general, they seek to limit, mislead, confuse, disrupt, delay, divert, destroy and isolate the vessel's cyber capabilities (Bodeau et al., 2013). Knowledge of the threat actor at hand may indicate their motivations, targets and capabilities.

Cyber threat actors are not equal in terms of capability and sophistication, and have a range of resources, training and support for their activities (Souppaya & Scarfone, 2013). An assessment of likelihood of attack occurrence and success is typically based on the adversary's intent, target and capability (National Institute of Standards and Technology, 2011). These actors may operate on their own or as part of a larger organisation, such as a state intelligence or organised crime groups.

The nature of cyber threat actors, including their motivations, targets and TTPs (Boyes et al., 2020) is discussed below:

- Cyber criminals may operate on their own or as organisations that generally have a moderate level of sophistication. They are largely driven by information advantage, reputation enhancement, economic or financial gain. They target assets using techniques such as phishing, botnets, password attacks, exploit kits and malware.
- Cyber espionage are the most sophisticated threat actors, often with dedicated resources and personnel, extensive skills, planning and coordination. They usually target intellectual property from governments and organisations to gain an advantage over competitors. They may employ phishing, password attacks, data exfiltration and malware to conduct strategic campaigns.
- Hacktivists are activist groups and individuals typically at the lowest level of sophistication. They target governments, organisations or individuals to influence political, ideological or social change. They rely on widely available tools such as DDoS attacks, doxing and web defacement.
- Insider threats are often disgruntled contractors, employees or partners individuals within an organisation. They are driven by revenge or financial gain to target weak physical processes, technical gaps and poor design in organisations. They are particularly dangerous because they can misuse their access privileges or exfiltrate data.

- Cyber war/Cyber terrorists have capabilities that range from the lowest to highest levels of sophistication. They target individuals, criminals, states or military. However, they often rely on widely available tools that require little technical skill to deploy such as website defacement and claimed leaks. Their actions often seek to influence political, ideological or social change.

Cyber attacks on maritime ships

With automation, digitisation and integration driving the maritime sector, infrastructure relies increasingly on technology. Consequently, cybersecurity has been a major cause of alarm in the industry. Cyber-related incidents involving navigating, movement of cargo, and other processes threaten lives, environment, property, and considerably disrupt maritime trade movement because of cyber attacks. Cyber attacks in the maritime industry are grouped into three categories (Shaikh, 2017): attacks on enterprise and information assets, attacks on navigation systems and advanced persistent threats.

Attacks on enterprise and information assets

Enterprise cybersecurity refers to protection of an organisation's on-premise and cloud-based infrastructure, as well as vetting third-party providers and securing the endpoints connected to a network via the Internet of Things (IoT) (Chaudhry et al., 2012). Personal data, intellectual property, cyber infrastructure and business-critical applications can be compromised through network attacks using security lapses and vulnerable services. The impact of such attacks is ranked as low to medium, as enterprise systems may be breached, but they rarely include loss of life or physical disruption (Shaikh, 2017). Attacks on enterprise and information assets in the maritime industry are seen in Table 18.1.

Attacks on navigation systems

Recent GPS jamming and spoofing incidents have revealed serious security flaws in Integrated Bridge Systems (IBS) and Global Navigation Satellite Systems (GNSS) of vessels, including the Global Positioning System (GPS). *GPS spoofing* involves an attacker placing rogue transmissions that can mislead on-board navigation systems on fundamental calculations such as location, velocity and heading (Hassani et al., 2017). The impact of such cyber attacks is ranked as medium to high (Agrafiotis et al., 2018). Alongside data, procedural and operational breaches, they can result in physical damage such as paralysed shipping lanes, collisions and piracy incidents, as seen in Table 18.2.

Table 18.1 Cyber attacks on enterprise and information assets in the maritime industry

Year	Target	Attack vector	Impact
2020	Mediterranean Shipping Company (MSC)	Malware	Network outage
2020	Strait of Hormuz Port	Malware	Data infiltration Damaged operating systems
2018	COSCO Shipping	Ransomware	Network outage

Table 18.2 Cyber attacks on navigation systems in the maritime industry

Year	Target	Attack vector	Impact
2020	Chinese vessels	GPS spoofing	GPS outage and spoofing
2019	Eastern and Central Mediterranean Sea, and Suez Canal	GPS interference	Navigation disruption Operation disruption
2019	Strait of Hormuz	GPS spoofing	GPS outage and spoofing Navigation disruption

Advanced persistent threats

Advanced persistent threats (APTs) are hackers with high-value targets, such as nation-states or large corporations, whose ultimate goal is stealing information over an extended time (Kessler, 2019). Most APT attacks aim to achieve and maintain ongoing access to the targeted network. The impact of such an attack is high: They result in maximum damage, including actual physical damage or loss of life. Table 18.3 shows two known APT attacks.

Overcoming cyber threats to vessels

Existing cyber risk frameworks

There exists a plethora of cybersecurity challenges faced by the maritime industry, one of which is awareness (Drougkas et al., 2019). This includes identifying vulnerable systems which must be made resilient and maintain functionality when a failure occurs. Ideally, these systems will employ fault tolerance, defence control and monitoring functions to oversee critical services and systems. Evolving technologies and threats make them difficult to maintain, and cyber risks cannot be addressed through technical standards alone.

A risk-based approach to managing cyber threats can be used by organisations to assess vessel cybersecurity. Cyber risk frameworks exist to recommend cyber risk management strategies that are resilient and exist as a natural extension of safety and security management practices. A consolidated list of guidelines on international cyber risk management is offered in Table 18.4.

Where frameworks fall short

The varied nature of cybersecurity threats means that no single approach can address all risks. Evolving technology and the steady flow of serious vulnerabilities in operating systems, software libraries and applications, means that any strategy needs to be kept under regular review.

Table 18.3 Advanced persistent threats (APTs) in the maritime industry

Year	Target	Attacker	Impact
2018	Maritime operations Satellite systems	Chinese Anchor Panda (APT 14)	Information theft Espionage
2017	Maritime sector	Chinese Leviathan (APT 40)	Information theft

Cybersecurity and Disruptive Technologies

Table 18.4 Existing guidelines on international cyber risk management

Year	Document
2021	IMO Resolution MSC.428(98): Maritime Cyber Risk Management in Safety Management Systems (International Maritime Organization (IMO), 2017)
This resolution encourages administrations to ensure cyber risks are addressed in existing safety management systems (as per the ISM Code) by the first verification of company compliance in 2021.	
2018	BIMCO Guidelines on Cyber Security Onboard Ships (BIMCO et al., 2018)
This addresses the requirement to incorporate cyber risks in a ship's safety management system (Jorgensen, 2018). It also reflects a deeper experience with risk assessments of OT and provides guidance for dealing with cyber risks that arise from the supply chain.	
2018	NIST Cybersecurity Framework for Improving Critical Infrastructure (National Institute of Standards and Technology, 2018)
A revised version of a 2014 framework to improve critical infrastructure cybersecurity, the voluntary framework includes standards, guidelines and practices to reduce cyber risks to critical infrastructure.	
2013	ISO/ IEC – 2700 Series (International Organization for Standardization, 2013)
This family of standards help organisations secure information assets. The ISO/IEC 27001:2013 standard provides requirements for an information security management system, which are implemented by the maritime industry.	

While Table 18.4 focuses on public resources used widely on the international level, other national and even corporate guidelines are also often applied. This helps to explain the discrepancies, and at times the duplicity, which characterise existing cyber risk frameworks. Equally, not one authority applies to all vessels, especially regarding incidents in international waters. Overcoming threats requires the integrated assessment of cyber security standards and practice.

Towards a legal framework for maritime cybersecurity

The uses and abuses of a borderless cyberspace impinge on vital maritime security. The security issues that arise from cyberspace extend far beyond the domain of internal affairs of any state (Betz, 2017). The oceans outside of state authority make up the global commons and no state may legitimately subject any part of the high seas to its sovereignty (Litfin, 1997). Balancing issues of collective interest and state sovereignty, namely territorial integrity and political independence, is the main aim of maritime security (Feldt et al., 2013). As a result, international laws such as the United Nations Convention for the Law of the Sea (UNCLOS) exist to maintain peace and order in the maritime environment (Guruswamy, 1998). Operationally, states strive to enforce their national laws and international law but are challenged by the threat of non-state actors seeking to exploit the seas where jurisdiction is unclear (Stahl, 2011).

A legal framework conferring universal jurisdiction over some acts of cyber aggression may help to resolve some of the jurisdictional issues raised by attacks (Stahl, 2011). Universal jurisdiction could be extended to cyber-crime if the international community recognises it as a universal offence. Additionally, the establishment of an international cyber-crime tribunal would encourage cooperation on the development of international norms relating to cyber-crime. This tribunal will allow nations to retain some level of autonomy in the development and enforcement of domestic cybersecurity policy (Stahl, 2011).

Cyber power in the maritime environment

Maritime cyber power is the ability to use cyberspace to create advantages and influence events in maritime operational environments and across the instruments of power (Kuehl, 2009). Cyberspace has a physical infrastructure layer that follows the economic laws of rival resources and political laws of sovereign justification and control (Nye, 2011). This cyberspace layer is critical in the political sphere because the state is deeply embedded in it. Cyber power includes both physical and informational instruments and ramifications within and beyond cyberspace (Nye Jr, 2010). Threat actors may also attempt to project cyber power by controlling leverage, access and force in international and domestic settings in ways that threaten security.

Cyber power provides the benefit of extending and accentuating existing forms of military power (Healey, 2016). It helps shape the landscape through control of systems, intelligence, surveillance and reconnaissance activities, especially in facilitating military effects that were previously only achievable through kinetic means. Moreover, cyber power is a unique political instrument.

Although cyber power brings advantages, it also exposes the maritime community to the same risks and vulnerability to attack as their land-based counterparts. Furthermore, cyber conflicts arise as a result of conflicting interest and in extreme cases, cyber war (Siedler, 2016). In contrast to optimising a state actor's military force, cyber power undermines an opponent state's capability by attacking its cyber elements.

Cyber risk management

Cyber risk management refers to the process of identifying, analysing, assessing and communicating cyber-related risk and accepting, avoiding, transferring or mitigating it to an acceptable level considering costs and benefits of actions taken to stakeholders (International Maritime Organization, 2019a). The goal of maritime cyber risk management is to support safe and secure shipping that is operationally resilient to cyber risks (BIMCO et al., 2018).

Effective cyber risk management should start at the top tiers of an organisation. Executive management must foster a culture of cyber risk awareness, thus ensuring a holistic and flexible cyber risk management regime (Refsdal et al., 2015). This is a continuous operation and is constantly evaluated and refined through effective feedback mechanisms.

Organisations can comprehensively assess and compare their current and desired cyber risk management postures to achieve the above (Tucci, 2017). Such assessments may reveal gaps that can be addressed to achieve risk management objectives through a prioritised cyber risk management plan. This risk-based approach will enable an organisation to best apply its resources.

There are five functional elements that encompass the activities and desired outcomes of effective cyber risk management: identify, protect, detect, respond and recover (National Institute of Standards and Technology, 2018). These may be applied to vessels and their critical systems that facilitate maritime operations and information exchange.

Risk strategy for maritime vessels

Risk strategy is fundamental to secure shipping operations. Risk management has traditionally been focused on operations in the physical domain, but greater reliance on digitisation, integration, automation and network-based systems has created an increasing need for cyber risk management.

Stakeholders can take the necessary steps to safeguard shipping from threats related to digitisation, integration and automation of processes and systems in shipping (International Maritime Organization, 2019a). Effective cyber risk management considers safety and security impacts resulting from the exploitation of vulnerabilities in information technology systems (Polatidis et al., 2018). Organisations should consider control options for cyber risk management such as management controls, operational or procedural controls and technical controls (Jensen, 2015).

Although each of these considerations is important, it is not enough for an organisation to practice proactive cybersecurity. Breaches are inevitable, and while risk can be managed, it can no longer be eliminated. Therefore, risk strategy for maritime vessels should also include cyber incident preparedness. Some factors that can contribute to incident preparedness are training, cyber insurance and transparency in reporting.

Training

Learning to respond to entire interconnected systems is challenging and that is evident in the training offered. It is likely the lack of adequate cyber training has resulted in poor classification of cyber attacks due to human error (Rothblum, 2000). For instance, a study led by Plymouth University's Maritime Cyber Threats Research Group suggests operators could easily mitigate against such dangers by providing better training for crews (Jones et al., 2016).

It is often mentioned that the weakest link in cybersecurity is the human link. Therefore, training is a fundamental aspect of cyber risk management. Some existing training methods include videos, courses and simulations, which involve creating a hypothetical environment where decision-makers respond to incidents, which emulate real cyber-incidents.

Cyber insurance

Insurance has traditionally saturated the maritime sector and is a significant regulating force for its role in compliance. While traditional offerings are well established, cyber insurance is a new concept. All insurance considers a degree of uncertainty, but cyber incidents are unique to insure, as they are highly uncertain and dependent on rapidly shifting technology. This is one reason the maritime sector has been slow to incorporate cyber insurance. Other reasons include lack of experience with cyber incidents, confusion around premiums, the issue of accumulated risk, undefined threat metrics and challenges around governance (Kuhn, Vasudevan, et al., 2020).

A 2019 report found the insurance industry loses just under 9% of the total economic loss associated with maritime cyber attacks, which shows this type of attack is highly underinsured (Cambridge Centre for Risk Studies, 2019). Despite this, and increasingly, cyber insurance is a defining aspect of cyber risk management for maritime vessels.

Transparency in reporting

While the shipping giant Maersk quickly made the 2017 Not-Petya ransomware attack they suffered public knowledge (Greenberg, 2018), their decision went against the norm. Maritime organisations often do not report cyber attacks and do not release information publicly to prevent customers' loss (Allianz Global Corporate and Specialty SE, 2016).

The attacks listed in this chapter are all public knowledge. They vary across state and sector, and collectively serve as a stark reminder that cyber incidents can disrupt critical services, cause glaring economic loss and threaten national security. Further transparency in the reporting on cyber attacks on maritime vessels will lead to more shared knowledge and improved, updated cyber risk frameworks that are a relevant tool for organisations to incorporate into their cyber risk strategy.

Conclusion

As long as vessels navigate the ocean, they will face cybersecurity risks. While traditional threats are well understood, cyber attacks are shrouded in uncertainties that have not yet been accounted for. More must be done to address cybersecurity and disruptive technologies that characterise the modern maritime vessel.

While cyber attacks cannot be treated like traditional attacks, we can use response to traditional attacks as a starting point from which to address them. Like traditional threats, cybersecurity can be overcome through the increased and continuous refinement of cyber risk frameworks, associated strategies and tools. Likewise, uncertainty can be accounted for through initiatives that lead to development of technology or discovery of information.

While cybersecurity is widely applicable, it is especially relevant to the maritime sector where the damage that can result from a cyber attack is unprecedented. In 2019, a study proposed significant economic losses, upwards of $110 billion, associated with a potential cyber attack on 15 ports (Cambridge Centre for Risk Studies, 2019). Maritime industries are an important engine for growth, and are a vibrant, dynamic and indispensable element of the global economy. In acknowledging the vital value of the sea to the global economy, it is clear to see the sea is an area worth fighting to control.

Maritime cyber power is poignant and increasingly relevant. Nations that depend on cyberspace are at risk of exploitation of cyber power for political effects. Yet, despite its weight, the maritime sector has not demonstrated proportionate effort to understand cyber attacks, and therefore remains exposed to them. In today's environment, cybersecurity is about managing risks – not eliminating them. There is a need for effective cyber risk management to improve preparedness to respond to cyber attacks. More must be done to address cybersecurity and disruptive technologies.

The ability to project power in the cyber domain remains an important source of influence alongside economic, military, informational and diplomatic leverage. In order to effectively address the challenges presented to maritime cybersecurity, the maritime sphere requires extensive national, jurisdictional and public–private coordination.

References

Agrafiotis, I., Nurse, J. R., Goldsmith, M., Creese, S., & Upton, D. (2018). A taxonomy of cyber-harms: Defining the impacts of cyber-attacks and understanding how they propagate. *Journal of Cybersecurity*, 4(1). 10.1093/cybsec/tyy006

Allianz Global Corporate and Specialty SE. (2016). *Safety and shipping review 2016*. Allianz Global Corporate and Specialty. https://www.agcs.allianz.com/content/dam/onemarketing/agcs/agcs/reports/AGCS-Safety-Shipping-Review-2016.pdf

Allianz Global Corporate and Specialty SE. (2020). *Allianz risk barometer: Identifying the major business risks for 2020*. https://www.agcs.allianz.com/content/dam/onemarketing/agcs/agcs/reports/Allianz-Risk-Barometer-2020.pdf

Betz, D. J. (2017). *Cyberspace and the state: Towards a strategy for cyber-power*. Routledge.

BIMCO et al. (2018). *The guidelines on cyber security onboard ships – version 3*. https://www.ics-shipping.org/wp-content/uploads/2020/08/guidelines-on-cyber-security-onboard-ships-min.pdf

Bodeau, D., Graubart, R., & Heinbockel, W. (2013). *Characterizing effects on the cyber adversary: A vocabulary for analysis and assessment* (Report no: MTR130432). MITRE Corporation. https://www.mitre.org/sites/default/files/publications/characterizing-effects-cyber-adversary-13-4173.pdf

Cybersecurity and Disruptive Technologies

Boyes, H., Isbell, R., & Luck, A. (2020). Good practice guide: Cyber security for ports and port systems. *Institution of Engineering and Technology*. https://assets.publishing.service.gov.uk/government/uploads/system/uploads/attachment_data/file/859925/cyber-security-for-ports-and-port-systems-code-of-practice.pdf

Brinkmann, M., & Hahn, A. (2017). Testbed architecture for maritime cyber physical systems. *2017 IEEE 15th International Conference on Industrial Informatics (INDIN)*, 923–928.

Cambridge Centre for Risk Studies. (2019). *Shen attack: Cyber risk in Asia pacific ports.* https://risk-studies-viewpoint.blog.jbs.cam.ac.uk/2019/10/30/shen-attack-cyber-risk-scenario-up-to-110-billion-at-risk-from-maritime-malware-attack/

Cardenas, A. (2018). *Cyber-physical systems security knowledge area* (Report no: 0.1). The Cyber Security Body of Knowledge. https://www.cybok.org/media/downloads/Cyber_Physical_Systems_KA_-_Issue_1.0_September_2019.pdf

Carrapico, H., & Barrinha, A. (2017). The EU as a coherent (cyber) security actor? *JCMS: Journal of Common Market Studies, 55*(6), 1254–1272. 10.1111/jcms.12575

Chaudhry, P. E., Chaudhry, S. S., Reese, R., & Jones, D. S. (2012). Enterprise information systems security: A conceptual framework. *Re-conceptualizing enterprise information systems* (pp. 118–128). Springer.

Drougkas, A., Sarri, A., Kyranoudi, P., & Zisi, A. (2019). *Port cybersecurity: Good practices for cybersecurity in the maritime sector.* European Union Agency for Cybersecurity (ENISA). https://www.enisa.europa.eu/publications/port-cybersecurity-good-practices-for-cybersecurity-in-the-maritime-sector

Electronics Notes. (2019). *What is RTTY for amateur radio.* https://www.electronics-notes.com/articles/ham_radio/digimodes/what-is-rtty-radio-teletype.php

Feldt, L., Roell, P., & Thiele, R. D. (2013). *Maritime security – Perspectives for a comprehensive approach* (Report no: 222). ISPSW. https://www.files.ethz.ch/isn/162756/222_feldt_roell_thiele.pdf

Greenberg, A. (2018). *The untold story of NotPetya, the most devastating cyberattack in history.* Wired. https://www.wired.com/story/notpetya-cyberattack-ukraine-russia-code-crashed-the-world/

Guruswamy, L. (1998). The promise of the United Nations Convention on the Law of the Sea (UNCLOS): Justice in trade and environment disputes. *Ecology LQ, 25*(2), 189–227.

Harry, C., & Gallagher, N. (2018). Classifying cyber events. *Journal of Information Warfare, 17*(3), 17–31.

Hassani, V., Crasta, N., & Pascoal, A. M. (2017). Cyber security issues in navigation systems of marine vessels from a control perspective. *ASME 2017 36th International Conference on Ocean, Offshore and Arctic Engineering, 7B.* https://asmedigitalcollection.asme.org/OMAE/proceedings-abstract/OMAE2017/57748/V07BT06A029/281549

Healey, J. (2016). Winning and losing in cyberspace. *2016 8th International Conference on Cyber Conflict (CyCon)*, 37–49. IEEE.

International Chamber of Shipping. (2020). Shipping and world trade: Top containership operators. https://www.ics-shipping.org/shipping-fact/shipping-and-world-trade-top-containership-operators/

International Maritime Organization. (2017). *Resolution Mscfal.1/circ.3, guidelines on maritime cyber risk management.* https://wwwcdn.imo.org/localresources/en/OurWork/Security/Documents/MSC-FAL.1-Circ.3%20-%20Guidelines%20On%20Maritime%20Cyber%20Risk%20Management%20(Secretariat).pdf

International Maritime Organization. (2019a). *Maritime cyber risk.* https://www.imo.org/en/OurWork/Security/Pages/Cyber-security.aspx

International Maritime Organization. (2019b). *Strategy for the development and implementation of e-navigation.* https://www.imo.org/en/OurWork/Safety/Pages/eNavigation.aspx

International Organization for Standardization. (2013). *ISO/IEC 27001:2013 — Information security management systems.* https://www.iso.org/standard/54534.html

Jensen, L. (2015). Challenges in maritime cyber-resilience. *Technology Innovation Management Review, 5*(4), 35–39.

Jones, K. D., Tam, K., & Papadaki, M. (2016). Threats and impacts in maritime cyber security. *Engineering & Technology Reference, 1*(1), 1-12. 10.1049/etr.2015.0123

Jorgensen, R. N. (2018). Container ship design. https://www.bimco.org/news/%20priority-news/20181207-industry-publishes-improved-cyber-guidelines

Kessler, G. C. (2019). Cybersecurity in the maritime domain. *USCG Proceedings of the Marine Safety & Security Council, 76*(1), 34.

Kuehl, D. T. (2009). From cyberspace to cyberpower: Defining the problem. *Cyberpower and National Security, 1*, 26–28.

Kuhn, K., Kipkech, J., & Shaikh, S. (2020). Maritime ports and cybersecurity. *Maritime transport and its solutions in port logistics* (In–press). Institution of Engineering Technology.

Kuhn, K., Vasudevan, S., & Carr, M. (2020). Cyber insurance and risk management: Challenges and opportunities. https://www.riscs.org.uk/cyber-insurance/

Lee, E., & Seshia, S. (2016). *Introduction to embedded systems: A cyber-physical systems approach.* MIT Press.

Litfin, K. T. (1997). Sovereignty in world ecopolitics. *Mershon International Studies Review, 41*(Supplement 2), 167–204.

Monostori, L. (2018). Cyber-physical systems. In S. Chatti & T. Tolio (Eds.) *Cirp encyclopedia of production engineering* (pp. 1–8). Springer. 10.1007/978-3-642-35950-7_16790-1

National Institute of Standards and Technology. (2011). *Special publication 800-39 managing information security risk: Organization, mission, and information system view.* https://nvlpubs.nist.gov/nistpubs/Legacy/SP/nistspecialpublication800-39.pdf

National Institute of Standards and Technology. (2018). *Framework for improving critical infrastructure cyber-security.* https://nvlpubs.nist.gov/nistpubs/CSWP/NIST.CSWP.04162018.pdf

New Jersey Department of State. (2017). *Environmental protection: Air quality, energy, and sustainability –Division of air quality.* https://www.nj.gov/dep/rules/adoptions/adopt_20171106b.pdf

Nye, J. S. (2011). Nuclear lessons for cyber security. *Strategic Studies Quarterly, 5*(4), 18–38.

Nye, J. S., Jr. (2010). *Cyber power.* Harvard University. https://apps.dtic.mil/sti/pdfs/ADA522626.pdf

Oram, R. (1965). The port. In R. Oram (1st ed.), *Cargo handling and the modern port* (pp. 1–16). Pergamon.

Polatidis, N., Pavlidis, M., & Mouratidis, H. (2018). Cyber-attack path discovery in a dynamic supply chain maritime risk management system. *Computer Standards & Interfaces, 56*, 74–82.

Polemi, N. (2017). *Port cybersecurity: Securing critical information infrastructures and supply chains.* Elsevier.

Refsdal, A., Solhaug, B., & Stølen, K. (2015). Cyber-risk management. *Cyber risk management* (pp. 33–47). Springer.

Rothblum, A. M. (2000). Human error and marine safety. *National Safety Council Congress and Expo, Orlando, FL,* (s 7).

Shaikh, S. (2017). Future of the sea: Cyber security. *Foresight, Government Office for Science, London, United Kingdom.*

Siedler, R. E. (2016). Hard power in cyberspace: CNA as a political means. *2016 8th International Conference on Cyber Conflict (CyCon)*, 23–36. IEEE.

Souppaya, M., & Scarfone, K. (2013). *NIST special publication 800-83 revision 1: Guide to malware incident prevention and handling for desktops and laptops.*

Stahl, W. M. (2011). The uncharted waters of cyberspace: Applying the principles of international maritime law to the problem of cybersecurity. *The Georgia Journal of International and Comparative Law, 40*, 247.

Tam, K., & Jones, K. (2018). Cyber-risk assessment for autonomous ships. *2018 International Conference on Cyber Security and Protection of Digital Services (Cyber Security)*, 1–8. IEEE.

Tam, K., & Jones, K. (2019). MACRA: A model-based framework for maritime cyber-risk assessment. *WMU Journal of Maritime Affairs, 18*(1), 129–163.

Tucci, A. (2017). Cyber risks in the marine transportation system. *Cyber-physical security* (pp. 113–131). Springer.

UK Government. (2016). *National cyber security strategy 2016–2021.* https://assets.publishing.service.gov.uk/government/uploads/system/uploads/attachment_data/file/567242/national_cyber_security_strategy_2016.pdf

United Nations Conference on Trade and Development (UNCTAD). (2018). *Review of maritime transport 2018.* https://unctad.org/system/files/official-document/rmt2018_en.pdf

United Nations General Assembly. (2008). *Report of the secretary general oceans and the law of the seas.* https://documents-dds-ny.un.org/doc/UNDOC/GEN/N08/266/26/PDF/N0826626.pdf?OpenElement

White House. (2005). *The national strategy for maritime security.* https://georgewbush-whitehouse.archives.gov/homeland/maritime-security.html

19
THE NEXUS BETWEEN NATURAL RESOURCE GOVERNANCE AND TRANSNATIONAL MARITIME CRIME

Lisa Otto

The link between natural resource abundance, its management, economic decline, and conflict and insecurity is well-established with a plethora of scholarship, detailed below, illustrating how this has played out in various countries around the world. Likewise, connections between natural resource governance and criminal activity, when understood as a sub-form of conflict and insecurity, can also be demonstrated, as this chapter contends. Transnational maritime crime (TMC), it could be extrapolated, may itself have a relationship to the governance of natural resources, and it is this that this chapter explores.

It begins by examining the key concepts and literature, notably maritime crime and the nexus between natural resource governance and conflict, insecurity, and crime. With this framework in place, the chapter turns to its case study, Nigeria, where it interrogates the relationship between the oil industry and TMC. The research on which this chapter is based employed a mixed-methods approach, utilising primary and secondary sources, interviews, and an extensive dataset of maritime criminal activity in the Gulf of Guinea.

The Nigerian case is relevant for a number of reasons. First, the Gulf of Guinea has become the hotspot for piracy and other maritime criminal activity in Africa since the decline of Somali piracy and Nigeria has been the locus of this hotspot, with maritime criminal activity spilling out from here into other parts of the region. Second, the maritime criminal problem in Nigeria, and in other parts of the sub-region, has a clear relationship with the oil industry, as will be detailed in this chapter. Furthermore, because the problem of maritime insecurity has spread from Nigeria throughout the sub-region, its contours and the solutions brought to combat it have implications for states beyond Africa and for a continent as a whole.

The chapter underscores that the relationship between natural resource governance and TMC is evident in the Nigerian case and is likely to have wider application in understanding the nature of TMC in resource-rich environments and how it may be combatted.

Conceptualisation

"Maritime crime" is often used as a catch-all descriptor but is rarely clearly defined. A brief survey of the ways in which the term is used shows that it is often employed either in reference

DOI: 10.4324/9781003001324-22

to maritime insurance or maritime piracy and the plethora of other activities often associated with it. Perhaps this is because, as I have written before (Otto, 2018), maritime piracy remains poorly defined under international law and this means that the series of crimes that are commonly referred to as piracy in fact constitute a number of differently defined crimes. This has led researchers (see Bateman, 2010; Mak, 2013; Percy, 2016) to use the term "maritime crime" as a substitute for speaking of this family of crimes. It has also been helpful in referencing the fact that most criminal groups often engage in a series of different criminal activities (Bateman, 2010). For the purposes of this chapter, however, it seems pertinent to preface the discussion with an explanation of what maritime crime is.

Maritime crime is often explained as transnational organised crime at sea, herein referred to as TMC. This is because the nature of the crimes that are referred to under the umbrella terminology tend to be both organised and transnational in nature.

Organised crime is another concept for which there is no generally accepted definition (Obasi, 2011, p. 56). It is difficult to define and gather empirical research on given that it exists in a turbid underworld that is perhaps entirely impenetrable. However, the Palermo Convention of 2000 holds that:

> organised criminal groups shall mean a structured group of three or more persons existing for a period of time and acting in concert with the aim of committing one or more serious crimes or offences... in order to obtain, directly or indirectly, a financial or other material benefit.
>
> *(UNODC, 2004, p. 5)*

Goredema and Botha (2004, p. 6) note that these serious crimes include participation by individuals in an organised criminal grouping, laundering the profits of criminal activity and corruption, as well as the obstruction of justice. Albanese (2000, p. 411) identifies four common features that often occur across various definitions: continuing organisation; an organisation that operates under rational conditions for the purpose of profit; making use of force, threats or control; and co-opting corrupt public officials to avoid arrest or prosecution. TMC can therefore be understood as including the crimes of maritime piracy, armed robbery at sea, kidnap-for-ransom at sea, illegal, unreported and unregulated fishing, as well as smuggling and trafficking activities.

Meanwhile, the idea that there is a link between resource abundance, poor economic growth and conflict or insecurity, which crime can be understood to be a type of, is popularly accepted. Various scholars have posited a variety of arguments for why this is so.

Sachs and Warner (1995) have been instrumental in providing insight into how resource abundance may, counter-intuitively, have a negative impact on economic growth – a phenomenon that has come to be known as the "resource curse". Economic analyses of this inverse relationship are summarised by Green and Otto (2014, p. 10) who note three primary arguments: one, trade theory which holds that "with time the price of primary commodities will decrease in relation to manufactured goods, resulting in countries specialising in primary commodity exports experiencing a detrimental economic effect"; two, the theory of volatile markets which suggests that economic growth may be damaged by volatility in the price of commodities; and three, the idea of "Dutch disease" which indicates that when an economy relies too heavily on one resource commodity, other economic sectors may become stifled.

Since these arguments have been floated, emerging theories offer more nuanced approaches to natural resource abundance and its governance, particularly with respect to Africa. In the stead of economics, socio-political arguments are offered and the quality of institutions is regarded as key. Here, practices of patronage and rent-seeking highlight the need for good governance and regulation (Green & Otto, 2014, p. 10).

Le Billon (2000, p. 25) notes the various perverse consequences that a state may suffer as a result of its resource wealth. These include: substandard economic growth; a disregard for non-resource sectors; growing inequality; increased corruption; inefficient economic policy; budgetary mismanagement; an increase in debt as a result of overconfident forecasts and the use of revenues as collateral to obtain loans; and high levels of vulnerability to commodity price and currency shocks. When one considers a scenario of poor governance, weak economic growth and insufficient regulation, it is plain to see that some form of grievance and conflict may result. Indeed, this has been seen in many countries in Africa and Latin America, for example.

Collier (2007, pp. 38–39) further notes the difficulty that poorer states have had in translating their resource wealth into development and growth, resulting in nearly a third of the world's billion poorest people living in countries whose economies are reliant on resource wealth – a phenomenon he calls the natural resource trap. Ultimately, Collier (2007, p. 42) argues that the rents received from resources contribute to income inequalities within a society, which, with the variety of maladies associated with this, including grievance expressed by the community and corruption within the state, can cause a state to malfunction. This can be seen to be happening in Nigeria.

Clover (2004, p. 8) highlights how high levels of poverty and inequality in resource-rich environments can spur conflict, which is then only exacerbated when degradation is caused by the extraction of resources, given the implication of the loss of livelihood this has for locals. Indeed, Ross (2004, p. 2) echoes this sentiment, noting that where average levels of income are low in a country with abundant resources, conflict characterised by violence is more likely to occur. As will be shown herein, the Niger Delta is an apt example of this reflecting in practice.

In this regard, Ross (2004, pp. 9–18) calls attention to a number of risk factors for conflict in the context of resource wealth. He describes poverty as the most crucial factor in this regard, noting that civil wars are more likely to occur in poor countries. Peripheries are another factor of importance, given that "peripheral regions are more likely to harbour people who identify themselves as ethnically or linguistically distinct", and the relative ease of access to weapons in these areas makes the development of separatist movements in peripheries more common. The case of the Biafran war can be evoked as an example here: in 1967 the region of Biafra declared unilateral independence from Nigeria, largely due to ethno-religious differences and control over oil resources, leading to a protracted civil war in which Biafra eventually surrendered (see Aremu & Buhari, 2017; Kirk-Greene, 1975).

Conflict, violence and upheaval are likely to occur when the populace considers their grievances to be sufficiently severe to justify such behaviour (Collier & Hoeffler, 2004, p. 564). However, rebellion can be profitable and insurgents may be "indistinguishable from bandits or pirates" – a kind of rebellion that is motivated by greed rather than grievance (Grossman, cited by Collier & Hoeffler, 2004). "Thus, the political science and economic approaches to rebellion have assumed both different rebel motivation – grievance versus greed – and different explanations – atypical grievances versus atypical opportunities".

As put by Bodea (2012, pp. 9–12), the problems posed by the relationship between resource abundance, conflict, and violence can be compounded by state weakness. This is because the excluded and the marginalised – often those who suffer the consequences of income inequality – also "bear the costs of the worst institutional and distributional outcomes associated with the presence of … resources without necessarily enjoying the benefits", as elites fail to share the rents received, even if only by means of delivering services.

Exploring the Nexus in the Gulf of Guinea: Nigeria in Focus

Nigeria falls at the centre of the geo-strategic region of the Gulf of Guinea, deemed an alternative oil gulf for a number of reasons. It has prolific on-, offshore and deep offshore oil reserves that are low in sulphur and therefore easily refined. Further, being near Western oil markets and refining facilities, holding large amounts of investment in oil from Western multinationals, and given regimes that produce relatively friendly investment climates, this sentiment is bolstered (Obi, 2011, p. 102).

While commercial quantities of oil were first discovered in 1956 with exports beginning in 1959, the boom that led to Nigeria's oil reliance and subsequent qualification as a petro-state only came in the 1970s, and today foreign multi-national corporations dominate the sector (Obi, 2011, p. 107). The Nigerian National Petroleum Corporation (NNPC) is the state-owned monopoly that these multinationals are required to cooperate with, via joint ventures, given that the federal government is the legal owner of the country's mineral resources (Gillies, 2009; Orogun, 2010, pp. 459–507). Human Rights Watch (1999, p. 26) suggests that oil deals have been structured this way due to "insufficient indigenous expertise" and a dearth of available funds for operating expenses; circumstances that have not changed much in the many decades since the discovery of oil.

Other national actors include the Ministry of Petroleum, which oversees the NNPC and plays the lead role in policy-making, while the Department of Petroleum Resources acts as the industry regulator. The latter is an independent entity, and its mandate includes the allocation of oil blocks, collection of royalties and the enforcement of regulations (Gillies, 2009, p. 2).

The nature of the relationship between these companies and state institutions can be characterised as bipolar and vacillating. The multinationals tend to be highly sophisticated and powerful firms that "leverage more power and resources in their hands, often at the expense of the poor oil producing communities", taking the view that the state is weak and unable to deliver political goods or maintain stability. Yet, these two parties "are wedded together in transnational extraction and sharing of oil profits" (Obi, 2011, pp. 107–108).

As such, it is not surprising that the governance of oil in Nigeria is considered weak. Aside from the fact that the spending of oil revenues has not resulted in tangible economic development in Nigeria as a whole (or in the areas from whence the resource comes), the state has neither had success in saving and investment in order to offset the depletion of natural resources with the accumulation of assets. Ajakaiye et al. (2011, pp. 238–240) describe this as "undoubtedly the most comprehensive decision failure" on the part of the government and indicate that between 1970 and 2003 Nigeria been unsuccessful in accumulating funds for precautionary savings and instead accumulated debt using its oil reserves as collateral. The Stabilisation Fund that was established during this period was considered "little more than token" as it invested the paltry sum of 0.5% of proceeds; monies that were subject to endemic problems of mismanagement, resulting in the closure of the fund in 2002. Conditions improved somewhat from 2003 onwards, as rents began to be accumulated while foreign debt was reduced dramatically, and gross fixed investment rose six-fold between 2003 and 2006 (Ajakaiye et al., 2011, pp. 241–242).

To combat the perception of weak resource governance, Nigeria has become involved in global oil-governance initiatives, key amongst which is the Extractive Industries Transparency Initiative (EITI) – an internationally accepted standard that works at promoting revenue transparency locally (Yates, 2009). Nigeria became EITI compliant in 2011 (EITI, 2020) and launched a national division in 2004, known as the NEITI (Yates, 2009, p. 12). The NEITI (2020) has produced a comprehensive audit of the petroleum industry in Nigeria and promotes transparency in the extractive industry. It has also helped uncover financial discrepancies to the tune of billions of dollars, highlighting industry corruption.

Nonetheless, Nigeria still ranks poorly in various iterations of the Resource Governance Index (2017, pp. 5, 55), and received a composite ranking of weak in 2017. Meanwhile, the 2019 Corruption Perceptions Index shows Nigeria has slipped further down the ranking, scoring 26/100 on a scale where zero indicates "highly corrupt" and 100 indicates "very clean" (Transparency International, 2020).

This comes as a result of continued multimillion-dollar corruption scandals in the sector. In the interest of brevity, I do not elaborate on these, but suffice to say there have been numerous incidents reported in the media in the last decade alone, many of which have implicated high-ranking officials.

Challenges in the Oil Industry

Not surprisingly, challenges in the oil industry in Nigeria are many and stem from conditions of weak governance and the disproportionate distribution of oil revenues which has served to marginalise the peoples of the oil-rich Niger and engender grievance as a consequence of the rapacity displayed by oil companies and the political elite.

Environmental Degradation

The extraction of oil has led to massive environmental degradation in the Niger Delta, which has threatened the traditional livelihoods of locals and endangered their health, while also imperilling the region's biodiversity and fragile ecosystems. This is despite Nigeria being signatory to several international environmental conventions (Chinweze et al., 2012).

In fact, companies have not complied with legal standards and have often linked spills to sabotage, which does not require compensation, and claims are rarely investigated. Further, oil companies tend not to "publish regular, comprehensive reports of allegations of environmental damage, sabotage, claims for compensation, protest actions, or police or military action carried out on or near their facilities" (Human Rights Watch, 1999, pp. 3–6).

Yet, crude oil spills, gas flaring and generalised pollution have been and continue to be responsible for the "progressive decimation of aquatic life and depletion of agro-forestry related vegetation", thereby removing agriculture, fisheries and lumbering as sustainable income-generating activities for locals, while also affecting the price of fish at market, and thus impacting on the region's food security (Orogun, 2010, p. 477). The extent of oil leaching and pollution in the region has been documented over decades, with several reports (such as by Human Rights Watch in 1999, Amnesty International in 2009, and the United Nations Environment Programme in 2011) noting the Niger Delta as one of the most polluted places on earth. Chinweze et al. (2012, pp. 3, 5) indicate that more than 13,000 oil spills were recorded between 1976 and 2010 leading to 3.2 million barrels of spillage. Current data is largely based on companies self-reporting and onshore spills are considered under-reported, however, Amnesty International (2018) notes that government had recorded nearly 1,400 spills associated with Shell between 2011 and 2018, and nearly 1,700 associated with ENI between 2014 and 2018.

This has held severe health implications for inhabitants of the Delta states. Water sources are so badly polluted that even underground water is affected, making it difficult for communities to avoid the use of contaminated water (Chinweze et al, 2012, pp. 5–6). Among the common maladies faced by locals are: reduced fertility and lowered birth rates, diminished life expectancy, a rise in birth defects in children, malnutrition, and a rise in cancers. As Orogun (2010, pp. 478–479) notes, this "vividly encapsulates the resource curse dilemma".

Illegal onshore oil theft, termed bunkering, ironically also plays a role in environmental degradation. While oil bunkering has emerged, in part, as a result of the poor distribution of oil revenues with groups stealing oil for resale on the black market, pipeline vandalism and bunkering have been associated with recklessness and pollution (Wilson, 2014, pp. 69–81).

Corruption in the Oil Industry

Oil, and the potential for political elite to benefit from it, has been a dominating factor in Nigeria's post-independence political milieu. Corruption has been considered one of the major features of state weakness in Nigeria. Given that oil is central to the Nigerian economy, as an easily extractable resource that requires little productive effort from the side of the government, it is not surprising that this industry is then subject to corrupt practices (Akpabio & Akpan, 2010, pp. 111–122).

According to a source that worked for an American oil company in Nigeria, corruption and collusion in the oil industry is both rife and blatant. Although unsubstantiated, the source refers to wells commonly known as "Mr. P" and "Mrs. P", because their profits went to the then-president and his wife.

Gillies (2009, pp. 2–4) describes the main risks for corruption in Nigeria's oil industry as follows: awarding of licenses and contracts given substantial government control over this process; bottlenecks and inefficiencies causing delays and thus creating opportunities for bribery; bunkering, given the widely held belief that oil companies, government elites and security officials are involved in these activities; and exporting crude and importing refined products, as "export and import transactions yield high levels of fungible returns, and the lack of transparency surrounding them creates considerable opportunities for corruption".

Resource Abundance, Conflict and Political Violence in Nigeria

The link between resource abundance and social dissatisfaction (which often leads to conflict) thus evidently comes into play in the Nigerian context. Suffering from the "paradox of plenty", Nigeria fits the various theses around the nexus between resource wealth and instability: the resource curse and rentier statism. Linked to the latter is "rentier mentality", where elites are unproductive and mismanage state funds for the purposes of prestige projects, patronage and entrenching political power. Relevant to this is "that oil increases the risk of institutional weakness, political instability, violent conflict, and blocks democracy and development". This implies conditions of corruption, state weakness and poverty may be present amidst abundant resource wealth (Yates, 2009, p. 8; Obi, 2011, pp. 104–105; Green & Otto, 2014, p. 11).

Jostling for political power as a means to acquire control over economic power has long characterised the Nigerian landscape, but, when referring specifically to how this has manifested in relation to oil wealth, there have been numerous instances where the local population has protested against the rentier mentality, seeking to effect a more equitable division of resources at least, and control over oil resources at most. As such, resource abundance in Nigeria has begot conflict, violence and crime.

Examples of this include the Biafran war and the formation of groups like Movement for the Emancipation of the Niger Delta (MEND) and the Movement for the Survival of the Ogoni People, the latter of which was known by its leader Ken Saro-Wiwa, his peaceful approach, and ensuing execution (Human Rights Watch, 1999; Courson, 2009). Subsequently, several other ethnic minority resistance movements surfaced, burgeoning in the late 1990s. Not all have adopted Saro-Wiwa's strategy of non-violence; many have taken aggressive and militant approaches to their resistance (Courson, 2009, pp. 14–15; Obi, 2011, p. 104). Indeed, militancy has been "precipitated by a governance crisis arising from grievances over a lack of popular participation, marginalisation, exclusion, alienation and exploitation of a vast majority of the populace in terms of resource allocation cum distribution or development promotion" (Aghedo & Osumah, 2014, pp. 1–15). Obi (2011, p. 106) echoes this sentiment.

Collier's thesis of greed versus grievance is evidently implied here, with greed referring to a desire to control a resource and grievance relating the sentiment of marginalisation and deprivation by sectors of the population (Yates, 2009, pp. 8–9). While Collier argues that greed rather than grievance inspires militancy, Aghedo and Osumah (2014, p. 4) suggest that greed and grievance more often have a reinforcing relationship.

Despite the constancy of protest around the governance of oil resources, successive regimes have failed to alter the discourse by acknowledging and addressing the grievance raised by these various groups over the years. Instead, the military has often used lethal force to repress dissent, which has left the region embroiled in conflict (Courson, 2009, p. 14; Chinweze et al, 2012, pp. 8–9). Obi (2011, p. 107) suggests that the government has seen local protests as "acts of economic sabotage to the main source of national revenues and a challenge to its power in the Niger Delta". Omotola (2007, pp. 73–89) notes the establishment of the Oil Mineral Producing Area Development Commission and the Niger Delta Development Commission, established in 1992 and 2000 respectively, as being the only concrete measures by government, but which still leave much to be desired in producing outcomes.

Complicating matters further, criminal groups have often co-opted or infiltrated local resistance movements, using political ideology as a front for profit-seeking. As such, it has been problematic to distinguish between criminal groups, rebel movements and other coterie that may be politically motivated. These groupings often fall within several of categories, or orbit between categories over time in what constitutes an intricate relationship between oil companies, the state, locals, militia, violence and criminality (Orogun, 2010, p. 461).

Ultimately, given the magnitude of criminality and militancy in the delta, "events [there] … provide empirical validation of the environment-conflict thesis"; environmental insecurity and mismanagement of oil resources have played a decisive role in communities resorting to agitation, protest and criminality (Omotola, 2007, p. 78).

Maritime Crime in Nigeria

These challenges, alongside rampant poverty and high levels of unemployment, in the context of a society where violence has been a normalised form of expression and method for conflict resolution, and where criminality flourishes unabated, it is unsurprising that an illicit economy has emerged around the oil industry. This has come mostly in two forms: bunkering and piracy.

Bunkering

Bunkering in Nigeria occurs mainly under three categories. The first are small-scale operations, around 30,000 barrels per day, obtained by local gangs through theft, and then smuggled for resale within Nigeria and countries in the sub-region, particularly Benin and Niger. Often petroleum condensate rather than oil is stolen, as this is more profitable, removing the need for refining. The second type is more high-brow and although varying monthly, may be equivalent to as much as 10% of the country's total exports, obtained by hot tapping (piercing pipelines) or uncorking wellheads and siphoning oil into barges which offload the product to trawlers offshore. Trawlers then make delivery to international markets. The third involves the use of fraudulent documentation to lift crude oil above amounts licensed. This happens thanks to collusion at high levels of the NNPC and major oil companies (Von Kemedi, 2006; Obasi, 2011, p. 60).

This indicates the wide array of local and international actors involved in bunkering. Locally, young men from the Delta carry out bunkering operations, "the boys", while they report back to their bosses, "the barons", who consist of an elite from various parts of the country, no doubt also aided by international stakeholders. These actors are supported by host communities from whence the bunkered oil comes, as well as passage communities, whose homeland through which bunkered oil must pass to reach the open seas, both of which receive payment for their cooperation. Police and military officials, who publicly are strongly opposed to oil bunkering activities, are also said to be complicit, whether this is through turning a blind eye to it or wilfully participating and receiving payment for services rendered (Obasi, 2011, pp. 60–62; Wilson, 2014, pp. 69–81).

Furthermore, oil companies have aided bunkerers and are often involved in the practice of diverting oil from NNPC pipelines by tampering with metres. Foreigners have also formed part of organised criminal networks, with sailors from abroad shipping oil products (Katsouris & Sayne, 2013). Lastly, the actors at the local and international destinations for the illicit oil provide a market for the product, and local illegal refineries have sourced their crude from the barons (Obasi, 2011, pp. 60–62; Wilson, 2014, p. 73). Aside from arriving in neighbouring countries, bunkered oil also makes it into the international market to places as far afield as Venezuela and Greece (Obasi 2011, pp. 58–59).

Von Kemedi (2006, p. 19) notes that to become a bunkerer one must be a "union member", which means an individual is required to pay a fee in order to be granted access. Logistics are negotiated with the navy, with agreements reached that are also acceptable to nearby villages in whose domain the activities are to take place. There is thus local buy-in and assurance from security forces that the intruders will be allowed to conduct their business undisturbed.

Bunkering activities have become so rampant that the scope thereof was estimated in 2012 to run to US$1 billion monthly in revenues diverted from the formal economy (Wallis, 2012). Von Kemedi (2006, p. 21) also notes that violence and conflict have in turn created conditions that further mask bunkering activities, thus allowing for the crime to flourish.

Obasi (2011, pp. 58–59) indicates a number of contributory factors to the thriving existence of organised crime in Nigeria, with particular reference to oil bunkering. The complex geography of the Delta is difficult to police, while high levels of poverty and a lack of community stake-holding make the area vulnerable to criminal activity. Further, erratic supply of petroleum products to local markets creates a black-market demand, bolstered by established illicit markets in the sub-region and internationally. A deficient maritime governance regime, alongside a general ambience of anarchy, complicated by a long-standing history of militant agitation and protest create conditions for maritime crime to occur low-risk. These conditions are then only worsened by a dearth of monitoring and accountability measures that allow corrupt practices and collusion to take place, in a context of entrenched patronage-clientelism with political elites being known to be connected to organised criminal activity.

Accordingly, the practice is conducted in a startlingly overt manner with accounts from oil industry operatives suggesting that oil companies assist criminals in bunkering safely by providing valves and the like, effectively benefitting from both the formal and informal economies. Moreover, locals believe the oil belongs to the people of the Delta who should thus be free to benefit from its extraction and thus have no qualms in purloining oil (Von Kemedi 2006, p. 16).

Piracy

Piratical acts have been taking place in Nigerian waters for many decades as trade expanded enormously after the oil boom, leading to an increase in the number of merchant vessels making their way through the port of Lagos. The number of vessels exceeded the capacity of the port itself, and as such many found themselves queuing up for days, making them vulnerable to opportunists (Villar, 1985, p. 16); circumstances that still ring true today.

Incidents started as small-scale and petty crimes that were generally spontaneous and disorganised. Attacks gradually became more sophisticated and organised, and by the 1990s the criminal focus had shifted to include kidnap-and-ransom and activities that were more clearly targeted to the commodity of oil.

According to Otto's (2016) typology of maritime criminal activity in Nigeria in the form of "piracy" and armed robbery at sea, which uses Murphy's (2013, p. 43) typology as a starting point, at least five different categories of piracy occur in the Gulf of Guinea:

- Category A, inland assaults that generally present as petty theft, usually targeting vessels that are at berth or awaiting berth.
- Category B, coastal shipping assaults which mainly involve the theft of money, personal items of the crew, equipment of stores, and take place when vessels are underway, adrift, or at anchor offshore, constituting armed robbery at sea.
- Category C, coastal shipping assaults that comprise the same kind of theft as in Category B but also involve selective kidnap-for-ransom.
- Category D, hijack of vessels either at anchor, in port, inland, or offshore, which are then usually redirected and where the cargo of the vessel (notably oil and petroleum products) is stolen, or the vessel may be used as a mother-ship.
- Category E, installation assaults or targeted cargo theft that does not involve hijacking, making use of high degrees of prior intelligence.

Sophistication of the crimes and the tools and weaponry used in their execution increase with each category. For example, in Category D attacks, International Crisis Group (2012, pp. 15–17) estimates, based on information on incidents in Benin, that between US$2 million and US$6 million worth of oil or petroleum products are typically lost per incident.

While there are certainly organised criminal groups perpetrating these more sophisticated attacks, "there is evidence that MEND and other rebel groups are financing their operations through black market oil bunkering and other activities" (Whiteneck, 2011, p. 42). Local resistance groups use political motives to explain these activities, but this has also been co-opted by organised criminal entities (Otto, 2014, p. 325) thus melding their motives together. The engagement of organised criminal groups has meant established cross-border linkages in the black market have been used to facilitate the movement of oil and petroleum products between countries within the sub-region and to international markets (Otto, 2014, p. 320).

While most prominent in Nigerian waters, the impacts of TMC have also spilled over into the sub-region, although notably these crimes are mostly committed by groups operating from Nigeria. Countries affected include Togo, the Ivory Coast, Cameroon and Benin, while isolated incidents also occur in the waters of other West African countries. Vreÿ (2013, pp. 1–23) explains this by noting the porosity of borders that make it easy for criminal gangs and separatist groups to move freely between countries in the sub-region. Furthermore, with the limited capacity of many states to patrol their waters, pirates have been able to conduct their activities with impunity, while the prevalence of cross-border organised crime has only served to exacerbate this.

Problems with underreporting suggest a far higher incidence than currently determined by existing data, but nonetheless, annual costs of West African piracy were estimated in 2016 to be US$793.7 million (Oceans Beyond Piracy, 2016).

Case Summary

The people of the Delta states have often taken responsibility for their own economic fortunes in the context of a reality marred by corruption, unchecked marginalisation, the feeling of powerlessness, poverty, ethnic tension and the tendency for the violent paths to resolution of conflict. This has been a political move of locals taking back the power (as they see it) and forcibly taking a cut of the oil revenue that rarely sees its way back to the Delta otherwise. With economic opportunities often also being limited, opportunities for income via criminality has been an obvious choice. Moreover, the deficient capacity (and also willingness) of state authorities to respond to criminal acts, as well as the opportunity crime provides for the self and the community act as additional pull factors. Further, piracy and bunkering have been characterised here by an incestuous enmeshment of actors spanning ideologically inspired locals, the criminal underworld, oil majors and the political elite, making it a highly complex problem to solve.

The oil industry and the presence, nay prevalence, of piracy and bunkering in Nigerian waters are thus inextricably linked. While this is material for separate analysis in its own right, the relationship in question here hints to the challenges that exist also for bringing to an end TMC. Indeed, the appetite for criminal activity will be ever-present as long as corruption and state weakness in Nigeria flourish also.

Conclusion

What the Nigerian case aptly demonstrates is that the linkage between natural resource governance and conflict and insecurity can be extrapolated to crime, transnational organised crime and TMC. The theoretical elements discussed in the early parts of the chapter illustrate how greed, grievance, poverty and inequality can manifest these forms of insecurity. What's more, the case is relevant for wider discussion on this nexus given that it is characterised by insecurity that has spilled over into the sub-region and brought implications that stretch beyond the confines of its own borders.

Might we see a clear link between resource governance and TMC in other parts of the world, however? Further research and comparative analysis can bring attention to how this nexus arises in other geographical locations affected by TMC. Questions such as why countries like Angola and Ghana, which also have high levels of poverty alongside rich reserves in oil and gas, have not seen a similar development of TMC are pertinent. Does the element of grievance remain yet underdeveloped, or does the quality and nature of governance play a role? On the continent's eastern seaboard similar questions are now being asked about whether Mozambique is at risk of a TMC problem as the country's resource-rich northern reaches have become subject to an insurgency which has targeted seaside towns and their infrastructure. Will this group turn to piracy or smuggling to fund their operations, and to what extent can grievance over the governance of resources be implicated in the group's emergence? It seems evident that the resource governance-crime nexus is reinforced, but that the nuances hereof require closer investigation.

In terms of policy application and practice, better understanding this linkage and the causal relationship it implies can provide a lens through which these challenges can be contemplated and, correspondingly, a framework from which to address them. This becomes important not only for states to develop and apply domestic measures but to be better poised to take forward multilateral cooperation to combat problems that have a transnational nature. By working together and sharing information and experiences, states will be better able to address the challenges of both poor resource governance and TMC.

References

Aghedo, I., & Osumah, O. (2014). Insurgency in Nigeria: A Comparative Study of Niger Delta and Boko Haram Uprisings. *Journal of Asian and African Studies*, *29*(4), 1–15.

Ajakaiye, O., Collier, P., & Ekpo, A. H. (2011). Management of Resource Revenue in Nigeria. In P. Collier & A. J. Venables (Eds.), *Plundered Nations? Successes and Failures in Natural Resource Extraction* (pp. 231–261). Palgrave Macmillan.

Akpabio, E. M., & Akpan, N. S. (2010). Governance and Oil Politics in Nigeria's Niger Delta: The Question of Distributive Equality. *Journal of Human Ecology*, *30*(2), 111–122.

Albanese, J. (2000). The Causes of Organized Crime: Do Criminals Organize around Opportunities for Crime or Do Criminal Opportunities Create New Offenders? *Journal of Contemporary Criminal Justice*, *16*(4), 409–423.

Amnesty International. (2018). *Niger Delta Negligence.* https://www.amnesty.org/en/latest/news/2018/03/niger-delta-oil-spills-decoders/#:~:text=Swimming%20in%20oil,about%20seven%20Olympic%20swimming%20pools

Aremu, J. O., & Buhari, L. O. (2017). Sense and Senselessness of War: Aggregating the Causes, Gains and Losses of the Nigerian Civil War, 1967–1970. *IAFOR Journal of Arts & Humanities*, *4*, 61–79.

Bateman, S. (2010). Confronting Maritime Crime in Southeast Asian Waters: Re-examining "Piracy" in the 21st Century'. In B. A. Ellerman, A. Forbes & D. Rosenberg (Eds.), *Piracy and Maritime Crime: Historical and Modern Case Studies* (pp. 137–156). Naval War College Press.

Bodea, C. (2012). Natural Resources, Weak States and Civil War. *Policy Research Working Paper* 6071. World Bank.

Chinweze, C., Abiola-Oloke, G., Onyeri, I., Kennedy-Echetebu, C., & Jideani, C. (2012). Oil and Gas Activities and the Nigerian Environment. Paper presented at the *IAIA12 Conference, Energy Future: The Role of Impact Assessment.* Oporto, 27 May – 1 June 2012.

Clover, J. (2004). Conflict and Human Security. In J. Clover & R. Cornwell (Eds.), *Supporting Sustainable Livelihoods: A Critical Review of Assistance in Post-Conflict Situations* (pp. 7–22). Monograph No. 102, Institute for Security Studies.

Collier, P. (2007). *The Bottom Billion: Why the Poorest Countries Are Failing and What Can Be Done about It.* Oxford University Press.

Collier, P., & Hoeffler, A. (2004). Greed and Grievance in Civil War. *Oxford Economic Papers*, *56*, 563–595.

Courson, E. (2009). Movement for the Emancipation of the Niger Delta (MEND): Political Marginalization, Repression and Petro-Insurgency in the Niger Delta. *Discussion Paper* No. 47. NordiskaAfrikainstitutet.

EITI. (2020). *Nigeria.* EITI. http://eiti.org/Nigeria

Gillies, A. (2009). Reforming Corruption out of Nigerian Oil? Part One: Mapping Corruption Risks in Oil Sector Governance. *U4 Brief*, February 2009 – 2, Anti-Corruption Resource Centre.

Goredema, C., & Botha, A. (2004). *African Commitments to Combating Organised Crime and Terrorism: A Review of Eight NEPAD Countries*, African Human Security Initiative.

Green, C., & Otto, L. (2014). Resource Abundance in Mozambique: Preventing Conflict, Ensuring Prosperity. *Occasional Paper*, 173, South African Institute of International Affairs.

Human Rights Watch. (1999). *The Price of Oil: Corporate Responsibility and Human Rights Violations in Nigeria's Oil Producing Communities.* Human Rights Watch.

International Crisis Group. (2012). The Gulf of Guinea: The New Danger Zone. *Africa Report*, 195. International Crisis Group.

Katsouris, C., & Sayne, A. (2013). *Nigeria's Criminal Crude: International Options to Combat the Export of Stolen Oil.* Chatham House.

Kirk-Greene, A. H. M. (1975). *The Genesis of the Nigerian Civil War and the Theory of Fear*, The Scandinavian Institute of African Studies.

Le Billon, P. (2000). The Political Economy of Resource Wars. In J. Cilliers & C. Dietrich (Eds.), *Angola's War Economy: The Role of Oil and Diamonds* (pp. 21–42), Institute for Security Studies.

Mak, J. N. (2013). NGOs, Piracy and Maritime Crime in Southeast Asia. *Asia Pacific Bulletin*, 228, East-West Center.

Murphy, M. (2013). Petro-piracy: Oil and Troubled Waters. *Orbis*, *57*(3), 424–437.

NEITI. (2020). *About NEITI*. Retrieved from http://neiti.org.ng/index.php?q=pages/about-neiti

Obasi, N. K. (2011). Organised Crime and Illicit Bunkering: Only Nigeria's Problem. In *Fuelling the World – Failing the Region? Oil Governance and Development in Africa's Gulf of Guinea*. Friedrich Ebert Stiftung. https://library.fes.de/pdf-files/bueros/nigeria/08607.pdf

Obi, C. (2011). Democratising the Petro-State in West Africa: Understanding the Challenges. In M. Roll & S. Sperling (Eds.), *Fuelling the World – Failing the Region? Oil Governance and Development in Africa's Gulf of Guinea* (pp. 102–120). Friedrich Ebert Stiftung.

Oceans Beyond Piracy. (2016). *The State of Maritime Piracy 2016: Assessing Economic and Human Cost*. Retrieved from http://oceansbeyondpiracy.org/reports/sop

Omotola, J. (2007). From the OMPADEC to the NDDC: An Assessment of State Responses to Environmental Insecurity in the Niger Delta, Nigeria. *Africa Today*, *54*(1), 73–89.

Orogun, P. S. (2010). Resource Control, Revenue Allocation and Petroleum Politics in Nigeria: The Niger Delta question. *GeoJournal*, *75*(5), 459–507.

Otto, L. (2014). Westward Ho! The Evolution of Maritime Piracy in Nigeria. *Portuguese Journal of Social Science*, *13*(3), 313–329.

Otto, L. (2016). *The Gulf of Guinea's Troubled Waters: The Evolution of Piracy and Other Maritime Crimes in Nigeria*. Unpublished Thesis. University of Johannesburg.

Otto, L. (2018). Defining Maritime Piracy: The Problem with the Law. *Acta Criminologica*, *31*(2), 134–148.

Percy, S. (2016). Maritime Crime and Naval Response. *Survival*, *58*(3), 155–186.

Resource Governance Index. (2017). *The 2017 Resource Governance Index*. https://api.resourcegovernanceindex.org/system/documents/documents/000/000/046/original/2017_Resource_Governance_Index.pdf?1498599435

Ross, M. (2004). Mineral Wealth and Equitable Development. *World Bank Development Report 2006*. World Bank.

Sachs, J., & Warner, A. (1995). Natural Resource Abundance and Economic Growth. *Working Paper* 5398, National Bureau of Economic Research.

Transparency International. (2020). *Corruption Perceptions Index 2020*. https://www.transparency.org/cpi2019

UNODC. (2004). *United Nations Convention Against Transnational Organized Crime and the Protocols Thereto*. http://www.unodc.org/documents/treaties/UNTOC/Publications/TOC%20Convention/TOCebook-e.pdf

Villar, R. (1985). *Piracy Today: Robbery and Violence at Sea Since 1980*. Conway Maritime Press.

Von Kemedi, D. (2006). Fuelling the Violence: Non-State Armed Actors (Militia, Cults, and Gangs) in the Niger Delta. *Niger Delta Economies of Violence Working Papers Paper*, 10, Our Niger Delta.

Vreÿ, F. (2013). Turning the Tide: Revisiting African Maritime Security. *Scientia Militaria*, *41*(2), 1–23.

Wallis, W. (2012, June 26). *Nigeria Losing $1bn a Month to Oil Theft*. Financial Times. http://www.ft.com/intl/cms/s/0/61fb070e-bf90-11e1–00144feabdc0.html

Whiteneck, D. J. (2011). *Piracy Enterprises in Africa*, CAN Corporation.

Wilson, G. (2014). The Nigerian State and Oil Theft in the Niger Delta Region of Nigeria. *Journal of Sustainable Development in Africa*, *16*(1), 69–81.

Yates, D. (2009). Enhancing the Governance of Africa's Oil Sector. *Affairs Occasional Paper*, 51, South African Institute of International.

20

FISHERIES CRIMES, POVERTY AND FOOD INSECURITY

Cornelia E. Nauen and Simona T. Boschetti

The World Bank's report "The sunken billions revisited" (2017) illustrates that the fisheries sector is weighing in way below its economic potential owing to weak governance and widespread illicit practices. Beyond the moral aspects of labour rights violations, including its extreme form of modern slavery, and other human rights violations, these and other illicit practices can be understood as cost-cutting mechanisms of a global competitive market for fish and fisheries products (Tickler et al., 2018). Fisheries products are the most globally traded food commodities in the world (Bellmann et al., 2016), characterised by often complex transnational supply chains, which make it virtually impossible for consumers to trace the fish or seafood they buy. Long confinement at sea and unclear or non-existing redress mechanisms provides the breeding ground for higher profits of beneficial vessel owners at the expense of labourers often recruited from particularly disadvantaged areas in developing countries (Marschke & Vandergeest, 2016). Rosello (2020) focuses mainly on two security implications of IUU fishing: the impact on human communities affected, including through loss of income and food security, and the operational synergies with crime.

Industrial illegal, unreported and unregulated (IUU) fishing is driven by overcapacity, government subsidies, and weak national and regional governance combined with missing cooperation between countries, as well as adaptive strategies of boat owners responding to attempts to enforce rules in one place by, for instance, changing flag state, vessel name, ports for laundering IUU catches; making hard to identify who has jurisdiction on the vessel (Witbooi et al., 2020). These and other techniques show high criminal energy in illegal fishing operations, particularly when associated with international organised crime (Österblom et al., 2010; UNODC, 2011; Sall & Nauen, 2017a; Okafor-Yarwood, 2019; Witbooi et al., 2020). They contribute to maritime insecurity as observed for example in the Malacca Strait (Raymond, 2009) and the Gulf of Guinea, where rampant industrial overfishing poses acute threats to local small-scale fisher's livelihoods (Okafor-Yarwood, 2019) and makes industrial trawlers themselves targets for kidnapping to extract ransom (GEMLAWS Africa, 2021). The fact that marine living resources are 93.8% fully exploited or already overexploited and/or collapsed (FAO, 2020a) exacerbates competition for access and aggravates territorial disputes.

In the following, we explore the key conditions evoked in the title and discuss the nexuses between them. We conclude with possible responses that take advantage of the global consensus on the interdependent Sustainable Development Goals which, even without full

DOI: 10.4324/9781003001324-23

implementation on the ground by their target date 2030, have potential for redressing currently worsening trends.

Fisheries Crimes

Illegal, unreported and unregulated fisheries cover a range of characteristics most pronounced in industrial and distant water fisheries. *Illegal fishing* pertains to activities in breach of existing laws and regulations, such as fishing in protected areas, illegal by-catch, including of protected species, falsifying papers, including technical specifications and disguising beneficial ownership, corruption, illegal transhipment at sea and other criminal offences in any part of the fisheries value chain in contravention of national or international legislation. Transhipment at sea involves typically the unloading of the catch of a (smaller) fishing vessel to a (larger) refrigerated reefer which then lands the combined catches in a port. This may lead to mixing legitimate and illegal catches and counters efforts at traceability of catches. In combination with provision of bunker oil and victuals by supply ships this extends the fishing capacity of a fleet extensively. *Unreported fisheries* typically entail falsifying logbooks and under-declaration of catches to avoid taxes and levies in contravention of national legislation and regulations or those of regional fisheries management organisations (RFMOs). In combination with transhipment at sea, this deprives countries additionally of reliable data for management as it falsifies stock assessments by underestimating extractions. *Unregulated fisheries* occur by vessels without nationality or flagged to countries not party to RFMOs or in regions or on stocks without established management schemes, when fishing is conducted in a "manner inconsistent with State responsibilities for the conservation of living marine resources under international law" (FAO, 2001).

The need to end or at least curb destructive practices has triggered key policy developments over several decades in the international arena. At the end of 1991, the UN General Assembly adopted Resolution 46/215 against large-scale pelagic drift net fishing (UN, 1991). In December 2017, in its annual resolution on sustainable fisheries, it proclaimed 5 June as the "International Day for the Fight Against Illegal, Unreported and Unregulated Fishing" (UN, 2017).

The basic instrument is the Code of Conduct for Responsible Fisheries, adopted by the FAO Committee of Fisheries in 1995. This Code sets out principles and international standards for responsible practices supporting the sustainable exploitation and production of living aquatic resources. It remains as relevant today as it was in 1995 (FAO, 2021).

Several international agreements and international plans of action (IPOA), such as the IPOA-IUU (FAO, 2001) have been initiated as a result. The most significant is the legally binding Port State Measures Agreement, which specifically targets IUU fishing and entered into force in 2016. It adds to complementary treaties and agreements within the frameworks of the International Maritime Organisation (IMO) and the International Labour Organisation (ILO) (FAO, 2020b). Moreover, FAO's Global Record of Fishing Vessels, Refrigerated Transport Vessels and Supply Vessels[1] is a data repository supporting states coordinating to fight IUU fishing. INTERPOL established a dedicated Environmental Security Programme (ENS) in 2010 and has ever since raised awareness and helped build capacities in countries' law enforcement and pursuit of increasingly sophisticated crimes associated with IUU fishing (INTERPOL, 2020).

Several states and regional organisations, such as the EU and the African Union through the African Maritime Safety and Security Agency (AMSSA) have explicitly included IUU as a threat in their maritime security strategies. Maritime actors rely on a mix of traditional security measures (e.g., naval presence, inspections at sea) but also new maritime domain awareness, electronic surveillance, and information sharing technologies to curb IUU fishing and a growing number of countries collaborate with Global Fishing Watch to fight IUU fishing.

The large seafood import markets in the USA, European Union, Japan and other wealthy Asian countries, are expected to be prone to illegal or dubious supply chains (Sumaila et al., 2020). In the case of the US, Pramod et al. (2014) estimate a range of 20% to 32% of illegal imports out of a total of 2.3 million tons in 2011. While difficult to study, a systematic analysis of illegal fishing for Patagonian toothfish (marketed as Chilean seabass) in the Southern Ocean between 1995 and 2008 showed three phases. Initially, it recorded high levels of illegal catches outside the management regime of the countries party to the Convention on the Conservation of Antarctic Marine Living Resources (CCAMLR) up to 1999 and lower illegal catches when countermeasures were taken by CCAMLR countries to protect their own legitimate fisheries up to 2004. Records showed yet lower, but persistent illegal catches in the period since, as perpetrators have become increasingly sophisticated and have adapted their strategies to enforcement efforts through changes to flags of convenience, vessel name and other measures to conceal beneficiary owners (Österblom et al., 2010). The authors are unsure whether the reduced illegal activity in the last observed phase is the result of sustained enforcement efforts or due to the degradation of the resource from extensive overfishing. A similar consideration is voiced by Pauly and Zeller (2016) observing a gradual reduction in fishing discards as global catches decline since the mid-90s. According to the global IUU fishing index[2] China, Taiwan, Cambodia, Russia and Vietnam are the top five out of 152 countries assessed in terms of their responsibility for their flagged vessels, coastal zones, ports and general obligations.

Note, however, that significant unreported catches concern small-scale fisheries, where countries do not have the capabilities and resources to document their often widely scattered and informal activities. The magnitude of underestimating small-scale fisheries was quantified for the first time through independent researchers collaborating under the umbrella of the Sea Around Us initiative[3] (Pauly & Zeller, 2016) with a view to improve fisheries statistics and management. As catches of small-scale commercial and subsistence fishers are predominantly serving direct human consumption and employment (Daniels et al., 2016), improving the understanding and quantification of their production is of high interest. This is to ensure poverty eradication and food security as stipulated by the Voluntary Guidelines for Sustainable Small-Scale Fisheries (VGSSF) (FAO, 2015).

IUU fishing is also a major problem for fisheries assessment and management as it leads to often grossly erroneous statistics and other data underpinning resource conservation, management and investment decisions. It delegitimises institutions and deprives developing countries, in particular, with limited surveillance and enforcement means of significant legitimate income, estimated at hundreds of millions of USD. For instance, for West African countries, a region suffering heavily from IUU fishing (Belhabib et al., 2015; Petrossian, 2015; Daniels et al., 2016; Doumbouya et al., 2017). IUU fishing is also increasingly associated with organised crime, for example in relation to human trafficking, labour abuse, drug trafficking, corruption, people smuggling and large-scale fraud (UNODC, 2011; Rosello, 2020; Witbooi et al., 2020).

Fisheries crimes have long been underestimated and framed as mere transgressions of administrative rules. Accordingly, levied fines were inconsequential compared to the gains from the illicit activity (Daniels et al., 2016; Doumbouya et al., 2017). While fishers are often used in such operations because of their skills and experience, they are rarely the drivers and masterminds of IUU fishing in conjunction with other criminal activities (UNODC, 2011). Key vulnerabilities to fisheries crime tend to be associated with one or more of the following conditions.

First, the global reach of high seas fishing vessels and the significant excess capacity created by harmful public subsidies create opportunities to conceal illicit activities next to legitimate ones. This is compounded by transhipment in the high seas or outside the reach of coastal surveillance which effectively eliminates traceability of catches, hampers law enforcement and provides breeding grounds for transnational organised crime. Flag states with vessel registries may be unable or unwilling to establish and enforce their criminal law jurisdiction and ensure transparency about beneficial ownership and a ship's track record (flags of convenience) (Österblom et al., 2010; Konar & Sumaila, 2019; FAO, 2020a; Long et al., 2020).

Second, corruption, lack of enforcement of existing rules in fisheries, weak overall governance and lack of international cooperation, create enabling conditions for organised crime to use fisheries for a host of other unlawful practices, thus jeopardising maritime security in general (Österblom et al., 2010; Petrossian et al., 2014; Rosello, 2020).

Third, widespread overfishing leading to loss of income and sustenance of coastal fisherfolk may make these and other disadvantaged populations vulnerable to poverty, forced labour and pressed into criminal activities (UNODC, 2011; Okafor-Yarwood, 2019; Rosello, 2020).

Petrossian et al. (2014) identify a set of conditions which make some ports hotspots for illegal landings or "ports of convenience" while the majority of others may experience low or no levels of crime. These conditions frequently entail the following: species concerned are mostly high value with low to modest quantities landed in high-frequency ports which make concealment of illicit catches easy. In conjunction with lax inspections, rule enforcement and corruption, this permissive context is among the best predictors of illegal landings and other illegal traffic.

Poverty

It is inaccurate to assume that fishing communities are generally characterised by, or associated with, poverty in a simple economic notion of financial income below the poverty line of the respective country measured through income and consumption patterns. When the World Bank first focused on poverty in the World Development Report (Ahmad et al., 1990), its approach was two-pronged: stimulating labour-intensive development and economic growth, even though it expected that the number of people living on one dollar a day would increase. Since 2015, the threshold of extreme poverty is set at US$ 1.90 a day in terms of 2011 purchasing power parity (PPP) by the World Bank, while great efforts are put into making the estimates comparable in time and between countries and regions (Ferreira et al., 2015). While income and consumption can be quantified, such data do not provide insights into the causes and the dynamic of poverty (Baulch, 1996). Generic economic growth is also no guarantee for reducing poverty and well-being if income and power distribution are heavily skewed and advances are primarily captured by entrenched elites (Wilkinson & Pickett, 2010). This is a strong pointer to poverty and associated vulnerabilities being more than an economic phenomenon. While quantifications, such as private consumption and access to common-pool resources together with generic provisions of public social services, provide helpful indicators at national policy level and may facilitate international comparison, they do not capture perceptions about well-being and livelihood at individual, family or community levels (Baulch, 1996).

The results of sociological and development studies have been found to apply to small-scale fishing communities as well. There is often no question of a dominant and general sense of income poverty, but rather of not having a voice and not being recognised. From field research, it is clear that in the past, small-scale fishers and their families, including the leading women in traditional fishing families, were often better off than their peers in agriculture, as documented, for example, by Sall and Nauen (2017a, 2017b) and by Sall (2018) in Senegal and Guinea. Similar conditions have been observed in other regions with rich fishery resources, such as the west coast of Latin America (Christensen et al., 2014, De la Puente et al., 2020). In the face of high population densities and ever more intensive resource use and overuse, in combination with often weak or absent social support structures and services, many small-scale fisheries communities in developing countries are, however, increasingly confronted with vulnerability and poverty. But how to characterise poverty?

Béné (2004) challenges the previously common notions of poverty in small-scale fisheries in developing countries as being attributed either to demographic growth (an endogenous issue) or conversely as an open-access problem of the resource (an exogenous issue), leading in both cases to low income and poverty. He points out that communities themselves, when given the chance to express their views, point more to lacking voice and entitlements than to income, as recently confirmed by Gaoussou Gueye of CAOPA (Confédération Africaine des Organisations de Pêche Artisanale) in West Africa in a statement at the FAO Symposium on Fisheries Sustainability, November 2019. Béné (2004) comments:

> the concept of poverty was redefined [by the ILO] to include other basic needs such as health and education, clean water and other services required to sustain livelihoods. [...] This basic needs model was the premise of a multi-dimensional definition of poverty which later led to the Human Development model of the UNDP.

Nayak et al. (2014) take the argument one step further by conceptualising poverty as a social-ecological system. Referring to field research in small-scale fisheries in coastal lagoons in India and Brazil, they look at it "as cycles of human-environment connections and disconnections that are crucial to understanding poverty and broader disempowerment processes in societies that are primarily dependent on natural resources for survival".

It is important to note in this context that there are fundamental differences between industrial and small-scale fisheries. Industrial fisheries, which are highly capital and fossil intensive, are driven mostly by the imperative to ensure a competitive financial return on investment. They operate according to a sector logic enabled by dedicated policies, which in the case of industrial and middle-income countries mobilise significant sums of harmful subsidies per year (Sumaila et al., 2019) to keep long-distance fleets going despite their questionable profitability, poor climate and environmental and social record.

Conversely, small-scale fisheries are not characterised by such a sector logic and instead are deeply embedded in the social fabric of their communities, often combining a wide range of other activities with fishing and post-harvest processing and marketing, including growing vegetables in the off-season, keeping livestock and engaging in hawking and petty trade to secure the livelihood of the (extended) family. This is why it is most appropriate to conceptualise small-scale fisheries as a social-ecological system, a term that arose later but which resonates well with the earlier concept of (sustainable) livelihood as defined by Chambers and Conway (1991). They place the emphasis on resilience, the ability to maintain or enhance capabilities and assets, now and for future generations.

In other words, poverty is not only, and in some cases not even primarily, a matter of financial shortfalls, but can encompass, in addition, a host of limitations preventing sustainable livelihoods. Among the most obvious are illness and need to look after sick dependents, relatives and neighbours, lack of social services, including health and education, weak or absent entitlements and other assets, poor social organisation engendering political invisibility and the ensuing marginalisation and disenfranchisement. Thus, recovering fishery resources to a healthy level is a necessary but not sufficient condition for sustainable livelihoods in small-scale fishing with an emphasis on eradicating poverty. This will have to include setting up and enforcing very large marine protected areas across all marine and coastal ecosystems (Sala et al., 2021). Unless this goes hand in hand with good management ensuring access to artisanal local operators and abolishing harmful subsidies which predominantly support industrial long-distance fisheries together with other measures increasing equity, the stated objectives of reducing or even eradicating poverty will remain elusive.

Other dimensions of poverty are also associated with low educational attainment and mental health issues (Oduro & Aryee, 2003), or to the nexus between poverty, hunger and reduced life expectancy (Pool et al., 2008). Poverty thus has social, political and ethical dimensions rather than purely economic ones (Bailey & Jentoft, 1990).

Food Insecurity

Food security, as defined by the United Nations' Committee on World Food Security, means that all people, at all times, have physical, social, and economic access to sufficient, safe, and nutritious food that meets their food preferences and dietary needs for an active and healthy life.[4]

This definition rightly places the emphasis on the socio-economic context of access, rather than on food production for human consumption as a physical output. The latter is typically used as an argument to justify industrialisation of agriculture, fisheries and aquaculture when global population projections are confronted with a presumed need for quantitative increases. As a matter of fact, global food production has more than kept pace with human demographics in recent decades, even though the absolute number of people suffering food insecurity and even hunger is not declining proportionately. Indeed, famines as an extreme case of hunger and food insecurity do mostly not occur as a result of complete unavailability of food, but due to the political invisibility of marginalised populations, poor logistics and other human factors (Sen, 1981). Such projections tend not to take into account postharvest losses and other wastage, currently estimated at 1.3 billion tons of foods produced for human consumption, or about a third of the total. This breaks down to 30% of cereals, 20% of dairy products, 20% of meat, 35% for fish and seafood, 45% of fruits and vegetables, 22% of oilseeds and pulses, and 45% of roots and tubers (FAO et al., 2020).

The concept has been further developed to take into account temporal features and to distinguish between short-term and longer-term structural food insecurity, often associated with protracted conflict and compounded by drought, crop failures and combinations of human and natural causes (FAO, 2006).

Current estimates suggest that nearly 690 million people are hungry, or 8.9% of the world population – an increase of nearly 60 million in five years. The number of people affected by severe food insecurity, which is another measure that approximates hunger, shows a similar upward trend. In 2019, close to 750 million – or nearly one in ten people in the world – were exposed to severe levels of food insecurity (FAO et al., 2020) and all the gains in the past in terms of reducing food insecurity and hunger have been lost by the SARS-CoV 2 pandemic in 2020.

Considering the total population affected by moderate or severe food insecurity, including on a short-term basis, an estimated 2 billion people on Earth did not have regular access to safe, nutritious and sufficient food in 2019 (FAO et al., 2020). This also squanders water, land, energy and labour, and contributes significantly to climate change. Reducing wastage and increasing efforts at greater equity in access to food, in line with the human right to nutritious food, as enshrined in the 1948 Human Rights Declaration, would go a long way to address widespread food insecurity and meeting Sustainable Development Goal 2: Zero Hunger.

Studies of food (in)security moreover, need to pay attention to adequate nutrition. This has been unpicked in an important paper by Hicks et al. (2019) about fish and fisheries products, which play an important role in balancing diets. They estimate, that Africa is a net exporter of nutritious foods, despite the fact that several countries and regions are affected by severe food insecurity. A global analysis of current food and feed production, trade and food availability for human consumption in relation to projected human population growth concluded that with more equitable distribution current production would be sufficient to the estimated human population of approximately 9.7 billion in 2050 (Berners-Lee et al., 2018). This would, however, require at least some reduction in waste and a shift towards more plant-based diets. Should current continue in middle-income populations in industrial countries, and increasingly in developing countries, the authors estimate that production – and distribution and access – would have to more than double by 2050.

Such a global assessment helps to focus on orders of magnitude and increases awareness about the undesirability or even impossibility of business-as-usual scenarios that avoid catastrophic increases in inequality and conflict. What is required for populations suffering food insecurity is a more fine-grained approach, sensitive to the social, cultural, economic, institutional and power relationships that make them vulnerable. The extent of global trade in fisheries products, the highest and most valuable of any food commodity means that the most valuable resources will go to where the highest purchasing power is. The biggest markets for imports of fish and fishery products are the EU, the US, Japan and the rising purchasing power of developing countries' middle classes following increasingly behind (Swartz et al., 2010; EUMOFA, 2018; FAO, 2020a).

Routes to Addressing These Often-Interdependent Challenges

The last two or more decades have brought significant advances in quantifying effective catches, illegal operations, poverty and food insecurity. These have been driven by independent research, non-governmental organisations and efforts of UN organisations who agree on the need to improve the often under-resourced national and international statistical databases and transparency. Although falling prices and new technologies have contributed to Big Data becoming more accessible and enabling new types of analysis, it does not flow automatically that patterns of unsustainable and harmful practices cease in the short-term, nor that privileges of elites get redistributed to those in need (McGee & Gaventa, 2011; Kempeneer, 2021).

The hard-won advances in quantification have the merit of showing the real challenge on many dimensions. Reliable employment statistics are not available in the vast majority of countries but the global estimates demonstrate that half the labour force along fisheries and aquaculture value chains are women (FAO, 2020a). These figures need to be complemented by questions concerning blue justice, fairness, gender equity, transparency and accountability. In particular, for each of the three main concepts in the title – fisheries crimes, poverty and food insecurity – it is known that vulnerable groups, generally women and minority people, sustain most of the negative effects and tend to be more weakly considered in allocations of entitlements and opportunities, including education, health care and market access (Sen 1981; Chambers & Conway, 1991; Williams et al., 2005; UNODC, 2011; Asche et al., 2015). More detailed understanding of the multi-faceted interactions is essential to take effective remedial action.

Where national policies are primarily informed by neoliberal economic models, it is essential to demonstrate that (a) such assumptions do not coincide with decision criteria of real people in many real-life situations, such as when they invest in their children's education even at the expense of forgoing some immediate consumption, and that (b) the primary challenge in most marine and coastal fisheries is at the moment to rebuild the resource to a state that it can produce the internationally mandated maximum sustainable yield (MSY) and thus increase the "cake to be distributed instead of fighting over a shrinking cake". How to achieve such gains and distribute them fairly so that compliance with rules can be more readily achieved? Experience suggests that a mix of hard and soft measures are most likely to increase maritime security, by identifying and addressing the socio-economic drivers of criminal activities (Witbooi et al., 2020). Seven measures stand out to enable the transition within the broader context of the interdependent Sustainable Development Goals (SDGs) and other specific measures:

- Reinforce maritime monitoring, control and surveillance and associated judicial enforcement capacity and enhance understanding and capabilities of national authorities to address IUU fishing with particular attention to its many ramifications into organised crime;
- Encourage more countries and get all RFMOs to prohibit transhipment in the waters under their purview and slapping more serious penalties on vessels when obstructing transparency and breaking the rules;
- Phase-out harmful subsidies in the WTO – estimated at USD 22 billion per year, 85% of which go to industrial fleets, including vessels with a track record of IUU fishing (Sumaila et al., 2019) – as this would make a substantial part of these fleets uneconomical, make them stop and reduce high levels of overcapacity in global fleets while at the same time move in the direction of a more level playing field between industrial and small-scale fisheries operations;
- Deny market access to IUU catches more effectively through more international cooperation among the different agencies and institutions, and strengthening their capacities to enforce existing rules, including more proactive use of registers/blacklisting of IUU vessels and making it easier for legitimate market participants to thrive;
- Invest in social services for local fishing communities to create attractive livelihood opportunities whether in fishing or other sources of income or suitable combinations further enabled through truly participatory forms of marine area management. Protect at least 30% of the ocean by 2030, so as to cover all types of marine and coastal ecosystems to allow restoring degraded ones;[5]
- Implement the FAOs Voluntary Guidelines for securing sustainable small-scale fisheries (FAO, 2015) in order to enable more than 90% of those working along fisheries and aquaculture value chains, men and women, to contribute to local and regional food security and poverty eradication.

Broad-based information campaigns about the challenges and opportunities in contemporary fisheries by civil society organisations on mainstream and social media have raised worldwide awareness about resource depletion and its causes. Nevertheless, the extent of IUU fishing and its nexus of poverty, food insecurity and broader maritime insecurity remains less known. As we have argued throughout this chapter, a more fine-grained questioning about how poverty and food insecurity unfold in real people's lives is much needed, in line with further research on the evolving strategies of IUU fishing. Governments must take more responsibility for hard law enforcement against drivers of maritime insecurity, but they must also play a role in ensuring generally accessible health, education and other social services. This would reduce the vulnerability of marginalised people drawn into criminal activities. Civil society organisations already play an important role in "soft interventions" and should further step-up efforts to empower vulnerable groups and support for a voice of men and women in small-scale fisheries. This needs to go hand-in-hand with a truly participatory approach to planning and decision-making processes, which will counter the tendency for decision-makers in disciplinary silos, large corporations and technical experts to decide policies. Examples of this are seen in, e.g., marine spatial planning (Flannery & McAteer, 2020), in maritime research and in national planning and policy processes (Sall & Nauen, 2017b). The effects of top-down measures are typically those people who will be exposed to the consequences but rarely sit at the negotiating table. A participatory process of consensus-building and social acceptance is a critical prerogative for the implementation of the necessary measures and achievement of proclaimed objectives. The process itself can be seen as a step towards greater fairness and equitable treatment once those previously excluded are recognised and supported with the means for a substantive participation (Chambers & Conway, 1991; Flannery & McAteer, 2020).

Under a sustainability scenario, addressing IUU fishing, poverty and food insecurity, incorporating a broader concept of maritime security, means extra efforts are needed to account for an ever-increasing human population.

Notes

1 See The FAO Global Record of Fishing Vessels, Refrigerated Transport Vessels and Supply Vessels, http://www.fao.org/global-record/en/
2 See the IUU Fishing Index at http://iuufishingindex.net/
3 See The Sea Around Us project at https://www.seaaroundus.org
4 See Committee on World Food Security, http://www.fao.org/cfs/en/
5 Global Ocean Alliance 30by30 is a UK-led initiative. Its aim is to protect at least 30% of the global ocean as Marine Protected Areas (MPAs) and Other Effective area-based Conservation Measures (OECMs) by 2030. See https://www.gov.uk/government/topical-events/global-ocean-alliance-30by30-initiative/about

References

Ahmad, E., Ayres, R. L., Fields, G., Ribe, H., Squire, L., Suridberg, M., Dominique, V. D. W., Jacques, V. D. G., & Walton, M. (1990). *World Development Report 1990: Poverty (English)*. World Development Report no. 13. World Bank Group.

Asche, F., Bellemare, M. F., Roheim, C., Smith, M. D., & Tveteras, S. (2015). Fair enough? Food security and the international trade of seafood. *World Development, 67*, 151–160.

Bailey, C. & Jentoft, S. (1990). Hard choices in fisheries development. *Maritime Policy, 14*(4), 333–344.

Baulch, B. (1996). Editorial. The new poverty agenda: A disputed consensus. *IDS Bulletin 27*(1), 1–10.

Belhabib, D., Sumaila, U. R., & Pauly, D. (2015). Feeding the poor: Contribution of West African fisheries to employment and food security. *Ocean and Coastal Management, 111*, 72–81.

Bellmann, C., Tipping, A., & Sumaila, U. R. (2016). Global trade in fish and fishery products: An overview. *Maritime. Policy, 69*, 181–188.

Béné, C. (2004). When fishery rhymes with poverty: A first step beyond the old paradigm on poverty in small-scale fisheries. *World Development, 31*(6), 949–975.

Berners-Lee, M., Kennelly, C., Watson, R., & Hewitt, C. N. (2018). Current global food production is sufficient to meet human nutritional needs in 2050 provided there is radical societal adaptation. *Elements Science of the Anthropocene, 6*(1), 1–14.

Chambers, R., & Conway, G. R. (1991). *Sustainable Rural Livelihoods: Practical Concepts for the 21st Century*. Institute of Development Studies Discussion Paper.

Christensen, V., De la Puente, S., Sueiro, J. C., Steenbeek, J. G., & Majluf, P. . (2014). Valuing seafood: The Peruvian fisheries sector. *Marine Policy, 44*, 302–311.

Daniels, A., Gutiérrez, M., Fanjul, G., Guereña, A., Matheson, I., & Watkins, K. (2016). *Western Africa's missing fish. The impacts of illegal, unreported and unregulated fishing and under-reporting catches by foreign fleets*. ODI Report.

De la Puente, S., López de la Lama, R., Benavente, S., Sueiro, J. C., & Pauly, D. (2020). Growing into poverty: Reconstructing Peruvian small-scale fishing effort between 1950 and 2018. *Frontiers in Maritime Science, 7*, 1–14.

Doumbouya, A., Camara, O. T., Mamie, J., Intchama, J. F., Jarra, A., Ceesay, S., Guèye, A., Ndiaye, D., Beibou, E., Padilla, A., & Belhabib, D. (2017). Assessing the effectiveness of Monitoring, control and surveillance of illegal fishing: The case of West Africa. *Frontiers in Maritme Science*, *4*, 1–10.

EUMOFA. (2018). The EU fish market 2018 edition. Brussels, European Commission, Directorate-General for Maritime Affairs and Fisheries, Director-General.

FAO. (2001). *International Plan of Action to Prevent, Deter and Eliminate Illegal, Unreported and Unregulated Fishing*. Food and Agriculture Organisation.

FAO. (2006). FAO policy brief food security. FAO, Issue 2. http://www.fao.org/fileadmin/templates/faoitaly/documents/pdf/pdf_Food_Security_Cocept_Note.pdf

FAO. (2015). *Voluntary Guidelines for Securing Sustainable Small-Scale Fisheries in the Context of Food Security and Poverty Eradication*. Food and Agriculture Organization.

FAO. (2020a). *The State of World Fisheries and Aquaculture 2020. Sustainability in Action*. Food and Agriculture Organization.

FAO. (2020b). *Joining Forces to Shape the Fishery Sector of Tomorrow. Promoting Safety and Decent Work in Fisheries through the Application of International Standards*. Food and Agriculture Organization.

FAO. (2021). *Implementation of the Code of Conduct: Trends over last 25 years*. Food and Agriculture Organization.

FAO, IFAD, UNICEF, WFP & WHO. (2020). *The State of Food Security and Nutrition in the World 2020. Transforming Food Systems for Affordable Healthy Diets*. Food and Agriculture Organization on the United Nations, the International Fund for Agricultural Development, the United Nations Children's Fund, World Food Programme and the World Health Organization.

Ferreira, F., Jolliffe, D. M., & Prydz, E. D. (2015, October 4). *The international poverty line has just been raised to $1.90 a day, but global poverty is basically unchanged. How is that even possible?* World Bank Blog "Let's Talk Development". https://blogs.worldbank.org/developmenttalk/international-poverty-line-has-just-been-raised-190-day-global-poverty-basically-unchanged-how-even

Flannery, W., & McAteer, B. (2020). Assessing marine spatial planning governmentality. *Maritime Studies*, *19*, 269–284.

GEMLAWS Africa. (2021). Gulf of Guinea: Maritime piracy graphics 2020. *Maritime Governance Brief*, *2*(2). 10 p.

Hicks, C. C., Cohen, P. J., Graham, N. A. J., Nash, K.L., Allison, E. H., D'Lima, C. , Mills, D. J., Roscher, M., Thilsted, S. H., Thorne-Lyman, A. L., & MacNeil, M. A. (2019). Harnessing global fisheries to tackle micronutrient deficiencies. *Nature*, *574*(7776), 95–98.

INTERPOL. (2020, December 7). *Fighting illegal, unreported and unregulated fishing*. https://www.interpol.int/News-and-Events/News/2020/Fighting-illegal-unreported-and-unregulated-fishing

Kempeneer, S. (2021). A big data state of mind: Epistemological challenges to accountability and transparency in data-driven regulation. *Government Information Quarterly*, *38*(3), 1–8. https://doi.org/10.1016/j.giq.2021.101578

Konar, M., & Sumaila, U. R. (2019). *Illicit trade in marine resources keeps billions out of Pacific economies every year*. World Resources Institute. https://www.wri.org/insights/illicit-trade-marine-resources-keeps-billions-out-pacific-economies-every-year

Long, T., Widjaja, S., Wirajuda, H., & Juwana, S. (2020). Approaches to combatting illegal, unreported and unregulated fishing. Nature Food 1, 389–391. https://doi.org/10.1038/s43016-020-0121-y

Marschke, M., & Vandergeest, P. (2016). Slavery scandals: Unpacking labour challenges and policy responses within the off-shore fisheries sector. *Maritime Policy*, *68*, 39–46.

McGee, R., & Gaventa, J. (2011). Shifting power? Assessing the impact of transparency and accountability initiatives. *IDS Working Papers 2011*, 383: 39p, 1–39.

Nayak, P. K., Oliveira, L. E., & Berkes, F. (2014). Resource degradation, marginalization, and poverty in small-scale fisheries: Threats to social-ecological resilience in India and Brazil. *Ecology and Society*, *19*(2), 13 pages. http://dx.doi.org/10.5751/ES-06656-190273

Oduro, A., & Aryee, I. (2003). *Investigating Chronic Poverty in West Africa*. Chronic Poverty Research Centre Working Paper, 28.

Okafor-Yarwood, I. (2019). Illegal, unreported and unregulated fishing, and the complexities of the sustainable development goals (SDGs) for countries in the Gulf of Guinea. *Maritime Policy*, *99*, 414–422.

Österblom, H., Sumaila, U. R., Bodin, Ö., Hentati Sundberg, J., & Press, A. J. (2010). Adapting to regional enforcement: Fishing down the governance index. *PLOS ONE*, *5*(9). e12832. 8 pages. https://doi.org/10.1371/journal.pone.0012832

Fisheries Crimes, Poverty, Food Insecurity

Pauly, D., & Zeller, D. (2016). Catch reconstructions reveal that global marine fisheries catches are higher than reported and declining. *Nature Communications, 7,* 1–9.

Petrossian, G. A. (2015). Preventing illegal, unreported and unregulated (IUU) fishing: A situational approach. *Biological Conservation, 189,* 39–48.

Petrossian, G. A., Marteache, N., & Viollaz, J. (2014). Where do "undocumented" fish land? An empirical assessment of port characteristics for IUU fishing. *European Journal of. Criminal Policy Research, 21*(3), 337–351.

Pool, I., Navaneetham. K., Dharmalingam, A., & Caselli, G. (2008). Mortality, poverty and hunger nexus: Synthesis and policy implications. In K. Navaneetham, A. Dharmalingam & G. Caselli (Eds.), *Poverty, Nutrition and Mortality: A Comparative Perspective* (pp. 287–303). Committee for International Cooperation in National Research in Demography.

Pramod, G., Nakamura, K., Pitcher, T. J., & Delagran, L. (2014). Estimates of illegal and unreported fish in seafood imports to the USA. *Maritime Policy, 48,* 102–113.

Raymond, K. Z. (2009). Piracy and armed robbery in the Malacca Strait. A problem solved? *Naval War College Review, 62*(3), 31–42.

Rosello, M. (2020). Illegal, unreported and unregulated (IUU) fishing as a maritime security concern. In L. Otto (Ed.), *Global Challenges in Maritime Security. An Introduction* (pp. 33–48). Springer Nature.

Sala, E., Mayorga, J., Bradley, D., Cabral, R. B. , Atwood, T. B. , Auber, A., Cheung, W., Costello, C., Ferretti, F., Friedlander, A. M., Gaines, S. D., Garilao, C., Goodell, W., Halpern, B. S., Hinson, A., Kaschner, K., Kesner-Reyes, K., Leprieur, F., McGowan, J., ... & Lubchenco, J. (2021). Protecting the global ocean for biodiversity, food and climate. *Nature, 592,* 397–402.

Sall, A. (2018). Entretien avec Madame Khady SARR au port de pêche artisanale de Hann. https://www.mundusmaris.org/index.php/fr/projets/entre/2001-khadysarr-fr

Sall, A., & Nauen, C. E. (2017a). *Criminal fisheries practices and their perverse effects in West Africa.* Poster presented at the EGU Conference, Vienna, 23–28 April 2017.

Sall, A., & Nauen, C. E. (2017b). Supporting the small-scale fisheries guidelines implementation in Senegal: Alternatives to top-down research. In S. Jentoft, N. Franz, M. J. Barragan Paladines & R. Chuenpagdee (Eds.), *Unpacking the Voluntary Guidelines for Securing Sustainable Small-Scale Fisheries - From Rhetoric to Action* (pp. 609–634). Springer.

Sen, A. (1981). *Poverty and Famines: An Essay on Entitlement and Deprivation.* Clarendon Press.

Sumaila, U. R., Ebrahim, N., Schuhbauer, A., Skerritt, D. , Li, Y., Kim, H. S., Mallory, T. G., Lam, V. W. L. & Pauly, D. (2019). Updated estimates and analysis of global fisheries subsidies. *Marine Policy, 109,* 103695.

Sumaila, U. R., Zeller, D., Hood, L., Palomares, M. L. D., Li, Y., & Pauly, D. (2020). Illicit trade in marine fish catch and its effects on ecosystems and people worldwide. *Science Advances, 6*(9), 6:eaaz3801 7 p. 10.1126/sciadv.aaz3801.

Swartz, W., Sumaila, Y. R., Watson, R., & Pauly, D. (2010). Sourcing seafood for the three major markets: The EU, Japan and the USA. *Marine Policy, 34*(6), 1366–1373.

Tickler, D., Meeuwig, J. J., Bryant, K., David, F. , Forrest, J. A. H., Gordon, E., Larsen, J. J., Oh, B., Pauly, D., Sumaila, U. R. & Zeller, D. (2018). Modern slavery and the race to fish. *Nature Communications, 9,* 4643, 10.1038/s41467-018-07118-9.

UN. (1991). *UN General Assembly Resolution 46/215 (1991) on Large-Scale Pelagic Drift Net Fishing and its Impact on Living Marine Resources of the World's Oceans and Seas.*

UN. (2017). Sustainable fisheries, including through the 1995 Agreement for the Implementation of the Provisions of the United Nations Convention on the Law of the Sea of 10 December 1982 relating to the Conservation and Management of Straddling Fish Stocks and Highly Migratory Fish Stocks, and related instruments. Resolution adopted by the UN General Assembly on 5 December 2017.

UNODC. (2011). *Transnational Organized Crime in the Fishing Industry. Focus on: Trafficking in persons, smuggling of migrants and illicit drugs trafficking.* United Nations Office on Drugs and Crime.

Wilkinson, R., & Pickett, K. (2010). *The Spirit Level: Why Equality is Better for Everyone.* Penguin Books.

Williams, S. B., Hochet-Kibongui, A.-M., & Nauen, C. E. (Eds.). (2005). *Gender, Fisheries and Aquaculture: Social Capital and Knowledge for the Transition towards Sustainable Use of Aquatic Ecosystems. ACP-EU Fisheries Research Reports,* 16. Office for Official Publications of the European Communities.

Witbooi, E., Ali, K. D., Santosa, M. A., Hurley, G., Husein, Y., Maharaj, S., Okafor-Yarwood, I., Quiroz, I. A.,. & Salas, O. (2020). Organized crime in the fisheries sector threatens a sustainable ocean economy. *Nature, 588*(7836), 48–56.

World Bank. (2017). *The Sunken Billions Revisited: Progress and Challenges in Global Marine Fisheries. Environment and Development.* World Bank.

21

SMALL ISLAND DEVELOPING STATES AND MARITIME SECURITY

Christian Bouchard

While oceans play a key role in everyone's lives, no one is more dependent on them than the small, vulnerable and isolated island developing states surrounded by the seas. [...]

We are the ocean people, so to speak: we live off and by the oceans and to varying degrees on and for them as well. The oceans define who we are and the coastal and marine environment is an integral part of our island lifestyle.

Our islands may be small in land area, but we morph into large ocean states when our exclusive economic zones are factored in.

Ronny Jumeau (2013), Seychelles Ambassador for Climate Change and SIDS Issues

Island societies, as well as small island developing states (SIDS), are children of the sea. The importance of the ocean for these societies has fluctuated over time and remains variable from one island state to another, yet the ocean emerges today as a fundamental dimension of any small island state, particularly in terms of territory, natural resources, connectivity, constraints and challenges. The emergence of the concept of SIDS itself and the establishment of an international action group for such states were both related to the sea from the outset, as they happened in the wake of the Small States Conference on Sea Level Rise, held in Malé, Maldives, in November 1989. From this first collective meeting and the creation of the Alliance of Small Island States (AOSIS) in 1990, ocean matters have always been of main significance to SIDS. Moving beyond their original primary focus on climate change and sustainable development, they are now getting deeply involved and showing leadership in the fast-developing Global Ocean international agenda (blue economy and blue growth, sustainable development goal #14, conservation and sustainable use of marine biological diversity of areas beyond national jurisdiction, etc.).

There is, in fact, an existential relation between the islands and the waters surrounding them, and this relation brings both opportunities and challenges. The ocean is paramount for the small island developing states, as it is a key factor for their current and future social, economic and even political development. With the wide diversity and significance of ocean-related threats and risks, such as sea level rise, marine pollution and criminality at sea, "for SIDS, there is a clear and undeniable maritime dimension to their security. Indeed, it can be argued that SIDS

250

DOI: 10.4324/9781003001324-24

Small Island Developing States

security and maritime security are in many ways indistinguishable" (Malcolm, 2017, p. 238). However, if some specific issues have been considered with more or less constancy since the 1990s in most of the SIDS, such as coastal erosion, illegal fishing and drug trafficking, maritime security has not usually been addressed in a comprehensive manner, nor has it been explicitly formalised as a SIDS collective priority. This is not to say that many ocean-related threats and risks were not clearly identified and addressed by the island states in some way, but until now, they have been mainly considered independent from one another in the different priority areas developed under the Barbados Programme of Actions for the Sustainable Development of the Small Island Developing States (1994), the Mauritius Strategy for the Further Implementation of the Programme of Action for the Sustainable Development of SIDS (2005) and the SIDS Accelerated Modalities of Action (SAMOA) Pathway (2014).

As formalised within the United Nations system, the list of SIDS currently includes 38 UN member states, to which another 20 non-UN member small island countries and territories are linked as associate members of one of the three SIDS Regional Commissions[1] (UN OHRLLS, 2020). In this chapter, we will consider a group of 29 SIDS located in the Caribbean, the African Atlantic Region, the Indian Ocean, and the Pacific Ocean (Table 21.1). From the UN list of 38 SIDS, we have extracted the four continental states (Belize, Guinea-Bissau, Guyana and Suriname), the three island states that have a land area over 30,000 km^2 (Papua New Guinea, Cuba and the Dominican Republic), as well as Bahrain and Singapore, which are quite distinct in nature from the rest of the group and present considerable differences in regard to maritime security. Altogether, the remaining 29 SIDS cumulate a land area of 146,000 km^2, 23.8 million inhabitants and 185 billion dollars of GDP (in purchasing power parity), but their cumulative maritime domains cover some 20.8 million km^2 (as defined here to be the ocean space from their coastline up to the outer limit of the EEZ). Therefore, they are definitively small in land territory (average of 5,029 km^2), in population (average of 820,000), and in economic terms (average GDP in PPP of 6.4 billion dollars), but they all have a much larger maritime domain than their land domain (average of some 718,000 km^2). The sea-to-land ratio varies from 4.48:1 for Haiti to 28,910:1 in Tuvalu,[2] for an average of 143:1 for all 29 SIDS.

In this chapter, as each national case is distinct, maritime security in the small island developing states is examined in a general manner. The first part discusses the existential link between the islands and their surrounding waters under a political perspective that considers sovereignty and territoriality at sea. The Southwest Indian Ocean serves as a case study to showcase the challenges related to defining SIDS maritime domains. The second part explores the diverse ocean threats and risks faced by SIDS in relation to the four dimensions of maritime security and to their quest for sustainable development. As SIDS lack sufficient capacity to address the maritime insecurities they are facing, capacity-building in regard to maritime security emerges as a complex and transformative process. The third and last part of the chapter investigates some of the national, regional and international ramifications and implications that relate to coping with maritime security in SIDS. Overall, small island developing states are now granted vast maritime domain that they plan to fully exploit as they embark on developing a successful blue economy. But to do so, they need to live, operate and develop in a healthy, safe and secure oceanic environment. In this context, maritime security is emerging as a pressing security matter in SIDS.

SIDS as [Large] Ocean States: The Maritime Domain

Addressing maritime security issues and challenges in SIDS begins by investigating and defining their maritime dimension in politico-spatial terms (spaces, zones, areas, borders and limits). It

Christian Bouchard

Table 21.1 SIDS selected for this chapter. GDP/PPP: Gross domestic product in purchasing power parity. Maritime domain: the ocean area from coastline to the outer limit of the exclusive economic zone. Data sources: CIA (2020; land area, population, GDP/PPP, coastline) and Pauly et al. (2020; maritime domain)

SIDS	Location	Land area km²	Population 2020	GDP/ PPP (M$) 2019	Coastline km	Maritime domain km²	Sea to land ratio
Antigua and Barbuda	Caribbean	443	98,179	2,128	153	107,939	244
Bahamas	Caribbean	10,010	337,721	13,937	3,542	628,026	63
Barbados	Caribbean	430	294,560	4,489	97	183,773	427
Cabo Verde	Atlantic Ocean	4,033	583,255	3,944	965	796,555	198
Comoros	Indian Ocean	2,235	846,281	2,622	340	164,643	74
Dominica	Caribbean	751	74,243	873	148	28,593	38
Fiji	Pacific Ocean	18,274	935,974	12,329	1,129	1,281,703	70
Grenada	Caribbean	344	113,094	1,931	121	26,133	76
Haiti	Caribbean	27,560	11,067,777	19,473	1,771	123,525	4
Jamaica	Caribbean	10,831	2,808,570	28,780	1,022	263,284	24
Kiribati	Pacific Ocean	811	111,796	268	1,143	3,437,132	4,238
Maldives	Indian Ocean	298	391,904	10,043	644	916,011	3,074
Marshal Islands	Pacific Ocean	181	77,917	227	370	1,992,022	11,006
Mauritius	Indian Ocean	2,030	1,379,365	29,098	177	1,272,765	627
Micronesia (Fed. St. of)	Pacific Ocean	702	102,436	391	6,112	2,992,415	4,263
Nauru	Pacific Ocean	21	11,000	146	30	308,506	14,691
Palau	Pacific Ocean	459	21,685	324	1,519	604,253	1,316
Saint Kitts and Nevis	Caribbean	261	53,821	1,392	135	10,209	39
Saint Lucia	Caribbean	606	166,487	2,824	158	15,472	26
Saint Vincent and the Grena	Caribbean	389	101,390	1,379	84	36,304	93
Samoa	Pacific Ocean	2,821	203,774	1,284	403	131,535	47
Sao Tome and Principe	Atlantic Ocean	964	211,122	852	209	165,345	172
Seychelles	Indian Ocean	455	95,981	2,837	491	1,331,964	2,927

(*Continued*)

Small Island Developing States

Table 21.1 (Continued)

SIDS	Location	Land area km²	Population 2020	GDP/ PPP (M$) 2019	Coastline km	Maritime domain km²	Sea to land ratio
Solomon Islands	Pacific Ocean	27,986	685,097	1,586	5,313	1,596,464	57
Timor-Leste	Pacific Ocean	14,874	1,383,723	4,039	706	77,051	5
Tonga	Pacific Ocean	717	106,095	647	419	664,751	927
Trinidad and Tobago	Caribbean	5,128	1,208,789	36,515	362	79,798	16
Tuvalu	Pacific Ocean	26	11,342	50	24	751,672	28,910
Vanuatu	Pacific Ocean	12,189	298,333	943	2,528	827,626	68
Total	-------	145,829	23,781,711	185,351	30,115	20,815,469	143
Average	-------	5,029	820,059	6,391	1,038	717,775	2,542
Median	-------	751	203,774	1,931	403	308,506	93

brings us to consider the phenomenon of maritime territorialisation by which coastal states extend their sovereignty or some sovereign rights and national jurisdiction over maritime areas that they essentially claim as theirs. This maritime domain finds its legal basis in the rules set by the United Nations Convention on the Law of Sea (UNCLOS, 1982), related national legislation (which incorporates UNCLOS in the national legal order) and the treaties and legal decisions defining their maritime borders. Accordingly, the national territory of any island state is necessarily partly maritime with the establishment of a territorial sea (up to 12 nautical miles beyond the baselines) where the coastal state exercises its sovereignty (subject to UNCLOS provisions and other rules of international law). Beyond this area of sovereignty, the coastal state maritime domain extends outward and includes a contiguous zone (up to 24 nautical miles from the baselines), an exclusive economic zone (up to 200 nautical miles from the baselines), and even in specific circumstances a continental shelf extending beyond the EEZ (up to 350 nautical miles from the baselines or 100 nautical miles from the 2,500-metre isobath on the outer edge of the continental margin). In several cases, island states also have inland waters (inward of the baselines) or archipelagic waters (delimited by archipelagic baselines).

What draws our attention here is the size of these national maritime domains. As shown in Table 21.1, if we consider the marine space extending from the coastline to the outer limit of the EEZ (and thus excluding any extended continental shelf), all of our 29 SIDS here have a maritime domain much greater than their land area. This ranges from 10,500 km² for Saint Kitts and Nevis to 3,437,000 km² for Kiribati, which correspond to respective sea-to-land ratios of 39:1 and 4,238:1. In 21 out of 29 cases (72.4%), the maritime domain is more than 50 times larger than the land area. In terms of area, half of the SIDS considered (14 out of 29) have a maritime domain that extends over 600,000 km², making them unquestionably large ocean states. The maritime domain and the sea-to-land ratio is even greater when considering the extensions of the continental shelf beyond the EEZ, which is relatively common situation in SIDS as in other coastal states (CLCS, 2020; Suarez-de Vivero, 2013).

Another dimension of maritime territorialisation that should be emphasised here is that of the establishment of maritime borders. These must be negotiated between states whose maritime domain may overlap, or else determined by international legal procedures to which the parties have acquiesced. This is an important question because the fixing of these inter-state borders makes it possible to determine with precision the extent of the maritime domain of the coastal states, and therefore the rights and obligations of all the users of the sea in this limited and zoned ocean space. Sovereignty disputes over certain islands (sometimes only rocks or low-tide elevations), conflicting relations between neighbouring states, as well as a lack of resources and/ or interest to establish a treaty explain that many maritime borders remain undefined. For those unfamiliar with this subject, it does not appear as an issue as the usual maps simply draw virtual borders in the absence of officially delimited borders (especially large-scale maps: world, ocean basins, continents, regions). But these virtual borders have no legal value and above all are often based on questionable claims or debatable interpretations of the rules established by UNCLOS.

Finally, the length of the coastline and the territorial configuration are two other geographical aspects that should be examined when considering territorial issues and maritime security in SIDS. The territorial sea area and the length of its outer limits[3] are a function of the length of the coastline. Being a part of the national territory, the territorial sea needs to be secured from illegal entries and activities (mainly illegal migrations and smuggling). More generally, it is in the coastal areas where human settlements, economic activities, and maritime security issues usually concentrate. Average length of coastline for our 29 SIDS is 1,038 km, ranging from 30 km in Nauru to 6,112 in the Federated States of Micronesia. These two states also exemplify the two extremes in terms of territorial configuration: one being a single island state and the other an archipelagic state made of a multitude of islands spread over a large oceanic space. The Federated States of Micronesia is comprised of 607 small islands stretching out over almost 2,700 km from East to West. In this case, the lengthy coastline and complex territorial configuration present great challenges for the effective surveillance and control of its coastal areas and territorial sea.

The Southwest Indian Ocean is an excellent case study to showcase the challenges of maritime territorialisation in SIDS. It is comprised of three SIDS, namely Comoros, Mauritius and Seychelles, as well as the French overseas departments and regions of Reunion and Mayotte (claimed by Comoros), a set of five small island entities grouped together by France in the Scattered Islands[4] (Bassas da India, Europa, Juan de Nova, Gloriosos Is., which are claimed by Madagascar, and Tromelin, which is claimed by Mauritius), the Chagos Archipelago (currently administered by the United Kingdom as the British Indian Ocean Territory, but claimed by Mauritius) and Madagascar (Figure 21.1). In this island region, there are many cases of contested sovereignty and of debatable maritime claims regarding the exclusive economic zone. Considering the usual representation of the region, very small islands such as Tromelin or Juan de Nova have disproportionate EEZ if a certain degree of proportionality (depending in particular on the area of the islands and the length of the coasts facing each other) was to be considered instead of applying the sole rule of equidistance between facing coasts. In addition, Bassas da India atoll[5] does not qualify as an island pursuant to UNCLOS rules and therefore France should not be able to establish there neither a territorial sea nor an exclusive economic zone. However, France claims and implements an EEZ of 127,300 km^2 from the atoll (TAAF, 2016).

In this maritime region, Seychelles and Mauritius represent archetype cases of SIDS being large ocean states. In both states, the maritime domain is still not entirely defined insofar as (1) two sovereignty conflicts prevent the formalising of the national territory and maritime domain of Mauritius, and (2) several maritime borders have not yet been fixed, a situation which is only partly due to the sovereignty issues. Where the Republic of Mauritius might be able to exercise its sovereignty over the Chagos Archipelago in the future,[6] the outcome of its claim to the island of

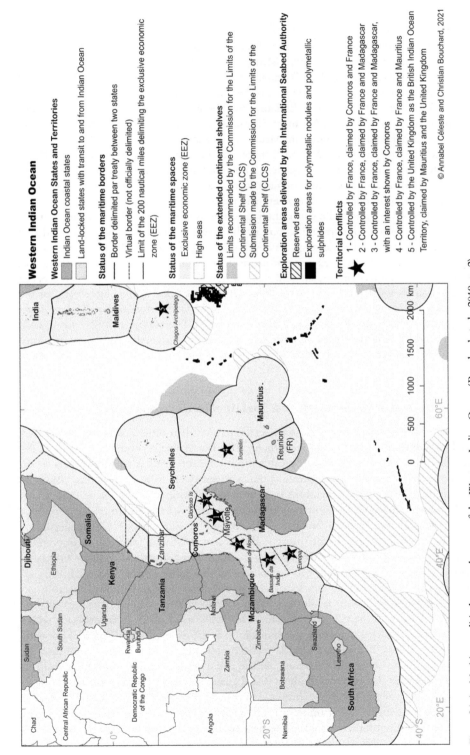

Figure 21.1 Maritime political geography map of the Western Indian Ocean (Bouchard et al., 2019, p. 2).

Tromelin is much uncertain.[7] Mauritius maritime domain now includes some 1.273 Mkm^2 within the limits of its EEZ, without considering neither the Chagos (EEZ of 640,000 km^2) and Tromelin (EEZ of 270,000 km^2). Added to this are the extended continental shelf areas of the Region of Rodrigues, the Mauritius-Seychelles Joint Management Area (administered jointly with the Seychelles) and the Chagos Archipelago Region, for an additional area of some 700,000 km^2 of continental shelf beyond the EEZ. In the case of Seychelles, its maritime domain now includes some 1.332 Mkm^2 within the limits of its EEZ to which should be added the extended continental shelf areas of Aldabra Island Region, Northern Plateau Region and the Mauritius-Seychelles Joint Management Area (administered jointly with Mauritius), an additional area of some 438,000 km^2 of continental shelf beyond the EEZ. We can therefore see here the very importance for SIDS to clearly establish their maritime domain. The areas at stake and the issues associated with them are of prime significance for small states which are now increasingly looking to the sea to support their current and future socio-economic development and national well-being.

In short, SIDS now consider their surrounding waters as their own. This maritime domain brings multiple economic opportunities, but it also needs to be efficiently protected and managed. The regulatory and physical spaces develop by states to govern the maritime (Bueger et al., 2020a; Ryan, 2019), their exercise of national sovereignty at sea, as well as the global ocean governance initiatives, interrelate and shape a new way of framing SIDS as true ocean states, many even being large ocean states. This reminds us "that considerable parts of the world's oceans and living resources are under the jurisdiction of erstwhile small island states with tiny populations and landmasses" (Chan, 2018, p. 537). Therefore, for SIDS, the ocean is an area of political expansion regarding both national territory (sovereignty) and international influence (ocean governance). It also brings tremendous opportunities and numerous challenges.

Maritime Security and Sustainable Development

Globally, SIDS are facing the same maritime security issues than other coastal states, but they generally lack sufficient capacity to address them. This is a problem commonly found in developing countries, but it is often of a greater magnitude for small states that possess a vast maritime domain. While there is obviously much diversity in national contexts, SIDS are greatly concerned by all four dimensions or domains of maritime security as identified and discusses by Bueger and colleagues, namely national security, marine environment, economic development and human security (Bueger, 2015; Bueger & Edmunds, 2017; Bueger et al., 2019). Taking a holistic approach, the threats and risks associated with maritime security in the small island developing states arise within each of these dimensions and in their numerous interrelations (Figure 21.2). Overall, SIDS responses to these threats and risks are mainly influenced by state capacity, human and social capital, business sector and external relations.

In SIDS, maritime aspects of traditional national security firstly involve the surveillance, protection and defence of the maritime domain. This firstly concerns the territorial sea, with a clear current focus on illegal migration and smuggling, as the issue of naval warfare is presently inexistent in the islands. It may also include maritime terrorism which is currently listed as a low-level threat in the small island nations. As the resources are usually quite limited, SIDS often have a single unit that performs both navy and coastguard tasks. Operational capacities are generally weak, especially in terms of maritime domain awareness (MDA) and activities at sea in the EEZ. Relations with the other three maritime security dimensions include, among others, enforcement of the environmental and fishing legislations, protection of maritime transportation, cruise ships and offshore infrastructures, search and rescue operations, humanitarian

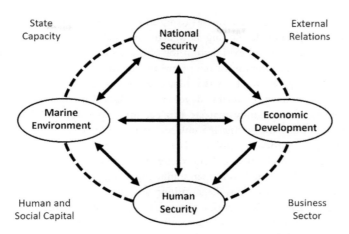

Figure 21.2 Maritime security domains matrix (ovals and arrows), and main drivers influencing the SIDS responses to maritime security threats and risks.

assistance and disaster relief, as well as the naval forces or coastguard units' economic significances and environmental impacts.

Maritime security threats and risks related to the marine environment are several and of chief importance to SIDS. Their national economy and well-being are very much dependent on a healthy ocean and enjoyable coastal environments providing several fundamental resources, ecosystem services and assets such as halieutic resources, beaches, coral reefs and mangroves. Relations with the other dimensions include, to name a few, the exploitation of marine energies (waves, currents, heat, etc.), offshore gas, oil and mineral resources, and marine genetic resources, as well as water desalinisation which is increasingly important to secure potable water alimentation in many islands. In brief, the marine environment provides the natural resources most of. But the ocean also brings its share of constraints and threats such as storms and cyclones, as well as coastal inundation and costal erosion. For some small and low-laying islands, sea level is even framed as an existential threat as they may become unhabitable or even be washed away. Marine environment and especially the coastal ecosystems are fragile and prone to pollution, physical degradation and destruction, climate change impacts such as warming ocean temperature and sea level rise, ocean acidification, etc. In this context, the protection and conservation of the marine environment and biodiversity are increasingly being recognised as a maritime security matter of prime importance, especially with regards to the efficient management of resources exploitation, particularly the fish stocks, and the creation of maritime protected areas (MPAs).

In the context of the SIDS small economies that have limited opportunities for economic growth, the ocean already offers a lot, especially for those who have been able to develop successful tourism and fisheries sectors. SIDS are also very dependent on maritime transport (ships, infrastructures and services) for their international trade as well as, in the case of archipelagoes, for their inter-island connections. Maritime safety for ships, crews and the environment is therefore an important issue that also relates to the three other domains of maritime security. This includes maritime piracy which can adversely impact SIDS economy as it was documented in the case of Seychelles in the peak of the Somali piracy crisis between 2008 and 2012[8] (Hardy, 2020; Marie & Bueger, 2020). Therefore, exploiting and cruising the sea requests safe and secure conditions to operate. Today the blue economy or blue growth is about pushing the economic exploitation of the sea to another level, expanding the traditional oceanic activities when possible, and developing new activities such as aquaculture, exploitation of marine energies, prospection and exploitation for offshore gas, oil and minerals, installation of communication cables, introduction of new touristic activities at sea, development of marine biotechnologies, etc. As promoted by SIDS, blue economy is supposed to be a green economy that will help them to achieve sustainable development[9] (UN & WB, 2017). It is thus vital for the islands to be able to efficiently manage this economic push at sea, limiting as much as possible any adverse effects on the marine environment and biodiversity.

Finally, the human security dimension relates to the maritime insecurities experienced by individuals and local communities, as either direct victims or been indirectly affected. It covers a wide array of threats and risks such as human trafficking, drugs and arms smuggling, other illicit traffics and unlawful activities such as illegal fishing and marine pollution, as well as threats to the safety of seafarers and to the security of coastal populations, economic activities and infrastructures. In this case again, there are numerous links with the other dimensions of maritime security, as for example SIDS clearly consider illegal fishing, inadequate fish stocks management and marine environment degradation as threats to their food security. Proneness and vulnerability to ocean-related natural hazards (high swell episodes, storms, tropical cyclones and tsunamis) and to climate change marine manifestations (sea level rise, warming sea temperatures, ocean acidification, etc.) is also a serious issue for SIDS. For some small low-laying islands such as atolls and sand keys, it is even their very physical existence or their habitability that are directly threatened by the sea-level rise and its related risks such as coastal inundation, coastal erosion and saltwater intrusion in their tiny freshwater table. Protecting the coastal island communities, or sometimes entire islands, against the aggression of the sea is another central aspect of human security in many SIDS.

In this holistic perspective, there is a large and even growing number of maritime security threats and risks that the SIDS now need to address. However, maritime security has not yet been explicitly identified as a collective priority by SIDS, even if almost all maritime insecurities are recognised in their sustainable development international agenda. In the context of SIDS, maritime security is essentially framed at national and regional levels in relation to their quest for sustainable development and related human security (Malcolm, 2017). Therefore, marine insecurities affecting the national economy, the island society and the environment can be understood as a threat to their future development. Given the fact that even large maritime powers of the world are unable to eradicate most of the identified maritime insecurities in their own maritime domain and maritime region, it is obvious that SIDS lacks the capacity and resources to comprehensively cope with all ocean-related threats and risks they are facing.

As other coastal states, SIDS responses to maritime security challenges is a function of their "institutions, practical activities, and procedures including its [their] governance structure and legal texture" (Bueger et al., 2020a, p. 12). Hence, these are areas where capacity-building is most needed, which can be concretised by "the building of new institutions, forms of coordination, writing of laws, creating of new forces, or training and enhancing existing ones, or the investment in new equipment, buildings, or vessels" Bueger et al. (2020a, p. 4). In the context of SIDS, capacity-building is strongly related to foreign assistance provided firstly by friendly states, but also by international institutions (such as United Nations Office on Drugs and Crime, and Interpol), as well as increasingly by international nongovernmental organisations (NGOs), foundations and even research projects. This foreign assistance can provide education, training, equipment, infrastructure, knowledge and expertise, financial support, personnel and services. Foreign states often provide operational security assistance such as independent or joint maritime patrol operations.

Small Island Developing States

We further suggest that SIDS responses to maritime insecurities are also influenced by their human and social capital and business sector. The former relates to the knowledge, skills, competencies and attributes that allow people to contribute to national well-being, including their community involvement, behaviours and mobilisation towards the ocean. The latter concerns the economic actors as main stakeholders and even often direct actors of maritime safety and security. Therefore, communities, civil society interest groups, education systems, artists, medias and the business sector can each contribute to develop an awareness for a healthy, safe and secure ocean.

Coping with Maritime Security: Internal, Regional and International Implications

More than just a buzzword, maritime security is a developing matter and a growing field of activity in SIDS. On this subject, the small islands are said to be vulnerable and to lack capacity. As they embrace the blue economy and develop an awareness for ocean-related threats and risks, they are embarking on a much need process of capacity-building to cope with maritime security issues. As the latter are interconnected and sometimes interdependent, liminal, commonly transnational and cross-jurisdictional in nature (Bueger et al., 2019), capacity-building and coping with maritime security is a complex and transformative process for SIDS. It has numerous internal (institutions, legislation, finance, planning, infrastructures, operational capacities at sea, and even political life), regional (cooperation with neighbours and foreign states), and international ramifications and implications (international relations and geopolitics).

In a recent report, Bergin et al. (2019) "examines how Pacific Island countries and Indian Ocean island states are managing and prioritising their maritime challenges". They provide a set of recommendations for both the Indo-Pacific island states as well as for what they call the "like-minded countries" working with Indo-Pacific island states (providing maritime security assistance). Table 21.2 presents these recommendations that we believe also fit well the other

Table 21.2 Bergin et al. (2019) recommendations for maritime security in the Indo-Pacific island states

For Indo-Pacific island states
- Strengthen national resilience through building national institutions.
- Develop and implement national maritime security strategies.
- Build maritime surveillance capabilities.
- Develop a formal tasking programme for the patrolling of remote islands and coastal areas.
- Build national maritime domain awareness systems.
- Strengthen institutional resilience through regional norms.
- Review interagency operational and staff training for maritime security.
- Collate relevant maritime laws, and ensure that they are easily accessible and understood.

For Australia, Japan and other like-minded countries working with Indo-Pacific island states
- Give coastguards a key role in maritime security and safety cooperation in the Indian Ocean.
- Establish a "Quad" of coastguards to coordinate regional capacity building.
- Step up Australia's maritime security capability-building efforts among selected IO island states.
- Assist the development of national and regional MDA systems.
- Develop framework disaster management arrangements.
- Shape the narrative on environmental security.
- Help strengthen regional institutions for Indo-Pacific island states.
- Provide support for infrastructure development.
- Build capacity for the blue economy.

SIDS of the Caribbean and the African Atlantic Region. In these two cases, SIDS work closely with European states (mainly France, United Kingdom, the Netherlands, Spain and Portugal) and the United States. Matching what small islands should do with how their foreign partners should contribute is quite indicative of how a growing community of security actors (navies, coastguards, analysts, commentators, researchers, defence and security firms) finds a very fertile ground within SIDS maritime security issues. However, it should not be forgotten that foreign assistance to maritime security represents only one aspect of the larger multi-scale and multi-facetted cooperation framework for SIDS needs in terms of sustainable development in general and blue economy in particular.

At the national level, the development and implementation of a national integrated maritime strategy and of a national maritime security strategy will help identifying and prioritising the needs and responses. In terms of best practices of maritime territorialisation and ocean management, the maritime domain should be entirely and formally delimited (at least when possible), baselines and maritime zones should be established in accordance with UNCLOS, marine protected areas should fulfil and even surpass international commitments, and integrated coastal zone management (ICZM) and marine spatial planning (MSP) should be implemented. As for best practices for maritime security and maritime affairs more broadly, they rely primarily on international norms (such as those adopted under the framework of the International Maritime Organization), as well as they should comply to regional and national codes of conduct (when these exist).

However, maritime security issues are frequently transnational in nature and are often best framed within a regional rather than a national perspective. Regional cooperation is necessary to cope with those issues that are shared between neighbouring costal state maritime domains and in the high seas, such as maritime piracy, illegal, unreported and unregulated (IUU) fishing, fish stocks management, and in some cases maritime pollution. Cooperation frameworks can be numerous in the same region as their state memberships depends on the problems to be dealt with, the objectives to be achieved, and the involved stakeholders. For example, several co-operation frameworks are simultaneously operating in the Western Indian Ocean such as the Maritime Security regional programme (MASE) which aims to promote safety and security at sea for the Eastern and Southern Africa and Indian Ocean (ESAO-IO) countries, and the Code of Conduct concerning the Repression of Piracy and Armed Robbery against Ships in the Western Indian Ocean and the Gulf of Aden (referred to as the Djibouti Code of Conduct). In this region, regarded by Bueger et al. (2020b, p. 240) as a crucible of innovation in maritime security capacity-building, foreign security assistance and regional cooperation is enriched by several multilateral operations (such as the EU Operation Atalanta and the US-led international Combined Task Forces CTF-150 and CTF-151), as well as by individual foreign national operations (noticeably by France, India and China). Therefore, capacity-building must notably be considered in its regional dimension.

Another characteristic of some SIDS regional environments in which collective maritime security is currently developing is the mix of neighbouring islands states and non-sovereign small island territories that is found in the Caribbean, the Southwest Indian Ocean and the Pacific Ocean. In island studies, these territories are often identified as sub-national island territories or SNIJs (Baldacchino & Milne, 2006; Randall, 2020). Consequently, efficient regional cooperation must also include these neighbouring territories with whom the SIDS share the same characteristics in terms of small land area, small population, small economy and vast maritime domain. The multilateral cooperation between SIDS and SNIJs is complicated by the fact that security issues are essentially a state prerogative, and thus have to be addressed with the island territories' larger nation-state parents (sovereign state to which island territories are attached: France, UK, USA, etc.). However, there is also a positive aspect in this situation as the parent-states usually develop a quite significant local maritime security capacity in their SNIJs as well as a vibrant defence and security cooperation with their neighbouring SIDS. In other words, these parent-states are legitimate regional stakeholders (as coastal states) as well as long-time security assistance providers to neighbours. France seems to be the best example of this as it is greatly involved in SIDS regional maritime security in each of the three island regional communities identified earlier (through bilateral and multilateral cooperation).

Finally, regarding SIDS maritime domain and maritime security, international ramifications and implications go way further than the regional cooperation just discussed. First, from a SIDS perspective, the relation between sovereignty and security deepens with the increasing territorialisation of the sea, evolving from the now usual UNCLOS-related zones to the newly established large marine protected areas, and considering their strong interest in the ocean management of the areas beyond national jurisdiction. As noted by Chan (2018, p. 549), "the emerging discourse and self-identification of the large ocean state reflects the new sovereign bargain that these states are engaging in to assert sovereign control over their EEZs in the context of global biodiversity conservation and oceans protection". Secondly, sea-level rise remains a chief maritime threat to the territorial integrity of SIDS, in terms of both land and maritime domains. This climate change-related issue has multiple international implications, especially as fundamental questions arise about the continuation of a state in the eventuality of the vanishing of its land territorial basis, the integrity of the maritime domain in the context of receding coastline, and the status of international climate refugees. Lastly, maritime security issues are of growing significance in SIDS international relations. This has already been discussed regarding capacity-building and regional cooperation, but there is also a growing global geopolitical implication that needs to be better studied and understood.

As much as the small island states can be considered as needing, asking and welcoming foreign assistance, they are also generally seen by major powers as geostrategic locations, where the latter need to secure or want to expand their political influence. In this context, maritime security arises as a natural area for cooperation, but also for large power competition. As noted by Bergin et al. (2019, p. 15),

> The [Indo-Pacific] island states are seeking to leverage their enhanced importance by drawing in the major powers to assist with their maritime security concerns. In that way, maritime security is in part redefining the greater geopolitical game with respect to the island states.

But navigating in an environment of increasing strategic competition is not an easy task and SIDS need to manoeuvre carefully under growing interest and pressure from rising powers such as China in the Indo-Pacific islands and India in the Indian Ocean islands, and long-time involved major powers in these same islands such as the USA, France, Australia, etc. Hardy (2020, p. 151), discussing the case of the Seychelles – which are often depicted as a very successful SIDS in navigating through the great geopolitical games of the large powers – concludes by reminding us that "in the end, the cold reality of geopolitics is that small island states are small island states, no more nor less". "A friend of all and an enemy of none" foreign policy (balancing policy), as well as not picking overtly a side in the strategic competition, has certainly work for many SIDS in the previous decades, but deepening security relations with everyone is only possible up to a certain limit of engagement with one another.

Conclusion

Small island developing states are intrinsically linked to the maritime space which traverses and surrounds them. In the wake of the adoption of UNCLOS in 1982 and of its entry into force in 1994, SIDS have embarked in a transformative ocean venture that morphs them into truly ocean states, often large ocean states. They now are granted vast maritime domains, over which they have sovereign rights for the purpose of exploring and exploiting, conserving and managing natural resources, as well as jurisdiction with regard to the establishment and use of artificial islands, installations and structures, marine scientific research, and the protection and preservation of the marine environment. This brings both tremendous opportunities that they now plan to fully exploit, and numerous challenges that they need to cope with, including sustainable exploitation of the sea, marine protection and conservation, as well as other ocean-related threats and risks such as maritime criminality and the ocean-related impacts of climate change. As a consequence, maritime security has recently emerged as a pressing national security matter for SIDS. For Bergin et al. (2019, p. 13), looking at the Indo-Pacific island states, "maritime security lies at the heart of their national wellbeing and existence".

After looking at maritime security in small island developing states at a macro-level and in a general manner, seven main observations can be made:

1   SIDS are still in the process of expanding and formalising their respective maritime domain, a process that implies the resolution of their lasting island sovereignty disputes, the establishment of all maritime borders, and the formalisation of their extended continental shelves.
2   Ocean threats and risks in SIDS arise from all four dimensions of maritime security, namely national security, marine environment, economic development and human security (Bueger, 2015, pp. 160–161), as well as their interconnections.
3   However, maritime security in SIDS is much less about traditional military issues and the survival of state (hard security) than about soft security which focuses on political, social, economic and environmental concerns, as well as on non-state actors.
4   In this specific small island's context, maritime security is to be framed in their respective sustainable development agenda in general and blue economy strategy in particular.
5   As SIDS currently lack the capacity to address the maritime insecurities they are facing, capacity-building in regard to maritime security emerges as an urgent and significant need, as well as a complex and transformative process.
6   As most of the maritime security concerns are either transnational or, when more locally bound, are shared between neighbouring states and territories, SIDS also must develop and participate in comprehensive regional maritime security frameworks.
7   Consequently, maritime security is a matter of foreign policy and international relation for SIDS. This becomes more evident and of great significance when foreign assistance is factored in, as an indispensable contribution to today's SIDS maritime security practice and capacity-building.

As small island developing states are acquiring sovereignty rights and national jurisdiction over vast maritime zones, they are now more than ever intimately linked to the ocean. In the future, the ocean will be fundamental to their socio-economic development and well-being, as well as to their identity and influence on the global arena. The ocean will however continue to bring numerous challenges, and in some cases, it may even threaten their very existence. Consequently, in the foreseeable future, SIDS will need to cope with numerous maritime insecurities over vast expanses of ocean, and with related issues pertaining to regional co-operation, foreign assistance, foreign policy and international relations. This is a lot to handle for states that remain small in many ways.

Notes

1 The Caribbean, the Pacific, and the Atlantic, Indian Ocean and South China Sea (AIS).
2 This value of sea-to-land ratio for Tuvalu, as some other ratios in Table 21.1, is very different than the 17,510:1 presented by Chan (2018, p. 541). This difference is mainly due to the land area data that are used. After verification, we find that that 26 km^2 is the usually recognised number for Tuvalu, and it is confirmed by the data provided by Albert et al. (2016, Table 1). Other land area data in our Table 21.1 are consistent with SIDS national publications.
3 The outer limit of the territorial sea is a border only when this line of demarcation separates the national territories of two states.
4 Administered as one of the five districts of the French Southern and Antarctic Territories.
5 According to French authorities responsible for the Scattered Islands, "the atoll is almost totally im-mersed at high tide. Consequently, development of any shape of aerial land life is prevented. Likewise, human settlement on the territory is impossible" (TAAF, 2016, p. 38).
6 "On 25 February 2019, the ICJ opined that the U.K.'s separation of the Chagos Archipelago from Mauritius in 1968 was not done in accordance with international law and the U.K. 'is under an obligation to bring to an end its administration of the Chagos Archipelago as rapidly as possible. Following this February advisory opinion, the UNGA in May passed resolution number 73/295 demanding that the U.K. withdraw its administration from the Archipelago within six months. These two high-profile developments challenge the status quo on Diego Garcia and the legitimacy of the BIOT" (Bashfield, 2020, p. 171).
7 For André Oraison (2012), France has strong arguments to defend her sovereignty over Tromelin.
8 This impact is well captured in a Seychelles presidential speech: "In 2009, our conservative estimates indicate a loss of 4% of our GDP due to piracy. Insurance costs have ballooned by 50%. Port and fisheries receipts have dropped by 30%. And we are spending over 2.3 million Euros per year on our anti-piracy patrols and surveillance." (Speech by President James A. Michel, Opening of the International Symposium on Piracy, Mahe, Seychelles, 12 July 2010)
9 For the United Nations and the World Bank (2017, p. vi), "the blue economy concept seeks to promote economic growth, social inclusion, and the preservation or improvement of livelihoods while at the same time ensuring environmental sustainability of the oceans and coastal areas".

References

Albert, S., Leon, J. X., Grinham, A. R., Church, J. A., Gibbes, B. R., & Woodroffe, C. D. (2016). Interactions between sea-level rise and wave exposure on reef island dynamics in the Solomon Islands. *Environmental Research Letters, 11*(5). 10.1088/1748-9326/11/5/054011

Baldacchino, G., & Milne, D. (2006). Exploring sub-national Island Jurisdictions: An editorial in-troduction. *The Round Table, 95*(386), 487–502.

Bashfield, S. M. (2020). Mauritian sovereignty over the Chagos Archipelago? Strategic implications for Diego Garcia from a UK-US perspective. *Journal of the Indian Ocean Region, 16*(2), 166–181.

Bergin, A., Brewster, D., & Bachhawat, A. (2019). *Ocean horizons: Strengthening maritime security in Indo-Pacific island states.* The Australian Strategic Policy Institute (ASPI).

Bouchard, C., Osman, S., & Rafidinarivo, C. (2019) Southwest Indian Ocean islands: Identity, devel-opment and cooperation. *Journal of the Indian Ocean Region, 15*(1), 1–6.

Bueger, C. (2015). What is maritime security. *Marine Policy, 53*(2015), 159–164.

Bueger, C., & Edmunds, T. (2017). Beyond seablindness: A new agenda for maritime security studies. *International Affairs, 93*(6), 1293–1311.

Bueger, C., Edmunds, T., & McCabe, R. (Eds.). (2020a). *Capacity building for maritime security: The Western Indian Ocean experience.* Palgrave Macmillan.

Bueger, C., Edmunds, T., & McCabe, R. (2020b). Into the sea: Capacity-building innovations and the maritime security challenge. *The World Quarterly, 41*(2), 228–246.

Bueger, C., Edmunds, T., & Ryan, B. J. (2019). Maritime security: The uncharted politics of the global sea. *International Affairs, 95*(5), 971–978.

Chan, N. (2018). "Large ocean states": Sovereignty, small islands, and marine protected areas in global oceans governance. *Global Governance, 24*(4), 537–555.

CIA. (2020). *The world factbook. Central intelligence agency.* Retrieved November 2020 from https://www.cia.gov/library/publications/the-world-factbook/

CLCS. (2020). "Submissions and recommendations" and "preliminary information." *United nations: Commission on the limits of the continental shelf.* Retrieved November 2020 from https://www.un.org/Depts/los/clcs_new/clcs_home.htm

Hardy, D. (2020). Seychelles: A small island state in a troubled sea. *Seychelles Research Journal, 2*(1), 137–154.

Jumeau, R. (2013). Small islands developing states, large ocean states (Declaration). Expert Group Meeting on Oceans, Seas and Sustainable Development: Implementation and follow-up to Rio+20, United Nations Headquarters, 18–19 April 2013.

Malcolm, J. A. (2017). Sustainability as maritime security: A small island developing state perspective? *Global Policy, 8*(2), 237–245.

Marie, A., & Bueger, C. (2020). Seychelles: Island solutions and capacity building successes. In C. Bueger, T. Edmunds, & R. McCabe (Eds.), *Capacity building for maritime security: The Western Indian Ocean experience* (pp. 199–221). Palgrave Macmillan.

Oraison, A. (2012). Radioscopie critique de la querelle franco-mauricienne sur le récif de Tromelin. *Revue Juridique de l'Océan Indien, 14*, 5–118.

Pauly, D., Zeller, D., & Palomares M. L. D. (Eds.). (2020). *Sea around us.* Retrieved November 2020 from http://www.seaaroundus.org/

Randall, J. E. (2020). *An introduction to island studies.* Island Studies Press at UPEI / Rowman & Littlefield.

Ryan, B. J. (2019). The disciplined sea: A history of maritime security and zonation. *International Affairs, 95*(5), 1055–1073.

Suarez-de Vivero, J. L. (2013). The extended continental shelf: A geographical perspective of the implementation of article 76 of UNCLOS. *Ocean & Coastal Management, 73*, 113–126.

TAAF. (2016). *Livret de découverte des Îles Éparses.* Terres australes et antarctiques françaises.

UNCLOS. (1982). United Nations Convention on the Law of the Sea. https://www.un.org/Depts/los/convention_agreements/texts/unclos/unclos_e.pdf

UN OHRLLS. (2020). List of SIDS. *United Nations: Office of the High Representative for the least developed countries, landlocked developing countries and small island developing states.* https://www.un.org/ohrlls/content/list-sids

UN & WB. (2017). *The potential of the blue economy – increasing long-term benefits of the sustainable use of marine resources for SIDS and coastal least developed countries.* United Nations/World Bank Group.

22

MARITIME SECURITY AND THE BLUE ECONOMY

Anja Menzel

Ocean-based resources and services are crucial to the global economy. More than 80% of the world trade volume is carried by sea, and it is estimated that 60 million people worldwide are employed in the primary sector of fisheries and aquaculture, most of them in small-scale fisheries in developing countries (FAO, 2020a, pp. 36–37). With a conservatively estimated annual economic value of US$2.5 trillion (UNEP, 2020), it becomes clear that the oceans economy is not only a substantial contribution to human livelihoods, but also offers promising business opportunities. Indeed, the oceans are increasingly coined "the new frontiers for economic development" (Gamage, 2016). Alongside established ocean industries, the trend of expansion and acceleration of human activity in and around the oceans is fuelled by emerging activities such as offshore renewable energy, deep seabed mining and marine biotechnology, which are expected to bring new growth, jobs and greater diversity to the oceans economy (EIU, 2015, p. 5). However, rapid unsustainable growth can lead to environmental risks and an erosion of the oceans' natural capital, resulting in threats to economic markets and human security (UNEP, 2020).

Alongside growing awareness for the potential damage of the ocean ecosystems through excessive economic activities, the "Blue Economy" is emerging as a relatively new and popular concept to describe a sustainable use of the oceans. The concept is heavily promoted by international organisations such as the United Nations (UN) and the World Bank, as well as regional powers like the European Union (EU). Due to its connection to human development and security, the concept of the Blue Economy also gathers the growing attention of academics and practitioners working in the realm of maritime security. In fact, the Blue Economy and the maritime security agendas are deeply intertwined. To disentangle the relationship, this chapter introduces different understandings of the concept of the Blue Economy, scrutinises maritime security and the Blue Economy as mutual enablers, examines existing national, regional and international Blue Economy strategies, and critically discusses the potential of the Blue Economy agenda for securing the maritime domain.

The Blue Economy

The term "Blue Economy" is often used interchangeably with the term "oceans economy", but has to be conceptually distinguished. Ocean economy focuses on any "portion of the economy

DOI: 10.4324/9781003001324-25

265

which relies on the ocean as an input to the production process or which, by virtue of geographic location, takes place on or under the ocean" (Kildow & McIlgorm, 2010, p. 368). The Economist Intelligence Unit broadly differentiates between four types of ocean economy activities and their corresponding sectors: the harvesting of living resources (fishing, aquaculture, marine biotechnology), the extraction of non-living resources (seabed mining, oil and gas, renewable energies), commerce and trade (shipping, port infrastructure, tourism) and the response to ocean health challenges (monitoring and surveillance, coastal protection, waste disposal) (EIU, 2015, p. 6). By way of contrast, it is widely agreed on that the Blue Economy describes an *appropriate* economic use of the oceans (Voyer et al., 2018a, p. 599). As such, the Blue Economy is synonymous to a *sustainable* ocean economy, meaning the economic activity is in balance with the long-term capacity of ocean ecosystems to support this activity and remain resilient and healthy (EIU, 2015, p. 7).

The term "Blue Economy" first gained widespread attention as a concept within environment and development politics after the 2012 UN Conference on Sustainable Development in Rio de Janeiro (UN Environment Programme, 2012). Similarly to the concept of the green economy, the UN Blue Economy Concept Paper from 2014 describes Blue Economy as an ocean economy that aims at the improvement of "human well-being and social equity, while significantly reducing environmental risks and ecological scarcities", and specifically highlights the role of coastal and island developing countries in these tasks (United Nations, 2014). Likewise, the World Bank defines the Blue Economy as a concept that "seeks to promote economic growth, social inclusion, and the preservation or improvement of livelihoods while at the same time ensuring environmental sustainability of the oceans and coastal areas" (World Bank, 2017, p. iv).

Despite these relatively specific notions, the Blue Economy perfectly encapsulates what Bueger (2015) calls an international "buzzword" that draws attention to a new challenge: the ambiguous umbrella term allows diverse actors to coordinate their efforts, but at the same time the buzzword also generates endless and irresolvable disagreements about what it might mean in practice (Bueger, 2015, p. 160). Indeed, the concept of the Blue Economy is being engrossed by a variety of actors with often competing agendas and objectives (Silver et al., 2015), and depending on the lens that is being applied, the tools deployed and the sectors included into the Blue Economy differ considerably. The main line can broadly be drawn between a discourse that promotes the "protection of ocean resources" and discourses that put emphasis on "development and growth" (Lee et al., 2020).

Different Perspectives on the Blue Economy

The protection perspective entails the understanding of the "oceans as natural resources". Advocates of this perspective argue that the assets of intact marine environments, such as the climate-regulating functions of coastal ecosystems ("blue carbon"), should be better accounted for (Silver et al., 2015, p. 143). The main objective of this notion of the Blue Economy is thus the protection and restoration of marine habitats, which is often deployed by nongovernmental organisations (NGOs) and conservation agencies calling for recognition of the economic benefits of environmental protection such as eco-tourism and the creation of Marine Protected Areas (Voyer et al., 2018a, p. 606).

The development perspective is characterised by the understanding of the "oceans as livelihoods". Often championed by development agencies and Small Island Developing States (SIDS), the focus lies on poverty alleviation and food security, especially provided by food-producing sectors such as small-scale fisheries and aquaculture, but also tourism (Voyer et al., 2018a, p. 605).

These efforts are being increasingly viewed within the context of the UN Sustainable Development Goals (SDGs) (Lee et al., 2020). Particularly SDG 14 ("Life Below Water") places the oceans more centrally on the development agenda and aims at helping small-scale fisheries, ending overfishing and illegal fishing practices, and increasing economic benefits to small island states (Roberts & Ali, 2016, pp. 13–14). From this perspective, the Blue Economy may also play an important part in addressing other SDGs such as "No Poverty" or "Zero Hunger".

Finally, the growth perspective understands the "oceans as good business". This perspective is mostly applied by the industry and large global economies such as the United States (US), the EU, and China, with the main goal of creating economic growth and employment opportunities through the Blue Economy. To this end, multinational, high-value sectors like oil and gas, high-scale fisheries and shipping are pivotal. The idea of the oceans as drivers of innovation also comes into play here: New and emerging industries, such as marine biotechnology, renewable energies, ocean observing technologies and potentially deep seabed mining can also contribute to the Blue Economy (Cogan, 2018, p. 48). Innovation, investment and partnerships between the public and private sector are seen as key drivers of this so-called "Blue Growth" (Voyer et al., 2018a, p. 606).

Conflict and Communalities between Perspectives

The variety of perspectives on the Blue Economy concept means that there is potential for conflict, as different interpretations put emphasis on certain actors and sectors, while excluding others. Industries that can potentially harm the environment, such as the carbon intensive oil and gas industries or deep seabed mining, are good examples for inherent conflict potential. Advocates of the protection perspective would reject an inclusion of these industries into the Blue Economy as "bluewashing" and instead support the expansion of renewable energies, whereas advocates of the growth perspective would argue that it is important to include all sectors to be able to account for both the economic benefits and the environmental externalities of these industries (Voyer et al., 2018a, p. 611). Some observers argue that there has been a shift in priorities over time, and that the Blue Economy has developed from a concept that originally implied socially equitable and sustainable development to an agenda increasingly seeking to encapsulate international interest in the growth of ocean-based economic development (Bennett et al., 2019, p. 991). However, all perspectives share the notion that it is important to quantify the value of the natural capital provided by the oceans, and that the Blue Economy is characterised by a *sustainable* use of ocean resources – the question up to interpretation is whether this sustainability is considered to be mainly of social, environmental or economic nature.

Maritime Security and the Blue Economy

It is exactly this question that also determines which dimensions of maritime security are in focus when scrutinising the interconnections between the Blue Economy and maritime security. As maritime security contributes to the conduct of the Blue Economy and the Blue Economy at the same time requires a certain degree of maritime security, different and inconsistent understandings of the Blue Economy matter for the maritime security agenda. This section explores the linkages between maritime security and the Blue Economy agendas in detail, and discusses implications of the interconnections for maritime security governance. In doing so, it refers to the concept of "maritime security" put forward by Bueger, which spans between the dimensions of marine environment, economic development, national security and human security (Bueger, 2015, p. 161).

Maritime Security as an Enabler of the Blue Economy

Insecurities in the maritime domain threaten the potential of the Blue Economy. One of the most significant threats to blue growth is Illegal, Unregulated and Unreported (IUU) fishing. Fishery crimes undermine national and regional efforts to manage fisheries resources sustainably, and also hamper the conservation of marine biodiversity (FAO, 2020b). Economically, the costs of IUU fishing cannot easily be quantified, while recent data is lacking. An older, but influential study estimates the yearly economic damage between US$10 and US$23.5 billion (Agnew et al., 2009). As there is a correlation between weak indicators of governance in coastal states and IUU fishing, particularly small-scale fisheries in low-income countries are disrupted by fishery crimes, and work and food security may be impacted (Le Manach et al., 2012). Maritime security actors can therefore contribute to strengthening fisheries governance by monitoring, controlling and surveilling (Rosello, 2020, p. 44), as well as enforcing relevant laws and regulations on IUU fishing (Voyer et al., 2018b, p. 37).

Furthermore, crimes like piracy, terrorism and smuggling put maritime commerce and trade around the world at risk. The most striking example is probably the threat piracy poses to chokepoints such as the Strait of Malacca and the Gulf of Aden. In the former case, a spike in piracy attacks in 2005 prompted the global insurance company Lloyd's to list the Strait of Malacca as a "war-risk-zone", and in the latter case, rampant piracy off the coast of Somalia since 2011, often including hijackings of crew, caused major disruptions for the shipping industry (Bensassi & Martínez-Zarzoso, 2012). Due to the concomitant rise in insurance rates, cargo vessels, fishing boats and cruise ships were redirected, creating massive costs for the global shipping industry. However, both cases show how coordinated efforts by maritime security actors help to limit the impacts of piracy attacks on maritime trade. In the Strait of Malacca, the patrols of littoral states contain piracy attacks on an acceptable level, and off the coast of Somalia, a coalition of navies, coastguards, international organisations and private maritime security personnel succeeded in oppressing piracy almost entirely (Bueger & Edmunds, 2017).

Maritime security also matters for the protection and management of ecosystems pivotal to the Blue Economy. First, this applies to the combat of environmental crimes such as the dumping of hazardous materials at sea and the enforcement of respective laws and regulations. Second, this also entails the need for maritime security agencies to prevent and respond to natural or human induced disasters at sea (Voyer et al., 2018b, p. 40). The important role of security operations in maritime disaster response and prevention was recently underlined by the 2020 oil spill off the coast of Mauritius. As national agencies were insufficiently prepared, a disaster unfolded that is threatening the region's vulnerable ecosystem, local fisheries and the country's profitable tourist sector (Bueger, 2020). Additionally, maritime security agencies such as navies can themselves pose a threat to marine ecosystems, e.g., through the disposal of waste or sonar activities, and there is increasing recognition that an active management of the environmental impact of these actions is required (Voyer et al., 2018b, p. 42). Thus, maritime security actors perform many functions that help safeguarding the health of the natural assets that form the basis of the Blue Economy.

Finally, the Blue Economy is put at risk by maritime insecurities such as inter-state disputes and unresolved maritime borders which can negatively impact the extraction of non-living and living marine resources. Here, blue management and growth requires clear articulation and resolution of jurisdictional questions (Voyer et al., 2018b, pp. 34–36). Prominent examples where an overlap of maritime claims hampers economic extraction include disputes over the delimitation of the continental shelf in the Arctic (Nordquist et al., 2016), and the securitisation of fisheries in the South China Sea following heavy Chinese engagement in the region (Zhang & Bateman, 2017).

The added value of border dispute resolution for blue growth can be observed in the Bay of Benghal, where littoral countries such as Bangladesh now have the opportunity of expanding offshore fisheries in previously sparsely exploited areas after settling maritime boundaries with India and Myanmar (Hussain et al., 2018).

The Blue Economy as an Enabler of Maritime Security

The connection between the maritime security and the Blue Economy agendas goes both ways: Not only does the Blue Economy need maritime security to provide a secure environment for economic development to occur; maritime security relies on a stable Blue Economy, too. If the Blue Economy cannot provide coastal populations with sufficient opportunities to support their livelihoods or even increases poverty by causing environmental degradation, there is a high risk that marginalised peoples turn to illicit maritime activities as alternative sources of employment (Bueger, 2017, p. 118). Indeed, the causal mechanism between fisheries scarcity and conflicts (Pomeroy et al., 2016), and overfishing and piracy (Biziouras, 2013; Denton & Harris, 2021) is well-documented.

To prevent maritime insecurities, an important task of the Blue Economy agenda is to ensure that the revenues of economic activities are not monopolised by transnational elites, but that coastal communities, particularly in less developed countries, profit directly from conducting business with the oceans. As sustainable economic growth, responsible fisheries management, and the protection of fragile ecosystems contribute to preventing economic grievances that may drive individuals into criminal activities in the maritime domain, the Blue Economy agenda has the potential to secure or improve the livelihoods of coastal populations by creating jobs in fisheries, tourism or renewable energies (Menzel & Otto, 2020, p. 234).

Maritime Security as a Part of the Blue Economy

Lastly, the connection between the maritime security and Blue Economy agendas goes beyond a mutually enabling relationship. An important, but often overlooked, connection is that maritime security is a sector within the Blue Economy, and thus itself a source of economic development and growth in the maritime domain. Along with a proliferation of the Blue Economy agenda comes an increasing demand for maritime security services offered by navies, coastguards and private security agencies, such as the policing of maritime crimes, monitoring and surveillance, and search and rescue operations (Voyer et al., 2018b, p. 44). For instance, the expansion of maritime trade triggers significant investments in port and shipping infrastructures, accompanied by an increased demand for private maritime security personnel to guard important shipping routes (Cullen & Berube, 2012), while maritime crimes such as piracy also spur the need for the development of new surveillance and information sharing technologies, as well as training and capacity-building activities (Bueger et al., 2020).

Overall, the maritime security and Blue Economy agendas are deeply intertwined and mutually enable each other. In fact, it has become clear that the co-dependence cuts across all four dimensions of maritime security proposed by Bueger (2015, p. 161): national security, the marine environment, economic development and human security are equally linked to the Blue Economy agenda. At its intersections, the maritime security and Blue Economy agendas therefore have the same goal – to provide a stable environment for sustainable development and economic growth, thus reinforcing maritime safety and security. How is this mutual co-dependency reflected in current Blue Economy strategies and policies?

Anja Menzel

International, Regional and National Blue Economy Strategies

Against the backdrop of the mutual co-dependency between maritime security and the Blue Economy agendas, policymakers on the international, regional and national level increasingly focus on blue growth strategies. This section introduces programmes and policies of selected states and organisations, and scrutinises the way they relate to the maritime security agenda.

International Blue Economy Initiatives

On the international level, the United Nations play the key role in setting the framework for a global Blue Economy agenda. The UN's agenda setting function is particularly obvious in the 2016 SDGs, in which SDG 14 ("Life Below Water") highlights the importance of sustainable ocean development and acts as a reference point for many subsequent Blue Economy initiatives (Lee et al., 2020). In the same vein, the establishment of the UN Ocean Conference series in 2017, the declaration of the 2021–2030 UN Decade of Ocean Science for Sustainable Development, and the influential 2017 report "The potential of the Blue Economy", which lays out the benefits of a sustainable use of marine resources for SIDS and coastal least developed countries, all bear witness of the range of attention the UN create for the Blue Economy agenda. UN sub-agencies such as the UN Environment Programme (UNEP), which hosts the Sustainable Blue Economy Finance Principles, or the UN Food and Agriculture Organization (FAO), through its Blue Growth Initiative, play an important role in implementing the UN's Blue Economy agenda.

As the leading international actor in the field of development financing and the Blue Economy, the World Bank (WB) wants to globally end extreme poverty and increase the income and welfare of the poor. The key focus of the WB's Blue Economy strategy thus lies on food security through sustainable fisheries management. As of 2020, the WB has an active Blue Economy portfolio around US$5 billion, with the prospects of a further US$1.65 billion replenishment (World Bank, 2020). With PROBLUE, an umbrella multi-donor trust fund aimed at managing fisheries and aquaculture, reducing marine pollution, developing oceanic sectors such as tourism and shipping, and capacity-building for governments, the WB supports the implementation of SDG 14. This also includes the Global Program on Fisheries (PROFISH), which heavily endorses investment in sustainable aquaculture to increase food security in developing countries.

Another notable international initiative is the High-Level Panel for a Sustainable Ocean Economy (Ocean Panel) that was established in 2018. Its unique structure is made up of serving heads of states and governments from Australia, Canada, Chile, Fiji, Ghana, Indonesia, Jamaica, Japan, Kenya, Mexico, Namibia, Norway, Palau and Portugal, supported by the UN Secretary-General's Special Envoy for the Ocean. The Ocean Panel works with governments, businesses, the science community and civil society to develop an action agenda for transitioning to a sustainable ocean economy and relies on the expertise of an interdisciplinary group of scientists to inform its agenda (World Resources Institute, 2020). The topics covered by the Ocean Panel broadly range from ocean finance, fisheries crime, energy, biodiversity and climate change to the role of data and technology for a sustainable Blue Economy. As the initiative is relatively new, the Ocean Panel constitutes a policy window to draw attention to the Blue Economy agenda, but its policy outcomes remain to be seen (Bennett et al., 2019, p. 993).

Generally, Blue Economy strategies and initiatives on the international level centre considerably around the role of ocean health for sustainable economic development. A nexus between the Blue Economy and maritime security is often implied, but seldom addressed explicitly. When security aspects are in focus, attention is predominantly paid to human security, meaning the protection of livelihoods and food security, particularly in developing countries.

Regional Blue Economy Initiatives

The Blue Economy concept is also increasingly invoked by regional organisations. In 2012, the EU published its so-called "Blue Growth" strategy, in which it considers the maritime domain to be an important factor for innovative economic growth (European Commission, 2012). In its definition of the Blue Economy, the EU aims at establishing a new type of economic sector by highlighting how different industries engaged with the oceans are interdependent, and due to this very reason, hold significant potential for economic growth (Bueger, 2021, p. 7). In homogenising blue industries, the EU's focus does not lie on sustainability nor maritime security, but instead on developing a strategy for economic growth and the mobilisation of market forces alone. More recent strategic EU documents support this assessment. Even though the EU's fisheries and maritime policies narrative repeatedly emphasises the importance of sustainability, economic growth remains the main and principal driver of its Blue Economy strategy (Hadjimichael, 2018, p. 163), and maritime security concerns are merely mentioned with regard to IUU fishing in the Mediterranean Sea and the role of coastguards and navies in the protection of the EU's maritime borders (European Commission, 2017, pp. 25–26).

The African continent particularly champions the potential of the Blue Economy for development. In 2014, the African Union (AU) adopted its influential "African Integrated Maritime Strategy" (AIM Strategy), which provides a broad framework for the protection and sustainable exploitation of the African maritime domain for wealth creation. Although the strategy clearly aims at economic development, interestingly the document does not provide a definition of the Blue Economy, but only lists a range of different sectors contributing to it. Instead, the AIM Strategy emphasises how the Blue Economy is understood as a security concern: The document calls for the Blue Economy to be "secured", and draws attention to a broad array of potential security threats that could inflict widespread economic harm to African states (African Union, 2014, p. 10). The 2016 follow-up "African Charter on Maritime Security and Safety and Development in Africa", also coined "Lomé Charter", provides a legally binding, albeit rather general, definition of the "Blue/Ocean Economy" (African Union, 2016, p. 7). The Charter is outstanding in the way it clearly links the prospects of utilising marine spaces and resources as the key driver for social and economic development to maritime security and safety (Egede, 2017). As such, the African Blue Economy concept rests mainly on the notion of "security" (Childs & Hicks, 2019).

As the Indian Ocean Rim Association (IORA)'s 22 member states are all Indian Ocean littorals, it is not surprising that the Blue Economy is one of the so-called IORA "focus areas", and that the IORA members are keen on placing emphasis on the potential of mutual cooperation for blue growth (Doyle, 2018). With the 2015 Mauritius and the 2017 Jakarta Declarations on Blue Economy, the IORA member states recognise the importance of sustainability when developing their Blue Economy sectors, particularly for their coastal communities. In the documents, maritime security is in focus with regard to preventing fisheries crimes and safeguarding food (IORA, 2017). Other world regions, in contrast, do not have comparably comprehensive strategies. The Americas lack a high-level coordinated approach, as does the Association of Southeast Asian Nations (ASEAN), despite the region having considerable potential in developing its Blue Economy (Gamage, 2016).

Overall, regional organisations set different priorities in their Blue Economy strategies. While the EU does not address the role of maritime security for blue growth explicitly, the AU's Blue Economy strategy stands out in that it strongly emphasises the link between sustainable economic development and maritime security.

National Blue Economy Initiatives

The Blue Economy concept is also increasingly put into practice by national governments. In this regard, China's Maritime Silk Road (MSR) is considered the most striking blue growth strategy with widespread global implications. The MSR is a major component of the Chinese "Belt and Road Initiative" and aims at expanding and upgrading maritime trade routes of the South China Sea, the Indian Ocean and the Mediterranean to foster seaborne trade between China and Southeast Asia, Europe and, particularly, Africa. The MSR does not only encompass the development of hard infrastructure, such as upgrading key ports along the route and on-site investment in the shipping, construction and energy sectors, but also the removal of trade barriers through trade agreements renegotiations and the conclusion of bilateral investment treaties (Blanchard & Flint, 2017, p. 227). Observers note that China's vigorous activities to sustain and boost its blue economic growth are motivated by larger geo-strategic motivations and have economic and political implications beyond China's Blue Economy (Funaiole & Hillman, 2018). In this larger context, China does not focus on maritime security, but on reshaping international trade in its national economic interests.

Other countries with a pronounced interest in their national Blue Economy development include, among others, India, Australia and South Africa (Potgieter, 2018). However, the countries pushing forward their Blue Economy agendas most are SIDS such as Seychelles or Maldives. Early on, many SIDS recognised the potential of their large ocean jurisdictions and the importance of ocean industries to their national economies and enthusiastically embraced the concept of the Blue Economy (Silver et al., 2015). Reframing their place in the global economy as "large ocean states" instead of small island states, the Blue Economy has provided them a greater role at the international negotiating table and has repositioned SIDS as areas of economic opportunity (Voyer et al., 2018a, p. 598). The case of Seychelles as a successful campaigner for the Blue Economy is particularly remarkable, as the Blue Economy became the central guide for the national policy of the island state, and Seychelles is now widely recognised as an innovator in ocean governance (Bueger & Wivel, 2018, p. 171). In its understanding of the Blue Economy, Seychelles promotes a concept concerned with economic growth, environmental sustainability and social equity (Michel, 2016; Schutter & Hicks, 2019) and pays less attention to maritime security matters.

In summary, the different objectives of the introduced initiatives and policies have underlined that many diverging perspectives on concept of the Blue Economy exist. As a consequence, the attention paid towards the nexus between maritime security and the Blue Economy in international, regional, and national strategies also differs. What does this empirical variety mean for maritime security governance?

Potential and Limits of the Blue Economy Agenda for Maritime Security Governance

While it is undeniable that maritime security and the Blue Economy are mutual enablers, there are limits to the potential of the Blue Economy agenda for securing the maritime domain. First, the lack of coherence between perspectives on the Blue Economy is likely to have negative

Maritime Security and the Blue Economy

implications for maritime security governance. Critics note that the "oceans as good business" perspective, as championed by the EU and many national blue growth initiatives, frames the oceans too positively as spaces of opportunity, and that despite the alleged focus on sustainability, substantial risks can arise both for people and the environment if the focus on economic profits is too narrow (Hadjimichael, 2018). It is criticised that multinational corporations and investors often one-sidedly utilise the concept to gain control over ocean resources (Barbesgaard, 2018), leading to exclusionary decision-making processes, spurring social injustice and economically discriminating against coastal communities such as small-scale fishers and indigenous peoples (Bennett et al., 2020a). These issues directly affect maritime security, as marginalised people are more likely to turn to illicit activities to support themselves. To reconcile between perspectives, it is important to acknowledge that different uses of ocean space have environmental and social implications, and to create inclusive governance tools to ensure that coastal populations directly benefit from the Blue Economy.

Second, observers demand that Blue Economy policies should integrate maritime security considerations in a holistic manner (Bueger, 2017, p. 2), but the review of Blue Economy strategies conducted above has revealed that maritime security considerations are often fragmented and not adequately represented in relevant policy documents. Where they are taken into consideration (e.g., in the rather ambitious African context), stakeholder resources and expertise are regularly lacking, and therefore coordination between the variety of agencies involved as well as effective implementation on the national level prove to be problematic (Walker, 2017). Appropriate law enforcement structures, regional cooperation and capacity-building are therefore essential for securing the Blue Economy agenda, particularly to make it less vulnerable against externalities. Evidently, the main foreseeable game changer is climate change and its ramifications for ocean and human well-being, which greatly impact the conduct of the Blue Economy. However, the recent oil spill off the coast of Mauritius or the economic damage to fisheries and shipping due to the COVID-19 pandemic have also underlined how the Blue Economy can be negatively affected by external shocks (Bennett et al., 2020b), and how this effect can be reinforced if overarching security considerations are lacking.

In conclusion, both the Blue Economy and the maritime security agendas are multifaceted, but they rely on each other to thrive. It is thus essential to not understand the two in isolation, but to conceive the oceans as an integrated space in need of coordination and cooperation between diverse security and economy agents to realise the full potential of a sustainable Blue Economy for maritime security governance.

References

African Union. (2014). *2050 Africa's integrated maritime strategy*. African Union.

African Union. (2016). *African charter on maritime security and safety and development in Africa (Lomé Charter)*. African Union.

Agnew, D. J., Pearce, J., Pramod, G., Peatman, T., Watson, R., Beddington, J. R., & Pitcher, T. J. (2009). Estimating the worldwide extent of illegal fishing. *PLoS One, 4*(2), e4570. 10.1371/journal.pone.0004570

Barbesgaard, M. (2018). Blue growth: Savior or ocean grabbing? *The Journal of Peasant Studies, 45*(1), 130–149. 10.1080/03066150.2017.1377186

Bennett, N. J., Cisneros-Montemayor, A. M., Blythe, J., Silver, J. J., Singh, G., Andrews, N., Calò, A., Christie, P., Di Franco, A., Finkbeiner, E. M., Gelcich, S., Guidetti, P., Harper, S., Hotte, N., Kittinger, J. N., Le Billon, P., Lister, J., López de la Lama, R., McKinley, E., Scholtens, J., Solås, A., Sowman, M., Talloni-Álvarez, N., Teh, L. C. L., Voyer, M., & Sumaila, U. R. (2019). Towards a sustainable and equitable blue economy. *Nature Sustainability, 2*, 991–993. 10.1038/s41893-019-0404-1

Bennett, N. J., Blythe, J., White, C., & Campero, C. (2020a). Blue growth and blue justice. *Working Paper 02*(2020). University of British Columbia: Institute for the Oceans and Fisheries.

Bennett, N. J., Finkbeiner, E. M., Ban, N. C., Belhabib, D., Jupiter, S. D., Kittinger, J. N., Mangubhai, S., Scholtens, J., Gill, D., & Christie, P. (2020b). The COVID-19 pandemic, small-scale fisheries and coastal fishing communities. *Coastal Management, 48*(4), 336–347. 10.1080/08920753.2020.1766937

Bensassi, S., & Martínez-Zarzoso, I. (2012). How costly is modern maritime piracy to the international community? *Review of International Economics, 20*(5), 869–883. 10.1111/roie.12000

Biziouras, N. (2013). Piracy, state capacity and root causes: Lessons from the Somali experience and policy choice in the Gulf of Guinea. *African Security Review, 22*(3), 111–122. 10.1080/10246029.2013.790318

Blanchard, J.-M. F., & Flint C. (2017). The geopolitics of China's Maritime Silk Road Initiative. *Geopolitics, 22*(2), 223–245. 10.1080/14650045.2017.1291503

Bueger, C. (2015). What is maritime security? *Marine Policy, 53*, 159–164. 10.1016/j.marpol.2014.12.005

Bueger, C. (2017). "We are all islanders now" – Michel's blue economy kaleidoscope and the missing link to maritime security. *Journal of the Indian Ocean Region, 14*(1), 117–119. 10.1080/19480881.2017.1317500

Bueger, C. (2020, August 12). The Mauritius disaster: Overlooked dimensions of maritime security. *The Diplomat*. https://thediplomat.com/2020/08/the-mauritius-disaster-overlooked-dimensions-of-maritime-security/

Bueger, C. (2021). Concepts in practice: The case of the "Blue Economy". In P. Ish-Shalom (Ed.), *Concepts at work: On the linguistic infrastructure of world politics*. Michigan University Press. https://www.academia.edu/30005888/Concepts_in_practice_The_case_of_the_Blue_Economy

Bueger, C., & Edmunds, T. (2017). Beyond seablindness: A new agenda for maritime security studies. *International Affairs, 93*(6), 1293–1311. 10.1093/ia/iix174

Bueger, C., Edmunds, T., & McCabe, R. (2020). Into the sea: Capacity-building innovations and the maritime security challenge. *Third World Quarterly, 41*(2), 228–246. 10.1080/01436597.2019.1660632

Bueger, C., & Wivel, A. (2018). How do small island states maximize influence? Creole diplomacy and the smart state foreign policy of the Seychelles. *Journal of the Indian Ocean Region, 14*(2), 170–188. 10.1080/19480881.2018.1471122

Childs, J. R., & Hicks, C. C. (2019). Securing the blue: Political ecologies of the blue economy in Africa. *Journal of Political Ecology, 26*(1), 323–340. 10.2458/v26i1.23162

Cogan, C. S. (2018). The Blue Economy. Theory and strategy. In V. N. Attri & N. Bohler-Muller (Eds.), *The blue economy handbook of the Indian Ocean Region* (pp. 38–63). Africa Institute of South Africa.

Cullen, P., & Berube, C. (Eds.). (2012). *Maritime private security: Market responses to piracy, terrorism and waterborne security risks in the 21st century*. Routledge.

Denton, G. L., & Harris, J. R. (2021). The impact of illegal fishing on maritime piracy: Evidence from West Africa. *Studies in Conflict & Terrorism, 44*(11), 938–957. 10.1080/1057610X.2019.1594660.

Doyle, T. (2018). Blue economy and the Indian Ocean rim. *Journal of the Indian Ocean Region, 14*(1), 1–6. 10.1080/19480881.2018.1421450

Egede, E. (2017, 16 July). Africa's Lomé Charter on maritime security: What are the next steps? *Piracy Studies.org*. http://piracy-studies.org/africas-lome-charter-on-maritime-security-what-are-the-next-steps/

EIU. (2015). The blue economy. Growth, opportunity and a sustainable ocean economy. https://eiuperspectives.economist.com/sites/default/files/images/Blue%20Economy_briefing%20paper_WOS2015.pdf

European Commission. (2012). Blue Growth. Opportunities for marine and maritime sustainable growth. *Communication from the Commission to the European Parliament, the Council, the European Economic and Social Committee and the Committee of the Regions*. COM(2012) 494. Publications Office of the European Union.

European Commission. (2017). Report on the Blue Growth Strategy. Towards more sustainable growth and jobs in the blue economy. *Commission Staff Working Document*. SWD(2017) 128.

FAO. (2020a). *The State of World Fisheries and Aquaculture 2020. Sustainability in action*. FAO.

FAO. (2020b). *Illegal, unreported and unregulated (IUU) fishing*. http://www.fao.org/iuu-fishing/en/

Funaiole, M., & Hillman, J. (2018). China's Maritime Silk Road Initiative. *CSIS Brief*. http://csis-website-prod.s3.amazonaws.com/s3fs-public/publication/180717_FunaioleHillman_ChinaMaritimeSilkRoad.pdf

Gamage, R. N. (2016). Blue economy in Southeast Asia: Oceans as the new frontier of economic development. *Maritime Affairs: Journal of the National Maritime Foundation of India, 12*(2), 1–15. 10.1080/09733159.2016.1244361

Hadjimichael, M. (2018). A call for a blue degrowth: Unravelling the European Union's fisheries and maritime policies. *Marine Policy, 94*, 158–164. 10.1016/j.marpol.2018.05.007

Hussain, M. G., Failler, P., Karim, A. A., & Alam, M. K. (2018). Major opportunities of blue economy development in Bangladesh. *Journal of the Indian Ocean Region*, *14*(1), 88–99. 10.1080/19480881.2017.1368250

IORA. (2017). *Declaration of the Indian Ocean Rim Association on the Blue Economy in the Indian Ocean Region*. Indian Ocean Rim Association (IORA).

Kildow, J. T., & McIlgorm, A. (2010). The importance of estimating the contribution of the oceans to national economies. *Marine Policy*, *34*(3), 367–374. 10.1016/j.marpol.2009.08.006

Le Manach, F., Gough, C., Harris, A., Humber, F., Harper, S., & Zeller, D. (2012). Unreported fishing, hungry people and political turmoil: The recipe for a food security crisis in Madagascar? *Marine Policy*, *36*(1), 218–225. 10.1016/j.marpol.2011.05.007

Lee, K. H., Noh, J., & Khim, J. S. (2020). The Blue Economy and the United Nations' sustainable development goals: Challenges and opportunities. *Environment International*, *137*(105528). 10.1016/j.envint.2020.105528

Menzel, A., & Otto, L. (2020). Connecting the dots: Implications of the intertwined global challenges to maritime security. In L. Otto (Ed.), *Global challenges in maritime security* (pp. 229–243). Springer.

Michel, J. A. (2016). *Rethinking the oceans: Towards the blue economy*. Paragon House.

Nordquist, M. H., Moore, J. N., & Long, R. (Eds.). (2016). *Challenges of the changing Arctic: Continental shelf, navigation, and fisheries*. Brill.

Pomeroy, R., Parks, J., Mrakovcich, K. L., & LaMonica, C. (2016). Drivers and impacts of fisheries scarcity, competition, and conflict on maritime security. *Marine Policy*, *67*, 94–104. 10.1016/j.marpol.2016.01.005

Potgieter, T. (2018). Oceans economy, blue economy, and security: Notes on the South African potential and developments. *Journal of the Indian Ocean Region*, *14*(1), 49–70.

Roberts, J. P., & Ali, A. (2016). The blue economy and small states. *Commonwealth Blue Economy Series 1*. http://www.cpahq.org/cpahq/Cpadocs/The%20Blue%20Economy%20and%20Small%20States.pdf

Rosello, M. (2020). Illegal, unreported and unregulated (IUU) fishing as a maritime security concern. In L. Otto (Ed.), *Global challenges in maritime security* (pp. 33–47). Springer. 10.1007/978-3-030-34630-0_3

Schutter, M. S., & Hicks, C. C. (2019). Networking the blue economy in Seychelles: pioneers, resistance, and the power of influence. *Journal of Political Ecology*, *26*(1), 425–447. 10.2458/v26i1.23102

Silver, J. J., Gray, N. J., Campbell, L. M., Fairbanks, L. W., & Gruby, R. L. (2015). Blue economy and competing discourses in international oceans governance. *The Journal of Environment & Development*, *24*(2), 135–160. 10.1177/1070496515580797

UN Environment Programme. (2012). A green economy in a blue world. Synthesis report. *UN Environment Programme*. https://www.undp.org/content/dam/undp/library/Environment%20and%20Energy/Water%20and%20Ocean%20Governance/green_economy_blue_world_synthesis_report.pdf

United Nations. (2014). *Blue economy concept paper*. https://sustainabledevelopment.un.org/content/documents/2978BEconcept.pdf

UNEP. (2020). Sustainable blue finance. *UN Environment Programme*. https://www.unepfi.org/blue-finance/

Voyer, M., Quirk, G., McIlgorm, A., & Azmi, K. (2018a). Shades of blue: What do competing interpretations of the blue economy mean for oceans governance? *Journal of Environmental Policy & Planning*, *20*(5), 595–616. 10.1080/1523908X.2018.1473153

Voyer, M., Schofield, C., Azmi, K., Warner, R., McIlgorm, A., & Quirk, G. (2018b). Maritime security and the blue economy: Intersections and interdependencies in the Indian Ocean. *Journal of the Indian Ocean Region*, *14*(1), 28–48. 10.1080/19480881.2018.1418155

Walker, T. (2017). Reviving the AU's maritime strategy. *ISS Policy Brief 96*. https://media.africaportal.org/documents/policybrief96.pdf

World Bank. (2017). The potential of the blue economy. Increasing long-term benefits of the sustainable use of marine resources for Small Island Developing States and Coastal Least Developed Countries. *World Bank*. https://openknowledge.worldbank.org/bitstream/handle/10986/26843/115545.pdf?sequence=1&isAllowed=y

World Bank. (2020). The World Bank's Blue Economy Program and PROBLUE: Supporting integrated and sustainable economic development in healthy oceans. *World Bank*. https://www.worldbank.org/en/topic/environment/brief/the-world-banks-blue-economy-program-and-problue-frequently-asked-questions

World Resources Institute. (2020). High level panel for sustainable ocean economy. World Resources Institute. https://oceanpanel.org/

Zhang, H., & Bateman, S. (2017). Fishing militia, the securitization of fishery and the South China Sea dispute. *Contemporary Southeast Asia*, *39*(2), 288–314.

23

SECURING MARITIME IDENTITIES: THE NEW PRACTICES OF MARITIME CULTURAL HERITAGE

Eliseu Carbonell

In summer 2020, in the midst of the COVID-19 pandemic, I was involuntarily involved in a conflict between owners of traditional vessels and the municipal authorities in the coastal town where I live. As in many small towns that do not have a port, the fishing boats used to be moored on the sand on the beach, on top of poles covered in grease that were used to slide the boats down to the water. Getting the boats into and out of the sea required a certain amount of skill, the execution of some old gestures, with backs pushing the boat towards the sea (Figure 23.1).

In this town of around 5,000 inhabitants, situated around 50 km from the city of Barcelona, there are no longer any fishermen. But there is an active group of people who restore and sail old lateen fishing boats and organise other activities on the town's fishing past, under the auspices of a cultural association for the conservation of maritime heritage. All these elements of tangible and intangible heritage are located on or close to the beach opposite the town centre, in front of the train station that connects this town with the city. Due to its easy access, this beach is frequented by a large number of bathers in the summer.

As a health measure to prevent infections, in summer 2020 the town hall prohibited the use of the traditional boats between 10 am and 6 pm. It was argued that the operation of launching and mooring the boats on the beach took up a space that the town hall wanted to keep clear so that bathers could keep a suitable distance from each other, in accordance with the health authorities' instructions. The owners of the boats protested because, in practice, this time restriction meant they could not sail. At the request of my friends in the cultural association and drawing on my experience as a researcher in maritime heritage, I tried to convince the local authorities, without success, that a traditional vessel is basically a boat that sails, that needs to be sailed. And that these vessels play an important role in local identity.

As we will see in this chapter, maritime heritage conservation has been popularised in recent years and no longer only concerns experts. New heritage practices are directly related to the domain of maritime security politics, for various reasons. First, through these practices, maritime sectors that are in crisis are reappraised. Examples are wooden boat building or small-scale fishing, which is defended because of its lower environmental impact. The consumption of local foods from the sea is revived, and these products are given a heritage value. The new

276   DOI: 10.4324/9781003001324-26

Figure 23.1 Beaching of a replica of a traditional fishing boat, April 2010 (Photo: author).

practices in maritime heritage point towards sustainable development and provide alternatives to the exclusive focus on sun and sea tourism, which has caused great imbalances. In addition, heritage plays a notable educational role. Through it, communities become aware of their maritime past. Cultural heritage promotes recognition and respect for cultural diversity. Finally, the new heritage practices make communities more resilient as, by taking an active part in the protection of maritime heritage, they become more confident in themselves, promote cooperation with other communities and contribute to developing a collective maritime identity.

The Institutionalisation of Maritime Heritage

Generally speaking, the protection of heritage began to be institutionalised internationally in the period between the two world wars, with the Athens Charter of 1931 that focused on the protection of artistic and archaeological heritage. Years later, in 1964, the Venice Charter was drawn up that was centred more on the conservation and restoration of buildings. However, it was not until the 1970s that the notion of heritage was expanded to other domains beyond monuments, to address the many and varied areas that it includes today, including that of maritime heritage (Peron, 2003). Maritime heritage is a relatively recent concept associated with the appearance of other types of heritage, such as industrial heritage, as in essence we are talking about artefacts and cultures of work over time. Apart from constructions (piers, fortresses, shipyards, lighthouses, tide mills, fishers' houses and fish markets, among others), maritime heritage can be divided into three areas: underwater heritage, floating heritage and intangible maritime cultural heritage (Alegret & Carbonell, 2015; for a detailed typology of maritime heritage see Menanteau, 2014). At the level of legislation and international protection, underwater heritage has received the most attention, while floating heritage has been protected more recently and the practice has not really been very effective. Finally, there is intangible maritime heritage that, although at a later stage, has benefitted from the interest aroused by the UNESCO "Convention for the Safeguarding of the Intangible Cultural Heritage" of 2003, which has been adhered to by governments and cultural institutions as well as civil society in many coastal areas of the planet.

The Athens Charter and the Venice Charter did not specifically mention maritime heritage and much less vessels. We would have to wait until 1982 with the approval of the "United Nations Convention on the Law of the Sea" (UNCLOS) to find a specific reference to this heritage: "States have the duty to protect objects of an archaeological and historical nature found at sea and shall cooperate for this purpose" (Article 303). Later on, international legal texts would appear that were focused on maritime heritage, basically to protect underwater heritage, such as the "European Convention on the Protection of the Archaeological Heritage" (Council of Europe, 1992), or the "Charter on the Protection and Management of Underwater Cultural Heritage" (ICOMOS, 1996). However, up to that point maritime heritage seemed to be limited to archaeological sites.

That is why, after the celebration in 2001 of the Fourth European Maritime Heritage Congress, it was decided to write the Barcelona Charter of 2002 or the "European Charter for the Conservation and Restoration of Traditional Ships in Operation". In the Barcelona Charter, the concept of "floating maritime heritage" was defined to encompass historical ships such as classic sailing boats, as well as more modest vessels associated with seafaring occupations that have gained cultural significance with the passage of time. One of the most notable aspects of this Charter is that it considers that traditional boats must be operational to survive. In other words, they can be used to sail. This implies their constant maintenance and the transmission of knowledge and skills needed for their conservation and use. In another paper (Carbonell, 2015), I presented the results of a survey administered to members of various maritime heritage associations. It emerged that the first condition to consider a boat a "traditional vessel" was precisely the fact that it could still be used to sail. That is, preservation in a dry dock or a museum was not considered sufficient guarantee of the conservation of floating heritage. This is fully aligned with the spirit of the UNESCO Convention for the Safeguarding of Intangible Cultural Heritage, which stresses the living conservation of aspects such as the knowledge, skills, language, beliefs and festivals of communities, and in our case maritime communities.

The Less Visible Faces of Maritime Heritage

The heritage of maritime communities is threatened today by factors such as urban pressure (Atkinson et al., 2002) and climate change (Harvey & Perry, 2015), which accelerate the degradation of elements exposed to environmental conditions that are in themselves unfavourable for the conservation of materials, whether they are wood, stone, ceramic, metal or others. Therefore, it is not surprising that UNESCO's "List of World Heritage in Danger" includes notable sites of maritime heritage, such as the port areas of Liverpool in the United Kingdom and that of Coro in Venezuela, impressive ceremonial centres such as Nam Madol in Micronesia or zones of exceptional ecological interest such as the East Rennell atoll in the Solomon Islands. However, beyond monuments, sites and natural environments, we can find a rich intangible maritime heritage that is not mentioned on this UNESCO list although it is equally at risk of disappearance and is of great importance to understand maritime cultures in their full dimension. Below we refer to some of these intangible faces of the complex reality that encompasses the concept of maritime heritage.

If the force of the sea is capable of eroding stone, what can it do to vessels and the people who sail in them? The relationship between humans and the sea is associated with exploration of the planet and the effort to connect distant places in the world that we live in. The liquid space between the port of origin and the port of destination was a dangerous barrier that had to be crossed as fast as possible (Cabantous & Buti, 2018). In Western imagination, the ocean that stood in the way of these two points of land was seen as an unknown, threatening space, the antithesis of the terrestrial space, a space of anti-humanity (Connery, 2006). Specialists in classical antiquity tell us that, faced with the possibility of a journey by sea, the people of the time felt the same fear that sick people may feel when faced with possible death (Romero, 2012). This fear seems to be justified if we consider the number of shipwrecks described by historians. For example, Alain Cabantous (2005) calculated that, in its two centuries of history, the Dutch East India Company lost almost 6% of its fleet in shipwrecks. According to UNESCO[1] estimations, there are around three million sunken ships in the world. If we look at more recent times, according to the International Labour Organization,[2] fishing is one of the most dangerous of all professions. In Denmark, in the 1990s, it was calculated that the fatality rate in fishing was 20–30 times higher than for jobs on land, and in the United States it was found that the fishing industry had a fatality rate 16 times higher than the professions of fire fighter or police officer.

Of course, people were scared of the sea. From this fear have arisen over time a series of supernatural beliefs, whether they are imaginary (sea gods, mermaids, giant serpents, kraken, leviathan or kappa, among others), magical prescriptions, taboos, rituals and narrations in the form of myths, popular tales and songs. This is a universal phenomenon and heritage. The renowned anthropologist Bronislaw Malinowski dedicated part of his book *Argonauts of Western Pacific* to the magic of the canoes and the flying witches that fed on the shipwrecked, in ethnographic descriptions that have fascinated anthropology students for a century. If we focus on the Western tradition, we can find, from the Bronze Age in the Aegean Sea, a great profusion of votive offerings of a seafaring nature that illustrate this fear of dying in the sea: miniature models of vessels, rigging of boats (anchors, oars, etc.) and ivory plaques reproducing maritime scenes. Through Cicero (*De natura deorum*, III, 37, 89), we even know of the existence of painted votive tablets offered to the gods by people who had survived a shipwreck (Figure 23.2).

This type of tablets was very common in the Christian world of the Baroque and a large number have survived decorating the walls of small, obscure chapels where they were carried by sailors who had survived accidents at sea. These polychrome tablets, known as "ex-voto", reproduce in the central part the situation that was experienced, which was often a storm on the high seas, some men overboard, a fire on a boat or a collision. At one end of the tablet, within a halo of light, is shown the apparition of the divine being that was invoked to save the life, often the saint or the virgin to whom the sanctuary is dedicated that is closest to the sailor's place of residence. Finally, in the bottom part, there is usually a brief description of the events. Ex-votos may also consist of an object from the saved ship, for example an oar or the ship's lantern, as well as a model of the same ship that hung from the roof of the chapel. Ex-votos show an attempt to make a pact with the great beyond, a negotiation in which the aim was to achieve salvation in exchange for keeping a promise made to the divinity. Apart from the artistic value of the polychrome tablets, this act of negotiation with the other side constitutes real intangible heritage as it informs us of the beliefs, fears and imagination of seafaring people.

However, the risks that sailors were exposed to cannot only be attributed to natural phenomena. Alain Cabantous (2005) reports that the violence of the natural elements was only a small part of the causes of maritime disasters. Contrary to what could be expected, most shipwrecks did not take place on the high seas in the midst of a storm, but close to the coast due

Figure 23.2 Ex-voto showing a shipwreck in front of Cabo Tiñoso (Spain) on the night of 24 February 1868. © Museu Marítim de Barcelona (641F).

to the poor measuring instruments and rough maps, at least until the end of the eighteenth century. They were often attributable to the fatigue of a long journey and all the hard work it entailed.

Regarding natural disasters, experts (Hastrup, 2011; Torry, 1972; Wisner et al., 2004) have shown that disasters cannot only be interpreted as natural accidents that would come to disturb the stability of a harmonic social order. To a certain extent, they represent the culmination of a system of social inequalities that are also expressed in levels of vulnerability to natural catastrophes (Hastrup, 2011, p. 5). Throughout history, fishers and seafarers have faced the sea with precarious technology, with very few safety systems on board and with a lack of port infrastructure for shelter that would provide a safe layover. The technology and infrastructure were not equal to the risks that sailors were exposed to and this made them more vulnerable to the fates of nature. The intangible heritage that has been transmitted by fishing communities talks of precisely this vulnerability.

We finish this section by referring to one of the most widespread oral traditions of intangible maritime heritage. This is a story told in the form of a legend in many places of the world over the centuries. It describes a sailor who, tired of his life of weariness, decided to set out inland to find a place where nobody recognised the oar he was carrying on his back, and to settle there to start a new life and forget the hardship experienced at sea. The first written reference to this story can be found, of course, in Homer's Odyssey. Book 9 mentions the offering of an oar to Poseidon when Tiresias invited Odysseus to carry an oar to the land that knows nothing of the sea. The story has been transmitted orally over time and space. This is demonstrated by the fact that, at the start of the twentieth century, various folklorists heard it from their informants in places as far apart as Greece, England or Catalonia. In 1905, the Catalan poet Jacint Verdaguer heard this story in his folklorist expeditions to the Pyrenees, specifically in a country house called "El Mariner" (The Sailor) in which a schooner can still be seen engraved over the lintel at the entrance, and where allegedly a sailor had settled after suffering a terrible shipwreck, following in the steps of Odysseus. He walked for several days towards the interior of the country carrying an oar, until, in response to his question of what the object was, an old man replied that it was a pole to move corn within a pot (Bosch i Rodoreda, 1992). William Hansen (2014) has compiled around 20 versions of this story in several countries. Although the profile of the main character and other details change, the essence of the principal elements of the story are maintained: fleeing from life at sea.

The strength and vitality of intangible maritime heritage could be seen in this story that William Hansen (2004) heard in 1975 told by a sailor of 35 years, who in turn had heard it during his service in the marines. The story is situated on the east coast of the USA where an old sailor from the US Navy decided to retire. He lifted an oar onto his shoulder and started walking. The people he bumped into asked him: "Where're you going with that oar over your shoulder?" but he paid no attention. He went through New Jersey, Ohio and Indiana and everybody asked the same question. Many days after starting his journey he reached Nebraska where he came across someone who said to him: "Hey, mister, what on earth are you carrying that piece of lumber over your shoulder for?" And it was there, where maritime culture had faded, that the old seaman would settle down.

The Fading of Maritime Cultures

Eric Hobsbawm (1995, p. 9) maintains that the most significant event in the twentieth century was the end of seven or eight millennia of history in which the immense majority of humanity subsisted on agriculture and livestock farming. Fishing, which is an older human activity as it dates back to the Upper Palaeolithic, clearly entered into a phase of crisis at the end of the twentieth century and global decline that affected above all the small-scale fishing sector (Crean & Symes, 1996; McGoodwin, 1990). Experts in small-scale fishing agree that the causes of this fishing crisis were the pollution of oceans caused by toxic waste and the massive urban coastal growth, as well as overexploitation of fishing resources due to technological development and expansion into new marine ecosystems (Freire & García-Allut, 2000; Pascual-Fernández et al., 2020).

In general terms, the global fishing fleet has grown continuously. Between 1950 and 2015, the number of fishing boats in the world doubled (Rousseau et al., 2019). However, in contrast, if we analyse specific areas of the Western world such as the European Union,[3] we can see that in recent decades the fishing fleet has diminished significantly. Between 2008 and 2019, the European fishing fleet dropped by 10,000 vessels, which represents a reduction of almost 12%. If we look at the data in more detail, the figures show that the small-scale fishing fleet, which is what provides work for most fishers in smaller boats, is by far the most affected by this reduction. For example, in Spain,[4] the number of employees in the fishing sector decreased between 2002 and 2020 by over a third.

A similar situation can be found in maritime transport. Globally the figures show constant growth, as maritime transport in the world has almost tripled in the last 40 years (UNCTAD, 2020). However, when we focus on specific regions of the West, we can see that small shipping along coastal routes, which was so important in the past and provided jobs for a large number of sailors, has declined considerably. For example, in Canada at the start of the twentieth century there were around a hundred schooners dedicated to shipping goods along the estuary of the Saint Lawrence River. They disappeared without trace when transport by road in lorries was developed in the 1970s (Tondreau, 1982).

Therefore, we can see that in the Western world maritime activities, including fishing and commercial transport, which often provided work for many members of the same family and even for entire small towns, have declined gradually and very significantly in recent decades. In many cases, they have disappeared completely in towns without a port. While this was happening, another economic activity increased exponentially on the coasts. This was sun and beach tourism, which from the 1960s has been the sector that has generated the greatest flow of tourists internationally (Shaw & Williams, 1994). The tertiarisation of the economy provided less dangerous, more stable jobs. Gradually, traditional societies were transformed, leaving behind customs, beliefs and pre-Fordism ways of working. Urban growth did the rest. The coastal landscape was transformed dramatically and where previously there had been fishing boats, engine oil, remains of fishing nets and decomposing fish, now there was clean sand, showers and beach bars for the tourists. The only nets that have remained on these beaches are those used to play volleyball. But when it seemed that everything had been forgotten, the phenomenon of recovering maritime heritage emerged.

In the Catalan town that I referred to at the start of this chapter, on the same beach where today a movement to recover maritime heritage is flourishing, in the winter of 1990 the mayor ordered to burn the last wooden ship in town. It was a "barca de bou" (a trawling system imported from France in the last third of the nineteenth century), abandoned on the beach since the last captain retired. The argument was that the beach should be "clean" for when the summer tourists arrived. This put a terribly sad end to a history of several centuries in which the inhabitants of the town had lived basically from fishing. It seemed as if the entire community had followed the steps of the legendary sailor who, carrying his oar on his shoulder, had decided to leave his previous life behind (Figure 23.3).

Recovering Maritime Culture through Heritage: A Hopeful Future?

At the beginning of the twenty-first century, coinciding with the approval of the UNESCO Convention for the Safeguarding of Intangible Cultural Heritage of 2003, cultural initiatives have emerged in many parts of the world to recover maritime culture and heritage. Before then, the recovery of maritime heritage had focused above all on underwater heritage and was therefore reserved for museums and social scientists. Since then, the recovery and promotion of maritime heritage has been focused mainly on intangible heritage and has become a more open, participatory activity (Bender, 2014). The new processes of heritagisation that occurred at the start of the twenty-first century have been interpreted as a "production of locality": a strategy of local communities to reconstruct their own identities and distinguish themselves in the context of globalisation (Frigolé & Roigé, 2006). In addition, this phenomenon could be interpreted in terms of "revitalising heritage" in the sense referred to by Jeremy Boissevain (1992) when he talked of the revitalisation of certain traditions that had been asleep for decades that were suddenly restored or resuscitated.

In recent decades, initiatives have emerged in the Western world to recover maritime culture and heritage. Although the list below is not exhaustive, it contains as an example some of the paradigmatic initiatives that have been carried out in the last two or three decades in relation to maritime heritage:

Figure 23.3 Burning the last fishing boat on 15 December 1990 (Photo: P. Sauleda archive).

- *Meetings of traditional vessels:* Some of the most spectacular initiatives are events relating to traditional vessels, such as the festival held in the port of Brest (France) every four years. These kinds of meetings are held in many other ports of Europe and America. These are not just displays of ships, but above all involve sailing together, to experience in your own body the sensations, risks and emotions of sailing in the past, and seeing similar vessels around you. It is an ephemeral reconstruction of the marine horizon of the past.
- *Recovery of sailing techniques:* Another case associated with the above would be the recovery of traditional sailing techniques, for instance the use of lateen sails in Mediterranean countries, where they had disappeared from the landscape almost a century ago. In Sardinia (Italy) an important lateen sail regatta is held in the town of Stintino every year at the end of August. Some schools in various countries are including learning traditional sailing in their educational programmes.
- *Recovery of small-scale trades:* We should also mention the recovery of traditional boat building techniques. In many places, workshop schools have emerged to teach the trade of traditional wooden boat building. One example is the recovery of techniques for producing plant-based sails from the pandamus tree in Melanesia, through programmes for training young people with the advice of old people and the recovery of local memory about the construction of traditional boats. This is promoted by the Vanuatu Cultural Centre, in Port Vila (Republic of Vanuatu).
- *Repair and construction of replicas:* Linked to the above, the activity of repairing old vessels is increasingly widespread. It is often carried out by retired people as a hobby or a life project. This activity involves the idealisation of pre-Fordism forms of work, in which processes are carried out from start to finish (Jalas, 2006). In addition, we should mention the reconstruction of replicas of traditional boats in recent years, which has generated doubts and discussions among experts (Apraiz, 2014; Laurier, 1998).

- *Heritagisation of foods and gastronomy:* Another interesting example is the heritagisation of foods from a marine origin, as for instance has occurred in recent years with the eel and the Gulf sturgeon in the estuary of Saint Lawrence in Canada (Doyon, 2017). Another similar case is the recovery of traditional sailors' cooking, which is given a heritage meaning. The "Fish Space" in the fishing port of Palamós (Spain) is a programme that uses show cooking to highlight the value of species of fish that are consumed less and are therefore cheaper. The aim is to help small-scale fishermen by promoting domestic consumption of fish, particularly among the younger generations (Alegret, 2014).
- *Heritagisation of fishing methods:* Finally, another curious case is the heritagisation of small-scale fishing systems that are no longer used, such as the "mattanza" of tuna in Sicily, for example in Tonnar's museum in Scopello. In Spain, in various coastal towns, fishing demonstrations are carried out with a sweep net. The net is set from a boat that moves in a semicircle from the beach and many people pull on the two ends of the net from the beach, to catch the fish within it. This system is currently prohibited because of the damage it causes to the seabed, but it is curiously carried out as a heritage activity (Carbonell, 2014). In addition, an activity that is increasingly widespread in Europe, America and Asia, are demonstrations of fishing or even the invitation to participate in professional fishing activities through what is known as "fishing tourism" (Moreno, 2018). That is another way of giving a heritage value to fishing.

These are just some of the many examples that could be mentioned that demonstrate the drive-in maritime heritage in recent decades, particularly in the area of intangible heritage.

Towards the Construction of New Maritime Identities

We will end on the same beach on which we started this chapter. We have seen a sample of activities to recreate maritime heritage that are taking place in different parts of the world; now we will look at heritage practices on the same beach close to Barcelona.

On the beach where in 1990 the last wooden fishing boat was burnt because it was considered a nuisance, today a replica can be seen that is similar to this last boat. The replica was built in 2008 from a model of an 11-metre fishing boat called *Saint-Pierre,* which was constructed in 1909 in Sète (France) and declared a "Monument historique" in 2010. This is a type of vessel that is called "catalane" in France and was designed for fishing oily fish: sardine, anchovy and mackerel. A mould was made from the *Saint Pierre* that has been used to create various replicas, including that shown in Figure 23.1.

In terms of materiality, this new old boat does not have great heritage value. However, its construction has served to promote a large number of activities that have been carried out (before COVID-19) on this beach, including the following: demonstration of the trade of "paler" (from "pal" or pole) who were fishermen in charge of carrying out the complicated operation, particularly in strong waves, of launching boats and getting them back onto the beach by supporting them on greased poles; demonstration of traditional fishing systems that have disappeared today, specifically the sweep net explained above in which many people from the town participated and then took home a bag containing some of the catch as a reward; demonstration of a traditional fish sale on the beach with bid calling, as until the 1970s fish were sold on the beach next to the boats through Dutch-style auctions; meeting of lateen sail boats such as those held in many towns, as normally inviting another town entails the commitment of attending their boat meeting; plays by a local amateur theatre group on the world of traditional fishing, performed on the beach with real traditional boats as props; a competition of Habaneras (traditional sailor's songs); fairs of

Securing Maritime Identities and Heritage

handcrafts and gastronomical products from the sea; talks and presentations of documentaries on ethnology and marine biology; and guided visits through the streets of the town to show its fishing past; among others. All these activities are promoted by a group of people, some of whose parents or grandparents were fishermen, who formed an "association for the recovery of maritime heritage" in 2001. The boats are a small part of their activity to recover maritime heritage. All of these activities serve to recuperate tangible and intangible maritime heritage and, in turn, to reconstruct the maritime identity of a town that lived from the sea in the past, but where for over the last 30 years there are no more professional fishermen.

These heritage practices, and many others that are carried out in coastal towns of the world, point towards the construction of new maritime identities. They are inspired in the seafaring past within which elements are sought to reshape contemporary identities. Restoring a vessel or a tradition involves seeking in the past a meaning for current life. It entails trying to answer the eternal question of who we are and where we come from. The fears of our ancestors that led to a cultural imaginary have given way to other new fears. They have not disappeared. It is no longer unpredictable meteorological phenomena or fearsome marine monsters that prevent us from sailing, but new fears such as that of catching a virus or losing the identity of a place in a globalised world. The new practices of maritime heritage seem designed to prevent the past from fading entirely, from us forgetting that what we are carrying on our back is an oar.

Notes

1 UNESCO. (2020). *Underwater Cultural Heritage.* Retrieved October 15, 2020, from http://www.unesco.org/new/en/culture/themes/underwater-cultural-heritage/underwater-cultural-heritage/wrecks/

2 ILO. (1999, December 13). *Fishing among the most dangerous of all professions, says ILO.* https://www.ilo.org/global/about-the-ilo/newsroom/news/WCMS_071324/lang--en/index.htm

3 Eurostat. (2020). *Fishing fleet, number of vessels.* Retrieved October 15, 2020, from https://ec.europa.eu/eurostat/databrowser/view/tag00116/default/table?lang=en

4 Gobierno de España, Ministerio de Agricultura, Pesca y Alimentación (2020). *Estadísticas pesqueras.* Retrieved October 15, 2020, from https://www.mapa.gob.es/es/estadistica/temas/estadisticas-pesqueras/2020_01_trabajadores_afiliados_tcm30-121836.pdf

References

Alegret, J. L. (2014). Seafaring heritage production in neo-museographical contexts. Palamós Fish Space and the heritage creation process of "low-priced fish". In J. L. Alegret & E. Carbonell (Eds.), *Revisiting the coasts: New practices in maritime heritage* (pp. 181–190). Documenta Universitaria.

Alegret, J. L., & Carbonell, E. (2015). Maritime heritage conservation. In H. Smith, J. L. Suárez, & T. S. Agardy (Eds.), *Routledge handbook of ocean resources and management* (pp. 408–421). Routledge.

Apraiz, J. A. (2014). The gimmicky transformation of seafaring tradition into cultural heritage. In J. L. Alegret & E. Carbonell (Eds.), *Revisiting the coasts. New practices in maritime Heritage* (pp. 21–44). Documenta Universitaria.

Atkinson, D., Cooke, S., & Spooner, D. (2002). Tales from the Riverbank: Place-marketing and maritime heritages. *International Journal of Heritage Studies, 8*(1), 25–40.

Bender, J. (2014). Intangible heritage in the maritime realm: The pedagogy of functional preservation. *Narodna umjetnost, 51*(1), 7–27.

Boissevain, J. (1992). *Revitalizing European rituals.* London: Routledge.

Bosch i Rodoreda, A. (1992). Estudi introductori. In J. Verdaguer(Ed.), *Rondalles.* Barcino.

Cabantous, A. (2005). Los riesgos del mar. In A. Corbin & H. Richard (Eds.), *El mar, terror y fascinación.* Paidós Ibérica.

Cabantous, A., & Buti, G. (2018). *De Charybde en Scylla. Risques, périls et fortunes de mer du XVIe siècle à nos jours.* Éditions Belin/Humensis.

Carbonell, E. (2014). Opportunities and contradictions in maritime heritage and small-scale fishing. A case study of Catalonia. *Collegium Antropologicum, 38*(1), 289–296.

Carbonell, E. (2015). What is a traditional boat? The continuity of Catalan traditional boats. In S. Lira, R. Amoeda, & C. Pinheiro (Eds.), *Sharing cultures 2015. Proceedings of the 4th International Conference on Intangible Heritage* (pp. 339 – 348). Green Lines Institute for Sustainable Development.

Connery, C. (2006). There was no more sea: The supersession of the ocean, from the Bible to cyberspace. *Journal of Historical Geography, 32*(3), 494–511.

Council of Europe. (1992). *European convention on the protection of the archaeological heritage.* https://www.coe.int/en/web/culture-and-heritage/valletta-convention

Crean, K., & Symes, D. (Eds). (1996). *Fisheries management in crisis.* Blackwell Science.

Doyon, S. (2017). Mise en marché et certification de l'anguille argentée et de l'esturgeon noir de l'estuaire du St-Laurent: des "vendredis maigres" aux produits fins. *Canadian Food Studies, 4*(1), 87–107.

Freire, J., & García-Allut, A. (2000). Socioeconomic and biological causes of management failures in European artisanal fisheries: The case of Galicia (NW Spain). *Marine Policy, 24*(5), 375–384.

Frigolé, J., & Roigé, X. (Eds.). (2006). *Globalización y localidad: Perspectiva etnográfica.* Publicacions de la UB.

Hansen, W. (2004). Cognition and affect in oral narration. In S. Des Bouvrie (Ed.), *Myth and symbol II: Symbolic phenomena in ancient greek culture.* Papers from the Norwegian Institute at Athens (13–24). Norwegian Institute at Athens.

Hansen, W. (2014). Odysseus and the oar: A comparative approach to a Greek legend. In L. Edmunds (Ed.), *Approaches to Greek myth* (2nd ed., pp. 247–279). Johns Hopkins University Press.

Harvey, D. C., & Perry, J. (Eds.). (2015). *The future of heritage as climates change: Loss, adaptation and creativity.* Routledge.

Hastrup, F. (2011). *Weathering the world: Recovery in the wake of the tsunami in a Tamil fishing village.* Berghan Books.

Hobsbawm, E. (1995). *Age of extremes: The short twentieth century 1914–1991.* Abacus.

ICOMOS. (1996). *Charter on the protection and management of underwater cultural heritage.* https://www.icomos.org/en/faq-doccen/179-articles-en-francais/ressources/charters-and-standards/161-charter-on-the-protection-and-management-of-underwater-cultural-heritage

Jalas, M. (2006). Making time. The art of loving wooden boats. *Time and Society, 15*(2/3), 343–363.

Laurier, E. (1998). Replications and restauration. Ways of making maritime heritage. *Journal of Material Culture, 3*(1), 21–50.

McGoodwin, J. R. (1990). *Crisis in the world's fisheries – people, problems and policies.* Stanford University Press.

Menanteau, L. (2014). Typology and recognition of maritime heritage: A comparative study of Atlantic Andalusia and Brittany. In J. L. Alegret & E. Carbonell (Eds.), *Revisiting the coasts: New practices in maritime heritage* (pp. 109–134). Documenta Universitaria.

Moreno, D. (2018) Contribution to the concepts of fishing tourism and pesca-tourism. *Cuadernos de turismo, 42,* 655–657.

Pascual-Fernández, J. J., Pita, C., & Bavinck, M. (2020). Small-scale fisheries take centre-stage in Europe (once again). In *Small-scale fisheries in Europe: Status, resilience and governance* (pp. 1–22). Springer.

Peron, F. (2003). *Le Patrimoine Maritime.* Presses Universitaires de Rennes.

Romero, M. (2012). Recetas para tratar el miedo al mar: las ofrendas a los dioses. In E. Ferrer, M. C. Marín, & A. Pereira (Eds.), *La religión del mar. Dioses y ritos de navegación en el Mediterráneo Antiguo* (pp. 107–118). Publicaciones de la Universidad de Sevilla.

Rousseau, Y., Watson, R. A., Blanchard, J. L., & Fulton, E. A. (2019). Evolution of global marine fishing fleets and the response of fished resources. *Proceedings of the National Academy of Sciences of the United States of America, 116*(25), 12238–12243.

Shaw, G., & Williams, A. M. (1994). *Critical issues in tourism: A geographical perspective.* Blackwell.

Tondreau, J. (1982). *Coque de bois. Coque d'acier. Historique du cabotage motorise sur le Saint-Laurent.* Production M.T. Marine.

Torry, W. (1972). Anthropology studies in hazardous environment: Past trends and new horizons. *Current Anthropology, 20*(3), 517–540.

UNCTAD. (2020). *Review of maritime transport 2019.* United Nations Conference on Trade and Development. https://unctad.org/system/files/official-document/rmt2019_en.pdf

Wisner, B., Blaikie, P., Cannon, T., & Davis, I. (2004). *At risk: Natural hazards, people's vulnerability and disasters.* Routledge.

24

NON-STATE AND HYBRID ACTORNESS AT SEA: FROM NARCO-SUBS TO DRONE PATROLS

Brendan Flynn

International relations literature has in general fetishised the so-called Westphalian state system, assuming states are the primary actors in international politics when reality has always been more complex (Osiander, 2001). Moreover, the Westphalian privileging of states as *primus inter pares* was never very clear-cut at sea.

For example, state backed trading companies routinely employed armed forces at sea. Privateers were non-state vessels that enjoyed government permission to engage in "legitimate" piracy. Moreover, states have frequently fought non-state actors at sea, notably campaigns against pirates or slave traders (Grindal, 2016). Long before the Westphalian reification of the state became problematic on land, it had never been useful at sea.

In fact, hybrid actorness is common at sea, for example seen in the claims by China of sovereignty over large parts of the South China Sea, supported by their navy, coastguard and maritime militias, but augmented by commercial activities of civilian Chinese fishing fleets or offshore oil and gas firms (Buszynski, 2019). Whether the latter are truly non-state actors (NSAs) is questionable, given extensive supervisory Chinese state power. Nonetheless, they routinely present themselves as commercial actors and are often "self-motivated economic players" with a surprising degree of autonomy, rather than being simply puppets for the Chinese state (Zhang & Bateman, 2017, p. 66).

Moreover, while UNCLOS has clarified territorial seas and exclusive economic zones for states, it also guarantees free movement of commercial shipping, and even for warships in territorial waters.[1] The requirement that commercial vessels have a "flag" state, has been entirely circumvented by registering with "flags of convenience" (de Nevers, 2015, p. 598). UNCLOS does not either grant state vessels permissive powers to stop, search or seize vessels in EEZs or international waters (Murphy, 2007, p. 73). In summary, while states are privileged actors under UNCLOS, they are less legally powerful at sea than upon their land territory. For NSAs then, the sea would appear to be replete with opportunities.

DOI: 10.4324/9781003001324-27

Brendan Flynn

Beyond Binaries: Mapping Non-state Actors across the Maritime Security Policy Cycle

It is important to have a non-binary understanding of how states and NSAs interact, because the line between both is often blurred at sea across diverse maritime security practices. NSAs themselves can play varied security roles, supplementing states, providing alternatives but sometimes offering opposition to state authority.

Indeed, the argument of this chapter is that a hybrid type agency for NSAs is both more commonplace in shaping maritime security politics than has traditionally been appreciated. This agency is hybrid because it often works with but can also be in opposition to states. When it does challenge state power at sea, this often confirms and justifies state actors' roles. It is also a hybrid agency given that some non-state actors can act like states at sea, for example whenever they are designing policies, providing maritime law enforcement, surveillance, monitoring and even (rarely) use of lawful force at sea. The fact that this is often in co-operation with state actors, reinforces such hybridity.

Yet for other NSAs, their agency takes forms of resistance, opposition, subversion and can range from overt acts of protest to covert and highly organised criminality. The latter sometimes involve technology, finance or violence that traditionally only states were thought capable of. Even when non-state actors are described as maritime security threats (pirates, smugglers, terrorists, etc.), any social construction is often complex and contested. For example, irregular migrants have perhaps surprising levels of agency to negotiate with smugglers or state authorities, notwithstanding their desperate plight (Mainwaring, 2016), and even Somali pirates have attempted to justify themselves with "Robin Hood" counter-narratives (Schneider & Winkler, 2013). In summary, state actors make use of, shape and co-operate with NSAs, who in turn influence, co-opt and sometimes rival them, in what becomes the co-construction of maritime security.

Examining this hybrid agency over the maritime security "policy cycle" offers one way to understand the impact of non-state actors upon maritime security politics. Traditionally "policy cycles" have involved identifying discrete stages of agenda-setting, allocation of resources, legislation and, finally, implementation and enforcement (Howlett et al., 2009). However, a simpler triangular positioning is employed here: firstly, non-state actors described as a maritime threat or victim; secondly, non-state actors who "perform" maritime security offering practical solutions which blends NGO activism with private enforcement; thirdly, non-state actors who lobby, influence and shape maritime security policies.

Examples of the first category would include the well explored examples of pirates, terrorists and even illegal, unreported and unregulated (IUU) fishers, but the case examined here is the less well-understood phenomenon of specialist maritime drug smugglers using "narco-submarines". They appear to be in stark opposition to states given their illegality and sophistication. While private maritime security contractors are often cited as the best example of NSAs engaged in privatised coercion, the case examined here is how many conservation NGOs are providing IUU monitoring and enforcement capabilities, especially via novel technologies and typically for weak states that may lack such means. Finally, some NSAs seek to "shape" problems, set agendas and raise awareness of maritime security problems. These are NGOs, research foundations, lobbies and also protest groups.

Figure 24.1 provides a simplified representation of this tripartite mapping, where it should be noted that NSAs can move between roles: from setting the agenda to being framed as a threat or victim, to even performing maritime security at sea. Some non-state actors, for example Greenpeace, have adopted all three positions at various times. They have variously engaged in

Non-state and Hybrid Actorness at Sea

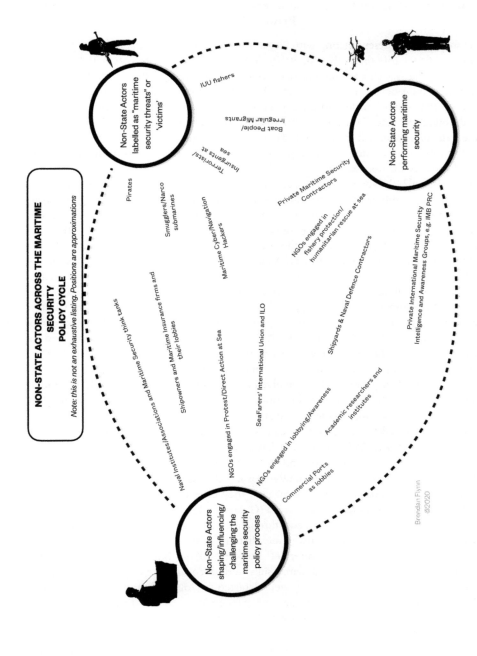

Figure 24.1 Non-state actors across the maritime security policy cycle.
(Source: author)

protests at sea, resulting in their members being arrested and jailed, alongside detailed policy lobbying and research, but they have provided vessels for fishery protection and monitoring.

Maritime Smuggling and Narco-Submarines: A Non-state Challenge to State Primacy?

Maritime smuggling represents, along with illegal fishing and piracy, probably one of the oldest forms of maritime security threat (Karras, 2010). As the Westphalian state system itself emerged, maritime smuggling was an endemic practice, which both challenged states but also did much to further their bureaucratic machinery for collection of customs, excise and supervision of borders. In a way, states "made" smuggling through perverse economic incentives or prohibition and smugglers "made" the state (respond) (Thai, 2018; Thomson, 1994; Wheeler, 2011). The same dynamics are arguably at work today when we examine narco-submarines which are just one form of maritime drug smuggling, albeit a trend that suggests an intriguing level of agency and capacity for non-state actors.

For example, on 24th November 2019, alarmed reports emerged off the coast of Galicia, of a 20-plus metre narco-submarine being intercepted in European waters, suggesting that drug cartels have now matured a means of moving literally tons of cocaine directly to Europe employing a technology that traditionally only navies have had access to (Giles, 2019).

In fact, as Sutton (2020) has observed, this was not the first-time narco-subs have made it to European waters: one was intercepted near Vigo in 2006. Moreover, for all their exoticism, narco-submarines are just one method used to smuggle drugs by sea, and a great deal of maritime drug smuggling uses regular merchant shipping container traffic (Guerrero, 2019, pp. 38, 48). One estimate for 2012, suggests that 80% of Andean drug flows were taking a maritime route to North America and of this perhaps 30% of that was shipped via narco-subs (Ramirez & Bunker, 2014). More recent US Coastguard figures suggest that the flow of specifically maritime trafficked cocaine has risen from 1,254 metric tons in 2015 to 2,827 in 2018, in effect doubling and reducing their interdiction rate (DHS-OIG, 2019, p. 3). Moreover, the actual level of technology involved combines the sophisticated with the crudely improvised and has evolved in several iterations from an earlier method of maritime drug smuggling using fast motorboats (Guerrero, 2019, pp. 45–46).

Narco-subs originated from Columbian cartels seeking to move drugs in quantity towards the United States, often to Mexico or other Latin American countries. They evolved in response to improved interdiction efforts and the first examples date back to the early 1990s, while by the mid-1990s they were hesitantly crossing the Atlantic (Guerrero, 2019, p. 47). Carrying between one and ten tonnes of cocaine, they offer economies of scale, despite the costs (US$2–5 million) and a high loss rate at sea (Guerrero, 2019, pp. 45, 49). They also confer more control over the valuable contraband throughout its journey and bypass port security measures, but the main attraction is lower interdiction: as many as three out of every four shipments may go undetected (Ramirez & Bunker, 2014). Nonetheless, by 2013 the Columbian authorities had seized 83 narco-subs and discovered over 20 illicit boatyards (Guerrero, 2019, p. 43). In 2019 alone, 36 were detected in Columbia, and it is estimated that about 200 could be in operation at any one time (StrategyPage, 2020). Today, they are built well inland and make staged journeys to sea with Cape Verde and the Azores likely stopping off points (Sutton, 2020).

The actual building of the vessels appears to be handled by a distinct group of independent illegal contractors who engage in peer competition to innovate (Guerrero, 2019, pp. 49, 92).

Indeed, narco-subs reflect a type of non-state actorness which is seemingly a rival for state actors as regards its instrumental rationality, access to finance and ability to mobilise social networks.

Although drug cartels are not insurgents, involvement is alleged by Columbia's FARC rebels and ex-guerrillas have likely been involved in the production of narco-submarines (Jacome, 2016). More generally, however, the phenomenon of narco-submarines reflects the observation on how disorder at sea often has deep social roots on land. Guerrero notes that the Columbian regions in which narco-submarine construction emerged, are marginal, lawless zones with long histories of resistance to central state control, which has been historically a perverse mix of authoritarian and weak (2019, pp. 48–49).

It is however possible to overstate the agency of drug cartels using the example of narco-submarines. This is not least because other less dramatic forms of maritime smuggling may be more pervasive and cost-effective (Harney, 2017, pp. 51–63), but also because the expedient of smuggling under water reflects as much the power and reach of state law enforcement agencies, improvements in surveillance technologies, and a desire on the part of the drug smugglers to avoid confrontations with more powerful state forces.

For states, maritime smuggling generally represents either a hard-headed loss of revenue or it can also represent a sovereignty challenge. Narcotics are not just a valuable consumable but create significant public bads and the enormous revenues generated can usurp state power through corruption. Such concerns were at the heart of Chinese opposition to official British state-sanctioned opium smuggling in the nineteenth century, which eventually led to two inter-state wars between China, Britain and later France, as part of a wider pattern of state-backed trade in narcotics across colonial Asia (Haijian, 2016, pp. 75–78; Kim, 2020).

That states, or their agents, have in the part engaged in systematic maritime drug smuggling should alert us to the possibility they could do so today, and this has been alleged in relation to North Korea (Perl, 2004; Wang & Blancke, 2014). We should also be aware of a more complex spectrum of possibilities whereby drug cartels can simply "buy" weak and corrupt local elites to create "narco-states". Guinea-Bissau has been cited as a primary example with Cape Verde more recently identified as being at risk (Mouhamadou, 2019), although the influence of drug cartels has extended along much of the West Africa Coast with varying degrees of intensity (Chabal & Green, 2016).

Some non-state actors involved in maritime drug smuggling therefore have the power to co-opt weak states through elite capture and corruption, although when faced with more powerful state adversaries it is clear their strategy is to avoid confrontation. Narco-submarines illustrate the dramatic scope and agency that some criminal non-state actors can have at sea and also reveal how drawing sharp distinctions between state and non-state power at sea can occlude a more complex reality.

Performing Security at Sea: The Hybrid Actorness of NGO IUU Enforcement

NGOs offering fisheries protection services provide a maritime security service normally delivered by states, occasionally augmented in some cases by private firms.[2] However, rather than attempting to replace states, they usually seek hybrid partnerships with maritime authorities. Their objective is often to embarrass states to step up their fishery protection role at sea. They also tend to specialise in helping small and weak states who lack resources.

Enjoying extensive media attention for their campaigns against whaling, the Sea Shepherds are probably the best-known group. However, whaling is a relatively small part of global fishing and the Sea Shepherds have used extreme "direct action" methods up to an including low-level violence (Nagtzaam, 2014). In recent years they have broadened their IUU focus, deploying their fleet of no less than ten vessels against illegal tuna, toothfish and shark finning practices.[3] They have signed co-operative agreements with Ecuador, Costa Rica, Senegal, Gabon (Schatz, 2018, pp. 7–10) and hosted Tanzanian fisheries officials to effect a search and arrest at sea.[4]

In 2017, a Greenpeace vessel (*Esperanza*) toured Cape Verde and Mauritania to raise awareness of IUU problems, and partnering with the Fisheries Surveillance Department of Guinea Bissau, made several arrests, including at least one Chinese fishing vessel (FCWC, 2017). What Greenpeace, and in some cases, the Sea Shepherds are offering here is a vessel as a fishery protection platform, but they are careful to work with local states; uniformed and armed Guinea Bissau personnel were aboard. The non-state actor here is simply providing the means for a weak state to go to sea, and as such this represents the epitome of hybrid state/non-state agency.

While Sharman and Eilstrup-Sangiovanni (2019, pp. 6, 10) are bullish about the prospects for NGO's abilities to enforce international law, this is likely to be problematic for some maritime security issues at sea, given that pirates, arms and narco-traffickers can be violent.[5] Clearly there are limits to the agency of non-state actors in such roles although they can perform the roles of detection and collection of evidence, autonomously of states.

Moreover, the legalities of such operations are far from clear-cut, for even if UNCLOS does suggest some scope for states to delegate enforcement roles to private actors, the overall legal regime for fisheries remains strongly state dependent with NGOs requiring clear state authorisation (Guggisberg, 2019, p. 321; Guilfoyle, 2009, pp. 98–100). This reinforces observations made here about the importance of hybrid actorness. Even if Greenpeace vessels have onboard local naval or coastguard personnel, it is unclear if that constitutes identifiable "government" status under maritime law (Schatz, 2018, p. 14). A situation could well arise where a fishing vessel refuses to stop, and in the March 2017 operation off the coast of Guinea Bissau, two Chinese ships fled the scene.

Apart from providing a vessel, foreign NGOs engage in local capacity building, which is vital to encourage small states to tackle the fishing vessels of more powerful countries that may be engaged in IUU fishing. Chinese, South Korean, Russian and EU fishing fleets have repeatedly sought access to West African waters, either through negotiated arrangements involving intense political pressure and economic side payments, but sometimes illegally. As Standing (2015) explains in the context of Senegal, local elites can often collude with industrialised fishing interests, so international NGOs provide a useful counterbalance by supporting local NGOs to challenge state fishing policy (2015, pp. 179, 186). The UK-based Environmental Justice Foundation (EJF) has been engaged in capacity building and information sharing in various West African states and cite as progress recent examples of refusals by Senegal and Liberia to grant fishing licenses to Chinese supertrawlers (EJF, 2020).[6]

NGOs are also embracing drones or remote sensing platforms to uncover IUU fishing. ATLAN Space,[7] an NGO startup partially funded by Microsoft, National Geographic and Morocco[8] offers state authorities imagery and GPS references to facilitate interception. Another cooperative project, FishGuard, involved the Seychelles Air Force, the Seychelles Fisheries Protection Agency and the Norwegian NGO Trygg Mat Tracking,[9] which provided specialist maritime data analytics, while the Norwegian NGO Grid-Arendal[10] provided funding (Bonnelame, 2018; UNEP, 2018). The Fish-i-Africa project[11] was funded by a mixture of charitable and state sources, and focused on data sharing of ship movements with eight East African partner nations (Tullis, 2017). Global Fishing Watch[12] also uses satellite and remote sensor technologies, although this often requires agreement from national authorities, for example Indonesia who allowed access to Vessel Monitoring System data of their national fleet.[13]

A different, "disruptive style" of operation is evidenced by the German-based Blackfish Foundation, whose core personnel originated from Greenpeace. Now known as FishAct,[14] they employ "citizen inspectors" to expose illegal fishing practices off Sicily, Tunisia, Morocco and Croatia. They have also trained activists for monitoring in German, Norwegian, Swedish and British waters. This NGO adopts a more critical and challenging position towards state agencies, by engaging in an independent monitoring of state fisheries regulation.

Shaping Security Policy at Sea: From Naval Institutes to Kayaktivists

Non-state actors can also try to directly influence maritime security policies either by awareness raising and problem definition, or more traditionally via lobbying, all with the aim of securing state action, funds or legislative changes. However, an important distinction lies here between policy "insiders", often very close to state actors, versus policy "outsiders" who are viewed by state agencies as marginal, extremist or challengers (Maloney et al., 1994).

Obviously, different institutional configurations provide variable opportunities for influence, protest and agenda-setting, not least the basic distinction between whether a state is democratic or authoritarian. Yet across many states, security think-tanks, and especially nationally embedded shipyards and defence contractors, can exert considerable influence on what could be termed the traditional statist agenda which privileges naval capabilities.

However, maritime commercial interests, notably insurers, and merchant shipping lines have in recent years played an important role in highlighting piracy, terrorism and cyber-attacks (Kapalidis, 2020). In this way, they have generally reinforced a much broader conception of maritime security. For example, in the United Kingdom, home to much of the global maritime insurance industry, Lloyd's of London has both lobbied for action on piracy and used "war risk" pricing to create powerful economic effects (Valdron, 2016, pp. 165–172). Denmark, home to the largest global shipping firm Maersk, has seen intense domestic lobbying by this firm during the height of the piracy problem off Somalia (Hansen, 2011; Smed & Wivel, 2017, p. 83). This is hardly a new phenomenon, as shipping firms and merchant navies have had long historical associations with state colonial and naval power projection (Lucas, 2019), meaning they have a hybrid blend of commercial interest mixed with some concerns for state power and security agendas.

Non-commercial NSAs are examined here using the specific example of the United States, because of that country's geostrategic importance and the diversity of non-state actors it offers. The US Naval Institute provides a clear-cut example of a non-commercial policy influencer that is emphatically an insider. As its name implies, it enjoys a close association with the US Navy, having many former and current personnel among its *circa* 50,000 members.[15] It remains influential, especially via publications, internet news, blogs and by running policy-related events. Unsurprisingly, it advocates for strong American naval power, although it also raises awareness of maritime piracy, terrorism and even IUU fishing as threats.

Another think tank shaping American views on maritime security is the explicitly more policy-focused Center for Naval Analyses (CNA), which describes itself as a "non-profit research and analysis organization"[16] with over 500 staff. It is more accurately described as a public-private partnership, having a subsidiary with the status of a federally funded research centre. While their focus has been on rather traditional naval great power rivalry and much wider military issues, in recent years they have embraced diverse maritime security debates, including piracy, climate change as a security challenge and even the maritime impacts of COVID-19 (CNA Military Advisory Board, 2014; Tallis et al., 2020).

These actors are regarded as more impartial than the more aggressive professional lobbies of shipyards and associated naval systems contractors (Nicander, 2016) who target congressional decision makers, forming classic "insider" networks adept at skewing the US defence budget to their own ends (Sapolsky et al., 2014, p. 169). There are also more generalised but partisan think tanks, who adopt conservative, centrist or liberal positions on American maritime security issues. For example, the liberal-oriented Center for International Policy argues for a significant reduction in US Navy size and weapons acquisition (CIP, 2019, pp. 43–44).[17] The conservative Heritage Foundation predictably canvasses for a larger force (Spoehr, 2020). The more centrist and bipartisan Center for a New American Security (CNAS) articulates the need for a more effective US Navy without the obsession on numbers of vessels (Estep, 2019).[18]

By way of sharp contrast from this "beltway politics", or the focus on traditional naval power, there are much smaller "outsiders" who prefer protest and direct action at sea. Their concerns are the environmental and human rights aspects of maritime security. For example, the so called "Kayaktivist" phenomenon in the United States involves small groups of water sports enthusiasts joining forces with environmental protestors to physically impede oil rigs or ships carrying coal and fracked gas. As Grossman (2019, pp. 47, 55) explains, such Kayaktivists have blocked ships in the Pacific North West after identifying ports as a strategic Achilles' heel, imposing huge costs on fossil fuel firms and gaining publicity.

The origins of this idea go back to anti-war and anti-nuclear weapons protestors (Taylor, 2013). However, probably the biggest and most visible protest occurred in May–July 2015 when Kayaktivists attempted to embarrass the Obama administration by blocking oil drilling rigs headed for Alaskan waters, at Puget Sound and Portland (Holthaus, 2015; Westerman, 2017). Ultimately, the exploration companies involved cancelled their plans. The tactic remains part of the repertoire of grassroots type groups, such as the Backbone Campaign[19] but also larger American environmental organisations such as 350.org,[20] who have promoted training in "Kayaktivism".[21]

Such protests at sea should not be dismissed as trivial in their agency, as they are often led by a small number of semi-professional activists who are savvy in exploiting the opportunities of new social media, in particular the "David versus Goliath" visual narratives of tiny kayaks versus huge vessels (Latimer, 2017; Westerman, 2017, p. 116).

This sort of "direct action" also means that the profile of protestors evolves from being merely agenda shapers. For police and coastguards, they become a low-order maritime security threat albeit within the limits of legitimate protest. With this example, we see how NSAs can change their actorness across the marine security problem cycle: they can shift from being a problem shaper, to problem maker, to problem responder, and all points in between.

Conclusion: Agency, Shape-Shifting and the Fetish of Non-state Status

It is important to acknowledge that the selection of non-state actors examined here is necessarily partial. Yet whether NSAs are motivated by profit or principle, or even whether they employ violence or not, are all distinctions that in practice become less clear-cut at sea. Moreover, we should avoid drawing sharp binaries between state and non-state actors, assuming contrasts between them are always stark, or that each is an inexorable rival. Both types of actor routinely co-exist, are often co-dependent and sometimes co-constitutive as regards their production of maritime security. Given that hybrid relationships are so very common for shipping navigation, safety, rescue and ports, we should not be greatly surprised by a significant degree of hybridity in how states and NSAs interact as regards maritime security.[22]

Non-state and Hybrid Actorness at Sea

What remains less clear-cut is the efficacy of NSAs: are they mostly marginal bit-players compared to states and their institutions, foremost navies and coastguards? This has been the rather traditional view within much of international relations scholarship, albeit moderated in recent decades with an increasing awareness of both their greater role and a debate about declining state power (Halliday, 2001, p. 27). Yet historical awareness that such actors have always been present (and sometimes powerful) has often been missing from academic accounts (Halliday, 2001).

If we conceive of actors' power and agency in a more relational way, rather than as a fixed static property of a given actor's set of material resources, then NSAs have the ability to be sometimes decisive. This does not mean they usurp states, but rather that they co-exist and innovate around the realities of state power, which for much of the world is anyhow rather limited to what in effect is a "hybrid state" (Boege et al., 2008), which is not in reality a privileged actor. If there is a problem here it lies more with the conceptual academic bias of a certain Western view of the state, as actor *primus inter pares*, a view that the complexities of the maritime world does much to moderate (de Nevers, 2015, p. 600). Moreover, the power and agency of non-state actors is surely not trivial whenever they can deploy resources that rival states (as for example narco-submarines illustrate) or when they can co-opt weak states, evident in the cases of IUU practices and the narco-state phenomenon.

A great deal of future maritime conflict and insecurity will likely feature amorphous maritime security crises and central to these will be NSAs, in all their diversity. They will manifest as the security problem itself, but also provide solutions and responses, or sometimes shape agendas and policymaking, while also probably operating in complex, hybrid ways, both alongside and in opposition to states.

Notes

1 Articles 17–20 UNCLOS.
2 An example of privatised fishery protection would be the use by the Scottish Fishery Protection Agency of aerial monitoring provided by Airtask group Ltd (https://www.airtask.com/). More controversially, private security companies offered maritime enforcement "services" during Sierra Leone's and Liberia's civil wars and off the coast of Somalia in the late 1990s and early 2000s (Cullen, 2012).
3 See: https://seashepherd.org/our-story/
4 https://www.seashepherd.org.uk/news-and-commentary/news/taiwanese-captain-sentenced-20-years-for-shark-finning-in-tanzania.html
5 This might not be a problem for private security companies, although the legal implications could be very serious.
6 See: https://ejfoundation.org/what-we-do/oceans/ending-pirate-fishing
7 See: http://www.atlanspace.com/ and https://twitter.com/AtlanSpace
8 See https://www.aiforsdgs.org/all-projects/atlan-space
9 See: https://www.tm-tracking.org/
10 See https://www.grida.no/about and https://www.grida.no/activities/275
11 https://stopillegalfishing.com/initiatives/fish-i-africa/
12 https://globalfishingwatch.org/about-us/. The latter was also known as *SoarOcean* (http://soarocean.org/project-details/). Other NGOs that do similar "remote enforcement" are *SeaScope* (https://www.seascopefisheries.co.uk/), and *SkyTruth* (https://skytruth.org/).
13 https://globalfishingwatch.org/vms-transparency/
14 See: https://fishact.org/about-us/our-story/
15 https://www.usni.org/about-us/mission-and-vision
16 https://www.cna.org/about/
17 https://www.internationalpolicy.org/about-us. Until 2013 this think tank was branded as Project on Defence Alternatives with funding from the non-profit Commonwealth Institute. See: http://comw.org/ and http://comw.org/pda/

18 https://www.cnas.org/mission
19 https://www.backbonecampaign.org/kayaktivism
20 https://350.org/about/
21 https://trainings.350.org/resource/paddle-power-manual-the-theory-and-tactics-of-kayaktivism/
22 Many maritime search and rescue agencies are private actors, sometime funded by states, for example the RNLI in the UK, DGzRS in Germany, SNSM in France. In the UK and Ireland, navigation providers, specifically lighthouses, have been partly funded by private light dues levied on shipping together with state subvention, managed by maritime charities, such as Trinity House. Many of the largest global ports, notably Shanghai and Singapore, are commercial entities but with state/municipal shareholding.

References

Boege, V., Brown, K., & Nolan, A. (2008). *On hybrid political orders and emerging states: State formation in the context of "fragility"*. Berghof Research Center.

Bonnelame, B. (2018, September 18). *Project FishGuard: Seychelles to monitor illegal fishing with unmanned drones*. Seychelles News Agency. http://www.seychellesnewsagency.com/articles/9754/Project+FishGuard+Seychelles+to+monitor+illegal+fishing+with+unmanned+drones

Buszynski, L. (2019). The South China Sea: An arena for great power strategic rivalry. In T. T. Thuy, J. B. Welfield, & L. T. Trang (Eds.), *Building a normative order in the South China Sea* (pp. 68–91). Edward Elgar.

Chabal, P., & Green, T. (Eds.). (2016). *Guinea-Bissau: Micro-state to "narco-state"*. Hurst.

CIP [Center for International Policy]. (2019). *Sustainable defense: More security, less spending*. Final Report of the Sustainable Defense Task Force of the Center for International Policy. June. CIP. https://comw.org/pda/sustainable-defense-more-security-less-spending

CNA Military Advisory Board. (2014). *National security and the accelerating risks of climate change*. Alexandria, VA: CNA Corporation. https://www.cna.org/cna_files/pdf/MAB_5-8-14.pdf

Cullen, P. (2012). Privatized maritime security in governance in war-torn Sierra Leone. In C. Berube & P. Cullen (Eds.), *Maritime private security: Market responses to piracy, terrorism and waterborne security risks in the 21st century* (pp. 101–112). Routledge.

de Nevers, R. (2015). Sovereignty at sea: States and security in the maritime domain. *Security Studies, 24*(4), 597–630.

DHS-OIG/Department of Homeland Security/Office of Inspector General. (2019, March 9). *Review of the U.S. Coastguard's Fiscal Year 2018 Drug Control Performance Summary Report*. Washington, D.C.: DHS-OIG. https://www.oig.dhs.gov/sites/default/files/assets/2019-03/OIG-19-27-Mar19.pdf

Environmental Justice Foundation [EJF]. (2020, October 12). Liberia protects small-scale fishers from chinese supertrawler threat. https://ejfoundation.org/news-media/liberia-protects-small-scale-fishers-from-chinese-super-trawler-threat

Estep, C. (2019, May 22). What Congress should do with the 2020 Defense Budget. CNAS Press Release. https://www.cnas.org/press/press-release/what-congress-should-do-with-the-2020-defense-budget

FCWC. (Fisheries Committee West Central Gulf of Guinea) (2017, March 31). Guinea Bissau: Joint fishing patrol snags 4 illegal fishing vessels off Guinea Bissau. https://fcwc-fish.org/other-news/guinea-bissau-president-boards-greenpeace-ship-to-focus-on-illegal-fishing

Giles, C. (2019, November 28). *Spanish tow narco-sub to port*. Navy Times. https://www.navytimes.com/news/your-navy/2019/11/28/spanish-tow-narco-sub-to-port/

Grindal, P. (2016). *Opposing the slavers: The Royal Navy's campaign against the Atlantic Slave Trade*. I.B. Tauris.

Grossman, Z. (2019). Native/non-native alliances challenging fossil fuel industry shipping at Pacific northwest ports. In J. Clapperton & L. Piper (Eds.), *Environmental activism on the ground: Small green and indigenous organizing* (pp. 47–72). University of Calgary Press.

Guerrero, J. C. (2019). *Narcosubmarines: Outlaw innovation and maritime interdiction in the war on drugs*. Springer.

Guggisberg, S. (2019). The roles of nongovernmental actors in improving compliance with fisheries regulations. *Review of European, Comparative & International Environmental Law 28*(3), 314–327.

Guilfoyle, D. (2009). *Shipping interdiction and the law of the sea*. Cambridge University Press.

Haijian, M. (2016). *The Qing Empire and the Opium War: The collapse of the Heavenly Dynasty*. Cambridge University Press.

Halliday, F. (2001). The romance of non-state actors. In D. Josselin & W. Wallace (Eds.), *Non-state actors in world politics* (pp. 21–37). Palgrave Macmillan.

Hansen, F. E. (2011, May 10). *Maersk raises piracy surcharge*. G-captain website. https://gcaptain.com/maersk-raises-piracy-surcharge/

Harney, S. M. (Lt. USN). (2017). *By land, sea, or air: A comparative analysis of cartel smuggling strategies*. MA Thesis. Naval Postgraduate School Monterey United States. https://apps.dtic.mil/sti/pdfs/AD1046400.pdf

Holthaus, E. (2015, May 19). *Kayaktivism: These boats protesting oil drilling are the perfect symbol of climate change activism*. The Slate. https://slate.com/technology/2015/05/protest-against-shell-drilling-in-the-arctic-kayaks-and-boats-near-seattle-in-puget-sound.html

Howlett, M., Ramesh, M., & Perl, A. (2009). *Studying public policy. Policy cycles and policy subsystems*. Oxford University Press.

Jacome, M. J. (2016). The revolutionary armed forces of Colombia (FARC) and the development of narco-submarines. *Journal of Strategic Security*, *9*(1), 49–69.

Kapalidis, P. (2020). Cybersecurity at sea. In L. Otto (Ed.), *Global challenges in maritime security. Advanced sciences and technologies for security applications* (pp.127–143). Springer.

Karras, A. L. (2010). *Smuggling: Contraband and corruption in world history*. Rowman & Littlefield.

Kim, D. S. (2020). *Empires of vice: The rise of opium prohibition across Southeast Asia*. Princeton University Press.

Latimer, C. (2017, November 24). Experience: I am a kayaktivist. *The Guardian*. https://www.theguardian.com/environment/2017/nov/24/experience-i-am-a-kayaktivist

Lucas, E. R. (2019). Public goods, club goods, and private interests: The influence of domestic business elites on British counter-piracy interventions in the South China Sea, 1921–35. *Security Studies*, *28*(4), 710–738.

Mainwaring, C̣. (2016). Migrant agency: Negotiating borders and migration controls. *Migration Studies*, *4*(3), 289–308.

Maloney, W. A., Jordan, G., & McLaughlin, A. M. (1994). Interest groups and public policy: The insider/outsider model revisited. *Journal of Public Policy*, *14*(1), 17–38.

Mouhamadou, K. (2019, June 4). "Is Cape Verde doomed to become a narco-state?" ENACT/ISS [Enhancing Africa's Response to Transnational Organized Crime/ South Africa Institute for Security Studies].

Murphy, M. N. (2007). The blue, green, and brown: Insurgency and counter-insurgency on the water. *Contemporary Security Policy*, *28*(1), 63–79.

Nagtzaam, G. (2014). Gaia's navy: The Sea Shepherd Conservation Society's battle to stay afloat and international law. *William & Mary Environmental Law and Policy Review*, *38*(3), 613–694.

Nicander, L. (2016). The recipe for think tank success: The perspective of insiders. *International Journal of Intelligence and Counter-Intelligence*, *29*(4), 738–759.

Osiander, A. (2001). Sovereignty, international relations, and the Westphalian myth. *International Organization*, *55*(2), 251–287.

Perl, R. F. (2004). State crime: The North Korean drug trade. *Global Crime*, *6*(1), 117–128.

Ramirez, B., & Bunker, R. (2014, August 2). *Narco-submarines: Drug Cartels' innovative technology*. Centre for International Maritime Security. http://cimsec.org/narco-submarines-drug-cartels-innovative-technology/12314

Sapolsky, H. M., Gholz, E., & Talmadge, C. (2014). *US defense politics: The origins of security policy* (2nd ed.). Routledge.

Schatz, V. J. (2018). Marine Fisheries Law Enforcement Partnerships in Waters under National Jurisdiction: The Legal Framework for Inter-State Cooperation and Public-Private Partnerships with Non-governmental Organizations and Private Security Companies. *Ocean Yearbook Online*, *32*(1), 329–375.

Schneider, P., & Winkler, M. (2013). The Robin Hood narrative: A discussion of empirical and ethical legitimizations of Somali pirates. *Ocean Development & International Law*, *44*(2), 185–201.

Sharman, J. C., & Eilstrup-Sangiovanni, M. (2019). Enforcers beyond borders: Transnational NGOs and the enforcement of international law. *Perspectives on Politics*, *19*(1), 131–147.

Smed, U. T., & Wivel, A. (2017). Vulnerability without capabilities? Small state strategy and the international counter-piracy agenda. *European Security*, *26*(1), 79–98.

Spoehr, T. (2020, February 13). *Why the US Navy needs at least 355 ships*. The Heritage Foundation. https://www.heritage.org/defense/commentary/why-the-us-navy-needs-least-355-ships

Standing, A. (2015). Mirage of pirates: State-corporate crime in West Africa's fisheries. *State Crime Journal*, *4*(2), 175–197.

StrategyPage. (2020, March 20). *Submarines: Trans-Atlantic narco-subs*. StratgeyPage.com. https://strategypage.com/htmw/htsub/articles/20200320.aspx#startofcomments

Sutton, H. I. (2020, August 31). Ghost gliders: Spanish narco-submarines. *Small Wars Journal*. https://smallwarsjournal.com/jrnl/art/ghost-gliders-spanish-narco-submarines

Tallis, J., Overfield, C., Inks, K., & Rosenblum, C. (2020). *Adrift: COVID-19 and the safety of seafarers*. October, CSI-2020-U-028490-Final. CNA. https://www.cna.org/CNA_files/PDF/CSI-2020-U-028490-Final.pdf

Taylor, R. K. (2013). *Blockade: A guide to nonviolent intervention*. Wipf and Stock.

Thai, P. (2018). *China's war on smuggling: Law, economic life, and the making of the modern 1842–1965*. Columbia University Press.

Thomson, J. E. (1994). *Mercenaries, pirates and sovereigns: State building and extra-territorial violence in early modern Europe*. Princeton University Press.

Tullis, P. (2017, November 21). *How data sharing is stopping illegal fishing in the Indian Ocean*. Pacific Standard. https://psmag.com/economics/using-data-to-combat-illegal-fishing

UNEP/United Nations Environment Programme. (2018). *Intelligent drones crack down on illegal fishing in African waters*. https://www.unenvironment.org/news-and-stories/story/intelligent-drones-crack-down-illegal-fishing-african-waters

Valdron, T. (2016). Economic security: An analysis of the strait of Malacca. In A. J. Masys (Ed.), *Exploring the security landscape: Non-traditional security challenges* (pp. 159–176). Springer.

Wang, P., & Blancke, S. (2014). Mafia state: The evolving threat of North Korean narcotics trafficking. *The RUSI Journal, 159*(5), 52–59.

Westerman, W. (2017). Kayaktivism: The anthropology of protest, craft, and the imagination. *Martor: Revue d'Anthropologie du Musée du Paysan Roumain, 22*, 109–126. http://martor.muzeultaranuluiroman.ro/archive/martor-22-2017/

Wheeler, C. (2011). Maritime subversions and socio-political formations in Vietnamese history: A look from the marginal center (mien Trung). In M. A. Aung-Thwin & K. R. Hall (Eds.), *New perspectives on the history and historiography of Southeast Asia: Continuing explorations* (pp. 141–156). Routledge.

Zhang, H., & Bateman, S. (2017). Fishing militia, the securitization of fishery and the South China Sea dispute. *Contemporary Southeast Asia, 39*(2), 288–314.

25

THE PRIVATISATION OF MARITIME SECURITY: IMPLICATIONS FOR INTERNATIONAL SECURITY

Eugenio Cusumano and Stefano Ruzza

Between 2008 and March 2012, Somali pirates hijacked over 170 vessels in the maritime area embracing the Gulf of Aden, the Horn of Africa, and the Western Indian Ocean. As the international military missions deployed in the region proved unable to immediately stop attacks, the shipping industry has increasingly resorted to onboard armed personnel. Although precise figures are unavailable, at least 50% of the merchant ships crossing the Gulf of Aden in 2012–2013 employed armed protection, using around 2,700 guards (Brown, 2012, p. 6). Not all these personnel were private military and security companies (PMSC) contractors. Some countries did not initially authorise the presence of private armed guards, requiring merchant ships flying under their flag to resort to vessel protection detachments (VPDs) consisting of military personnel. By 2020, however, all flag states with a sizeable registry had accepted the presence of private guards on ships (Cusumano & Ruzza, 2020, 2018).

This trend, combined with the end of military operations in Iraq and Afghanistan, prompted most PMSCs to seek new business opportunities in the maritime domain. Owing to the decrease in pirate attacks occurred over the last few years, however, the maritime private security bubble bursted, causing many companies to close their doors or merge. As of 2019, there were still at least 50 PMSCs worldwide offering vessel protection services. The largest, Ambrey, has purportedly secured over 10,000 transits across the high-risk area and protects up to 124 vessels per day, still employing almost 900 guards (Cusumano & Ruzza, 2020).

The widespread reliance on PMSCs as providers of vessel protection stands in glaring contrast with the long-standing practice of discouraging the presence of weapons onboard civilian ships and states' commitment to uphold and enforce a monopoly of violence. For centuries, the most powerful states in the international system sought to limit private violence on land and at sea alike, marginalising the use of actors like mercenaries and privateers as dangerous, unlawful aberrations (Percy, 2007; Thomson, 1994). Why have countries worldwide departed from such norms and turned to PMSCs as to protect ships from pirates operating in the Gulf Aden and Western Indian Ocean? This chapter seeks to answer this question by examining the private security policies of the states hosting the three largest shipping registries worldwide: Panama, Liberia and the Marshall Islands.

DOI: 10.4324/9781003001324-28

299

As they currently account for 40% of worldwide tonnage, these countries shape the most widely applied policies in the shipping sector. Maritime private security is no exception. The fact that Panama, Liberia and the Marshall Islands alike all rapidly authorised the use of PMSCs as providers of vessel protection marked a turning point in the privatisation of maritime security worldwide, urging most states to allow for the presence of armed guards aboard ships. Despite their negligible military capabilities and economic wherewithal, Panama, Liberia and the Marshall Islands have been crucial in reshaping the state monopoly of violence at sea. Consequently, these cases highlight how even small and micro-states can play a crucial role in maritime security governance.

The chapter is structured as follows. The next section provides a brief overview of the rise of Somali piracy and the challenge it has posed to international shipping. After briefly reviewing the institution of open registries, the third section examines each of the three cases in greater details, starting with the largest registry, Panama. It then zooms into the case of Liberia, the second largest registry worldwide during the peak of Somali piracy. The final part of the third section covers the flag of the Marshall Islands. The fourth section and the ensuing conclusions analyse the reasons underlying the increasing privatisation of vessel protection, the role played by small flag states in shaping this trend, and its implications.

International Shipping and the Rise of Piracy

By the late twentieth century, the maritime domain was tightly regulated by long-standing international norms, institutionalised and codified in various treaties and conventions that protected maritime trade. Privateers were relegated to history books and the lack of weapons on merchant vessels had become an accepted practice, allowing merchant vessels to fully benefit from the "innocent passage" principle. Yet, maritime crime and piracy in particular have not disappeared. Notably, three areas have been plagued by piracy up until now: Southeast Asian seas, the Gulf of Guinea and the Gulf of Aden.

Somali piracy has been the most disruptive for the international shipping industry. In 2008 and 2009, a Somali pirate attack was taking place every 30 hours on average (Chalk, 2016, p. 123). In order to make profits, pirates systematically resorted to kidnap and ransom. In 2012 only, 589 hostages were being detained, 349 of whom captured in that very year. The World Bank estimated that between April 2005 and December 2012 Somali pirates hijacked 179 ships, collecting between US$339 and 413 million in ransoms (World Bank, 2013).

Given its magnitude and its ability to disrupt trade across the Suez Canal – a chokepoint of global importance – Somali piracy had a serious economic impact on the international shipping industry. About 23,000 ships transit through the Gulf of Aden annually, carrying roughly 50% of the world's containers (EUNAVFOR, 2012). Ship owners crossing the Suez Canal have therefore faced a number of hurdles, including the payment of large ransom in case of kidnapping, higher insurance costs, re-routings, increased speed and additional labour and security measures. Due to these reasons, Somali piracy imposed a very heavy toll on international shipping, costing up to US$7 billion per year (OBP, 2018).

In May 2008, with Resolution 1814, the UN Security Council authorised states to enter Somali territorial waters in order to fight piracy and armed robbery at sea (UN, 2008; UNSC, 2008). Since then, multilateral military missions aimed at curbing piracy gained momentum. Three major international naval missions were deployed, also known as the "Big Three", which took up the largest share of military counter-piracy efforts against Somali piracy. These "Big Three" include EUNAVFOR Atalanta, Combined Task Force 151 (CTF-151), and NATO Ocean Shield.

The shipping industry did not just pressure governments to launch naval missions but also took independent initiatives. The most relevant of these is the introduction and update of the so-called "Best Management Practices" (BMPs), a set of guidelines on how to deter pirates and to protect ships and seafarers when transiting across the High Risk Area (HRA) affected by Somali pirate attacks. Since their first inception in 2009, the BMPs have been updated four times, with their latest edition (the fifth) released in 2018. According to the BMP3, the HRA "defines itself by where the piracy attacks have taken place", and was originally "bounded by Suez to the North, 10°S and 78°E" (BMP3, 2010, p. 3). The physical extension of the HRA was later revised. Nonetheless, construing the HRA as a securitised space was a form of "zonation" that enabled exceptional measures usually prohibited or discouraged in other areas, including the use of PMSCs (Bueger, 2018; Ryan, 2019).

The first three versions of the BMPs only recommended passive security measures like electrical fences and armoured citadels where the crew could find shelter and retain control of the ship. The combination of passive security measures and international military missions failed to deliver immediate results in curbing pirate attacks, which continued unabated until 2011. Consequently, the fourth edition of these best practices published in August 2011 (BMP4) foresees the possibility for ship owners to resort to armed protection aboard. Specifically, Section 8.15 of BMP4 drops previous caveats against security personnel, stating that ship operators have the option to consider armed guards as an additional layer of security. The document, however, expresses a preference for military vessel protection detachments (VPDs) over private security teams (BMP4, 2010, pp. 39–40).

Open Registries and International Shipping

Around 70% of worldwide tonnage currently flies the flag of a country different from its own. This figure was only slightly smaller when Somali piracy was at its peak (UNCTAD, 2012, p. 45, 2013; p. 55; 2017, p. 32). Three states in particular – Panama, Liberia and the Republic of the Marshall Islands – host the largest open naval registries (UNCTAD, 2019). Panama's flag flies on the largest merchant fleet worldwide in terms of deadweight tonnage (DWT), followed by the Marshall Islands, which in 2018 overtook Liberia, still the third largest flag (UNCTAD, 2019–2008). Panama, Liberia and the Marshall Islands have developed the largest shipping registries worldwide by adopting laws and regulations that closely resonate with the desiderata of the international shipping industry. Their policies, however, are not identical, as each of these flags has specialised in serving a specific segment of the industry. As the remainder of the chapter will show, important differences can also be found with respect to how these countries regulate the provision of maritime security.

According to the *United Nations Convention on the Law of the Sea* (UNCLOS, 1982), any ship should sail under a state's flag. It is such a flag that determines to which laws and regulations a vessel adheres. Consequently, ship owners have developed a strong tendency to register their ships in specific countries, often referred to "flags of convenience" (FoCs). Flying such flags entails a number of benefits, including lighter taxation, and looser labour, safety and environmental legislation. The need to protect vessels from pirates has introduced another factor in ship owners' preference for a flag over another: the perceived clarity and efficiency of the regulations concerning the use of armed personnel onboard.

Given the large number of ships flying their flags, as illustrated by Table 25.1, Panama, Liberia and the Marshall Islands were heavily hit by piracy. As shown by Table 25.2, a sizeable number of these attacks consisted in successful hijacking by Somali pirates.

Table 25.1 Pirate attacks against Panamanian-, Liberian- and Marshallese-flagged vessels 2007–2013

	2007	2008	2009	2010	2011	2012	2013
Panama	42	52	69	82	71	49	32
Liberia	28	19	38	57	57	45	43
Marshall Islands	16	15	29	36	45	21	31

Source: IMB (2008–2014).

Table 25.2 Hijackings of Panamanian-, Liberian- and Marshallese-flagged vessels by Somali pirates, 2007–2013

	2007	2008	2009	2010	2011	2012	2013
Panama	1	8	6	11	6	3	0
Liberia	0	3	0	3	2	2	0
Marshall Islands	0	1	2	4	2	0	0

Source: IMB 2008–2014

Attacks dropped after 2011, when each of these countries had enacted policies authorising the presence of armed guards. Although they all consisted of the use of PMSCs, these policies display some differences, which will be examined below.

Panama

Historical reasons, such as the Prohibition or German owners' willingness to avoid having their ships attacked and apprehended during the Second World War, made the Panamanian flag very popular since the first half of the twentieth century. Today, Panama accounts for the largest share of merchant ships worldwide and its flag flies on 17% of the global tonnage. The country also occupies the second position globally for number of ships, with almost 8,000 vessels in 2019 (8.4% of the world total).

Since Panama's flag flies on the largest worldwide fleet, it is unsurprisingly that it has been affected by an outstanding number of pirate attacks. Between 2007 and 2013, the Panamanian fleet fell victim to 35 successful hijackings by Somali pirates, which peaked between 2008 and 2011 (see Tables 25.1 and 25.2). Panama's status as a demilitarised country made it impossible to deploy VPDs on ships, forcing to default on private contractors. As the absence of national armed forces also limited the capabilities of Panamanian private security companies, the list of PMSCs accredited with Panamanian authorities to provide maritime security services outlined in circular MMC-245 is dominated by British and Greek PMSCs (Panama Maritime Authority, 2012b).

The use of armed guards onboard Panamanian-flagged vessels was first regulated in August 2011 with Merchant Marine Circular 228 (MMC-228) (Panama Maritime Authority, 2011), published right after the international shipping industry gave its blessing to the presence of armed personnel aboard vessels by publishing the BMP4. According to MMC-228, guards have to be supernumerary to maintain a clear distinction between the security team, the crew and their respective functions. In 2012, the Merchant Marine General Bureau of the Panama Maritime Authority perfected the general regime regulating the use of PMSCs with the issuing of Resolution No. 106-13-DGMM. The regulations contained therein detailed the process allowing PMSCs to be accredited by the General Directorate of the Merchant Marine for the delivery of onboard security, including armed protection. More specifically, the document states that, in order to be accredited, a PMSC ought to provide proof of insurance for damage to third parties, perform adequate checks on the expertise of the personnel they employ, have clear procedures for the handling and inventory of weapons onboard ships (including transport, shipment and disembarkation) and abide to international quality standard (Panama Maritime Authority, 2012a). Furthermore, Resolution No. 106-13-DGMM indicates that the "General Directorate of the Merchant Marine may establish and clarify concepts and additional details regarding the requirements and procedures for the authorisation of the private security companies by means of Merchant Marine Circulars", it is to say MMCs (Panama Maritime Authority, 2012a, p. 5).

The Panamanian regulation on armed onboard protection has indeed been expanded through several of MMC circulars and resolutions which did not alter the substance of the regulatory framework, but outlined further details. Notably, Resolution No. 106-85-DGMM requires PMSCs to provide the list of security personnel operating onboard and sets the fees to be paid, namely a lump sum of 1,000 Panamanian Balboas (corresponding to US$1,000) to apply for authorisation and an annual fee of 5,000 Panamanian Balboas (US$5,000) to maintain the accreditation. Resolution No. 106-85-DGMM also clarifies the cases in which authorisation for maritime PMSCs can be revoked. The list includes crime, misconduct, technical deficiencies and failure in corresponding fees, but also states that a company will lose authorisation if it does not perform any transit for a period of two years.

The introduction of private security on vessels flying the Panamanian flag had positive effects for their security when transiting through the HRA. Already in 2011, the number of successful hijackings by Somali pirates decreased, inverting the trend of the previous years. 2012 registered only three successful hijackings, which dropped to zero from 2013 on. According to maritime and security professionals, Panama's regulatory regime of maritime PMSCs is relatively simple and therefore quite popular among ship owners and operators.[1] Circular MMC-245 contains a list of all the PMSCs accredited to work on Panamanian-flagged vessels. According to a Peter Cook, co-founder of (now dissolved) SAMI, Circular MMC-245 used to contain around a hundred names.[2] However, the decreasing threat of Somali piracy led to a natural reduction in numbers. The May 2014 version of the document listed only 79 companies, which further decreased to 59 in July 2017 (Panama Maritime Authority, 2012b).

Liberia

After the Second World War, former US Secretary of State Edward Stettinius decided to launch a corporate form of economic aid to Liberia which included the creation of a shipping registry. As of today, the Liberian registry is managed by the Liberian International Ship & Corporate Registry (LISCR), an US-based corporation (de Sombre, 2006; IRI, 2020a; Liberian registry, 2020; Stopford, 2009). The Liberian registry has been the second largest for tonnage globally up until 2018, when it was surpassed by the Marshall Islands. In 2019, the Liberian flag accounted for 12% of global tonnage and around 3,500 vessels (more than 3.6% of the world's total).

As one of the largest worldwide, and the second largest at the peak of Somali piracy, Liberia's fleet has suffered from a large number of piracy-related incidents. The worst period was between 2008 and 2013, when ten vessels were hijacked by Somali pirates (see Tables 25.1 and Table 25.2). It was impossible for Liberia to address piracy via military means, as the country has a small military, but lacks a navy. Moreover, Liberia has very restrictive firearms laws, a legacy of the devastating civil wars that plagued the country. Liberian gun laws are not only very restrictive in general, but also prohibit PMSCs from arming their personnel (GunPolicy.org, 2020). Notwithstanding Liberia's restrictive firearms regulation on land, there are no specific limits about weapons and onboard Liberian-flagged vessels, permitted at the owner and master's discretion (Liberian Bureau of Maritime Affairs, 2011b). The very large size of the Liberian-flagged fleet, the restrictive gun laws and an underdeveloped local private security industry meant that the private provision of onboard counter-piracy security could not be sourced locally, but had to be provided by foreign PMSCs.

Regulation of onboard armed teams was clarified with the Maritime Security Advisory 03/2011 (MSA 03/2011) by the Liberian Bureau of Maritime Affairs in May 2011 (Liberian Bureau of Maritime Affairs, 2011a). MSA 03/2011 is pretty minimalistic, outlining only few restrictions and obligation for PMSCs and their employers. First, the document states that ship operators willing to resort to armed teams should submit a ship security plan (SSP) to the Maritime Administration. This plan should describe the procedures pertaining to application of additional counter-piracy measures; watch keeping and vigilance; communication procedures with the PCASP [armed team]; use of defensive measures; use of passive/non-lethal devices; authority of the Master (PCASP embarked on the vessel are at all times subject to the authority of the vessel's Master); activation of PCASP and the risk of escalation. (Liberian Bureau of Maritime Affairs, 2011a, pp. 1–2). MSA 03/2011 also requires ship operators to verify the background and experience of the PMSCs they employ; to take care of proper onboard accommodation and of the safety of the security personnel; to verify the ability of the crew and the armed team to cooperate; to agree rules for the use of force with the security company; and to guarantee full compliance with BMPs. Each of these points is addressed in few lines of text without providing additional details, which leaves owners and operators ample leeway. The permissiveness of Liberia's approach is apparent in the lack of any list of Liberian-licensed PMSCs, which leaves ship owners the freedom to resort to any private security provider at their own risk.

Notwithstanding the large size of Liberia's fleet, hijackings dropped to zero in 2013, consistent with the trend experienced by other large flags worldwide. This result was partially due to the use of armed teams. In October 2011, for instance, boarding attempt on the Liberian-flagged cargo *Lara Rickmers* was successfully thwarted by armed private security guards (IMB, 2012).

The Marshall Islands

The Republic of the Marshall Islands (RMI) is a micro-state spreading across more than a thousand islands that cover a total surface of only 181 square kilometres. From 2007 to 2018, the Marshall Islands' aggregate GDP hovered between US$150 and 220 million. As showcased by these modest figures, the Marshall Islands do not have a self-sustaining economy. Imports consistently exceed exports, and the largest contribution to the national GDP comes from US assistance and lease payments for the military use of the Kwajalein Atoll (CIA, 2020). It is easy to understand why a large shipping registry is essential to the Marshall Islands and the US alike. For a microstate lacking a significant domestic economy like the RMI, a naval registry is a fundamental source of revenues. As for the US, the availability of a naval registry in a formally sovereign but *de facto* subordinated state (Veenendaal, 2017) guarantees all the advantages of a FoC without the attached risks and reputational costs.

The advantages attached to the Marshallese flag enabled a steady growth in the size of its registry. In 2018, the Marshallese flag accounted for more than 12% of the global deadweight tonnage and for about 3,500 vessels in 2019 (more than 3.6% of the world total) (UNCTAD, 2019). The value of the Marshallese fleet – one of the youngest worldwide – increased even faster than its size, including a large number of "high-value liquefied natural gas tankers, off-shore drill ships and other specialised vessels" (UNCTAD, 2017, p. 32). Moreover, the Marshallese registry recently diversified its customer base as well, with Greece supplanting the United States as the first country of ownership (IRI, 2020b; UNCTAD, 2019–2008).

Vessels flying the flag of the Marshall Islands have been hijacked by Somali pirates a grand total of nine times between 2007 and 2013, just once less than those flying Liberia's flag. Four hijackings occurred in 2010 only (see Tables 25.1 and 25.2), but no attacks occurred after 2012.

For obvious reasons, the Marshall Islands – themselves dependent on US military protection – could not resort to military personnel to protect their merchant fleet. At times, however, its vessels used military personnel provided by other states, a possibility explicitly envisaged by Marshallese maritime security regulations. In addition, the Marshall Islands' also encouraged the resort to passive security measures. Along with Panama, Liberia and the Bahamas (the fourth major flag of convenience), the Marshall Islands publicly committed to the BMPs during CGPCS meetings (CGPCS, 2009; Weitz, 2011). Moreover, the Marshall Islands financially supported the so-called "Djibouti Code of Conduct", created to help coastal states face the Gulf of Aden to fight piracy, via its trust fund (IMO, 2009).

Firearms regulations of the Marshall Islands are extremely restrictive. According to the 1971 Weapons Control Act (then revised in 2004) and the 1983 Firearms Control Act, civilian ownership of firearms is banned altogether. The Marshall Islands' regulation of armed teams' onboard civilian vessels is also more articulated and thorough than its Panamanian and Liberian counterparts. The main guidelines are contained in Marine Notice No. 2–011-39, published by the Republic of the Marshall Islands Maritime Administrator in 2011. Since then, the policy has been updated several times (the last in April 2019). The Marshallese policy clearly defines the two main criteria for private protection: the kind of ship and the need to transit through a risky area. As for the type of vessel, the Marshall Islands' vessel protection policy applies to passenger ships, cargo or special purpose ships of a gross tonnage of 500 or above and self-propelled mobile offshore drilling units capable of travelling. In terms of geographic scope, the policy does not apply exclusively to the HRA defined in the BMPs, but also to several other maritime regions plagued with maritime crime (e.g., the Gulf of Guinea and Southeast Asian seas).

The guidelines provided by MN 2–011-39 include a standardised set of indications, including requests to draft a comprehensive risk assessment and a ship security plan (SSP) as well as ensuring that the PMSCs to be employed for onboard protection have relevant maritime experience, certifiable procedures and adequately vetted personnel. This basic set of guidelines has been present since the inception of the policy and remains in place to date (Republic of the Marshall Islands, Maritime Administrator, 2019, 2013 and 2011). Their most important feature is that compliance with all the elements listed above is compulsory, not just recommended. The presence of weapons onboard is allowed for as long as the ship is "not trading within internal, archipelagic, or territorial waters of the Republic of the Marshall Islands" (Republic of the Marshall Islands, 1971, p. 5). The maximum number of allowed weapons is three per guard, with an ammunition cap currently set at 250 rounds each (previously 300). Weapons need to be owned and licensed for export, transport and use by the PMSC, and only the employees of said PMSC can use them. Private armed teams are required to be supernumerary and distinct from the crew to maintain a clear distinction between guards and seafarers. The original policy did not state any required minimum number of guards, but this requirement was later updated to three (Republic of the Marshall Islands, Maritime Administrator, 2019, 2013 and 2011).

The policy contained in MN 2–011-39 requires private armed teams to follow clear rules for the use of force. The Republic of the Marshall Islands has been directly involved in the establishment of such rules. In cooperation with the International Chamber of Shipping (ICS) and the Baltic and International Maritime Council (BIMCO), the Marshall Islands have drafted code known as *The 100 Series Rules: An International Model Set of Maritime Rules for the Use of Force*, published in May 2013.[3] Accordingly, the Marshall Islands have advocated the 100 Rules as a standard to follow for all PMSCs operating aboard its merchant fleet. Moreover, the Marshallese regulatory framework also requires compliance with International Standardization Association (ISO) standards. Since January 2016, ship owners and operators are therefore obliged to rely exclusively on PMSCs that have been certified as ISO 28007 compliant (Republic of the Marshall Islands, Maritime Administrator, 2019, 2013 and 2011).

Once the Marshall Islands Maritime Administrator finds the request to have PMSCs on vessels in compliance with existing regulations, it then issues a "letter of non-objection" (LONO). LONOs are valid for a single voyage and do not represent a blanket authorisation for onboard armed security. Details to be provided when asking for a LONO include all the elements that allow for a clear identification of the vessel, as well as the names of the master, the company security officer (CSO) and the vessel operator or agent. In 2012, more than 1,000 were granted, but this number grew in the following years. This increase proves that – despite the drop in Somali piracy – the use of armed guards' onboard merchant vessels has been mainstreamed as a new normal.[4]

Open Registries and Maritime Security Privatisation

The fleets of Panama, Liberia and the Marshall Islands account for about 40% of worldwide tonnage. As FoCs, these countries developed policies that are clearly informed by the preferences of the global shipping industry. Consequently, when the global shipping industry started supporting armed protection, the resort to PMSCs became a widespread practice across each of these three countries, which drafted their maritime security regulations accordingly. Since protected transits are generally not recorded (with the Marshall Islands as an exception to this general rule), it is impossible to pin down how many vessels flying FoCs have resorted to commercial vessel protection. The figures on the LONOs provided by the Marshallese registry, however, suggest that armed onboard protection has become a standard practice of the global shipping industry. According to security professionals, one whole generation of seafarers has now grown used to the presence of armed guards onboard, and the concern they had initially expressed about the presence of armed guards on merchant ships at the beginning of the 2010s has now waned.[5]

The maritime private security policies of Panama, Liberia and the Marshall Islands have been quickly formulated in response to the demands of the global shipping industry and have been only been slightly polished over time. Since no major widely publicised incident occurred, there has been no significant pressure for a substantial overhaul of these arrangements in any of the three cases considered. While they have all authorised private armed teams, the three countries considered here have quite different regimes. At one extreme, the Marshall Islands have a very thorough authorisation process, incorporating the best international standards and practices as soon as these became available. At the other extreme, Liberia ultimately allows ship operators to do as they please at their own risk. Panama falls somewhere in the middle, although the requirements to operate on Panamanian-flagged vessels are closer to Liberian than Marshallese standards. The permissive maritime private security policies developed by Liberia and Panama may have problematic consequences. Due to the difficulty to monitor the activities of private guards in the high sea, enforcing tight professional standards and reporting mechanisms is of crucial importance to avoid abuses in the use of force against suspect pirates and a host of other incidents.

But why has the privatisation of vessel protection been so pervasive in the largest shipping registries and worldwide despite its potentially problematic consequences? Private security scholars have identified four main drivers of security privatisation: functionalist explanations explain the use of PMSCs as the outcome of financial as well as strategic material constraints and incentives; ideational explanations link the decision to (not) privatise security to international as well as domestic norms and cultures; political explanations stress the convenience of privatisation as a way to circumvent the political costs and constraints attached to the deployment of soldiers abroad; organisational explanations focus on the preferences and cultures of foreign policy and security bureaucracies, which tend to resist the outsourcing of activities seen as part of their core mission but welcome the privatisation of unwelcome, peripheral tasks (Cusumano & Ruzza, 2020; Kinsey & Patterson, 2012; Kruck, 2014).

Functionalist explanations play a key role in accounting for the increasing resort to commercial providers of vessel protection. Due to the size and nature of the maritime milieu, it is difficult for states to control the sea, which inevitably enables the proliferation of transnational threats. The ability to police maritime shipping lanes is further hindered by problems of collective action and inter-operability. Consequently, protecting merchant fleets is a major challenge even for great powers. The comprehensive commercialisation of vessel protection has been further magnified by the unique configuration that the institution of sovereignty has assumed in the maritime domain. Under the international law of the sea, ships on the high seas are considered under the jurisdiction of flag states, which ensures a right of innocent passage and protection from unauthorised boarding. The creation of open registries, however, has caused a mismatch between countries' military and diplomatic capabilities, and the size of their merchant fleet (de Nevers, 2015). Owing to the creation of open registries, countries with very small or even no military capabilities, such as Panama, the Marshall Islands and Liberia, fly their flags over a very large number of vessels that cannot be protected by their military capabilities. The rise of maritime piracy in the international waters off the Horn of Africa has rendered this mismatch apparent. In this context, PMSCs have served as a surrogate for the protection that small flag states have been unable to provide. Owing to their limited military capabilities, small states with large shipping registries had no choice but delegating their sovereign power to protect ships to the private sector. Far from remaining the preserve of small flags of convenience, this strategy has also proved appealing to larger countries. Ultimately, the extensive commercialisation of vessel protection is at least in part as an unintended by-product of the very tenuous link between merchant ships and their flag states.

The fact that both small states with large shipping registries and large naval powers like the United States and the United Kingdom opted for commercial vessel protection mainstreamed the use of PMSCs at sea into a new normal, encouraging other countries to engage in a process of emulation and use of armed contractors to circumvent the logistical hurdles and political costs attached to deploying their own military personnel aboard merchant ships (Cusumano & Ruzza, 2018).

Conclusion

The privatisation of security in expeditionary military operations has often proved problematic, causing abuses and externalities that have been detrimental to achieving the objectives of counterinsurgency and state-building missions like those in Iraq and Afghanistan (Cusumano, 2016; Kruck, 2014). Commercial vessel protection, on the other hand, provides a more encouraging picture. As no vessel protected by armed guards has been hijacked by Somali pirates, the shipping and insurance industries have credited PMSCs for being effective maritime security providers. Even the Security Council of the United Nations (UN) has praised armed guards as crucial to deter pirate attacks (UNSC, 2018).

To be sure, evidence of PMSCs' effectiveness against piracy is sketchier and less conclusive than often assumed. Far from being caused by PMSCs alone, the drop in pirate attacks was the combined outcome of several factors, including military missions in the Indian Ocean, capacity-building initiatives on African mainland and the wider set of BMPs devised by the shipping industry. Moreover, contracted teams did not always possess sufficient training, nor have they always displayed discipline and restraint. These caveats notwithstanding, PMSCs have generally been capable of protecting merchant vessels at lower costs than VPDs. Although somewhat simplistic, this widespread perception has played an important role in encouraging the commercialisation of vessel protection, vindicating the argument that privatisation can generate effective security at reduced costs.

This belief may spill over into the land domain as well, accelerating the resort to PMSCs for the provision of a number of other tasks. Consequently, the case of vessel protection policies examined in this chapter confirms that the maritime arena serves as "a crucible for change and innovation in global politics as a whole" (Bueger & Edmunds, 2017, p. 1311). Rather than being a replica of the governance arrangements in place for the privatisation of security on land, the institutional frameworks developed by flag states to authorise PMSCs on ships display several unique features. Indeed, the regulation of PMSCs at sea significantly departed from the provisions in place for private guards on land, often permitting the use of weaponry usually not allowed by flag states on their domestic territory.

Due to the institution of open registries, even small and micro-states like those examined in this chapter can therefore play a major role not only in maritime security, but also in re-designing the state monopoly of violence and the institution of sovereignty at large.

Notes

1 Interview with British private security professional (21 May 2019); Interview with Cristiano Aliperta, Alternate Permanent Representative of Italy to the IMO 2011-16 (31 May 2019); interview with Peter Cook, co-founder of SAMI (24 and 25 June 2019).
2 Interview with Peter Cook, co-founder of SAMI (24 and 25 June 2019).
3 Interview with Peter Cook, co-founder of SAMI (24 and 25 June 2019).
4 Email exchanges with anonymous source, March 2020.
5 Interview with Peter Cook; email exchange with a designated person ashore from a Ship Management Company involved in seafarer hostage negotiation, March 2020.

References

BMP3. (2010, June). *Best management practices 3: piracy off the coast of Somalia and Arabian Sea area*. Witherby Publishing Group.
BMP4. (2011, August). *Best management practices for protection against Somalia-based piracy*. Witherby Publishing Group.
Brown, J. (2012). Pirates and privateers: Managing the Indian Ocean's Private Security *Boom*. *Lowy Institute for International Policy*. Retrieved 12 September 2019 from https://archive.lowyinstitute.org/sites/default/files/brown_pirates_and_privateers_web_0.pdf
Bueger, C. (2018). Territory, authority, expertise: Global governance and the counter-piracy assemblage. *European Journal of International Relations*, *24*(3), 614–637.
Bueger, C., & Edmunds, T. (2017). Beyond seablindness: A new agenda for maritime security studies. *International Affairs*, *93*(6), 1293–1311.
CGPCS [Contact Group on Piracy off the Coast of Somalia]. (2009, May 29). Communiqué.

Chalk, P. (2016). The privatization of counter-piracy: Implications for order at sea. In S. Ruzza, A. P. Jakobi, & C. Geisler (Eds.), *Non-state challenges in a re-ordered world* (pp. 122–138). Routledge.

CIA [Central Intelligence Agency]. (2020). *Marshall Islands*. Updated: 7 February 2020. Retrieved 8 February 2020 from https://www.cia.gov/library/publications/the-world-factbook/geos/pm.html

Cusumano, E. (2016). Bridging the gap. Mobilisation constraints and contractor support to US and UK military operations. *Journal of Strategic Studies, 33*(1), 94–119.

Cusumano, E., & Ruzza, S. (2018). Piracy and the commercialisation of vessel protection. *International Relations, 32*(1), 80–103.

Cusumano, E., & Ruzza, S. (2020). *Piracy and the privatization of vessel protection*. Palgrave.

de Nevers, R. (2015). Sovereignty at sea: States and security in the maritime domain. *Security Studies, 24*(4), 597–630.

de Sombre, E. R. (2006). *Flagging standards: Globalization and environmental, safety, and labor regulations at sea*. The MIT Press.

EUNAVFOR. (2012, May 12). European Union naval force Somalia operation Atalanta. Presentation EU Open Day.

GunPolicy.org. (2020). Retrieved 9 February 2020 from https://www.gunpolicy.org

IMB [International Maritime Bureau]. (2008, 2009, 2010, 2011, 2012, 2013, 2015, 2016, 2017, 2018, 2019). *Piracy and armed robbery against ships*.

IMO [International Maritime Organization]. (2009, 29 January). *The code of conduct concerning the repression of piracy and armed robbery against ships in the Western Indian Ocean and the Gulf of Aden* (Djibouti Code of Conduct).

IRI [International Registries Inc.]. (2020a). https://www.register-iri.com

IRI [International Registries Inc.]. (2020b). *Fleet highlights*. https://www.register-iri.com/info-center/fleet-highlights

Kinsey, C., & Patterson, M. H. (Eds.) (2012). *Contractors and war: The transformation of United States' expeditionary operations*. Stanford University Press.

Kruck, A. (2014). Theorising the use of private military and security companies: A synthetic perspective. *Journal of International Relations and Development, 17*, 112–141.

Liberian Bureau of Maritime Affairs. (2011a, May 24). *Maritime security advisory 03/2011* (MSA 03/2011).

Liberian Bureau of Maritime Affairs. (2011b). *Piracy: Guidance for liberian flagged vessels regarding 3rd party security teams*.

Liberian registry. (2020). https://www.liscr.com

OBP [Oceans Beyond Piracy]. (2018). The state of maritime piracy 2017. One Earth Future Foundation. http://oceansbeyondpiracy.org/reports/sop/summary.

Panama Maritime Authority. (2011). *MMC-228 – Use of armed security personnel on board Panamanian flagged vessels (online application)*. Updated: December 2019.

Panama Maritime Authority. (2012a). MMC-238 – *Ship protection measures for vessels transiting high risk areas*. Updated: March 2014.

Panama Maritime Authority. (2012b). *MMC-245 – Authorized private maritime security companies (PMSC) transiting high risk areas (online application)*. Updated: July 2017.

Percy, S. (2007). *Mercenaries: The history of a norm in international relations*. Oxford University Press.

Republic of the Marshall Islands, Maritime Administrator. (1971). *Weapons Control Act*.

Republic of the Marshall Islands, Maritime Administrator. (2011, November). *Marine Notice No. 2-011-39 – Use of Privately Contracted Armed Security Personnel (PCASP)*.

Republic of the Marshall Islands, Maritime Administrator. (2013, February 14). Marine Notice No. 2-011-39—Use of Privately Contracted Armed Security Personnel (PCASP). Rev.

Republic of the Marshall Islands, Maritime Administrator. (2019). Marine notice No. 2-011-39—Piracy, Armed Robbery, and the Use of Armed Security.

Ryan, B. (2019). The disciplined sea: A history of maritime security and zonation. *International Affairs, 95*(5), 1055–1073.

Stopford, M. (2009). *Maritime economics*. Routledge.

The 100 Series Rules: An International Model Set of Maritime Rules for the Use of Force (RUF) (2013).

Thomson, J. E. (1994). *Mercenaries, pirates and sovereigns*. Princeton University Press.

UN [United Nations]. (2008, June 2). Security Council Condemns Acts of Piracy, Armed Robbery Off Somalia's Coast, Authorizes for Six Months "All Necessary Means" to Repress Such Acts. Retrieved 20 March 2019 from https://www.un.org/press/en/2008/sc9344.doc.htm

UNCLOS. (1982). United Nations Convention on the Law of the Sea. https://www.un.org/Depts/los/convention_agreements/texts/unclos/unclos_e.pdf

UNCTAD [United Nations Conference on Trade and Development]. (2008, 2009, 2010, 2011, 2012, 2013, 2014, 2015, 2016, 2017, 2018, 2019). *Review of maritime transport.* https://unctad.org/en/Pages/Publications/Review-of-Maritime-Transport-(Series).aspx

UNSC [United Nations Security Council]. (2008, May 15). Resolution 1814. On the relocation of the UN Political Office for Somalia (UNPOS) from Nairobi to Somalia(S/RES/1814). https://digitallibrary.un.org/record/626781?ln=en

UNSC [United Nations Security Council]. (2018, October). *The situation with respect to piracy and armed robbery at sea off the coast of Somalia* (S/2018/903). https://www.securitycouncilreport.org/atf/cf/%7B65BFCF9B-6D27-4E9C-8CD3-CF6E4FF96FF9%7D/s_2018_903.pdf

Veenendaal, W. P. (2017). Analyzing the foreign policy of microstates. The relevance of the international patron-client model. *Foreign Policy Analysis, 13*(3), 561–577.

Weitz, R. (2011). War and governance: international security in a changing world order. Praeger.

World Bank. (2013). "Pirate trails" tracks dirty money resulting from piracy off the horn of Africa. https://www.worldbank.org/en/news/press-release/2013/11/01/pirate-trails-tracks-dirty-money-resulting-from-piracy-off-the-horn-of-africa

26

NATO AND MARITIME SECURITY IN THE NORTH ATLANTIC

Gavin E. L. Hall and Mark Webber

In June 2016 Vice Admiral James Foggo, Commander of the US Sixth Fleet, declared the "Fourth Battle of the Atlantic" to be underway (Foggo & Fritz, 2016). The North Atlantic is once again an arena of strategic competition after a period of transient stability since the end of the Cold War. This chapter explores the key elements of that competition. First, it provides the context for maritime (in)security in the region by defining the geographic parameters of the North Atlantic and identifying the institutional configurations in place there. Second, the chapter analyses the interactions between different Atlantic actors. Third, potential future developments are assessed. Through the lens of strategic competition, the North Atlantic is characterised as a site for the deployment of advanced military power.

Context of Maritime (In)Security – Institutional Configurations and Ocean Policies

The North Atlantic was a key theatre of maritime military operations in the twentieth century. Significant activity was evident in both the Great War and the Second World War. The Battle of the Atlantic spanned almost the entirety of the Second World War, was pivotal to the British war effort and confirmed the essential material connection between the US and Canada on the one hand, and the European allies on the other. The North Atlantic Treaty of 1949 (which gave rise to NATO) was an expression of that trans-Atlantic link – one subsequently reinforced by the exigencies of East-West rivalry (see next section). With the end of the Cold War, the strategic standing of the North Atlantic waned – a process that spanned the 1990s and early 2000s as the historic tensions between NATO and Russia abated. That situation, however, has been in reverse since 2008 (the year of the Russo-Georgia war). And from 2014 (the year of Russia's annexation of Crimea), NATO and individual allies have once again come to regard Russia as a strategic rival (Roberts, 2019).

The strategic importance of the North Atlantic is determined by the number of different oceans and seas to which it connects: the Arctic, Mediterranean, Baltic, Norwegian and Caribbean. It is a gateway ocean that is constrained by chokepoints especially on its eastern side (Hamre & Conley, 2018). The International Hydrographic Organisation (IHO) (1953) identifies the North Atlantic as the area between the eastern seaboard of the United States across to southern Greenland, and then following a line across to Iceland and the Northern waters of the

DOI: 10.4324/9781003001324-29

311

United Kingdom (UK), stretching down the west coast of the UK, Ireland, Europe and Africa until it reaches the equator. The CIA World Factbook (Central Intelligence Agency, 2020) goes further by including the Caribbean and Gulf of Mexico, the Mediterranean, the Gulf of Guinea, the North Sea, the Baltic and the Northern Passage up to the Norwegian island of Svalbard. The North Atlantic Treaty, meanwhile, sets the boundaries for the application of its collective defence provisions (Article V of the treaty) as essentially the same as the IHO's *Limits of Oceans and Seas*, but specifically identifies the Tropic of Cancer as the southern boundary (NATO, 1949). Proceeding from that definition, the focus of this chapter is on the North Atlantic up to the Greenland-Iceland-UK (GIUK) Gap, excluding the High North, Arctic, North Sea and the Baltic (although these northern latitudes are seen as connecting to Atlantic contingencies).

Beyond NATO, there are few international institutional apparatuses focused on the North Atlantic, bar occasional bilateral fisheries treaties covering specific sections of the ocean. The United Nations Law of the Sea Convention (UNCLOS), signed in 1982, established freedom of navigation rights and established 12 nautical mile territorial boundaries as well as exclusive economic zones (EEZ) 200 nautical miles out from the states in question. Compared to the bordering Arctic Ocean, the North Atlantic is not the site of significant territorial disputes. This state of affairs is due to the geographic separation of interested parties, something that limits contestation to the boundaries of EEZ. A case in point here is the dispute over Rockall – a once *terra nullius* islet formally annexed by the UK in 1972. This rocky outcrop is situated some 162 nautical miles to the west of Scotland's Outer Hebrides and 263 nautical miles north-west of Ireland. London and Dublin signed a bilateral EEZ boundary agreement in November 1988, although Ireland does not recognise the UK jurisdiction of the rock. Both Iceland and Denmark meanwhile, dispute this delineation (but unlike Ireland neither claims sovereignty to Rockall itself). All four nations have utilised the conflict resolution mechanisms within the UNCLOS, and whilst unresolved to the satisfaction of all parties, the lack of political capital invested in the dispute suggests it is not a source of fundamental disagreement.

Territorial dispute, then, is not a marker of the North Atlantic's security status. That stems rather from the position of the ocean as a site of strategic manoeuvre. As one observer (Nordenman, 2019, p. 12) has noted, "[a] war in Europe will not be won in the North Atlantic, but it can surely be lost there".

Interactions between Actors

Security competition in the North Atlantic is determined overwhelmingly by the relationship between the NATO allies and Russia. NATO is, however, dispersed and differentiated. The navies of Germany, Poland and the Netherlands, lacking easy access to the Atlantic, are concentrated on coastal defence. The navies of Norway and Denmark prioritise the Arctic; those of Greece, Italy and Turkey look primarily to the Mediterranean. Turkey, along with Romania and Bulgaria, is also oriented towards the Black Sea. Among NATO's Atlantic-facing members, Spain Portugal, Canada, and France retain a significant presence in the ocean (this includes Atlantic submarine patrols of French strategic nuclear forces), but two allies are key to NATO's Atlantic position: the US and the UK. That said, because NATO acts as a collective expression of maritime strategy, doctrine and deployment, it is worth regarding it as a distinct actor in its own right. This section thus begins with an overview of the Alliance as such. It then turns to the positions of the US and the UK, and then to NATO's principal rival, Russia.

NATO, since its inception in 1949, has been premised on the indivisibility of security in the Euro-Atlantic Area. "The North Atlantic Alliance", the 2014 declaration on "The Transatlantic

Bond" notes, "binds North America and Europe in the defence of [...] common security" (NATO, 2014, paragraph 1). To deliver that goal, requires political cohesion among a large group of allies (a constant work in progress in NATO) and a planning assumption that a major reinforcement in the European theatre would require a reliable supply route by air and sea across the Atlantic. During the Cold War, NATO plans aimed at countering Soviet aggression through conventional means were premised on Western Europe benefitting from a major injection of forces from North America (Canada figured here, but US forces were clearly crucial). This meant transiting across the North Atlantic and required sufficient local infrastructure in order to manage the embarkation and de-embarkation of personnel and material. Between 1969 and 1993 annual Return of Forces to Germany (REFORGER) exercises provided forceful demonstration of a collective resolve to furnish this "transcontinental reinforcement" (Blackwill & Legro, 1989, p. 70). In the post-Cold War period, these contingencies fell out of NATO's planning cycles. They have been revived since 2014 (see next). The Trident Juncture exercises in 2015 and 2018, as well as Defender 2020, are REFORGER's latter-day equivalents (Judson, 2019).

The centrality of the North Atlantic to NATO was underlined by the establishment of Allied Command Atlantic in 1952. In June 2003, however, the Command was disbanded to be replaced by Allied Command Transformation. In parallel, Allied Command Europe was replaced by Allied Command Operations. NATO's two strategic commands thus moved from a geographic to a functional focus. This reflected NATO's post-Cold War orientation towards crisis management, counterterrorism and stabilisation (evident in the Balkans, Afghanistan and Libya). Here, the traditional tasks of collective defence assumed a lesser importance. NATO's maritime configuration in the decade or so after 2003 was geared towards support for these more important missions or towards small-scale naval engagements (counter-piracy missions off East Africa and counter-terrorism patrols in the Mediterranean). NATO's Allied Maritime Component Command operated between 2004 and 2010, before being replaced by Allied Maritime Command (MARCOM), based at Northwood near London. MARCOM became the sole maritime component for NATO with the deactivation of Allied Maritime Command Naples in March 2013 and operated under Joint Force Command Brunssum. The operational remit of MARCOM extended to leading the four NATO Standing Maritime Groups; two frigate groups (SNMG1 and SNMG2) and two mine countermeasures groups (SNMCMG1 and SNMCMG2).

The downgrading of trans-Atlantic defence in NATO's organisational hierarchy was felt acutely in Eastern Europe. Jolted by the Russo-Georgia war of 2008, political leaders in the region complained that the US, and NATO more broadly, were neglecting their security interests (Webber et al., 2014, pp. 778–779). Things changed decisively in 2014. Russia's annexation of Crimea that year and Moscow's follow-on military campaign in eastern Ukraine occasioned a major strategic rethink in NATO (Sperling & Webber, 2017) while also rendering moot key documents agreed in previous years (including the NATO Maritime Strategy of 2011) (NATO, 2011). Measures to restore credible deterrence in Europe were taken forward at the Wales and Warsaw Summits of 2014 and 2016 (Moore & Coletta, 2017). It was not, however, until the Brussels Summit of July 2018, that NATO formally acknowledged the importance of the North Atlantic in these new circumstances. At that meeting the allies agreed to reinforce NATO's "maritime posture", "reinvigorate [its] collective maritime warfighting skills" and "ensure support to reinforcement by and from the sea" across the Atlantic (NATO, 2018, paragraph 19). NATO also agreed to establish a new strategic maritime command. Joint Force Command Norfolk (JFC-NF) was duly declared operational in September 2020, with MARCOM maintaining responsibility for day-to-day operations. The purpose of these reforms was clearly spelled out at the time by the NATO Secretary General, Jens Stoltenberg (cited in NATO, 2020a) – to "ensure [that] crucial routes for reinforcements and supplies from North America to Europe remain secure".

The American approach to the North Atlantic mirrors NATO's. The US Second Fleet was established in February 1950 tasked with providing security in the North Atlantic. By the mid-2000s altered strategic circumstances meant that Cold War subordinate command groups, such as Striking Fleet Atlantic, began to be disbanded. The Second Fleet itself was formally dissolved in September 2011. Just as NATO no longer viewed the North Atlantic as a strategic theatre of competition, so too the US decided that its maritime security efforts were better directed towards higher-priority programmes. However, acknowledgment of what the Pentagon referred to as "great power competition" in the Atlantic "prompted by a resurgent Russia" (Browne, 2018) led in August 2018 to the formal re-establishment of the Second Fleet. Significantly, at that point it was established that the commander of the Second Fleet would double up as commander of JFC-NF, so combining the American and NATO commands.

The revival of the Second Fleet should be seen within broader developments in US naval strategy. The *Cooperative Strategy for Twenty-First Century Seapower* of 2007 was described as America's first ever "unified maritime strategy", integrating the sea power of the US with the maritime capabilities of its allies (Conway et al., 2008, p. 7). The 2020 update (United States Department of the Navy, 2020, p. 6) noted similarly that "allies, partners and alliances such as NATO support America's enduring asymmetric advantage over [its] rivals [...] generat[ing] naval power, and provid[ing] access to valuable strategic maritime positions". Since the end of the Cold War, the US has been seeking to apply the principles of Alfred Mahan to the modern era. Specifically, the broader notion of maritime security has been placed alongside forward presence, deterrence, sea control and power projection. That strategy emphasises the importance of cooperative relationships in the development of maritime security. The particular challenge for the US here – something reflective of its position at the centre of a web of international alliances – is to exercise the leadership commensurate with its global interests and military weight while at the same time taking account of the regional interests of its allies. NATO is the transatlantic expression of that challenge (Raap-Hooper, 2020).

Among America's NATO allies, the UK has, in the maritime domain, been crucial. However, that importance has diminished as British maritime assets have contracted. The Royal Navy no longer operates separate geographic commands – the Western and Eastern Fleets were dissolved in 1971. Its operational headquarters are located at Northwood alongside MARCOM, and the Royal Navy seeks to maintain suitable capability to meet operational requirements as and when crises emerge. UK surface vessels and submarines, for instance provided support for Operation Allied Force in the Balkans 1999 and Operation Unified Protector against Libya in 2011. In addition to the tasks of coastal defence, longer-term deployments are global in reach. Vanguard submarines are the basis of the UK's continuous at sea nuclear deterrent. The Royal Navy as of 2020 was deployed in the Pacific, Indian and Arctic Oceans as well as in the Mediterranean and Black Seas. It also retained a presence in the South Atlantic (including a standing commitment to the Falkland Islands). These deployments sound impressive but are thinly spread. This is especially the case in the North Atlantic, a situation best illustrated by the lack of maritime patrol aircraft (MPA), used for anti-submarine and anti-surface warfare, search and rescue and intelligence gathering. The retirement by the Royal Air Force of the Nimrod MR2 aircraft in 2011 (and a decision by the Ministry of Defence not to purchase the replacement MRA4) left the UK with "no current or planned MPA capability" (House of Commons Defence Committee, 2012, p. 12). The Nimrod had a long operational history. Deployed in the Falklands War, both Gulf Wars as well as to Afghanistan, it was also crucial to patrols over contiguous British waters including the North Atlantic. The replacement Poseidon MRA Mk 1 has had numerous problems and was only declared at Initial Operating Capability in April 2020, with two aircraft deployable and a further seven on order. Air Vice Marshal A. L. Roberts (rtd.) suggested in June 2018, that "however, capable the [Poseidon] may be, the number of aircraft planned is undoubtedly inadequate to fulfil even the highest priority tasks likely to be assigned to the force in tension and hostilities" (Roberts cited in Allison, 2018). And the issue of capability is not limited to MPA. The Chair of the Defence Select Committee, Dr Julian Lewis MP referred in July 2019 to the "present pathetic total" of warships available to the Royal Navy (13 frigates and six destroyers) (cited in Bunkall, 2019). The problem here is not necessarily resolved by the decision to construct the two Queen Elizabeth II class aircraft carriers. A UK carrier force could, of course, be deployed to the North Atlantic along with allied naval support (perhaps tellingly, Carrier Strike's first operational deployment, scheduled for 2021, was with the US Marine Corps). However, the Carrier Strike Force is designed for global deployment and so is likely as not to be somewhere other than the North Atlantic. The force also requires surface and submarine protection – and even if allies join in, home assets will still be crucial, so drawing upon the Royal Navy's limited resources (House of Commons Public Accounts Committee, 2020).

The 2021 Integrated Review of Security, Defence, Development and Foreign Policy (HM Government, 2021) held out some hope of salvaging this situation. The headline reporting of the Review tended to focus on the UK's ambition to ensure a naval presence "East of Suez in the Indo-Pacific region". However, as Malcolm Chalmers (2021, p. 17) has noted the Review's provision for a major naval rebuilding programme (doubling surface fleet tonnage by 2030 compared to its 2015 position) was focused mainly on deployment to the UK's traditional area of concern – the "Euro-Atlantic neighbourhood". That level of ambition and projected investment was clearly pleasing to the Royal Navy (Radakin, 2021) and appeared to mark a return to the UK's role as a maritime power. Reaching the necessary level of ambition, however, was seen as likely to take several years. In the interim the UK would retain a fleet that was "relatively old" and over-stretched (Mark Francois MP transcribed in House of Commons Defence Committee, 2021, Q105). In short, therefore, at the time of the Integrated Review the Royal Navy's force posture remained a not entirely reliable provider of maritime security in the North Atlantic – a far cry from the great maritime organisation envisaged by Winston Churchill (1952, p. 10) where the US and the UK perceived "with increasing aptitude each other's capabilities and limitations".

The UK's faltering posture contrasts markedly to that of Russia. The Russian navy has expanded its capability in the North Atlantic with continued modernisation of the Northern Fleet, in line with the State Armaments Programme 2020 – launched in 2010 and since extended to 2027 (Connolly & Boulègue, 2018). Further, "The Atlantic Priority Area" is formally identified in Russia's 2015 maritime doctrine. Distinct from the Arctic, the Atlantic is specified in the document as a key site of rivalry with NATO and, accordingly, grounds for "strengthening the naval potential of the Russian Federation [...including] the Northern Fleet" (US Naval War College, 2015, paragraphs 52 and 60b). The International Seabed Authority, which organises and controls mineral-resources activity as part of UNCLOS, is also identified as an important partner for Russia in pursuit of its strategic interests. Russia's approach, therefore, is to promote its ability to exploit the natural resources within its EEZ under the auspices of United Nations frameworks, whilst trying to ensure it has the military capability to prevent NATO members from encroaching onto its periphery, as it argues the Alliance has done in Eastern Europe since 1991. These considerations apply most obviously to the Baltic and Barents Seas and the Arctic Ocean. These maritime territories, of course, abut the Atlantic.

Russia's strategic objective, therefore, is to demonstrate a capability, or perception of capability, sufficient to deny NATO members the ability to operate in the Eastern North Atlantic, so weakening Alliance cohesion and credibility.

In this regard, developments in cruise missile technology and associated launch platforms gives Russia the ability to adopt an Anti-Access/Area Denial (A2/AD) posture off the Kola Peninsula in the Arctic, one with the potential to negate the command and control that NATO, via the US, has in the North Atlantic. Russia has also been increasing its forward operating presence in and around the GIUK Gap. The objective here is to demonstrate an ability to interdict transatlantic resupply efforts. More specifically, Russia has been deploying upgraded *Kilo* class submarines capable of launching upgraded *Kalibr* cruise missiles (of the sort Russia has launched from the Caspian Sea into Syria).

Submarine capabilities are of particular significance. Russia does not have a modern, or large enough surface fleet to be able to compete with NATO members. Its submarine fleet, however, stands up well to combined NATO assets. The Russian navy in 2020 possessed 62 submarines compared to 68 held by the US navy (and of NATO's Atlantic allies, ten submarines were held by the UK, nine by France, four by Canada, three by Spain and two by Portugal). Two-thirds of Russian submarines are assigned to the Northern Fleet – when on mission, deployed to the Atlantic and Arctic Oceans. While the British and US navy's own fleets have benefitted from modernisation (through the commissioning of Astute and Seawolf-class submarines), Russia has also made equivalent steps (upgrades to the Kilo-class submarine and the deployment of at least one Lada-class vessel). Concerns at Russian submarine advance were the principal reason behind the revival, noted above, of the US Second Fleet (LaGrone, 2019). That decision has since been justified by reference to ongoing Russian activity. A Russian undersea naval exercise in 2019 involving approaches to the US eastern seaboard prompted alarm in NATO militaries. The commander of the US Second Fleet suggested in February 2020 that the east coast was no longer a "safe haven" and that the Atlantic was now a "contested space" (Vice Admiral Andrew Lewis cited in Mabeus, 2020).

Future Developments

The main issues that will shape future maritime security in the North Atlantic include defence investment, technological innovation, Chinese encroachment and climate change. Whilst there is some crossover between these four categories, each is important enough to be analysed in its own right.

Defence Investment

Defence budgets are currently more uncertain than at any point since the end of the Cold War owing to the economic consequences of the COVID-19 pandemic. That said, while governments have absorbed unprecedented drops in economic activity (and huge increases in public borrowing to match), one lesson of the pandemic is that defence, at least for some governments, retains a protected status.

The US maintains the world's largest military and its defence expenditure dwarfs every other nation on earth. According to the Stockholm International Peace Research Institute (2020), in 2019 America's defence budget was nearly three times that of China's and more than 11 times the size of Russia's. The Trump administration's defence budget request for 2021 was largely flat compared to 2020. During the 2020 election campaign Joe Biden alluded to the need for reductions in defence spending, but as a number of analysts have pointed out, there should be no automatic assumption that spending will fall as a consequence of a change of president or because of the impact of a COVID-19 recession (Cancian, 2020). Indeed, upon assuming office the Biden administration's first defence budget request to Congress reflected levels largely unchanged from the last year of the Trump presidency (Mehta & Gould, 2021).

Geographic priorities also showed a certain continuity. The US had made clear, under President Obama, that a refocusing of American strategic priorities required a "pivot" to Asia (Cha, 2016). President Trump's "America First" Policy reaffirmed that position, albeit in cruder terms (Anton, 2019), and early signs from the Biden administration did not suggest a deviation from the focus on China notwithstanding a parallel intention to restore civility with the NATO allies following the transatlantic tensions of the Trump period (Baer, 2020).

The American pivot to Asia – now a process that spans at least three administrations – carries two implications. First, that defence budget constraints will impact more on America's commitment to Europe than to its engagement in the Asia-Pacific, and second that in consequence the European allies need to stump up more for their own defence. The latter, indeed, was the purpose of the defence spending pledge agreed at the 2014 NATO summit in Wales – and, more obviously, of Trump's constant admonitions that the allies were "delinquent" in their commitment to defence spending targets. The budget trends in Canada and Europe do not suggest that the allies will be able any time soon to compensate for lowered American commitment. There has been much talk of European "strategic autonomy", but this is a narrative directed towards the EU (not NATO) and for missions that do not include maritime presence in the North Atlantic. Some scenarios (Posen, 2020) paint a picture of European allies able to defend themselves against Russian destabilisation (the standard scenario being a conflict that envelops the Baltic States), but these do not extend to a maritime conflagration where in the Atlantic NATO would remain critically dependent upon US forces.

Without the US, NATO's maritime capability deficit is thus stark. Some small comfort might be obtained by a consideration of the UK position. In November 2020, Prime Minister Boris Johnson announced an intention to uphold the position of the Royal Navy as Europe's most powerful maritime force (Rayner, 2020). Importantly, that announcement contained a commitment to thirteen new frigates – although it was unclear how many of these were additional to, or replacements for, existing ships. Equally, Johnson's announcement foresaw an extra £24 billion for defence over a four-year period. The Integrated Review (see earlier) confirmed the UK's maritime ambition albeit proceeding from a much-diminished position.

How does this compare with the Russian position? Between 2010 and 2019, its defence expenditure increased in real terms by approximately 30%. That, according to some estimates, still only placed Russia alongside medium-sized powers such as the UK and France – and hardly made it a peer competitor of the US. This may not, however, be the whole story. Measuring expenditure in terms of purchasing power parity, inflates the Russian commitment at least threefold (and by this measure the US outpaces Russia by a factor of just four not eleven as noted above). Such a calculation explains why, according to Kofmann and Connolly (2019), "Russian procurement dwarfs that of most European powers combined" – and why, relatedly, Russia is able to maintain an ocean-going navy that, bar the US, outstrips that of all other NATO allies.

Technological Innovation

Here there are three significant game changers: maritime-based missile defence, cruise missiles and maritime autonomous vehicles or drones. On the first, in November 2020, the US navy demonstrated that it could shoot down an Intercontinental Ballistic Missile (ICBM) using a missile intercept from a warship. Although the test took place in the Pacific with North Korea in mind, its wider impact on Terminal High Altitude Area Defence (THAAD) cannot be overstated.

Specifically, the utility of the North Atlantic in providing a component of the NATO missile defence shield, in support of the active layered *Aegis* capable warships, has been significantly enhanced. However, this in turn, incentivises Russia to place an even greater emphasis on cruise missile technology.

In December 2015 an upgraded *Kilo* class, became the first Russian submarine to fire cruise missiles in anger. Though the target was Raqa in Syria, the potential of the *SS-N-30A Kalibr* cruise missile to impact security in the North Atlantic was clear. Whilst cruise missiles can be deployed from a range of air and land platforms, it is a submarine's ability to remain undetected close to a target that is particularly appealing (and worrying) to defence planners. Further, Russia is keen to deploy the *Kalibr* across a range of different platforms, in addition to the *Kilo*. Three *Yasen* class SSNs, able to carry up to 40 missiles, have entered into service with a further six planned. The *Kalibr-M*, meanwhile, is reportedly in development, with a range up to 4,500 km, as part of Russia's 2027 rearmament programme (TASS, 2019). Even with its more limited range, the *Kalibr* in service today can be fired from submarines off the Kola Peninsula at targets including European ports capable of receiving resupply across the Atlantic. The Northern Fleet, therefore, no longer needs to break through the GIUK Gap into the open sea of the North Atlantic in order to achieve its strategic objectives.

The place of the third technological development of note is set out in a 2016 US Department of Defence report, *Autonomous Undersea Vehicle Requirement for 2025*. This made the case for Autonomous Undersea Vehicles (AUV) or drones being a key part of the Third Offset Strategy – that is, the US response to the development of A2/AD capabilities being developed by potential adversaries (Chief of Naval Operations, 2016). Three missions were noted: Intelligence, Surveillance, and Reconnaissance (ISR), Seabed Warfare, and Deception. Further, the report suggested that the autonomy of the AUV "with the minimum [of] human interaction" will increase over time, so furthering an overall aim of expanding AUVs "into far forward operations" and increasing "the number of tasks that can be performed". The North Atlantic, especially is likely to see an increase in the deployment of AUVs to take forward existing missions. ISR, for instance, is not a new task. Anti-submarine sensors integrated into the Sound Surveillance System (SOSUS) were installed as far back as the 1950s. SOSUS has recently been upgraded and now forms part of the US Integrated Undersea Surveillance System (IUSS), which also incorporates the new Deep Reliable Acoustic Path Exploitation System (DRAPES) (Stashwick, 2016). The continued development of IUSS is, however, matched by Russian seabed warfare capabilities – described by one US think tank report as "the most developed [...] in the world" (Metrick & Hicks, 2018, p. 7). The focus of NATO members' concerns here has been on the potential for Russia to interfere with undersea communication cables (Stavridis, 2017). Consequently, the US Navy, according to its Chief of Naval Operations (2016, p. 4), "must develop the capability to deny potential adversaries the benefit of seabed systems and simultaneously exploit concealment" executing a "diverse set of missions from inside an adversary's [A2/AD] envelope". The US, therefore, is specifically planning to utilise AUVs around the Kola Peninsula inside the Russian defence bastion.

China

Speculation on a Chinese interest in the North Atlantic derives from a number of concerns. First, China has already demonstrated a global maritime ambition. Since the mid-2000s, the Chinese navy has been regularly deployed to the northern Indian Ocean, the Gulf of Aden and the Central and Western Pacific. Since 2014, it has made regular forays into the South Atlantic (Martinson, 2019). While a presence in the North Atlantic has yet to materialise, China has obtained increasing influence in contiguous areas. This is most evident in the Arctic. China has been on observer in the Arctic Council since 2013, published an Arctic Strategy in 2018 and has major investments in energy projects in Arctic waters (Lino, 2020). But it is Chinese activities in Europe that have really caught the eye. China is a key investor in a number of European ports (Kynge et al., 2017). Piraeus in Greece, and Trieste in Italy have attracted the most attention, but Chinese companies also have stakes in Antwerp, Barcelona, Felixstowe, Hamburg, Le Havre, Rotterdam and Zeebrugge. It is easy to exaggerate the strategic significance of these moves. Chinese investment, for instance, often sits alongside significant national control arrangements (as in Trieste) or involvement by major European investors (Ghiretti, 2020). Nonetheless, Chinese commercial intrusion into Europe has increased rapidly – and with it has come a degree of political influence (evident in Belt and Road agreements with Italy and Greece, a bourgeoning security relationship with Serbia, and the "17 + 1" format that embraces China plus states in Eastern Europe and the Balkans).

These intrusions have certainly worried the EU. The European Commission (cited in Von Der Burchard, 2019) has branded China a "systemic rival" – a country that is "an economic competitor", a sponsor of "an alternative model of governance" and with "ambitions to become a leading global power". NATO too has woken up to China. The London Declaration of December 2019 (NATO, 2019, paragraph 6) referred to the "challenges" posed by "China's growing influence and international policies". The "rise of China" was addressed by NATO Foreign Ministers at their meeting in December 2020 (NATO, 2020b). And *NATO 2030* – an expert report commissioned by the NATO Secretary General (Reflection Group Appointed by the NATO Secretary General, 2020, pp. 16, 27) – referred to China as "a full-spectrum systemic rival" noting its role in cyber-attacks, acquisitions of infrastructure in Europe ("which have a potential bearing upon communications and interoperability") and intellectual property theft ("with implications for Allied security"). The report went on to note that China had developed "deepening defence ties with Russia", had made extensive investments in its military (including the pursuit of an ocean-going navy) and had expanded "its military reach" into the Atlantic as well as the Arctic and Mediterranean. The US Department of Defence (2020, p. 15) has raised similar issues – noting that China's investment in European port infrastructure should be placed in strategic context – as a means to "pre-position the necessary logistics support to sustain naval deployments" in distant waters, the Atlantic included.

Climate Change

Climate change is increasingly shaping the security concerns of nations. Since 2007, the UN Security Council has held five open debates (in 2007, 2011, 2018, 2019 and 2020) on the climate-security nexus. A Concept Note prepared by the German Presidency of the Security Council for the July 2020 meeting noted that "climate-related security risks" in the shape of "severe weather phenomena", as well as floods, droughts and sea-level rise, were already "a daily reality for millions of people". It added that "the security implications of climate change will rise [...], aggravate[ing] existing vulnerabilities and conflict drivers [and] contribut[ing] to the emergence of new and unprecedented risks" (United Nations Security Council, 2020, p. 3). As an influential report of 2014 (King, 2014, p. 4) had already noted, such risks included greater "rivalry between states" over natural resources and disputed national boundaries. The latter is already evident in the Arctic, where Russian territorial claims have alarmed the US. Two other NATO nations – Denmark and Norway – have their own claims. All these allies, as well as Canada, meanwhile, are also wary of China's increasing interest in the region (Shea, 2019). Similar concerns have also been focused further south. A shrinking of the Arctic ice cap – and with it, an opening of the Northwest Passage and Northern Sea Route – has raised the possibility of a future Chinese naval presence in the North Atlantic (Melia et al., 2017). Such worries aside, climate change has other maritime security implications. Desalination caused by polar ice melt can affect the accuracy of navigation and detection systems that rely on underwater sound speed, so undermining the reliability of both the IUSS system as well as of AUVs as they enter service (Ainslie, 2010, pp. 513–571). This not only increases the risk of underwater accidents but can lead to false readings so heightening tensions between the NATO countries and Russia.

Conclusion

This chapter has focused on the military dimensions of security, something that has a clear and enduring importance in the North Atlantic given the ocean's overlap with NATO's area of responsibility and the dynamic of competition with Russia. Although closely linked to maritime security in the Arctic, the North Atlantic has its own specific security dynamics. The sustainment of this ocean as a zone of rivalry has historical echoes – emanating from both the Cold War and the two World Wars of the twentieth century. The new factors that now set it apart are the emergence of China as an interested party in the region and the long-term consequences of climate change. Both these developments are so far largely unmediated. The lack of institutional bodies, other than the United Nations, that can deescalate, or limit, tensions is notable. To make matters worse, NATO-Russia rivalry has contributed to an evident de-institutionalisation of relations. The NATO-Russia Council, which had had some focus on maritime security, has been largely inactive since the 2014 Crimea crisis. NATO currently has no mechanism for security dialogue with China. The North Atlantic thus remains both contested and unregulated as a site of military security.

References

Ainslie, M. (2010). *Principles of sonar performance modelling*. Springer.

Allison, G. (2018, July 18). *Planned force of nine Poseidon aircraft "Insufficient to Guarantee Continuous Cover"*. UKDJ. https://ukdefencejournal.org.uk/planned-force-of-nine-p-8-poseidon-aircraft-insufficient-to-guarantee-continuous-cover/

Anton, M. (2019, April 20). The Trump doctrine. *Foreign Policy*. https://foreignpolicy.com/2019/04/20/the-trump-doctrine-big-think-america-first-nationalism/

Baer, D. (2020, November 6). America under Biden won't go soft on China. *Foreign Policy*. https://foreignpolicy.com/2020/11/06/biden-china-trump-election/

Blackwill, R. D., & Legro, J. W. (1989). Constraining ground force exercises of NATO and the Warsaw Pact. *International Security*, *14*(3), 68–98.

Browne, R. (2018, May 5). *US Navy re-establishes Second Fleet amid Russia tensions*. CNN Politics. https://edition.cnn.com/2018/05/04/politics/us-navy-second-fleet-russia-tensions/index.html

Bunkall, A. (2019, July 27). *Size of Royal Navy's warship fleet is pathetic, says chairman of the Defence Select Committee*. Sky News. https://www.julianlewis.net/selected-news-coverage/4916:size-of-royal-navy-s-warship-fleet-is-pathetic-says-chairman-of-the-defence-select-committee

Cancian, M. F. (2020). *Military forces in FY2021. The budgetary and strategy overview: Four challenges and a wild card*. Centre for Strategic and International Studies. https://www.csis.org/analysis/military-forces-fy-2021-budget-and-strategy-overview-four-challenges-and-wild-card

Central Intelligence Agency. (2020). Atlantic Ocean. *The World Factbook*. https://www.cia.gov/library/publications/the-world-factbook/geos/zh.html

Cha, V. (2016, September 6). The unfinished legacy of Obama's pivot to Asia. *Foreign Policy*. https://foreignpolicy.com/2016/09/06/the-unfinished-legacy-of-obamas-pivot-to-asia/

Chalmers, M. (2021). The integrated review: The UK as a reluctant middle power?. *RUSI Occasional Paper*. https://www.rusi.org/sites/default/files/rusi_pub_281_chalmers_final_web_version_0.pdf

Chief of Naval Operations. (2016, February 18). *Report to Congress: Autonomous undersea vehicle requirement for 2025*. Undersea Warfare Directorate. https://news.usni.org/wp-content/uploads/2016/03/18Feb16-Report-to-Congress-Autonomous-Undersea-Vehicle-Requirement-for-2025.pdf

Churchill, W. (1952). *The Second World War: Volume 5 – Closing the ring*. Cassell & Co.

Connolly, R., & Boulègue, M. (2018, May). Russia's new state armament programme: Implications for the Russian armed forces and military capabilities to 2027. *Chatham House Research Paper*. https://www.chathamhouse.org/sites/default/files/publications/research/2018-05-10-russia-state-armament-programme-connolly-boulegue-final.pdf

Conway, J. T., Roughead, G., & Allen, T. W. (2008). A cooperative strategy for 21st century seapower. *Naval War College Review, 61*(1). 7–13.

Foggo, J., & Fritz, A. (2016). The Fourth Battle of the Atlantic. *Proceedings of the US Naval Institute, 142*(6). https://www.usni.org/magazines/proceedings/2016/june/fourth-battle-atlantic

Ghiretti, F. (2020, October 15). Demystifying China's role in Italy's Port of Trieste. *The Diplomat*. https://thediplomat.com/2020/10/demystifying-chinas-role-in-italys-port-of-trieste/

Hamre, J., & Conley, H. (2018). The centrality of the North Atlantic to NATO and US strategic interests. In J. Olsen (Ed.), *NATO and the North Atlantic: Revitalising collective defence*. Royal United Services Institute.

HM Government. (2021). *Global Britain in a competitive age: The integrated review of security, defence, development and foreign policy*. https://assets.publishing.service.gov.uk/government/uploads/system/uploads/attachment_data/file/975077/Global_Britain_in_a_Competitive_Age-_the_Integrated_Review_of_Security__Defence__Development_and_Foreign_Policy.pdf

House of Commons Defence Committee. (2012). *Future maritime surveillance*. House of Commons. https://publications.parliament.uk/pa/cm201213/cmselect/cmdfence/110/110.pdf

House of Commons Defence Committee. (2021, April 13). *Oral evidence: Defending global Britain, HC 133*. House of Commons. https://committees.parliament.uk/oralevidence/2006/pdf/

House of Commons Public Accounts Committee. (2020, September 28). *Oral evidence, carrier strike, HC 684*. House of Commons. https://committees.parliament.uk/oralevidence/1006/default/

International Hydrographic Organisation. (1953). *Limits of oceans and seas* (3rd ed.). https://epic.awi.de/id/eprint/29772/1/IHO1953a.pdf

Judson, J. (2019, October 7). *Reforger Redux? Defender 2020 to be 3rd largest exercise in Europe since Cold War*. Defence News. https://www.defensenews.com/land/2019/10/07/reforger-redux-defender-2020-exercise-to-be-3rd-largest-exercise-in-europe-since-cold-war/

King, G. W. (2014). *Climate change: Implications for defence*. Global Military Advisory Council on Climate Change. https://static.s123-cdn-static-d.com/uploads/2385729/normal_5d3c7f594d326.pdf

Kofmann, M., & Connolly, R. (2019, December 16). *Why Russia's military expenditure is much higher than commonly understood (as is China's)*. War on the Rocks. https://warontherocks.com/2019/12/why-russian-military-expenditure-is-much-higher-than-commonly-understood-as-is-chinas/

Kynge, J., Campbell, C., Kazmin, A., & Bokhari, F. (2017, January 12). *How China rules the waves*. Financial Times. https://ig.ft.com/sites/china-ports/

LaGrone, S. (2019, December 31). *US fleet created to counter Russian subs now fully operational*. USNI News. https://news.usni.org/2019/12/31/u-s-fleet-created-to-counter-russian-subs-now-fully-operational

Lino, M. R. (2020, February 20). *Understanding China's Arctic activities*. International Institute for Strategic Studies Analysis. https://www.iiss.org/blogs/analysis/2020/02/china-arctic#:~:text=China%20published%20its%20own%20Arctic,km)%20from%20the%20Arctic%20Circle

Mabeus, C. (2020, February 4). Navy 2nd Fleet commander: Atlantic Ocean is a "Battle Space". *Navy Times*. https://www.navytimes.com/news/your-navy/2020/02/05/navy-2nd-fleet-commander-atlantic-ocean-is-a-battle-space/#

Martinson, R. D. (2019). China as an Atlantic naval power. *The RUSI Journal, 164*(7), 18–31.

Mehta, A., & Gould, J. (2021, April 9). *Biden requests $715b hinting at administration's future priorities*. Defense News. https://www.defensenews.com/breaking-news/2021/04/09/biden-requests-715b-for-pentagon-hinting-at-administrations-future-priorities/

Melia, N., Haines, K., & Hawkins, E. (2017). *Future of the sea: Implications from opening Arctic Sea routes*. Foresight, Government Office for Science. https://assets.publishing.service.gov.uk/government/uploads/system/uploads/attachment_data/file/634437/Future_of_the_sea_-_implications_from_opening_arctic_sea_routes_final.pdf

Metrick, A., & Hicks, C. H. (2018). *Contested seas: Maritime domain awareness in Northern Europe*. Washington DC: Centre for Strategic and International Studies. https://csis-website-prod.s3.amazonaws.com/s3fs-public/publication/180328_MetrickHicks_ContestedSeas_Web.pdf

Moore, R., & Coletta, D. (Eds.). (2017). *NATO's return to Europe: Engaging Ukraine, Russia, and Beyond.* Georgetown University Press.

NATO. (1949, April 4). *The North Atlantic Treaty.* NATO. https://www.nato.int/cps/en/natolive/official_texts_17120.htm

NATO. (2011, March 18). *Alliance Maritime Strategy.* NATO. https://www.nato.int/cps/en/natohq/official_texts_75615.htm

NATO. (2014, September 5). *The Wales Declaration on the Transatlantic Bond.* NATO. https://www.nato.int/cps/en/natohq/official_texts_112985.htm

NATO. (2018, July 11). *Brussels Summit Declaration.* NATO. https://www.nato.int/cps/en/natohq/official_texts_156624.htm?selectedLocale=en

NATO. (2019, December 4). *London Declaration.* NATO. https://www.nato.int/cps/en/natohq/official_texts_171584.htm

NATO. (2020a, December 17). *NATO's New Atlantic Command Declared Operational.* NATO. https://www.nato.int/cps/en/natohq/news_178031.htm

NATO. (2020b, December 2). *NATO foreign ministers discuss China's rise, security in the Black Sea region.* NATO. https://www.nato.int/cps/en/natohq/news_179806.htm#:~:text=NATO%20foreign%20ministers%20met%20virtually,the%20European%20Union%20High%20Representative

Nordenman, M. (2019). *The new battle for the Atlantic: Emerging naval competition with Russia in the far north.* Naval Institute Press.

Posen, B. (2020). Europe can defend itself. *Survival, 62*(6), 7–34.

Raap-Hooper, M. (2020). *Shields of the republic: The triumph and peril of America's alliances.* Harvard University Press.

Radakin, T. (2021, March 23). *First Sea Lord's message on integrated review.* Royal Navy. https://www.royalnavy.mod.uk/news-and-latest-activity/news/2021/march/23/1sl-message-on-integrated-review

Rayner, G. (2020, November 18). Boris Johnson to end "Era of Retreat" with £24 billion armed forces spending pledge. *The Daily Telegraph.* https://www.telegraph.co.uk/politics/2020/11/18/boris-johnson-end-era-retreatwith-24bn-armed-forces-spending/

Reflection Group Appointed by the NATO Secretary General. (2020). *NATO 2030: United for a new era.* https://www.nato.int/nato_static_fl2014/assets/pdf/2020/12/pdf/201201-Reflection-Group-Final-Report-Uni.pdf

Roberts, P. (2019, November 6). NATO vs Russia at 70. *RUSI Commentary.* https://rusi.org/commentary/nato-vs-russia-70

Shea, N. (2019, May 8). *Scenes from the new Cold War unfolding at the top of the world.* National Geographic. https://www.nationalgeographic.com/environment/2018/10/new-cold-war-brews-as-arctic-ice-melts/

Sperling, J., & Webber, M. (2017). NATO and the Ukraine crisis: Collective securitisation. *European Journal of International Security, 2*(1), 19–46.

Stashwick, S. (2016, November 4). US Navy upgrading undersea sub-detecting sensor network. *The Diplomat.* https://thediplomat.com/2016/11/us-navy-upgrading-undersea-sub-detecting-sensor-network/

Stavridis, J. (2017). The United States, the North Atlantic and maritime hybrid warfare. In J. A. Olsen (Ed.), *NATO and the North Atlantic: Revitalising collective defence.* Routledge.

Stockholm International Peace Research Institute. (2020). Trends in world military expenditure, 2019. *SIPRI Fact Sheet* (April). https://www.sipri.org/sites/default/files/2020-04/fs_2020_04_milex_0.pdf

TASS. (2019, January 8). *New Kalibr-M cruise missile with range of over 4,500 km in development in Russia.* TASS, Russian News Agency. https://tass.com/defense/1039123

United Nations Security Council. (2020). *Letter dated 18 July 2020 from the permanent representative of Germany to the United Nations addressed to the Secretary-General.* https://www.securitycouncilreport.org/atf/cf/%7B65BFCF9B-6D27-4E9C-8CD3-CF6E4FF96FF9%7D/s_2020_725.pdf

United States Department of the Navy. (2020). *Advantage at sea: Prevailing with integrated all-domain naval power.* https://news.usni.org/2020/12/17/u-s-maritime-strategy-advantage-at-sea#more-82207

US Department of Defence. (2020). *Military and security developments involving the People's Republic of China 2020.*

US Naval War College. (2015). *Maritime doctrine of the Russian federation* (translated by Anna David). Russia Maritime Studies Institute.

Von Der Burchard, H. (2019, March 12). *EU slams China as "Systemic Rival" as trade tensions rise.* Politico. https://www.politico.eu/article/eu-slams-china-as-systemic-rival-as-trade-tension-rises/

Webber, M., Hallams, E., & Smith, M. A. (2014). Repairing NATO's motors. *International Affairs, 90*(4), 773–793.

27

MARITIME SECURITY IN THE SOUTH ATLANTIC

Érico Esteves Duarte

This chapter examines the South Atlantic Ocean according to a minimalist definition of maritime security – the provision of law on the sea – which results from the confluence of maritime activities of state and non-state actors in complying with an established set of norms (Duarte & Moura, 2019). However, given the lack of an ultimate authority to coordinate the network of maritime activities, the law of the sea is enforced by the distribution of power among the states surrounding an ocean and the types of regimes established for stewarding the sea. Conversely, maritime security can be disturbed and corroded by more capable states' lack of will or means to ensure compliance with such norms as well as inter-state rivalry, which leave unopposed all kinds of maritime criminal organisations.

This analysis draws on a structural realist approach of international relations (Waltz, 1979), which explains the international order as a result of great power politics (Mearsheimer, 2019). Great powers create and govern several types of bounded/thick and international/thin institutions to help them manage their interactions with weaker states and other great powers; they abandon and replace security regimes when their interests are not served or to deal with new rivals. This structuralist approach, however, is both restricted and complemented by the recursive interaction between contextual factors (such as the environment, economic crises and pandemics) and state-level decision-making (Flint & Dezzani, 2018; Goertz, 1994; Tilly & Goodin, 2006).

Accordingly, the South Atlantic can be seen as an underdeveloped international political subsystem. An international subsystem is composed of "groups of units within an international system that can be distinguished from the whole system by the particular nature or intensity of their interactions/interdependence with each other" (Buzan & Little, 2000, pp. 68–69). The ocean stretching from the Caribbean to Antarctica and bordered by West Africa and South America was governed by European countries and the United States' navy from the New World's colonisation until the twentieth century. After the Second World War and African decolonisation, new security interactions and regimes emerged and defined the South Atlantic as a subsystem, but this process was shaped by the Cold War's bipolarity. On the one hand, security was configured by the capabilities and interests of the region's larger navies. For instance, Brazil and South Africa privileged anti-submarine warfare against the Soviet Navy over coastal patrolling (Eisenberg, 2012; Vidigal, 1985). On the other hand, the creation of a South Atlantic Treaty Organisation was initially proposed by South American and African pundits and

DOI: 10.4324/9781003001324-30

decision-makers (Hurrell, 1983; Mattos, 1980). This idea gained weight from the systemic dynamics in world politics that ended and replaced the Cold War, which opened up brief windows of opportunity for regional security initiatives. However, these were wasted owing to the absence of a sponsor – a regional power or coalition of countries – with sufficient capacity to consolidate a maritime security regime.

The first opportunity to build a South Atlantic maritime community occurred in the 1980s. In this heightened period of the Cold War, US President Ronald Reagan showed interest in the proposal for a South Atlantic Treaty Organisation as a bounded maritime security regime. However, the 1982 Falklands War resulted in cleavages that removed the conditions for it, and the United States focused its security imperatives in Eurasia. This void encouraged the formation of the first block of countries around the Zone of Peace and Cooperation of the South Atlantic (ZPCSA, also known by its Portuguese acronym, ZOPACAS). During this brief historical period, African countries enjoyed relative political stability, and Brazil sponsored the enterprise (Viegas, 2016). Unfortunately, the debt crisis during the so-called "lost decade" during the 1980s consumed the attention of South American governments, overshadowing other priorities. During the 1990s, civil wars ravaged Africa, while the United States "war on drugs" agenda dominated South America.

The second window of opportunity opened in the 2000s, when the United States waged war in Afghanistan, Iraq, and elsewhere against terrorist groups. This time, South American and African countries as well as their regional coalitions proved more resourceful and engaged in more substantial South-South cooperation (da Silva, 2017, p. 28). This also provided the momentum for the ZPCSA to have a second chance. However, the national economic and institutional crises following the 2008 recession and the global redistribution of power terminated the experiment of the South Atlantic maritime security regime. The systemic effects of international multipolarity in the South Atlantic increased bilateral rivalries, weakened regional security arrangements, and led to contests between the United States, Russia, China and the European Union (Wills, 2020, p. 38).

This chapter outlines with some pessimism the conditions for maritime security in the South Atlantic. The next section presents the available data indicating the escalation of drug trafficking, illegal fishing and piracy. This web of maritime criminality has been caused by (1) the increasing rivalry of great powers; (2) the recrudescence of regional security initiatives in South America and the shortcomings of those in West Africa; and (3) the lack of a reliable regional power to sponsor a South Atlantic maritime security regime. The chapter ends by addressing two potential hotspots at risk of descending further into crisis in the South Atlantic.

The State of Maritime Insecurity in the South Atlantic

The South Atlantic lacks a regime to steward maritime activities during the globalisation of its countries' "blue economies". In this section, it shall be demonstrated how a lack of government regulation and oversight had made the economic integration of South America and West Africa vulnerable. Reduced operational costs in the global value chain have motivated new forms of ocean-based organised crime and political–criminal nexuses.

This section presents data on illegal maritime activities in the South Atlantic, with a focus on cocaine trafficking, illegal fishing and piracy. The data analyses show that these activities are expanding and becoming endemic. South Atlantic transnational criminal organisations have not shown the regular cyclical pattern of the "balloon effect" (UNODC, 2020a, pp. 9–10, 25), which suggests they are entrenched in more stable organisational and societal bases.

Drug Trafficking

South American cartels hold a monopoly on cocaine production. Since 2010, when the United States, the European Union and Mexican anti-drug operations began targeting maritime shipment routes and final destinations, the South Atlantic has become the current transhipment area for trafficking cocaine from South America to Europe and Asia. The new routes proved to be cheaper and allowed for more successful evasion of anti-narcotics operations and agencies than previous waterways. The drug cartels discovered a more available workforce and complicity from local governments in Brazil, Argentina and West Africa (Duarte et al., 2019).

Recent reports estimate that South American production of cocaine reached 1,410 tonnes in 2016 and 1,976 in 2017 (UNODC, 2018, p. 28; UNODC, 2019, p. 8). However, while they accurately assessed cocaine cultivation in Colombia (which doubled from 2015 to 2017) but not the expansion of production in Peru and Bolivia (UNODC, 2020b, pp. 23–26), the real volume is probably much greater. In these two countries, cartels have succeeded in establishing coca bush cultivation closer to the borders of Argentina and Brazil to reduce shipment costs.

The United Nations Office on Drugs and Crime (UNODC) provides little information on the quantity of drugs trafficked by vessels and those intercepted. Therefore, to supplement this information, official reports from the few national law enforcement agencies in South Atlantic states that publish updated drug apprehension reports were accessed, such as the Brazilian Federal Police, the Argentine Ministry of Security and the Uruguayan Ministry of Interior. For this reason, it is possible to appraise the trafficking of cocaine from South America but only roughly estimate the tonnage shipped to West Africa, Europe and Asia. Although insufficient, our research shows an increase in cocaine enforcement in Argentina and Brazil of 100% and 300%, respectively, between 2015 and 2018. In the latter case, the preliminary report of 2020 revealed that 92.5 tonnes of cocaine were apprehended just in the first six months, out of which 60% was seized in the largest Brazilian port of Santos (Agencia Brasil, 2020) (Tables 27.1 and 27.2).

The data suggests cartels' bases of operations have moved closer to ports in Southern America and Venezuela. On the one hand, the predominance of seizures involving coca leaves over paste and salt in Argentina confirmed that this country evolved within the cocaine trafficking network from a consumer and pathway country to an area of refinement, supplying the hub of shipments straight to Europe from Argentina and Brazil. On the other hand, it can be seen that Venezuela has become the main route to Europe and Asia through West Africa (Sampó, 2019, pp. 193–195).

Illegal Fishing

Documenting illegal fishing is a daunting task, as information is scarce and not adequately provided by any national or international public agency. The global fishing interactive map of the Global Fishing Watch is the closest to a report.[1] However, while this shows the evolution of

Table 27.1 Most significant cocaine seizures in the South Atlantic, 2012–2016 (kg)

Country	2012	2013	2014	2015	2016
Argentina (leafs)	94,702	87,088	118,088	113,732	115,640
Brazil (salts)	19,875	41,710	33,858	27,223	41,472
Nigeria (salts)	132	290	226	260	302
Venezuela (salts)	27,458	20,462	25,929	65,389	34,919

Source: UNODC, Annual Drug Seizures: https://dataunodc.un.org/drugs/seizures. Accessed 17th April 2020.

Table 27.2 Cocaine seizures in Argentina, Brazil and Uruguay, 2015–2018 (tons)

	Argentina	*Brazil*	*Uruguay*
2015	6.9	27.5	0.20
2016	8.4	41.5	0.28
2017	15.7	48	0.17
2018	11.9	79.2	0.75
2019	–	93	1.75

Sources: Argentina. Estadísticas Criminales. Ministerio de Seguridad [Buenos Aires] 2019. Disponível em: https://estadisticascriminales.minseg.gob.ar; Brazilian Federal Police. Estatística de Drogas Apreendidas – Atualizados até maio/2019: http://www.pf. gov.br/imprensa/estatistica/drogas; URUGUAY. Evolución de incautación de drogas (2005–2019). Ministerio del Interior. Montevideo, 2019: https://www.minterior.gub. uy/images/2019/PDF/Cuadro_drogas_2005_-_2019.pdf. Accessed 17th April 2020.

worldwide fishing activities between 2012 and 2020, it only gives a rough impression of the phenomenon, without providing systematic statistics.

First, patterns of illegal fishing can be identified on the limits of the Exclusive Economic Zones (EEZ) between Suriname and French Guiana, Angola and Namibia, as well as Argentina and the Falklands/Malvinas Isles (Clarín, 2020; Hartman, 2017; Mbewa, 2019; Moritán, 2020). This indicates that the illegal fishing industry is sufficiently risk-sensitive to avoid areas with high coastguard activity levels.

Second, illegal fishing is entangled with piracy and other maritime crimes because transnational crime organisations reach out to the same coastal populations for labour and sanctuary (Jacobsen, 2017). In Nigeria, for instance, some studies have identified a causal relationship between illegal fishing's negative socioeconomic impacts and higher levels of hiring by piracy and trafficking organisations in fishing communities (Okafor-Yarwood, 2020, pp. 9, 16).

Armed Robbery and Piracy

The International Maritime Organization provides more informative and reliable reports on piracy and armed robbery at sea. However, most shipping companies consensually omit incidents to avoid bad publicity and the rise of insurance fees (Table 27.3).

The analysis of these data points to a rise in incidents of piracy and armed robbery in the South Atlantic, predominantly in the Gulf of Guinea (Jeong, 2018, p. 11). Similar to drug trafficking, piracy is related to a population's poverty and its susceptibility to co-optation by militias and criminal organisations that provide welfare in place of the local government (Biberman & Turnbull, 2018).

The Rivalry of the Great Powers in the South Atlantic

The United States played a leading role in sponsoring maritime security cooperation in the South Atlantic until the late 1990s during its "war on drugs" (Carrier et al., 2012; Mabry, 1988). Aside from its uncertain results, the campaign lost momentum after the United States directed most of its military resources and attention to the Persian Gulf during the Bush administration. This trend continued during Barack Obama's redeployment of naval and coastguard assets to the Indo Pacific and the more recent interest of the Trump administration in the Baltic Sea (Bruns, 2019, p. 8). The current US National Security Strategy (US, 2017) remains

Maritime Security in the South Atlantic

Table 27.3 Piracy and armed robbery in West Africa and South
America, 2010–2020

Year	West Africa	South America
2010	47	40
2011	61	29
2012	64	21
2013	54	17
2014	45	9
2015	27	4
2016	62	25
2017	48	23
2018	81	22
2019	70	15
2020	14	3

Source: IMO, Piracy and Armed Robbery Reports. http://
www.imo.org/en/OurWork/Security/PiracyArmedRobbery/
Reports/Pages/Default.aspx. Accessed 17th April 2020.

heavily focussed on Russian and Chinese threats, rather than on enhancing maritime security cooperation and capacity-building.

Another factor we must take into account when examining the United States' dismissal of a maritime security role is its Navy's warfighting strategic culture (Libel, 2020). Since the end of the Cold War, there has been a "mismatch between the platforms designed for warfighting and [the] day-to-day tasks orientated towards diplomacy and statecraft" (McFate, 2020, p. 43), which are imperative for the stewardship of maritime security. This was demonstrated by the deactivation in 2014 of the Maritime Civil Affairs and Security Training Command (MCAST) (McFate, 2020, p. 55).

Consequently, most of the United States' recent maritime security measures in the South Atlantic have been reactions against naval competitors. For instance, in 2018, Colombia became a NATO "Global Partner" to operate as a net maritime security provider and exporter in the region (Neira, 2020). This move, however, was more instrumental in exerting pressures on Venezuela's government (due to its close association with Russia) rather than turning the Colombian Navy into a South American sea control force. Unsurprisingly, the United States set up a security assistance agreement with Argentina the same year. In addition to galvanising further support against Venezuela, the initiative aimed to respond to the China-Argentina military agreement of 2015 but made no mention of maritime security (Wilson, 2015). Finally, most US operations in the Gulf of Guinea aim to tackle illegal activities that finance terrorist groups, without providing a reasonable capacity building package in coastal patrolling. Therefore, the United States plays a minimal role in providing good order in the South Atlantic, which is recognised as a debilitating factor when faced with great power competition (Tallis, 2020).

An increasing number of Chinese and Russian military activities have taken place around the South Atlantic. Naval exercises involving Russia, China and South Africa between November and December 2019 stand out as illustrative examples (Mastro, 2020; Panda, 2019). Moreover, Russia and China have undertaken military ventures in South America and Africa. In South America, Russia traded hard currency and military assistance to Venezuela for access to bases and ports where it showcased two Blackjack nuclear-capable bombers and a naval task force for the first time in the Western Hemisphere. Some outlets recognised the critical role of Russian private military companies played in the survival of Nicolás Maduro's regime's in Venezuala, and Russian defence authorities have since assessed Venezuelan infrastructure for more extensive deployments (Poggio Teixeira & Da Silva Nogueira de Melo, 2019, p. 91; The Guardian, 2019; Zverev & Tsvetkova, 2019). In Africa, Russia has resumed Soviet-era ties and regained its position as the region's largest arms supplier. Since 2015, Russia has put into effect defence agreements with Cameroon, Nigeria and Sierra Leone and secured access to Guinea's airbases. Agreements with Ghana, Gambia and Niger are under negotiation, and Russian private military companies operate in the Central African Republic and Mozambique. It therefore seems unlikely that Russia will change its projected course of power in the South Atlantic (Adibe, 2019; Hedenskog, 2018; Schmitt & Gibbons-Neff, 2020).

China holds a complete set of assets for influencing South Atlantic countries. Although its military ambitions in South America are yet limited to a space station in Argentina's Patagonia, China has substantial investments, infrastructure projects and defence cooperation agreements in Africa. Its modus operandi has been to set up companies that pour investments into local economies before entangling them in more strategic agendas (Hanauer & Morris, 2013; Nantulya, 2020). China has thus established defence and security cooperation ties with South Africa in 2000 and updated with Namibia and Angola agreements extant since their independence wars (Campos & Vines, 2008). Although Chinese presence in Africa predates the Belt and Road Initiative, this project paved the way for positioning Africa as the barometer for a global security governance system headed by China (Nantulya, 2019). With pace and patience, China became an Africa's main weapon supplier and the sponsor of the China-Africa Defence and Security Forum, which as of 2019 had gathered "nearly 100 senior representatives from the defence departments of 50 African countries and the African Union, including 15 defence ministers and chiefs of general staff, to discuss new approaches of China-Africa security cooperation in the new era" (Yi, 2019). The so-called "Vision for Maritime Cooperation under the Belt and Road Initiative" has even more extensive reach. It promises blue partnerships for the "exploration of marine resources, maritime industries, and maritime safety" as well as the control of illegal activities at sea (Medeiros & Benvenuto, 2020, p. 12). The initiative aims to establish 12 ports as Strategic Maritime Distribution Centres (SMDC), five of which would be located in the South Atlantic: Mar del Plata in Argentina, Salvador in Brazil, Libreville in Gabon, Tema in Ghana, and Dakar in Senegal (do Nascimento, 2020, pp. 30–35). Finally, China's (not so) informal leadership of BRICS can help it buffer its interests in the region (Silva, 2020, p. 100).

The great power rivalry in the South Atlantic also involves European countries acting as security proxy sponsors for the United States or looking to fill the void of power (Duarte, 2019). The European Union has advanced a maritime security plan with a less militarised approach for the Gulf of Guinea that has nevertheless been undermined somewhat by some of its members' more ambitious unilateral agendas.

The European Union sponsored the Cocaine Route Programme (CRP) and the Critical Maritime Routes in the Gulf of Guinea Programme (CRIMGO), which evolved into the Gulf of Guinea Action Plan for 2015–2020. Since 2016, most of the European Union's projects and programmes on the South Atlantic focused on training and capacity building, intelligence sharing and multi-national operational coordination (Cabral, 2017; Jesperson, 2017). Such initiatives include, for example, the Critical Maritime Routes Monitoring, Support and Evaluation Mechanism (CRIMSON), the Gulf of Guinea Inter-Regional Network (GoGIN) and the Support to West Africa Integrated Maritime Security (SWAIMS).

However, there is a trade-off between those projects and support for maritime security policies to guarantee the safe passage of oil and gas, the related growing market around the Gulf of Guinea, and the temptation to expand or consolidate influence over African countries.

For instance, Portugal had many opportunities to express its intention to redirect NATO and national efforts towards the restoration of its historical maritime leadership within any sort of South Atlantic governance (Beirão & da Silva Ramos, 2019; Poggio Teixeira & Da Silva Nogueira de Melo, 2019, pp. 82, 92; Thomashausen & Graça, 2015, p. 74). The current French military operations in West Africa display striking continuities with historical patterns of intervention in the region (Diallo, 2019).

The Setback of the South Atlantic Maritime Security Regimes

The rivalry of great power politics has eroded the South American and West African regional security regimes without replacing them with a functional international one. The self-help logic of each great power project with South Atlantic countries has resulted in regional misperceptions and polarisation. Consequently, the South Atlantic countries that hold more capabilities – Brazil, South Africa and Nigeria – have been unable to put forth a collective maritime security agenda.

In South America, the once active and expanding Southern Common Market (Mercosur) and the Union of South American Nations (UNASUR) have lost their force and relevance. Polarisation among South American countries split these organisations apart, which hold limited significance today. Not surprisingly, ZPCSA never had a chance to engage with these alliances and play a relevant role, even in South America (Duarte & Kenkel, 2019, pp. 8–9).

The ultimate dividing force is arguably Brazil's inconstant role in maritime security, which dates back to the three United Nations conferences on the Law of the Sea (da Silva, 2017, p. 25). Brazil never revised its Cold War geopolitical perspective towards the South Atlantic (Duarte & Kenkel, 2019). The Brazilian purpose of ZPCSA has been to block extra-regional great powers, rather than build a real maritime security regime, as explicitly stated in its most recent National Security Strategy (Brasil, 2016, p. 26). Moreover, most Brazilian security initiatives followed an historical trend of prioritising bilateral ties to guarantee predominance over its neighbours (Duarte, 2016; Espach, 2019, pp. 140–144; Malamud, 2011). Under the far-right populist government of Bolsonaro, Brazilian foreign policies became increasingly reactive and opposed liberal international norms and regional organisations, which signals that Brazil is likely to remain, for a long time to come, an unreliable regional player in terms of supporting any collective efforts towards South Atlantic maritime security governance.

The advancements in maritime security cooperation in Africa developed from subregional organisations and foreign donors' support. They are remarkable achievements; however, they face relevant challenges.

The starting point was the creation of the Gulf of Guinea Commission in 2001. It supported the conception of the Maritime Trade Information Sharing Centre and the Regional Maritime University at Accra, Ghana, in 2014. During the same period, the Southern African Development Community (SADC) implemented the most ambitious maritime agenda in the South Atlantic, based on previous comprehensive security plans and legally binding agreements. The SADC designed its Maritime Security Strategy in 2011 to address piracy and illegal fishing. This was followed by a far-reaching regional blue economy plan four years later (Duarte & Kenkel, 2019, pp. 9–12). The African Union's 2050 Integrated Maritime Strategy (AIM), adopted in January 2014, aimed to streamline all these initiatives. Two years later, the African Charter on Maritime Security and Safety and Development (also known as the Lomé Charter) was published under the auspices of the African Union.

The impressive track of the regionalisation of maritime security in Africa was nevertheless unable to overcome noteworthy limits. First, most of the agreements and projects were sound only on paper and failed to address West African countries' structural deficits in conducting effective maritime security operations (Silva, 2019). For instance, only two boats, both lacking surveillance radar, are responsible for all 250 km of Ghana's coast. The capabilities of Senegal, Angola, Togo, the Ivory Coast and Mali are reduced to token navies, while Guinea Bissau has no coastguard at all (Correa, 2019, p. 189; Sampó, 2019, p. 190).

Second, even West African countries failed to translate most maritime security agreements into actual practice. For example, Nigeria "has no functional piece of legislation for managing, coordinating ocean governance under the UNCLOS" (Anozie et al., 2019, p. 193), which hampered the operational compliance with such agreements (Obi-Nwosu et al., 2014).

Third, a general problem in the region is sea blindness (Bueger & Edmunds, 2017). African countries face multiple domestic crises which often prevents them from prioritising maritime security concerns (Jacobsen, 2017; Okafor-Yarwood, 2020). Consequently, their national and collective maritime security programmes are constantly menaced by a lack of long-term political will and investment (Potgieter, 2018, p. 8). That is the case of South Africa, where the Navy's ongoing condition of marginalisation and obsolescence constrains the increasing demand for coastal patrolling operations to attend to SADC's commitments (Neethling, 2019). Furthermore, the business-oriented approach of its Operation Phakisa project, which is seeking to unlock the economic potential of South Africa's oceans, is likely to result in limited progress, without improving coastal populations' resilience against "blue crimes" (Bueger & Edmunds, 2020).

This pattern also plagues European donors in the Gulf of Guinea, as they favour capacity building in national security and the blue economy over developmental or human security aspects. Without whole-of-government solutions to address local populations' insecurity and poverty, inter-regional maritime security programmes will continue to have limited impact (Brits & Nel, 2018, p. 8).

Conclusion

The political context and most recent data on maritime crime in the South Atlantic produce a dark forecast. Unlike current agendas in the Mediterranean Sea and West Indian Ocean, ocean governance has low prospects for progress among South American and West African countries. The failure or suspension of national and regional state-building projects has reduced the number and effectiveness of public policies. Consequently, these regions have been plagued by frail coastal populations, powerful transnational criminal organisations, and wrecked political institutions (Cockayne, 2016). Two cases stand out as potential hotspots at risk of descending further into crisis.

In South America, Venezuela's current situation is severe because state failure is entangled within regional divides and great power rivalry. While criminal activities are unleashed from its coasts and across the South Atlantic, the involvement of the United States and Russia in Maduro's regime has polarised the region. Consequently, Venezuela cannot count on functional support for the restoration of its governmental capacity. In West Africa, the European Union's aid in fostering maritime security will shrink owing to the stark economic effects of COVID-19 and Brexit. The web of maritime criminality in the Gulf of Guinea will possibly increase and make West African countries even more dependent on China and Russia's security sponsorships, escalating great power rivalry to the detriment of that region's maritime regimes.

Note

1   See https://globalfishingwatch.org/map-and-data

References

Adibe, J. (2019, November 14). *What does Russia really want from Africa?* Brookings. https://www.brookings.edu/blog/africa-in-focus/2019/11/14/what-does-russia-really-want-from-africa

Agencia Brasil. (2020, June 26). *Governo divulga balanço sobre apreensão de drogas e* combate ao *tráfico no País.* Governo do Brasil. https://www.gov.br/pt-br/noticias/justica-e-seguranca/2020/06/governo-divulga-balanco-sobre-apreensao-de-drogas-e-combate-ao-trafico-no-pais

Anozie, C., Umahi, T., Onuoha, G., Nwafor, N., & Alozie, O. J. (2019). Ocean governance, integrated maritime security and its impact in the Gulf of Guinea: A lesson for Nigeria's maritime sector and economy. *Africa Review, 11*(2), 190–207.

Beirão, A. P., & da Silva Ramos, B. V. A. (2019). The possibility of NATO and Portuguese presence in the South Atlantic Ocean. In É. Duarte & M. Correia de Barros (Eds.), *Maritime security challenges in the South Atlantic* (pp. 79–104). Springer International Publishing.

Biberman, Y., & Turnbull, M. (2018). When militias provide welfare: Lessons from Pakistan and Nigeria. *Political Science Quarterly Wiley-Blackwell, 133*(4), 695–727.

Brasil. (2016). *Estratégia Nacional de Defesa.* Ministerio da Defesa.

Brits, P., & Nel, M. (2018). African maritime security and the Lomé Charter: Reality or dream? *African Security Review, 27*(3–4), 226–244.

Bruns, S. (2019). From show of force to naval presence, and back again: The U.S. Navy in the Baltic, 1982–2017. *Defense & Security Analysis, 35*(2), 117–132.

Bueger, C., & Edmunds, T. (2017). Beyond seablindness: A new agenda for maritime security studies. *International Affairs, 93*(6), 1293–1311.

Bueger, C., & Edmunds, T. (2020). Blue crime: Conceptualising transnational organised crime at sea. *Marine Policy, 119*. 10.1016/j.marpol.2020.104067. http://www.ncbi.nlm.nih.gov/pubmed/104067

Buzan, B., & Little, R. (2000). *International systems in world history: Remaking the study of international relations.* Oxford University Press.

Cabral, I. M. (2017). *The E.U. as a security actor in the Gulf of Guinea.* Master's Dissertation, Instituto Universitário de Lisbon, Escola de Sociologia e Políticas Públicas.

Campos, I., & Vines, A. (2008). *Angola and China: A pragmatic partnership.* Center for Strategic and International Studies.

Carrier, N., Klantschnig, G., Honwana, A., de Waal, A., Dowden, R., & Kitchen, S. (Eds.). (2012). *Africa and the War on Drugs.* Zed Books.

Clarín. (2020, May 18) *Aguas de nadie: Los 400 barcos extranjeros que depredan el Mar Argentino en el Sur.* Clarín. https://www.clarin.com/sociedad/aguas-nadie-400-barcos-extranjeros-depredan-mar-argentino-sur_0_K75JRhOJb.html

Cockayne, J. (2016). *Hidden power: The strategic logic of organized crime.* Oxford University Press.

Correa, M. (2019). Conclusion. In E. Duarte & M. Correa (Eds.), *Navies and maritime policies in the South Atlantic* (pp. 187–195). Palgrave Macmillan.

da Silva, A. P. (2017). Brazil's recent agenda on the sea and the South Atlantic contemporary scenario. *Marine Policy, 85*, 25–32. 10.1016/j.marpol.2017.08.010

Diallo, M. A. (2019). The impacts of neo-colonial security frameworks in the South Atlantic: The case of French presence in Western Africa. In É. E. Duarte & M. C. Barros (Eds.), *Maritime security challenges in the South Atlantic.* (pp. 41–78). Palgrave Macmillan.

do Nascimento, L. Gd. (2020). The Beijing Consensus and the New Silk Road in Africa: Chinese investments in new disputes of hegemony. *Conjuntura Internacional, 17*(1), 27–38.

Duarte, É. (2016). Brazil, the blue economy and the maritime security of the South Atlantic. *Journal of the Indian Ocean Region, 12*(1), 97–111.

Duarte, É. (2019). Introduction. In É. Duarte & M. C. Barros (Eds.), *Navies and maritime policies in the South Atlantic* (pp. 1–12). Palgrave Macmillan.

Duarte, É., Marcondes, D., & Carneiro, C. (2019). Facing transnational criminal organisations in the South Atlantic. In E. Duarte & M. Correia de Barros (Eds.), *Maritime security challenges in the South Atlantic* (pp. 11–40). Palgrave Macmillan.

Duarte, E., & Moura, G. (2019). Os Fins e os Meios Navais no Âmbito da Zona Econômica Exclusiva. *Revista Brasileira de Estudos de Defesa, 6*(2), 39–61.

Duarte, É. E., & Kenkel, K. M. (2019). Contesting perspectives on South Atlantic maritime security governance: Brazil and South Africa. *South African Journal of International Affairs, 26*(3), 395–412.

Eisenberg, R. (2012). *Reexamining the Global Cold War in South Africa: Port usage, space tracking, and weapons sales*. Master dissertation, Portland State University.

Espach, R. (2019). Reflections on the ends, ways, and means of maritime security cooperation in the South Atlantic. In É. E. Duarte & M. C. Barros (Eds.), *Maritime security challenges in the South Atlantic* (pp. 129–153). Palgrave Macmillan.

Flint, C., & Dezzani, R. (2018). Defining and operationalizing context through structural political geography for international relations. In W. Thompson (Ed.), *The Oxford encyclopaedia of empirical international relations theory* (pp. 429–450). Oxford University Press.

Goertz, G. (1994). *Contexts of international politics*. Cambridge University Press.

Hanauer, L., & Morris, L. (2013). *Chinese engagement in African drivers, reactions, and implications for the U.S. policy*. Rand Corporation.

Hartman, A. (2017, September 11). Illegal fishing vessels are reported to Angola. *IUU Watch*. http://www.iuuwatch.eu/2017/09/illegal-fishing-vessels-reported-angola/

Hedenskog, J. (2018). *Russia is stepping up its military cooperation in Africa*. Swedish Defense Research Agency.

Hurrell, A. (1983). The politics of South Atlantic security: A survey of proposals for a South Atlantic Treaty Organization. *International Affairs, 59*(2), 179–193.

Jacobsen, K. L. (2017). Maritime security and capacity building in the Gulf of Guinea: On comprehensiveness, gaps, and security priorities. *African Security Review, 26*(3), 237–256.

Jeong, K. (2018). Diverse patterns of world and regional piracy: Implications of recurrent characteristics. *Australian Journal of Maritime and Ocean Affairs, 10*(2), 118–133.

Jesperson, S. (2017). Responding to drug trafficking: A question of motives. In L. B. Reitano, R. B. Lugo, & S. Jesperson (Eds.), *Militarised responses to transnational organised crime: The war on crime*. Palgrave.

Libel, T. (2020). Rethinking strategic culture: A computational (social science) discursive-institutionalist approach. *Journal of Strategic Studies, 43*(5), 686–709.

Mabry, D. U. S. (1988). The US military and the war on drugs in Latin America. *Journal of Interamerican Studies and World Affairs, 30*(2–3), 53–76.

Malamud, A. (2011). A leader without followers? The growing divergence between regional and global performance of Brazilian foreign policy. *Latin American Politics and Society, 53*(3), 1–24.

Mastro, O. (2020). *Russia and China team up on the Indian Ocean*. Lowy Institute. https://www.lowyinstitute.org/the-interpreter/russia-and-china-team-indian-ocean

Mattos, C. M. (1980). Atlântico Sul: Sua Importância Estratégica. *A Defesa Nacional* 67(688), 72–90.

Mbewa, D. O. (2019, September 24). *Namibia pledges at $2.7 million to fight illegal fishing*. CGTN Africa. https://africa.cgtn.com/2019/09/24/namibia-pledges-2-7-million-to-fight-illegal-fishing/

McFate, M. (2020). Being there: US Navy organisational culture and the forward presence debate. *Defense and Security Analysis, 36*(1), 42–64.

Mearsheimer, J. J. (2019). Bound to fail: The rise and fall of the liberal international order. *International Security, 43*(4), 7–50.

Medeiros, S. E., & Benvenuto, L. M. (2020). The Chinese belt and road initiative and possible repercussions to BRICS and Brazil. *Journal of China and International Relations*, 8, 1–22. Special Edition: BRICS.

Moritán, R. (2020, May 14). *La complicidad uruguaya en la pesca ilegal China en el Mar Argentino*. Clarín. https://www.clarin.com/politica/complicidad-uruguaya-pesca-ilegal-china-mar-argentino_0_eUMMfHy2r.html

Nantulya, P. (2019). *Chinese hard power supports its growing strategic interests in Africa*. Africa Center for Strategic Studies: https://africacenter.org/spotlight/chinese-hard-power-supports-its-growing-strategic-interests-in-africa/.

Nantulya, P. (2020). *Chinese security contractors in Africa Carnegie-Tsinghua*. Africa Center for Strategic Studies. https://carnegietsinghua.org/2020/10/08/chinese-security-contractors-in-africa-pub-82916.

Neethling, T. (2019). The South African navy and regional maritime security: The dilemma of political-strategic objectives and financial constraints. In É. Duarte & M. Correa (Eds.), *Navies and maritime policies in the South Atlantic* (pp. 41–68). Palgrave Macmillan.

Neira, R. (2020). *Boats, budget, and boots: The Colombian Navy's challenges in international cooperation*. Center for International Maritime Security. http://cimsec.org/boats-budget-and-boots-the-colombian-navys-challenges-in-international-cooperation/45583

Obi-Nwosu, H., Nwafor, C., & Joe-Akunne, C. (2014). Cognitive restructuring: A panacea for good governance and national security in Nigeria. *Social Science Research, 2*(2), 99–109.

Okafor-Yarwood, I. (2020). The cyclical nature of maritime security threats: Illegal, unreported, and unregulated fishing as a threat to human and national security in the Gulf of Guinea. *African Security, 13*(2), 116–146.

Panda, A. (2019, November 27). *Chinese, Russian, South African navies conduct trilateral naval exercises.* The Diplomat. https://thediplomat.com/2019/11/chinese-russian-south-african-navies-conduct-trilateral-naval-exercises/

Poggio Teixeira, C. G., & Da Silva Nogueira de Melo, D. (2019). NATO and South Atlantic. *Conjuntura Austral, 10*(51), 82–108.

Potgieter, T. (2018). Oceans economy, blue economy, and security: Notes on the South African potential and developments. *Journal of the Indian Ocean Region, 14*(1), 49–70.

Sampó, C. (2019). El Tráfico de cocaína entre América Latina y África occidental. *URVIO. Revista Latinoamericana de Estudios de Seguridad, 24*(24), 187–203.

Schmitt, E., & Gibbons-Neff, T. (2020, January 28). *Russia exerts a growing influence in Africa, worrying many in the West.* The New York Times. https://www.nytimes.com/2020/01/28/world/africa/russia-africa-troops.html

Silva, I. (2019). The African way of warfare and its challenge to South Atlantic security. In É. Duarte & M. C. Barros (Eds.), *Maritime security challenges in the South Atlantic* (pp. 155–192). Palgrave Macmillan.

Silva, M. (2020). Brazil and China's interests in Atlantic Africa. *Journal of China and International Relations, 8*, 98–132. Special Edition: BRICS. 10.5278/jcir.v8iSE.4241

Tallis, J. (2020). *Maritime security and great power competition: Maintaining the US-led international order.* Center for Naval Analysis. https://apps.dtic.mil/sti/citations/AD1101486

The Guardian. (2019, January 25). *Russian mercenaries reportedly in Venezuela to protect Maduro.* The Guardian. http://www.theguardian.com/world/2019/jan/25/venezuela-maduro-russia-private-security-contractors

Thomashausen, A., & Graça, P. Q. (2015). Security and governance in the extended continental shelf zones of the Lusophone South. In P. Borges Graça (Ed.), *New challenges of the Atlantic: An approach from Portugal.* Institute of Social and Political Sciences of the University of Lisbon.

Tilly, C., & Goodin, R. (2006). It depends. In C. Tilly & R. Goodin (Eds.), *The Oxford handbook of contextual political analysis* (pp. 1–31). Oxford University Press.

UNODC. (2018). *World drug report.* United Nations.

UNODC. (2019). *World drug report.* United Nations.

UNODC. (2020a). *World drug report. Booklet 1.* United Nations.

UNODC. (2020b). *World drug report. Booklet 3.* United Nations.

US. (2017). *National security strategy of the United States.* The White House.

Vidigal, A. (1985). *A evolução do pensamento estratégico naval brasileiro.* Biblioteca do Exército.

Viegas, J. (2016). A Segurança do Atlântico Sul e as Relações com a África. FUNAG. http://funag.gov.br/loja/download/1180-a-seguranca-do-atlantico-sul-e-as-relacoes-com-a-africa.pdf.

Waltz, K. (1979). *Theory of international politics* (1st ed.). Addison-Wesley Publishing Company.

Wills, S. (2020). These aren't the SLOC's you're looking for: Mirror-imaging battles of the Atlantic will not solve current Atlantic security needs. *Defense and Security Analysis, 36*(1), 30–41.

Wilson, J. (2015). *China's military agreements with Argentina: A potential new phase in China–Latin America defence relations.* US-China Economic and Security Review Commission, Staff Research Report. https://www.uscc.gov/research/chinas-military-agreements-argentina-potential-new-phase-china-latin-america-defense

Yi, X. (2019). *Overview of 1st China-Africa Peace and Security Forum – Ministry of National Defense.* China Military Online. http://eng.mod.gov.cn/news/2019-07/17/content_4846012.htm

Zverev, A., & Tsvetkova, M. (2019, January 25). *Exclusive: Kremlin-linked contractors help guard Venezuela's Maduro – Sources.* Reuters. https://www.reuters.com/article/us-venezuela-politics-russia-exclusive-idUSKCN1PJ22M

28

MARITIME SECURITY IN THE MEDITERRANEAN

Michela Ceccorulli

Introduction

Reviewing the literature, one is puzzled by the paucity of books exploring maritime security in the Mediterranean compared to the ink spent on other sea spaces (see for example Bueger et al., 2019; Guan & Skogan, 2007; Percy, 2018). This is surprising given the importance this basin has played for centuries in terms of trade and energy flows, transportation of goods and persons and cultural connections (Adler et al., 2006; Gillespie & Volpi, 2019).

The Mediterranean is the theatre of multiple, synchronised and connected events, which urgently need fresh input and governance (see Chapter 6). The so-called "refugee crisis" of 2015, for instance, is only one of many events that have attracted widespread attention, along with energy disputes in the eastern Mediterranean and the protracted political instability in the Middle East and North Africa region. Other challenges such as illicit trade in narcotics and weapons, traffic in human beings, and severe environmental degradation, are further affecting the region. From an academic point of view, untangling this knot and investigating the role of maritime security requires shedding light into how the Mediterranean is understood, as often the region and the sea have overlapped in the public debate, with the former overpowering the latter. The distinction does not need to be neat though, if one recognises that the sea and the region are inevitably connected. However, so far, the scholarly debate has scarcely considered the role of the sea and the ways to cope with challenges and capitalise on the opportunities of this water basin.

The aim of this chapter is to consider how maritime security in the Mediterranean has been recently framed and the related implications. If the Mediterranean has topped the agenda of the Euro-Atlantic community – of the European Union (EU) foremost – this has been mainly due to discernible and often overlapping securitisation processes (see Chapter 8), which have often yielded to a geopolitical re-bordering of the area. Differently put, the sea has attracted increasing attention mostly because of its divisive, unruly and difficult to govern nature (Biscop, 2017; Gentry, 2020); inevitably, this is the conception of "maritime security" that has prevailed when discussing the Mediterranean. The interplay between a wide array of state and non-state actors (Taufer, 2015) portrays the Mediterranean as a distinct context of maritime security interactions. The increasing intrusion of non-Mediterranean actors with regional or global ambitions and the rising assertiveness of Mediterranean ones, have brought back debates about a revival of "naval realism" as the essence of maritime security, reflecting past understandings of

334

DOI: 10.4324/9781003001324-31

the term (Germond, 2015, pp. 10, 36; McCabe et al., 2020). Less traditional challenges such as irregular immigration, criminal activities and energy quarrels have also revealed escalating tensions related to maritime use and governance (Germond, 2015, p. 84). This, however, is only part of the story, for there is growing acknowledgement that the sea connects bordering areas and their future in an indivisible knot, forcing an understanding of maritime security that goes beyond short-term considerations and that requires deep and comprehensive coordination.

The first section briefly looks at how the sea has progressively gained space in conventional understandings of the Mediterranean region. The second section explores the relevance the Mediterranean has acquired for the security of the EU, while the third section discusses a series of sea-related challenges perceived as urgent by scholarly and policymaking circles. The fourth section introduces a different conception of maritime security that extends beyond the immediate (Euro-centric) security concerns and relates to the sustainability and the ability to face more challenging global threats in the foreseeable future. The concluding section wraps up and suggests potential avenues for further research.

Re-drawing the Mediterranean: From Land to Sea

In recent years, several authors have made clear how the Mediterranean basin has become a context to be studied per se, for its relevance as a "permissive" environment or "milieu" (Germond, 2015, p. 16), or as a quasi "political" space or a "sea-region" with its own dynamics, with critical implications for regional and international security (Kuru, 2021). Before this, scholars have examined the Mediterranean as a common space of interaction mirroring a regional security community (Korkmaz, 2008) while often neglecting its "blue" aspects. The construction of the Mediterranean in different institutional settings, such as the 1995 Euro-Mediterranean Partnership and the EU's neighbourhood policy launched in 2003, was expected to provide policy coherence for participating countries and favored the naïve image of a cohesive political space (Barbé & Surrallés, 2010). The EU-led efforts geared towards region-building, however, had already lost much substance with the launch of the Union for the Mediterranean in 2008 and the progressive revision of the neighbourhood policy, with ambitions cut short and the cohesiveness of the Mediterranean region questioned in practice (Bicchi, 2011).

A wide range of literature has also pointed to the "paternalistic" construction of the Mediterranean and the lack of mutual understanding and co-ownership among partners in an extremely complex region (Gillespie, 2013). Over time, a series of political, security and humanitarian issues produced a crisis-triggered interest in the Mediterranean (Kuru, 2021, p. 20). A number of tipping moments accelerated this process, such as the 9/11 terrorist attacks which focused attention on potential security threats travelling via the Mediterranean, the Arab Springs of 2011, the Libyan quagmire, or the "refugee crisis" of 2015 (MEDRESET, 2017). This shift had a two-fold implication. First, the adoption of a geopolitical approach translated into an exercise of narrative "spatialisation" of world politics (Germond, 2015, p. 11), which contributed to framing the Mediterranean as a fragmented and torn space. Rather than a connecting bridge, the Mediterranean kept apart continents, religions, cultures and political systems, demarcating spaces of security and insecurity (Cobarrubias, 2018; Huber et al., 2018; Korkmaz, 2008). Second, the framing of the sea as critical for security. The rising economic and military presence of major regional and global players and their differing approaches towards the Mediterranean further added to the securitisation of the space, annulling the idea of a "single monolithic cartography" (Ehteshami & Mohammadi, 2017). The Mediterranean was thus depicted as a space to be "secured" rather than "protected", which affected the prevailing understanding of maritime security in the area.

Michela Ceccorulli

The EU and Maritime Security in the Mediterranean

The EU's first Maritime Security Strategy (EUMSS) was adopted in 2014 and explicitly added a maritime dimension to the security of the Union (European Council, 2014a). The sea was described as key to the EU's growth and prosperity, and thus had to remain "open, protected and secure" (European Council, 2014a, p. 2).

This understanding of maritime security extended beyond "sea domination", including a wide range of topics and issues, from protecting European economic interests at sea, to maintaining the freedom of navigation, fighting organised crime, to countering risks associated with the harmful exploitation of marine resources, environmental disasters, and climate change (European Council, 2014a; European Union, 2016). The securitisation of the maritime domain, however, often took precedence over other priorities such as blue economic growth or marine health preservation, with the EU becoming a key security provider in the area (Germond, 2015, p. 124). Consequently, maritime security became integrated within the wider Common Foreign and Security Policy (CFSP) framework, accompanying development cooperation, political dialogue and capacity building. In this regard, scholars have recently focused on the maritime dimension of the Union's foreign and security policy as a new and substantial turn in the EU's external policies (Bosilca, 2017; Molnár & Takács, 2021; Riddervold, 2018, 2021). The fact that the largest Common Security and Defence Policy (CSDP) military operations of the EU have been deployed at sea is a case in point.

The EUMSS and subsequent implementation plan highlighted a wide range of maritime security threats and risks at sea: the smuggling of migrants and trafficking activities and threats to free-trade flows were mentioned as the greatest challenges to be faced in adjacent waters (European Council, 2014b), together with lack of agreement on maritime zones (European Commission, 2014). The years to come would reveal the Mediterranean's centrality for such challenges. The escalation of insecurity in Libya coupled with a soaring number of irregular arrivals on European shores and migrants' deaths in the Mediterranean drew instantaneous attention to this theatre (see Chapter 14). Operation EUNAVFOR MED Sophia, launched in 2015 and unprecedented due to its military character in response to migration, was intended to offer a concrete contribution to maritime security (European Union, 2016) focusing on curbing migrant smuggling, training and sharing information with the Libyan coastguard and navy, and supporting the implementation of the UN weapons embargo on the high seas off Libya. In this sense, it aimed to complement different land-based strategies adopted to decrease insecurity, including the civilian mission assisting Libyan authorities in improving the country's border security (EUBAM Libya) as well as a number of bilateral cooperation programmes (Ceccorulli & Coticchia, 2020; Lehti, 2018). Coordination with FRONTEX, the European Border and Coast Guard Agency, was also critical for enhancing maritime security, clearly linking the EU security with developments at sea.

Beginning with 2015, a number of documents were released, which explicitly connected the internal and external EU security dimensions and thus turned the sea into a critical space for European security (Germond, 2015). These included, for instance, the Agenda on Migration and the European Agenda on Security, the EU Action plan against migrant smuggling, the revised Neighbourhood policy and the EU Global Strategy. The 2017 report on the implementation of the EUMSS action plan further emphasised the risks and threats at and from the sea, while clearly linked them to the deteriorating situation in the neighbourhood (European Commission, 2017). It listed five areas within the "EU's political priority" (European Commission, 2017, p. 5), including the Central Mediterranean, with smuggling and irregular flows issues coupled with the situation of insecurity in Libya.

Maritime surveillance activities were prioritised accordingly and promoted through the Seahorse Mediterranean Network, engaging some EU Member States and some North African countries (European Council, 2017) and the FRONTEX "Common patrols" projects (European Commission, 2017, p. 33). Permanent deployments in African states to support the fight against smuggling and trafficking were also urged, while reference was made to the Shared Awareness and De-confliction in the Mediterranean forum (SHADE MED) to discuss new coordinated efforts to crack down on irregular migration in the Mediterranean Sea (Bueger & Edmunds, 2017; European Commission, 2017, p. 32).

The revised 2018 EUMSS implementation plan not only insisted on such priorities but also highlighted maritime security as a requirement for the stability and "resilience" of southern riparian states and unstable neighbouring areas (Cusumano & Hofmaier, 2020; European Council, 2018). For example, the new mandate of operation EUBAM Libya, tasked to train the Libyan coast guard, also foresaw assisting Libyan authorities in drafting a maritime security strategy as well as a national strategy of border and security management (Nielsen, 2020).

This section has shown how the EU's understanding of maritime security has been largely moulded by what have been perceived as urgent security challenges. Alongside migration, other challenges have heated up the Mediterranean waters as discussed next.

Maritime Security in the Mediterranean

Whereas maritime security, as discussed at length in the second part of this chapter and as shown in this handbook, is much broader than "good order at sea" (Taufer, 2015, p. 50), recent events have reinforced the security connotation of the term. Overall, this has produced concrete effects, resulting in a growing militarisation of the sea.

An Overcrowded Area: Powers at Play

The literature on the Mediterranean has noted how the sea has turned into a political space, where not only local but also geographically distant countries are jockeying for position. The growing influence of states such as China and Russia, for instance, has been largely seen as a disturbing factor, which could potentially affect Western control over the sea (Linden, 2018; Siddi, 2020).

China's abundant economic investments in key ports and infrastructure in states including Italy, Spain, Greece and Turkey have been interpreted as supporting the country's economic expansion plans, much like its increasing military presence in the region. For some observers, Europe and China share a common interest in the Mediterranean's stability and hence ac-commodating one another is deemed as mutually beneficial, with Beijing propping up the EU's sluggish progress on infrastructure and making substantial investments in the region (Prodi, 2015). Additionally, the two actors have aligned interests related to various non-traditional challenges, as seen in the case of antipiracy efforts in the Indian Ocean (Dossi, 2015). Other views point instead at China's rising ambitions in the region as illustrated by its joint naval exercises with Russia in the eastern Mediterranean and the growing importance of the region for its Belt and Road Initiative (Paul, 2019). Russia's re-emergence as a maritime power in the Mediterranean in 2015 and the reactivation of its naval base in the Syrian port of Tartu raised even more serious concerns. The country's central role in the protracted Syrian conflict has seen a significant military deployment at sea, consisting of submarines, ships and air and sea bases along the Syrian coast. Russia has also intruded into the chaotic situation of Libya through private military contractors, conducting what seems like hybrid warfare and antagonising

Western attempts to simmer down tensions (Cristiani, 2020). The Syrian and Libyan powder kegs have not only disrupted the geopolitical equilibria in the area, but have contributed to the securitisation of the Mediterranean via an increased military presence.

From Sophia to Irini: Human Maritime Insecurity Neglected but Not Gone

As seen above and at length in Ferreira (Chapter 14), migration has been increasingly seen as a security concern in the Mediterranean. Various initiatives geared towards "the fight against human smuggling" were set up to deflate the number of irregular crossings and save the lives of migrants (Ceccorulli & Lucarelli, 2018). Paradoxically, human security at sea has declined and the migrants' death toll has increased following the intensified military presence at sea (Cusumano, 2017). Even the more robust commitment to fight human smuggling that had initially prompted the EU military deployment gradually lost its edge; as a result, the EU-led maritime operation EUNAVFOR MED *Irini*, taking over from *Sophia*, centred its entire efforts on the enforcement of the UN arms embargo at sea off Libya, avoiding the question of saving migrants' lives altogether. By now it has become widely accepted that given the overall context of insecurity surrounding the Mediterranean and the lack of reform in the asylum system of the EU, migration requires more a complex fix than patrolling and capacity-building exercises. Moreover, the very rationale of these activities has been questioned: most of the arms supplied to Libya do not transit by sea but rather on land (Megerisi, 2019).

Overheating in the Eastern Mediterranean

The Mediterranean represents a vital transit hub for oil and gas destined to the EU and the US markets from other seas (the Persian Gulf and the Caspian Sea) and states (Russia) via the Suez Canal, the Dardanelles and the Bosphorus Straits (Sartori, 2015). Additionally, the production of oil and gas is also becoming increasingly relevant; the discovery of gas fields beginning with 2009 in the Eastern Mediterranean off the coasts of Israel, Cyprus and Egypt prompted a number of scholars to develop the concept of the "East Med" as a sub-region (Sartori & Bianchi, 2019).

These developments were crucial in many ways, due to the recent emphasis on decarbonisation policies, new shipping possibilities of liquefied gas and decreasing dependence on foreign supplies, among others. This surging interest in energy resources triggered widespread debates on whether these discoveries, their connecting infrastructures and long-term contracts could engender prospects for cooperation between regional actors, cushioning against possible disruptions (Colombo & Dentice, 2020; Rubin & Eiran, 2019; Sotirious, 2020). This type of argument seems to be confirmed by the establishment in 2019 of the Eastern Mediterranean Gas Forum (EMGF) between Italy, Egypt, Israel, Cyprus, Greece and the Palestinian Authority, with the ambition of creating a regional gas market. From a western point of view, increasing opportunities for cooperation were a way to decrease dependence on Russia, with the Eastmed pipeline project between Greece, Cyprus and Israel connecting the EU and the Eastern Mediterranean being warmly greeted by the EU and the US alike (Colombo & Dentice, 2020).

By contrast, some maintain that energy concerns would not only add fuel to already present tensions in the Mediterranean, but also cripple Western cohesion (Grigoriadis, 2014). At play are not only considerations regarding energy security, but also the diplomatic use of energy by some actors, notably Turkey. In the case under analysis the issue concerns territorial disputes over exclusive economic zones and sea-border delimitation. On the one hand, Turkey has denied recognition of contracts signed by Cyprus with international energy companies, alluding to the sovereign rights of the Turkish Republic of Northern Cyprus. On the other hand, the country has started drilling off the coast of Cyprus, infringing on its economic zone. Adding to Turkey's manoeuvres in the East is the 2019 agreement with Tripoli's government to delimit Turkey's and Libya's reciprocal exclusive economic zones. Turkey's claimed rights (hydrocarbon drilling included) are an impediment to any gas activity in the Central and Eastern Mediterranean which aims at excluding the Anatolian state, while the expected control over zones claimed by Greece can ignite new tensions at any moment.

Turkey's actions are not only troubling for European countries but also for other Mediterranean states such as Egypt and Israel, with which confrontation is manifest both on energy issues in the Eastern Mediterranean and the civil conflict in Libya (Scazzieri, 2020). As a by-product of the generalised malaise, military deployments at sea have sat alongside arms purchases (quite a salient point given years of cuts in defence budgets), while the widespread militarisation of the Mediterranean has triggered fears of possible accidents. At the end of August 2020 Greece, Italy, France and Cyprus engaged in joint drills codenamed Eunomia in the Eastern Mediterranean as a clear sign of commitment to keeping the rule of law in that part of the sea (Ansaldo, 2020). Escalation is perceived as a concrete likelihood in view of provocatory exercises, such as Turkey's recent deployment of warships in Greek waters (Axt, 2021; Karakasis, 2019). As an alternative to the risk of being embroiled in the spiral of insecurity in southern Mediterranean countries, offshore production has started to be taken into consideration; however, this option too could soon be affected by security tensions in the area (Sartori, 2015).

Terrorism and Organised Crime

Terrorism is similarly entangled with perceptions of maritime security in the Mediterranean. The sea has been considered a vehicle for terrorist infiltration, for instance along migration corridors that lead from North Africa, the Middle East and the Balkans to the EU. Consequently, sea patrolling has become one of the chief activities undertaken to enhance security. The maritime operation *Active Endeavour* launched by NATO under article 5 in the aftermath of the 9/11 terrorist attacks and superseded by operation *Sea Guardian* in 2016 are cases in point, with the latter having wider mandate including situational awareness and capacity building. The sea could also offer a base from which to run counter-terrorism operations in riparian states south of the Mediterranean and in closer regions, where terrorist formations have their stronghold (Isaac & Kares, 2017).

Illegal activities such as drug trafficking and human smuggling at sea potentially being used to finance terrorist networks is another matter of concern (Achilli & Tinti, 2019; Cornell, 2012). Moreover, direct attacks on ports, pipelines or shipping in the Mediterranean are another key threat for maritime security (Taufer, 2015; Taylor, 2019), albeit potentially less likely (Lesser, 2016).

Maritime Security in the Mediterranean Updated

All the challenges discussed above depict the Mediterranean as a dangerous and unstable place. Yet this picture is only partial for two related reasons. First, the concept of maritime security acquires new nuances when less publicly debated challenges are considered. The less vocal discussions about sustainability and blue growth in the region, for instance, offer an image of a less divided geographical area, where no space is available for zero-sum calculations and instead, the need for deep coordination is widely recognised. Second, many of the threats that rank high on the Mediterranean political agenda are caused and magnified by the neglect of a comprehensive understanding of maritime security.

As maritime security is being conceptually broadened to include a wider array of challenges, scholarly and policy literature has started to pay increasing attention to how Mediterranean countries perform against the 2030 Agenda for Sustainable Development and its Sustainable Development Goals (SDGs), including in the maritime dimension (Riccaboni et al., 2020).

Environmental challenges in this geographical spot are considered significant and the acknowledgement is widely shared that broad transnational partnerships of governments, businesses, stakeholders and citizens are to be offered as a recipe to cope.

Of all the environmental challenges, climate change is a particularly worrisome indicator. Global warming as a facet of climate change is underlined as a severe challenge for the Mediterranean region, with an impact second only to the Arctic region. Without additional mitigation efforts, the temperature of the region is expected to increase by 2.2°C by 2040 (MedECC, 2019). Many factors are simultaneously related to this challenge and need in-depth consideration as potential amplifiers, such as water (and also seawater) and agriculture management and energy sustainability, dubbed in the specialised literature as the "water–energy–food nexus" (Saladini et al., 2018). The Mediterranean, and, in particular, the Middle East and North Africa are visibly affected by these developments (Schilling et al., 2020). The challenge is not only related to inland areas, but also to the sea and coastal regions. Climate change is expected to reduce available water resources, increase the likelihood of extreme events and, just as important, result in rises in the general level of the sea triggering land movements and saline intrusion into fertile lands, thus increasing food insecurity. For some highly populated geographical spots such as the Nile delta, this means a massive security disruption.

Water quality (also of the sea) is another issue of relevance, and here again the assessment is not particularly encouraging for the MENA region. Contributing to the bleak scenario are massive tourism, population growth, new industries and rapid urbanisation coupled with poor results in terms of adaptation (Riccaboni et al., 2020). Heavily populated coastal areas, already subject to resource stress and rapid alterations in habitat, are particularly affected (MedECC, 2019, p. 17). According to the MedECC report, around 150 million people live close to the sea; events related to climate change, first and foremost rising sea levels, are anticipated to have devastating impacts on these areas, such as the likely risk of flooding for at least 15 ports in various countries (MedECC, 2019, p. 19). Furthermore, many cultural world heritage sites identified by UNESCO are currently at risk (MedECC, 2019).

Shifting back to the sea and its sustainability, untenable methods can be traced largely to fisheries, with overfishing figuring prominently: by 2050 current fish stocks are expected to be reduced by half (Riccaboni et al., 2020). This would not only affect coastal economies engaged in fishing, aquaculture and related activities, but would also increase the likelihood of quarrels over legitimate fishing rights among states, as already shown by multiple events in the Mediterranean (D'Ignoti, 2020). Sea populations are also likely to change as cold-water species move towards cooler waters and warm-water ones start to inhabit the Mediterranean, often with devastating consequences in the case of invasive species disturbing the ecosystem (MedECC, 2019, p. 10). Sea warming, together with water acidification, is also expected to lead to the extinction of many species in the Mediterranean and affect the entire marine ecosystem (ibid).

Environmental considerations are crucial when attached to prospects for stability in the Mediterranean region. Adverse climate effects are projected to impact already fragile countries, where resource scarcity is often exploited by competing factions to alter conflict dynamics, and where demographic figures act as amplifiers (Daoudy, 2020; Mastrojeni & Pasini, 2020;

Scheffran & Battaglini, 2011). The displacement of people within and across borders is one of the most problematic outcomes of these developments (UNHCR, 2020). The scarcity of and conflict over resources are further worsening the situation of the most vulnerable displaced in the Sahel region and the Middle East. Moreover, environmental challenges make the prospect of refugees and displaced persons returning to their home territories an even more remote possibility, having important implications for the flux of sea crossings in the Mediterranean.

Institutional frameworks such as the Mediterranean Action Plan, working on marine and coastal degradation within the United Nations Environmental Programme, have been specifically set up to advance political dialogue and promote instruments and policies to deal with the potential challenges facing this basin, with a view to increasing its sustainability.

That specific framework led to the Convention for the Protection of the Marine Environment and the Coastal Region of the Mediterranean (Barcelona Convention) and added Protocols (UNEP, 2019), emphasising the need for cooperation to preserve the sea, the coasts and their richness. For example, recent work has been done to encourage cleaner shipping.[1] With a particular focus on promoting the sustainable development goals (SDGs), the contracting parties of the Barcelona Convention adopted the Mediterranean Strategy for Sustainable Development (MSSD 2016–2025) (UNEP/MAP, 2016). Moulded around six objectives (including the promotion of sustainable development in marine and coastal areas; management of sustainable cities and shipping, mitigation of and adaptation to climate change and transition towards a green and blue economy), the strategy calls for common objectives, stakeholder involvement, and solidarity and equity among others, and proposes strategic directions accordingly.

The Union for the Mediterranean also aims to foster regional dialogue among countries of the European Union and other Mediterranean countries to the east and south. Efforts are focused on mitigating climate-related effects using various tools – such as offshore renewable energies, green shipping and transport, smart ports and sustainable value chains – for a sustainable blue economy in the Mediterranean, including the context of the COVID-19 pandemic (Union for the Mediterranean, 2021). For its side, the EU has recently released a communication on a new approach for a sustainable blue economy, which outlines a holistic view that integrates ocean policy into its broader economic policies within the context of the European Green Deal and the Recovery Plan for Europe (European Commission, 2021). This approach aims to protect the EU's natural capital while reducing net greenhouse gas emissions so as to sustain a modern, competitive, and resource-efficient economy. The objective to drastically reduce pollution in the Mediterranean is clearly stated, an effort which entails coping with the decarbonisation and depollution of maritime transport, ports and energy production (European Commission, 2021, p. 4). Significant attention is devoted to the proper management of fisheries, which requires an inclusive approach bringing together all stakeholders.

Regional cooperation is thus emphasised as vital for facing the common challenges that affect states sharing the same sea basin. Guidance and support for regional states on fisheries and ecosystem conservation, shipping, transportation and trade, sustainable energy, environmental sustainability climate change and coastal infrastructure is also at the centre of the 2019 Africa Blue Economy Strategy (African Union, 2019). Harnessing the potential of water resources for "socio-economic emancipation and industrialization" in Africa in a sustainable way is clearly reiterated as a way to overcome challenges related to poor governance and climate and environmental change (African Union, 2019, p. ix).

As seen above, maritime security has recently been framed beyond traditional understandings to include challenges that can be tackled only through a regional or global approach; rather than being a divisive, zero-sum concern, securing the sea and coastal areas entails close cooperation and coordination among a broad range of stakeholders at all levels.

Conclusion

This chapter has explored different yet interrelated understandings of maritime security in the Mediterranean. The analysis above has revealed two key aspects. First, for both the policy and scholarly community at large, the understanding of maritime security has mostly translated into the idea of the Mediterranean as a space to be secured. According to this interpretation, the sea is both a battleground where different actors (and related interests) clash and a shield to guard against potential challenges coming from unstable spaces. The focus on this understanding and the perception of imminent challenges to be faced have led to the profound militarisation of this maritime arena, which risks diverting attention away from impending problems such as climate change and environmental issues, as well as the opportunities that the sea could offer. The geopolitical approach mentioned in this chapter has placed the sea back in a central position in perceptions of the Mediterranean region but has seemingly clouded the fact that the EU's security and that of the Mediterranean region at large depends on acknowledging the complexity, diversity and magnitude of the challenges ahead.

However, and here comes the second aspect, a still minoritarian but increasingly vocal field of interdisciplinary research is drawing attention to how the safety of the Mediterranean is of key value for all actors engaged in the region and beyond. In this case the known scenario of tensions, insecurity and disputes underlining the potential for generalised instability is replaced by a scenario were challenges acknowledgement invites to more cooperation. The sustainability of the Mediterranean Sea as a space where not only security but also development and prosperity are preserved and magnified requires coordinated action as well as convergent understanding of the challenges that tie together the fate of Mediterranean communities. While experts, practitioners and policymakers are part of this slow but growing realisation, the scholarly community seems to be lagging behind with poor interdisciplinary work in the field. As a matter of fact, the literature seems much more disposed to describe fragmentation than attempts at coordination and fails, hence, to make sense of and provide advice to cope with a fast-changing reality. A much more robust effort in this direction is thus strongly needed, taking stock of and further exploring the growing scientific literature on the matter and global attempts at broadening the understanding of urgent security challenges.

Note

1 https://www.rempec.org/en/news-media/rempec-news/regional-expert-meeting-on-the-possible-designation-of-the-mediterranean-sea-as-a-whole-as-an-emission-control-area-for-sulphur-oxides-med-sox-eca-pursuant-to-marpol-annex-vi-press-release

References

Achilli, L., & Tinti, A. (2019). Debunking the smuggler-terrorist nexus: Human smuggling and the Islamic state in the Middle East. *Studies in Conflict & Terrorism*, 1–16.

Adler, E., Bicchi, F., Crawford, B., & Del Sarto, R. A. (Eds.). (2006). *The convergence of civilizations: Constructing a Mediterranean region* (Vol. 1). University of Toronto Press.

African Union. (2019). Africa blue economy strategy. Retrieved 24 March 2021 from https://osf.io/3vy94/?view_only=ea6924dc03bd4f728f5635e81ee6bfc6

Ansaldo, M. (2020, August 26). Mediterraneo, Erdogan ad Atene: "ci riprenderemo quello che è nostro. Non fate errori. Sarà la vostra rovina". *La Repubblica.* https://www.repubblica.it/esteri/2020/08/26/news/mediterraneo_al_via_le_esercitazioni_congiunte_grecia_italia_francia_e_cipro-265504242/

Axt, H. J. (2021). Troubled water in the Eastern Mediterranean. Turkey challenges Greece and Cyprus regarding energy resources. *Comparative Southeast European Studies*, *69*(1), 133–152.

Barbé, E., & Surrallés, A. H. (2010). Dynamics of convergence and differentiation in Euro-Mediterranean relations: Towards flexible region-building or fragmentation? *Mediterranean Politics, 15*(2), 129–147.

Bicchi, F. (2011) The Union for the Mediterranean, or the changing context of Euro-Mediterranean relations. *Mediterranean Politics 16*(1), 3–19.

Biscop, S. (2017). *Euro-Mediterranean security: A search for partnership: A search for partnership.* Routledge.

Bosilca, R. L. (2017). *Maritime security policy in the making: The case of military CSDP operations at sea.* PhD dissertation. Bucharest/Oslo: National University of Political Studies and Public Administration.

Bueger, C., & Edmunds, C. (2017). Beyond seablindness: A new agenda for maritime security studies. *International Affairs, 93*(6), 1293–1311.

Bueger, C., Edmunds, T., & McCabe, R. (2019). Into the sea: Capacity-building innovations and the maritime security challenge. *Third World Quarterly, 41*(2), 228–246.

Ceccorulli, M., & Coticchia, F. (2020). "I'll take two". Migration, terrorism, and the Italian military engagement in Niger and Libya. *Journal of Modern Italian Studies, 25*(2), 174–196.

Ceccorulli, M., & Lucarelli, S. (2018). Securing borders, saving migrants: The EU's security dilemma in the twenty-first century. In S. Economides & J. Sperling (Eds.), *EU security strategies: Extending the EU system of security governance* (pp. 162–180). Routledge.

Cobarrubias, S. (2018). Beyond the European Union's neighbourhood: Liberation geographies in the Mediterranean. *Geopolitics, 25*(4), 887–915.

Colombo, M., & Dentice, G. (2020, February 21). *Approfondimento: l'accordo Turchia-GNA sui confini marittimi.* ISPI. https://www.ispionline.it/it/pubblicazione/approfondimento-laccordo-turchia-gna-sui-confini-marittimi-25158

Cornell, S. E. (2012). The interaction of drug smuggling, human trafficking, and terrorism. In A. Jonsson (Ed.), *Human trafficking and human security* (pp. 60–78). Routledge.

Cristiani, D. (2020). Framing Russia's Mediterranean return: Stages, roots and logics. IAI commentaries 20/59. https://www.iai.it/en/pubblicazioni/framing-russias-mediterranean-return-stages-roots-and-logics

Cusumano, E. (2017). Emptying the sea with a spoon? Non-governmental providers of migrant search and rescue in the Mediterranean. *Marine Policy, 75*, 91–98.

Cusumano, E., & Hofmaier, S. (2020). Introduction. In E. Cusumano & S. Hofmaier (Eds.), *Projecting resilience across the Mediterranean* (pp. 1–16). Springer.

Daoudy, M. (2020). *The origins of the Syrian conflict. Climate change and human security.* Cambridge University Press.

D'Ignoti, S. (2020, November 23). *Sicilian fishermen's capture escalates "red prawn war" between Italy and Libya.* Politico. https://www.politico.eu/article/sicilian-fishermen-capture-red-prawn-war-italy-libya/

Dossi, S. (2015). The EU, China and non-traditional security: Prospects for cooperation in the Mediterranean region. *Mediterranean Quarterly, 26*(1), 77–96.

Ehteshami, A., & Mohammadi, A. (2017). The key powers' construction of the Mediterranean. MEDRESET Policy Papers 2. https://www.iai.it/en/pubblicazioni/key-powers-construction-mediterranean

European Commission. (2014). For an open and secure global maritime domain: Elements for a European Union maritime security strategy. JOIN (2014) 9 final, Brussels. 6 March.

European Commission. (2017). Joint staff working document. Second report on the implementation of the EU maritime security strategy action plan. SWD (2017) 238 final, Brussels. 14 June.

European Commission. (2021). On a new approach for a sustainable blue economy in the EU. Transforming the EU's blue economy for a sustainable future. COM (2021) 240 final. Brussels, 17 May.

European Council. (2014a). European Union maritime security strategy. 11205/14, Brussels. 24 June.

European Council. (2014b). European Union maritime security strategy (EUMSS) action plan. 17002/14, Brussels. 16 December.

European Council. (2017). Council conclusions on global maritime security. 10238/17, Luxembourg. 19 June.

European Council. (2018). Council conclusions on the revision of the European Union maritime security strategy (EUMSS) action plan. 10494/18, Brussels. 26 June.

European Union. (2016). A global strategy for the European Union's foreign and security policy. Brussels, 28 June.

Gentry, B. (2020). Regional and global impacts of post-Gaddafi Libya. In M. R. Anderson & S. S. Holmsten (Eds.), *Political and economic foundations in global studies* (pp. 120–132). Routledge.

Germond, B. (2015). *The maritime dimension of European security.* Palgrave.

Gillespie, R. (2013). The challenge of co-ownership in the Euro-Mediterranean space. *Geopolitics, 18*(1), 178–197.

Gillespie, R., & Volpi, F. (Eds.). (2019). *Routledge handbook of Mediterranean politics*. Routledge.

Grigoriadis, J. (2014). Energy discoveries in the Eastern Mediterranean: Conflict or cooperation? *Middle East Policy, XXI*(3), 124–133.

Guan, K. K. C., & Skogan, J. (Eds.). (2007). *Maritime security in Southeast Asia*. Routledge.

Huber, D., Nouira, A., & Paciello, M. C. (2018). The Mediterranean: A space of division, disparity and separation. *MEDRESET Policy Papers 3*.

Isaac, S. K., & Kares, H. E. (2017). American discourses and practices in the Mediterranean since 2001: A comparative analysis with the EU. MEDRESET Working Papers 4. June.

Karakasis, V. P. (2019). The 2017 incidents in the Aegean and Turkish foreign policy: Using Q-methodology to examine Greek viewpoints. *Southeast European and Black Sea Studies, 19*(3), 451–472.

Korkmaz, V. (2008). Constructing the Mediterranean in the face of new threats: Are the EU's words really new? *European Security, 17*(1), 141–160.

Kuru, D. (2021). Not international relations' "mare nostrum": On the divergence between the Mediterranean and the discipline of international relations. *Mediterranean Politics, 26*(2), 145–167.

Lehti, J. (2018). "…in these exceptional and specific circumstances…": The EU military operation against human smuggling and trafficking in the Southern Central Mediterranean. In J. Schildknecht, R. Dickey, M. Fink, & L. Ferris (Eds.), *Operational law in international straits and current maritime security challenges* (pp. 181–194). Springer.

Lesser, I. (2016, June 21). *Terrorism and Mediterranean security: A net assessment*. Blog Post. German Marshall Fund. https://www.gmfus.org/news/terrorism-and-counter-terrorism-mediterranean

Linden, R. H. (2018). *The new sea people: China in the Mediterranean*. Istituto Affari Internazionali (IAI).

Look, J. (2019, August 21). Egypt, China conduct joint naval drill in the Mediterranean Sea. *Maritime Security Review*. http://www.marsecreview.com/2019/08/egypt-china-conduct-joint-naval-drill-in-mediterranean-sea/

Mastrojeni, G., & Pasini, A. (2020). *Effetto serra, effetto guerra* (New edition). Chiarelettere.

McCabe, R., Sanders, D., & Speller, I. (2020). Conclusion. In R. Mc Cabe, D. Sanders, & I. Speller (Eds.), *Europe, small navies and maritime security* (pp. 199–201). Routledge.

MedECC. (2019). *Risk associated to climate and environmental changes in the Mediterranean region*. Retrieved 11 November 2020 from https://ufmsecretariat.org/wp-content/uploads/2019/10/MedECC-Booklet_EN_WEB.pdf

MEDRESET. (2017). *The EU and geopolitics in the Mediterranean*. European Policy Brief. September. https://www.iai.it/sites/default/files/medreset_pb_2.pdf

Megerisi, T. (2019). EU's Irini Libya mission: Europe's operation Cassandra. Commentary. European Council on Foreign Relations. https://ecfr.eu/article/commentary_the_eus_irini_libya_mission_europes_operation_cassandra/

Molnár, A., & Takács, L. (2021). The European Union's response to mass migration through Mediterranean: A shift from humanitarian foreign policy actor towards a pragmatist foreign policy actor?. In A. Tsiampiris & F. Asderaki (Eds.), *The new Eastern Mediterranean transformed* (pp. 199–217). Springer.

Nielsen, N. (2020, September 18). *EU to help draft Libya's strategy on border security*. EU Observer. https://euobserver.com/migration/149468

Paul, M. (2019). *Partnership on the high seas. China and Russia's joint naval manoeuvres*. SWP Comment 26. https://www.swp-berlin.org/publications/products/comments/2019C26_pau.pdf

Percy, S. (2018). Maritime security. In A. Gheciu & W. C. Wohlfort (Eds.), *The Oxford handbook of international security* (pp. 607–621). Oxford University Press.

Prodi, R. (2015). A sea of opportunities. *Mediterranean Quarterly, 26*(1), 1–4.

Riccaboni, A., Sachs, J., Cresti, S., Gigliotti, M., & Pulselli, R. M. (2020). *Sustainable development in the Mediterranean*. Report 2020: Transformations to achieve the Sustainable Development Goals. Sustainable Development Solutions Network Mediterranean (SDSN Mediterranean).

Riddervold, M. (2018). *The maritime turn in EU foreign and security policies*. Palgrave Macmillan.

Riddervold, M. (2021). Heading forward in response to crisis: How the Ukraine crisis affected EU maritime foreign and security policy integration. In M. Riddervold, J. Trondal, & A. Newsome (Eds.), *The Palgrave handbook of EU crises* (pp. 569–584). Palgrave Macmillan.

Rubin, A., & Eiran, E. (2019). Regional maritime security in the eastern Mediterranean: Expectations and reality. *International Affairs, 95*(5), 979–997.

Saladini, F., Betti, G., Ferragina, E., Bouraoui, F., Cupertino, S., Canitano, G., Gigliotti, M., Autino, A., Pulselli, F. M., Riccaboni, A.,Bidoglio, G., & Bastianoni, S. (2018). Linking the water-energy-food nexus and sustainable development indicators for the Mediterranean region. *Ecological Indicators, 91*, 689–697.

Sartori, N. (2015). Il Mediterraneo e la sicurezza energetica. In A. Marrone & M. Nones (Eds.), *La Sicurezza nel Mediterraneo e l'Italia* (pp. 53–72). Edizioni Nuova Cultura.

Sartori, N., & Bianchi, M. (2019). From findings to market: Perspectives and challenges for the development of gas resources in the East Med. Global Turkey in Europe Working Paper 22. IAI. https://www.iai.it/sites/default/files/gte_wp_22.pdf

Scazzieri, L. (2020). Gas heats up the Eastern Mediterranean. Insight. Centre for European Reform. https://www.cer.eu/insights/gas-heats-eastern-mediterranean

Scheffran, J., & Battaglini, A. (2011). Climate and conflicts: The security risks of global warming. *Regional Environmental Change, 11*(1), 27–39.

Schilling, J., Hertig, E., Tramblay, Y., & Scheffran, J. (2020). Climate change vulnerability, water resources and social implications in North Africa. *Regional Environ Change, 20*(15). 10.1007/s10113-020-01597-7

Siddi, M. (2020). The Mediterranean dimension of West-Russia security relations. In A. Futter (Ed.), *Threats to Euro-Atlantic security* (pp. 165–177). Palgrave Macmillan.

Sotirious, S. (2020). Creating norms around the Eastern Mediterranean energy resources as a necessary means of security. *European Security, 29*(2), 235–253.

Taufer, M. (2015). The evolution of maritime security in the Mediterranean Sea. *Strategic Studies, 35*(4), 45–60.

UNEP. (2019). Convention for the protection of the marine environment and the coastal region of the Mediterranean and its protocols. https://wedocs.unep.org/bitstream/handle/20.500.11822/31970/bcp2019_web_eng.pdf

UNEP/MAP. (2016). Mediterranean strategy for sustainable development 2016–2025. Plan Bleu, Regional Activity Centre. https://wedocs.unep.org/bitstream/handle/20.500.11822/7097/mssd_2016_2025_eng.pdf

UNHCR. (2020). Strategic framework for climate action. UNHCR. https://www.unhcr.org/604a26d84.pdf

Union for the Mediterranean. (2021). *Towards a sustainable blue economy in the Mediterranean region.* https://ufmsecretariat.org/wp-content/uploads/2021/01/UfM-Towards-a-Sustainable-Blue-Economy-in-the-Mediterranean-region-EN_v2.pdf

Wolff, S. (2012). *The Mediterranean dimension of the European Union's internal security.* Palgrave Macmillan.

29

MARITIME SECURITY IN SOUTHEAST ASIA

Kwa Chong Guan and Collin Koh

The issues and concerns of Southeast Asia's nine littoral states over their maritime security today are grounded on colonial legacies of undefined sea boundaries and porous borders which traders, smugglers and pirates crossed with impunity and fishermen, nomadic communities and migrants ignored. The post-colonial states emerging out of the decolonisation of Southeast Asia after the Second World War struggled to define their marine boundaries as integral to the sovereignty of the nation-states they were building. This chapter of the handbook traces the efforts by Southeast Asian littoral states to manage, if not resolve their contentious sea boundaries within the evolving frameworks of international law relating to the sea to minimise disputes with neighbours.

This chapter also reviews the strategies of maritime forces developments as well as the promotion of confidence and security building measures and other practical security co-operation adopted by Southeast Asia's littoral states to establish the security of their maritime domains. The chapter also reviews Southeast Asian government responses to the old traditional maritime security problems of piracy and armed robbery, smuggling, irregular human migration as well as illegal, unreported and unregulated fishing.

The Colonial Roots of Southeast Asia's Maritime Security

The significance of Southeast Asia's seas and its straits is that they were, and are, the connectors between the trading world of the Indian Ocean and that of the South China Sea. The waterways of Southeast Asia were, however, more than a critical junction on the "Maritime Silk Road", which the nineteenth century geographer Ferdinand Freiherr von Richthofen (1833–1908) recognised as complementing the overland Silk Road he proposed linked Rome to Han China. Along the waterways and riverine systems of Southeast Asia also flowed the spices, aromata and pharmacopeia to the principal emporia on the Strait of Malacca and port-settlements on the other coasts of Southeast Asia for traders and shippers to take onboard their vessels to markets in China or South and West Asia and onwards to European markets. In 2013, Chinese President Xi Jinping appropriated this idea of a Maritime Silk Road to frame China's new foreign policy initiatives its international supply and value chains. The Strait of Malacca was identified as the Achilles's heel of China's expanding supply chains (Lai, 2007). Seven centuries earlier the Portuguese also identified the Straits of Malacca and Singapore as its

346

DOI: 10.4324/9781003001324-32

Achilles heel on its sailing routes to East Asia and planned to establish forts on Singapore to protect its Achilles heel, as historian Peter Borschberg (2010) has documented.

Sixteenth and seventeenth century Iberian intervention in the East Indies, as Southeast Asia was known in the early modern era, was about extending forms of Mediterranean maritime *imperium* to establish a monopoly of the lucrative spice trade and control of sailing through the Malacca Strait to East Asia. But this Iberian grasp for *imperium* over Southeast Asian seas and its trade was challenged by the Dutch and the British (Borschberg, 2010). Local response from the Malay sultans of the Malacca Strait, the Sulu Sea and Southern Philippines to European intervention ranged from collaboration to resistance, which was labelled "piracy" and its suppression was a driver of nineteenth century historical developments in the region. The 1824 Anglo-Dutch Treaty effectively divided the old Malay world between the Dutch and the British with the Strait of Singapore as their boundary. But for the communities on either side of the Straits of Malacca and Singapore, that colonial boundary was alien as they continued to crisscross the straits to trade, smuggle arms, drugs and other contraband goods, including counterfeit currency and illegal labour. It was a pattern that repeats in the Gulf of Tonkin and the Sulu Sea (Amirell, 2019). The emergence of long-distance raiding by the Iranun, "lanun", or "Moro" from 1768 to 1878 was, according to historian James Warren (2007), a consequence of an early cycle of globalisation that integrated the Sulu Sultanate into an emerging global economy. Access to European weapons and technology from traders in Hong Kong and Macau enabled the Iranun and Balangingi to build and arm their raiding expeditions for slaves to collect and harvest the sea and jungle products of the Sulu Sea which were in increasing demand in regional markets. For the Royal Navy tasked to establish law and order in the Straits of Malacca and Singapore to protect and promote the trade upon which the prosperity of expanding British influence in the peninsula and Borneo depended, these annual raiding expeditions of the Iranun and Balangingi were not "privateering" authorised by the Sultans of Sulu. They were "pirates" who had to be suppressed along with the remnants of the sea nomad warriors turned sea robbers. Suppression of piracy in the Straits of Malacca and Singapore became the justification for increasing colonial intervention and expansion by the British into the Malay Peninsula from the 1870s, the Spanish in Mindanao and the French in the Gulf of Tonkin (Amirell, 2019). James Warren (2007) sees analogies between the emergence of piracy in the eighteenth and nineteenth centuries responding to cycles of globalisation of the global economy and the resurgence of piracy at the end of the twentieth century also in response to new cycles of globalisation and deglobalisation.

Delimiting Maritime Boundaries

The ten nation-states which emerged out of the decolonisation of Southeast Asia after the Second World War were defined by their colonial boundaries.[1] The twentieth century anti-colonial nationalist struggle for independence was about land and its peoples. The priority was to claim the borders of the old colonial state under the principle of *uti possidetis juris* (Latin for "as you possess under the law") for the new nation. Negotiating and demarcating territorial borders to define a nation state took higher priority than demarcating porous borders on an open sea. Further, to the extent that maritime boundaries were never clearly delimited, much less demarcated by the old colonial powers, then the nation-states of Southeast Asia today could not apply the principle of *uti possidetis juris* to claiming maritime domains (Mak, 2008). All they inherited was the colonial demarcation of a claim to the traditional three nautical miles offshore sea. This proved inadequate (as it did for the colonial powers, as historian Eric Tagliacozzo, 2005 has documented) for the new nation-states to manage shipping, trade, travel and fishing while policing piracy, smuggling, human trafficking and other illegal activities including subversive political activists illegally crossing borders to escape arrest and detention (Cribb & Ford, 2009; on Indonesia's maritime security challenges). The coastal states were also driven to expand their maritime jurisdiction to assert rights over fisheries and seabed resources (as other countries led by the US were doing after the Second World War).

The consequence is that delimiting maritime boundaries is very much a work still in progress in Southeast Asia today (Forbes, 2001). International law rules and principles, especially the 1982 UNCLOS III, have been the basis of Southeast Asian delimiting of its maritime boundaries and rights and duties of Straits' states (Koh, 2020). Indonesia and the Philippines as archipelagic states (Indonesia comprises five major islands with 17,500 other islands while the Philippines comprises 7,646 islands) have had difficulties defining their maritime boundaries. Indonesia's claims to be recognised as an archipelagic state, first made in 1957, was finally recognised by the Law of the Sea ratified in 1992 (UNCLOS III) (Butcher & Elson, 2017). The Philippines has yet to resolve its colonial demarcation of its maritime boundaries that are not in line with international law practice (Bautista, 2011).

Between 1969 and 2009, Southeast Asia's coastal states concluded 37 maritime boundary arrangements. These include 29 delimitation agreements where a boundary was agreed upon and eight provisional arrangements where no boundary could be agreed upon and forms of joint exercise of jurisdiction and management of resources were agreed to (Davenport, 2014). That these delimitation agreements and provisional arrangements could be reached must in large part be attributed to the formation of the Association of Southeast Asian Nations (ASEAN) in 1967, which promoted a new era of regional cooperation. Two maritime disputes, however, could not be resolved in the "ASEAN fashion" and were referred to the International Court of Justice (ICJ). These were the dispute between Singapore and Malaysia over *Pedra Branca* (Beckman & Schofield, 2009; Mohamad, 2008) and between Malaysia and Indonesia over Sipadan and Ligitan Islands (Ranjit Singh, 2020). Malaysia and Indonesia continue to dispute overlapping claims to the potentially oil rich Ambalat region in the Sulawesi Sea off the east coast of Sabah. The dispute has been the most controversial between the two countries since the end of Indonesian Confrontation of Malaysia in 1966. There were minor skirmishes in 2005, which could have escalated if ASEAN diplomatic practices and protocols for managing disputes among its neighbours had not prevailed (Druce & Baikoeni, 2016). Other than these two cases submitted to the ICJ, Myanmar is the only other case of a Southeast Asian country submitting its disputed maritime claim in the Bay of Bengal with Bangladesh to the International Tribunal for the Law of the Sea in 2009 for arbitration (Faruque, 2012).

UNCLOS III has facilitated Southeast Asian coastal states delimit their maritime boundaries of a territorial sea of 12 nm and an EEZ up to 200 nm, and where it is entitled, to a continental shelf beyond its 200 nm EEZ. UNCLOS III enabled Indonesia's recognition as an archipelagic state and Malaysia and Vietnam to submit in December 2019 a claim of an extended continental shelf in the South China Sea. Under this convention, provisions for a 200 nm EEZ and further claims to a continental shelf, however, also opened a new series of overlapping claims to maritime zones, especially EEZs, between Southeast Asia's coastal states and with China in the South China Sea. However, UNCLOS III with all its ambiguities remains the overarching framework for managing conflicting claims to sovereignty over offshore islands and other maritime disputes in Southeast Asia (Bateman, 2007; Bautista, 2014).

Building Naval Assets

As independent nation-states the coastal countries of Southeast Asia had to develop their naval assets to assert their jurisdiction over maritime spaces they were claiming, secure the sea lines of

Maritime Security in Southeast Asia

Table 29.1 Maritime defence and security capacities of selected Southeast Asian countries

Country	Land area (sq. km)	Maritime zones (sq. km)	Maritime/land area ratio	Total no. of ships[1]	Total no. of planes[2]
Brunei Darussalam	5,765	24,352	4.2	20	1
Cambodia	181,041	55,564	0.3	14	0
Indonesia	1,904,342	5,409,981	2.8	254	32
Malaysia	332,649	475,727	1.4	308	5
The Philippines	300,000	1,891,247	6.3	147	12
Singapore	588	343	0.6	130	5
Thailand	414,001	324,812	0.6	197	3
Vietnam	332,556	722,337	2.2	140	6

Source: Data compiled from various materials including The Military Balance 2020, International Institute of Strategic Studies.
Notes: 1. Surface combat and patrol vessels only, includes maritime law enforcement agencies (MLEAs). 2. Fixed-winged maritime patrol aircraft only, includes MLEAs.

communications (SLOCs) in their waters and resist naval pressure from their neighbours and extra-regional naval powers. These naval assets were also deployed for constabulary operations against pirates, smugglers and other organised clandestine organisations, and for Humanitarian Assistance Disaster Relief (HADR). Thailand justified its acquisition of an aircraft carrier for HADR operations. Southeast Asia's navies are essentially, "general-purpose fleets". Their development since the 1960s, when the imperative to expand maritime space started, has been disjointed for a variety of structural factors and contingent circumstances (Till & Chan, 2013). The major structural challenge confronting not only the region's navies, but also other Maritime Law Enforcement Agencies (MLEAs) is the disproportionately large maritime zones with respect to their countries' land areas which they are responsible for the security of (Table 29.1).

Varying national defence doctrines and strategies on how to defend the nation's marine domain, budgetary constraints, interservice rivalry and bureaucratic politics all work to ensure that the region's navies are unlikely to develop blue water capability to defend their nation's wider maritime interests. The structure of Southeast Asian's "general purpose fleets" is dominated by coastal and inshore assets (see Figure 29.1) optimised to operate within the 12 nm territorial sea limits:

The acquisition of high-powered assets, in particular submarines (Till & Koh, 2017), and also corvettes and guided missile frigates by Southeast Asian navies are highly selective and without the logistic system and support vessels, unlikely to provide their navies the capability to operate at the further reaches of their 200 nm EEZs.

Instituting Maritime Security Cooperative Mechanisms

The end of the Cold War provided new opportunities for ASEAN's members to reach out to extra regional powers to build new maritime cooperative mechanisms and regimes (Bateman, 2007). Three regional mechanisms are highlighted here. The first is the Regional Forum, set up by ASEAN in 1993, to consolidate its bilateral dialogues with its ten regional partners. The ASEAN Regional Forum (ARF) initiated in 2009 a series of "Inter-Sessional Meetings" on

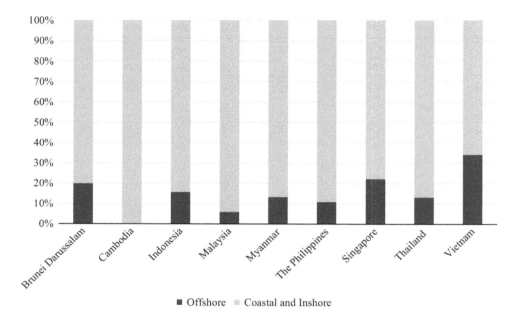

Figure 29.1 Patrol and combat vessels of maritime forces in Southeast Asia.

Source: Data compiled from various materials including The Military Balance 2020, International Institute of Strategic Studies.

Maritime Security to specifically discuss maritime security. The second is the Maritime Forum established by ASEAN in 2010 for its members to discuss maritime security, and two years later, expanded to include extra-regional members. The third, and probably most significant, is the annual ASEAN Defence Ministers Meeting (ADMM) since 2006 to develop trust and confidence for practical defence cooperation. The meeting was expanded in 2010 to include ASEAN's dialogue partners. These forums and meetings have been criticised as nothing more than "talk shops" which do not generate any actionable policy recommendations (Bateman, 2011). But they are useful, if not necessary, to build the confidence, trust and transparency which may lead to practical maritime security cooperation, which is dependent upon how much risk regional governments are prepared to take in sharing information with others in which could reveal their own national weaknesses and potentially sensitive assessments of the maritime environment. As a result, the Republic of Singapore Navy in 2009 initiated a regional "Information Fusion Centre" which brings together 24 navies to facilitate and catalyse information sharing and enhancing collective Maritime Domain Awareness (Koh, 2019).

Practical security cooperation means walking the talk – going beyond mere "talk shop" to engage in actual activities between policymakers and maritime practitioners such as regional navies and maritime law enforcement agencies. Towards this end, the ADMM+ has spawned a multilateral joint training series – the Maritime Security Field Training Exercise (MS-FTX), the fourth iteration of which was co-organised by Singapore and South Korea in late April–May 2019. The MS-FTX is essentially a platform to explore issues of information sharing and interoperability between 18 very diverse militaries with a wide range of capabilities. ASEAN conducted its first Multilateral Naval Exercise (AMNEX) for its own navies in November 2017 and joined with the US to conduct the first ASEAN-US Maritime Exercise in October 2019.

ASEAN members have, however, conducted more bilateral military exercises among its own members and with external militaries. Thailand has conducted Exercise Cobra Gold with the US since 1982. The exercise has now been opened to 27 other militaries. Other bilateral exercises include Indonesia and Malaysia series of "*Malindo Darsasa* Exercises". Such military exercises and exchange of information are the bricks upon which other initiatives in maritime security cooperation can be build, one of which is joint action against piracy and smuggling.

Supressing Piracy and Clandestine Groups

The end of the twentieth century and the beginning of the twenty-first century witnessed a resurgence of piracy (Frécon, 2003), as at the start of the nineteenth century, when the cycles of globalisation and deglobalisation were shifting, unleashing forces of uncertainty and disorder to drive a new cycle of not only smuggling and piracy, but also transnational terrorism and other transnational organised crimes (Hastings, 2010). Figure 29.2 charts the rise of reported incidents of piracy and armed robbery at the turn of the century and its decline as Southeast Asian countries rose to the challenge of tackling the problem:

The three Malacca Straits' states were pushed to act when Lloyd's Joint War Risk Committee announced its intent to declare the waterway a "high-risk war zone" in 2005, and so increase insurance for ships transiting the Straits and the US announced it may patrol the Straits under its 2004 "Regional Maritime Security Initiative" (Kyodo News, 2004). It was to pre-empt the US and other extra-regional powers intervening in the Malacca Strait that galvanised Indonesia, Malaysia, Singapore and Thailand to launch the Malacca Straits Patrols (MSP). The latter were a series of coordinated, rather than integrated sea patrols, building on

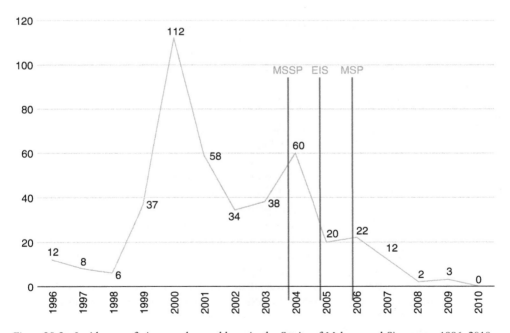

Figure 29.2 Incidences of piracy and sea robbery in the Straits of Malacca and Singapore, 1996–2010.

Source: Data compiled from successive International Maritime Organization Annual Reports: Report on Acts of Piracy and Armed Robbery Against Ships, 1996–2010.

pre-existing bilateral coordinated patrols between the three Malacca Straits' states, with no provisions for "hot pursuit" beyond territorial waters and into the territorial waters of the other two Malacca Straits, which would raise issues of sovereignty and jurisdiction. An aerial surveillance component, "Eye in the Sky (EiS)" was added to complement the coordinated patrols in 2006.

Continuing incidents of piracy, extending to hijacking ships in the Sulu Sea prompted Indonesia, Malaysia and the Philippines to launch a "Trilateral Cooperative Arrangement" (TCA) to police the Sulu Sea (Febrica, 2014). It was modelled on the Malacca Straits Patrols of coordinated sea and air patrols of the Sulu Sea (Bernama, 2016). As with the Malacca Straits Patrols, the Trilateral Cooperative Arrangement was a qualified success in suppressing piracy in the Sulu Sea. Both the MSP and the TCA demonstrate that ASEAN members can rise above issues of sovereignty over their territories to cooperate against the common threat of piracy and when challenged by external powers to do something (Storey, 2009).

The prevalence of piracy and armed robbery, as well as its potential link with terrorism, called for a larger-scale response to address the continued concerns of the international community. A multilateral government-to-government anti-piracy and armed robbery Information Sharing Centre, the Regional Cooperation Agreement on Combating Piracy and Armed Robbery against Ships in Asia (ReCAAP), was established in September 2006. The centre, with offices in Singapore, brings together 14 member countries, including eight of the ten ASEAN countries (excluding Indonesia and Malaysia) who fund and staff the centre to operate an information sharing system to collate and disseminate information on piracy and other crimes on the seas (Ho, 2009; Win et al., 2016). ReCAAP represents a transition from primarily local to increasingly regional efforts to address these issues of piracy and sea robbery.

The South China Sea Imbroglio

UNCLOS III provided justification for four Southeast Asian littoral states, Vietnam, Philippines, Brunei and Malaysia, to claim overlapping EEZs in the South China Sea and consolidate earlier claims to islands and reefs surveyed and staked out by colonial powers. These disputes were however managed in the "ASEAN Way" of talking around and co-existing with the disputes through the 1990s. A series of inconclusive workshops explored ways of joint development of resources in the overlapping EEZs. But China's strident reassertion of its historic right to much of the South China Sea has changed the rules of the game (Chachavalpongpun, 2014; Kassim, 2017; Storey & Lin, 2016).

Escalating tension between China and Southeast Asian littoral states claims to the South China Sea led ASEAN to propose a "Declaration of Conduct" that the members of ASEAN and China, according to Article 4 of the Declaration, "resolve their territorial and jurisdictional disputes [in the South China Sea] by peaceful means, without resorting to the threat or use of force" (ASEAN Secretariat, 2002). That Declaration, concluded in 2002, was to lead to a more binding "Code of Conduct" which in 2020 is still being negotiated. The reasons for these 20-year negotiations are complicated, ranging from China's coercive diplomacy towards ASEAN and ASEAN's lack of cohesion and solidarity. In 2012, these divisions in ASEAN over the South China Sea became public when the ASEAN foreign ministers at their annual meeting in Phnom Penh failed, for the first time in the association's 45 years of history, to issue a joint communique about their meeting because of disagreements on the South China Sea. In 2013, the Philippines filed with the UN Tribunal for the Law of the Sea for arbitration over China's claims to historic rights over the South China Sea. The Tribunal's 2016 decision against China's claims to historic rights was a turning point in the South China Sea disputes.

ASEAN's push back against China's claims to the South China Sea has become mired in complex geopolitical issues of responding to China's very rapid rise to global power status; push back from extra regional powers – Australia, India, Japan and the US (forming a Quad) – opposing China's claims to the South China for different geostrategic reasons from ASEAN's push back against China; and the fallout from a widening Sino-US rivalry. ASEAN's negotiations with China over a Code of Conduct have become quagmire in a widening complex debate over what kind of a Rule Based Order (RBO) should prevail in the Asia Pacific. On this trajectory, negotiations for a Code of Conduct in the South China Sea may be in the works for some time. Until then ASEAN can hope for the best but prepare to manage a crisis from the next unplanned encounter between Southeast Asian and Chinese vessels in the South China Sea (Kwa, 2010).

Conclusion: Regionalising Maritime Security

This chapter has sought to root Southeast Asia's maritime security problems in a series of undefined colonial maritime boundaries, resulting in porous sea borders which the colonial powers and the succeeding nation states struggled to govern. The failure of the colonial powers to delimit the maritime boundaries of their colonies was a consequence of their priorities to demarcate *terra firma* boundaries for colonial administration. This was further aggravated by the acceptance of a Grotian *mare liberum* which challenged the reality of ungovernable maritime borders, and the need for some kind of stewardship of the seas as a global common as advocated by Grotius' critic, Selden, for a *mare clausum* (Thornton, 2006). This chapter has outlined how delimiting their maritime boundaries to minimise, if not avoid, disputes with neighbouring states continues to be a work in progress among Southeast Asia's littoral countries. UNCLOS III has been the overarching framework for Southeast Asian delimiting of its maritime boundaries and managing disputes. The chapter has also suggested that the large maritime domain Southeast Asian littoral states have carved out and are entitled to under UNCLOS has however posed severe challenges to their inadequate navies and maritime law enforcement agencies to secure and police.

Southeast Asian littoral states' conclusion of 29 delimitation agreements of their disputed maritime boundaries between 1969 and 2009 was not only because UNCLOS III provided a foundation for the negotiation of these agreements, but equally, these littoral states had evolved a set of norms and diplomatic protocols associated with ASEAN, to manage their differences and pre-empt their escalation into disputes. The "ASEAN Way" (Capie & Evans, 2007, pp. 9–20) has become associated with very low-key informal diplomacy which talks and manoeuvres around conflict, very often never resolving it, but never allowing it to spillover to wider cooperative arrangements between ASEAN members. In the 1990s ASEAN extended its "ASEAN Way" to engage the major and other regional powers it had been having annual dialogues with, to an ARF to promote cooperative security in the Asia Pacific. The vision is that the ARF and other regional forums, such as the Western Pacific Naval Symposium, will put in place the Confidence Building Measures (Capie & Evans, 2017, pp. 87–93), which will lead to practical maritime security cooperation in creating information sharing centres to enhance cooperative maritime domain awareness and joint exercises which will build up the interoperability between different naval forces for joint surveillance and patrols against common maritime threats.

This strategy of reaching out to engage and enmesh the region's navies and extra-regional navies in cooperative security worked well in the now 50-year old Five Power Defence Arrangements (Storey et al., 2011), which brought together the armed forces Australia,

Malaysia, New Zealand, Singapore and the United Kingdom to form a multilateral agreement for their joint defence against common threats. The challenge for ASEAN today is whether its "ASEAN Way" can reach out to engage and enmesh the regional navies to build a regional cooperative security regime.

Note

1 The nine states (excluding Thailand, which was not colonised) that emerged from the decolonisation of Southeast Asia after the Second World War are:

1 Indonesia (17 August 1945)
2 Vietnam (2 September 1945)
3 Philippines (4 July 1946)
4 Burma/Myanmar (4 January 1948)
5 Cambodia (9 November 1953)
6 Malaya (31 August 1957)/Malaysia Federation with Sarawak and Sabah (16 September 1963)
7 Singapore (9 August 1965)
8 Laos (2 December 1975)
9 Brunei (1 January 1984)

References

Amirell, S. E. (2019). *Pirates of empire; colonisation and maritime violence in Southeast Asia*. Cambridge University Press.

ASEAN Secretariat. (2002, November 4). Declaration on the conduct of parties in the South China Sea. https://asean.org/?static_post=declaration-on-the-conduct-of-parties-in-the-south-china-sea-2

Bateman, S. (2007). Building good order at sea in Southeast Asia: The promise of international regimes. In C. G. Kwa & J. Skogan (Eds.), *Maritime security in Southeast Asia* (pp. 111–130). Routledge.

Bateman, S. (2011). Solving the "wicked problems" of maritime security: Are regional forums up to the task? *Contemporary Southeast Asia, 33*(3), 1–28.

Bautista, L. B. (2011). Philippines territorial boundaries: Internal tensions, colonial baggage, ambivalent conformity. *Journal of Southeast Asian Studies, 16*, 35–53. http://ro.uow.edu.au/lhapapers/768

Bautista, L. B. (2014). Dispute settlement in the Law of the Sea Convention and territorial and maritime disputes in Southeast Asia: Issues, opportunities and challenges. *Asian Politics & Policy, 6*(3), 375–396.

Beckman, R., & Schofield, C. (2009). Moving beyond disputes over island sovereignty: ICJ decision sets stage for maritime boundary delimitation in the Singapore Straits. *Ocean Development & International Law, 40*(1), 1–35.

Bernama (2016, August 24). Top brass of ASEAN navies call on Sultan of Selangor. *Malay Mail*. https://www.malaymail.com/news/malaysia/2016/08/24/top-brass-of-asean-navies-pay-courtesy-call-on-sultan-of-selangor/1190893

Borschberg, P. (2010). *The Singapore and Melaka Straits: Violence, security and diplomacy in the 17th century*. NUS Press.

Butcher, J. G., & Elson, R. E. (2017). *Sovereign and the sea: How Indonesia became an archipelagic state*. NUS Press.

Capie, D., & Evans, P. (2017). *The Asia-Pacific security lexicon* (Updated 2nd ed.). ISEAS Publishing.

Chachavalpongpun, P. (Ed.) (2014). *Entering uncharted waters: ASEAN and the South China Sea*. ISEAS Publishing.

Cribb, R., & Ford, M. (Eds.) (2009). *Indonesia beyond the water's edge: Managing an archipelagic state*. Institute of Southeast Asian Studies.

Davenport, T. (2014). Southeast Asian approaches to maritime boundaries. *Asian Journal of International Law, 4*(2), 309–357.

Druce, S. C., & Baikoeni, E. Y. (2016). Circumventing conflict: The Indonesia-Malaysia Ambalat block dispute. In M. Oishi (Ed.), *Contemporary conflicts in Southeast Asia: Towards a new ASEAN Way of conflict management* (pp. 137–156). Springer Science & Business Media.

Faruque, A. A. (2012). Judgment in maritime boundary dispute between Bangladesh and Myanmar: Significance and implications under international law. *Asian Yearbook of International Law, 18*, 62–84.

Febrica, S. (2014). Securing the Sulawesi Seas from maritime terrorism: A troublesome cooperation? *Perspectives on Terrorism, 7*(3), 64–83.

Forbes, V. L. (2001). *Conflict and cooperation in managing maritime space in semi-enclosed seas.* Singapore University Press.

Frécon, E. (2003). *Pavillon Noir sur l'Asie du Sud-Est: Histoire d'une Résurgence de la Piraterie Maritime.* L'Hartmattan.

Hastings, J. V. (2010). *No man's land: Globalization, territory and clandestine groups in Southeast Asia.* Cornell University Press (NUS Press reprint).

Ho, J. (2009). Combating piracy and armed robbery in Asia: The ReCAAP Information Sharing Centre (ISC). *Marine Policy, 33*(2), 432–434. 10.1016/j.marpol.2008.08.007

Kassim, Y. R. (Ed.) (2017). *The South China Sea disputes: Flashpoints, turning points and trajectories.* World Scientific.

Koh, S. L. C. (2019). Chapter 3. Beyond information fusion and sharing: The IFC and the future of Southeast Asian maritime security governance. In C. Bueger & J. Chan (Eds.), *Paving the way for regional maritime domain awareness: Information Fusion Centre* (pp. 20–27). S. Rajaratnam School of International Studies.

Koh, T. (2020). *Building a new legal order for the oceans.* NUS Press. 10.2307/j.ctv136c5rx

Kwa, C. G. (2010). Cooperation and confidence building: A Southeast Asian perspective. In S. Bateman & J. Ho (Eds.), *In Southeast Asia and the rise of Chinese and Indian naval power* (pp. 243–247). Routledge.

Kyodo News. (2004, May 11). *U.S. proposes initiative for maritime security in Asia-Pacific.* Kyodo News.

Lai, H. H. (2007). China's oil diplomacy: Is it a global security threat? *Third World Quarterly, 28*(3), 519–537.

Mak, J. N. (2008). Sovereignty in ASEAN and the problem of maritime cooperation in the South China Sea. *RSIS Working Paper No. 156.* https://www.rsis.edu.sg/wp-content/uploads/rsis-pubs/WP156.pdf

Mohamad, A. K. (2008). *Pacific settlement of disputes based on international law: Malaysia's experiences at the International Court of Justice.* Institute of Diplomacy and Foreign Relations, Ministry of Foreign Affairs. https://www.kln.gov.my/pbp-icj/images/book/IDFR_Occasional_Paper_1_of_2008.pdf

Ranjit Singh, D. S. (2020). *The Indonesia-Malaysia dispute concerning sovereignty over Sipadan and Ligitan islands: Historical antecedents and the International Court of Justice.* ISEAS Publishing.

Storey, I. (2009). Maritime security in Southeast Asia: Two cheers for regional cooperation. In D. Singh (Ed.), *Southeast Asian affairs 2009* (pp. 39–58). ISEAS Publications.

Storey, I., Emmers, R., & Singh, D. (Eds.). (2011). *The five power defence arrangements at forty.* ISEAS Publishing.

Storey, I., & Lin, C. (Eds.) (2016). *The South China Sea dispute: Navigating diplomatic and strategic tensions.* ISEAS Publishing.

Tagliacozzo, E. (2005). *Secret trades, porous borders: Smuggling and states along a Southeast Asian Frontier, 1865–1915.* Yale University Press.

Thornton, H. (2006). John Selden's response to Hugo Grotius: The argument for closed seas. *International Journal of Maritime History, XVIII*(2), 105–127.

Till, G., & Chan, J. (2013). *Naval modernisation in South-East Asia: Nature, causes and consequences.* Routledge.

Till, G., & Koh, C. S. L. (2017). *Naval modernisation in Southeast Asia, part two: Submarine issues for small and medium navies.* Palgrave-Macmillan.

Warren, J. F. (2007). A tale of two centuries: The globalisation of maritime raiding and piracy in Southeast Asia at the end of the eighteenth and twentieth centuries. In J. F. Warren (Ed.), *A world of water* (pp. 309–333). University of Western Australia Press.

Win, K. H., Ahmed, H., Ansari, A. H., Masum, A. & Jan, N. I. (2016). Critical analysis of the efficacy of the ReCAAP in combating piracy and armed robbery against ships in Asia. *Journal of the Indian Law Institute, 58*(2), 160–188.

30

MARITIME SECURITY IN THE SOUTH CHINA SEA

Chris Rahman

The South China Sea undoubtedly is the most politically contentious body of water on the planet at present. Within a single semi-enclosed sea area, it exhibits multiple types of maritime security problems. Overwhelmingly, such problems relate to the underlying political disputes over territory, maritime claims and marine resources, and to the detrimental impact of claimant state actions upon existing international rules, norms, expectations of peaceful resolution of disputes and good order at sea. At the heart of these issues is the overweening geostrategic impact of China, both in terms of the geopolitical implications of its regional ambitions, and the consequences of its actions. This chapter will, first, establish both the bounds of the South China Sea and why this area is so important; second, distinguish between different categories of dispute; and third, conclude by identifying the centrality of strategic factors for maritime security.

What Is the South China Sea, and Why Is It Important?

Such are the political sensitivities surrounding this body of water that even determining the limits of the South China Sea for technical, hydrographic purposes can be difficult. The International Hydrographic Organization (IHO) has been trying to update its outdated 1953 third edition S-23 technical publication, which names and establishes limits of seas and oceans, since the mid-1980s; but to no avail. Even though the document is explicitly technical rather than legal or political in purpose, East Asian states are often rigidly sensitive both to limits and naming of regional seas. Although the South China Sea is not the primary reason holding up adoption of the updated 2002 S-23 fourth edition, China nevertheless unsuccessfully proposed to subsume the Natuna Sea within the South China Sea (IHO, 2012, Annex B). The Natuna Sea's depiction as a separate body of water is one of three main changes to the South China Sea limits incorporated into the draft fourth edition; the others being exclusion also of the waters of the Taiwan Strait and Gulf of Tonkin (IHO, 2002, p. 6–6). The Gulf of Thailand already had been described as a separate body of water. Even in terms of its diminished extent in the 2002 draft, the South China Sea still encompasses a substantial body of water. Due to different approaches taken in the presumption of the Sea's limits, sources variously describe it in a range, from the world's sixth to tenth largest body of water. Either way, it undoubtedly is the world's largest semi-enclosed sea area. It is that semi-enclosed character, bounded by eight states – Vietnam, China, Taiwan, the Philippines, Malaysia, Brunei, Indonesia and, marginally,

356

DOI: 10.4324/9781003001324-33

Maritime Security in the South China Sea

Singapore – and encompassing several groups of disputed territorial features, which generates the now globally infamous, intractable dilemmas of the world's most contested maritime political geography.

The 2002 draft S-23 limits are employed in this chapter as the most sensible for modern conditions and are generally accepted, if not yet officially adopted, by states within the IHO. However, it should be noted that the data used to evaluate different aspects of maritime security herein often either assume different limits, or are sufficiently vague as to raise questions about which waters, specifically, are being referred to: such are the inherent geographical hazards of South China Sea analysis. Although the Sea's precise limits can be debated, its name is not controversial. In their own languages, China refers to it as the South Sea, and Vietnam refers to it as the East Sea. Manila has adopted the name West Philippine Sea to refer to the extent of its own maritime claims in the area, and in 2017 Indonesia renamed the part of the Sea it claims as its exclusive economic zone (EEZ) as the North Natuna Sea. Such measures serve national political and, perhaps, emotional purposes, but are of no strategic or legal consequence.

The South China Sea is a major maritime thoroughfare connecting Europe, Africa, Atlantic-coast South America, the Middle East, South Asia, Southeast Asia and Australasia, with the major markets and manufacturing hubs of Northeast Asia. The South China Sea's semi-enclosed character also determines that entry into, and exit from, those waters by maritime traffic sailing from/to points beyond the Sea's own shores or those of the Gulfs of Thailand or Tonkin, requires passage through one or more of a number of chokepoints, or very narrow sea areas. Applying the limits established by the 2002 S-23 draft, the most notable entry/exit points comprise, to the north, the Taiwan Strait between Taiwan and mainland China; and to the northeast, the Luzon Strait, comprising the Bashi and Balintang Channels, between Taiwan and the main Philippine island of Luzon. To the east, passages are either through the Philippine archipelago, via the Mindoro Strait linking to the Sulu Sea or the Verde Island Passage linking both to the Sulu Sea and to the Philippine Sea–Pacific Ocean via the San Bernadino Strait; or via the Balabac Strait linking to the Sulu Sea, between the Philippine island of Palawan and the East Malaysian state of Sabah. To the south, there are numerous routes through the islands of Indonesia's geographically dispersed Riau Archipelago, which separate the South China Sea from the Natuna Sea. Most importantly for international trade, to the southwest, the Singapore Strait is a very narrow sea passage linking to the Port of Singapore and, via the interlinked Malacca Strait, to the Indian Ocean and points beyond. The most important sea lines of communication (SLOC) pass through the middle of the South China Sea, linking the Singapore Strait with both the Taiwan and Luzon Straits, well away from the navigationally dangerous areas of disputed territorial features. Other important SLOC include the routes between: the Singapore Strait and points northeast via the sea lane east of the Spratly islands and west of Borneo, Palawan and Luzon, which also connects to the Balabac and Mindoro Straits; the Singapore Strait and the Thai ports in the northern Gulf of Thailand; the Singapore Strait and Saigon; the Singapore Strait and northern Vietnam/southern China via the Gulf of Tonkin; the Mindoro Strait and Guangdong province, southern China; and the Luzon Strait and China.

The seaborne trade which plies these SLOC is globally important, particularly in terms of its overall value to the world economy and its economic importance to individual states. Further, the trade in oil, other essential mineral resources and petroleum product have an added significance, both economically and strategically, especially for the import-dependent large economies of Northeast Asia. Although statistics on trade volumes and values circulate publicly, including those often repeated by governments, these are based on crude guestimates only. The actual value of this trade is simply impossible to calculate accurately. Whilst acknowledging the limitations of our knowledge, one recent analysis makes a plausible effort to calculate a representative value for seaborne trade flowing through South China Sea SLOC: estimated at US$3.37 trillion in 2016, it accounted for just over one-fifth of the value of all international trade. Unsurprisingly, those Southeast Asian littoral states without alternative routes, and the straits states, were most dependent upon these SLOC: as a percentage of total national trade, South China Sea routes accounted for a range between a high of 86% for Vietnam, to 58% for Malaysia. These SLOC were also calculated to be particularly important for South Korea, at 47%, and China, accounting for almost 40% of its total trade in goods. Indeed, China plus Hong Kong accounted for over 27% of the total trade passing through the South China Sea, with South Korea and Singapore sporting the next largest shares, at just over, and just under, 6%, respectively (CSIS ChinaPower Project, 2017). In terms of the oil trade, in 2016 more than 30% of world crude oil trade by volume transited the South China Sea, accounting for around 90% of the crude imports each of China, Japan and South Korea (EIA, 2018). Similarly, in the same year almost 40% of world liquefied natural gas (LNG) trade transited the Sea, accounting for 90% of Taiwan's LNG imports, about two-thirds each of China's and South Korea's, and over half of Japan's (EIA, 2017).

The sheer value of this trade alone ensures that the safety and security of shipping is a high priority interest not just for regional states but for all states and entities with stakes in the global system of maritime trade. Ships are especially vulnerable in narrow sea areas or other points close to land, whether from natural hazards such as rocks or shallows, or from criminally motivated actors or terrorists. The main sea routes through the South China Sea mostly lie beyond such natural hazards, which are concentrated at the entry/exit points, or in navigationally dangerous areas avoided by merchant shipping. Therefore, the main day-to-day safety issue may well be one of traffic management in highly traversed waters. In terms of security threats to shipping, Southeast Asia as a whole continues to suffer from numerous terrorist and insurgent threats. None appear to be active in the waters of the South China Sea, although the prospect of terrorist threats to shipping will continue to be a risk factor. Ship security is also most at risk in locations closer to land, especially in or near chokepoints. Piracy and armed robbery at sea have been persistent regional problems for three decades, but the specific threat has changed over time and in respect to location (Liss & Biggs, 2017). The South China Sea has not been a major locus for piracy over this period, with two exceptions. Firstly, there were attacks reported in the so-called Hong Kong-Luzon-Hainan triangle in the mid-1990s (Chalk, 2008, p. 16). Over the past decade, however, there have been attacks in the waters near the Riau Archipelago, often near Bintan or the Anambas islands. These attacks became noteworthy around 2009 and peaked in 2014, often targeting petroleum products (ReCAAP, 2007–2020). Some of this activity may have occurred within Indonesian territorial waters, but several attacks did take place beyond territorial waters, and thus legally examples of piracy under the Law of the Sea Convention. This is quite unusual for Southeast Asia, making the South China Sea the only area within the region where piracy, strictly defined by international law, has occurred in recent years.

The South China Sea is also important as a source of marine resources for littoral countries, the most critical of which is fish. As was the case with trade data, reliable fisheries statistics do not exist, particularly when it comes to stock assessments. Much of the available data is based on catch reports, themselves inconsistent and unreliable. However, the significance of fisheries to littoral states, as established in the semi-scientific literature, can be summarised without recourse to the specifics of sometimes questionable data. South China Sea fisheries undoubtedly are significant on a global scale, probably one of the world's five largest areas for marine capture fish production, although annual catch levels may have peaked in 2003 (Teh et al., 2019, p. 9). Catch rates have also been reported as declining for most of the Sea's fisheries. In addition to the generic difficulty of "counting fish" at sea, some states possibly may be over-reporting catches. On the flip side, catches could be underestimated, for example, due to illegal, unreported and unregulated (IUU) fishing, although attributing what is truly "illegal" in waters under dispute, where enforcement is inherently problematic, is not always possible. However, it has been estimated that unreported fish catches, including those generated by small-scale commercial, subsistence and recreational fishing, could add another 60% to the reported landings (Pauly & Liang, 2020; Teh et al., 2017, p. 62).

The most intense fishing activity occurs around the littoral areas, rather than in the middle part of the Sea or around the disputed territories, although specific species are targeted in almost all parts of the broader area. The South China Sea as a whole is intensively fished, with few, if any, underexploited stocks; with China alone accounting for an estimated one-third of the catch. It is generally believed that fishing effort has been increasing, but with takings largely stable, and with the share of non-targeted species and juvenile fish growing, the sustainability of South China Sea fisheries is of real concern (Pauly & Liang, 2020). Because seafood contributes to a relatively high proportion of the animal protein consumed by many of the communities living adjacent to the South China Sea, any precipitous decline in production could generate food security problems, especially for subsistence fishing and other poorer coastal communities. That more intensive fishing effort and greater demand for fish, caused by growing populations, rising incomes and consumer preferences, trade, industry subsidies and policy directives, thus makes effective management of fish stocks which pay no heed to political or legal boundaries in the water, even where such imaginary lines exist at all, increasingly fraught. Article 123 of the Law of the Sea Convention encourages cooperation amongst the littoral states of semi-enclosed seas, raising an expectation that they will coordinate marine living resource management and protection and preservation of the marine environment. Such injunctions are quixotic in the contexts of the South China Sea, where political and strategic geography, and a complicated history, have conspired to ensure an atmosphere, not of cooperation, but of dispute, tension and conflict; thereby exaggerating rather than ameliorating tragedy of the commons dilemmas.

The stability of fisheries and related downstream industries are also affected by the health of South China Sea ecosystems, which are challenged not just by alleged overfishing in some parts, but also by destructive fishing practices, other forms of environmental degradation, climate change and acidification. Island building in disputed archipelagos, especially by China, also has caused further damage, including potentially to spawning grounds which produce stocks for numerous fisheries. The socio-economic importance of fisheries extends beyond just the fish, with estimates that well over half-a-million small-scale and commercial boats are active in the South China Sea. An estimated 2.7 million people are employed in the area's fisheries, but that number is likely to be significantly understated (Teh et al., 2017, p. 64). When employment in ancillary industries is taken into account, fisheries take on much greater salience still. Therefore, any major reduction in catches could affect not just food security, but also employment, trade and, consequently, economic growth, in some littoral states. In the worst-case scenario of a rapid decline in stocks, or denial of access to regular fishing grounds by more powerful state actors, it is not too hard to envisage such impacts generating social instability within vulnerable coastal communities and a greater likelihood of violent clashes at sea; whether between fishing boats, or between fishing boats and enforcement vessels, or between enforcement vessels or even navies of different states. Fisheries thus constitute a central part of the South China Sea maritime security equation.

The other marine resources of note are the Sea's hydrocarbon reserves. US estimates of the area's proved or "probable" reserves have been assessed as approximately 11 billion barrels of oil and 190 trillion cubic feet of natural gas. However, some commercial estimates are much lower.

In addition, the US Geological Survey has estimated undiscovered reserves to be 5–22 billion barrels of oil and 70–290 trillion cubic feet of gas. It is not at all clear how much might be economically exploitable, although China has demonstrated a willingness elsewhere to pay above world market prices to improve the diversity and security of its supplies of vital commodities. These estimates are significant, especially for gas, but still rather minor on a global scale; for gas this equates only to about 3% of world resources. China, on the other hand, has estimated higher levels of undiscovered resources, but these have not been independently verified. According to the US Energy Information Administration, no oil and only small quantities of gas are known to exist in the disputed Spratly archipelago, with no oil and even less gas in the Paracel archipelago, although the latter may contain natural gas hydrates. Most current exploitation activities instead take place in relatively shallow waters closer to the coasts of littoral countries. Nonetheless, about one-fifth of undiscovered gas reserves may be present in or close to the Spratlys, especially in the Reed Bank area in the northeast section (EIA, 2013a, 2013b). This is important to the Philippines, in particular, which had been counting on Reed Bank resources to replace those from its dwindling Malampaya gas field, to the northwest of Palawan; but it was forced to desist from drilling activities by Chinese coercion. However, fisheries are the more vital resource. If unexploited hydrocarbon reserves remain untouched, this does not equate to an actual loss, merely missed opportunities for anticipated future gains; whereas any significant reduction in fisheries will be painful, with immediate consequences.

The Disputes

One common error is to refer to the South China Sea "dispute", singular, rather than "disputes", plural. In truth, there are at least four distinct, albeit interrelated, types of dispute. The first three have both political and, at least nominally, legal characters. These involve disputes over territory; disputes over maritime jurisdiction, particularly over marine resources; and disputes over other aspects of the law of the sea, especially regarding military operations. The fourth is the strategic one concerning China's attempt to exert geopolitical control over the entire area, which will be dealt with in the concluding section.

Of the first type of dispute, it is important to understand that "territory" in this context refers to terrestrial features. In the case of the South China Sea disputed territories consist of small islands, reefs, atolls and cays, sandbanks, shoals and rocks. "Territory" does not refer to the surrounding sea areas. The defining geophysical characteristic must be either terrestrial or maritime space; it cannot be both. Moreover, in the South China Sea there is not a single territorial dispute, but several, each with different sets of claimants. There are, however, two common factors: both China and Taiwan claim all disputed features. It should be noted also that the post-War claims of China and Taiwan are historically identical, as the People's Republic inherited the old inchoate Republic of China claim and a vague 1947 "dashed-line" map incorporating all territorial features and much of the Sea's waters (Elleman, 2009, p. 44; Samuels, 1982). However, it is no longer altogether clear whether their respective evolving interpretations of the claim are the same. This chapter takes no position on the veracity of specific modern territorial claims, but suggests that none are overwhelmingly convincing. None of the assertions of claims antedating the Second World War seem to have merit, and the vagueness of China's 1947 map is not particularly enlightening. In many ways the modern disputes are a direct result of the 1951 San Francisco Peace Treaty, the formal settlement of the Pacific War, in which Japan was required to renounce any claim, but no successor sovereign was named for any of the land features. It thus was incumbent upon claimants to take active measures to assert their sovereignty. In the Spratly archipelago, this began by the permanent occupation of the largest island in the group, Itu Aba (Taiping), by Taiwan in 1956. Other states followed suit over the succeeding decades, taking possession of, or exerting effective control over, individual territorial features.

China's claim now groups the disputed features into four archipelagos: *Dongsha Qundao* (Pratas island group); *Xisha Qundao* (Paracel island group); *Zhongsha Qundao* (incorporating otherwise unconnected Macclesfield Bank, Scarborough Shoal and three other shoals); and the *Nansha Qundao* (Spratly island group). The Pratas group is located in the northern part of the Sea southeast of Hong Kong and southwest of Taiwan, and is only claimed by Beijing and Taipei, with Pratas Island itself occupied by Taiwan. The Paracels consist of two archipelagos: the Amphitrite group and the Crescent group, and is claimed by China, Taiwan and Vietnam. China occupies and controls the entire Paracel group, having forcibly expelled South Vietnam from the Crescent group in January 1974. Of the *Zhongsha Qundao* features, Scarborough Shoal is the only actual territorial one, as the others remain completely submerged even at low tide, and thus cannot be subject to territorial claim under international law. Scarborough Shoal is located west of Luzon, and is claimed by China, Taiwan and the Philippines. It was nominally controlled by Manila until 2012, when China wrested control in a stand-off between their respective coast guards. The Spratlys consist of over 100 separate features, located west of Palawan, west of Borneo and east of Vietnam. The Spratly features are claimed wholly by China, Taiwan and Vietnam, and in part by the Philippines and Malaysia. Brunei implicitly claims one feature but has not made a formal statement to that effect. Currently over 60 features are occupied: China occupies around 20 in the Paracels and seven in the Spratlys; Vietnam 21 in the Spratlys plus a number of platforms built on submerged features; the Philippines nine; Malaysia five; and Taiwan one. Extensive island building has occurred, with China, in particular, creating over 3,200 acres of new territory in the Spratlys, along with further expansion works in the Paracels. Other states have also expanded the extent of their holdings, most notably Vietnam, but none on the scale, or of the consequence, of China (AMTI, 2020).

The second category of dispute, maritime jurisdiction, is a primary reason why states have exerted sovereignty over territorial features. A basic principle of international law is that the land dominates the sea; that is, sovereignty over territory provides the basis for claims to maritime jurisdiction generated from that territory. In the context of the 1982 Law of the Sea Convention, the regimes of the EEZ and continental shelf in effect encouraged the occupation of territorial features in order to assert rights over marine resources found in zones of jurisdiction claimed from such features. Not only do claimants to disputed territory also clash over maritime jurisdiction, but claims of jurisdiction from disputed features also overlap the EEZ and continental shelf claims drawn from the metropolitan territories of littoral states. All such claims overlap with the nine-dashed line claim of China and Taiwan. This has led to many clashes at sea. It is noteworthy that in this second category, Indonesia is also a party to the disputes, as its South China Sea EEZ claim drawn from its archipelagic baselines around the Natuna islands lacks agreed EEZ boundaries with its neighbours and, most notably, also overlaps the nine-dashed line. Beijing issued its first official version of the nine-dashed line map in 2009, in response to a joint Malaysia-Vietnam submission to the United Nations Commission on the Limits of the Continental Shelf (CLCS) (People's Republic of China, 2009). China's note to the United Nations elicited responses from other states, most notably, for the first time, Indonesia, which in July 2010 contested both the legal basis for the map, and EEZ and continental shelf claims generated from small, insignificant features (Republic of Indonesia, 2010).

Over the past decade China has been particularly effective, not to mention aggressive, in asserting what it calls "maritime rights protection" within the area of the nine-dashed line, using both its People's Armed Forces Maritime Militia (PAFMM), and rapidly expanded and recently integrated China Coast Guard (CCG), supported explicitly by the People's Liberation Army (PLA) Navy, for that purpose (Erickson & Martinson, 2019). As China's at-sea footprint has grown, so too has its assertiveness. There have been a number of incidents, for example, beginning in May 2010, involving Chinese enforcement vessels coercing out-muscled Indonesian enforcement vessels to release arrested Chinese fishing boats within the area of overlap between Indonesia's EEZ claim and the nine-dashed line. Such incidents, however, are not solely the result of Chinese activities: there have been similar incidents involving Vietnam and Indonesia, in 2017 and 2019. In an April 2019 incident Vietnamese enforcement vessels shouldered an Indonesian Navy ship, but unlike in the China incidents Indonesia is not so easily overmatched by a fellow ASEAN state. Increasingly, China uses its coast guard to escort its fishing fleets and hydrocarbon exploration platforms in disputed waters, including within legitimate littoral state exclusive economic zones, while CCG and PAFMM vessels have established a semi-permanent presence near some of the most contested territorial features. This has led to fears that Chinese fishing fleets so protected may be unsustainably harvesting the Sea, in many cases illegally, including targeting endangered species such as marine turtles and giant clams. In the most sustained crisis over jurisdiction thus far, in mid-2014 China sent an oil exploration platform, *Haiyang Shiyou 981*, to drill in waters off the Paracels also claimed by Vietnam. Vietnam sent civilian enforcement vessels and fishing boats to protest, leading to clashes between the two similar flotillas, involving bumping and grinding, ramming and the use of water cannon. One Vietnamese fishing boat was rammed, and subsequently sank, and many other vessels were damaged. Although the larger Chinese flotilla had the better of the encounters, Hanoi's sustained pressure eventually led China to withdraw the rig. However, as frustrations and tensions continue to mount, dangerous at-sea activity is becoming more common: for example, in April 2020 a CCG vessel rammed and sank a Vietnamese fishing boat. And new PAFMM vessels operating out of Sansha, Woody Island, in the Paracels, have been constructed with reinforced hulls and armed with water cannon: optimised for rights protection duties they do little or no fishing (Kennedy & Erickson, 2017, p. 10).

The Philippines in 2013 pursued a different route, lodging a case against China's jurisdictional claims with the International Tribunal for the Law of the Sea, which established an Arbitral Tribunal under the Annex VII dispute resolution process of the Law of the Sea Convention. China refused to participate and does not recognise the legitimacy of the process or the Tribunal's decisions, which heavily favoured the Philippines, even though, in theory, Beijing is bound by the outcome under international law. Not all of the Tribunal's Award is uncontroversial, but at least it has brought clarity to several legal issues. Among other things, the Award ruled against China's claims to historic rights to marine resources within the nine-dashed line beyond those established by the Convention; that all territorial features in the Spratlys above water at high tide were merely "rocks" and thus not capable of generating EEZs or continental shelves; that the Spratlys could not collectively as a unit generate maritime zones; that certain features, as low-tide elevations, were part of the Philippine EEZ and continental shelf, to which China has no legitimate claim under the Convention; that Chinese island building and fishing activities had caused large-scale, irreparable damage to the marine environment; and that Chinese vessels had breached international rules on safe navigation in the 2012 crisis over Scarborough Shoal (Award, 2016). A further Malaysian CLCS submission in December 2019 elicited the obligatory Chinese response and subsequent rebuttals from other claimants. Less expected were the diplomatic notes from non-claimants: in 2020 the United States, Australia, the United Kingdom, France and Germany each rejected some or all of China's claims, and lent support for full implementation of the Award. None of this diplomatic pressure, however, has changed China's behaviour.

The third type of dispute relates primarily to military operations in the exclusive economic zone (Bateman, 2020). It must be noted that, with the exceptions of Brunei and Singapore, all littoral states have at least some rules on the navigation of foreign warships which are inconsistent with the Law of the Sea Convention. But of these, China is the one that has taken an actively aggressive stance, resulting in incidents in or over China's EEZ, such as the EP-3E airborne collision in 2001 and the 2009 USNS *Impeccable* incident, both off Hainan, as well as numerous lesser incidents elsewhere and constant challenges to foreign warships and military aircraft. The Convention is unambiguous on this matter: China's actions are entirely inconsistent with international law and, indeed, hypocritical; not only because China is a party to the Convention and rules governing international airspace, but because its own warships, military aircraft and enforcement vessels operate with increasing regularity in and over the EEZs of other states. Speculation has mounted, furthermore, that Beijing will try to implement an air defence identification zone over the South China Sea, as it has in the East China Sea (Pilger, 2016, pp. 7–12), although such zones are, in practice, unenforceable against foreign military aircraft. And, in a June 2018 draft negotiating text of the ASEAN-China Code of Conduct in the South China Sea, which would, in theory, be binding on parties once concluded, China inserted a clause which would have given it an effective right of veto over any military exercise in the Sea between an ASEAN state and an extra-regional power.

The sum of Beijing's actions amounts to a wholesale, paradoxical rejection of the rules, norms and accepted behaviours of the same liberal international system that has enabled, even encouraged, China's rise. The implications of China's actions are thus much broader than just undermining maritime security in a single confined, albeit large, sea space. Further, it seems sensible to conclude that any Code of Conduct which legitimises the status quo of Beijing's dominant position, and its controversial behaviour to coerce ASEAN claimants to share resources to which China is not legitimately entitled, is contrary to their interests.

Strategic Factors Dominate

A number of factors can, in part, account for the salience of the South China Sea as an area of great maritime security concern, including littoral state actions to maximise jurisdiction and access to resources for food security, energy security and economic development; safeguard claims to sovereignty, at once reflecting, assuaging and stoking domestic nationalism; and satisfy the institutional needs of navies and other organisations. However, added to these largely universal factors, in China's case, is the geostrategic imperative to recover its international greatness and traditional dominance over its periphery, including maritime Southeast Asia, to extend its defensive perimeter to the point where it can effectively control adjacent seas; thus making potential military interventions by hostile forces costly or impossible, and allowing China itself to project strategic influence out into the oceans beyond (Rahman, 2016, pp. 94–98). To get to the nub of the strategic question it would be difficult to improve upon the assessment of Marwyn Samuels almost 40 years ago: "… the modern contest for the islands is itself but one act in the larger drama of a new and more powerful Chinese presence at sea" beginning in the early 1970s. He continued, explaining that:

> [T]he changing role of China as a maritime power everywhere conditions the meaning of the contest for the South China Sea … [as] inferred by China's expanding commercial interests at sea, as well as by the growth of Chinese naval power. Similarly, it is also indicated by the emergence of an assertive ocean policy aimed to defend and extend China's maritime frontiers. But, the most dramatic indication of

that changing role has come in the context of China's claims to the islands ... [which] affirm the growth of China as a major maritime power in Asia, one of whose principal goals is to reassert an historic presence in the southern maritime frontier. (Samuels, 1982, pp. 112, 150)

Even accounting for its seemingly at times opportunistic and reactive behaviour, it is probable that the ambition, policy and strategy for China's current dominant posture was established at least a half-century ago. Beijing's expansion throughout the South China Sea, whilst not a linear process, has nonetheless been inexorable since January 1974, spreading into the Spratlys in 1987, with a decisive military action against Vietnamese forces in 1988, further occupation and military construction from late 1994, a new wave of activity from the mid-2000s, with rapid expansion of coast guard and PAFMM "gray zone" operations from 2009 and intensive island building from 2014, through to the operationalisation and increasing militarisation of airstrips on the artificial islands built on Fiery Cross, Subi and Mischief Reefs in 2016–2018. Together with expansion of facilities in the Paracels, especially its longstanding base on Woody Island, and the Yulin naval base at Sanya, Hainan province, China has established a permanent presence sufficient to intimidate, harass, unlawfully extract resources, and prevent other littoral states from exploiting resources to which they are legally entitled. In geostrategic terms, though, one underlying weakness to Beijing's approach is its attempt to territorialise that which cannot alchemically be transformed into territory. This "continentalist", land-centric approach to the sea, especially such a large area as the South China Sea, is inherently flawed: China thus will likely continue to be frustrated in its attempts to convert its improved strategic position into exclusive geopolitical control.

Furthermore, the international reaction has been building, especially since the Tribunal's Award. In July 2020, US secretary of state, Mike Pompeo, issued a new policy statement not only supportive of the Philippines, but which also applied the Award's principles to reject China's encroachment on waters under the jurisdiction of Brunei, Indonesia, Malaysia and Vietnam, stating that "The world will not allow Beijing to treat the South China Sea as its maritime empire" (Pompeo, 2020). The arbitration, perhaps ironically, may have provided the legal justification for more concerted political-strategic counter-action. Were China not such a central actor, there would still be multiple maritime security problems in the South China Sea, not least amongst the other claimant states. But such is its central role that most maritime security problems have become subsumed within the malign consequences of Beijing's geopolitical covetousness: meaningful amelioration of the primary symptoms of the maritime security disease will therefore require an elusive curative for great power strategic ambition.

References

AMTI [Asia Maritime Transparency Initiative]. (2020). Occupation and island building. https://amti.csis.org/island-tracker/

Award. (2016, July 12). In the matter of the South China Sea arbitration before an Arbitral Tribunal constituted under Annex VII to the 1982 United Nations Convention on the Law of the Sea between the Republic of the Philippines and the People's Republic of China.

Bateman, S. (2020). *Freedoms of navigation in the Asia-Pacific region: Strategic, political and legal factors*. Routledge.

Chalk, P. (2008). *The maritime dimension of international security: Terrorism, piracy, and challenges for the United States*. RAND Corporation.

CSIS ChinaPower Project. (2017). How much trade transits the South China Sea? https://chinapower.csis.org/much-trade-transits-south-china-sea/

EIA [U.S. Energy Information Administration]. (2013a, April 3). Contested areas of South China Sea likely have few conventional oil and gas resources. Retrieved 7 September 2021 from https://www.eia.gov/todayinenergy/detail.Php?id=10651

EIA. (2013b, February 7). South China Sea. Retrieved 7 September 2021 from https://www.eia.gov/international/analysis/regions-of-interest/South_China_Sea

EIA [U.S. Energy Information Administration]. (2017, November 2). Almost 40% of global liquefied natural gas trade moves through the South China Sea. Retrieved on 7 September 2021 from https://www.eia.gov/todayinenergy/detail.php?id=33592

EIA [U.S. Energy Information Administration]. (2018, August 27). More than 30% of global maritime crude oil moves through the South China Sea. Retrieved 7 September 2021 from https://www.eia.gov/todayinenergy/detail.php?id=36952

Elleman, B. A. (2009). Maritime territorial disputes and their impact on maritime strategy: A historical perspective. In S. Bateman & R. Emmers (Eds.), *Security and international politics in the South China Sea: Towards a cooperative management regime* (pp. 42–57). Routledge.

Erickson, A. S., & Martinson, R. D. (2019). *China's maritime gray zone operations*. Naval Institute Press.

IHO [International Hydrographic Organization]. (2002, June). *Names and limits of oceans and seas*. Special Publication No. 23 (4th ed.). Final Draft. International Hydrographic Bureau.

IHO [International Hydrographic Organization]. (2012, February – revised June). Final Report of S-23 Working Group to Member States.

Kennedy, C. M., & Erickson, A. S. (2017, March). China's third sea force, the people's armed forces maritime militia: Tethered to the PLA. *China Maritime Report* No. 1. China Maritime Studies Institute, U.S. Naval War College.

Liss, C., & Biggs, T. (2017). *Piracy in Southeast Asia: Trends, hot spots and responses*. Routledge.

Pauly, D., & Liang, C. (2020). The fisheries of the South China Sea: Major trends since 1950. *Marine Policy, 121*(Nov 2020), 1–7.

People's Republic of China. (2009, May 7). CML/17/2009. Note *Verbale* to the Secretary-General of the United Nations with reference to the Joint Submission by Malaysia and the Socialist Republic of Viet Nam dated 6 May 2009, to the Commission on the Limits of the Continental Shelf. https://www.un.org/Depts/los/clcs_new/submissions_files/submission_mys_12_12_2019.html

Pilger, M. (2016, March 2). ADIZ update: Enforcement in the East China Sea, prospects for the South China Sea, and implications for the United States. U.S.-China Economic and Security Review Commission Staff Research Report.

Pompeo, M. R. (2020, July 13). U.S. position on maritime claims in the South China Sea. https://www.state.gov/u-s-position-on-maritime-claims-in-the-south-china-sea/

Rahman, C. (2016). People's Liberation Army Navy (PLAN). In C. Waters (Ed.), *Navies in the 21st century* (pp. 93–104). Seaforth Publishing.

ReCAAP [Regional Cooperation Agreement on Combating Piracy and Armed Robbery against Ships in Asia]. (2007–2020). *Annual reports*. ReCAAP Information Sharing Centre.

Republic of Indonesia. (2010, July 8). No. 480/POL-703/VII/10. Note *Verbale* to the Secretary-General of the United Nations with reference to the circular note of the Permanent Mission of the People's Republic of China number CML/17/2009. https://www.un.org/Depts/los/clcs_new/submissions_files/submission_mys_12_12_2019.html

Samuels, M. S. (1982). *Contest for the South China Sea*. Methuen.

Teh, L. S. L., Cashion, T., Alava Saltos, J. J., Cheung, W. W. L., & Sumaila, U. R. (2019). Status, trends, and the future of fisheries in the East and South China Seas. *Fisheries Centre Research Reports volume, 27*(1), University of British Columbia Institute for the Oceans and Fisheries.

Teh, L. S. L., Witter, A., Cheung, W. L., Sumaila, U. R., & Yin, X. (2017). What is at stake? Status and threats to South China Sea marine fisheries. *Ambio, 46*(1), 57–72.

31

MARITIME SECURITY IN THE ARCTIC

Amund Botillen and Marianne Riddervold

With the ice melting due to climate change, the Arctic has gained increased attention in international relations, maritime security and maritime governance studies. The Arctic is warming faster than any other area of the world today. This has broad environmental, economic and geopolitical consequences, as well as implications for the living conditions of indigenous peoples in the region. Perhaps of particular relevance for understanding changes in the region, while previously difficult to exploit, the prospects of strategically and economically important new sea lines and untapped natural resources potentially create conflicts between states who want territorial control or equal access to previously inaccessible areas. Arctic state Russia, in particular, has become increasingly assertive in the area, claiming this to be of particular strategic and economic importance. It is, however, telling of the Arctic's increasing international relevance that not only the Arctic states, but also China, Japan and India – states that at the outset may seem rather distant to the Arctic – have shown a strong interest in the area, e.g., by having achieved observer status in the Arctic Council (Battarbee & Fossum, 2014; Germond, 2015; Huebert et al., 2012; Riddervold & Cross, 2019; Tonami, 2019). Also the European Union (EU) has recently developed its policies towards the region (Huebert et al., 2012; Riddervold, 2018; Riddervold & Cross, 2019; Wegge, 2012). Not surprisingly, the Arctic states – Canada, Denmark (including Greenland and the Faroe Islands), Finland, Iceland, Norway, Russia, Sweden and the United States – are active in a more accessible Arctic region. However, the emergence of other actors such as the EU and China is more puzzling (Riddervold & Cross, 2019). For China, the Arctic is far away from its traditional, regional sphere of interest, focused mainly on the South and East China Seas. Although Sweden, Denmark and Finland are members of the EU, the opposition towards developing a distinct EU Arctic policy has traditionally been strong in several EU states for various reasons, including sensitivity towards Russia (Riddervold, 2018; Riddervold & Cross, 2019). So why, then, are we witnessing this development? Does the increasing number of actors and claims made towards the region suggest that the Arctic is becoming an area of great power competition?

To contribute to a better understanding of the changing dynamics of international relations and maritime security in the Arctic, this chapter explores the EU, China, US and Russia's main policies towards the governance of the Arctic, discussing whether there is evidence to suggest an increasing level of geopolitical conflict over contested domains in the area. Due to a high level of common institutions and interdependence, the Arctic has traditionally been perceived as an area of relative stability. Recent studies, however, suggest that this may be changing in a more volatile and

366   DOI: 10.4324/9781003001324-34

uncertain global environment, not least due to Russian aggression in Ukraine and beyond (Byers, 2017), a growing and more assertive China, and a changing US foreign policy. But there are few newer studies systematically exploring potentially increasingly tense relations amongst all these four actors (exceptions include, among others chapters in Gjørv et al., 2020; Coates & Holroyd, 2020).

The chapter is organised as follows. First, we provide some background on the Arctic, discussing various environmental, geopolitical, economic and minority rights aspects of the region in light of recent developments. Second, we develop and operationalise two alternative hypotheses of actors' perspectives and policies of the future governance of these areas. We also briefly discuss our methodological approach. Thereafter follows the analysis, where we discuss the relevance of our two hypotheses for understanding each of the four actors – the US, EU, China and Russia – main strategies and perspectives on the Arctic. We do this by focusing on the arguments they use when justifying their policies, their perspectives on the role of international governance structures and their military deployments to the area, hence providing insights into the international relations and maritime security issues of the region more broadly. Our analysis suggests that there indeed seems to be more potential for conflict in the Arctic area than previously. However, despite a more geopolitical volatile environment, the Arctic has remained peaceful, characterised by a dense network of institutionalised international cooperation.

The Arctic: Geopolitics, Economic Interests, Indigenous Peoples and the Environment

Ice melting in the Arctic region has huge geopolitical, environmental and economic consequences, with big implications also for Arctic indigenous peoples. Studies show that the Arctic is warming two to three times faster than the rest of the planet (Kraska & Baker, 2014), and that it may become nearly ice-free within the next 40 years. Ice melting in the Arctic directly leads to sea-level rise across the globe and it is changing the seabeds. This rapid warming also threatens endemic species and the Arctic's importance as a vast carbon and ice storage (Crawford, 2021; Vincent, 2020, p. 507).

According to Huebert et al. (2012, p. 1), the Arctic is a "bellwether for how climate change may reshape geopolitics in the post–Cold War era". Geopolitically, new strategic shipping routes and access to strategically salient geographical positions are of interest both to bordering states and to states with international ambitions. Of particular importance, the increasing level of tensions between Russia and the West since 2014 following Russian aggression in and beyond Ukraine has added fuel to potential geopolitical conflicts in the region. Economically, the ice melting opens up new and much more efficient routes for international sea-based trade and access to energy resources, which is also attractive from an energy-security perspective. The Arctic is estimated to hold 13% of the world's undiscovered/untapped oil and 30% of undiscovered/untapped gas supplies (Crawford, 2021; Riddervold & Cross, 2019).

Because of these changes, both states and non-state actors are now making claims to these areas, including Arctic indigenous peoples, shipping companies, multinational corporations, state-owned enterprises and different non-state organisations (Riddervold & Newsomek, 2021). Many states have recently developed or revised their Arctic strategies, in addition to or instead of their maritime strategies, and several states, not least Russia, have started rebuilding their Arctic military capabilities (Huebert et al., 2012). Most of the Arctic is within the Arctic states' territorial sovereignty (Crawford, 2021), but also the high seas areas in the Arctic are becoming increasingly accessible. Once the territorial waters and exclusive economic zones of the major players are accounted for, surrounding the North Pole is the so-called "donut hole", which is defined as international waters. These are areas that belong to no one state and are in principle global collective goods. This is why they are referred to as "global commons" and the UN refers to them as a "human heritage". According to Crawford (2021), the Arctic's importance for life on earth also makes it a vital part of the global commons. In principle, both territorial and high seas areas are regulated by international law. Only one UN Law of the Seas (UNCLOS, since 1994) – Article 234 – refers directly to the Arctic (Koivurova et al., 2020, pp. 413–414). But UNCLOS is a key framework for international relations in all sea areas, and together with other binding and non-binding treaties, bodies and norms in international law, including the Convention on Climate Change (UNFCCC) and the Arctic Council, form the main legal basis of Arctic relations (Wallace, 2020, p. 351). As in all other areas of the world, the rules of war and conflict are governed by the Hague and Geneva conventions (Magnússon & Norchi, 2020). There is however disagreement on how far out Arctic states can make territorial claims in accordance with UNCLOS. In some cases, claims overlap, and with the ice melting, the seabeds and thus the borders themselves are moving, making discussions even more complicated. Canada, Russia, Norway, Denmark and Greenland have for example all submitted continental shelf claims to the Commission on the Limits of the Continental Shelf. Since it is not a signatory to UNCLOS, the US has not presented any territorial claims (Kolås, 2015, p. 423).

The Arctic Council discusses all common relevant issues except for security, although this indirectly has reached the agenda with the broader term "security issues linked to climate change". The eight Arctic member states are permanent members. Underlining the Arctic's increased international importance, 12 countries have also gained observer status in the Arctic Council: France, Germany, the UK, the Netherlands, Italy, Poland, Spain, China, Japan, Korea, Singapore and India. Thirty additional observers include several intergovernmental organisations such as various UN agencies, including the International Maritime Organisation, the UN Environment Programme (UNEP) and the UN Development Programme (UNDP), the Red Cross, and non-governmental organisations including indigenous peoples and environmental protection NGOs. A final implication of climate change in the Arctic is linked to indigenous peoples, whose way of living has been strongly affected directly due to ice melting and indirectly by states and other actors' often competing economic and geopolitical interests. Indigenous peoples, sometimes referred to as Circumpolar peoples or Arctic peoples, make up around 10% of the total population living in the Arctic areas and comprise more than 40 different ethnic groups (Arctic Centre, 2021). Non-traditional security issues such as human and cultural security have gained attention through national and international indigenous rights laws. Their unique knowledge of Arctic challenges has been acknowledged as an important contribution by scientific communities and the Arctic Council (Crawford, 2021). Through national and international indigenous rights laws, the Arctic Council Indigenous Peoples Secretariat, organisations and forums, indigenous people can potentially impact Arctic policies as stakeholders (Newman, 2020; Wilson, 2020). However, resolutions such as the United Nations Declaration on the Rights of Indigenous Peoples (UNDRIP), aimed at indigenous peoples' rights, are not legally binding. There are significant national differences regarding the implementation of these legal governance rights across Arctic states. When adopted in 2007, Russia abstained from voting, and the US and Canada voted against the resolution. Rather than being treated as an Arctic issue proper, questions linked to indigenous peoples' rights have predominantly been dealt with within national structures and processes (Vincent, 2020, p. 2).

Analytical Framework, Methods and Operationalisation

Drawing on key international relations (IR) perspectives one can envisage two main options for managing international relations in the Arctic: an international regulatory regime to secure equal but controlled access to various resources and sea lines as one would expect following a neoliberal perspective (1); or territorial control and balancing by a few states, in line with a neorealist perspective (2).

Until recently, the Arctic has best fit the first of these descriptions, with a high level of stability due to a high level of complex interdependence and interaction in and respect for common institutions and norms (Byers, 2017; Coates & Holroyd, 2020; Wegge, 2012). This is in line with a neoliberal perspective on international relations. Rather than linking behavior to a quest for absolute gains and power, scholars applying neoliberal perspectives focus on how cooperation might increase everyone's gain in the long term, i.e., on the absolute gain of cooperation as well as on the role of non-state actors in international relations (Goldstein et al., 2001; Keohane & Nye, 2012). In modern, interdependent societies, states seek power and influence instrumentally through other means, mainly linked to economic interests and influence via international institutions. Accordingly, neoliberal scholars predict that states may cooperate when this is perceived necessary or advantageous to promote their foremost economic interests, which in this case is to secure access to resources and sea lines and rational management of these resources for economic purposes. Once common institutions and rules are established, they are also expected to affect the likelihood of further cooperation. Such institutions provide information channels on other actors' preferences and positions and increase the credibility of actors' commitment to future cooperation (Goldstein et al., 2001; Keohane & Nye, 2012).

In a more uncertain and volatile international environment, one might however also expect the Arctic to develop into a more competitive environment. A basic neorealist assumption is that foreign policy actors operate in an anarchical environment where they engage in a zero-sum game, aiming to increase their relative security by all available means (Walt, 1998; Waltz, 2000). In short, realist scholars assume that states' preferences are ranked towards security and territorial control, that force is their most important instrument, and that institutions at best are arenas for state's power competition. This is the opposite of a liberal multilateral institutionalised system characterised by "an absence of hierarchy among issues, the presence of transgovernmental and transnational channels of contact, and the near irrelevance of military force" (Byers, 2017). Are we moving in this direction in the Arctic? If so, following Byer's framework, we should expect: (1) that the actors' policy preferences are focused towards security/energy security and the balancing of other powers; (2) increased reference to the need to deploy military means, and/or an increase in such deployment; and (3) that international regulations and organisations are perceived as unnecessary or of not much relevance for dealing with conflicts and challenges in the Arctic.

Towards More Conflict in the Arctic?

To study the relevance of these two hypotheses, particularly exploring whether there is evidence that the Arctic is moving towards a neorealist model, the analysis below compares the Arctic strategies and preferences of the four main global actors, Russia, the US, China, and the EU.

Russia

In territorial terms, Russia is the biggest Arctic state and one of the Arctic Council's founding members. It controls more than 53% of the Arctic coastline, including vast unexploited natural resources and most of the Northern Sea Route (Ananyeva, 2019). To Russia, the Arctic is of great economic and strategic importance, accounting for 22% of its exports and 20% of its GDP, mainly from natural resources. A total of 25% of the world's reserves in hydrocarbon resources is within the Russian Arctic territory. Equally significant, the Arctic provides Russia with its "strategic deterrent" and "second-strike" ability. The Northern Fleet is based in Severomors and the ballistic missile submarine (SSBN) force on the Kola Peninsula (Rumer et al., 2021). It is also increasing its operational presence in the North Arctic and European Arctic.

Russia's new Development Strategy for the Arctic (2020–2035, from 2020) draws on past strategies but stresses the impact of climate change in the region. While the ice and harsh Arctic climate used to function as a natural defence, ice melting now leaves Russia more vulnerable, but also provides a number of new economic and strategic opportunities. By 2035, Russia for example aims to increase its regional presence and influence by developing new vessels, airports, seaports and railroads (Brzozowski, 2020). Observers also expect further militarisation and more cooperation with China in the Arctic. Environmental protection is, according to Kluge and Paul (2020), not a likely Russian priority. The overall implications of Russia's policy change are a combination of tackling the climate crises and a response to the former and latter US administrations Arctic policy.

After the Cold War, the potential for a Russian-Western confrontation in the Arctic was low (Sergunin, 2020, p. 130). From a realist perspective, one would expect tension between Russia and the West to grow from 2014, with conflicts in Ukraine and Syria spilling over to the Arctic, thus adding fuel to potential geopolitical conflicts in the region (Byers, 2017). Although tensions have increased somewhat, studies, however, show that "the annexation of Crimea did not cause Arctic international relations to move far across the spectrum towards the realist ideal type. Instead, Arctic international relations shifted to the middle of the spectrum, demonstrating characteristics of both ideal types" (Byers, 2017, p. 394).

Official documents and other studies after 2017 confirm this view. Russia has a "preference for soft power instruments", through "multilateral institutions" and has thus remained engaged in international cooperation in the Arctic (Gjørv et al., 2020, p. 6). However, Russia has systematically linked its economic and strategic interests in the region, with a clear preference for a bilateral approach on "hard" issues and a multilateral approach on "softer" ones (Ananyeva, 2019; Fondahl et al., 2020; Sergunin, 2020). Russia is actively engaged in several multilateral institutions such as the Arctic Council, the Northern Dimension policy cooperation and the Barents Euro-Arctic Council (BEAC). It is particularly engaged in discussions on Arctic transborder logistical routes and longer-term issues such as research, climate change, and search and rescue. Since the US does not participate in the Northern dimension or BEAC, these institutions also provide platforms free of US influence (Ananyeva, 2019).

Russia prefers to engage bilaterally in discussions that directly relate to its core national strategic and economic interests – territorial control and accesses to resources – and systematically avoids dealing with such issues in multilateral forums. Bilaterally, the economic sanctions imposed by the EU and the US have made Russia engage more closely with Asian states such as China to pursue its primary objectives through economic and technological cooperation. A systematic literature review conducted by Ananyeva (2019, pp. 89–91) found that while only 1% of Russian official documents and literature mention the Arctic in the context of Russian-American relations, both Russian and Chinese documents underline the importance of a strong bilateral Russian-Chinese partnership in the region. This is also followed by practice. As discussed below, in cooperation with Russia, China seeks to develop a Polar Silk Road and is deeply involved in the Russian oil and gas buildout.

Undoubtedly, Russia has a strong military presence that underlines its sovereignty and control of large parts of the area (Sørensen & Klimenko, 2017). Rather than confronting or seeking to balance other powers, however, Sergunin (2020, p. 129) argues that the Russian fleet is there "to demonstrate and ascertain Russia's sovereignty (…) to protect its economic interests in the High North (…) [and] to demonstrate (…) its great-power status and (…) world-class military capabilities". According to other scholars, the worry amongst some that sanctions and increased Sino-Russian cooperation might lead to a militarised Russian presence in the Arctic has not materialised (Gjørv et al., 2020, p. 9). Unlike what we have seen in many other regions, Russia does not seem to have an interest in engaging in military conflict or escalating tensions in the Artic. Russia is the biggest Arctic state and already has control over substantial resources and potential shipping lanes. There is also an established institutional structure that gives Russia a strong voice in discussions on the region's issues. At least for the moment, most scholars thus suggest that it is Russia's interest to play "the long game" in the Arctic, seeking to position itself as a major power by participating in regional governance, development and cooperation, and by following rules and multilateral agreements (Ananyeva, 2019; Sergunin, 2020).

The US

Historically, the US has not attached much importance to the Arctic region as a national security point or a region where the US faces a potential territorial security threat (Corgan, 2020, p. 152). Instead, according to Germond (2015, p. 178), since the Cold War, the US "continues to regard the region as a strategic zone". The region's strategic importance is linked to its submarine fleet and increasingly to strategic considerations linked to its defence missile programme. In recent years, the Arctic has gained more attention in official US documents, but this has, according to Corgan (2020), not been matched by a de facto policy allocation of resources to the region. Neither the Arctic nor the near-Arctic areas of the US in Alaska have ranked high on the US national agenda, which, according to Haycox (2020, p. 233), is why the US has never fully developed an Arctic policy. Although often arguing in favour of free passage and respect for the freedom of navigation principles in the Arctic and beyond, the US is the only Arctic council member who has not ratified the UN Convention of the Law of the Seas (UNCLOS). It is, therefore, not engaged in any territorial disputes in the region (Crawford, 2021). With some exceptions, the US accepts the principles of international law and acknowledges UNCLOS and the Arctic Council as a basis for Arctic governance (Battarbee & Fossum, 2014, p. 71), together with other basic international laws and principles like the Hague and Geneva conventions linked to the use and presence of force.

The first US Arctic strategy under President Clinton was never published and had little real impact. The US released a comprehensive Arctic strategy in 2009, "elucidating the state's interest in protecting the region's environment, developing its natural resources, and maintaining national security". This was followed by the National Strategy for the Arctic Region in 2013, setting out the main aim of a "secure and stable region where U.S. national interests are safeguarded, the U.S. homeland is protected, and nations work cooperatively to address challenges" (Corgan, 2020, p. 156; Department of Defense, 2013; Huebert et al., 2012, p. 33). In practice, however, US foreign policies were focused on other areas of the world, implying that "nothing was going to happen soon, despite the growing understanding that the environment in the region was changing and that economic activity was increasing" (Corgan, 2020, p. 157).

The Russian annexation of Crimea and China's increased interest in the area has led to a more assertive US in the Arctic, including increased military engagement. Rather than building forces in the area, the US however mainly engages in the area via NATO members and other allies in the region – Canada and the Scandinavian states (Ananyeva, 2019, p. 93). Examples include stationary troops and the NATO exercise Trident Juncture in Norway.

As in other areas of US foreign policy, unilateralism under Trump also affected US Arctic policies. The withdrawal from the Paris climate accord sent a clear signal that the US would not prioritise environmental policies in the region and beyond. In line with Trump's broader security strategies and discourse, the also US took on a more confrontational tone with Russia and China, including in the Arctic (Corgan, 2020, p. 161). The US Navy, for example, started patrolling the Barents Sea in 2020. Much of the Barents Sea is part of the Russian economic zone, and Russia has a significant submarine presence in the area (Crawford, 2021). The Trump administration also substantially changed its rhetoric regarding China's engagement in the Arctic, raising concerns about the increasing Sino-Russian cooperation.

Biden has so far signalled a clear break with his predecessor's Arctic policies, although an US Arctic policy according to Stronski and Kier (2021) is still in the making. Climate change and the restoration of trust and cooperation with US' partners are central to the new administration, with the US for example returning to the Paris climate accords and clearly embracing NATO and the EU. Accordingly, the Biden administration's approach is "to treat the Arctic as a zone where multilateral and cooperative approaches" is central (Stronski & Kier, 2021). Although continuing a harsh stance on China in particular, the Biden administration is also seeking cooperation with Russia and China to combat climate change (Holm, 2021). Whether the US, together with its European partners, will be able to cooperate with China in some areas when geopolitical and economic tensions are increasing in others however remains to be seen. The Biden administration is also perhaps less trusted than previous administrations – after all, both allies and strategic rivals now know that changes made under the current administration might be revered by successive presidents (Riddervold & Newsome, 2021).

China

China, who signed the Svalbard treaty in 1925, has engaged in various Arctic research projects since the 1990s and been involved in the Arctic council since 2007 – with an observer status since 2013. Although located 1,500 km away, China describes itself as a "near-Arctic state" in their first "Arctic Policy" published in 2018 (The State Council the People's Republic of China, 2018). This is an "indicator of China's strategic interest in the region and a step towards a more confident Arctic policy" (Mariia, 2019, p. 95). According to Gjørv et al. (2020, p. 9), China's main strategy is "to become an Arctic insider through a multilayered policy approach aimed at creating an Arctic identity, regardless of geography", by defining Arctic regional governance as an international affair with relevance to non-Arctic states.

Accordingly, China seeks to justify its engagement in the Arctic based on international law and scientific grounds, referring to parts of the Arctic as a Global Common where there is a need for joint research, exploration, governance and cooperation (Tonami, 2019, p. 56). According to China, the Svalbard treaty grants the contracting parties access and entry to certain Arctic areas and its resources (The State Council the People's Republic of China, 2018). China also refers to the UNCLOS freedom of the seas and innocent passing principles when justifying its maritime presence in the region. Besides having the right to "scientific research, resource exploration and exploitation, shipping and security", Chinese scholars such as Woon (2020, p. 1) also argue that "climate change and its potential consequences on the region are expected to affect much of the world, which thereby warrants Beijing's rightful concern with Arctic affairs". However, many of the open waters in the Arctic are within the Arctic states' internationally recognised national jurisdictions. While China argues that the Arctic waterways are international waters, "both Russia and Canada claim sovereignty over two of these waterways, the Northwest Passage and the Northern Sea Route, and they believe they have the legal right to block others from entering" (Crawford, 2021).

China marked a clear presence and claim to the area by being the first nation to send a vessel through the North Sea Route, the Arctic Ocean, and the Northwest Passage of Canada. The Chinese Polar Institute sent a second icebreaker on an Arctic expedition through the Northern Sea Route in 2020 (Tonami, 2019). Although China justified these expeditions by pointing to scientific ambitions, observers agree that its engagement in the Arctic is mainly economically and strategically motivated, underlined amongst other things by its many bilateral oil and gas agreements with Russia (Tonami, 2019, pp. 55–56).

Economically, China's engagement in the region is linked to developing shipping routes, thus governing the area's resources. China wants to develop a "Polar Silk Road", "linking Europe to China via the Northern Sea Route [NSR], thus connect it with the belt and road initiative [BRI] states" Woon (2020, p. 2). China "formally added the Arctic Ocean to the list of maritime regions essential to China's Belt and Road trade initiatives in 2017" (Lanteigne, 2020, p. 312). Later that year, China further stressed that access and development of sea routes in the greater Arctic Ocean are crucial for Chinese maritime trade (Lanteigne, 2020).

In strategic terms, the Arctic officially became an area of Chinese national security when The National Security Act of 2015 defined the polar region as a national security domain (Mariia, 2019; Tonami, 2019, p. 56). China's white paper expresses a strong interest in a peaceful and internationally governed Arctic (Grieger, 2018). According to Doshi et al. (2021, p. 11), China therefore officially downplays its aim to be a great Arctic power. Unofficially it is however increasingly concerned with securing its strategic and economic interests and is aware of the potential for conflict, with observers expecting a revision of its military-strategic capacity (Doshi et al., 2021). Currently, China relies on oil and gas shipped through the somewhat unstable Middle East and will gain from a stable, shorter shipping route via the NSR. The same goes for the Polar Silk Road. Through its bilateral cooperation with Russia, these passages can, for the most part, be adopted for shipping beyond US influence (Lanteigne, 2020, p. 313).

In line with this, China has not made territorial claims to areas in the Arctic, nor has it directly attempted to militarise its presence in the region (Tunsjø, 2020, p. 145). Instead, to access resources and strategic shipping routes, China has established strong military, economic, technological and diplomatic bilateral ties with Russia, which it perceives as a gatekeeper to the area (Lanteigne, 2020; Sørensen & Klimenko, 2017; Tunsjø, 2020). China also takes advantage of a weakened Russian position under the Crimea sanctions to get a better foothold, economically and politically, in the region (Gjørv et al., 2020). Simultaneously, China is careful not to interfere with Russian domestic affairs – a concern the two states share in international affairs more broadly. Contrary to a realist balancing hypothesis, and key to understanding its soft approach, China does not want to confront the US directly or via its cooperation with Russia (Sørensen & Klimenko, 2017, pp. 11–12). In this sense, as Crawford (2021) notes, China's position is ambiguous, on the one hand acknowledging the Arctic states' territories while on the other hand justifying its right to access it based on international law.

The European Union (EU)[1]

EU's Arctic policies go back to the adoption of a Northern Dimension policy in 2000. With the enlargement to Sweden and Finland in 1995, the EU gained a common border with Russia. The two states have been the strongest champions of a Northern security focus, together with the Baltic states. Since 2008, the European Commission has applied several times for an observer status in the Arctic Council, but this has not been granted due to opposition from permanent members: from Canada linked to the import of seal fur (until 2014) and since 2014 from Russia over EU sanctions linked to Ukraine and oil projects in the Russian Arctic (Depledge, 2015). Thus, the EU participates as an observer in the Arctic Council on an ad hoc basis, meaning that the Commission has to apply to attend the meetings.

Since 2014, the EU has become an increasingly active player in the Arctic. In terms of balance of power/territorial claims, the EU does not directly have a sovereignty-based claim to the area. According to Riddervold and Cross (2019), three factors are key to understanding the EU's engagement: Russia's aggression in the Arctic and Ukraine, the EU's concern for environmental protection and an interest in the principle of free navigation, including gaining access to the trade routes that are opening up as a result of global warming. First, EU Arctic policies have developed in response to geopolitical events linked to Russian behaviour, most notably the annexation of Crimea in 2014. In response to the Russian flag-planting in 2007/2008, the Commission and the High Representative of the Union for Foreign Affairs and Security Policy (HR/VP) published a report on "Climate change and international security" calling for member states to develop a common EU Arctic policy – a report that "was dominated almost exclusively by security and geopolitical rhetoric that stressed the importance of interstate disputes, conflicts over natural resources" (Weber & Romanyshyn, 2011, p. 852). However, member states did not follow these initiatives until Russia annexed Ukraine, which placed security high on the European agenda. In response, member states agreed to move forward with "the further development of an integrated and coherent Arctic Policy" in "a region of growing strategic importance" (European Council, 2014).

Although also driven by geopolitical events in other parts of the world, and very much aware of the Arctic's increased strategic importance, the EU's main justification for seeking influence over Arctic developments is the need "to assist in addressing the challenge of sustainable development in a prudent and responsible manner" (European Council, 2014). The European External Action Service (EEAS) outline three main policy objectives for the Arctic: "(1) protecting and preserving the Arctic in cooperation with the people who live there (2) promoting sustainable use of resources (3) international cooperation" (EEAS, 2015). The EU is also very much concerned with securing free navigation of the sea in line with UNCLOS, including its own access to new navigation routes in the North. The EU has a significant merchant fleet, most of its freight trade is transported by sea, and it wants to participate in the energy policy of future Arctic governance (Riddervold & Cross, 2019). That being said, the EU only recently developed a common Arctic policy, even though the impact on climate change was known long before 2014. Riddervold and Cross (2019) argue that the EU saw the need to react following Russian aggression, but its main aim is to contribute to sustainable development through international cooperation. The fact that parts of the Arctic belong to the high seas Global Commons is moreover key to understanding the EU's policies in the region, with the EU seeking to play a particular leadership role in trying to prevent "the tragedy of the commons", through promoting modes of governance that will protect the environment and prevent over-exploitation (Riddervold & Cross, 2019). In contrast to Russia, the EU is also the actor that perhaps most explicitly seeks to take indigenous peoples' particular rights and knowledge into consideration when engaging in the region, both at the EU and member state levels, particularly in Denmark (Coates & Holroyd, 2020).

The EU has not deployed military means to the area. This is not surprising, given the EU's main focus on civilian foreign policy means, its clear preference for multilateral solutions in the Arctic and beyond, and the fact that only Denmark – who does not participate in the EU's security and defence policies – is the only Arctic state among its members. The EU's preference

Maritime Security in the Arctic

for the Arctic is thus in line with the neoliberal model developed above. The EU wants a seat at the table but prefers strong international regulations multilateral regimes, and sustainable development is a main concern (Bretherton & Vogler, 2006; Falkner, 2007). Undoubtedly, the freedom of navigation, including access to the Northern sea routes as they open due to climate change, is key to the EU. At the same time, the EU's main concern in the area is to secure a sustainable development of these areas and revert the negative climate changes as much as possible. The EU seeks to "ensure that the Arctic remains a zone of low tension and peaceful cooperation, where issues are solved through constructive dialogue" (European Commission, 2020). The EU launched a public consultation on EU Arctic policies in 2020, with the aim of revising and updating its policies (European Commission, 2020).

Conclusion

While a higher level of conflict might be expected in the Arctic as resources and shipping lanes become more accessible and territorial claims remain unsettled, we find that the Arctic has mainly remained cooperative. The potential for conflict is greater than before, not least between Russia and the US, in the longer term between China and the US, as their relationship tenses elsewhere. Russia has established a strong military presence and controls large parts of the area. Contrastingly to the cases of Ukraine and Syria, Russia does not seem interested in escalating tensions in the Artic. Instead, most scholars suggest that Russia's interest is to play "the long game", positioning itself through international cooperation.

The US has become more active in the Arctic than it has been traditionally: While it was very vocal towards China and Russia and their increasingly strong Arctic cooperation under Trump, Biden has endorsed a more cooperative approach not least due to the administration's climate focus. Compared to other areas of the world, the US has not developed a strong and assertive policy in the Arctic. It has increased its military presence in the North, but to a large degree through its allies. Overall, its foreign policy focus remains elsewhere, also under Biden. However, observers expect US Arctic policies to be largely oriented towards climate change and security in a broader environmental context, implying a continued US preference for increased international cooperation in the region.

Climate change may also be one of the areas where China and the US can cooperate in institutionalised settings, more independently of broader geopolitical issues. China is presenting itself as a "cautious partner", seeking not to increase tensions with the US, while cooperating closely with Russia to access resources and important sea lines. In general, scholars agree that China also has an interest in maintaining peaceful relations through international cooperation in the region, and securing a stable environment to achieve its economic interests.

The EU's priorities clearly suggest a liberalist policy. As argued elsewhere, the EU has recently developed into a more confident, state-like actor in relation to the Arctic, with member states joining forces to increase their common international strength against a changing international context (Riddervold & Cross, 2019). At the same time, the EU's main goal is not to gain power per se, but rather to protect the environment through regime building. It also has a strong interest in keeping open sea lines in the area.

In sum, international relations in the Arctic can still be described as an area of multilateral cooperation and increasingly a combination of the two models (Byers, 2017). Alternatively, in the words of Govella (2021) and Crawford's (2021), the Arctic is best described as a "grey area", in the sense that it is peaceful but filled with activity, competition and disputes that strain interstate relations. Although not completely insulated from developments elsewhere in the world, the Arctic is still an island of cooperation in a rougher sea.

Note

1 This part of the analysis is based on Riddervold and Cross (2019). Several of the EU member states have developed their own Arctic policies (Huebert et al., 2012). Here, however, we refer to the common EU policies conducted towards the Arctic, decided within the framework of the EU's Common Foreign and Security Policy, the CFSP.

References

Ananyeva, E. (2019). Russia in the Arctic region: Going bilateral or multilateral? *Journal of Eurasian Studies*, *10*(1), 85–97. 10.1177/1879366518814655

Arctic Centre. (2021). *Arctic indigenous peoples*. University of Lapland. https://www.arcticcentre.org/EN/arcticregion/Arctic-Indigenous-Peoples

Battarbee, K. J., & Fossum, J. E. (Eds.). (2014). *The Arctic contested*. P.I.E. Peter Lang.

Bretherton, C., & Vogler, J. D. (2006). *The European Union as a global actor* (2nd ed.). Routledge.

Brzozowski, J. (2020). Mixed embeddedness of immigrant entrepreneurs and community resilience: Lessons for the Arctic. In N. Yeasmin, W. Hasanat, J. Brzozowski, & S. Kirchner (Eds.), *Immigration in the circumpolar north* (pp. 162–175). Routledge.

Byers, M. (2017). Crises and international cooperation: An Arctic case study. *International Relations*, *31*(4), 375–402. 10.1177/0047117817735680

Coates, K., & Holroyd, C. (Eds.). (2020). *The Palgrave handbook of Arctic policy and politics*. Palgrave Macmillan.

Corgan, M. T. (2020). US security policy in the American Arctic. In G. H. Gjørv, M. Lanteigne, & H. Sam-Aggrey (Eds.), *Routledge handbook of Arctic security* (pp. 152–164). Routledge.

Council of the European Union. (2014, May). Council conclusions on developing a European Union policy towards the Arctic region. *Council of the European Union, Foreign Affairs Council, 14 May 2014*, 1–3.

Crawford, B. (2021). Explaining Arctic peace: A human heritage perspective. *International Relations*, *35*(x), forthcoming.

Department of Defense. (2013). *Arctic strategy*. Secretary of Defense. https://dod.defense.gov/Portals/1/Documents/pubs/2013_Arctic_Strategy.pdf

Depledge, D. (2015). Hard security developments. In J. Jokela (Ed.), *Arctic security matters* (pp. 59–68) European Union Institute for Security Studies, report no. 24.

Doshi, R., Dale-Huang, A., & Zhang, G. (2021, April). Northern expedition: China's Arctic ambition and activism. *Foreign Policy at Brookings*. The Brookings Institution. https://www.brookings.edu/wp-content/uploads/2021/04/FP_20210412_china_arctic.pdf

EEAS. (2015). *EU Arctic policy*. http://eeas.europa.eu/arctic_ region/index_en.html

European Commission. (2020, July 20). Arctic policy: EU opens consultation on the future approach. *European Commission Press Release*. https://ec.europa.eu/commission/presscorner/detail/en/IP_20_1318

Falkner, R. (2007). The political economy of a "normative power" Europe: EU environmental leadership in international biotechnology regulation. *Journal of European Public Policy*, *14*(4, May), 507–526.

Fondahl, G., Espiritu, A. A., & Ivanova, A. (2020). Russia's Arctic regions and policies. In K. Coates & C. Holroyd (Eds.), *The Palgrave handbook of Arctic policy and politics* (pp. 195–216). Palgrave Macmillan.

Germond, B. (2015). *The maritime dimension of European security: Seapower and the European Union*. Springer.

Gjørv, G. H., Lanteigne, M., & Sam-Aggrey, H. (Eds.). (2020). *Routledge handbook of Arctic security*. Routledge.

Goldstein, J. L., Kahler, M., Keohane, R. O., & Slaughter, A. M. (2001). *Legalisation and world politics*. MIT Press.

Govella, K. (2021) China's challenge to the global commons: Cooperation, contestation, and subversion in the maritime and cyber domains. *International Relations*, *35*(3), 446–468.

Grieger, G. (2018). China's Arctic policy: How China aligns rights and interests. *European Parliament Think Tank*. https://www.europarl.europa.eu/thinktank/en/document.html?reference=EPRS_BRI(2018)620231

Haycox, S. (2020). Arctic policy of the United States: An historical survey. In K. Coates & C. Holroyd (Eds.), *The Palgrave handbook of Arctic policy and politics* (pp. 233–250). Palgrave Macmillan.

Holm, A. O. (2021, June 18). Biden–Putin summit groundbreaking for Arctic co-operation. *High North News*. https://www.highnorthnews.com/en/biden-putin-summit-groundbreaking-arctic-co-operation

Huebert, R., Exnen-Pirot, H., Lajeunesse, A., & Gulledge, J. (2012). *Climate change & international security: The Arctic as a bellwether*. Center for Climate and Energy Solutions.

Keohane, R., & Nye, J. (2012). *Power and interdependence* (4th ed.). Longman.

Kluge, J., & Paul, M. (2020). Russia's Arctic strategy through 2035. *Stiftung Wissenschaft Und Politik*, *57*(C). 10.18449/2020C57

Koivurova, T., Kleemola-Juntunen, P., & Kirchner, S. (2020). Emergence of a new ocean: How to react to the massive change? In K. Coates & C. Holroyd (Eds.), *The Palgrave handbook of Arctic policy and politics*. Palgrave Macmillan.

Kolås, A. (2015). The Arctic contested. *International Affairs*, *91*(2, March), 423–424. 10.1111/1468-2346.12256

Kraska, J., & Baker, B. (2014, March). Policy brief: Emerging Arctic security challenges. *Center for a New American Security Policy Brief, March 2014*, 1–16.

Lanteigne, M. (2020). Considering the Arctic as a security region: The roles of China and Russia. In Gjørv G. H., Lanteigne, M. & Sam-Aggrey, H. (Eds.), *Routledge handbook of Arctic security*. Routledge.

Magnússon, B. M., & Norchi, C. H. (2020). Geopolitics and international law in the Arctic. In Gjørv G. H., Lanteigne, M. & Sam-Aggrey, H. (Eds.), *Routledge handbook of Arctic security*. Routledge.

Mariia, K. (2019). China's Arctic policy: present and future. *The Polar Journal*, *9*(1), 94–112. 10.1080/2154 896X.2019.1618558

Newman, D. (2020). International indigenous rights law and contextualized decolonization of the Arctic. In K. Coates & C. Holroyd (Eds.), *The Palgrave handbook of Arctic policy and politics* (pp. 427–437). Palgrave Macmillan.

Riddervold, M. (2018). *The maritime turn in EU foreign and security policies: Aims, actors and mechanisms of integration*. Palgrave Macmillan.

Riddervold, M., & Cross, M. (2019). Reactive power EU: Russian aggression and the development of an EU Arctic policy. *European Foreign Affairs Review*, *24*(1), 43–60.

Riddervold, M., & Newsome, A. (2021). Introduction. Cooperation, conflict and interaction in the global commons. *International Relations*, *35*(3), 365–383.

Rumer, E., Sokolsky, R., & Stronski, P. (2021, March). The return of global Russia: Russia in the Arctic – A critical examination. *Carnegie Endowment for International Peace*. https://carnegieendowment.org/files/Rumer_et_al_Russia_in_the_Arctic.pdf

Sergunin, A. (2020). Arctic security perspectives from Russia. In Gjørv G. H., Lanteigne, M. & Sam-Aggrey, H. (Eds.), *Routledge handbook of Arctic security* (pp. 129–139). Routledge.

Sørensen, C. T. N., & Klimenko, E. (2017). Emerging Chinese–Russian cooperation in the Arctic: Possibilities and constraints. *SIPRI Policy Paper* (46). https://www.sipri.org/sites/default/files/2017-06/emerging-chinese-russian-cooperation-arctic.pdf

Stronski, P., & Kier, G. (2021, May 17). *A fresh start on U.S. Arctic policy under Biden*. Carnegie Moscow Center – Carnegie Endowment for International Peace. https://carnegie.ru/commentary/84543?utm_source=rss&utm_medium=rss

The State Council the People's Republic of China. (2018). White paper: China's Arctic policy. http://english.www.gov.cn/archive/white_paper/2018/01/26/content_281476026660336.htm

Tonami, A. (2019). The rise of Asia and Arctic legal order-making: Political-economic settings. In Shibata Z. L., Sellheim, N. & Scopelliti, M. (Eds.), *Emerging legal orders in the Arctic: The role of non-Arctic actors* (pp. 27–41). Routledge.

Tunsjø, Ø. (2020). The great hype: False visions of conflict and opportunity in the Arctic. *Survival. Global Politics and Strategy*, *62*(5), 139–156. 10.1080/00396338.2020.1819649

Vincent, W. F. (2020). Arctic climate change: Local impacts, global consequences, and policy implications. In K. Coates & C. Holroyd (Eds.), *The Palgrave handbook of Arctic policy and politics* (pp. 507–526). Palgrave Macmillan.

Wallace, R. R. (2020). Canada and Russia in an evolving circumpolar Arctic. In K. Coates & C. Holroyd (Eds.), *The Palgrave handbook of Arctic policy and politics* (pp. 351–372). Palgrave Macmillan.

Walt, S. M. (1998). The ties that fray: Why Europe and America are drifting apart. *The National Interest*, *54*, 3–11.

Waltz, K. N. (2000). Structural realism after the Cold War. *International Security*, *25*(1), 5–41.

Weber, S., & Romanyshyn, J. (2011). Breaking the ice: The European Union and the Arctic. *International Journal*, *66*(4), 849–860.

Wegge, N. (2012). The EU and the Arctic: European foreign policy in the making. *Law and Politics*, *3*, 6–29.

Wilson, G. N. (2020). Indigenous internationalism in the Arctic. In K. Coates & C. Holroyd (Eds.), *The Palgrave handbook of Arctic policy and politics* (pp. 27–40). Palgrave Macmillan.

Woon, C. Y. (2020). Framing the "Polar Silk Road (冰上丝绸之路): Critical geopolitics, Chinese scholars and the (re)positionings of China's Arctic interests. *Political Geography*, *78*(April, 102141). 10.1016/j.polgeo.2019.102141

INDEX

Symbols

9/11 2, 4, 94–95, 98, 154, 157, 191, 198, 201, 208, 336, 340

Active Endeavour 34, 340
Afghanistan 108, 299, 307, 314–315, 325
Africa Blue Economy Strategy 342–343
Africa's Integrated Maritime Strategy 69–70, 273
African Charter on Maritime Security and Safety and Development in Africa 113, 271, 273
African Integrated Maritime Strategy 113, 271
African Union (AU) 111, 271
Alfred Thayer Mahan 38, 48, 60
Alliance of Small Island States (AOSIS) 250
Allied Command Atlantic 314
Allied Command Europe 314
Allied Command Operations 314
Allied Command Transformation 82, 314
Allied Maritime Command (MARCOM) 314
Angola 135, 236, 238, 327, 329, 331–333
anthropocene 139, 149, 247
anthropology 116, 118, 120, 125–126, 279, 286, 298
Anti-Access/Area Denial (A2/AD) 317
anti-narcotics operations 326
anti-piracy 3, 44, 71, 78, 99, 115, 181, 263, 353
anti-ship weapons 57
aquaculture 244–246, 248–249, 258, 265–266, 270, 274, 341
arbitration 37, 80–83, 89, 349, 353, 365
archipelagic states 349
Arctic 3, 55, 67–68, 70, 81, 99, 104, 225, 268, 275, 297, 312–313, 315–317, 320–323, 341, 367–378
Arctic Council 320, 367, 369–373, 375

Arctic governance 372, 375
Arctic Ocean 81, 313, 316, 374
Arctic policy 367, 371–373, 375, 377–378
Arctic strategy 320, 372, 377
Argentina 326–329, 334
armed protection 299, 301, 303, 306
armed robbery 4, 11–12, 66, 72, 75–77, 80, 127, 135, 138, 157, 162, 177, 181–183, 185, 187, 228, 235, 249, 260, 300, 309–310, 327–328, 347, 352–353, 356, 359, 366
arms smuggling 258
arms trafficking 128, 137
artificial islands 68, 262, 365
ASEAN 70, 77, 82, 100–101, 104, 271, 349–356, 363–364
Asia Pacific 81, 104, 215, 225, 238, 354
assemblage theory 6, 30, 35, 122, 124
Association of Southeast Asian Nations (ASEAN) 271, 349 1
assurance 77–78, 234
asylum 27, 34–35, 102–103, 105, 109–110, 114–115, 169–172, 174–175, 339
Atlantic 4–5, 10, 13, 22, 24, 26, 46–47, 54, 60, 67, 71, 81–82, 111, 140, 144–145, 149–150, 175, 199, 212, 251–252, 260, 263, 286, 290, 296, 298, 312–335, 346, 358
Atlantic Ocean 54, 140, 144, 150, 321–322, 324, 332
Australia 10, 53, 76, 81, 84, 93, 95, 100–105, 109–110, 115, 141, 143, 150, 162, 171–172, 175, 181, 206, 259, 261, 270, 272, 354, 356, 363
Australian Navy 61, 203
Automatic Identification System (AIS) 216
autonomous vessels 217

Index

Bahrain 36, 251
Balkans 314–315, 320, 340
ballooning effects 129–130, 132–133, 135, 137
Baltic and International Maritime Council (BIMCO) 306
Baltic Sea 60, 327
Bangladesh 172, 174, 269, 275, 349, 356
Barbados 251–252
Barcelona Charter 278
Barcelona Convention 342
Barents Euro-Arctic Council (BEAC) 371
Barents Sea 373
Belt and Road Initiative 46, 272, 329, 333, 338, 374
Benin 44, 132–133, 135, 138, 233, 235
Biden 317–318, 321–322, 373, 376–378
biodiversity conservation 261
biological, chemical or nuclear weapons (BCNWs) 94
Black Sea 5, 12, 313, 323, 345
blue crime 9, 332
blue economy 5, 66–68, 72, 74, 82, 139, 184–185, 215, 250–251, 257–260, 262–275, 330–332, 334, 342–344, 346
blue growth 177, 185, 250, 257, 267–274, 340
blue industries 271
blue water 143, 183, 350
bluewashing 267
boat migrants 101, 103–104, 171–172, 174; boat people 102–103, 105, 170–171, 175; border control 103, 108, 114, 166
border dispute resolution 269; border management 172, 174; border regime 110
border security 102, 109–110, 146, 337, 345
border surveillance systems 166
Brazil 24, 26, 54, 60, 243, 248, 324–327, 329–330, 332–334
BRICS 329, 333–334
Brundtland Report 2
Brunei 350, 353, 355, 357, 362, 364–365
Bulgaria 313

Cambodia 241, 350, 355
Cameroon 36, 132, 235, 329
Canada 11, 26, 47, 270, 282, 284, 311–314, 317–318, 320, 367, 369, 373–375, 378
capacity-building 3, 70, 119, 121, 128–129, 136–137, 180, 184, 186, 251, 258–262, 264, 269–270, 274, 328, 339, 344
cargo vessels 146, 268
Carl Schmitt 20
cartography 32, 139–140, 142, 144, 148, 150, 336
Caspian Sea 211, 317, 339
Central Africa 72, 180–181, 187
Central African Republic 329
Central Mediterranean 108, 114, 337, 345

Charles Tilly 17–18, 25–26
Charter on the Protection and Management of Underwater Cultural Heritage 278, 286
Chile 50, 270
China 3, 5, 10, 12, 34–35, 37, 46–48, 51–56, 60–62, 67–68, 72, 76–77, 79–85, 89, 92, 94–95, 99–100, 104–105, 141–142, 144, 150, 179, 181, 183, 198–199, 201, 204, 208, 211–212, 241, 260–261, 263, 267–268, 272, 274–275, 287, 291, 296–298, 311, 317–323, 325, 328–329, 331–334, 338, 344–345, 347, 349, 353–374, 376–378
Chinese naval power 364; chokepoint 202, 211, 300; circumpolar peoples 369; civil rights movement 147
Clausewitz 50
climate change 5, 9, 34, 55, 62, 66, 184, 197, 244, 250, 257–258, 261–262, 270, 273, 278, 293, 296–297, 317, 320–322, 337, 341–344, 346, 360, 367–369, 371, 373, 375–378
climate refugees 261
coast guards 69, 163, 186, 362
coastal communities 4, 9, 62, 113, 128, 167, 178–179, 181, 183–185, 269, 271, 273, 360
coastal ecosystems 244, 246, 257, 266
coastal erosion 251, 258
coastal inundation 257–258
coastal populations 63, 258, 269, 273, 327, 331
coastal protection 266
coastal shipping 235
coastguards 35, 46, 57, 108–109, 162, 182, 201, 259–260, 268–269, 271, 294–295
cocaine 135, 138, 290, 325–327, 329
Cocaine Route Programme (CRP) 329
Code of Conduct for Responsible Fisheries 240
coercion 22, 25–26, 153, 155, 172–173, 288, 361
Cold War 1–2, 6–7, 28–29, 34, 42–43, 45, 47, 51–53, 55, 57–58, 60, 66, 99, 176, 182, 198, 312, 314–315, 317, 321–325, 328, 330, 333, 350, 368, 371–372, 378
collective action 69, 74–75, 78–79, 82, 84, 307
collective defence 60, 313–314, 322–323
Colombia 39, 297, 326, 328; colonial powers 348, 353–354; colonialism 21, 43–44, 139–140, 148
Columbia 70, 115, 162, 199, 274, 290–291, 298, 366
Combined Task Force 151 (CTF-151) 300
commerce raiding 51, 56, 176
Commission on the Limits of the Continental Shelf (CLCS) 362
Common Foreign and Security Policy (CFSP) 337
common heritage of humanity 63, 70
compellence 77–78
conflict management 62, 355; constabulary tasks 101, 103; constitution of the oceans 63; constructivist perspectives 7

Index

Contact Group on Piracy off the Coast of Somalia (CGPCS) 180

Container Security Initiative 2, 77, 82; contiguous zone 65, 76, 81–82, 253; continental shelf 36, 62, 65, 68, 75, 89–92, 204, 253, 256, 264, 268, 275, 334, 349, 362–363, 366, 369

Convention for the Protection of the Marine Environment of the North-East Atlantic (OSPAR) 67

Convention on the Conservation of Antarctic Marine Living Resources 241

Copenhagen School 105

corruption 9, 129, 132, 137, 179, 228–229, 231–232, 236–238, 240–242, 291, 297

cosmography 140, 143

counter-piracy 11, 30, 36, 70, 72, 104, 111–112, 115, 117–121, 124–130, 132, 135, 153, 159–162, 176–177, 179–181, 183–185, 187, 297, 300, 304, 308–309, 314

counter-piracy missions 153, 161, 314

counter-piracy operations 11, 30, 126, 160–162, 183

counter-securitisation 98

counter-terrorism 314, 340, 345

counterinsurgency 307

COVID-19 10, 273–274, 276, 284, 293, 298, 317–318, 331, 342

crime-terror nexus 195–196, 198

Crimea 46, 312, 314, 321, 371–372, 374–375

criminal activities 166, 173, 183, 185, 228, 241–242, 246, 269, 331, 336; criminal law 4, 87, 124, 161, 168, 242; criminal networks 112, 121, 167, 185, 189, 234

crisis management 52, 314

Critical Maritime Routes in the Gulf of Guinea Programme (CRIMGO) 329

critical national infrastructure 203, 206

cruise missile 57, 195, 317, 319, 323

Cuba 36, 43, 172, 251

cultural heritage 4, 9, 66, 276–278, 282, 285–286

cultural representation 7

customary international law 73, 78–79, 82, 86–87, 102, 156

cyber attacks 214–216, 218–220, 223–224

cyber espionage 218; cyber infrastructure 219; cyber insurance 223, 226

cyber power 215, 222, 224, 226

cyber risk management 215, 220–226

cyber security 8, 221, 224–226

cyber terrorism 197

cyber threats 214–215, 217, 220, 223

Cyprus 62, 211, 339–340, 343

deep seabed mining 265, 267; defence budget 294, 317–318; defence spending 317–318

democracy 2, 32, 35–36, 115, 131, 138, 232

Denmark 36, 55, 158, 279, 293, 313, 320, 367, 369, 375

desecuritisation 7, 98–99, 103

detection 57, 155, 173–174, 191, 292, 321

deterrence 39, 41–42, 53, 81, 84–85, 98, 103, 105, 108, 166, 169, 172–174, 179, 314–315

disarmament 28, 42, 63

disembarkation 110, 114, 169, 172, 303

dispute settlement 81, 83, 86, 88–89, 91, 95, 355

disputes resolution 62

disruptive technologies 214–215, 217, 219, 221, 223–225

dissuasion 166, 174

Djibouti Code of Conduct 66, 99, 180, 260, 305, 309

Dominican Republic 172, 251

dominium 3, 64

drug cartels 290–291, 297, 326

drug smuggling 290–291, 344

drug trafficking 101, 241, 251, 325–327, 333, 340

East Africa 68, 76, 80, 314

East Indies 140, 348

Eastern Europe 28, 314, 316, 320

Eastern Mediterranean 108, 204, 208, 211–212, 335, 338–340, 343, 345–346

eco-tourism 266

economic development 2, 66–67, 98, 186, 230, 256, 262, 265, 267, 269–272, 274–275, 364; economic sanctions 371; economic security 63, 298

education 9, 126, 243, 245–246, 258–259

empire-building 19, 22

energy resources 339, 343, 346, 368

England 19, 22–24, 26, 140, 147, 281; environmental conservation 65–66; environmental degradation 43, 82, 94, 231–232, 269, 335, 360

environmental protection 4, 63, 226, 266, 369, 371, 375; environmental risks 265–266; environmental security 63, 69, 240, 259

environmental sustainability 263, 266, 272, 342

equitable treatment 247; ethnic groups 369; ethnography 7, 116–126

EU Action plan against migrant smuggling 337

EU Arctic policy 367, 375, 377–378

EU Global Strategy 337

EUBAM Libya 337–338

EUNAVFOR Atalanta 300

EUNAVFOR MED Irini 339

EUNAVFOR MED Sophia 337

Euro-Atlantic 313, 316, 335, 346

European Agenda on Security 337

European Commission 119, 125, 248, 271, 274, 320, 337–338, 342, 344, 374, 376–377

European Convention on the Protection of the Archaeological Heritage 278, 286

Index

European Court of Human Rights 159, 173
European empires 20, 24–25
European External Action Service 375
European Green Deal 342
European Union (EU) 111, 139, 166, 265, 335, 367, 374
European Union Maritime Security Strategy (EUMSS) 112, 344
exclusive economic zone (EEZ) 65, 89, 358
exclusive interests 88

Falkland Islands 315
famine 146
Federated States of Micronesia 254
Fiji 36, 252, 270
Finland 367, 374
First World War 41, 45
Fish Stock Agreement 157, 163; fisheries crime 177, 183, 241, 270; fisheries governance 268
fisheries treaties 313
fishing communities 27, 242, 246, 274, 280, 327
flag state 92–93, 154, 156, 168, 200, 239
flags of convenience 92–93, 95, 168, 241–242, 287, 301, 307
food insecurity 9, 239, 241, 243–247, 249, 341
food security 2–3, 63, 74, 106, 128, 231, 239, 241, 244, 246–248, 258, 266, 268, 270–271, 275, 360, 364
foreign assistance 258, 260–263
France 22–23, 26, 29–30, 33, 36, 39, 77, 81, 83, 113, 159–160, 164, 254, 260–261, 263, 282–284, 291, 296, 313, 317–318, 340, 363, 369; free navigation 375; free trade 62
freedom from fear 140, 167
freedom from want 167
freedom of navigation 56, 60, 62, 65–66, 68, 74–76, 78–83, 85, 90–92, 95, 154, 165, 313, 337, 372, 376
freedom of the seas 33, 83, 90, 373
French Guiana 327
FRONTEX 102, 112, 172, 175, 337–338

G7++ 128–129, 137
Gabon 129, 132, 134–135, 292, 329
gender equality 112–113
gender-based violence 107, 109, 113
Geneva Convention on the High Seas 177
geopolitics 2, 40, 47–48, 83, 96, 98–99, 213, 259, 261, 274, 344–345, 368, 378
Germany 36, 42, 47, 51, 296, 313–314, 323, 363, 369
Ghana 36, 132, 134–136, 236, 270, 329–331
global commons 82–84, 221, 369, 375, 377–378
global economy 3, 76, 208, 217, 224, 265, 272, 348
global governance 36, 62, 70, 82, 104, 119, 124, 126, 182, 187–188, 264, 308

Global Navigation Satellite System (GNSS) 216
global order 20, 26, 65, 71
global political ethnography 116–117, 119–123, 125–126
Global South 3, 7, 29
global warming 3, 5, 9–10, 62, 341, 346, 375
globalisation 9, 21, 27, 32, 43, 45, 55, 67, 179, 188, 214, 282, 325, 348, 352, 356; good governance 64, 68, 132, 215, 229, 333; good order at sea 5, 7, 9–10, 29, 42–46, 52, 101, 105, 338, 355, 357
governance regime 65, 70, 73, 234
great power competition 6, 38, 43, 46, 53, 59, 198, 315, 328, 334, 367
Greece 62, 109, 147–148, 211, 234, 281, 305, 313, 320, 338–340, 343
green economy 258, 266, 275
Greenland 42, 312–313, 367, 369
Greenpeace 6, 28–29, 33–36, 288, 292–293, 296
Gulf of Aden 3, 11, 85, 100, 111, 125, 162, 171–172, 178, 187, 211, 260, 268, 299–300, 305, 309, 319
Gulf of Benin 44
Gulf of Guinea 5, 7, 11–12, 63, 66, 69–70, 76, 80, 82–83, 85, 101, 105, 127–129, 132, 137–138, 175–176, 178–187, 201, 204, 208, 210–211, 227, 230, 235, 237–239, 248, 274, 296, 300, 305, 313, 327–334
Gulf of Mexico 313
Gulf of Oman 200, 202, 208, 211
Gulf of Tonkin 348, 357–358

Hans Morgenthau 38
harbour 6, 23, 33, 167, 229
Hezbollah 56–57, 191, 194
High North 313, 372, 377
High Representative of the Union for Foreign Affairs and Security Policy 375
hijacking 3–4, 12, 94, 179, 193, 201, 211, 235, 353
Hong Kong 348, 359, 362
Horn of Africa 11, 69, 76, 115, 126, 137, 172, 180, 186–187, 299, 307, 310
Hovering Acts 64–65
Hugo Grotius 9, 73, 89, 356; human development 243, 265; human geography 150, 196, 198
human rights 2, 4, 8, 12, 28, 87, 105, 108, 118, 124–125, 153–163, 167–169, 173–175, 182, 187, 230–232, 237, 239, 244, 294
human rights at sea 8, 158–160, 162, 175
human rights protection 161
human security 7–8, 10, 63, 68, 71, 100, 107, 113–114, 143, 165–168, 174–175, 237, 256, 258, 262, 265, 267, 269, 271, 331, 339, 344
human smuggling 109, 166–167, 184, 339–340, 343, 345
human traffickers 3
humanitarian crisis 8, 60, 171, 174; humanitarian regime at sea 168–170; hunger 244, 249, 267

381

Index

hybrid actorness 9, 287, 289, 291–293, 295, 297
hybrid warfare 61, 76, 79, 201, 323, 338
hydrocarbon 340, 360–361, 363, 371

ice melting 367–369, 371
Iceland 36, 42, 312–313, 367
illegal fishing 4, 9, 34–35, 37, 44, 64–66, 88, 94,
    101, 184, 186, 239–241, 248, 251, 258, 267,
    273–274, 290, 293, 296, 298, 325–327, 330, 333
illegal migration 100, 108, 112, 166, 183, 256
illegal, unreported and unregulated (IUU) fishing
    128, 178, 239, 249, 260, 274–275, 360
illicit trafficking 11–12, 66, 68, 193; imperialism
    21–22, 141, 147–149; imperium 3, 19, 64, 348
inclusive interests 88
Indian Ocean 5, 11–13, 24–25, 37, 67–70, 72, 76,
    80, 83–85, 104, 114, 123–125, 161, 176,
    178–186, 199, 201, 251, 254–255, 259–261,
    263–264, 271–272, 274–275, 298–299,
    308–309, 319, 331–334, 338, 347, 358
Indian Ocean Rim Association (IORA) 271, 275
indigenous peoples 273, 367–369, 375, 377
Indo-Pacific 70, 76, 79, 81, 83, 212, 259,
    261–262, 316
Indochina 170–171
Indonesia 76, 114, 149, 181, 185, 270, 292,
    349–350, 352–353, 355–358, 362–363,
    365–366
inequality 106, 146, 229, 236, 245; informal
    governance 177, 182, 184–185; information
    sharing 3, 77, 162, 180–181, 187, 241, 269, 292,
    330, 351, 353–354, 356, 366
innocent passage 74–77, 80–82, 87, 89–92, 182,
    300, 307
intangible heritage 276, 279–280, 282, 284–286
intelligence, surveillance and reconnaissance
    155, 222
interception 102, 110, 154, 163, 169–170, 173,
    175, 292
Intercontinental Ballistic Missile (ICBM) 318
International Chamber of Shipping (ICS) 187, 305
international community 43, 64, 86–88, 90, 94,
    111, 121, 167, 170–171, 173–174, 178, 202,
    221, 274, 353
International Convention for the Safety of Life at
    Sea (SOLAS) 168
International Convention on Maritime Search and
    Rescue (SAR) 168
International Court of Justice 30, 36, 78, 81,
    349, 356
international criminal law 87, 168
international human rights law 4, 8, 87, 153, 157,
    162, 168
international law of the sea 95, 168, 307
International Maritime Bureau (IMB) 127,
    177, 187

international maritime law 11–12, 153, 168–169,
    173, 176, 226
International Maritime Organisation (IMO) 65,
    168, 170, 240
International Organisation for Migration
    (IOM) 170
international protection 169–170, 277
International Relations 1–2, 18, 20–21, 23, 25–26,
    28, 36–38, 41, 71, 104–106, 115–116, 118, 124,
    147, 176, 186, 259, 261, 263, 287, 295, 297,
    308–309, 324, 332–334, 345, 367–371,
    376–378
International Seabed Authority 316
International Ship and Port Facility Security (ISPS)
    Code 3
international shipping 134, 214, 217, 300–302
international trade 55, 247, 257, 272, 358–359
International Tribunal for the Law of the Sea 78,
    81, 156, 163, 349, 363
Internationally Recommended Transit Corridor
    (IRTC) 179
Internet of Things (IoT) 219
Interpol 199, 240, 248, 258
Iran 76, 79, 179, 191, 194, 201–203, 207, 211, 213
Iraq 27, 36, 108, 195, 201, 203, 207–208, 213, 299,
    307, 325
Ireland 296, 313
irregular maritime migration 100, 165–166, 175
Islamic State 195, 201, 213, 343
island disputes 99
Israel 36, 76, 194, 211, 339–340
Italy 108–109, 115, 158, 164, 171, 173, 175, 283,
    308, 313, 320, 322, 338–340, 344, 369
Ivory Coast 127, 132, 135, 138, 235, 331

Jamaica 24, 26, 36, 252, 270
James Cook 140
Japan 5, 48, 76, 81, 84, 95, 99, 181, 208, 213, 241,
    245, 249, 259, 270, 354, 359, 361, 367, 369
Joint Force Command Norfolk 314
Julian Corbett 38, 49, 52
jurisdictional claims 363

Kenya 29, 126, 183–184, 186, 270
Kerch Strait 3, 62
kidnapping 128, 133–134, 138, 167, 169, 179, 181,
    185, 195, 210, 239, 300–301
Kola peninsula 317, 319, 371

large ocean states 70, 250, 253–254, 256, 262,
    264, 272
Latin America 229, 243, 333–334
law enforcement 12, 42–43, 45, 86, 92–93,
    117–122, 124–125, 132, 134, 153–155, 157,
    159–163, 167, 179–180, 240, 242, 246, 273,
    288, 291, 297, 326, 350–351, 354

382

Index

law of the sea 4, 12, 29, 34, 36–37, 55, 60, 63–64, 69–73, 75, 78, 81, 83–87, 89–95, 102, 114, 126, 135, 138, 140, 150, 153, 155–158, 160, 162–164, 168, 177, 186, 188, 221, 225, 249, 264, 278, 296, 301, 307, 310, 313, 324, 330, 349, 353, 355, 359–365

League of Nations 43–44

Lebanon 56–57, 82, 211

legal studies 4, 118, 120, 162

letter of non-objection 306

Levantine groups 194

liberal approach 44, 62–67, 69, 71

Liberation Tigers of Tamil Eelam 56, 194, 201

Libya 56, 108, 114, 157, 173–175, 194, 203, 210, 213, 314–315, 337–340, 344–345

littoral defence 103

littoralisation 197

living resources 65–66, 91, 93, 239, 241, 256, 266

local fisheries 143, 268

Lomé Charter 113, 271, 273–274, 330, 332

Macau 348

Madagascar 254, 275

Malacca Straits 76, 181, 352–353

Malaysia 76, 100, 105, 181, 186, 206, 349–350, 352–353, 355–357, 359, 362, 365–366

Maldives 250, 252, 272

male gaze 7

Malta 171

Malvinas Isles 327

mare clausum 73, 90, 95, 354

mare liberum 73, 89, 95, 142, 148, 354

marginalisation 143, 179, 181, 233, 236, 243, 331

marine art 141

marine biodiversity 65, 268

marine biotechnology 265–267

marine environment 11, 63, 66–71, 166–167, 215, 250, 256–258, 262, 267, 269, 342, 346, 360, 363

marine genetic resources 67, 257

marine pollution 4, 11, 64, 67, 71, 250, 258, 270

marine protected areas 65, 70, 244, 247, 260–261, 264, 266

marine resources 11, 67, 142, 165, 240, 248–249, 264, 268, 270, 275, 329, 337, 357, 359–363

marine spatial planning 181, 247–248, 260; maritime commerce 5, 40–41, 50, 77, 84, 268; maritime commons 73–75, 81–82, 154; maritime crime 8, 12, 43, 127–130, 134, 137, 177, 181, 183–184, 188, 192, 195–196, 227–229, 231, 233–235, 237–238, 300, 305, 331

maritime culture 60, 281–282

maritime disputes 62, 71, 78, 81, 83, 94, 349, 355

maritime domain awareness 8, 33, 35, 77, 101, 193, 240, 256, 259, 322, 351, 354, 356

maritime enforcement 77, 79, 110, 173, 178, 183, 193, 295

maritime governance 6, 64, 68, 70, 73, 80, 116, 123, 180, 234, 248, 367

maritime heritage 276–278, 280–282, 284–286

maritime history 25–26, 28, 144, 356

maritime identities 276–277, 279, 281, 283–285

maritime industry 214–215, 219–221

maritime insecurity 8, 69, 116, 127–128, 130, 132, 135, 183, 191, 193, 197, 199, 210, 227, 239, 246, 325, 339

maritime jurisdiction 55, 95, 349, 361–362

maritime law enforcement 42–43, 153–155, 159, 162–163, 288, 350–351, 354

maritime museum 143–145, 150

maritime piracy 8, 11, 70, 80, 104, 124–126, 129, 137–138, 176–177, 179, 181–188, 228, 238, 248, 257, 260, 274, 293, 307, 309

maritime politics 7, 10, 28–30, 33, 35

maritime powers 3, 73–74, 76, 79–81, 84, 258

maritime regional security 96, 99

maritime research 247

maritime safety 65, 98, 180, 240, 257, 259, 269, 329

maritime securitisation 74, 96–101, 103–105, 166

maritime security actors 122, 268

maritime security governance 3, 11, 13, 73–75, 77–79, 81–83, 85, 116–123, 125, 174, 179, 185–186, 267, 272–273, 300, 330, 332, 356

maritime security regime 3, 68–70, 104, 325, 330

Maritime Security Regional Programme (MASE) 260

maritime security studies 11, 70, 116–117, 120–121, 123–124, 162, 186, 263, 274, 308, 332, 344

Maritime Silk Road (MSR) 272

maritime smuggling 290–291

maritime strategy 6, 13, 25, 38, 42, 44–45, 47–55, 57, 59–61, 69–71, 113, 115, 176, 260, 271, 273, 275, 313–315, 323, 330, 366

maritime surveillance 6, 77, 183, 259, 322, 338

maritime territoriality 73, 80

maritime terrorism 3–4, 8, 11, 44, 66, 98, 125, 167, 187, 189–199, 201, 256, 356

maritime trade routes 142, 272

maritime transport 63, 85, 225–226, 257, 281, 286, 310, 342

maritime zones 64–65, 86, 90, 92, 94, 179, 182, 185, 260, 262, 337, 349–350, 363

Marshall Islands 33, 149, 299–307, 309

Mauritius 125–126, 251–252, 254, 256, 263, 268, 271, 273–274

Médecins Sans Frontières 35

Mediterranean Action Plan 342

Mediterranean Sea 35, 109–110, 115, 172, 175, 220, 271, 331, 338, 343, 345–346; mercenaries 21, 26, 298–299, 309, 334; merchant fleet 39,

383

Index

301, 305–307, 375; merchant shipping 45, 290, 293, 359
Mexico 36, 213, 270, 290, 313
micro-state 296, 304
Middle East 10, 44, 335, 340–343, 345, 358, 374
migrant smuggling 12, 157, 163, 167, 170, 337
Migrant Smuggling Protocol 157, 163
migration flows 108, 166; migration management 167; migration-violence nexus 107; migratory crisis 165; militarised sea borders 108
military capabilities 55, 300, 307, 322, 368, 372
military deployments 340, 368; military personnel 299, 305, 307; military power 10, 42, 46, 65, 222, 312; military security 87, 100, 321
mineral resources 230, 257, 358
missile defence 41, 318–319
Missing Migrants Project 108, 114
mixed flows 165, 167
modern state security 64
Mozambique 135, 236–237, 329
MS Achille Lauro 194; multilevel cooperation 69; multinational corporations 273, 368
Myanmar 172, 269, 349, 355–356

Namibia 36, 270, 327, 329, 333
narco-submarines 290–291, 295, 297–298
nation-states 166, 220, 347–349
national jurisdiction 67, 70–71, 92–93, 250, 253, 261–262, 297
national oil companies (NOCs) 203
national security 2, 4, 13, 28, 31, 36, 75, 77–79, 85, 92, 143, 187, 198, 223, 225, 256, 262, 267, 269, 296, 327, 330–331, 333–334, 372, 374
National Strategy for the Arctic Region 372
NATO 3, 10–11, 31, 33–34, 36, 42, 46, 56, 60, 67, 71, 75–76, 78–80, 82–84, 101, 111, 125–126, 131, 179, 300, 312–323, 328, 330, 332, 334, 340, 372–373
NATO Secretary General 315, 320, 323
NATO Standing Maritime Groups 314
natural hazards 258, 286, 359
natural resource governance 227, 236
natural risks 66
naval doctrine 52–53, 61
naval operations 3, 12, 44, 69, 98, 174, 183, 319, 322
naval policy 38, 54–55, 58
naval warfare 13, 19, 47–53, 55, 57, 59–61, 87, 141, 188, 256; navigation rights 313; neighbourhood policy 336–337; neoliberal perspective 370; neorealist model 370
New Zealand 33, 37, 55, 72, 95, 162–163, 355
Niger Delta 129–131, 133–134, 136–138, 205, 229, 231–233, 237–238
Nigeria 76, 82, 128, 131–133, 135–138, 178, 180, 184–185, 187–188, 208, 227, 229–238, 326–327, 329–333; non-living resources 91, 266; non-refoulment 169

non-state actors 6, 9, 75, 78, 86–87, 92, 94, 99, 123, 125, 182, 192, 198, 221, 262, 287–295, 297, 324, 335, 368, 370
non-traditional security issues 96, 99, 369
North Africa 10, 76–77, 211, 335, 340–341, 346
North America 140, 290, 314–315
North Pole 368
North Sea 36, 313, 374
Northern Dimension policy 371, 374
Northern Sea Route 212, 321, 370, 374
Northwest Passage 321, 374
Norway 25, 55, 270, 313, 320, 367, 369, 373
nuclear, biological and chemical attacks 3

Obama 294, 318, 321, 327
ocean acidification 257–258
ocean governance 63, 70–72, 82–84, 114, 139, 148, 168, 256, 272, 331–332
ocean management 12, 260–261
Ocean Shield 179, 300
offshore gas 257–258
offshore renewable energy 265
oil bunkering 131–132, 134, 183, 196, 232, 234–235
oil industry 131, 178, 227, 231–234, 236
oil infrastructure 178, 202
oil spills 99, 231
Operation Unified Protector 315
Opium Wars 144
organised crime 7–8, 30, 66, 75, 100–101, 112, 218, 228, 234–239, 241–242, 246, 325, 332–333, 337, 340
overfishing 239, 241–242, 267, 269, 341, 360

Pacific Ocean 140, 142, 251, 260, 358
Palau 252, 270
Panama 9, 39, 43, 94, 299–303, 305–307, 309
pandemic 10, 244, 273–274, 276, 317, 342
Papua New Guinea 251
Paris Climate Accords 373
Pax Britannica 65, 71
peaceful resolution 357
Persian Gulf 76–78, 80, 200–201, 203–205, 207–208, 211–212, 327, 339
petro-state 230, 238
petroleum industry shipping 200
Philippines 36, 43, 179, 181, 185, 348–350, 353, 355, 357, 361–363, 365
piracy numbers 127–131, 133, 135, 137; pirate attacks 133, 299, 301–302, 308; place of safety 168–170
Polar Silk Road 371, 374, 378; policing of maritime crimes 269; political instability 167, 232, 335
political violence 191–192, 196–198, 232
politics of numbers 12, 127–130, 132, 135–137

384

Index

population growth 245, 341
port authorities 216
port infrastructure 199, 266, 280, 320
port security 4, 193, 290
Port State Measures Agreement 240
Portugal 22, 90, 139, 260, 270, 313, 317, 330, 334
Poseidon 109, 280, 316, 321
post-Cold War 2, 6, 29, 34, 60, 314, 368
post-imperial 142
post-Westphalian state 73, 78, 82
postcolonial states 4
poverty eradication 241, 246, 248
practices and norms 5–8, 151
prevention 64, 66, 71, 77, 108, 226, 268
private actors 28, 121, 292, 296
private military and security companies
    (PMSC) 299
private military companies 329
private security 66, 78–79, 177, 182, 186, 269, 274,
    295–297, 299–304, 306–308
privateering 19, 21–26, 176, 348
Privately Contracted Armed Security Personnel
    (PCASP) 180, 309
privatisation of vessel protection 300, 307
protectionism 45, 65
Protocol Against the Smuggling of Migrants by
    Land, Sea and Air 163, 170, 175
Protocol to Prevent, Suppress and Punish
    Trafficking in Persons, Especially Women and
    Children 170, 175
public agencies 66

qualitative methods 116

Rainbow Warrior 6, 28, 30, 33–35, 37
realism 13, 38–39, 41, 43, 45, 47–48, 335, 378
recession 318, 325
reconnaissance 155, 222, 319
Red Cross 162, 369
referent object 7, 97, 105, 171
refoulement 155, 157, 161
refugee crisis 4, 115, 149, 166, 335–336
refugee law 4, 168–169, 173
regional cooperation 68–69, 185, 187, 260–261,
    263, 273, 342, 349, 353, 356, 366
Regional Cooperation Agreement on Combating
    Piracy and Armed Robbery against Ships in Asia
    (ReCAAP) 353
Regional Fisheries Management Organisations
    (RFMOs) 67, 240
regional governance 73, 239, 372–373
regional organisations 3, 179, 240, 271–272, 330
rescue operations 108, 169, 173, 256, 269
resource curse 228, 232
resource governance-crime nexus 236; resource
    management 65, 114, 139, 360; rise of China 5, 320

risk management 5, 98, 103, 202, 213, 215,
    220–226
Romania 313
Royal Navy 43, 203, 296, 315–316, 318, 321,
    323, 348
rule of law 79, 87–88, 94–95, 154, 165, 340
Russia 3, 17, 39–40, 44, 46–47, 55, 62, 76, 79–81,
    84, 104, 179, 183, 187, 198–199, 206, 208, 212,
    225, 241, 312–323, 325, 328–329, 331–334,
    338–339, 344–346, 367–378
Russian Maritime Doctrine 54

Sahel 136–137, 342
sailing techniques 283
sanctions 56, 76, 78, 154, 201, 371–372, 374–375
Saudi Arabia 76, 202, 204, 207–208
Scandinavian states 373
Scotland 19, 144, 313
sea control 40, 44, 50–51, 53–56, 58–59, 61,
    315, 328
sea denial 40, 51, 55–56, 59
sea domination 337
sea lines of communication (SLOC) 74, 208, 358
sea-based trade 39–40, 43, 368
sea-level rise 258, 261, 263, 320, 368
Sea-Watch 35
seabed mining 265–267
seablindness 11, 70, 155, 158, 162, 179, 186, 263,
    274, 308, 332, 344
seaborne migration 139, 165–168, 170, 174
seaborne violence 20–24
seafarers 4, 23, 50, 102, 106, 115, 128, 141–143,
    183, 185, 258, 280, 298, 301, 305–306
seapower 6, 13, 19, 21, 23, 25, 42, 46–48, 52,
    60–61, 70, 98, 124, 139, 188, 315, 322, 377
search and rescue (SAR) 102, 168
Second World War 42, 63, 302–303, 312, 322,
    324, 347–349, 355, 361
securitisation theory 70, 96, 98, 105
security agenda 36, 65–69, 97, 106, 114, 140, 185,
    267, 270, 330
security at sea 4–5, 29, 34, 43, 45, 64, 66, 70, 72,
    90, 116, 209–210, 260, 288, 291, 339
security community 68–69, 336
security discourse 2, 7
security governance 3, 5, 11, 13, 73–75, 77–85,
    116–123, 125, 174, 179, 185–186, 267,
    272–273, 300, 329–330, 332, 344, 356
security practices 6, 35, 65, 97, 288
security referents 80
security regimes 62, 64, 100–101, 324, 330
security risk 165, 206–209, 211–212, 226
Security Studies 1, 11–12, 28, 31, 62, 64, 70–72,
    95, 104–106, 115–117, 120–121, 123–125, 137,
    158, 162, 176, 186, 188, 237–238, 263, 274,
    296–297, 308–309, 332, 344, 377

Index

security-humanitarianism-rights nexus 110
Senegal 36, 242, 249, 292, 329, 331
Seychelles 125–126, 250, 252, 254, 256–257, 261, 263–264, 272, 274–275, 292, 296
SHADE 180, 184, 338
SHADE MED 184, 338
ship hijackings 193
ship security plan (SSP) 304–305; ship-to-shore connection 215–216; shipping companies 66, 129, 327, 368
shipping industry 121, 178, 180, 182, 185, 217, 268, 299–302, 306, 308; shipping routes 269, 368, 374; shipwreck 150, 171, 279–281
Silk Road 272, 274, 332, 347, 371, 374, 378
Singapore 71, 76–77, 100, 105, 181, 185, 251, 296, 347–353, 355–356, 358–359, 364, 369
Sino-Russian cooperation 372–373
slave trade 65, 140, 296
Small Island Developing States (SIDS) 250, 266
small-scale fisheries 241, 243, 246–249, 265–268, 274, 286
smuggling of migrants 76, 109, 112, 157, 163, 167, 170, 173–175, 249, 337
social equity 266, 272; social exclusion 9; societal security 63
socio-economic maritime development 9
sociology 2, 21, 23, 25–26, 105, 116, 118
soft power 183, 371
Somali piracy 3, 98, 101, 105, 111, 117–120, 122–125, 129, 132, 178–180, 183, 186–187, 201, 227, 257, 300–301, 303, 306
Somalia 3, 7, 11–12, 34, 44, 66–67, 85, 101, 105, 108, 111–112, 114–115, 124–126, 129, 131, 135, 153, 157, 159–160, 162–163, 172, 178, 180, 182, 185–188, 197, 268, 293, 295, 308–310
South Africa 76, 272, 274, 297, 324, 328–333
South America 5, 29, 44, 211, 324–326, 328–331, 358
South Atlantic 5, 10, 82, 315, 319, 324–334
South Atlantic Treaty Organization 333
South China Sea 3, 5, 10, 34, 62, 67–68, 72, 76, 80–83, 85, 89, 92, 94–95, 99, 104–105, 141–142, 150, 204, 208, 211–212, 263, 268, 272, 275, 287, 296–298, 347, 349, 353–362, 364–366
South Korea 126, 208, 351, 359
Southeast Asia 10, 12, 44, 48, 55, 82, 99, 101, 104–105, 140, 176, 179, 181–185, 187–188, 201, 238, 272, 274–275, 297–298, 345, 347–352, 354–356, 358–359, 364, 366
Southwest Indian Ocean 251, 254, 260, 263
sovereign prerogatives 74, 76, 79–80, 82
Spain 22, 26, 39, 90, 139, 171, 260, 280–281, 284, 286, 313, 317, 338, 369
spice trade 348

state actors 6, 9, 29, 34, 75, 78, 86–87, 92, 94, 99, 117, 121, 123, 125, 182, 192, 197–198, 221, 262, 287–295, 297, 324, 335, 360, 368, 370
stowaways 4, 12, 168, 175
Strait of Hormuz 56, 77, 83, 219–220
Strait of Malacca 69, 181, 268, 298, 347
Strait of Singapore 348
strategic competition 83, 198, 261, 312
Strategic Studies 2, 47, 60, 72, 125, 163, 226, 309, 322, 333, 346, 350–351
SUA Convention 3, 94
SUA Protocol 157, 163
Suez Canal 208, 300, 339
Sulawesi Sea 349
Sulu Sea 187, 348, 353, 358
Suriname 251, 327
surveillance 6, 33, 35, 77, 101, 104, 155, 166, 173, 175, 180–181, 183, 222, 241–242, 246, 248, 254, 256, 259, 263, 266, 269, 288, 291–292, 319, 322, 331, 338, 353–354
Sustainable Development Goals (SDGs) 137, 246, 248, 267, 341–342
Svalbard treaty 373
Sweden 26, 55, 84, 367, 374
Syria 27, 56, 108, 201, 211, 317, 319, 371, 376

Taiwan 241, 357–359, 361–362
territorial disputes 62, 211, 239, 313, 339, 366, 372
territorial seas 34, 89–91, 287
territorial waters 65, 75–79, 81, 135–136, 177, 180, 205, 287, 300, 305, 353, 359, 368
territorialisation 56, 150, 253–254, 260–261
terrorism 3–4, 7–8, 11, 30, 33, 44, 52, 57, 66, 68, 75, 82, 86, 88, 93–94, 98–101, 103, 105, 118, 124–125, 138, 157, 167, 178, 186–199, 201–202, 211, 237, 256, 268, 274, 293, 296, 314, 340, 343–345, 352–353, 356, 365
terrorist organisations 189, 191, 195–196
Thailand 76, 82, 171, 350, 352, 355, 357–358
the Caribbean 140, 171–172, 251, 260, 313, 324
the Faroe Islands 367
the Marshall Islands 33, 299–301, 303–307, 309
the Netherlands 22, 53, 126, 139, 260, 313, 369
the Philippines 36, 43, 179, 181, 185, 349–350, 353, 357, 361–363, 365
Thucydides 38, 48–49
tourism 143, 216, 257, 266, 269–270, 277, 282, 284, 286, 341
trade routes 142, 176, 272, 375; traditional threats 47, 55, 66–67, 224; traditional vessels 217, 276, 283; trafficking of human beings 112–113; transhipment 240, 242, 246, 326
transnational organised crime 75, 101, 228, 236, 242, 332–333
travel 21, 120, 174, 179, 348

386

Index

Treaty of Tordesillas 19, 23
Trident Juncture 314, 373
Trieste 320, 322
Triton 102, 109
Trump 84, 317–318, 321, 327, 373, 376
Turkey 62, 108–109, 114, 147–148, 211, 313, 338–340, 343, 346

Ukraine 54, 62, 199, 225, 314, 323, 345, 368, 371, 375–376
UN Convention Against Illicit Traffic in Narcotic Drugs and Psychotropic Substances 157
UN Decade of Ocean Science for Sustainable Development 270
UN Development Programme (UNDP) 369
UN Environment Programme (UNEP) 270, 369
UN Food and Agriculture Organization (FAO) 270
UN Security Council 101, 124, 157–158, 179–180, 188, 300, 320; unconventional threats 65–66, 69; underwater heritage 277–278, 282
Union for the Mediterranean 336, 342, 344, 346
United Kingdom 105, 143, 226, 254, 260, 278, 293, 307, 313, 355, 363
United Nations 2, 4, 12, 29, 43, 63, 65, 67, 70–73, 82, 85–86, 95, 102, 106, 111–112, 114, 126, 135, 138, 155, 162–164, 168, 170–171, 174–175, 177, 188, 214, 221, 225–226, 231, 238, 244, 248–249, 251, 253, 258, 263–266, 270, 275, 278, 286, 298, 301, 308–310, 313, 316, 320–321, 323, 326, 330, 334, 342, 362, 365–366, 369
United Nations Conference on Trade and Development (UNCTAD) 214, 226
United Nations Convention on the Law of the Sea 29, 63, 70, 72–73, 86, 95, 162–164, 168, 177, 188, 225, 249, 264, 278, 301, 310, 365
United Nations Declaration on the Rights of Indigenous Peoples (UNDRIP) 369
United Nations Office on Drugs and Crime (UNODC) 111, 326
United Nations Security Council 126, 155, 163, 174, 310, 320, 323
United States 2, 34–35, 39, 46, 51, 64, 89, 93–94, 145, 166, 179, 181, 186, 199, 202, 212, 260, 267, 279, 286, 290, 293–294, 297, 305, 307, 309, 312, 315, 323–329, 331, 334, 363, 365–367, 377
urbanisation 197, 341
Uruguay 327
US Arctic strategy 372
US Department of Defence 319–320, 323
US Marine Corps 316
US National Security Strategy 327
US Naval Institute 60–61, 293, 322
USS Cole 191, 195
USS The Sullivans 191, 194

Venezuela 234, 278, 326, 328, 331, 334
vessel protection 180, 186, 205, 299–301, 305–309
Vietnam War 46, 147, 171
violence at sea 25, 176, 192, 199, 238, 300
visual representations 139–149
Vladimir Putin 44
vulnerable groups 245–246

warship 121, 207, 318, 321
waste dumping 101
water-born improvised explosive devices (WBIEDs) 202
weapon smuggling 3
West Africa 101, 137, 180, 186–187, 212, 238, 243, 248–249, 274, 291, 298, 324–326, 328–331
West Asia 347
Western Indian Ocean 12, 37, 124, 176, 178–186, 255, 260, 263–264, 299, 309
women seafarers 106, 115
World Bank 79, 85, 237–239, 242, 247–249, 263–266, 270, 275, 300, 310
world trade 139, 214, 225, 265

Yaoundé Code of Conduct 63, 72, 128
Yemen 56–57, 60, 172, 199, 202, 204, 211

zoning of the sea 64

Milton Keynes UK
Ingram Content Group UK Ltd.
UKHW020641210624
444299UK00005B/14